THE LONGMAN
STANDARD HISTORY
OF ANCIENT
PHILOSOPHY

THE LONGMAN STANDARD HISTORY OF ANCIENT PHILOSOPHY

DANIEL KOLAK

William Paterson University of New Jersey

GARRETT THOMSON

College of Wooster

Routledge
Taylor & Francis Group

LONDON AND NEW YORK

First published 2006 by Pearson Education, Inc.

Published 2016 by Routledge
2 Park Square, Milton Park, Abingdon, Oxon OX14 4RN
711 Third Avenue, New York, NY 10017, USA

Routledge is an imprint of the Taylor & Francis Group, an informa business

Senior Cover Designer/Manager: Nancy Danahy

ISBN-13: 978-0-321-23513-8 (pbk)

Library of Congress Cataloging-in-Publication Data

Kolak, Daniel.
   The Longman standard history of philosophy / Daniel Kolak, Garrett Thomson.
      p. cm.
   Includes bibliographical references and index.
   ISBN 978-0-321-23511-4 (volume 6 (comprehensive) : alk. paper)—ISBN 978-0-321-23513-8
(volume 1 (ancient) : alk. paper)—ISBN 978-0-321-23512-1 (volume 3 (modern) : alk. paper)—
ISBN 978-0-321-23510-7 (volume 5 (20th century) : alk. paper)
   1. Philosophy—History. I. Title: Standard history of philosophy. II. Thomson, Garrett. III. Title.
B72.K635 2006
190—dc22
                                                                      2002010370

◆ CONTENTS ◆

III: ARISTOTLE　　273

◇PROLOGUE　　273

ARISTOTLE　　273

◆ PREFACE ◆

Philosophy may not be the oldest profession but it is the oldest discipline, the source of our views about reality, knowledge, and morality. To understand the revolutionary nature of the evolution of philosophy is to understand ourselves and our world anew. Inspired by the intellectual intimacy that philosophy affords, the mind is broadened and refreshed. In that sense philosophy is always anything but old: awash with new possibilities of inquiry and understanding, the illuminating questions of philosophy liberate us from the blinding obviousness of accepted answers, the blinders of our individual and collective biases.

Though philosophers build upon the work of their predecessors, they continually revise and often overthrow the views of their predecessors—sometimes, even those of their own teachers. One of the most famous examples is the sequence from Socrates to Plato to Aristotle. And yet throughout the evolution of thought that philosophy heralds much remains the same: the call to wonder, to dispute, to question, to liberate, to ponder, to inquire, to understand everything one can about the whole of our being—reality, knowledge, and morality—without becoming ourselves closed off. To behold the whole without being conquered by the wholeness of the vision, that is the sum and substance of the western intellectual tradition made possible by philosophy.

To see new wisdom in the old and old wisdom in the new is to be not just learned but wise. And to not just tolerate such expansive openness but to love it now and then is what it means to be a philosopher, then and now. This book may not make you a philosopher. But it will provide you with everything you need to become one. A big claim and, therefore, a big book: with 44 of the greatest works by 20 of the most important western philosophers from ancient times, this volume assembles into one book some of the most profound and edifying ideas in the history of human thought. In addition to 14 of the major dialogues of Plato and 10 of Aristotle's groundbreaking works, this volume contains a full selection of the Pre-Socratic philosophers and the Hellenistic and Roman schools of thought.

Suitable for a one-semester introduction to ancient philosophy, history of philosophy, history of ideas, or western intellectual history, this book is a covert assembly with a covert purpose, to bring philosophy to you but even more importantly: to bring you to philosophy.

We have structured the book to make this possible. The volume as a whole is divided into four standard divisions: "Section I, Early Ancient Greek Philosophy," "Section II, Plato," "Section III, Aristotle," and "Section IV, Hellenistic and Roman Philosophy." Each Section opens with a "Prologue", offering a context for specific philosophers, such as "Prologue to Plato," or to key schools of thought, such as "Prologue to Stoicism." These are designed to let you in on what has come before, so that you don't enter the conversation in the middle. Individual "Biographical Histories" give pertinent details about the life and times of each philosopher, such as "Aristotle: A Biographical History." The purpose is to show you that philosophers are neither divine demigods nor depersonalized thinking machines but individual human beings with a penchant for grappling with the perennial big questions. The purpose of the "Philosophical Overviews" to each philosopher is two-fold: first, to show how that philosopher's thinking about reality, knowledge and morality integrate into a coherent view; second, to integrate each particular philosopher into a broader philosophical context. Each reading selection comes with its own concise intro-duction designed to quicken your entry into the issues and prepare you for what is to come.

The selections themselves have been chosen for their profundity and edited to high-light the central importance, while leaving in the all-important methods, processes, and development of the views expressed therein. Where translations are involved, we have in each case selected the most lucid. The "Study Questions" at the end of each chapter, such as "Study Questions for Pre-Socratic Philosophy," provide comprehension questions as well as wider discussion questions; these are for you, to test yourself, to see how well you have understood what you have read. "The Philosophical Bridges" at the end of each chapter, such as "The Platonic Influence," summarizes the influence of each thinker on later gener-ations in order that you can appreciate the threads connecting different periods and see how philosophy's perennial questions lead to ever more evolving views.

Special thanks to each of the following reviewers, whose comments about one or more of the volumes in the "Longman Standard History of Philosophy" series helped to enhance each book.

Michael L. Anderson, University of Maryland
Marina P. Banchetti-Robino, Florida Atlantic University
David Boersema, Pacific University
Stephen Braude, University of Maryland Baltimore County
Cynthia K. Brown, Catholic University of America
Richard J. Burke, Oakland University
Marina Bykova, North Carolina State University
Jeffrey Carr, Christopher Newport University
James P. Cooney, Montgomery County Community College
Elmer H. Duncan, Baylor University
Christian Early, Eastern Mennonite University
Emma L. Easteppe, Boise State University
James E. Falcouner, Brigham Young University
Chris L. Firestone, Trinity International University
Merigala Gabriel, Georgia Southern University
Bruce Hauptli, Florida International University
Larry Hauser, Alma College
David J. Hilditch, Webster University
Mary Beth Ingham, Loyola Marymount University
Betty Kiehl, Palomar College
John H. Kulten, Jr., University of Missouri
Nelson P. Lande, University of Massachusetts
Dorothea Lotter, Wake Forest University
Charles S. MacKenzie, Reformed Theological Seminary

Thomas J. Martin, University of North Carolina Charlotte
D. A. Masolo, University of Louisville
Leemon B. McHenry, California State University, Northridge
John T. Meadors, Mississippi College
Glenn Melancon, Southeastern Oklahoma State University
Mark Michael, Austin Peay State University
Thomas Osborne, University of Nevada, Las Vegas
Walter Ott, East Tennessee State University
Anna Christina Ribeiro, University of Maryland
Stefanie Rocknak, Hartwick College
George Rudebusch, Northern Arizona University
Ari Santas, Valdosta State University
Candice Shelby, University of Colorado-Denver
Daniel Silber, Florida Southern College
Allan Silverman, Ohio State University
James K. Swindler, Illinois State University
David B. Twetten, Marquette University
Thomas Upton, Gannon University
Barry F. Vaughan, Mesa Community College
Daniel R. White, Florida Atlantic University
David M. Wisdo, Columbus State University
Evelyn Wortsman Deluty, Nassau Community College

We would like to thank the following people for their help. Brandon West of the College of Wooster for his sterling work as a student research assistant. Amy Erickson and Patrice Reeder of the College of Wooster for their unfailing secretarial help. Professors Martin Gunderson, Ron Hustwit, Henry Kreuzman, Adrian Moore, Elizabeth Schiltz, and Philip Turetzsky for their useful comments. Everyone at Longman for their very professional work, especially Priscilla McGeehon, who has supported the project with tireless energy and enthusiasm. Our wives, Wendy and Helena, for their help and understanding. Finally, we would like to dedicate this volume to our children: Julia, Sophia, Dylan, and Andre Kolak; and to Andrew, Frances, Verena, Susana, and Robert Thomson.

About 2,600 years ago, something remarkable occurred. Original thinkers appeared almost simultaneously around the globe. It was as if thinking had been discovered independently in different parts of the world. In China, there were Lao Tzu (604–510 B.C.) and Confucious (557–479 B.C.); in India, Gotma Buddha (563–483 B.C.) and Mahavira Jain (540–468 B.C.); and in Persia, Zoroaster (628–551 B.C.). The most fertile land for growing thinkers was Greece. Thales, Anaximander, Pythagoras, and Parmenides all flourished within one century. Between Thales (624–545 B.C.) and Socrates (470–399 B.C.), there is only about 150 years. Yet, during this short span, we can see many of the great ideas of western philosophy in embryonic form.

Ancient philosophy contains nearly all the major elements of western thought. Because of its simplicity, it is often more beautiful and edifying than later philosophical work, which tends to be cluttered with qualifications and which contains ideological debates, such as those surrounding Christian doctrine. The ancient Greek philosophers pioneered many of the great ideas of humanity, and by studying these thinkers we may hope to regain the original force, freshness, and clarity of their insights.

The intellectual culture of ancient Greece was optimistic and bold. In general, it lacked the cynicism and self-doubt that sometimes plague our age. The early Greeks in particular had an extraordinary confidence that they could understand the world in all of its aspects through the application of their own intellectual capacities. They discovered that we learn some of nature's secrets just by reasoning clearly and systematically based on empirical observation. This is probably humanity's greatest discovery. It was an extremely powerful, invigorating, and liberating breakthrough for the ancient Greeks. Probably for these reasons, ancient Greece gave birth to three of the greatest minds of all time: Socrates, Plato, and Aristotle.

When reading the ancient Greeks, it is important to remember that we take for granted a vast and complex background of accumulated knowledge and concepts that the ancient philosophers did not have. For example, we know that the moon is smaller than the sun, we assume that all animals and plants are classified into species, and we know how to explain the existence of clouds. In the ancient world, this complex web of background knowledge and concepts had yet to be discovered and formulated. For the Greeks, this presented itself as a challenge; there was a whole world to understand and explore.

A Brief Story

Any story is a simplification of what occurs. It is necessarily selective. Furthermore, scholars often dispute how the views of these thinkers should be understood. Nevertheless, the development of ancient philosophy is an interesting story that can be divided into four parts, which correspond to the sections of this first volume.

The Early Ancient Greek Philosophers

From about 580 B.C., in the eastern provinces of the Greek empire, the first pre-Socratic thinkers (Thales, Anaximander, and Anaximenes) tried to explain systematically the nature of the universe by identifying the basic stuff out of which all things are made, and by specifying the fundamental principles that order nature. Around 500 B.C., with the work of Heraclitus and Pythagoras, this philosophy became more metaphysically oriented.

Around 450 B.C., Parmenides threatened dramatically this whole enterprise. He denied the very possibility of science or natural philosophy. He and Zeno argued for the claim that the universe is an undivided whole in which change and plurality are impossible. In other words, they argued that natural philosophy was no more than a description of illusion. The problem was that their arguments appeared sound. Although later natural philosophers, such as Empedocles and Democritus, tried to ward off this threat and brought progress to natural philosophy, the challenge was not met decisively.

In about 420 B.C., a new and even more skeptical approach emerged: Sophism. Partly in reaction to the diversity of earlier metaphysical theories, the Sophists taught a form of relativism that spurned metaphysics and challenged the religious and moral views of the time. In general terms, the Sophists argued that there were no metaphysical and ethical truths to be learned. Instead, they taught their pupils to debate persuasively.

Socrates and Plato

In about 420 B.C., Socrates began to argue against Sophism. He took issue with its skeptical and relativist view of ethics. In order to refute such relativism decisively, Plato argued for the existence of universal Forms. These Forms, or Ideas, are abstract objects that define the essence of terms, such as 'justice' and 'goodness,' and their existence is required to explain knowledge and language. In his many dialogues, Plato expounds the implications of the theory of Forms for many areas of knowledge, such as epistemology, education, theology, ethics, art, and politics.

Plato also rejected the pre-Socratic tradition of natural philosophy, arguing that purely mechanical explanations never provide the reasons why things happen. The rejection of mechanism also indicates the need for the Forms. In other words, Plato saw the two options of pre-Socratic thought, that is, the physical mechanism of the Ionians and the relativism of the Sophists, as a false dichotomy. This points to the existence of universal Forms. It seemed that the deadlock of pre-Socratic philosophy had been resolved.

Aristotle

However, does the refutation of Sophism and mechanism really require the existence of universal Forms? Aristotle argued that it does not. He claimed that the denial of relativism does not require Platonic absolutism. Aristotle had a great interest in the natural world and the classification of species. He also classified uses of misleading philosophical terms, such as 'to be' and 'cause,' and this led him to conclude that things can be said to exist in different ways, which he calls categories. In particular, the category of 'substance' indicates what exists primarily, and other kinds of existence such as that of qualities or the Forms are derivative. In other words, Plato was mistaken to treat the Forms as if they were substances. Furthermore, Aristotle explained form and matter as two inseparable aspects of substance: the Form is its essence, and the matter is what it is composed of. This allowed Aristotle to transcend both Plato and the pre-Socratics, who respectively and mistakenly treat form and matter as if they were independent substances. Aristotle thought that universals exist, but that their existence is derivative or parasitic on natural substances. The forms are immanent in the natural world.

Hellenistic and Roman Philosophy

The period of brilliance in Greek philosophy did not end with Aristotle, even though the golden age of the city-states faded away. About 20 years after the death of Aristotle, there emerged three important new schools of philosophy: Epicureanism, Stoicism, and Pyrrhonean skepticism. As the Greece of small city-states declined and Rome became the central European power, these new systems gained strength, especially Stoicism. Around 170 A.D., the Stoic Roman emperor Marcus Aurelius gave grants to the four philosophical schools of Athens: Plato's Academy, Aristotle's Lyceum, Epicurus' Garden, and the Stoa of the Stoics. By this time, however, the philosophical originality of ancient Greece had been lost. Rome was already under the threat of invasion, and philosophy was about to decline. The revival of philosophy in the medieval period is the theme of Volume II of this collection.

Some Historical Background

Ancient Greece was not a single country but rather a collection of small city-states, spread throughout the Aegean, which shared a language and a culture. An important part of this common heritage was the mythology that Homer expressed in the *Iliad* and *Odyssey* in around 700 B.C. Another aspect of this shared culture was athletics; the Olympic Games, first held in 776 B.C., were also festivals in which people from all over the region participated. As its wealth increased, Greek civilization developed its distinctive drama, architecture, and other art forms, as well as the first scientific philosophy. As it spread eastward, this civilization came into conflict with the great and growing Persian Empire.

In 491 B.C., a Greek force of about 20,000 soldiers won the historic battle of Marathon against the Persian army of possibly more than 100,000. Then, in 480, after years of preparation, the Persian king Xerxes sent a huge army and navy against Greece. Remarkably, because Athens and Sparta worked together and because of their superior organization, the Greeks were able to resist this onslaught with an especially decisive sea battle at Salamis. These events mark an important turning point in European history, after which victorious Athens enjoyed a golden age of greatness. Because of its newfound wealth, stability, and self-confidence, Athens attained new intellectual and cultural heights. Pericles, who held political office from 467 to 428 B.C., led this process: he instituted many reforms that made Athens a democracy as well as an economic and cultural center. During this golden period, the arts flourished. In 447, Pericles initiated the construction of the Parthenon. This was the period of the great tragic plays of Aeschylus, Sophocles, and Euripides, and later the comedies of Aristophanes. This was also the time of the great philosophers such as Parmenides, Zeno, Democritus, Empedocles, Anaxagoras, the Sophists, and Socrates. In Periclean Greece, Herodotus and Thucydides produced their major historical works, and Hippocrates wrote his systematic medical texts.

However, under the leadership of Sparta, the other Greek city-states, such as Megara and Corinth, challenged Athens' military and economic supremacy. This initiated the Peloponnesian War (431–404 B.C.), which Sparta eventually won. The ensuing war led to the crowding of Athens' population into the city walls, and a devastating plague resulted. Pericles was blamed, convicted, and removed from office. That same year, in 429, he died. The turning point in the war was the Sicilian Expedition of 415–413. Under the leadership of Alcibiades, Athens hoped to capture the rich city of Syracuse on Sicily, which was a colony of Corinth, Athens' great commercial rival. In this debacle, Athens lost half of its military and naval power. This loss ignited a conflict between aristocracy and democracy in Athens, and, in 411, various oligarchic councils replaced the democratic assembly. Thereafter, Athens lost its fleet and its citizens suffered starvation during a blockade.

Athens' defeat in 404 marks the beginning of the end of the golden age of classical Greece. There was no stable peace under Spartan control. In 387, Sparta signed a pact with the Persians that gave Sparta the protection of the Persians but ceded all the Greek cities in Asia to Persian control. This led to discontent among the Greek city-states and Thebes won a famous victory against Sparta, which allowed Athens to regain supremacy of the region by around 360 B.C. However, even though it was home to Plato and Aristotle and despite its economic prosperity, Athens did not repeat the artistic and cultural achievements of its Periclean past.

SECTION

I

◆ EARLY ANCIENT ◆
GREEK PHILOSOPHY

PROLOGUE

The early ancient Greek, or pre-Socratic, philosophers were interested primarily in the study of nature. They tried to systematically describe and explain natural phenomena. This makes them both the first philosophers and scientists. Of course, no such distinction existed 2,500 years ago. The early ancients did not separate questions that are best answered conceptually through reasoning and those that are best addressed empirically through observation. Their philosophy was based on the assumption that nature is orderly and can be classified, explained, and understood systematically. They tried to make sense of nature without ad hoc appeals to the whims of the gods. The pre-Socratics assumed that nature is organized according to certain principles. Their main aim was to discover those principles.

This aim required the pre-Socratics to invent or form concepts that are now usually taken for granted. For example, they used the word 'cosmos' to stand for the universe as an orderly whole. They employed the word 'nature' (or *phusis*, from which we have derived 'physics') to stand for things that grow, as opposed to artifacts, which are made. The aim of explaining natural phenomena also requires the concept of natural essences. Natural things have certain fundamental properties or an essence, in terms of which their other properties can be explained. The pre-Socratic enterprise also employs the notion of systematic explanation: the idea of explaining as much as possible, assuming as little as possible.

These first thinkers tried to advance arguments in favor of their positions. For this reason, they deserve to be called the first philosophers, who discovered that careful reasoning can yield knowledge of nature. Such a discovery can belong only to those who distinguish reasoning from speculation. The idea of giving arguments for one's claims was novel. In this respect, we might contrast the pre-Socratic philosophers with the mythical stories of Hesiod's *Theogony*. Hesiod's poem, which was probably written in the eighth century B.C., charts the genealogy of the gods, starting with Chaos, Gaea (Earth), and Eros (Love). Its mythology became a generally accepted part of Greek culture. The poem personifies natural forces and objects, and tries to explain the origin of some natural phenomena, such as day and night, the mountains, the sea, and people. For example, it describes how the mating of Earth and her son, Uranus, the Heavens, produced the first race, the Titans.

Furthermore, the idea that claims about the nature of the universe and morality should be supported by some argument or reasoning destroys the assumption that they should be accepted because they are advanced by an authority. Arguments are revolutionary, because they allow for more freedom of thought than acceptance based on authority.

The Development of Early Ancient Greek Philosophy

Early ancient Greek philosophy first unfolds as a story of the conflict between various visions concerning the basic principles of nature. Philosophy was born in what is today Turkey. The first three philosophers, Thales (624–545 B.C.), Anaximander, and Anaximenes, lived in the coastal town of Miletus, which was in the Greek province of Ionia. To identify the basic principles around which the nature is organized, they studied many varied natural phenomena, from planets to plants.

In the second phase of pre-Socratic thought, Ionian philosophy became more metaphysical. Pythagoras (570–497 B.C.) taught that the soul is immortal and that it transmigrates even into the bodies of animals. He formed a school to teach people how to live in accordance with his semimystical views. Around 500 B.C., Heraclitus wrote a series of caustic and mystical aphorisms that express an intriguing metaphysics based on change and the duality of opposites.

In the third phase, Parmenides and his followers argued forcefully that the very idea of a science of nature was an error. These thinkers from Elea, the Eleatics, argued that there could not be a plurality of things. Parmenides wrote a poem arguing for the existence of a single, indivisible, changeless thing. Zeno supported this position with many arguments, including his famous so-called paradoxes. The works of Parmenides and Zeno constitute a fundamental objection to pre-Socratic naturalistic thought.

The fourth phase consists in various responses to Parmenides and in attempts to continue with the Milesian or Ionian tradition of natural philosophy. The main authors of this period are Empedocles, Anaxagoras, and Democritus. For example, Empedocles agreed with Parmenides that nothing can come into or go out of existence, but he argued that the eternal stuff of the universe, the four elements (earth, air, fire, and water), could change and intermingle. Democritus argued for the existence of indivisible atoms.

In the fifth phase, the Sophists embraced relativism and skepticism, and rejected the project of discovering truths about nature, substituting for it the aim of teaching the art of persuasion. In so doing, they set philosophy a fundamental challenge: 'Are there truths that can be discovered by reasoning?' The replies of Socrates and Plato to this question constitute Section II of this volume.

The Texts

The original works of the pre-Socratic philosophers have been lost. Our knowledge of their thought is based entirely on later reports, quotations, and commentaries. This means that the reliability of these sources is questionable and often disputed.

The Greek philosopher Aristotle (384–322 B.C.) discussed the views of many of the pre-Socratic thinkers, and so his writings are an important source of information, even though his interpretations may reflect his own reading of the development of thought. Aristotle's pupil, Theophrastus (371–287 B.C.), wrote a work called *On the Senses*, which discusses the views of several pre-Socratic philosophers. Plutarch (45–120 A.D.) wrote papers and treatises about history, biography, literature, and philosophy that contain quotations from the pre-Socratics. In the third century A.D., Diogenes Laertius wrote a work called the *Lives of the Philosophers*, which has survived and which is a valuable source of information about the pre-Socratics, even though some of its stories are probably false. Another very important source of many of the original texts is Simplicius' commentary on Aristotle's *Physics*, written in 530 A.D.

The fragments of the pre-Socratic philosophers, which were scattered in many later writings, were collected by Hermann Diels and Walther Kranz toward the end of the nineteenth century. His work, *Fragmente der Vorsokratiker*, was translated into English by Kathleen Freeman and published as *Ancilla to the Presocratic Philosophers*. The B numbers cited after each fragment refer to this text. However, there are later and better translations from the original Greek, which we have used in this collection. Also, the *Ancilla* does not contain the commentaries of later ancient thinkers, which are sometimes also useful.

There are considerable and unavoidable problems when translating these ancient texts. First, abstract terms such as '*logos*' have significantly different senses in different contexts. '*Logos*' can mean 'reason,' 'rational principle,' 'causal law,' or 'organizing idea' in different texts. Second, none of our English equivalent terms may capture well the nuances and ambiguities that the original Greek word may have had for an ancient reader. For example, '*logos*' has a connotation of the divine or godly that none of the earlier mentioned English words have. Third, additionally, all words come with a history of usage, and many of our English philosophical terms have a Christian ancestry. For this reason, it is not exactly correct to translate the Greek term '*psuché*' with the English 'soul,' or '*àreté*' with 'virtue.' For these reasons, readers should be careful in attributing contemporary meanings to the texts.

THE MILESIANS
PROLOGUE

Our first three philosophers come from the town of Miletus, a city in the Greek province of Ionia, located on what is now the western coast of Turkey. Sometimes, these philosophers are also called the Ionians. Miletus was a wealthy seaport, a focal point for commercial activity, and partly because of this, there was increased leisure time that permitted thought, discussion, and art. Miletus became a cultural center.

THALES (APPROX. 624–545 B.C.)
Biographical History

We do not know much about the life of Thales, and nothing of his work remains, if indeed he wrote, except fragments reported by later writers, such as Aristotle and Herodotus, the fifth century A.D. historian. However, he was named as one of the seven sages of the early ancient Greeks, and he was known not only as a philosopher and scientist, but also as a political advisor. He urged the Ionians to establish a single council located at the center of the province. During the Persian War, when the army of Croesus could not cross the River Halys, Thales ordered the digging of a channel and dam that diverted the river so that it was fordable. He was also an astronomer who allegedly predicted an eclipse of 585 B.C., as well as discovering some of the first theorems of geometry (such as that in every isosceles triangle, the angles at the base are equal). Reportedly he once fell in a ditch when looking at the stars. The woman he was with exclaimed, "Do you think, Thales, that you will learn what is in the heavens, when you cannot see what is in front of your feet?" In contrast, it is claimed that he wanted to show that it is easy for a philosopher to become rich: he foresaw a good early olive crop, and hired all the olive presses, which he rented out at great profit.

Philosophical Overview

Thales is famous for claiming that all things are made of water. Although this may sound like a ludicrous statement to us today, nevertheless it is important because Thales conjectured about the nature of the substance-stuff out of which everything is made. He introduced the idea of the fundamental composition of the world, and thereby launched one of humanity's great debates. In so doing, he saw that proposing the idea of one fundamental substance-kind would be the simplest way to explain all natural phenomena. The claim that there exists such stuff is potentially the most powerful and most economical way to systematically explain nature. Moreover, as far as historical sources allow us to tell, it seems that Thales advanced an argument for his position. He claimed that water is essential to life.

Thales is also well known for claiming that all things have a soul. His argument for this claim is that magnets can move iron and that anything that is capable of initiating movement is thereby animate. By definition, anything that is animate has a soul. The Greek word *psuché* (soul) comes from the word *empsuchos,* which means 'animate.' When reflecting on this thesis, we should not impose the Christian conception of the soul as a conscious spiritual substance on Thales. His idea is more that all things are to some degree animate and that, therefore, there is no strict dividing line between what is alive and what is not.

FRAGMENTS
Thales

As the selection shows, the most important fragments concerning the philosophy of Thales come from Aristotle, who lived some 250 years later. The wording of the first fragment, which is from Aristotle's *Metaphysics,* reveals how Aristotle reviews the thoughts of the early pre-Socratics in order to draw lessons for his own philosophy.

1.

Most of the first philosophers thought that principles in the form of matter were the only principles of all things. For they say that the element and first principle of the things that exist is that from which they all are and from which they first come into being and into which they are finally destroyed, its substance remaining and its properties changing. . . . There must be some nature—either one or more than one—from which the other things come into being, it being

---

Thales, from *Early Greek Philosophy,* translated by Jonathan Barnes, (Penguin Classics, Harmondsworth, 1987). Copyright © Jonathan Barnes, 1987. Reproduced by permission of Penguin Books Ltd.

preserved. But as to the number and form of this sort of principle, they do not all agree. Thales, the founder of this kind of philosophy, says that it is water (that is why he declares that the earth rests on water). He perhaps came to acquire this belief from seeing that the nourishment of everything is moist and that heat itself comes from this and lives by this (for that from which anything comes into being is its first principle)—he came to his belief both for this reason and because the seeds of everything have a moist nature, and water is the natural principle of moist things.

(Aristotle, *Metaphysics* 983b6–11, 17–27)

2.

Some say that [the earth] rests on water. This in fact is the oldest view that has been transmitted to us, and they say that it was advanced by Thales of Miletus who thought that the earth rests because it can float like a log or something else of that sort (for none of these things can rest on air, but they can rest on water)—as though the same must not hold of the water supporting the earth as holds of the earth itself.

(Aristotle, *On the Heavens* 294a28–34)

3.

He supposed that water was the first principle of all things, and that the world has a soul and is full of spirits. They say he discovered the seasons of the year and divided it into three hundred and sixty-five days.

Diogenes Laertius, *Lives of the Philosophers*, I 22–28, 33–40

4.

Some say that <soul> is mixed in the whole universe. Perhaps that is why Thales thought that everything was full of gods.

(Aristotle, *On the Soul* 411a7–8)

Thales, judging by what they report, seems to have believed that the soul was something which pro-duces motion, inasmuch as he said that the magnet has a soul because it moves iron.

(*ibid* 405a19–21)

5.

Aristotle and Hippias say that he ascribed souls to lifeless things too, taking the magnet and amber as his evidence.

(Diogenes Laertius, *Lives of the Philosophers*, I 22–28, 33–40)

6.

The following aphorisms are ascribed to him. Of existing things, god is the oldest—for he is ungenerated. The world is the most beautiful—for it is god's creation. Space is the greatest—for it includes everything. Mind is the swiftest—for it runs through everything. Necessity is the strongest—for it controls everything. Time is the wisest—for it discovers everything. He said that death is no different from life. 'Then why don't *you* die?' someone asked him. 'Because it makes no difference,' he replied. When someone asked him which came first, day or night, he answered, 'Night came first—by a day.' When someone asked him whether a man can escape the notice of the gods if he does wrong, he replied: 'Not even if he *thinks* of doing wrong.' An adulterer asked him if he should swear that he had not committed adultery: he replied, 'Perjury is no worse than adultery.' When asked what is difficult, he said, 'To know yourself'; what is easy, 'To give advice to someone else'; what most pleasant, 'Success'; what divine, 'What has neither beginning nor end'. When asked what was the strangest thing he had seen, he said: 'An old tyrant'. How can we bear misfortune most easily?—If we see our enemies faring worse. How can we live best and most justly?—If we do not ourselves do the things we blame others for doing. Who is happy?—One who has a healthy body, a well-stocked soul, and an educable nature.

Diogenes Laertius, *Lives of the Philosophers*, I 22–28, 33–40

STUDY QUESTIONS: THALES, FRAGMENTS

1. What does Thales mean by claiming that everything is made of water?
2. What does Thales mean by 'first principle'?
3. What is Thales' view of the soul?
4. Why is Thales considered to be a philosopher?

ANAXIMANDER (610–540 B.C.)

Biographical History

Anaximander was reportedly a student of Thales. He wrote an ambitious, wide-ranging work called *On Nature*, which included a cosmology; a natural history of the earth; a description of many kinds of natural phenomena, such as rain and wind; an account of the development of animals; and a geography, including a famous map of the world. Unfortunately, only a few sentences of this work have survived.

Philosophical Overview

Anaximander claimed that the fundamental constituent of the universe is something infinite or without limits. This is usually taken to mean something spatially infinite, eternal, and without determinate qualities, or something infinitely old and large and without definite properties. Anaximander probably held these views based on reasoning similar to that outlined below.

If the basic constituent of nature is something indefinite, as Anaximander argues, then it cannot be any of the four traditional elements: earth, water, air, and fire. Since these elements can change into one another, they cannot be basic. Furthermore, Anaximander also argued that the four elements have opposing qualities; for example, air is cold and fire is hot. If any one of these elements were unlimited, then it would have destroyed the others. Since none of the elements have been destroyed, we may conclude that the basic constituent of the universe is not one of these elements.

1. *The basic substance-stuff must be infinitely old.*
2. *If the basic substance-stuff were one of the elements, then it would have destroyed the other elements in an infinite amount of time.*
3. *All four elements can be observed to exist.*

---

4. *Therefore, the basic substance-stuff is not one of the elements.*

Anaximander is also famous for his ingenious explanation of the fact that the earth hangs in empty space without physical support and yet does not move. He argued that if the earth is midway between all other things, then there can be no reason for it to move one way rather than another. Consequently, if the earth is the center of the universe, then it must stay where it is. To give an idea of the range of his interests, we have also included passages that show Anaximander's account of the origin of species.

FRAGMENTS

Anaximander

The first selection outlines the basic points of Anaximander's philosophy. In the second selection, which is from Aristotle's *Physics*, we find Anaximander's argument for the need of an infinite first principle:

1. *Everything must either come from a first principle or itself be such a principle.*

2. *The unlimited cannot be derived from a principle, for then it would be limited by that principle.*

---

3. *Therefore, the unlimited itself must be a principle from which other things are derived.*

As the third selection (also from Aristotle) indicates, Anaximander probably also argued that the primordial substance-stuff of the universe is infinite in age because change is perpetual, and all change is the alteration of some preexisting substance.

The fourth fragment, which is quoted from Simplicius, is probably very close to Anaximander's original text, in which case it is the earliest surviving piece of written western philosophy. It gives an argument based on the premise that the basic stuff of the universe must underlie all changes. Since all of the so-called elements (earth, water, air, and fire) can change one into the other, none of them can be the basic substance of the universe.

1. *The basic substance-stuff underlies all change, and, therefore, it cannot change into something else.*
2. *The elements do change into the others.*

---

3. *Therefore, the basic substance-stuff of the universe is not one of the elements.*

1.

He said that a certain infinite nature is first principle of the things that exist. From it come the heavens and the worlds in them. It is eternal and ageless, and it contains all the worlds. He speaks of time, since generation and existence and destruction are determinate.

Anaximander said that the infinite is principle and element of the things that exist, being the first to call it by the name of principle. In addition, there is an eternal motion in which the heavens come into being.

Hippolytus, *Refutation of All Heresies* I vi 1–7

2.

It is with reason that they all make [the infinite] a principle; for it can neither exist to no purpose nor have any power except that of a principle. For everything is either a principle or derived from a principle. But the infinite has no principle—for then it would have a limit. Again, it is ungenerated and indestructible and so is a principle. For what comes into being must have an end, and there is an end to every destruction. Hence, as I say, it has no principle but itself is thought to be a principle for everything else and to govern everything. . . . And it is also the divine; for it is deathless and unperishing, as Anaximander and most of the natural scientists say.

(Aristotle, *Physics* 203b6–11)

3.

[A]gain, because generation and destruction will give out unless there is something infinite from which what comes into being is subtracted.

(Aristotle, *Physics* 203b6–11, 13–30)

4.

Of those who hold that the first principle is one, moving, and infinite, Anaximander, son of Praxiades, a Milesian, who was a successor and pupil of Thales, said that the infinite is principle and element of the things that exist. He was the first to introduce this word 'principle'. He says that it is neither water nor any other of the so-called elements but some different infinite nature, from which all the heavens and the worlds in them come into being. And the things from which existing things come into being are also the things into which they are destroyed, in accordance with what must be. For *they give justice and reparation to one another for their injustice in accordance with the arrangement of time* [12 B 1] (he speaks of them in this way in somewhat poetical words). It is clear that he observed the change of the four elements into one another and was unwilling to make any one of them the underlying stuff but rather chose something else apart from them. He accounts for coming into being not by the alteration of the

---

element but by the separating off of the opposites by the eternal motion.

(Simplicius, *Commentary on the Physics* 24.13–25)

5.

Anaximander, an associate of Thales, says that the infinite is the universal cause of the generation and destruction of the universe. From it, he says, the heavens were separated off and in general all the worlds, infinite in number. He asserted that destruction and, much earlier, generation occur from time immemorial, all the same things being renewed.

(Plutarch, *Miscellanies* fragment 179.2, in Eusebius, *Preparation for the Gospel*, I vii 16)

6.

The earth is aloft, not supported by anything but resting where it is because of its equal distance from everything.

(Hippolytus, *Refutation of All Heresies* I vi 1–7)

7.

Some say that [the earth] rests where it is because of the similarity (so, among the ancients, Anaximander). For there is no reason why what is situated in the middle and is similarly related to the edges should move upwards rather than downwards or sideways.

But it cannot move in opposite directions at the same time. So it necessarily rests where it is.

(Aristotle, *On the Heavens* 295b11–16)

8.

Anaximander says that the first animals were born in moisture, surrounded by prickly barks. As they grew older they emerged on to drier parts, the bark burst, and for a short time they lived a different kind of life.

([Plutarch], *On the Scientific Beliefs of the Philosophers* 908D)

9.

Animals come into being <from moisture> evaporated by the sun. Humans originally resembled another type of animal, namely fish.

(Hippolytus, *Refutation of All Heresies* I vi 1–7)

10.

Further, he says that originally humans were born from animals of a different kind, because the other animals can soon look after themselves while humans alone require a long period of nursing; that is why if they had been like this originally they would not have survived.

([Plutarch], *Miscellanies* fragment 179.2, in Eusebius, *Preparation for the Gospel* I vii 16)

STUDY QUESTIONS: ANAXIMANDER, FRAGMENTS

1. What is the first principle, according to Anaximander?
2. What is Anaximander's argument for claiming that the first principle must be infinite?
3. What prevents generation and destruction from 'giving out'?
4. What are Anaximander's two arguments for thinking that the first principle cannot be one of the four elements?
5. According to Anaximander, why does the earth float in space?
6. How does Anaximander account for animals coming into being?
7. What would Anaximander say about the principle of the conservation of energy?

ANAXIMENES (585–528 B.C.)

Biographical History

Anaximenes may have been a student of Anaximander. Apart from the fact that he was Milesian, very little else is known about his life.

Philosophical Overview

Like his two predecessors from Miletus, Anaximenes proposed that there is a single substance-stuff out of which everything is made. Anaximenes thought that Anaximander's views were not explicit enough in two crucial ways. First, Anaximenes claimed that the elemental substance-stuff is unlimited air. In other words, he substituted his teacher's indeterminate substance for something determinate and gaseous. Second, Anaximenes was more explicit than his predecessors concerning the processes through which ordinary things are generated from the one material principle; these are condensation and rarefaction. Through compression, air thickens and progressively becomes clouds, water, and earth. Through expansion, air becomes thinner and turns into fire. This view implies that the different properties of the things we observe (such as liquids and solids) are due to differences in their relative density.

FRAGMENTS

Anaximenes

The first selection describes the processes of condensation and compression by which all natural objects are formed out of invisible air, and how in this process hot and cold come into being. This first point is reinforced in the fourth fragment, and the last point (regarding hot and cold) is reinforced in the third one.

    The second fragment is important in part because of the claim that the soul is air and because of the parallel that it draws between air and breath. Anaximenes thought that air was the basic stuff of nature because it is the constituent of the soul.

1.

Anaximenes, son of Eurystratus, was also Milesian. He said that the first principle is infinite air, from which what is coming into being and what has come into being and what will exist and gods and divinities come into being, while everything else comes into being from its offspring. The form of the air is this: when it is most uniform it is invisible, but it is made apparent by the hot and the cold and the moist and the moving. It is always in motion; for the things that change would not change if it were not in motion. For as it is condensed and rarefied it appears different: when it dissolves into a more rarefied condition it becomes fire; and winds, again, are condensed air, and cloud is produced from air by compression. Again, when it is more condensed it is water, when still further condensed it is earth, and when it is as dense as possible it is stones. Thus the most important factors in coming into being are opposites—hot and cold.

(Hippolytus, *Refutation of All Heresies* I vii 1–9)

2.

Anaximenes, son of Eurystratus, a Milesian, asserted that air is the first principle of the things that exist; for everything comes into being from air and is resolved again into it. For example, *our souls*, he says, *being air, hold us together, and breath and air contain the whole world* ('air' and 'breath' are used synonymously). [B 2]

([Plutarch], *On the Scientific Beliefs of the Philosophers* 876 A B)

3.

Or should we, as old Anaximenes thought, treat the hot and the cold not as substances but rather as common properties of matter which supervene upon changes? For he says that matter which is concentrated and condensed is cold, while that which is rare and *slack* (that is the word he uses) is hot. [13 B 1]

(Plutarch, *The Primary Cold* 947F)

4.

Winds are generated when the air is condensed and driven along. As it collects together and is further thickened, clouds are generated and in this way it changes into water. Hail comes about when the water falling from the clouds solidifies, and snow when these same things solidify in a more watery form.

(Hippolytus, *Refutation of All Heresies* I vii 1–9)

STUDY QUESTIONS: ANAXIMENES, FRAGMENTS

1. What is the first principle, according to Anaximenes?
2. According to Anaximenes, what is the form of air?
3. Why does Anaximenes refuse to treat hot and cold as substances?
4. According to Anaximenes, how does air change into stones? What is the opposite process?
5. According to Anaximenes, what is the soul?
6. Are the Milesians scientists? How should one distinguish between science and philosophy?
7. Which of the Milesians has the most plausible view? Why is this?

Philosophical Bridges: The Milesian Influence

The Milesians introduced the fundamental concept of the substance-kind or -stuff out of which everything is composed, as well as the claim that all natural phenomena should be explained in terms of alterations to that substance. They were the first to take a systematic and unified approach to the explanation of natural phenomena. Much of later ancient philosophy, such as the influential atomism of Democritus and Epicurus, continued in this same tradition. Much of the rest of ancient thought, such as Plato's theory of Forms, can be considered in part as a reaction against the Milesian-inspired tradition of natural philosophy.

The revolution in thought that occurred during the sixteenth century, which gave birth to modern science, was inspired directly by the rediscovery of ancient thinkers. Toward the end of the medieval period and in the early Renaissance, ancient philosophers had considerable influence. The fact that some of the ancient Greeks had argued for materialistic scientific theories, including atomism, was profoundly liberating for the early scientists and scientific philosophers, such as Galileo Galilei and Francis Bacon. In this way, the Milesians were the forerunners of sixteenth- and seventeenth-century natural philosophy and, hence, of contemporary science. For example, the contemporary principle of the conservation of matter and energy has its roots in the Milesian tradition. You can see the idea passing on from Thales and Anaximander to the Epicureans and Stoics, and from them to modern scientific thinkers such as René Descartes and Galileo. In *The Critique of Pure Reason* (1781), Immanuel Kant argues explicitly for the Milesian claim that substance cannot be created or destroyed because all changes must be conceived as alterations to a single underlying substance or stuff. His argument of the First Analogy contends that this claim is a precondition of the unity of time and hence of all knowledge.

The Milesians were also the precursors of scientific enquiry because of the broad scope of their interest in nature. They initiated a long tradition that examined and tried to explain a wide range of natural phenomena, from stars to mountains and from plants to animals, as well as the tides, the wind, and the rain, in a unified and systematic manner. This tradition continued in the ancient period until *On the Nature of Things* by the great Roman poet Lucretius (99–55 B.C.). However, we can also see Descartes' book *The World* (1633) as a continuation of the same tradition because it seeks a unified account of all natural material phenomena, such as fire, light, the movements of the planets, the tides, and human physiology.

THE IONIANS

PROLOGUE

Although the next two philosophers are considered as Ionian in terms of their birth and tradition, their thought is significantly different from that of the earlier Milesians. The philosophies of Pythagoras and Heraclitus go beyond the scientific philosophy of nature of the Milesians because they both are also concerned with metaphysics and, to some extent, with ethics.

PYTHAGORAS (570–497 B.C.)

Biographical History

Pythagoras was born on the island of Samos in the eastern Aegean, located between Miletus and Athens. Around the age of 30, he moved to Croton in southern Italy, where he established a community of followers. The community grew and acquired political importance in the region. As a consequence of this, after about 20 years, there was an uprising against the Pythagoreans.

Pythagoras wrote nothing, but his later followers wrote much, attributing to him many views. It is from his followers that we have the picture of Pythagoras as a brilliant mathematician, who invented the theorem that, in any right-angled triangle, the square of the hypotenuse is equal to the sum of the square of the other two sides. He was portrayed as applying his mathematics to music and astronomy and, thereby, developing a metaphysical system based on numbers. However, it is difficult to define exactly what Pythagoras himself thought because the later Pythagorean schools tend to attribute to the master their own teachings. By the fourth century A.D., Pythagoras was considered the greatest of all philosophers, eclipsing even Plato and Aristotle because of his influence on both of these thinkers. As we shall see, Pythagoras had an especially important influence on Plato.

Philosophical Overview

After his death, his disciples split into two groups: the *mathematikoi* and the *akousmatikoi*. The first group was interested in the study of mathematics, music, and astronomy. The key to their ideas is that the universe consists of a harmony that should be studied mathematically. In this, they rejected the Ionian idea of trying to discover the basic stuff of the universe, replacing it with the study of form. In this study, the numerical ratios between sounds in the musical scales provided an analogy for the harmonious development of the whole universe. In other words, according to this group, we can understand the universe by knowing the numerical relations that express the harmonic ratios according to which everything changes.

The second Pythagorean School was called the *akousmatikoi*, and it followed Pythagoras' religious teaching concerning the soul and the right way to live. They regarded Pythagoras as a spiritual master who taught about the existence of the immortal soul that may be reborn in animal form. This doctrine of transmigration has two important implications. First, it implies that personal identity is constituted by the soul. A person literally is his or her soul. Second, it laid down some guidelines for the moral way of life or for a moral code. Pythagoras' doctrine of the soul means that we are not mortal beings but rather immortal souls, and that we are not really at home in our bodies. It also means that the animals are our kin, and, for this reason, the Pythagoreans considered the eating of flesh as a form of cannibalism. Pythagoras probably conceived of the world as divided into good and evil, and claimed that each person must struggle to be a good moral agent.

FRAGMENTS
Pythagoras

The first four passages quoted below are fragments from Philolaus, born in Croton around 470 B.C., who was the first Pythagorean to set down the teaching in writing. The other fragments are called the testimonies, which are later in origin. The religious aspect of Pythagoras' following is emphasized in selections 5–11. In contrast, the selections numbered 12–17 emphasize the Pythagorean conception of number as the fundamental harmony of the universe.

1.

(DK 44B14) The ancient theologians and prophets testify to the fact that the soul has been yoked to the body as a punishment of some kind and that it has been buried in the body as in a tomb.

(Philolaus [fr. 14 Diels/Kranz] in Clement, *Miscellanies* 2.203.11 Stählin/Früchtel)

2.

(DK 44B1; KRS 424) Nature in the universe was harmonized out of both things which are unlimited and things which limit; this applies to the universe as a whole and to all its components.

(Philolaus [fr. 1 Diels/Kranz] in Diogenes Laertius, *Lives of Eminent Philosophers* 8.85.13–14 Long)

3.

(DK 44B4; KRS 427) And everything which is known has number, because otherwise it is impossible for anything to be the object of thought or knowledge.

(Philolaus [fr. 4 Diels/Kranz] in John of Stobi, *Anthology* 1.21.7b Wachsmuth/Hense)

4.

(DK 44B6; KRS 429) On the subject of nature and harmony, this is how things stand: the being of things, *qua* eternal, and nature itself are accessible only to divine and not human knowledge—except that it is impossible for any of the things that exist and are known by us to have arisen without the prior existence of the being of the things out of which the universe is composed, namely limiters and unlimiteds. Now, since these sources existed in all their dissimilarity and incompatibility, it would have been impossible for them to have been made into an orderly universe unless harmony had been present in some form or other. Things that were similar and compatible had no need of harmony, but things that were dissimilar and incompatible and incommensurate had to be connected by this kind of harmony, if they are to persist in an ordered universe.

(Philolaus [fr. 6 Diels/Kranz] in John of Stobi,
Anthology 1.21.7d Wachsmuth/Hense)

5.

(DK 14A1; KRS 261) The Egyptians were also the first to claim that the soul of a human being is immortal, and that each time the body dies the soul enters another creature just as it is being born. They also say that when the soul has made the round of every creature on land, in the sea, and in the air, it once more clothes itself in the body of a human being just as it is being born, and that a complete cycle takes three thousand years. This theory has been adopted by certain Greeks too—some from a long time ago, some more recently—who presented it as if it were their own. I know their names, but I will not write them down.

(Herodotus, *Histories* 2.123.2–3 Hude)

6.

(DK 58B39) They [*Aristotle's predecessors*] try only to describe the soul, but they fail to go into any kind of detail about the body which is to receive the soul, as if it were possible (as it is in the Pythagorean tales) for just any old soul to be clothed in just any old body.

(Aristotle, *On the Soul* 407ᵇ20–3 Ross)

7.

(DK 14A8) Heraclides of Pontus says that Pythagoras used to say about himself that he had once been born as Aethalides and was regarded as a son of Hermes. Hermes told him that he could choose anything he wanted except immortality, and he asked to be able to retain, both alive and dead, the memory of things that had happened. He therefore remembered everything during his lifetimes, and when dead he still preserved the same memories. Later he entered into Euphorbus and was wounded by Menelaus. Euphorbus used to say that he had formerly been born as Aethalides and had received the gift from Hermes, and used to tell of the journeying of his soul and all its migrations, recount all the plants and creatures to which it had belonged, and describe everything he had experienced in Hades and the experiences undergone by the rest of the souls there. When Euphorbus died, his soul moved into Hermotimus, who also wanted to prove the point, so he went to Branchidae, entered the sanctuary of Apollo, and pointed out the shield which Menelaus had dedicated there. . . . When Hermotimus died, he became Pyrrhus, the fisherman from Delos, and again remembered everything, how he had formerly been Aethalides, then Euphorbus, then Hermotimus, and then Pyrrhus. And when Pyrrhus died, he became Pythagoras and remembered everything that has just been mentioned.

(Heraclides of Pontus [fr. 89 Wehrli] in Diogenes Laertius,
Lives of Eminent Philosophers 8.4–5 Long)

8.

(DK 58C3; KRS 275) In *On the Pythagoreans* Aristotle explains the Pythagorean injunction *to abstain from beans* as being due either to the fact that they resemble the genitals in shape, or because they resemble the gates of Hades (since it is the only plant which has no joints), or because they ruin the constitution, or because they resemble the nature of the universe, or because they are oligarchic, in the sense that they are used in the election of magistrates by lot. And the injunction *not to pick up things that have fallen* he explains as being an attempt to accustom them not to eat in immoderate quantities, or due to the fact that it signals someone's death. . . . The injunction *not to touch a white cock* is due to the fact that the creature is sacred to the New Month and is a suppliant. . . . The injunction *not to touch any sacred fish* is due to the fact that the same food should not be served to gods and men, just as free men and slaves should have different food too. The injunction *not to break a loaf* is due to the fact that in olden days friends used to meet over a single loaf.

(Aristotle [fr. 195 Rose] in Diogenes Laertius, *Lives of Eminent Philosophers* 8.34.1–35.2 Long)

9.

(KRS 434) Anticleides says that Pythagoras was particularly interested in the arithmetical aspect of geometry, and discovered the properties of the monochord. Nor did he neglect medicine either. Apollodorus the mathematician says that Pythagoras sacrificed a hecatomb when he discovered that the square on the hypotenuse of the right-angled triangle is equal to the squares on the sides which encompass the right angle.

(Anticleides [fr. 1 Jacoby] in Diogenes Laertius, *Lives of Eminent Philosophers* 8.11.10–12.5 Long)

10.

In his *Introduction to Music* Heraclides says that, according to Xenocrates, it was Pythagoras who discovered that the musical intervals also come about inevitably because of number, in the sense that they consist in a comparison of one quantity with another, and that he also looked into the question of what makes the intervals concordant or discordant, and in general what factors are responsible for harmony and disharmony.

(Xenocrates [fr. 9 Heinze] in Porphyry, *Commentary on Ptolemy's 'Harmonics'* 30.1–6 Düring)

11.

(DK 14A4) Pythagoras of Samos visited Egypt and studied with the Egyptians. He was the first to import philosophy in general into Greece, and he was especially concerned, more conspicuously than anyone else, with sacrifice and ritual purification in sanctuaries, since he thought that even if, as a result of these practices, no advantage accrued to him from the gods, they would at least gain him a particularly fine reputation among men. And this is exactly what happened. He became so much more famous than anyone else that all the young men wanted to become his disciples, while the older men preferred to see their sons associating with him than looking after their own affairs. And it is impossible to mistrust their opinion, because even now those who claim to be his followers are more impressive in their silence than those with the greatest reputation for eloquence.

(Isocrates, *Busiris* 28.5–29.9 van Hook)

12.

(KRS 279) In order to indicate this [*the importance of number in things*] the Pythagoreans are accustomed on occasion to say that 'There is a resemblance to number in all things', and also on occasion to swear their most characteristic oath: 'No, by him who handed down to our company the *tetraktys*, the fount which holds the roots of ever-flowing nature.' By 'him who handed down' they mean Pythagoras, whom they regarded as divine, and by the '*tetraktys*' they mean a certain number which, being composed out of the first four numbers, produces the most perfect number—that is, ten (for $1 + 2 + 3 + 4 = 10$). This number is the first *tetraktys* and it is called 'the fount of ever-flowing nature' because it is their view that the whole universe is organized on harmonic principles, and harmony is a system of three concords (the fourth, the fifth, and the octave), and the ratios of these three concords are found in the four numbers I have already mentioned—that is, in 1, 2, 3, and 4. For the fourth is constituted by 4 : 3, the fifth by 3 : 2, and the octave by 2 : 1.

(Sextus Empiricus, *Against the Professors* 7.94–6 Bury)

13.

(DK 58B4, B5; KRS 430) At the same time [*as Leucippus and Democritus*] and earlier than them were the so-called Pythagoreans, who were interested in mathematics. They were the first to make mathematics prominent, and because this discipline constituted their education they thought that its principles were the principles of all things. Now, in the nature of things, numbers are the primary mathematical principles; they also imagined that they could perceive in numbers many analogues to things that are and that come into being (more analogues than fire and earth and water reveal)—such-and-such an attribute of numbers being justice, such-and-such an attribute being soul and mind, due season another, and so on for pretty well everything else; moreover, they saw that the attributes and ratios of harmonies depend on numbers. Since, then, the whole natural world seemed basically to be an analogue of numbers, and numbers seemed to be the primary facet of the natural world, they concluded that the elements of numbers are the elements of all things, and that the whole universe is harmony and number. They collected together all the properties of numbers and harmonies which were arguably conformable to the attributes and parts of the universe, and to its organization as a whole, and fitted them into place; and the existence of any gaps only made them long for the whole thing to form a connected system. Here is an example of what I mean: ten was, to their way of thinking, a perfect number, and one which encompassed the nature of numbers in general, and they said that there were ten bodies moving through the heavens; but since there are only nine visible heavenly bodies, they came up with a tenth, the counter-earth. . . .

They hold that the elements of number are the even and the odd, of which the even is unlimited and the odd limited; one is formed from both even and odd, since it is both even and odd; number is formed from one and, as I have said, numbers constitute the whole universe. Other members of the same school say that there are ten principles, which they arrange in co-ordinate pairs: limit and unlimited; odd and even; unity and multiplicity; right and left; male and female; still and moving; straight and bent; light and darkness; good and bad; square and oblong.

(Aristotle, *Metaphysics* 985ᵇ23–986ᵃ26 Ross)

14.

(DK 58A8) The Pythagoreans spoke of two causes in the same way, but added, as an idiosyncratic feature, that the limited and the unlimited and the one were not separate natures, on a par with fire or earth or something, but the unlimited itself and the one itself were taken to be the substance of the things of which they are predicated. This is why they said that number was the substance of everything.

(Aristotle, *Metaphysics* 987ᵃ13–19 Ross)

15.

The Pythagoreans, as a result of observing that many properties of numbers exist in perceptible bodies, came up with the idea that existing things *are* numbers, but not separate numbers: they said that existing things consist of numbers. Why? Because the properties of numbers exist in musical harmony, in the heavens, and in many other cases.

(Aristotle, *Metaphysics* 1090ᵃ20–5 Ross)

16.

(DK 58B9; KRS 431) The Pythagoreans recognize only one kind of number, mathematical number, but they say that it is not separate, but that perceptible things are made up of it. For they construct the whole universe out of numbers—and not numbers made up of abstract units, but they take their numerical units to have spatial magnitude. But they apparently have no way to explain how the first spatially extended unit was put together.

(Aristotle, *Metaphysics* 1080ᵇ16–21 Ross)

17.

(DK 44A23; KRS 451) There is another theory about the soul that has come down to us, which many people find the most plausible one around. . . . They say that the soul is a kind of attunement (*harmonia*), on the grounds that attunement is a mixture and compound of opposites, and the body is made up of opposites.

(Aristotle, *On the Soul* 407ᵇ27–32 Ross)

STUDY QUESTIONS: PYTHAGORAS, FRAGMENTS

1. From where does harmony in nature originate, according to Pythagoras?
2. What role do the limited and the 'unlimited' play in the Pythagorean notion of numbers?
3. What reasons did the Pythagoreans give for the claim that number was the substance of everything?
4. How did Pythagoras discover the relationship between numbers and musical intervals?
5. When the Pythagoreans say that the unlimited and the one are the substance of things (14), what does this mean?
6. Explain the difference between the two Pythagorean schools.
7. What is the nature of the soul, according to the Pythagoreans?
8. What sort of injunctions did the Pythagoreans live by? Why did their community have such rules?
9. In what ways is Pythagoras' thought different from that of the Milesians? Do these differences tell us anything about the distinctions between science, religion, and philosophy?

10. Why did the Pythagoreans think that ten was the perfect number?
11. Are numbers a feature of things in the way that hot and cold are?

Philosophical Bridges: The Pythagorean Influence

By the fourth century A.D., Pythagoras was considered to be a philosopher of at least equal importance as Plato and Aristotle. First, his idea that the universe has numerical structure and harmony had an enormous impact on the later Plato and the neo-Platonic thinkers of the Roman Empire. Second, his mystical religious views concerning the importance and nature of the soul also influenced Plato. These two strands of Pythagoras' thinking also had a longer-term impact.

1. The rediscovery of Pythagorean ideas during the sixteenth century reignited the claim that the universe is inherently mathematical and harmonious, and, consequently, was vital to the birth of modern science. These ideas were seen as an illuminating and refreshing antidote to the Scholasticism of the middle and later medieval periods. For example, Copernicus (1473–1543) drew inspiration from this Pythagorean and neo-Platonic tradition in formulating his bold hypothesis that the earth orbits the sun. The Ptolemic hypothesis that the sun and planets orbit the earth had become increasingly complex to accommodate new observations, and Copernicus sought an alternative explanation because of his Pythagorean conviction that nature had to be simple. Johannes Kepler's great astronomical work had the Pythagorean title *The Harmony of the World* (1619). Having explained the orbits of the planets in terms of three simple laws, Kepler compared the speed of each orbit to a musical note and likened their combined effect to the music of the spheres in true Pythagorean tradition. Later, Galileo claimed that the universe is written in the language of mathematics. This general idea has support today among realists, who claim that the universe is inherently mathematical.

2. Pythagoras was the first western thinker to articulate clearly the idea of a soul distinct from the body, which found full expression in the works of Plato. Furthermore, like Plato after him, Pythagoras stressed the moral importance of the soul. These Pythagorean ideas became part of western culture because of the later marriage of neo-Platonism and Christianity through the works of Plotinus (205–270) and St. Augustine (354–430) (see the section below, 'Philosophical Bridges: The Platonic Influence').

HERACLITUS (540–480 B.C.)

Biographical History

Heraclitus was born in Ephesus, a town on the western coast of Ionia, between Miletus and Colophon. Heraclitus was of noble birth, but he gave up all of his political opportunities to pursue philosophy. He wrote his main philosophical work in about 500 B.C. Of this, over 120 fragments remain. These sayings are culled from other later writers, such as Sextus Empiricus, who quote Heraclitus. This means that we do not know the order of the short sayings of Heraclitus, except for the first two, which occurred near the beginning of the book. Of course, this order affects the interpretation of his philosophy, and consequently it is a contentious issue among scholars.

Philosophical Overview

Heraclitus was a polemical and enigmatic thinker, who was scornful of the popular beliefs of the many and who rejected the authorities of the time. He wrote in a playful, poetic style, sometimes using apparently paradoxical sentences and, at other times, employing memorable aphorisms. This, coupled with his rebellious attitude, makes Heraclitus a source of inspiration for many diverse later writers.

Heraclitus' philosophy ranges over many topics, including the nature of knowledge, theology, and ethics. However, the most influential aspect of his work is his philosophy of nature, which has three main features. First, he famously claims that everything is in flux, even when the change is imperceptible. Whether this implies that we should conceive of the universe as a process rather than as consisting of things or entities is a debatable point.

Second, Heraclitus affirms a doctrine of the unity of opposites, according to which everything is necessarily characterized by both of two opposing features, such as, 'The way up and down is one and the same' (B60). According to Heraclitus, this unity of opposites is a fundamental pattern of the universe. It is in these terms that we should understand the cosmos as a process.

Third, Heraclitus asserts a monism, according to which the underlying nature of the universe is fire. However, if Heraclitus means to assert that there are no permanent entities because everything is in flux, then it may be incorrect to think of fire as a permanent underlying substance out of which everything is composed. In such a case, Heraclitus' view would be probably that the cosmos is a process, rather than a static substance. The process would be one of burning and quenching, of heating up and cooling. It would be in this sense that everything is fire.

FRAGMENTS

Heraclitus

The first fragment quoted below claims that everything happens in accordance with a general law of nature (the Greek word is *logos*). The first set of fragments, up to selection 33, stresses the hidden or esoteric nature of real knowledge. From 34 to roughly 44, the fragments indicate Heraclitus' understanding of this general law of nature and his views on fire. Selections 38–51 state his views on change. The grouping from 34 to 52 form the basis of Heraclitus' natural philosophy. It is important for the reader to remember that the fragments do not come in any preordained order. They are grouped together by the translator and therefore reflect his interpretation.

The Art and Thought of Heraclitus: A New Arrangement and Translation of the Fragments by Charles H. Kahn. Reprinted with the permission of Cambridge University Press.

1.

Although this account holds forever, men ever fail to comprehend, both before hearing it and once they have heard. Although all things come to pass in accordance with this account, men are like the untried when they try such words and works as I set forth, distinguishing each according to its nature and telling how it is. But other men are oblivious of what they do awake, just as they are forgetful of what they do asleep.

(D. 1, M. 1) Sextus Empiricus,
Adversus Mathematicos VII.132

2.

Not comprehending, they hear like the deaf. The saying is their witness: absent while present.

(D. 34, M. 2) Clement, *Stromateis* V.115.3

3.

Although the account is shared, most men live as though their thinking were a private possession.

(D. 2, M. 23b) Sextus Empiricus,
Adversus Mathematicos VIII.133

4.

Most men do not think things in the way they encounter them, nor do they recognize what they experience, but believe their own opinions.

IV (D. 17, M. 3) Clement, *Stromateis* II.8.1.

5.

[[Men forget where the way leads. . . . And they are at odds with that with which they most constantly associate. And what they meet with every day seems strange to them. . . . We should not act and speak like men asleep.]]

(D. 71–3, M. 69b¹, 4, 3c, 1h¹) Marcus Aurelius IV.46

6.

[[The world of the waking is one and shared, but the sleeping turn aside each into his private world.]]

(D. 89, M. 24) Plutarch, *De Superstitione* 166C

7.

He who does not expect will not find out the unexpected, for it is trackless and unexplored.

(D. 18, M. 11) Clement, *Stromateis* II.17.4

8.

Seekers of gold dig up much earth and find little.

(D. 22, M. 10) Clement, *Stromateis* IV.4.2

9.

Men who love wisdom must be good inquirers into many things indeed.

(D. 35, M. 7) Clement, *Stromateis* V.140.5

10.

Nature loves to hide.

(D. 123, M. 8) Philo, Themistius, etc.

11.

Let us not concur casually about the most important matters.

XI (D. 47, M. 113) Diogenes Laertius IX.73

12.

In taking the poets as testimony for things unknown, they are citing authorities that cannot be trusted.

(D. A23, M. 6a¹) Polybius IV.40.2

13.

We should not listen like children to their parents.

(D. 74, M. 89) Marcus Aurelius IV.46 (following citation V above)

14.

Whatever comes from sight, hearing, learning from experience: this I prefer.

(D. 55, M. 5) Hippolytus, *Refutatio* IX.9.5

15.

Eyes are surer witnesses than ears.

(D. 101a, M. 6) Polybius XII.27.1

16.

Eyes and ears are poor witnesses for men if their souls do not understand the language.

(D. 107, M. 13) Sextus Empiricus,
Adversus Mathematicos VII.126

17.

Not knowing how to listen, neither can they speak.

(D. 19, M. 1g) Clement, *Stromateis* II.24.5

18.

Much learning does not teach understanding. For it would have taught Hesiod and Pythagoras, and also Xenophanes and Hecataeus.

(D. 40, M. 16) Diogenes Laertius IX.1

19.

The teacher of most is Hesiod. It is him they know as knowing most who did not recognize day and night: they are one.

(D. 57, M. 43) Hippolytus, *Refutatio* IX. 10.2

20.

[[Hesiod counted some days as good, others as bad, because he did not recognize that the nature of every day is one and the same.]]

(D. 106, M. 59) Plutarch, *Camillus* 19.1

21.

Homer deserves to be expelled from the competition and beaten with a staff—and Archilochus too!

(D. 42, M. 30) Diogenes Laertius IX.1

22.

Men are deceived in the recognition of what is obvious, like Homer who was wisest of all the Greeks. For he was deceived by boys killing lice, who said: what we see and catch we leave behind; what we neither see nor catch we carry away.

(D. 56, M. 21) Hippolytus, *Refutatio* IX.9.5

23.

Pythagoras son of Mnesarchus pursued inquiry further than all other men and, choosing what he like from these compositions, made a wisdom of his own: much learning, artful knavery.

(D. 129, M. 17) Diogenes Laertius VIII.6

24.

[[Pythagoras was the prince of imposters.]]

(D. 81, M. 18) Philodemus, *Rhetorica* I, coll. 57, 62

25.

Of all those whose accounts I have heard, none has gone so far as this: to recognize what is wise, set apart from all.

VII (D. 108, M. 83) Stobaeus III.1.174

26.

I went in search of myself.

(D. 101, M. 15) Plutarch, *Adversus Coloten* 1118C

27.

It belongs to all men to know themselves and to think well.

(D. 116, M 15f=23e) Stobaeus III.5.6

28.

Speaking with understanding they must hold fast to what is shared by all, as a city holds to its law, and even more firmly. For all human laws are nourished by a divine one. It prevails as it will and suffices for all and is more than enough.

(D. 114, M. 23a) Stobaeus III.1.179

29.

Thinking is shared by all.

(D. 113, M. 23d) Stobaeus III.1.179

30.

Thinking well is the greatest excellence and wisdom: to act and speak what is true, perceiving things according to their nature.

(D. 112, M. 23f) Stobaeus III.1.178

31.

The lord whose oracle is in Delphi neither declares nor conceals, but gives a sign.

(D. 93, M. 14) Plutarch, *De Pythiae Oraculis* 404D

32.

You will not find out the limits of the soul by going, even if you travel over every way, so deep is its report.

(D. 45, M. 67) Diogenes Laertius IX.7

33.

It is wise, listening not to me but to the report, to agree that all things are one.

(D. 50, M. 26) Hippolytus, *Refutatio* IX.9.1

34.

The ordering, the same for all, no god nor man has made, but it ever was and is and will be: fire everliving, kindled in measures and in measures going out.

(D. 30, M. 51) Clement, *Stromateis* V.103.6

35.

The reversals of fire: first sea; but of sea half is earth, half lightning storm.

(D. 31A, M. 53A) Clement, *Stromateis* V.104.3

36.

Sea pours out <from earth>, and it measures up to the same amount it was before becoming earth.

XXXIX (D. 31B, M. 53B) Clement, *Stromateis* V.104.5

37.

All things are requital for fire, and fire for all things, as goods for gold and gold for goods.

XL (D. 90, M. 54) Plutarch, *De E apud Delphous* 388D–E

38.

[[The death of fire is birth for air, and the death of air is birth for water.]]

XLI (D. 76, M. 66e¹) Plutarch, *De E apud Delphous* 392C

39.

[[The sun is overseer and sentinel of cycles, for determining the changes and the seasons which bring all things to birth.]]

(D. 100, M. 64) Plutarch, *Quaestiones Platonicae* 1007D–E

40.

[[There is a certain order and fixed time for the change of the cosmos in accordance with some fated necessity.]]

XLIIIB (D. A5) Simplicius, *in Physicorum* 23, 38

41.

The sun will not transgress his measures. If he does, the Furies, ministers of Justice, will find him out.

(D. 94, M. 52) Plutarch, *De Exilio* 604A

42.

The limits of Dawn and Evening is the Bear; and, opposite the Bear, the Warder of luminous Zeus.

(D. 120, M. 62) Strabo I.1.6

43.

[[If there were no sun, it would be night.]]

(D. 99, M. 60) Plutarch (?), *Aqua an ignis utilior* 957A

44.

[[The sun is the size of a human foot.]]

(D. 3, M. 57) Aetius II.21 (ed. Diels, *Doxographi Graeci* p. 352)

45.

[[The sun is new every day.]]

(D. 6, M. 58a) Aristotle, *Meteorologica* II.2 355a13

46.

Cold warms up, warm cools off, moist parches, dry dampens.

(D. 126, M. 42) Tzetzes, *Scholia ad Exegesin in Iliadem* p. 126

47.

As they step into the same rivers, other and still other waters flow upon them.

(D. 12, M. 40a) Arius Didymus fr. 39.2, ed. Diels, *Doxographi Graeci* p. 471, 4

48.

[[One cannot step twice into the same river, nor can one grasp any mortal substance in a stable condition, but it scatters and again gathers; it forms and dissolves, and approaches and departs.]]

LI (D. 91, M. 40c³) Plutarch, *De E apud Delphous* 392B

49.

[[It rests by changing.]]

(D. 84a, M. 56A) Plotinus IV.8.1 (text below)

50.

[[It is weariness to toil at the same tasks and be always beginning.]]

(D. 84b, M. 56B) Plotinus (reference above)

51.

The wise is one, knowing the plan by which it steers all things through all.

(D. 41, M. 85) Diogenes Laertius IX.1

52.

Human nature has no set purpose, but the divine has.

(D. 78, M. 90) Origen, *Contra Celsum* VI. 12

53.

[[The most beautiful of apes is ugly in comparison with the race of man; the wisest of men seems an ape in comparison to a god.]]

(D. 82–3, M. 92b) [Plato], *Hippias Major* 289A–B

54.

A man is found foolish by a god, as a child by a man.

(D. 79, M. 92a) Origen, *Contra Celsum* VI.12

55.

[[Human opinions are toys for children.]]

(D. 70, M. 92d) Iamblichus, *De Anima*, in Stobaeus II.1.16

56.

What wit or understanding do they have? They believe the poets of the people and take the mob as their teacher, not knowing that 'the many are worthless', good men are few.

(D. 104, M. 101) Proclus in *Alcibiades* I, p. 117 Westerink

57.

A fool loves to get excited on any account.

(D. 87, M. 109) Plutarch, *De Audiendis Poetis* 28D

58.

Dogs bark at those they do not recognize.

(D. 97, M. 22) Plutarch, *An Seni Respublica gerenda sit* 787C

59.

In Priene lived Bias son of Teutames, who is of more account than the rest.

(D. 39, M. 100) Diogenes Laertius I.88

59.

What the Ephesians deserve is to be hanged to the last man, every one of them, and leave the city to the boys, since they drove out their best man, Hermodorus, saying 'Let no one be the best among us; if he is, let him be so elsewhere and among others.'

(D. 121, M. 105) Strabo XIV.25 with Diogenes Laertius IX.2

61.

One man is ten thousand, if he is the best.

(D. 49, M. 98) Theodorus Prodromus, *Epistulae* 1 (Migne p. 1240A)

62.

The people must fight for the law as for their city wall.

(D. 44, M. 103) Diogenes Laertius IX.2

63.

It is law also to obey the counsel of one.

(D. 33, M. 104) Clement, *Stromateis* V.115.2

64.

It is not better for human beings to get all they want. It is disease that makes health sweet and good, hunger satiety, weariness rest.

(D. 110–11, M. 71 and M. 44) Stobaeus, III.1.176–7

65.

[[For god all things are fair and good and just, but men have taken some things as unjust, others as just.]]

(D. 102, M. 91) *Scholia Graeca in Homeri Iliadem* ed. H. Erbse, I (1969), p. 445, on *Iliad* IV.4 (=Porphyry, *Quaestiones Homericae*, p. 69 Shrader)

66.

If it were not for these things, they would not have known the name of Justice.

(D. 23, M. 45) Clement, *Stromateis* IV.9.7

67.

The sea is the purest and foulest water: for fish drinkable and life-sustaining; for men undrinkable and deadly.

(D. 61, M. 35) Hippolytus, *Refutatio* IX.10.5

68.

[[Asses prefer garbage to gold.]]

(D. 9, M. 37) Aristotle, *Nicomachean Ethics* X.5, 1176a6

69.

[[Swine delight in mire more than clean water; chickens bathe in dust.]]

(D. 13, M. 36a[1]) Clement, *Stromateis* I.2.2

70.

Doctors who cut and burn and torture their patients in every way complain that they do not receive the reward they deserve.

(D. 58, M. 46) Hippolytus, *Refutatio* IX.10.3

71.
The path of the carding wheels is straight and crooked.
(D. 59, M. 32) Hippolytus, *Refutatio* IX.10.4

72.
[[The counter-thrust brings together, and from tones at variance comes perfect attunement, and all things come to pass through conflict.]]
(D. 8, M. 27d¹=28c¹) Aristotle, *Nicomachean Ethics* VIII.1, 1155b4)

73.
All beasts are driven by blows.
(D. 11, M. 80) [Aristotle], *De Mundo* 6, 401a10

74.
[[Even the potion separates unless it is stirred.]]
(D. 125, M. 31) Theophrastus, *De Vertigine* 9

75.
They do not comprehend how a thing agrees at variance with itself; it is an attunement turning back on itself, like that of the bow and the lyre.
(D. 51, M. 27) Hippolytus, *Refutatio* IX.9.2

76.
The name of the bow is life; its work is death.
(D. 48, M. 39) *Etymologicum Magnum*, s.v.

77.
The hidden attunement is better than the obvious one.
(D. 54, M. 9) Hippolytus, *Refutatio* IX.9.5

78.
[[Homer was wrong when he said 'Would that Conflict might vanish from among gods and men!' (*Iliad* XVIII.107). For there would be no attunement without high and low notes nor any animals without male and female, both of which are opposites.]]
(D. A22, M. 28c²) Aristotle, *Eudemian Ethics* VII.1. 1235a25

79.
One must realize that war is shared and Conflict is Justice, and that all things come to pass (and are ordained?) in accordance with conflict.
(D. 80, M. 28) Origen, *Contra Celsum* VI.28

80.
War is father of all and king of all; and some he has shown as gods, others men; some he has made slaves, others free.
(D. 53, M. 29) Hippolytus, *Refutatio* IX.9.4

81.
What awaits men at death they do not expect or even imagine.
(D. 27, M. 74) Clement, *Stromateis* IV.144.3

82.
The great man is eminent in imagining things, and on this he hangs his reputation for knowing it all.
(D. 28A, M. 20) Clement, *Stromateis* V.9.3

83.
Incredibility escapes recognition.
(D. 86, M. 12) Plutarch, *Coriolanus* 38=Clement, *Stromateis* V. 88.4

84.
Justice will catch up with those who invent lies and those who swear to them.
(D. 28B, M. 19) Clement, *Stromateis* V.9.3

85.
Corpses should be thrown out quicker than dung.
(D. 96, M. 76) Strabo XVI.26=Plutarch, *Quaestiones Conviviales* IV.4.3, etc.

86.
Death is all things we see awake; all we see asleep is sleep.
(D. 21, M. 49) Clement, *Stromateis* III.21.1

87.
A man strikes a light for himself in the night, when his sight is quenched. Living, he touches the dead in his sleep; waking, he touches the sleeper.
(D. 26, M. 48) Clement, *Stromateis* IV.141.2

88.
[[Men asleep are laborers and co-workers in what takes place in the world.]]
(D. 75, M. 1h²) Marcus Aurelius VI.42

89.

Immortals are mortal, mortals immortal, living the others' death, dead in the others' life.

(D. 62, M. 47) Hippolytus, *Refutatio* IX.10.6

90.

The same . . . : living and dead, and the waking and the sleeping, and young and old. For these transposed are those, and those transposed again are these.

(D. 88, M. 41) Pseudo(?)-Plutarch, *Consolatio ad Apollonium* 106E

91.

Lifetime is a child at play, moving pieces in a game. Kingship belongs to the child.

XC (D. 52, M. 93) Hippolytus, *Refutatio* IX.9.4

92.

[[A generation is thirty years, in which time the progenitor has engendered one who generates. The cycle of life lies in this interval, when nature returns from human seed-time to seed-time.]]

(D. A19, M. 108b¹) Plutarch, *De Defectu Oraculorum* 415E

93.

Greater deaths are allotted greater destinies.

(D. 29, M. 95) Clement, *Stromateis* V.59.4

94.

The best choose one thing in exchange for all, ever-flowing fame among mortals; but most men have sated themselves like cattle.

(D. 25, M. 97) Clement, *Stromateis* IV.49.2

95.

Once born they want to live and have their portions; and they leave children behind born to become their dooms.

(D. 20, M. 99) Ibid. III.14.1

96.

[[The beginning and the end are shared in the circumference of a circle.]]

(D. 103, M. 34) Porphyry, *Quaestiones Homericae*, on *Iliad* XIV.200

97.

Gods and men honor those who fall in battle.

(D. 24, M. 96) Clement, *Stromateis* IV.16.1

98.

To the soul belongs a report that increases itself.

(D. 115, M. 112) Stobaeus III.1.180a

99.

For souls it is death to become water, for water it is death to become earth; out of earth water arises, out of water soul.

(D. 36, M. 66) Clement, *Stromateis* VI.17.2

100.

The way up and down is one and the same.

(D. 60, M. 33) Hippolytus, *Refutatio* IX.10.4

101.

One must quench violence quicker than a blazing fire.

(D. 43, M. 102) Diogenes Laertius IX.2

102.

It is hard to fight against passion; for whatever it wants it buys at the expense of soul.

(D. 85, M. 70) Plutarch, *Coriolanus* 22.2; cf. Aristotle, *Eudemian Ethics* II.7, 1223b22, etc.

103.

A man when drunk is led by a beardless boy, stumbling, not perceiving where he is going, having his soul moist.

(D. 117, M. 69) Stobaeus III.5.7

104.

[[It is better to hide one's folly; but that is difficult in one's cups and at ease.]]

(D. 95, M. 110a³) Plutarch, *Quaestiones Conviviales* 644F

105.

[[It is delight, not death, for souls to become moist.]]

(D. 77, M. 66d¹) Porphyry, *De Antro Nympharum* 10 (Numenius fr. 30 des Places=fr. 35 Theodinga)

106.

A gleam of light is the dry soul, wisest and best.

(D. 118, M. 68) Stobaeus III.5.8

107.

(. . .) to rise up (?) and become wakeful watchers of living men and corpses.

(D. 63, M. 73) Hippolytus, *Refutatio* IX.10.6

108.

[[Souls smell things in Hades.]]

(D. 98, M. 72) Plutarch, *De Facie in Orbe Lunae* 943E

109.

[[If all things turned to smoke, the nostrils would sort them out.]]

(D. 7, M. 78) Aristotle, *De Sensu* 5, 443a21

110.

[[The soul is an exhalation that perceives; it is different from the body, and always flowing.]]

CXIIIA (D. A15) Aristotle, *De Anima* I.2, 405a25
(cf. 404b9)

111.

Man's character is his fate.

(D. 119, M. 94) Stobaeus IV.40.23=Plutarch, *Quaestiones Platonicae* 999E, etc.

112.

The mysteries current among men initiate them into impiety.

(D. 14. M. 87) Clement, *Protrepticus* 22.2

113.

If it were not Dionysus for whom they march in procession and chant the hymn to the phallus, their action would be most shameless. But Hades and Dionysus are the same, him for whom they rave and celebrate Lenaia.

(D. 15, M. 50) Clement, *Protrepticus* 34.5

114.

They are purified in vain with blood, those polluted with blood, as if someone who stepped in mud should try to wash himself with mud. Anyone who noticed him doing this would think he was mad. And they pray to these images as if they were chatting with houses, not recognizing what gods or even heroes are like.

(D. 5, M. 86) *Theosophia* 68 (Erbse, *Fragmente griechischen Theosophien*, p. 184) plus Origen, *Contra Celsum* VII.62

115.

The wise is one alone, unwilling and willing to be spoken of by the name of Zeus.

(D. 32, M. 84) Clement, *Stromateis* V.115.1

116.

The thunderbolt pilots all things.

(D. 64, M. 79) Hippolytus, *Refutatio* IX.10.7

117.

(Fire is?) need and satiety.

(D. 65, M. 79 and 55) Hippolytus, *Refutatio* IX.10.7

118.

Fire coming on will discern and catch up with all things.

(D. 66, M. 82) Ibid.

119.

How will one hide from that which never sets?

(D. 16, M. 81) Clement, *Paedagogus* II.99.5

120.

The god: day and night, winter and summer, war and peace, satiety and hunger. It alters, as when mingled with perfumes, it gets named according to the pleasure of each one.

(D. 67, M. 77) Hippolytus, *Refutatio* IX.10.8

121.

Graspings: wholes and not wholes, convergent divergent, consonant dissonant, from all things one and from one thing all.

(D. 10, M. 25) [Aristotle], *De Mundo* 5, 396b20

122.

[[The fairest order in the world is a heap of random sweepings.]]

(D. 124, M. 107) Theophrastus, *Metaphysica* 15 (p. 16, Ross and Fobes)

STUDY QUESTIONS: HERACLITUS, FRAGMENTS

1. What does Heraclitus think people fail to comprehend?
2. How are we asleep, even while awake, according to Heraclitus?
3. What does Heraclitus mean by saying that 'the account is shared'? What does this have to do with being awake?
4. 'Whatever comes from sight . . . this I prefer.' What does Heraclitus mean? (14)
5. 'Eyes and ears are poor witnesses for men if their souls do not understand the language.' Why does he think that this is true?
6. What does Homer deserve, and why?
7. What does Heraclitus say about thinking well? What argument might he give for saying that?
8. He says that 'the ordering [is] the same for all.' What is this ordering in the universe, and why does he emphasize that it is the same for all persons? (34)
9. Why does Heraclitus claim 'the way up and down is one and the same'?
10. What is the *logos* or principle underlying all change, according to Heraclitus?
11. What does Heraclitus mean by asserting that one cannot step into the same river twice? What does he say immediately after this famous saying?
12. Does Heraclitus believe that there are substances? What would it mean to deny that any substances exist?
13. Quite apart from Heraclitus, what reasons are there for thinking that substances do not exist?
14. Why does Heraclitus claim that the thunderbolt steers or pilots all things?
15. Why does Heraclitus claim that 'asses prefer garbage to gold'? What do swine prefer?
16. What does Heraclitus say about attunement and the bow? What does the bow stand for?
17. Why was Homer wrong to wish for the end of conflict?

Philosophical Bridges: The Influence of Heraclitus

Heraclitus originated the ideas that there is a divine intelligence governing the universe and that a spark of this intelligence exists in human reason. His idea of fire as the divine aspect of the cosmos and man, and his claim that eternal laws govern the universe, had a decisive influence on Zeno of Citium, the founder of Stoicism. Stoic philosophy became very popular in ancient Rome, and the Roman Empire was receptive to Christianity in large part because of the Heraclitean aspects of Stoicism.

Heraclitus' paradoxical, rebellious, and aphoristic style had an important influence on the nineteenth-century philosopher Friedrich Nietzsche, who notoriously claimed that God is dead. Nietzsche was a classical scholar who argued vehemently against Christian and Platonic otherworldliness. In so doing, he employed a style and presented ideas that are often reminiscent of Heraclitus. For instance, like his predecessor, he dismissed the popular opinion of the herd and argued for a universe of constant flux (but without the order of *logos* postulated by Heraclitus) upon which the strong must impose their will.

Heraclitus' thesis that all is flux has been an inspiration to a long tradition of philosophers, such as the twentieth-century process thinker Alfred Whitehead, who have rejected the standard static ontology of objects and properties for failing to recognize the importance of time, and who have sought to replace it with a dynamic ontology based on processes and events. This tradition would also include the great German philosopher G. W. F. Hegel (1777–1831), who wrote his thesis on Heraclitus. It would also include the

French Nobel Prize winner Henri-Louis Bergson (1859–1941), as well as Karl Marx and Friedrich Engels, who regarded Heraclitus as a precursor of their dialectical materialism because of his conception of change through the conflict of opposites. Part of western metaphysics can be regarded as a debate between the Parmenidean claim that reality must be changeless and the Heraclitean thesis that reality must be ever changing. Whereas Parmenides' claim has tended to dominate much of the history of philosophy, Heraclitus' thesis has had more influence in the last 50 years.

Heraclitus' assertion that one cannot step into the same river twice, his idea of constant flux, has recently inspired more radical ideas. Following leads taken from Nietzsche, some contemporary French philosophers, such as Jacques Derrida and Luce Irigaray, have challenged the idea of the self-identity of an object. According to this challenge, the thesis that X is simply identical to itself is problematic because X is defined primarily by what it is not. Difference is more fundamental than identity in a way that makes repetition of the same thing through time impossible. Through such ideas, Derrida deconstructs the metaphysics of presence, which he claims has dominated most western philosophy.

THE ELEATICS

PROLOGUE

The Eleactics gave natural philosophy a tremendous shock. They challenged the very idea of such a project, and argued for a mystical, antinaturalistic view of the universe. What is surprising about their thought is the strength of their arguments. They appear to be sound.

PARMENIDES (515–445 B.C.)

Biographical History

Parmenides was born in Elea, a Greek city in southern Italy. He was reportedly a student of Xenophanes, and may have studied with the Pythagoreans, but he followed neither. He wrote a long poem in Homeric hexameters, of which about 150 lines have been recovered. This poem radically changed philosophy. It is divided into two parts: the first describes the Way of Truth, and the second the Way of Seeming, which characterizes a false and deceitful manner of thinking.

Philosophical Overview

In his poem, Parmenides journeys to the *House of Night*, where he meets the goddess of wisdom, who shows him the truth through argument. In the *Way of Truth*, the goddess argues for a seamless, changeless, finite universe. In effect, she argues that there can only be one thing or, in other words, that all plurality is an illusion. The argument for this conclusion is based apparently on the premise that we cannot speak of or think about that which does not exist. Every subject of inquiry and thought must exist. In contemporary terms, one cannot think about what does not exist because if one can refer to something, then it exists. From this conclusion, the goddess appears to argue that change is impossible because change requires either that something comes from nothing, or that something comes to not exist, both of which are impossible. The argument is as follows:

1. *The concept of the nonexistent is impossible.*
2. *The idea of change requires the concept of the nonexistent.*

---

3. *Therefore, change is impossible.*

As a consequence, what exists must be unchanging and eternal, possibly in the sense of being timeless. Furthermore, since it is impossible to think about what does not exist, the existent must be seamless or without gaps because the idea of gaps presupposes the nonexistent, which is impossible. In this way, Parmenides' goddess argues that the whole is not divisible.

Notice that Parmenides' poem does not contain an argument against the existence of empty space, from which also he could have concluded that motion is impossible. Such an argument was given in fact by his follower Melissus.

The second half of the poem (from 8.51 to 8.61 and 9 and 10) outlines the Way of Seeming, which describes the erroneous views of mortals, who mistake appearances for reality. Parmenides' position in the first part of the poem apparently implies that all sense perception is illusory and, furthermore, that the true nature of reality is revealed by reason. However, it is a contended point how one should understand the relation between the two parts of the work.

This poem was a watershed in the history of early western philosophy. It had great influence on later generations, but, of course, it apparently meant that the scientific investigation of nature is impossible, or at best is only a study of illusions. The great challenge was now to overcome the arguments in favor of Parmenides' strange position.

FRAGMENTS
Parmenides

In his poem, Parmenides journeys to the *House of Night*, where he meets the goddess of wisdom, who shows him the truth through argument. In the *Way of Truth*, the goddess argues for a seamless, changeless, finite universe. In effect, she argues that there can only be one thing or, in other words, that all plurality is an illusion.

The second half of the poem (from 8.51 to 8.61 and 9 and 10) outlines the Way of Seeming, which describes the erroneous views of mortals, who mistake appearances for reality. Parmenides' position in the first part of the poem apparently implies that all sense perception is illusory and, furthermore, that the true nature of reality is revealed by reason. However, it is a contended point how one should understand the relation between the two parts of the work.

1.

The mares that carry me, as far as impulse might reach,
Were taking me, when they brought and placed me upon the much-speaking route
Of the goddess, that carries everywhere unscathed the man who knows;

Thereon was I carried, for thereon the much-guided mares were carrying me,
5 Straining to pull the chariot, and maidens were leading the way.
The axle, glowing in its naves, gave forth the shrill sound of a pipe,
(For it was urged on by two rounded

Parmenides, from *Parmenides of Elea: Fragments*, translated by David Gallop. University of Toronto Press, 1984. Reprinted by permission of the publisher.

Wheels at either end), even while maidens, Daughters of
the Sun, were hastening

To escort me, after leaving the House of Night for the
light,

10 Having pushed back with their hands the veils from
their heads.

There are the gates of the paths of Night and Day,

And a lintel and a threshold of stone surround them,

And the aetherial gates themselves are filled with great
doors;

And for these Justice, much-avenging, holds the keys
of retribution.

15 Coaxing her with gentle words, the maidens

Did cunningly persuade her that she should push back
the bolted bar for them

Swiftly from the gates; and these made of the doors

A gaping gap as they were opened wide,

Swinging in turn in their sockets the brazen posts

20 Fitted with rivets and pins; straight through them at
that point

Did the maidens drive the chariot and mares along the
broad way.

And the goddess received me kindly, and took my right
hand with her hand,

And uttered speech and thus addressed me:

'Youth attended by immortal charioteers,

25 Who come to our House with mares that carry you,

Welcome; for it is no ill fortune that sent you forth to
travel

This route (for it lies far indeed from the beaten track
of men),

But right and justice. And it is right that you should
learn all things,

Both the steadfast heart of persuasive truth,

30 And the beliefs of mortals, in which there is no true trust.

But nevertheless you shall learn these things as well,
how the things which seem

Had to have genuine existence, permeating all things
completely.'

1–30: Sextus Empiricus, *Against the Mathematicians*
VII.111–14.

28–32: Simplicius, Commentary on *De Caelo*
(Comm. Arist. Gr. VII, 557)

2.

Come, I shall tell you, and do you listen and convey
the story,

What routes of inquiry alone there are for thinking:

The one—that [it] is, and that [it] cannot not be,

Is the path of Persuasion (for it attends upon truth);

5 The other—that [it] is not and that [it] needs must
not be,

That I point out to you to be a path wholly
unlearnable,

For you could not know what-is-not (for that is not
feasible),

Nor could you point it out.

1–8: Proclus, Commentary on *Timaeus* (Diehl, vol I, 345)
3–8: Simplicius, Commentary on *Physics*
(Comm. Arist. Gr. IX, 116)

3.

. . . because the same thing is there for thinking and
for being.

Clement *Miscellanies* VI.2, 23; Plotinus *Ennead* V.1.8

4.

Look upon things which, though far off, are yet firmly
present to the mind;

For you shall not cut off what-is from holding fast to
what-is,

For it neither disperses itself in every way everywhere
in order,

Nor gathers itself together.

Clement *Miscellanies* V.2, 15

5.

And it is all one to me

Where I am to begin; for I shall return there again.

Proclus, Commentary on *Parmenides* (Cousin 708)

6.

It must be that what is there for speaking and thinking
of is; for [it] is there to be

Whereas nothing is not; that is what I bid you consider,

For <I restrain> you from that first route of inquiry,

And then also from this one, on which mortals knowing
nothing

5 Wander, two-headed; for helplessness in their

Breasts guides their distracted mind; and they are
carried

Deaf and blind alike, dazed, uncritical tribes,

By whom being and not-being have been thought both
the same

And not the same; and the path of all is backward-
turning.

1–9: Simplicius, Commentary on *Physics*
(*Comm. Arist. Gr.* IX, 117)
8–9: Simplicius, Commentary on *Physics*
(*Comm. Arist. Gr.* IX, 78)

7.

For never shall this prevail, that things that are not are;
But do you restrain your thought from this route of
inquiry,
Nor let habit force you, along this route of much-
experience,
To ply an aimless eye and ringing ear
5 *And tongue; but judge by reasoning the very*
contentious disproof
That has been uttered by me.

1–2: Plato, *Sophist* 237a
1: Aristotle, *Metaphysics* N2, 1089a2
3–6: Sextus Empiricus, *Against the Mathematicians* VII.144

8.

A single story of a route still
Is left: that [it] is; on this [route] there are signs
Very numerous: that what-is is ungenerated and
imperishable;
Whole, single-limbed, steadfast, and complete;
5 *Nor was [it] once, now will [it] be, since [it] is, now,*
all together,
One, continuous; for what coming-to-be of it will you
seek?
In what way, whence, did [it] grow? Neither from
what-is-not shall I allow
You to say or think; for it is not to be said or thought
That [it] is not. And what need could have impelled it
to grow
10 *Later or sooner, if it began from nothing?*
Thus [it] must either be completely or not at all.
Nor will the strength of trust ever allow anything to
come-to-be from what
Besides it; therefore neither [its] coming-to-be
Nor [its] perishing has Justice allowed, relaxing her
shackles,
15 *But she holds [it] fast; the decision about these matters*
depends on this:
Is [it] or is [it] not? but it has been decided, as is
necessary,

To let go the one as unthinkable, unnameable (for it is
no true
Route), but to allow the other, so that it is, and is true.
And how could what-is be in the future; and how
could [it] come-to-be?
20 *For if [it] came-to-be, [it] is not, nor [is it] if at some*
time [it] is going to be.
Thus, coming-to-be is extinguished and perishing not
to be heard of.
Nor is [it] divisible, since [it] all alike is;
Nor is [it] somewhat more here, which would keep it
from holding together,
Nor is [it] somewhat less, but [it] is all full of what-is.
25 *Therefore [it] is all continuous; for what-is is in*
contact with what-is.
Moreover, changeless in the limits of great chains
[It] is un-beginning and unceasing, since coming-to-be
and perishing
Have been driven far off, and true trust has thrust
them out.
Remaining the same and in the same, [it] lies by itself
30 *And remains thus firmly in place; for strong Necessity*
Holds [it] fast in the chains of a limit, which fences it
about.
Wherefore it is not right for what-is to be incomplete;
For [it] is not lacking; but if [it] were, [it] would lack
everything.
The same thing is for thinking and [is] that there is
thought;
35 *For not without what-is, on which [it] depends, having*
been declared,
Will you find thinking; for nothing else <either> is or
will be
Besides what-is, since it was just this that Fate did
shackle
To be whole and changeless; wherefore it has been
named all things
That mortals have established, trusting them to be true,
40 *To come-to-be and to perish, to be and not to be,*
And to shift place and to exchange bright colour.
Since, then, there is a furthest limit, [it] is completed,
From every direction like the bulk of a well-rounded
sphere,
Everywhere from the centre equally matched; for [it]
must not be any larger
45 *Or any smaller here or there;*
For neither is there what-is-not, which could stop it
from reaching

[Its] like, nor is there a way in which what-is could be
More here and less there, since [it] all inviolably is;
For equal to itself from every direction, [it] lies
    uniformly within limits.
50 Here I stop my trustworthy speech to you and thought
About truth; from here onwards learn mortal beliefs,
Listening to the deceitful ordering of my words;
For they established two forms in their minds for naming,
Of which it is not right to name one—wherein they
    have gone astray—
55 And they distinguished opposites in body and established
    signs
Apart from one another: here, on the one hand,
    aetherial fire of flame,
Which is gentle, very light, everywhere the same as
    itself,
But not the same as the other; but on the other hand,
    that one too by itself
In contrast, dark night, a dense and heavy body;
60 All this arrangement I proclaim to you as plausible;
Thus no opinion of mortals shall ever overtake you.
> 1–52: Simplicius, Commentary on *Physics*
> (*Comm. Arist. Gr.* IX, 144)
> 1–14: Simplicius, Commentary on *Physics*
> (*Comm. Arist. Gr.* IX, 78)
> 50–61: Simplicius, Commentary on *Physics*
> (*Comm. Arist. Gr.* IX, 38)
> 53–59: Simplicius, Commentary on *Physics*
> (*Comm. Arist. Gr.* IX. 179)

9.

But since all things have been named light and night,
And these [have been applied] according to their
    powers to these things and to those,
All is full of light and obscure night together,
Of both equally, since for neither [is it the case that]
    nothing shares in them.
> Simplicius, Commentary on *Physics*
> (*Comm. Arist. Gr.* IX, 180)

10.

And you shall know both the nature of the aether and all
The signs in the aether, the destructive works of the
    splendid sun's
Pure torch, and whence they came-to-be,

And you shall learn the wandering works of the
    round-eyed moon,
5 And its nature, and you shall also know the
    surrounding sky,
Whence it grew and how Necessity did guide and
    shackle it
To hold the limits of the stars.
> Clement *Miscellanies* V. 14, 138

11.

How earth and sun and moon
And the common aether and Milky Way and the
    outermost heaven
And the hot strength of the stars did thrust forward
To come-to-be
> Simplicius, Commentary on *De Caelo*
> (*Comm. Arist. Gr.* VII, 559)

12.

For the narrower [rings] are filled with unmingled fire,
And those next upon them with night, and a portion of
    flame is sent forth;
In the midst of these is the goddess who steers all things;
For she rules over hateful birth and union of all things,
5 Sending female to mingle with male, and again conversely
Male with female . . .
> 1–3: Simplicius, Commentary on *Physics*
> (*Comm. Arist. Gr.* IX, 39)
> 2–6: Simplicius, Commentary on *Physics*
> (*Comm. Arist. Gr.* IX, 31)

13.

She devised Love first of all the gods. . . .
> Plato *Symposium* 178b; Aristotle *Metaphysics* A4, 984b23;
> Plutarch *Amatorius*756f; Simplicius, Commentary
> on *Physics* (*Comm. Arist. Gr.* IX, 39)

14.

Night-shiner, wandering around the earth, an alien light

> **Plutarch** *Reply to Colotes* 1116a

15.

Always looking towards the rays of the sun
> Plutarch *On the Face of the Moon* 929a; *Quaestiones
> Romanae* 282b

16.

For as each man has a union of the much-wandering
limbs,
So is mind present to men; for it is the same thing
Which the constitution of the limbs thinks,
Both in each and every man; for the full is thought.
Aristotle *Metaphysics* Γ5, 1009b21; Theophrastus *On Sense*
1–4 (*Dox. Gr.* 499–500)

17.

<She placed> young males on the right side [of the
womb], young females on the left.
Galen, *Commentary on Sixth Book of Hippocrates' Epidemics*
II.46 (Kuhn 1002; Wenkebach-Pfaff 119)

18.

When man and woman mingle the seeds of love
That spring from their veins, a formative power
Maintaining proper proportions moulds well-formed
bodies from this diverse blood.
For if, when the seed is mingled, the forces therein
clash

5 *And do not fuse into one, then cruelly*
Will they plague with double seed the sex of the
offspring.
Caelius Aurelianus *On Chronic Diseases* IV.9

19.

Thus according to belief, these things were born and
now are
And hereafter, having grown from this, they will come
to an end,
And for each of these did men establish a distinctive
name.
Simplicius, Commentary on *De Caelo* (*Comm. Arist. Gr.*
VII, 558)

20.

Cornford's Fragment

Such, changeless, is that for which as a whole the
name is: 'to be.'
Plato *Theaetetus* 180e; Simplicius, Commentary on *Physics*
(*Comm. Arist. Gr.* IX, 29, 16–18, 143, 10)

STUDY QUESTIONS: PARMENIDES, *FRAGMENTS*

1. What does Parmenides claim can be said of the 'One'? Why is it indivisible and changeless?
2. How does Parmenides distinguish being from nonbeing?
3. What does Parmenides mean by the 'nothing'? Why does he say that 'nothing is not'?
4. How does Parmenides answer the question 'How could what-is be in the future?' What is there to prevent it?
5. Why is the ordering of his words deceitful? (8. L. 52) Is there any way to avoid that?
6. Can the way the world is according to belief and the One be reconciled? Are they two separate worlds? Why not?
7. What does Parmenides mean by 'the aether'?
8. What is the basis of Parmenides' claim that all change is impossible?
9. How does Parmenides define 'change'?
10. What would Parmenides say to the Milesians' way of doing philosophy? To Pythagoras?
11. What implications does Parmenides' view have for the distinction and the relationship between philosophy and science?

Philosophical Bridges: The Parmenidean Influence

Perhaps surprisingly, Parmenides' thesis that everyone is an indivisible whole has had an enormous influence on philosophy. It introduced many fundamental new concepts to western thought, which have had a lasting effect. First, it is an early precursor of pantheism and deism. For instance, Plotinus conceived of God as the Parmenidian One and launched a pantheistic understanding of God as an alternative to mainstream Christian orthodoxy. Parmenides' claim that everything is a seamless whole is also echoed in the Stoic claim that the universe is one. This Stoic assertion influenced the seventeenth-century metaphysician Baruch de Spinoza, who argued for the existence of only one indivisible substance, namely, nature as a whole, which he called 'God.'

Second, Parmenides' thesis requires a sharp distinction between the realms of appearances and reality. Parmenides' assertion that reality is timeless and unchanging introduced a new idea to philosophy via Plato. With his theory of Forms, Plato adopted these Parmenidean claims and made them important themes throughout the history of philosophy. For example, we find echoes of Parmenides' thesis in Kant's phenomena/noumena distinction and in later versions of idealism.

Third, the sharp distinction between appearances and reality implies that sense-perception as a whole is systematically misleading; it cannot give us knowledge of reality but only of appearances. Plato made Parmenides' arguments for this idea even more powerful and, thereby, transformed philosophy. It has influenced not just Rationalist, transcendental, and idealist thinkers but also Empiricism. Rationalists employed such considerations to argue that real knowledge of the world cannot be gained through sense-experience. Idealists used such arguments to support the claim that there exists a realm of existence that transcends the objects we apparently perceive.

Fourth, if knowledge of reality cannot be gained through the senses, then it must be acquired by reasoning carefully, even when that reasoning runs against common sense. Once again, Plato took up this idea in his epistemology, and, through him, it entered into much medieval and later philosophy. This concept reappears in the seventeenth- and eighteenth-century philosophies of Spinoza and Gottfried Leibniz, both of whom argue that the true nature of reality can only be grasped by reason.

Fifth, to argue for his startling thesis, Parmenides introduced a new methodology and precision to western thought, namely, that of basing deductive arguments on a reflective analysis of key terms, such as 'is' and 'exists.' Given this, it is no wonder that Parmenides caused a revolution in ancient philosophy and that it required an intellect as great as Aristotle's to even begin to reply to his arguments. Of course, to attempt this in the *Categories* and *Metaphysics*, Aristotle had to employ the same kind of methodology used by Parmenides.

Given the above, we can see why Parmenides' assertion that one cannot refer to that which does not exist has continued to haunt philosophy. How can we refer to Santa Claus when he does not exist? How can we refer to the nonexistent? As an answer to this question, in the nineteenth century, Alexius Meinong argued for an ontology that included nonexistent objects. In the 1920s, Bertrand Russell formulated his theory of descriptions as an alternative and ontologically less extravagant answer to this question. In brief, Russell's idea was that sentences such as 'The present King of France is bald' are in fact a conjunction of three distinct sentences: (1) 'There is a thing that is the present king of France,' (2) 'There is only one of them,' and (3) 'That thing is bald.' However, even Russell thought that language must contain simple, logically proper names that cannot fail to refer (see Volume V).

Zeno (490–430 B.C.)

Biographical History

Zeno came from Elea. He was about 25 years younger than Parmenides, and they may have been lovers. In 450 B.C., they visited Athens together and probably met with Socrates, who was about 20 years old. Plato's dialogue *Parmenides* reconstructs these fascinating discussions. We know little else about Zeno's life except that, after participating in a rebellion to overthrow a tyrant, he was captured and, despite being tortured, he refused to betray his companions.

Philosophical Overview

With his so-called paradoxes, Zeno made the challenge of Parmenides even greater. 'Zeno's Paradoxes' are not really paradoxes at all; a paradox is an apparently inescapable contradiction. They are arguments, which are designed to prove the startling conclusion that motion is impossible. In this way, Zeno aimed to support Parmenides' conclusion that there is only one thing, and to deny the existence of a plurality. We are told that Zeno had 40 such arguments in his work *Attacks*, but of these only six survive. Four of these are his famous arguments against motion, stated by Aristotle in his *Physics*, quoted in the second passage below. The four arguments are the midway problem, Achilles, the arrow, and the stadium. Zeno's basic strategy is to show that the commonsense view that more than one thing exists leads to absurdities or contradictions, thereby supporting Parmenides' claim that only one thing can exist. The Achilles paradox is essentially similar in form to the midway problem, which we shall now examine.

The Midway Problem

Imagine that you have to cross a room by traveling half of the distance across it, then half of the remaining distance, half of the remaining distance, and so on. You will never actually cross the room. The journey cannot be completed. However, the argument applies to any journey, and, therefore, no journey or movement can even begin. In effect, he argues as follows:

1. *For anything to move requires its completing an infinite number of tasks.*
2. *It is impossible to complete an infinite number of tasks.*

3. *Therefore, movement is impossible.*

According to the first premise, moving requires an infinite number of tasks because space is continuous and hence infinitely divisible. This means that, between any two points, there are an infinite number of points. This in turn implies that to move between any two points requires completing an infinite number of steps or tasks. Concerning the second premise, it may seem that Zeno's point is that it is impossible to complete an infinite number of tasks in a finite time. However, his real point is rather that it is impossible to complete an infinite series because an infinite series has no last member.

The Arrow

Imagine an arrow flying through space. Zeno argues,

1. *At any moment, the arrow occupies a space that is equal to its own size.*
2. *Something that occupies a space equal to its own size is at rest.*

3. *Therefore, at any moment, the arrow is at rest.*

This conclusion can be generalized to show that no motion is possible.

The Stadium (or Moving Rows)

There are different interpretations of the details of this argument, but they agree on its basic form. There are three groups of blocks, all of equal size. Group A is stationary. The two remaining groups move with equal speed in opposite directions. Let us suppose that each group has two blocks, After a period of time (T), one of the B blocks has moved past all two C's and only one of the A's. Hence, the following argument applies.

1. *Block B1 moves past a single A in time T.*
2. *Block B1 moves past two Cs in time T.*
3. *Blocks A, B, and C are equal in size.*
4. *Blocks C and B move with equal speed.*
5. *Time = distance divided by velocity.*

6. *Therefore, T = 1/2 T.*

From this absurd consequence, Zeno concludes that motion is impossible.

The Other Arguments

There are other extant arguments of Zeno, among which the following is perhaps the most famous. Any thing X is the same as itself, and if something were to be added to it, then it would not be X but rather X + Y. Everything must have magnitude. However, anything with magnitude is divisible into parts, and whenever it is divided, there will remain a part still to be divided. Therefore, everything that exists is X + Y. This argument can be repeated indefinitely. Therefore, if there were many things, they would be either infinitely large or infinitely small.

FRAGMENTS

Zeno

The first fragment is from Plato's dialogue *Parmenides*. The second one is from Aristotle, who gives Zeno's four arguments. However, Aristotle contends that they are fallacious because they rely on the false view that time is composed of indivisible instants. It is a debated point whether this is a correct or fair way to understand Zeno's arguments.

1.

According to Antiphon, Pythodorus said that Zeno and Parmenides once came [to Athens] for the festival of the Great Panathenaea. Parmenides was already a very old man, white-haired but of distinguished appearance—he was about sixty-five years old. Zeno was then nearly forty, tall and pleasing to look at—he was said to have been Parmenides' lover. They were staying with Pythodorus, outside the city wall in the Ceramicus. There Socrates and a few others visited them, eager to hear Zeno's writings—for this was the first time they had been brought by them to Athens. Socrates was then very young.

Zeno himself read to them, while Parmenides happened to be out. There was only very little of the argument still left to be read, Pythodorus said, when he himself came back and with him Parmenides and Aristotle (who became one of the thirty tyrants); so they heard just a little of the writings—although Pythodorous himself had actually heard Zeno before.

When Socrates had heard him out, he asked Zeno to read again the first hypothesis of the first argument. When it had been read he said: 'Zeno, what do you mean? Are you saying that if more things than one exist, then they must be both only one thing then the argument leads to many absurd and contradictory conclusions. My book attacks those who say that several things exist, aiming to show that their hypothesis, that several things exist, leads to even more ridiculous results, if you examine it properly, than the hypothesis that only one thing exists. It was with that sort of ambition that I wrote it when I was young. After it was written someone stole it, so that I could not even consider whether it should be brought out into the light or not.'

(Plato, *Parmenides* 127A—128D)

2.

Zeno argues fallaciously. For if, he says, everything is always at rest when it is in a space equal to itself, and if what is travelling is always in such a space at any instant, then the travelling arrow is motionless. That is false; for time is not composed of indivisible instants—nor is any other magnitude.

Zeno's arguments about motion which provide trouble for those who try to resolve them are four in number.

The first maintains that nothing moves because what is travelling must first reach the half-way point before it reaches the end. We have discussed this earlier.

The second is the so-called Achilles. This maintains that the slowest thing will never be caught when running by the fastest. For the pursuer must first reach the point from which the pursued set out, so that the slower must always be ahead of it. This is the same argument as the dichotomy, but it differs in that the additional magnitudes are not divided in *half*. Now it follows from the argument that the slower is

not caught, and the same error is committed as in the dichotomy (in both arguments it follows that you do not reach the end if the magnitude is divided in a certain way—but here there is the additional point that not even the fastest runner in fiction will reach his goal when he pursues the slowest); hence the solution must also be the same. And it is false to claim that the one ahead is not caught: it is not caught *while it is ahead*, but nonetheless it *is* caught (provided you grant that they can cover a finite distance).

Those, then, are two of the arguments. The third is the one we have just stated, to the effect that the travelling arrow stands still. It depends on the assumption that time is composed of instants; for if that is not granted the inference will not go through.

The fourth is the argument about the bodies moving in the stadium from opposite directions, an equal number past an equal number; the one group starts from the end of the stadium, the other from the middle; and they move at equal speed. He thinks it follows that half the time is equal to its double. The fallacy consists in claiming that equal magnitudes moving at equal speeds, the one past a moving object and the other past a stationary object, travel for an equal length of time. But this is false.

For example, let the stationary equal bodies be AA; let BB be those beginning from the middle, equal in number and in magnitude to them; and let CC be those beginning from the end, equal in number and in magnitude to them and equal in speed to the Bs. It follows that, as they move past one another, the first B and the first C are at the end at the same time. And it follows that the C has travelled past all of them but the B past half of them. Hence the time is half—for each of the two is alongside each for an equal time. At the same time it follows that the first B has travelled past all the Cs; for the first C and the first B will be at opposite ends at the same time (being, as he says, alongside each of the Bs for a time equal to that for which it is alongside each of the As)—because both are alongside the As for an equal time. That is the argument, and it rests upon the falsity we have mentioned.

(Aristotle, *Physics* 239b5–240a18)

3.

But in his treatise, which contains many arguments, he shows in each case that anyone who says that several things exist falls into inconsistencies.

There is one argument in which he shows that if several things exist they are both large and small—so large as to be infinite in magnitude, so small as to have no magnitude at all. Here he shows that what has no magnitude, no mass, and no bulk, does not even exist. For, he says,

> if it were added to anything else, it would not make it larger. For if it is of no magnitude but is added, [the other thing] cannot increase at all in magnitude. Thus what is added will therefore be nothing. And if when it is subtracted the other thing is no smaller—and will not increase when it is added again—then clearly what was added and subtracted was nothing. [29 B 2]

Zeno says this not to do away with the one but in order to show that the several things each possess a magnitude—a magnitude which is actually infinite by virtue of the fact that, because of infinite divisibility, there is always something in front of whatever is taken. And he shows this having first shown that they possess *no* magnitude from the fact that each of the several things is the same as itself and one. Zeno seems rather to say that there do not exist several things.

From Simplicius, *Commentary on the Physics*, 138.3–6 138.29–140.6, 140.18–140.11

4.

Porphyry holds that the argument from dichotomy belonged to Parmenides who attempted to show by it that what exists is one. He writes as follows:

> Parmenides had another argument, the one based on dichotomy, which purports to show that what exists is one thing only and, moreover, partless and indivisible. For were it divisible, he says, let it have been cut in two—and then each of its parts in two. Since this goes on for ever, it is clear, he says, that either some final magnitudes will remain which are minimal and atomic and infinite in number, so that the whole thing will be constituted from infinitely many *minima*; or else it will disappear and be dissolved into nothing, and so be constituted from nothing. But these consequences are absurd. Therefore it will not be divided but will remain one. Again, since it is everywhere alike, if it is really divisible it will be divisible everywhere alike, and not divisible

in one place and not in another. Then let it have been divided everywhere. It is clear, again, that nothing will remain but that it will disappear; and if it is constituted at all, it will again be constituted from nothing. For if anything remains, it will not yet have been divided everywhere. Thus from these considerations too it is evident, he says, that what exists will be indivisible and partless and one. . . .

Porphyry is right here to refer to the argument from dichotomy as introducing the indivisible one by way of the absurdity consequent upon division; but it is worth asking whether the argument is really Parmenides' rather than Zeno's, as Alexander thinks. For nothing of the sort is stated in the Parmenidean writings, and most scholars ascribe the argument from dichotomy to Zeno—indeed it is mentioned as Zeno's in Aristotle's work *On Motion* [i.e. *Physics* 239b9]. And why say more when it is actually found in Zeno's own treatise? For, showing that if several things exist the same things are finite and infinite, Zeno writes in the following words:

> If several things exist, it is necessary for them to be as many as they are, and neither more nor fewer. But if they are as many as they are, they will be finite. If several things exist, the things that exist are infinite. For there are always others between the things that exist, and again others between them. And in this way the things that exist are infinite. [B 3]

And in this way he has proved infinity in quantity from the dichotomy. As for infinity in magnitude, he proved that earlier in the same argument. For having first proved that if what exists had no magnitude it would not even exist, he continues:

> But if it exists, it is necessary for each thing to have some bulk and magnitude, and for one part of it to be at a distance from the other. And the same argument applies to the protruding part. For that too will have a magnitude, and part of it will protrude. Now it is all one to say this once and to say it for ever. For it will have no last part of such a sort that there is no longer one part in front of another. In this way if there exist several things it is necessary for them to be both small

and large—so small as not to have a magnitude, so large as to be infinite. [B 1]

Perhaps, then, the argument from dichotomy is Zeno's, as Alexander holds, but he is not doing away with the one but rather with the many (by showing that those who hypothesize them are committed to inconsistencies) and is thus confirming Parmenides' argument that what exists is one.

(Simplicius, *Commentary on the Physics* 138.3–6, 138.29–140.6, 140.18–141.11)

5.

Zeno's argument seemed to do away with the existence of place. It was propounded as follows: If places exist, they will be in something; for everything that exists is in something. But what is in something is in a place. Therefore places are in places—and so *ad infinitum*. Therefore places do not exist. . . . Eudemus relates Zeno's view as follows:

Zeno's puzzle seems to lead to the same conclusion. For he claims that everything that exists is somewhere. But if places are among the things that exist, where will they be? Surely in another place—and that in another, and so on.

(Simplicius, *Commentary on the Physics* 562.3–6, 563.17–20)

6.

It is clear that nothing can be in itself as its primary place. Zeno's puzzle—that if places exist then they will be *in* something—is not difficult to resolve. For nothing prevents the primary place of a thing from being in something else—but not in it as in a place.

(Aristotle, *Physics* 210b22–25)

STUDY QUESTIONS: ZENO, FRAGMENTS

1. Could you refute Zeno's paradox of motion by walking across the room? Why?
2. What is the midway problem?
3. What is the paradox of Achilles?
4. According to Zeno, why is it impossible for an arrow to move?
5. Is Aristotle right to contend that Zeno assumes that time is composed of indivisible instants? How would Zeno's arguments hinge on such an assumption? How might they escape it?
6. In principle, could an argument prove that it is impossible for several things to exist? Could the senses be wrong in suggesting that there are many things? If the senses and reasoning were to conflict in this way, what should one do?
7. How does Zeno argue that if there are many things, then they will be both infinitely large and infinitely small?
8. Zeno argues that places do not exist. What is his argument for this claim? How does Aristotle try to counter this argument?
9. What was Parmenides' argument for the claim that nothing could be divisible?
10. What objections might there be to the claim that everything is one? Are these objections answerable?

Philosophical Bridges: The Influence of Zeno

Zenos' paradoxes apparently indicate a deep puzzle about the nature of infinitesimals, such as points in space and time. Does a line or a distance consist in an infinite number of dimensionless points? Does a period of time consist in an infinite number of moments? Zeno's influence can be seen in both the philosophy of mathematics and the metaphysics of space and time.

According to Aristotle, at least one of Zeno's arguments may have convinced the Greek atomists that indivisible atoms have to exist. In a similar vein, Leibniz (1646–1716), who invented the calculus based on infinitesimals, argued that matter could not be a substance because it must be infinitely divisible like the space that it is in. He spotted an apparently viscous infinite regress akin to Zeno's arguments: an infinitely divisible material object would depend for its existence on its spatial parts, which in turn would depend for their existence on their parts ad infinitum. Ultimately, there would be nothing to depend on. He concluded that reality must consist in nonmaterial and nonspatial substances, called 'monads.'

Henri Bergson (1859–1941) claimed that we usually misconceive time as analogous to a line composed of instants that are like dimensionless points. This mathematical analogy treats time falsely as if it were space and thereby generates Zeno's paradoxes. In effect, Bergson appeals to Zeno in order to argue for an alternative conception of time that sees duration as continuous without quantitative differentiations. In other words, according to Bergson, Zeno's arguments show us that space and time are not composed of infinitesimal points. The American pragmatist William James (1842–1910) and the process thinker Whitehead (1861–1947) advanced similar claims.

Like his teacher Parmenides, Zeno set a new standard of rigor in philosophical argument. To attempt to answer Zeno, Aristotle had to attain at least the same level of precision. However, Aristotle did not have the concept of a convergent series and Georg Cantor's notion of infinite sets, which are required to attempt a mathematically precise reply to Zeno's arguments. Briefly, the point is that we can calculate the sum of an infinitely long series of numbers if the series converges on some limit. The sum of an infinite convergent series of numbers will be finite. For example, the infinitely long series $1/2 + 1/4 + 1/8 + 1/2n \ldots$ has a sum, which is 1. This is given by the formula $S n = 2(1 - 1/2 n + 1)$.

In other words, concerning Zeno's midway problem, the sum of the half, plus the half of the half and so on, is 1, and so you are able to cross the room. The main point is that, to begin to answer Zeno's paradoxes, one requires mathematical concepts that were not developed until the seventeenth and nineteenth centuries.

In 1967, in his book *Modern Science and Zeno's Paradoxes*, the physicist/philosopher Arthur Grünbaum showed that a complete reply to Zeno's arguments depends not only on pure mathematics but also on the relation between mathematics and physical reality. Are space and time actually structured like a continuum? One can begin to see that Zeno's simple paradoxes are very deep.

THE PLURALISTS AND ATOMISTS

PROLOGUE

The next three philosophers, Empedocles, Anaxagoras, and Democritus, continued to think philosophically about nature, following the earlier Milesian tradition. To do so, they had to respond to the challenge of the Eleatics, Parmenides and Zeno. They did so in rather different ways.

Empedocles and Anaxagoras argued for a pluralistic view of substance. Although they were philosophers of nature who continued the Milesian tradition, they argued that there are several different kinds of substance-stuffs that constitute the world, rather than only one, as the Milesians claimed.

In contrast to the pluralists, Democritus, following his teacher Leucippus, advanced an atomistic theory of nature. The world consists of undividable physical atoms. Leucippus is said to have written two books, *On the Mind* and *The Great World System*, but no fragments of his work remain and almost nothing is known about his life. Nevertheless, his atomism was expounded by Democritus and is explained by Aristotle and other later ancient writers, such as Simplicius.

EMPEDOCLES (495–435 B.C.)

Biographical History

Empedocles came from a wealthy family in Acragas, Sicily. He himself had some political influence. He wrote several works, of which two poems survive in part: *On Nature* and *Purifications*. Several fragments of both poems exist, but they come from various sources, which generally do not indicate the order of the selection.

Philosophical Overview

Empedocles continued the tradition of natural philosophy started by the Milesians. He claimed that the universe consists of four basic elements, earth, air, fire, and water, which are operated on by two forces, love and strife, or attraction and repulsion. Empedocles believed that the development of the universe is cyclical and eternal. Under the influence of the attractive force, the universe forms itself into a unified seamless sphere. Under the influence of the repulsive force, strife, the universe splits into different objects and becomes the world we now live in. This process of union and division is repeated an infinite number of times for eternity.

These views constitute a response to Parmenides, who claimed that change was impossible given that we cannot refer to what does not exist. First, Empedocles answers Parmenides by agreeing that absolute creation and destruction are impossible and, consequently, that the basic elements have always existed and always will. Second, his response is that changes in the world are simply the reorganization of what already exists, namely, the four basic elements. In other words, such changes do not violate the Parmenidean principle that we cannot refer to what does not exist.

ON NATURE

This reading consists of parts of two poems by Empedocles. The first, *On Nature*, was reportedly 2,000 lines long, of which less than 400 lines have survived. In this poem, Empedocles describes many natural phenomena, including the working of the eye, the action of breathing, and the development of the universe. He tries to explain biological and psychological phenomena in terms of different effluences or liquids fitting, or failing to fit, different pores or inlets in parts of the body.

In his other poem, later called *Purifications*, Empedocles advances a Pythagorean-inspired view of human spirituality. For instance, he describes the fall of humankind.

Originally we were spirits who enjoyed a life of bliss. As a consequence of some error, we are destined to live as incarnate beings, reborn in animal and sometimes even plant form.

1.

The powers spread over the body are constricted, and many afflictions burst in and dull their meditations. After observing a small part of life in their lifetime, subject to a swift death they are borne up and waft away like smoke; they are convinced only of that which each has experienced as they are driven in all directions, yet all boast of finding the whole. These things are not so to be seen or heard by men or grasped with mind. But you now, since you have come aside to this place, will learn within the reach of human understanding. [B 2]

2.

But turn from my tongue, o gods, the madness of these men, and from hallowed lips let a pure stream flow. And I entreat you, virgin Muse, white-armed, of long memory, send of that which it is right and fitting for mortals to hear, driving the will-reined chariot from the place of reverence. [B 3]

3.

If for the sake of any one of mortal men, immortal Muse, (it pleased you) that our cares came to your attention, now once more, Kalliopeia, answer a prayer, and stand by as a worthy account of the blessed gods is being unfolded. [B 131]

4.

And you, Pausanias, son of wise Anchitos, hear me. [B 1]

5.

And do not let (it) compel you to take up garlands of glory and honor from men, on condition that you speak recklessly, overstepping propriety, and so then sit on the high throne of wisdom. But come, observe with every power in what way each thing is clear, without holding any seeing as more reliable compared with hearing, nor echoing ear above piercings of the tongue; and do not keep back trust at all from the other parts of the body by which there is a channel for understanding, but understand each thing in the way in which it is clear. [B 3]

6.

It is indeed the habit of mean men to disbelieve what is authoritative, but do you learn as the assurances of my Muse urge, after the argument has been divided within your breast. [B 4]

7.

Hear first the four roots of all things: bright Zeus and life-bringing Hera and Aidoneus and Nestis, whose tears are the source of mortal streams. [B 6]

8.

A twofold tale I shall tell: at one time it grew to be one only from many, and at another again it divided to be many from one. There is a double birth of what is mortal, and a double passing away; for the uniting of all things brings one generation into being and destroys it, and the other is reared and scattered as they are again being divided. And these things never cease their continual exchange of position, at one time all coming together into one through love, at another again being borne away from each other by strife's repulsion. (So, insofar as one is accustomed to arise from many) and many are produced from one as it is again being divided, to this extent they are born and have no abiding life; but insofar as they never cease their continual exchange, so far they are forever unaltered in the cycle.

But come, hear my words, for learning brings an increase of wisdom. Even as I said before, when I was stating the range of my discourse, a twofold tale I shall tell: at one time it grew to be one only from many, and at another again it divided to be many from one—fire and water and earth and measureless height of air, with pernicious strife apart from these, matched (to them) in every direction, and love among them, their equal in length and breadth. Contemplate her with the mind, and do not sit staring dazed; she is acknowledged to be inborn also in the bodies of men, and because of her their thoughts are friendly and they work together, giving her the name Joy, as well as Aphrodite. No mortal has perceived her as she whirls among them; do you though attend to the progress of my argument, which does not mislead.

All these are equal and of like age, but each has a different prerogative, and its particular character, and they prevail in turn as the time comes round. Moreover, nothing comes to birth later in addition to these, and there is no passing away, for if they were continuously perishing they would no longer exist. And what would increase this whole, and from where would it come? How would it be completely destroyed, since nothing is without them? No, these are the only real things, but as they run through each other they become different objects at different times, yet they are throughout forever the same. [B 17]

9.

It is impossible for there to be a coming into existence from that which is not, and for what exists to be completely destroyed cannot be fulfilled, nor is to be heard of; for when and where it is thrust, then and there it will be. [B 12]

10.

There is no part of the whole that is empty or overfull. [B 13]

11.

They are as they were before and shall be, and never, I think, will endless time be emptied of these two. [B 16]

12.

Here is another point: of all mortal things no one has birth, or any end in pernicious death, but there is only mixing, and separating of what has been mixed, and to these men give the name "birth."[B 8]

13.

When they have been mixed in the form of a man and come to the air, or in the form of the race of wild animals, or of plants, or of birds, then people say that this is to be born, and when they separate they call this again ill-fated death; these terms are not right, but I follow the custom and use them myself. [B 9]

14.

But come, if the form of my preceding argument was in any way incomplete, take note of the witnesses of these to what I have said before: sun with its radiant appearance and pervading warmth, heavenly bodies bathed in heat and shining light, rain everywhere dark and chill, and from earth issue firmly rooted solids. Under strife they have different forms and are all separate, but they come together in love and are desired by one another. From them comes all that was and is and will be hereafter—trees have sprung from them, and men and women, and animals and birds and water-nourished fish, and long-lived gods too, highest in honor. For these are the only real things, and as they run through each other they assume different shapes, for the mixing interchanges them. [B 21]

15.

As painters, men well taught by wisdom in the practice of their art, decorate temple offerings when they take in their hands pigments of various colors, and after fitting them in close combination—more of some and less of others—they produce from them shapes resembling all things, creating trees and men and women, animals and birds and water-nourished fish, and long-lived gods too, highest in honor; so let not error convince you in your mind that there is any other source for the countless perishables that are seen, but know this clearly, since the account you have heard is divinely revealed. [B 23]

16.

They prevail in turn as the cycle moves round, and decrease into each other and increase in appointed succession. For these are the only real things, and as they run through one another they become men and the kinds of other animals, at one time coming into one order through love, at another again being borne away from each other by strife's hate, until they come together into the whole and are subdued. So, insofar as one is accustomed to arise from many, and many are produced from one as it is again being divided, to this extent they are born and have no abiding life; but insofar as they never cease their continual exchange, so far they are forever unaltered in the cycle. [B 26]

17.
For what is right is worth repeating. [B 25]

18.
Strife was retreating from them to the extremity as they were coming together. [B 36]

19.
There the swift limbs of the sun are not distinguished. . . . [I]n this way it is held fast in the close covering of harmony, a rounded sphere, rejoicing in encircling stillness. [B 27]

20.
For two branches do not spring from his back, he has no feet, no swift knees, no organs of reproduction, but he is equal to himself in every direction, without any beginning or end, a rounded sphere, rejoicing in encircling stillness. [B 29/28]

21.
But when great strife had grown in the frame and leapt upward to its honors as the time was being completed, a time of exchange for them, which has been defined by a broad oath [B 30]

22.
For one by one all the parts of god began to tremble. [B 31]

23.
For all these—sun and earth and sky and sea—are one with the parts of themselves that have been separated from them and born in mortal things. In the same way, those that are more ready to combine are made similar by Aphrodite and feel mutual affection. But such as are most different from each other in birth and mixture and in the molding of their forms are most hostile, quite inexperienced in union, and grieving deeply at their generation in strife, in that they were born in wrath. [B 22]

24.
This is well known in the mass of mortal limbs: at one time, in the maturity of a vigorous life, all the limbs that are the body's portion come into one under love; at another time again, torn asunder by evil strifes, they wander, each apart, on the shore of life. So it is too for plants, and for fish that live in the water, and for wild animals who have their lairs in the hills, and for the wing-sped gulls. [B 20]

25.
Come now, I shall tell you from what sources, in the beginning, the sun and all those others which we now see became distinct—earth and swelling sea, moist air, and Titan sky, whose circle binds all things fast. [B 25]

26.
(Air) with deep roots sank down over the earth. [B 54]

27.
Earth increases its own bulk, and air increases air. [B 37]

28.
And many fires burn beneath the surface of the earth. [B 32]

29.
If the depths of earth, and extensive air, are without limit, as has come foolishly from the tongue of the mouths of many who have seen but a little of the whole . . . [B 39]

30.
But I shall turn back to the path of song I traced before, leading off from one argument this argument: when strife had reached the lowest depth of the whirl and love comes into the center of the eddy, in her then all these things unite to be one only; not immediately, but coming together from different directions at will. And, as they were being mixed, countless types of mortal things poured forth, but many, which strife still restrained from above, stayed unmixed, alternating with those which were combining, for it had not yet perfectly and completely stood out as far as the furthest limits of the circle, but part remained within and part had gone out of the frame. And, in proportion as it continually ran on ahead, a mild, immortal onrush of perfect love was continually pursuing it. Immediately what were formerly accustomed to be immortal became mortal, and formerly unmixed

things were in a mixed state, owing to the exchanging of their ways. And, as they were being mixed, countless types of mortal things poured forth, fitted with all kinds of forms, of wonder to see. [B 35]

31.

But as god mingled further with god they fell together as they chanced to meet each other, and many others in addition to these were continually arising. [B 59]

32.

And now hear this—how fire, as it was being separated, brought up by night the shoots of men and pitiable women, for the account is to the point and well informed. First, whole-nature forms, having a share of both water and heat, sprang up from the earth; fire, as it tended to reach its like, kept sending them up, when they did not as yet show the lovely shape of limbs, or voice or language native to man. [B 62]

33.

But if your belief about these things in any way lacked assurance, how, from the combining of water, earth, air, and sun came the forms and color of mortal things which have now arisen, fitted together by Aphrodite . . . [B 71]

34.

There are effluences from all things in existence. [B 89]

35.

With earth we perceive earth, with water water, with air divine air, with fire destructive fire, with love love, and strife with baneful strife. [B 109]

36.

All things are fitted together and constructed out of these, and by means of them they think and feel pleasure and pain. [B 107]

37.

There by the will of chance all things have thought. . . . [B 103]

38.

And earth, anchored in the perfect harbors of Aphrodite, chanced to come together with them in almost equal quantities, with Hephaistos and rain and all-shining air, either a little more, or less where there was more. From these came blood and the forms of different flesh. [B 98]

39.

This is the way in which all things breathe in and out: they all have channels of flesh, which the blood leaves, stretched over the surface of the body, and at the mouth of these the outside of the skin is pierced right through with close-set holes, so that blood is contained, but a passage is cut for air to pass through freely. Then, when the smooth blood rushes away from the surface, a wild surge of blustering air rushes through, and when the blood leaps up, the air breathes out again. It is like a girl playing with a clepsydra of shining bronze—when she puts the mouth of the pipe against her pretty hand and dips it into the smooth body of shining water, no liquid yet enters the vessel, but the mass of air pressing from within against the close-set perforations holds it back until she releases the compressed current, and then, as the air escapes, a due amount of water enters. Similarly, when she has water in the hollow if the bronze vessel, and the neck and passage are closed by human hand, the air outside, pressing inward, keeps the water in at the gates of the harsh-sounding strainer, controlling the defenses, until the girl releases her hand; then, the reverse of the former preocess—as the air rushes in, a due amount of water runs out before it. In the same way, when the smooth blood surging through the body rushes back and inward, a flooding stream of air at once comes pouring in, and when the blood leaps up, an equal amount (of air) in turn breathes back out again. [B 100]

40.

Happy the man who has gained the wealth of divine understanding, wretched he who cherishes an unenlightened opinion about the gods. [B 132]

41.

For he is not equipped with a human head on a body, [two branches do not spring from his back,] he has no feet, no swift knees, no shaggy genitals, but he is mind alone, holy and inexpressible, darting through the whole cosmos with swift thoughts. [B 134]

42.

If you push them firmly under your crowded thoughts, and contemplate them favorably with unsullied and constant attention, assuredly all these will be with you through life, and you will gain much else from them, for of themselves they will cause each thing to grow into the character, according to the nature of each. But if you yourself should reach out for things of a different kind, for the countless trivialities which come among men and dull their meditations, straightaway these will leave you as the time comes round, longing to reach their own familiar kind; for know that all things have intelligence and a share of thought. [B 110]

PURIFICATIONS

1.

My friends who live in the great town of the tawny Acragas, on the city's citadel, who care for good deeds (havens of kindness for strangers, men ignorant of misfortune), greetings! I tell you I travel up and down as an immortal god, mortal no longer, honored by all as it seems, crowned with ribbons and fresh garlands. Whenever I enter prospering towns I am revered by both men and women. They follow me in countless numbers, to ask where their advantage lies, some seeking prophecies, others, long pierced by harsh pains, ask to hear the word of healing for all kinds of illnesses. [B 112]

2.

My friends, I know that there is truth in the words which I shall speak, but indeed it comes hard to men, and the onrush of conviction to the mind is unwelcome. [B 114]

3.

Fools, for their meditations are not far-reaching thoughts, men who suppose that what formerly did not exist comes into existence, or that something dies and is completely destroyed. [B 11]

4.

But why do I lay stress on this, as if it were some great achievement of mine, if I am superior to many-times-dying mortal men? [B 113]

5.

A man who is wise in such matters would not surmise in his mind that men are, and good and ill befall them, for as long as they live, for a lifetime as they call it, and that before they were formed, and after they have disintegrated, they do not exist at all. [B 15]

6.

For before now I have been at some time boy and girl, bush, bird, and a mute fish in the sea.

7.

I wept and wailed on seeing an unfamiliar place. . . . [B 118]

8.

(a joyless place) where (there are) slaughter and hatred and hordes of other violent deaths (and parching fevers and consumptions and ?dropsy) . . . they wander in darkness over the field of Atē. [B 121]

9.

Alas, poor unhappy race of mortal creatures, from what strifes and lamentations were you born. [B 124]

10.

We have come under this roofed cave. [B 120]

11.

Alas that the pitiless day did not destroy me first, before I devised for my lips the cruel deed of eating flesh. [B 139]

12.

Will you not cease from the din of slaughter? Do you not see that you are devouring one another because of your careless way of thinking? [B 136]

13.

The father will lift up his dear son in a changed form, and, blind fool, as he prays he will slay him, and those who take part in the sacrifice bring (the victim) as he pleads. But the father, deaf to his cries, slays him in his house and prepares an evil feast. In the same way son seizes father, and children their mother, and having bereaved them of life devour the flesh of those they love. [B 137]

14.

Among animals they are born as lions that make their lairs in the hills and bed on the ground, and among fair-leafed trees as laurels. [B 127]

15.

And at the end they come among men on earth as prophets, minstrels, physicians, and leaders, and from these they arise as gods, highest in honor. [B 146]

STUDY QUESTIONS: EMPEDOCLES, *FRAGMENTS*

1. What are the elements, according to Empedocles?
2. Why does Empedocles say that there is a double birth of what is mortal?
3. In what way are things 'forever unaltered'? In what ways do things have no 'abiding life'? How does Empedocles reconcile these two claims?
4. Why is it impossible for there to be a coming into existence?
5. How would Empedocles explain the claim that there is no part of the whole that is empty or overfull?
6. What is strife? What are the effects of strife on nature?
7. What happens after things separate? Why does this happen?
8. What would Empedocles say in reply to Parmenides' views? Is this a strong reply to Parmenides? How would Parmenides himself answer?
9. In what ways might Empedocles' philosophy be considered an advance on that of the Milesians?
10. What is Empedocles' theory of effluences?
11. In *Purifications*, Empedocles says that, before now, he had at one time been what? Is his claim really plausible?
12. Why is Empedocles against slaughter?

ANAXAGORAS (500–428 B.C.)

Biographical History

Anaxagoras came from Ionia. Like the earlier philosophers from there, his main interest was in the philosophy of nature and the cosmos. At the age of 20, he moved to Athens, where he remained for 30 years. His book *On Nature* was proclaimed the greatest scientific work of the period. Only about 1,000 words of this work survive, mostly preserved by Simplicius. He wrote it in prose instead of poetry. It is said that he predicted the fall of a meteorite, and he claimed that the sun was a red-hot ball of stone rather than a god. He had a passion for astronomy. He was a friend and teacher of the famous statesman Pericles, who was the founder of democracy in Athens. He also taught the playwright Euripides. Anaxagoras' apparently materialist and antireligious views were unpopular, and he was charged with impiety by Pericles' opponents and was exiled from Athens.

Philosophical Overview

Unlike the previous natural philosophers that we have studied, Anaxagoras rejected the idea that there are basic elements out of which everything is composed. Indeed, he claimed that all substances are always intermingled. For example, a small piece of gold contains all of the other kinds of substances, and those tinier pieces of the other substances contain all of the others. In other words, the world is a thoroughgoing and infinitely divisible mixture. There are no basic elements because there is no smallest or largest portion of any substance-stuff. In this sense, everything is infinitely divisible, and infinite in quantity.

Anaxagoras argued for this conclusion on the basis of the observation that anything, or rather any kind of substance, can come from any other. For example, water can come from clouds, air can arise from fire, and wood can originate from water. Bones and flesh can come from a seed. In short, from any single substance-kind, any other stuff can be extracted. To this empirical observation, we must add the principle that if one can extract a substance from some object, then that object must contain some of that stuff. In short, Anaxagoras argued,

1. *From any substance-stuff, one can extract any other substance-kind.*
2. *If one can extract a substance-kind from some object, then that object must contain some of that kind of substance.*

---

3. *Therefore, any piece of a substance contains all other stuffs.*

Anaxagoras accepted the claim of Parmenides that creation and destruction are impossible. Consequently, nothing can come from nothing, and everything has always existed. However, like Empedocles, Anaxagoras rejected Parmenides' assertion that change and motion are impossible. All change is simply the reorganization or separation of what already exists.

According to Anaxagoras, the mind is separate from all material things. It is not intermingled with anything material, although it can be present in some physical things. The mind is infinite, all-knowing, and self-controlling. Moreover, it is initially responsible for the changes that occur in the physical universe. These changes comprise the continuing separation of the different materials of the universe from an undifferentiated mass. This view may be regarded as a reply to Parmenides' view that change is impossible. Anaxagoras argues that change requires the agency of mind.

FRAGMENTS
Anaxagoras

The first ten fragments outline Anaxagoras' views concerning the physical aspect of nature, such as the infinitely small and the mixing of the elements as described in the Philosophical Overview. Fragments 10 to 13 summarize Anaxagoras' pioneering views concerning the mind. Fragments 18–21 are more biographical, and they reveal the scope of his interests.

1.

Together were all things, infinite both in quantity and in smallness—for the small too was infinite. And when all things were together, none was patent by reason of smallness; for air and ether covered all things, being both infinite—for in all things these are the greatest both in quantity and in size. [59 B 1]

Simplicius, *Commentary on the Physics*, 155.21–157.24

2.

For air and ether are separating off from the surrounding mass. And what surrounds is infinite in quantity. [B 2]

Ibid., 155.21–157.24.

3.

For of the small, he says, there is no smallest, but there is always a smaller. For what is cannot not be. And again of the large there is always a larger, and it is equal to the small in quantity. But in relation to itself each thing is both large and small. [B 3]

Ibid., 164.14–165.5.

4.

This being so, one should believe that in everything that is combining there are present many things of every sort and seeds of all things having all kinds of shapes and colours and savours, and men were compacted and the other animals that possess soul. And the *men* possess inhabited cities and constructed goods, as with us and they have a sun and moon and the rest, as with us, and the earth grows many things of every sort for them, the most useful of which they gather into their houses and use. This I have said about the separating off, because it will not have occurred with us only but also elsewhere. [B 4a]

Ibid., 155.21–157.24.

But before these things separated off, when all things were together, not even any colour was patent; for this was prevented by the commixture of all things— of the wet and the dry and the hot and the cold and the bright and the dark and much earth present therein and seeds, infinite in quantity, in no way like one another. This being so, one should believe that all things were present in the whole. [B 4b]

Ibid.

5.

These things being thus dissociated, one should recognize that all things are neither fewer nor more numerous. For it is impossible for them to be more numerous than all, but all are always equal. [B 5]

Ibid.

6.

Now since there are equal shares of the great and of the small in quantity, for this reason too all things will be in everything; nor can they be separate, but all things possess a share of everything.

Since there cannot be a smallest, things cannot be separated or come to be by themselves, but as they were in the beginning so too now are all things together. In all things there are many even of the things that are separating off, equal in quantity in the larger and smaller. [B 6]

Ibid., 164.14–165.5.

7.

. . . so that we do not know the quantity either in word or in deed of the things that are separating off. [B 7]

Simplicius, *Commentary on On the Heavens*, 608.21–28.

8.

They have not been cut off by an axe, neither the hot from the cold nor the cold from the hot [B 8]

Simplicius, *Commentary on the Physics*, 175.11–15.

9.

As these things thus revolve and are separating off by force and speed (the speed produces the force), their speed is similar in speed to none of the things that now exist among men, but is certainly many times faster. [B 9]

Ibid., 34.18–35.21.

10.

In everything there is present a share of everything except mind—and in some things mind too is present. [B 11]

Ibid., 164.14–165.5.

11.

Mind is something infinite and self-controlling, and it has been mixed with no thing but is alone itself by itself. For if it were not by itself but had been mixed with some other thing, it would share in all things, if it had been mixed with any. For in everything there is present a share of everything, as I have said earlier, and the things commingled with it would have prevented it from controlling anything in the way in which it does when it is actually alone by itself. For it is the finest of all things and the purest, and it possesses all knowledge about everything, and it has the greatest strength. And mind controls all those things, both great and small, which possess soul. And mind controlled the whole revolution, so that it revolved in the first place. And first it began to revolve in a small area, and it is revolving more widely, and it will revolve yet more widely. And mind recognizes all the things which are commingling and separating off and dissociating. And mind arranged everything—what was to be and what was and what now is and what will be—and also this revolution in which revolve the stars and the sun and the moon and the air and the ether which are separating off. But the revolution itself made them separate them off. And the dense is separating off from the rare, and the hot from the cold, and the bright from the dark, and the dry from the wet. And there are many shares of many things, but nothing completely separates off or dissociates one from another except mind. All mind, both great and small, is alike. Nothing else is alike, but each single thing is and was most patently those things of which it contains most. [B 12]

Ibid., 155.21–24.

12.

And when mind began to move things, things were separating off from everything that was being moved, and everything that mind moved was dissociated. And as they were moving and dissociating, the revolution made them dissociate far more. [B 13]

Simplicius, *Commentary on the Physics*, 300.27–301.10.

13.

Mind, which always exists, now assuredly is where all the other things also are—in the surrounding mass and in the things that have associated and in the things that have separated off. [B 14]

Simplicius, *Commentary on the Physics*, 155.21–157.24.

14.

The dense and the wet and the cold and the dark congregated here where now is the earth, and the rare and the hot and the dry and the bright moved out to the farther part of the ether. [B 15]

Ibid., 178.33–179.10.

15.

In this way from these as they separate off earth is compacted; for water is separated off from the clouds, earth from the water, and stones are compacted from

the earth by the cold. And these move out further than the water. [B 16]

Ibid., 178.33–179.10.

16.

The Greeks do not have a correct notion of generation and destruction; for no things are generated or destroyed, but they are commingled and dissociated from things that exist. And for this reason they would be correct to call generation commingling and destruction dissociation. [B 17]

Ibid., 163.18–26.

17.

We are not capable of discerning the truth by reason of their feebleness, [B 21]

what appears is the sight of what is unclear, [B 21a]

Sextus Empiricus, *Against the Mathematicians*, VII 90, 140.

BIOGRAPHICAL REMARKS

18.

He was remarkable for his good birth and his wealth—and also for his generosity inasmuch as he ceded his inheritance to his friends. For when they accused him of neglecting it he said: 'Then why don't *you* look after it?' In the end he went into retirement and spent his time in scientific study, giving no thought to politics. When someone asked him if he had no care for his country, he replied: 'Be quiet—I have the greatest care for my country', pointing to the heavens.

Diogenes Laertius, *Lives of the Philosophers*, II 6–14.

19.

[S]omeone said that just as in animals so in nature mind is present and responsible for the world and its whole ordering: he appeared as a sober man compared to his predecessors who spoke at random.

Aristotle, *Metaphysics*, 984b15–18.

20.

I once heard someone reading from a book of Anaxagoras and saying that it is mind which arranges and is responsible for everything. This explanation delighted me and it seemed to me somehow to be a good thing that mind was responsible for everything—

I thought than in that case mind, in arranging things, would arrange them all, and place each, in the best way possible. So if anyone wanted to discover the explanation of anything—why it comes into being or perishes or exists—he would have to discover how it is best for it to be or to be acted upon or to act. . . . Now, my friend, this splendid hope was dashed; for as I continued reading I saw that the man didn't use his mind at all—he didn't ascribe to it any explanations for the arranging of things but found explanations in air and ether and water and many other absurdities.

Plato, *Phaedo*, 97 BC, 98 BC.

21.
Anaxagoras hit upon the old doctrine that nothing comes into being from what is not, and did away with generation, introducing dissociation in its place. For he said that all things have been mixed with one another and that as they grow they dissociate. For in the same seed there are hairs and nails and veins and arteries and tendons and bones, and they are invisible because of the smallness of their parts; but as they grow they gradually dissociate. For how, he says, could hair come into being from what is not hair, or flesh from what is not flesh? [B 10] And he says this not only of bodies but also of colours; for black is present in white and white in black. And he posited the same for weights, believing that the light was commingled with the heavy and *vice versa*. All this is false—for how can opposites co-exist?

Scholiast to Gregory of Nazianzus (*Patrologia Graeca*, XXXVI 911 BC).

STUDY QUESTIONS: ANAXAGORAS, FRAGMENTS

1. Why does Anaxagoras claim that things are infinite in quantity and smallness?
2. Explain why Anaxagoras says that there is no smallest but there is always a smaller. Why is the claim 'There is no smallest' important to his philosophy?
3. He says that one should believe that all things were present in the whole. Why?
4. What is his reason for thinking that 'all things possess a share of everything'? (6)
5. 'In everything there is present a share of everything,' except what? Why this is the exception? (10)
6. What role does mind play in the physical processes of the universe? Why does it play this role?
7. Why is mind self-controlling? What else does it control?
8. No things are generated or destroyed. Instead, they are what?
9. Does the mind's role in nature undermine the attempt to explain natural phenomena in natural terms? How would Anaxagoras answer this question?

DEMOCRITUS (470–360 B.C.)

Biographical History

Democritus was born in Abdera in Thrace in northern Greece. During his long life, he traveled widely in the ancient world, although the reports that he visited India are probably false. He was a pupil of Leucippus, who was the first atomist. The Greek word *'atomos'* means something that cannot be cut or divided. Allegedly, Democritus lived to the age of 110, and he was one year older than Socrates. He was a prolific writer. Diogenes Laertius lists over 60 works written by Democritus, including his famous *Maxims*. His interests extended far beyond natural philosophy and atomism. He discussed the nature of humans as cultural and social beings, what we would today call anthropological studies. He wrote treatises on poetry, mathematics, and various technical matters, such as farming, diets, medical judgment, and military tactics. He also wrote nine works on moral and political philosophy.

Philosophical Overview

According to Democritus, space is infinite in extent, and there are an infinite number of bodies. However, those bodies are not infinitely divisible; they are indivisible atoms. These atoms have a size and a shape, and they are solid. Sometimes, when they collide, the atoms cohere to form more complex compound bodies. In this way, they form the building blocks of everything we perceive. However, individual atoms lack properties such as taste, color, and smell (which John Locke later called the secondary qualities).

Democritus claimed that atoms cannot be destroyed and are unchangeable. In this respect, Parmenides was right. Each atom is like an unchanging Parmenidean world. However, in opposition to Parmenides, Democritus argued that these atoms are constantly moving and that, through this motion, they constitute our familiar world. To support this claim, Democritus argued directly against Parmenides' premise that we cannot refer to what does not exist. According to Democritus, the nonexistent is no more than empty space or a vacuum, about which we can speak and think. Everything that exists is composed of atoms that occupy and fill that otherwise empty space, and, because of this, anything that does not exist must be identical to empty space.

One of the most remarkable features of Democritus' philosophy is his theory of perception. Diogenes Laertius cites works by Democritus on flavors, colors, and shapes, as well as a general treatise on the senses. Democritus realized that his atomism has dramatic implications for perception. The only real things are atoms. Since these are colorless, color and other similar perceptual properties must be illusions. Consequently, our senses continually deceive us; the world itself is very different from how we perceive it to be.

FRAGMENTS
Democritus

This reading is divided into five sections. The first section outlines Democritus' atomism, which was summarized in the Philosophical Overview. Notice how our knowledge of Democritus' physics relies heavily on Aristotle and his later commentator, Simplicius (530 A.D.). The second section contains Democritus' views on knowledge and perception. The third, the fragments numbered 12 to 30, concerns his views on ethics. His famous maxims comprise the fourth section. Finally, there is a brief section on politics.

I. ATOMISM

1.

Democritus thinks that the nature of eternal things consists in small substances, infinite in quantity, and for them he posits a place, distinct from them and infinite in extent. He calls place by the names 'void', 'nothing' and 'infinite'; and each of the substances he calls 'thing', 'solid' and 'being'. He thinks that the substances are so small that they escape our senses, and that they possess all sorts of forms and all sorts of shapes and differences in magnitude. From them, as from elements, he was able to generate and compound visible and perceptible bodies. The atoms struggle and are carried about in the void because of their dissimilarities and the other differences mentioned, and as they are carried about they collide and are bound together in a binding which makes them touch and be contiguous with one another but which does not genuinely produce any other single nature whatever from them; for it is utterly silly to think that two or more things could ever become one. He explains how the substances remain together in terms of the ways in which the bodies entangle with and grasp hold of one another; for some of them are uneven, some hooked, some concave, some convex, and others have innumerable other differences. So he thinks that they hold on to one another and remain together up to the time when some stronger force reaches them from their environment and shakes them and scatters them apart. He speaks of generation and of its contrary, dissolution, not only in connection with animals but also in connection with plants and worlds—and in general with all perceptible bodies. [Aristotle, fragment 208]

(Simplicius, *Commentary on On the Heavens*
294.30–295.22)

2.

Leucippus and his colleague Democritus say that the full and the void are elements, calling the one 'being' and the other 'non-being'; and of these the full and solid is being, the void non-being (that is why they say that being no more exists than non-being—because void no more exists than body), and these are the material causes of the things that exist. And just as those who make the underlying substance single generate other things by its properties, making the rare and the dense origins of the properties, so these men say that the differences [among the atoms] are the causes of the other things. They say that the differences are three in number—shape, order, and position. For they say that beings differ only by 'rhythm', 'contact' and 'mode'—where rhythm is shape, contact is order and mode is position. The letter A differs from N in shape; AN differs from NA in order; and N differs from Z in position. As for motion (whence and how existing things acquire it), they too, like the others, negligently omitted to inquire into it.

(Aristotle, *Metaphysics* 985b4–20)

3.

Democritus seems to have been persuaded by appropriate and scientific arguments. What I mean will be clear as we proceed.

There is a difficulty if one supposes that there is a body or magnitude which is divisible everywhere and that this division is possible. For what will there be that escapes the division? If it is divisible everywhere, and the division is possible, then it might be so divided at one and the same time even if the divisions were not all made at the same time; and if this were to happen no impossibility would result. So if it is by nature everywhere divisible, then if it is divided—whether at successive mid-points or by any other method—nothing impossible will have come about. (After all, if it were divided a thousand times into a thousand parts, nothing impossible would result, even though no-one would actually so divide it.)

Now since the body is everywhere divisible, suppose it to have been divided. What will be left? A magnitude? That is not possible; for then there will be something that has not been divided, but we supposed it divisible everywhere. But if there is to be no body or magnitude left and yet the division is to take place, it will either consist of points and its components will have no magnitude, or else they will be nothing at all so that it would come to be, and be composed, from nothing and the whole body would be nothing but an appearance.

Similarly, if it is made of points it will not be a quantity. For when the points were in contact and were a single magnitude and were together, they did not make the whole at all larger. For if it is divided into two or more parts the whole is no smaller or larger than it was before, so that even if all the points are put together they will not make any magnitude.

If some sawdust, as it were, is created when the body is being divided, and in this way some body escapes from the magnitude, the same argument applies: how is *this* body divisible?

Perhaps it is not a body but a separable form or property which escapes, and the magnitude consists of points or contacts with such and such a property? But it is absurd to think that a magnitude consists of what are not magnitudes.

Again, where will these points be, and are they motionless or moving?

And a single contact always involves two things, so that there is something apart from the contact and the division and the point.

If one posits that any body of whatever size is everywhere divisible, all these things follow.

Again, if I divide a log or anything else and then put it together, it is again a unit of the same size. This is so at whatever point I cut the log. So it has potentially been divided everywhere. Then what is there apart from the division? Even if it has properties, how is the body dissolved into these and how does it come into being from them? And how are they separated? So if it is impossible for magnitudes to consist of contacts or points, necessarily there are indivisible bodies and magnitudes.

(Aristotle, *On Generation and Corruption* 316a13–b16)

4.

And even more in his second accusation [Colotes] fails to notice that he drives Epicurus out of life along with Democritus. For Democritus' claim—by convention colour and by convention sweet and by convention compounds, etc, in reality the void and the atoms [cf B 125]—was, he says, an attack on the senses; and he holds that anyone who sticks by this argument and uses it cannot even think that he is himself a man and alive.

But what does Democritus say?—That substances infinite in quantity, indivisible and indestructible, and also qualityless and impassive, are carried about scattered in the void. When they approach one another or collide or are entangled, the aggregates *appear* as water or fire or plants or men, but all things really *are* what he calls these indivisible forms and nothing else. For there is no generation from what does not exist, while from the things that exist nothing can be generated in virtue of the fact that, because of their hardness, the atoms neither are affected nor change. Hence no colour can emerge from things which are colorless, and no nature or soul from things which are qualityless and impassive.

(Plutarch, *Against Colotes* 1110F–1111A)

II. KNOWLEDGE

5.

Democritus sometimes does away with what appears to the senses and says that nothing of this sort appears in truth but only in opinion, truth among the things that exist lying in the fact that there are atoms and void. For he says:

> By convention sweet and by convention bitter, by convention hot, by convention cold, by convention colour: in reality atoms and void. [cf B 125]

That is to say, objects of perception are thought and believed to exist but they do not exist in truth—only atoms and void do.

In his *Buttresses*, although he undertakes to ascribe reliable power to the senses, he is found nonetheless condemning them. For he says:

> We in reality know nothing firmly but only as it changes in accordance with the condition of the body and of the things which enter it and of the things which resist it. [B 9]

And again he says:

> That in reality we do not know how each thing is or is not has been shown in many ways. [B 10]

And in *On Ideas* he says:

> And a man must recognize by this rule that he is removed from reality; [B 6]

and again:

> This argument too shows that in reality we know nothing about anything, but our belief in each case is a changing of shape; [B 7]

and again:

> Yet it will be clear that to know how each thing is in reality is a puzzle. [B 8]

Now in these passages he does away in effect with all knowledge, even if it is only the senses which he explicitly attacks. But in the *Rules* he says that there are two forms of knowledge, one by way of the senses and the other by way of the understanding. The one by way of the understanding he calls genuine, ascribing reliability to it with regard to the discrimination of truth; the one by way of the senses he names dark, denying that it is unerring with regard to the discernment of what is true. These are his words:

> There are two forms of knowledge, one genuine and the other dark. To the dark belong all these: sight,

hearing, smell, taste, touch. The dark, separated from this <. . .>. [B 11a]

Then, setting the genuine above the dark, he continues thus:

When the dark can no longer see more finely or hear or smell or taste or perceive by touch, *but something finer* <. . .>. [B 11b]

So according to Democritus, reason, which he calls genuine knowledge, is the standard of truth.
(Sextus Empiricus, *Against the Mathematicians* VII 135–140)

6.
. . . Democritus, who does away with qualities where he says:

By convention hot, by convention cold: in reality atoms and void. [cf B 125]
(Diogenes Laertius, *Lives of the Philosophers* IX 72)

7.
Everyone knows that the greatest charge against any argument is that it conflicts with what is evident. For arguments cannot even start without self-evidence: how then can they be credible if they attack that from which they took their beginnings? Democritus too was aware of this; for when he had brought charges against the senses, saying:

By convention colour, by convention sweet, by convention bitter: in reality atoms and void,

he had the senses reply to the intellect as follows:

Poor mind, do you take your evidence from us and then try to overthrow us? Our overthrow is your fall. [B 125]
(Galen, *On Medical Experience* XV 7–8)

8.
All these people presuppose that the primary element is qualityless, having no natural whiteness or blackness or any other colour whatever, and no sweetness or bitterness or heat or cold or in general any other quality whatever. For, says Democritus,

by convention colour, by convention bitter, by convention sweet: in reality atoms and void. [cf B 125]

And he thinks that it is from the congregation of atoms that all the perceptible qualities come to be—

they are relative to us who perceive them, and in nature there is nothing white or black or yellow or red or bitter or sweet. For by the term 'by convention' he means something like 'by custom', 'relatively to us', 'not in virtue of the nature of the things themselves'. This in turn he calls 'in reality', deriving the word from 'real' which means 'true'. So the sense of his theory, taken as a whole, will be this: Men think that there are white things and black things and sweet things and bitter things; but in truth everything is things and nothing—this is just what he said himself, calling the atoms 'things' and void 'nothing'. Now all the atoms, being small bodies, lack qualities. The void is a sort of space in which all these bodies move up and down for the whole of time, and either entangle with one another or strike and rebound, and in these meetings they dissociate and again associate with one another and from this they make all compounds, including our own bodies and their properties and perceptions.
(Galen, *The Elements according to Hippocrates* I 417–418 K)

9.

Man is what we all know. [B 165]
(Sextus Empiricus, *Against the Mathematicians* VII 265)

10.
Democritus does not state whether perception takes place by opposites or by likes. If he makes perceiving come about by alteration, then he would seem to have it take place by things that are different—for like is not altered by like. But if perceiving—and alteration in general—takes place by being affected, and if, as he says, it is impossible for things that are not the same to be affected (even if things which are different have an effect, they do so not insofar as they are they are different but insofar as they have something the same in common), then it would seem to take place by likes. So we can take him in either way.

He attempts to account for each of the senses in turn. He has sight occur by reflection, but he talks of reflection in a special way. The reflection does not take place immediately in the pupil; rather, the air between the eye and the seen object is imprinted when it is compressed by what is seen and what sees (for there are always effluences coming off everything). Then this air, which is solid and has a different colour, is reflected in the eyes, which are moist. What is dense does not receive it, but what is moist lets it pass through.

(Theophrastus, *On the Senses* 49–50)

11.

Democritus, so they say, used to claim that he would rather discover a single causal explanation than become king of the Persians [B 118]

(Dionysius, in Eusebius, *Preparation for the Gospel* XIV xxvii 4)

III. ETHICS

12.

If you are to be content you must not undertake many activities, whether as an individual or in concert with others, nor choose activities beyond your own power and nature; but you must be on your guard so that even when fortune strikes you and leads you to excess by your beliefs, you put it aside and do not attempt more than you can. For a modest cargo is safer than a great.

(Stobaeus, *Anthology* IV xxxix 25)

13.

If the body were to take the soul to court for the pains and sufferings it had endured throughout its life, then if he were to be on the jury for the case he would gladly cast his vote against the soul inasmuch as it had destroyed some parts of the body by negligence or dissipated them by drunkenness, and had ruined and ravaged other parts by its pursuit of pleasures—just as he would blame the careless user if a tool or utensil were in a bad condition. [B 159]

([Plutarch], *On Desire and Grief* 2)

14.

Happiness and unhappiness belong to the soul. [B 170]

(Stobaeus, *Anthology* II vii 31)

15.

From the same sources from which good things come to us we may also draw bad; but we may avoid the bad. For example, deep water is useful for many purposes, and then again it is bad—for there is danger of drowning. So a device has been discovered: teaching people to swim. [B 172]

(Stobaeus, *Anthology* II iv 1–5)

16.

For men bad things spring from good, when one does not know how to manage the good or to keep it resourcefully. It is not just to count such things bad: they are good, but it is possible, for anyone who wishes, to use good things for bad ends too. [B 173]

(Ibid.)

17.

There is surely intelligence among the young and lack of intelligence among the old; for it is not time that teaches good sense but timely upbringing and nature. [B 183]

(Ibid., II xxx 71–73)

18.

It is fitting for men to set more store by their souls than by their bodies; for perfection of soul rights wickedness of body, but strength of body without reasoning makes the soul no better at all.

(III i 27 = B 187 = B 36)

(Ibid., III i 27)

19.

The boundary of advantage and disadvantage is joy and absence of joy. [B 188]

(Clement, *Miscellanies* II xxi 130.45)

20.

It is best for a man to live his life with as much contentment and as little grief as possible; this will come about if he does not take his pleasures in mortal things. [B 189]

(III i 45–47)

(Stobaeas, *Anthology* III i 45–47)

21.

For men gain contentment from moderation in joy and a measured life: deficiencies and excesses tend to change and to produce large movements in the soul, and souls which move across large intervals are neither stable nor content. Thus you must set your judgement on the possible and be satisfied with what you have, giving little thought to things that are envied and admired, and not dwelling on them in your mind; and you must observe the lives of those who are badly off, considering what they suffer, so that what you have and what belongs to you may seem great and enviable and, by no longer desiring more, you may not suffer in your soul. For one who admires those who possess much and are deemed blessed by other men and who dwells on them every hour in his memory is compelled always to plan something new and, because of his desire, to set himself to do some pernicious deed that the laws forbid. That is why you must not seek certain things and must be content with others, comparing your own life with that of those who do worse and deeming yourself blessed, when you reflect on what they undergo, in faring and living so much better than they do. For if you hold fast to this judgment you will live in greater contentment and will drive away those not inconsiderable plagues of life, jealousy and envy and ill-will.

(Stobaeus, *Anthology* III i 210 = B 191)

22.

Desire for money, if it is not limited by satiety, is far heavier than extreme poverty; for greater desires create greater needs. [B 219]

(Ibid., III x 42–44)

23.

If you exceed the measure, what is most enjoyable becomes least enjoyable. [B 233]

(Stobaeus, *Anthology* III xvii 37–38)

24.

Men ask for health in their prayers to the gods: they do not realize that the power to achieve it lies in themselves: lacking self-control, they perform contrary actions and betray health to their desires.

(Stobaeus, *Anthology* III xviii 30 = B 234)

25.

For those who get their pleasures from their bellies, exceeding the measure in food and drink and sex, the pleasures are brief and short-lived, lasting as long as they are eating or drinking; but the pains are many. For they always have the same desire for the same

things; and when they obtain what they desire, the pleasure swiftly departs, there is nothing good in them but a brief joy, and they need the same things again.

(Ibid., III xviii 35 = B 235)

26.

It is hard to fight against anger: to master it is the mark of a rational man.

(Ibid., III xx 56 = B 236)

27.

Feel shame before others no more than before yourself: do wrong no more if no-one is to know about it than if all men are: feel shame above all before yourself and set this up as a law in your soul so that you may do nothing unsuitable. [B 204]

(Ibid., IV v 43–48)

28.

If you do not desire much, a little will seem much to you; for a small appetite makes poverty as powerful as wealth. [B 284]

(Ibid., IV xxxiii 23–24)

29.

It is irrational not to accommodate yourself to the necessities of life.

(Ibid., IV xliv 64 = B 289)

30.

Drive out by reasoning the unmastered pain of a numbed soul. [B 290]

(Ibid., IV xliv 67–70)

IV. MAXIMS

31.

He who chooses the goods of the soul chooses the more divine: he who chooses the goods of the body, the human. [B 37]

32.

Men flourish neither by their bodies nor by their wealth but by uprightness and good sense. [B 40]

33.

Refrain from error not out of fear but out of duty. [B 41]

34.

It is important to think as you should in times of misfortune. [B 42]

35.

Remorse for foul deeds is the salvation of life. [B 43]

36.

A man who does wrong is more wretched than one who is wronged. [B 45]

37.

Magnanimity is bearing wrongs lightly. [B 46]

38.

A man completely enslaved to money will never be just. [B 50]

39.

The unintelligent come to their senses by suffering misfortune. [B 54]

40.

One should emulate the deeds and actions of virtue, not the words. [B 55]

41.

For beasts, good breeding consists in bodily strength: for men, in grace of character. [B 57]

42.

Neither skill nor wisdom is attainable unless you learn. [B 59]

43.

It is better to examine your own mistakes than those of others. [B 60]

44.

If your character is orderly, your life too will be well-ordered. [B 61]

45.

To be good is not to refrain from wrong-doing but not even to want to commit it. [B 62]

46.

To praise someone for noble deeds is noble; for to praise for bad deeds is the mark of a cheat and a deceiver. [B 63]

47.

Many who have learned much possess no sense. [B 64]

48.

Men are reliable and unreliable not only on the basis of what they do but also on the basis of what wish. [B 68]

49.

Goodness and truth are the same for all men: for different men different things are pleasant. [B 69]

50.

Immoderate desire is the mark of a child, not of a man. [B 70]

51.

Inopportune pleasures give birth to pains. [B 71]

52.

Violent appetite for anything blinds the soul to everything else. [B 72]

53.

Rightful love is longing without violence for the noble. [B 73]

54.

It is pleasant to get nothing which is not to your advantage. [B 74]

55.

Without intelligence, reputation and wealth are not safe possessions. [B 77]

56.

Actions always planned are never completed. [B 81]

57.

Happy is the man who has property and sense; for he uses it nobly on what he should.

The cause of error is ignorance of what is better. [B 83]

58.

It is greedy to say everything and to want to listen to nothing. [B 86]

59.

Your enemy is not he who wrongs you but he who wishes to. [B 89]

60.

Small favours at the right time are very great for those who receive them. [B 94]

61.

A generous man is not one who looks to a return but one who has chosen to confer a benefit. [B 96]

62.

The friendship of one intelligent man is better than that of all the unintelligent. [B 98]

63.

A man who has not a single good friend does not deserve to live. [B 99]

64.

A man who loves no-one seems to me to be loved by no-one. [B 103]

V. POLITICS

65.

It is hard to be ruled by an inferior. [IV iv 27 = B 49]

66.

Ruling is by nature appropriate to the superior. [IV iv 19 = B 267]

67.

Use servants like parts of your body, one for one task and another for another. [IV xix 45 = B 270]

68.

Poverty and wealth are names for lack and satiety; so one who lacks is not wealthy and one who does not lack is not poor. [B 283]

STUDY QUESTIONS: DEMOCRITUS, FRAGMENTS

1. Why, according to Democritus, are being and nonbeing elements?
2. Why does he think that atoms are indivisible? Why are they infinite in number?
3. What is the absurd consequence if magnitude consist of points?
4. How do substances remain together, according to Democritus?
5. What are the three differences between atoms? How does Aristotle in his commentary employ the letters 'A,' 'N,' and 'Z' to illustrate these differences?
6. How does Democritus ascertain the properties of atoms?
7. If, as Democritus claims, only atoms and the void exist, what accounts for appearances?
8. Why does Democritus claim 'by convention sweet and by convention bitter'? What is the next part of this quotation?
9. What is Democritus' view of sense-perception?
10. What is the sense reply to the intellect?
11. Why does Democritus claim, 'Man is what we all know'?
12. What would happen if the body were to take the soul to court and the soul were on the jury? Why is that?
13. What happens if one does not desire much?
14. In what way are Democritus' beliefs regarding atoms different from contemporary atomic theory?
15. How would Democritus reply to the arguments of Parmenides? Are they adequate replies?

Philosophical Bridges: The Influence of Atomism

Democritus' atomism had a vital influence on the philosopher Epicurus and the later Epicurean Lucretius. During the sixteenth-century Renaissance, this atomism was an important source of inspiration to the early scientific thinkers of the time. Sir Francis Bacon (1561–1626), the great spokesman of early modern science, praised Democritus' materialism and, like Galileo, argued that natural phenomena, such as heat, should be explained in terms of the movement of corpuscles.

Strictly speaking, the corpuscles of these early modern scientists are not Democritus' atoms because they were conceived as divisible. They were so conceived because they are located in space, which is continuous and infinitely divisible. However, later scientists, such as Newton, saw wisdom in Democritus' original idea of indivisible atoms. This is because the assertion that matter is infinitely divisible is problematic. Anything made of bits or parts cannot transmit forces instantaneously, will not be perfectly rigid, and, thus, cannot satisfy the requirements of Newton's theory, which involves forces acting at a point. In short, Newton's theory of motion requires the existence of atoms that do not have parts.

Democritus' impact on the history of thought has been largely indirect through the influential writings of the Epicurean poet-philosopher Lucretius (see 'Philosophical Bridges: The Early Ancient Influence' and 'Philosophical Bridges: The Hellenistic and Roman Influence').

What we today call atoms are not indivisible particles. The atom has been split. Contemporary physical theories involve a multitude of subatomic particles, such as neutrons, protons, and electrons. Furthermore, protons and neutrons, which are called hadrons, are composed of quarks. The leptons, such as electrons, are not composed of quarks. Nevertheless, Democritus' idea of basic atoms remains alive as the search continues for fundamental particles that are not composed of anything further. Such fundamental particles would be indivisible, and they would constitute the ultimate constituents of all other nonfundamental particles, along the lines postulated by Democritus.

THE SOPHISTS

PROLOGUE

The Sophists do not constitute a school of thought in the way that the Milesians do. They are individual thinkers who shared a common general outlook rather than specific claims. It was more of a movement than a school. The Sophists included Protagoras, Gorgias, Hippias, and Antiphon, among many others. They had a critical attitude to prevailing moral and religious beliefs, and articulated cultural relativism. Sophists claimed that there are no objectively true moral claims, and that moral beliefs arise solely through social convention. They contrasted convention (*nomos*) with the objectivity of nature (*phusis*).

Sophism resulted in part because of the increasing prosperity and political sophistication of Athens in the fifth century B.C. This led to a demand for forms of education that went beyond the elementary training in literature, music, arithmetic, and gymnastics offered in the schools of the time. In response, the Sophists worked as travelling teachers, offering instruction in rhetoric and persuasion, and transmitting their analyses of morality and politics.

Following Plato, some writers tend to portray the Sophists as superficial thinkers, who taught for financial gain. However, the term 'Sophist' originally came from the word 'sophia,' meaning wisdom. The Sophists were regarded as people of wisdom. However, later the term 'Sophist' became associated with the word 'sophon,' which means cleverness. In this way, the Sophists came to be portrayed as purveyors of cleverness rather than philosophers, lovers of wisdom.

PROTAGORAS (490–420 B.C.)

Biographical History

Protagoras was the first Sophist. He came from Abdera, an Ionian colony on the coast of Thrace. As a child, he may have been educated by the Persians. As a young man, he went to live in Athens, and in 443 B.C., he was asked by Pericles to form a constitution for a colony in southern Italy. He knew Democritus. Although he probably wrote 18 works (12 of which are listed by Diogenes Laertius), there only remain a few sentences and phrases of these works. However, Plato discusses Protagoras' thoughts at length, especially in the dialogues *Protagoras* and *Theaetetus*. From these and other sources, it is possible tentatively to reconstruct his philosophy.

Philosophical Overview

Protagoras is well known for his claim that man is the measure of all things. This saying raises many questions of interpretation. Does it mean humans as a species or individual people? Does it mean *that* things are or *how* they are? Protagoras probably meant that the phenomenal qualities of a thing depend on the individual perceiver. This interpretation can be specified in three ways:

1. *That the very existence of a phenomenal object depends on the mind of the observer; for example, the water you see only exists in your mind.*
2. *That the object perceived exists independently of the perceiver, but its phenomenal qualities only exist in the mind of the perceiver (i.e., the water itself is neither hot nor cold, but if you perceive it as hot, then the heat exists only in your mind).*
3. *That the water itself is both hot and cold, and that perceived objects have contradictory properties.*

Protagoras thought that for every argument in favor of a proposition, there is another argument for the opposite statement. He taught his students how to make the apparently weaker argument stronger. Plato objected to this on the grounds that such a procedure teaches people to win a victory in a debate, but not how to discover truth. To what extent this is a fair representation of Sophists such as Protagoras is debatable. Consider that Protagoras also was a teacher of àreté or virtue. He trained his students to exercise good judgment in the management of their own lives and of the city. He taught them to act in a way that would have beneficial effects. Therefore, Protagoras' view was probably that, in debate, a wise person would use his or her oratory skills to promote the view that will have overall the most beneficial effects.

FRAGMENTS
Protagoras

In the first selected fragment, Diogenes Laertius, writing in the third century A.D., gives a broad overview of Protagoras' views. In several places, it paints Protagoras as a relativist. The second fragment highlights that the Sophists were perhaps the first philosophers to pay attention explicitly to language and argumentation. The third fragment, which is from Plato, emphasizes the political aspect of Sophism and the nonrelativist aspect of Protagoras' thought, namely, that he makes men into *good* citizens. This can be contrasted with the sixth selection, which is also from Plato and which emphasizes the apparently more relativist aspect of Protagoras' views. The fourth selection gives Aristotle's interpretation of the famous saying, 'Man is the measure of all things.'

1.

(DK 80AI) Protagoras was the first to claim that there are two contradictory arguments about everything, and he used them to develop the consequences of contradictory premises, being the first to use this argumentative technique. He began one of his books as follows: 'Man is the measure of all things—of the things that are, that they are, and of the things that are not, that they are not.' He used to say that the mind was nothing but the senses, as Plato says in *Theaetetus*, and that everything is true. He began another of his books as follows: 'Where the gods are concerned, I am not in a position to ascertain that they exist, or that they do not exist. There are many impediments to such knowledge, including the obscurity of the matter and the shortness of human life.' . . .

(Diogenes Laertius, *Lives of Eminent Philosophers* 9.51–3
Long)

2.

He was also the first to develop the kind of argument known as 'Socratic'. And, as Plato says in *Euthydemus*, he was the first to make use, in his talks, of the argument of Antisthenes which tries to prove that contradiction is impossible. He was also the inventor of methods of attacking any given position, as Artemidorus the dialectician reports in his *Against Chrysippus*. . . . He was the first to distinguish the following four kinds of speech: wishing, asking, answering, commanding.

(Ibid.)

3.

'I just want to check that I've understood what you're saying,' I said. 'You seem to me to be talking about political expertise, and to be promising to make men good citizens of their community.'

'Yes, Socrates,' he said. 'That is exactly the profession I make.'

(Plato, *Protagoras* 316b8–319a7 Burnet)

4.

(DK 80AI9) Protagoras said that man is the measure of all things, by which he meant that any impression a person receives is also securely true. From this it follows that the same thing both is and is not the case, and is bad and good and all other contradictories, because it often happens that something can appear beautiful to one lot of people and the opposite to another lot, but on Protagoras' view it is what appears to anyone that is the measure.

(Aristotle, *Metaphysics* 1062^{b}13–19 Ross)

5.

Protagoras says that the being of things that are consists in their being perceived. He says: 'If you are here with me, it is obvious that I am sitting, but this is not obvious to someone who is not here. Whether or not I am sitting is not clear.' And they say that everything that exists consists in being perceived. I see the moon, for example, while someone else does not see it; whether or not the moon exists is not clear. When I

Protagoras, from *The First Philosophers: The Presocratics and Sophists*, translated by Robin Waterfield. Copyright © 2000. Reprinted by permission of Oxford University Press.

am healthy the apprehension of honey that arises is that it is sweet, but someone else who has a fever apprehends it as bitter; whether it is sweet or bitter is therefore not clear. In this way they intend to assert the lack of objective apprehension.

(A fragment of Didymus the Blind, *Commentary on the Psalms*; text first published by M. Gronewald in *Zeitschrift für Papyrologie und Epigraphik*, 2 (1968), 1–2)

6.

(DK 80A22) [*Protagoras speaking*] I know of plenty of things which are harmful to people (they may be foods or drinks or drugs, or whatever), and others which are beneficial; and I know of things which are neither harmful nor beneficial to people, but which are to horses—or are only to cattle, or only to dogs. And then there are things which are neither harmful nor beneficial for any of these creatures, but are for trees; and things which are good for the roots of trees, but bad for their shoots, such as manure, which is good for all plants when it is applied to their roots, but deadly if put on their shoots and young branches. Or then there's olive oil, which is completely pernicious for all plants and ruins the hair of all non-human creatures, but is good for human hair and for the rest of their body too. Goodness is so diverse and varied that even in our case one and the same thing may be good for the outside of a human body, but awful for the inside.

(Plato, *Protagoras* 334a3–c2 Burnet)

7.

(DK 80A23) Protagoras of Abdera held a view that was identical in meaning to that of Diagoras, but he did not express himself in identical words, in order to avoid the excessive recklessness of the view. So he said that he did not know whether there were gods— but this is the same as saying that he knew there were no gods. For if in contrast to his first statement he had said, 'I certainly do not know that they do not exist.' . . .

(Diogenes of Oenoanda, fr. 11 Chilton, col. 2)

8.

(DK 80B10) Protagoras said that skill was nothing without practice, and practice nothing without skill.

(John of Stobi, *Anthology* 3.29.80 Wachsmuth/Hense)

STUDY QUESTIONS: PROTAGORAS, FRAGMENTS

1. What does Protagoras mean when he says, 'Man is the measure of all things'? How does the quotation finish? Is he right?
2. How does Protagoras describe his profession to Plato? Does this description accord with the claim that man is the measure of all things?
3. What does Protagoras claim about the mind?
4. What does Protagoras assert about the gods?
5. Name one of the argumentative methods developed by Protagoras.
6. What does Protagoras say about the being of things that are?
7. Protagoras says that goodness is diverse and varied. How does he support this claim?

GORGIAS (485–395 B.C.)

Biographical History

Gorgias was born in Leontinoi, an Ionian colony in Sicily. Around 427 B.C., Leontinoi was at war with the city of Syracuse. Gorgias was sent to Athens as part of an envoy from his native town to seek the support of Athens. Apparently, he astonished the Athenian assembly with his rhetorical skills, and he succeeded in winning the help of Athens for the war. He traveled throughout the Greek world, lecturing and teaching. In Athens, his teaching brought him great financial success.

Philosophical Overview

Of the 11 works that he wrote, we have only two summaries of Gorgias' book *On Nature*, or *On What Is Not*. In this work, Gorgias argued for three extraordinary claims, corresponding to the three parts of his treatise:

1. *That nothing exists.*
2. *Even if something does exist, we humans cannot know it.*
3. *Even if something does exist and can be known, it cannot be communicated.*

The extraordinary thesis that nothing exists is an attack on Parmenides, who claimed that we cannot refer to what does not exist. In response, Gorgias argues that both being and not-being do not exist. Concerning the second part, the basis of Gorgias' claim is that we cannot know things directly. Knowledge is always mediated by perception and language, and, therefore, we have no direct contact with reality. The third statement is probably based on the idea that words do not convey the things that they refer to. The word 'table' can never give one a table.

FRAGMENTS

Gorgias

The first three selected passages give some biographical and anecdotal context for the longer fourth passage, which explains the argumentation of Gorgias' lost book, *On What Is Not*. The longer passage, which is from Sextus Empiricus (175–225 A.D.), is divided into three parts along the lines explained in the Philosophical Overview.

1.

(DK 82A4) The delegation *[from Leontini to Athens, in 427 BCE]* was headed up by the orator Gorgias, who was by far the most skilful person of his generation at speaking. He was also the inventor of rhetorical techniques and, as a Sophist, was so far ahead of everyone else that he was paid 100 minas by his pupils. After arriving in Athens, he went before the popular Assembly and spoke to them about the possibility of entering into an alliance, and his speech impressed the Athenians, who were an intelligent and cultured people, with its innovative use of language.

(Diodorus of Sicily, *Universal History* 12.53.2–5 Vogel)

2.

(DK 82A25) Gorgias did the same, they say, in writing speeches designed to praise or criticize particular objects, because it was his opinion that it was especially relevant for an orator to be able to amplify a subject by praising it and, on the other hand, to deflate it by criticizing it.

(Cicero, *Brutus* 12.47.1–5 Friedrich)

3.

(DK 82A26) *[Protarchus, a pupil of Gorgias, speaking]* Well, Socrates, when I heard Gorgias speak he often used to say that the art of persuasion is easily the most outstanding science, the reason being that it enslaves everything in voluntary, unconstrained submission to itself; it is, in other words, the most noble science by a long way.

(Plato, *Philebus* 58a7–b2 Burnet)

4.

(DK 82B3) Gorgias of Leontini shared the starting-point of those who did away with the criterion, but did not follow the same line of attack as Protagoras. In his work entitled *On What Is Not* or *On Nature* he constructs arguments under three headings, one after another (1) that nothing has being; (2), that even if it did have being, no human being could apprehend it; (3) that even if it was apprehensible, still it could not be expressed or explained to our neighbour.

(1) His reasoning for the conclusion that nothing has being is as follows. If something has being, it is either something with being, or something without being, or both something with being and something without being. But (*a*) he will go on to establish that it is not the case that something with being has being; (*b*) he will show that something without being has no being either; (*c*) he will demonstrate that it is not the case that both something with being and something without being have being.

(*b*) First, then, that nothing without being has being. If something without being has being, it will simultaneously have and not have being, in the sense that *qua* conceived as not being it will not have being, but *qua being* something without being it will, on the other hand, have being. But since it is completely absurd for something simultaneously to have and not have being, it follows that nothing without being has being. Besides, if something without being has being, then something with being will not have being, since they are opposites to each other, and if being turns out to be an attribute of something without being, then not being will turn out to be an attribute of something with being. But in fact it is not the case that something with being does not have being, and so it is equally not the case that something without being will have being.

(*a*) But then again, something with being does not have being either. For if something with being has being, it must either be eternal or created or both eternal and created. But it is neither eternal nor created nor both, as we will show, and from this it fol-

lows that something with being does not have being. If it is eternal (taking this proposition first), it has no beginning, because anything created has a beginning, but *qua* uncreated something eternal has no beginning. Since it has no beginning, it is infinite, and since it is infinite, it is nowhere, because if it is somewhere, then that in which it is is different from it, and so something with being will no longer be infinite, given that it is contained within something. For the container is greater than the contained, but there is nothing greater than what is infinite, which means that something infinite cannot be anywhere. But neither is it contained within itself. For if this is so, the container and the contained will be identical, and the thing with being will become two, both place and body (the container being place and the contained being body). But this is absurd, and therefore something with being is not within itself either. The outcome of all this is that if something with being is eternal, it is infinite, and if it is infinite, it is nowhere, and if it is nowhere, it has no being. And so, if something with being is eternal, it has no being at all.

But neither can something with being be created. For if it was created, it came into being either from something with being or from something without being. But it did not come into being from something with being, because something with being already has being and does not come into being. And neither did it come into being from something without being, because nothing without being is capable of generating anything, since in order for anything to generate anything else it necessarily has to partake of existence. Therefore, something with being is not generated either.

By the same token, it is not both eternal and created at the same time, because these two are mutually exclusive, so that if something with being is eternal, it did not come into being, and if it came into being, it is not eternal. And therefore, if something with being is neither eternal nor created nor both, then something with being has no being.

Besides, if it has being, it is either single or multiple; but since it is neither single nor multiple, as will be demonstrated, then something with being does not have being. For if it is single, it is either a discrete quantity or a continuum or a magnitude or a body. But if it is any of these, it is not single: if it is a quantity it will be divisible, and if it is a continuum it will be severable. Likewise, if it is conceived as a magnitude, it will not be indivisible. And if it is in fact a body it will be threefold, because it will possess length, breadth, and depth. But it is absurd to say that something with being is none of these things, and from this it follows that something with being has no being. Nor is it multiple, because if it is not single, it is not multiple either, because anything multiple is a compound of singles. Therefore, if there is nothing that is single, there is nothing that is multiple either.

And so it is evident that neither does something with being have being, nor does something without being have being. (c) And, next, it is easy to work out that it is not the case that both something with being and something without being have being. For if something without being has being and something with being has being, then in respect of being something without being it will be identical to something with being. And this is why neither of them has being. For it is a given that something without being has no being, and it has been shown that something with being is identical to something without being, and so something with being will therefore have no being. Moreover, if something with being is identical to something without being, the two of them cannot have being. For if there are the two of them, they are not identical, and if they are identical, they cannot be two.

From all this it follows that nothing has being. For since neither something with being has being, nor does something without being have being, nor do both have being, and since nothing else can be conceived except for these, then nothing has being.

(2) Next it must be demonstrated that even if something does have being, it is unknowable and incomprehensible to any human being. For, Gorgias says, if the objects of thought are not things with being, then something with being is not an object of thought. And this makes sense, because if it were the case that objects of thought were white, it would also be the case that only white things were objects of thought, and by the same token if it were the case that objects of thought were things without being, it would necessarily be the case that things with being would not be objects of thought. Therefore it is perfectly sound and logical to say: 'If the objects of thought are not things with being, then something

with being is not an object of thought.' But objects of thought (to start with this) are not things with being, as we will show. And from this it follows that something with being is not an object of thought. Now, it is evident that objects of thought are not things with being. For if objects of thought were things with being, then everything that one thinks of, however one thinks of them, would have being. But this is nonsensical. For it is not the case that if one thinks of a man flying or a chariot being driven in the sea, then there immediately is a man flying or a chariot being driven in the sea. And so it is not the case that objects of thought are things with being.

Moreover, if objects of thought are things with being, then things without being will not be objects of thought. For opposites are characterized by opposite attributes, and being is opposite to not being. Hence it inevitably follows that if being thought is an attribute of being, not being thought is an attribute of not being. But this is absurd, because Scylla and Chimaera and plenty of things without being are thought of, and so it is not the case that something with being is the object of thought. Just as objects of sight are said to be visible because they are seen, and objects of hearing are said to be audible because they are heard, and it is not the case that we reject objects of sight because they are not heard, nor do we dismiss audible things because they are not seen (for each object should be assessed by its proper sense and not by any other), so also in the case of objects of thought, even if they are not seen by the eyes or heard by the ears, they will still have being, because they can be grasped by their proper criterion. So if one thinks of chariots being driven in the sea, even if one does not see them, one ought to believe that there are chariots being driven in the sea. But this is absurd. Therefore it is not the case that something with being is the object of thought and is apprehended.

(3) Even if it were to be apprehended, it could not be expressed to anyone else. If things with being are visible and audible and, in general, perceptible—that is, if they are external substances—and if those of them that are visible are apprehensible by sight and those of them that are audible are apprehensible by hearing, but not the other way round, then how could one communicate them to someone else? The spoken word is our means of communication, but the

spoken word is not the same as substantial things and things with being. Therefore, it is not the case that we communicate things with being to our neighbours; what we communicate is the spoken word, which is different from these entities. Just as something visible cannot become something audible, and vice versa, so since something with being is an external substance, it cannot become our spoken words, and since it is not the spoken word it cannot be explained to anyone else. Speech, according to Gorgias, is formed when external events—that is, perceptible things—impinge on us. It is from meeting with flavour that there arises in us the spoken word which is expressive of that quality, and the spoken word which is expressive of colour arises from encountering colour. But if this is so, it is not the spoken word that is indicative of something

external, but something external that becomes revelatory of the spoken word. Moreover, it is impossible to claim that the spoken word is the same kind of substantial entity as things which are visible and audible, and so that it is possible for substantial entities and things with being to be communicated as a result of its being a substantial entity and a thing with being. For even if the spoken word has substance, Gorgias says, it is still different from every other substantial entity, and there is an enormous difference between visible bodies and spoken words; that which is visible is grasped by one organ and the spoken word by another. Therefore, the spoken word cannot communicate most substantial entities, just as they too cannot demonstrate one another's natures.

(Sextus Empiricus, *Against the Professors* 7.65.1–86. II Bury)

STUDY QUESTIONS: GORGIAS, FRAGMENTS

1. According to Gorgias, what is the most outstanding science? Why?
2. What is the structure of Gorgias' argument for the conclusion that nothing has being?
3. How does he attempt to prove that something with being does not have being?
4. What is the next major conclusion that Gorgias tries to prove?
5. Objects of thought are not things with being. What does this mean? How does Gorgias prove this, and how does he use this in his argument?
6. Why is it that even if something could be apprehended, it could not be expressed?
7. What does Gorgias say about the spoken word? Could what he says be true given that he is saying it? How could Gorgias reply to that point?
8. Is Gorgias' skepticism plausible? What arguments might one give against it? How should one reply to these arguments?

Philosophical Bridges: The Sophist Influence

Protagoras' famous assertion that man is the measure of all things has articulated important historical changes in thought. For example, it was taken to express an idea that was vital to the development of humanism during the Renaissance of the fifteenth century. The saying indicates a shift of emphasis away from the standards of the Divine and of the otherworldly realm of Platonic Forms toward the human. This was a great insight of the Renaissance: we must understand things in human terms, and humanity should be devoted to the study of itself.

Some nineteenth-century pragmatists also saw Protagoras' saying as a way of articulating the claim that truth must be regarded in terms of usefulness for human purposes and cannot consist in a metaphysical correspondence between our beliefs and reality. Human knowledge is bound to be anthropocentric. In his book *Humanism* (1903), the English philosopher F. C. S. Schiller, who was influenced by William James, cites Protagaras with approval in his argument for the claim that all truth is human-made. In 1976, Reuben Abel, an expert on Schiller, wrote a philosophy textbook entitled *Man Is the Measure* (Free Press,

New York) premised on Protagoras' claim, which he says has never been 'fully grasped nor properly applied.'

Probably, the philosophy of Nietzsche (1844–1900) represents the pinnacle of the Sophist influence. Like the Sophists, Nietzsche rejected the idea that we can represent objectively truths about the world; what we call truths are useful and metaphorical claims, which necessarily reflect a perspective. Moreover, he also denied the objectivity of moral evaluations, which are relative and merely reflect the wishes of rulers. Like some Sophists, such as Thrasymachus, who appears in Book 1 of Plato's *Republic*, Nietzsche claimed that justice consists in the rules of those who have power. He rejected Christian morality as slavish and life-denying. Postmodernists, who were directly influenced by Nietzsche, are sometimes called contemporary Sophists because of their radical rejection of realistic conceptions of truth and representational epistemologies.

Philosophical Bridges: The Early Ancient Influence

In general terms, the works of the early ancient philosophers contain the seeds of much later thinking. In part, this is simply because they were the first philosophers. However, because of this, their historical impact is often indirect. It is also indirect because so little of their work survived the demise of the ancient civilizations of Greece and Rome. Consider, for example, Democritus. His atomism influenced Zeno of Citium, the Stoic, whose views had a profound effect on early modern science mainly through the later writings of Lucretius. In this way, Democritus' influence is mainly via two intermediaries (i.e., Zeno and Lucretius).

However, reviewing the extent of the influence of the early ancients reminds us that their thought was extraordinarily diverse and rich both in style and content. The fragments that remain from this period reveal many different styles of philosophical thinking and writing: scientific poems, paradoxical aphorisms, and wise sayings, as well as prose. They contain bright flashes of insight, detailed observations of nature and speculations, as well as sustained argument. In early ancient thought, we can find many of the perennial debates of philosophy: the senses versus reason, reality is timeless versus reality is ever changing, mathematics versus poetry, science versus religion, matter versus form, argument versus rhetoric, and the Absolute versus the relative. The pre-Socratics were the first to formulate concepts that are key to philosophy and other disciplines.

Some writers have claimed that early ancient thought is philosophy at its best. Nietzsche asserted that early ancient pagan thought is preferable to what he called the 'slave morality' of Christianity that denigrates this earthly life for the sake of an afterlife. He also condemns the emphasis on reason and virtue in Socrates, Plato, and Aristotle. In short, according to Nietzsche, the most brilliant period in the history of philosophy is the early ancient one.

Like Nietzsche before him, the twentieth-century philosopher Martin Heidegger (1889–1976) also claimed that philosophy took a wrong turn after and because of Plato. According to Heidegger, later philosophy, with its emphasis on reason, hides rather than discloses Being. In his later life, Heidegger found more illumination in the poetic style of thinking of some of the early pre-Socratics than in the lofty but rationalistic metaphysics of Plato.

BIBLIOGRAPHY

GENERAL

Primary

Barnes, J., *Early Greek Philosophy*, Harmondsworth, 1987

Freeman, Kathleen, *Ancilla to the Presocratic Philosophers*, Basil Blackwell, 1956

McKirahan, Richard, *Philosophy Before Socrates*, Hackett, 1994

Waterfield, Robin, *The First Philosophers: The Presocratics and Sophists*, Oxford University Press, 2000

SECONDARY

Barnes, J., *The Presocratic Philosophers*, Arguments of the Philosophers, Routledge, 1989

Guthrie, W. K. C., *A History of Greek Philosophy*, vols. 1 and 2, Cambridge University Press, 1965

Hussey, E., *The Presocratics*, London, 1972

Kirk, G. S., Raven, J. E., and Schofield, M., *The Presocratic Philosophers*, 2nd ed., Cambridge University Press, 1983

Long, A. A., ed., *The Cambridge Companion to Early Greek Philosophy*, Cambridge University Press, 1999

Taylor, C. W. W., ed., *From the Beginning to Plato*, Routledge History of Philosophy, vol. 1, Routledge, 1997

Milesians

Kahn, C. H., *Anaximander and the Origins of Greek Cosmology*, Columbia University Press, 1962

Pythagoras

Huffman, C., *Philolaus of Croton: Pythagorean and Presocratic*, Cambridge University Press, 1993

Heraclitus

Robinson, T. M., *Heraclitus Fragments*, University of Toronto Press, 1987

Kahn, C. H., *The Art and Thought of Heraclitus*, Cambridge University Press, 1979

Parmenides and Zeno

Cornford, F. M., *Plato and Parmenides*, Routledge, 1939

Gallop, D., *Parmenides of Elea: Fragments: A Text with an Introduction*, University of Toronto Press, 1984

Grünbaum, Arthur, *Modern Science and Zeno's Paradoxes*, Allen and Unwin, 1968

Mourelatos, A. P., *The Route of Parmenides*, Yale University Press, 1971

Salmon, W., ed., *Zeno's Paradoxes*, Bobbs Merrill, 1970

The Pluralists and Atomists

Furley, David, *Two Studies in the Greek Atomists*, Princeton University Press, 1967

Inwood, Brian, *The Poem of Empodocles: A Text and Translation with an Introduction*, University of Toronto Press, 1992

Schofield, Malcolm, *An Essay on Anaxagoras*, Cambridge University Press, 1980

Wright, M. R., *Empodocles: The Extant Fragments*, Yale University Press, 1981

The Sophists

de Romilly, J., *The Great Sophists in Periclean Athens*, Clarendon Press, 1992

Guthrie, W. K. C., *The Sophists*, Cambridge University Press, 1971

Kerferd, G. B., *The Sophistic Movement*, Cambridge University Press, 1981

SECTION II

◆ PLATO ◆

PROLOGUE

This prologue will concentrate on Socrates (469–399 B.C.), Plato's mentor, who is perhaps the most famous of all philosophers. Why is Socrates so well known? He was not the first philosopher; he did not write a philosophical treatise. Our knowledge of Socrates comes from four principle sources: Plato's dialogues, in 20 of which Socrates is the main character; Xenophon, who wrote the *Memorabilia*, which claims to record several Socratic conversations; Aristophanes, who wrote a comedy, the *Clouds*, featuring Socrates; and, finally, Socrates is mentioned many times by Aristotle. Socrates is portrayed best in the early dialogues of Plato, which reveal something of his extraordinary character.

Socrates' fame is due to the remarkable force of his personality, which is in many ways the embodiment of the philosophical approach. Socrates does not profess to have special knowledge. On the contrary, he claims to be ignorant. He is fascinated by philosophical questions, and, rather than forming fixed views, he asks brilliantly penetrating questions. He engages those around him in thinking, and, in these dialogues, he goads his interlocutor into offering a definition of a key idea, such as justice, courage, or knowledge. He persists with his questioning until either he arrives at a satisfactory answer or he has shown that the proposed theory cannot be true because it contains a hidden contradiction. Socrates' method, often called *elenchos*, or refutation, challenges us to face our ignorance and stimulates us to think more deeply. In summary, Socrates' way of being makes him the best-known of all philosophers.

This does not mean that Socrates did not advance any philosophical claims. His views are reflected in Plato's early dialogues, a point that is confirmed by the works of Xenophon and Aristotle. Among the early dialogues are the following: the *Laches, Charmides, Hippias Major, Euthyphro, Apology, Crito,* and *Protagoras,* as well as the *Gorgias,* which was probably the last work of this early period. Plato has no part himself in any of his works; Socrates usually takes the leading role, and in the early dialogues, Plato restricts himself to portraying Socrates' way of thinking and conveying the master's views. It is only in the dialogues of the middle and later periods that Plato argues for his own theories. As portrayed in the early dialogues, Socrates was almost exclusively concerned with the question 'How should a person live his or her life?' In the *Laches, Charmides, Hippias Major,* and *Euthyphro,* he searches for an answer to these questions, but the dialogues end inconclusively.

Socrates was concerned with virtue or excellence (àreté), regarding which he advances three main claims. First, he argues that knowledge of goodness is necessary and sufficient for virtue. This implies that no one does wrong intentionally: we always will what we perceive as good. As a consequence, there is no such thing as weakness of the will (akrasia). Second, Socrates argues for the unity of the virtues. A person who is virtuous cannot lack any of the virtues; for example, a just person must be also courageous and temperate. Third, Socrates argues that there can be no higher good than virtue: a virtuous person is bound to be happier than one who is not. Given these three claims, we can see why Socrates and Plato thought that study of the good was supremely important for our lives.

Socrates' questioning was perceived as threatening and rebellious. In 399 B.C., he was charged with corrupting the youth of Athens and not recognizing the gods of the city. Once convicted, he was condemned to drink the poisonous hemlock that killed him. These dramatic scenes are immortalized in some of Plato's dialogues. The *Euthyphro* portrays Socrates on his way to court; the *Apology*, the trial itself; the *Crito* shows Socrates' refusal to escape from prison; and the later *Phaedo*, the last conversation and death of the old master.

PLATO (427–347 B.C.)

Biographical History

Plato was only 28 when his beloved teacher, Socrates, was condemned to death. These events affected profoundly the young philosopher, who left Athens shortly afterward. For nearly ten years, he traveled in southern Italy and Sicily, where he began writing his famous dialogues.

Plato came from a prominent aristocratic Athenian family. His mother was a descendent of Solon, the great seventh-century B.C. poet and statesman, who initiated constitutional reforms, wrote many of Athens' laws, and celebrated Athenian democracy in popular poems. Plato received the best education available to prepare him for a great political career. He excelled in poetry, music, and wrestling. However, he grew up during the 27-year Peloponnesian War between Athens and Sparta, and when Athens surrendered in 404 B.C., the young Plato grew disillusioned. He spurned the idea of a life dedicated to politics. Instead, he turned to philosophy, having been influenced by the Sophist Cratylus, and having studied the Eleatics, Protagoras, and Heraclitus. Finally, he became a pupil of Socrates.

After his stay in Sicily following the death of Socrates, Plato returned to Athens and established his famous school, the Academy, a center for the advancement of wisdom and learning. At around the age of 60, Plato received an invitation to train the newly appointed king of Syracuse, Dionysius, to become a philosopher-king, following the model of Plato's work, the *Republic*. When the political climate of Syracuse became unfavorable, Plato was sent away. Four years later, he returned to Syracuse, but had to flee again because of political intrigues.

Philosophical Overview

Plato is the first philosopher to have an integrated view of philosophy as a separate discipline. He combines all of the elements of philosophy discussed by the pre-Socratics and Socrates, and more besides, into one global vision, which encompasses the theory of knowledge, metaphysics, the philosophy of language, mind, mathematics, science, art, education, morality, and politics. Philosophy reveals the existence of and the need for objects that are inaccessible to the senses, and these Forms show us how we should transform our own individual lives and the politics of the state. From this vision, philosophy emerges as the most important of all disciplines. This grand vision is based foremost on the existence of the Forms. These are abstract, eternal, and changeless entities that exist independently of us but can be known through thought, and that define the essence of things in the world. A question such as 'What is Justice?' seeks to understand the Form of Justice. The basis of morality and wisdom is to know the Form of the Good. The existence of the Forms in a way synthesizes Heraclitus and Parmenides. The world of appearances or of the senses is in flux, but the world of the eternal Forms is changeless.

There are 26 surviving dialogues by Plato. They are usually divided into three periods: the early, middle, and late. The early dialogues reflect the thinking and style of Socrates. Plato develops his own philosophical system in the middle period.

The Early Period

The early dialogues are remarkable for their portrayal of the extraordinary personality of Socrates. They show Socrates philosophizing, examining, and challenging views, and they demonstrate how we can deepen our philosophical understanding without necessarily settling on a definitive answer. From this early period we have selected the *Euthyphro*, the *Apology*, the *Crito*, and important excerpts from the *Protagoras* and *Gorgias*.

The Middle Period

Around 386 B.C., when Plato was in his early forties, he developed his own system of thought. The center of this philosophy is the theory of Forms. According to Plato, there exist abstract, nonmaterial objects or entities, called Ideas or Forms. These Forms make worldly objects what they are. Whenever a predicate term, which classifies reality into different types, is applied to many things, there is a Form corresponding to that term. For example, all square things are squared because they participate in the Form of Squareness. Wisdom consists in understanding this realm of Forms, especially the Form of the Good. Knowledge of this Form will make a person happy and virtuous, and, thereby, such knowledge is valuable for the political life of the community. In the *Republic*, Plato tries to show the benefits of leading a virtuous life, quite independent of any of the implications for the afterlife. Plato's mature philosophy is above all a theory of the Forms.

There are a few dialogues that some scholars classify as transitional, in which Plato's own thought begins to emerge but does not yet attain the full maturity of the middle period. Among this transitional group, the most important are the *Meno* and the *Phaedo*, which we have included in the selections. In the *Meno*, Plato argues that learning is really the recollection of knowledge that the soul acquired prior to birth. In the *Phaedo*, Plato also argues for the immortality of the soul, thinking that the true benefits of living virtuously can only be received after the death of the body.

The middle period dialogues include the *Symposium*, *Republic*, *Phaedrus*, *Parmenides*, and *Theaetetus*. The *Symposium* is famous for its discussion of the nature of love. The *Republic* is Plato's most famous and complete work. The *Parmenides* and *Theaetetus* mark Plato's transition to the later period. The *Theaetetus* contains his theory of knowledge, and the *Parmenides* apparently contains his own criticisms of his theory of Forms.

The Late Period

Around 367 B.C., Plato became aware of deficiencies with his own theory of Forms, and he tried to modify the theory. For example, in the *Statesman*, he clarifies that there are not Forms corresponding to every predicate. Forms exist only for natural classifications, and not for arbitrary human divisions, such as the distinction between Greek and non-Greek.

Late-period dialogues include the *Timeaus*, *Critias*, *Sophist*, *Statesman*, *Philebus*, and *Laws*. With the exception of the *Philebus*, Socrates plays only a minor role in these later six dialogues. This is perhaps because the later Plato wanted to signal that his later views were different from those of the middle period. In the *Sophist*, Plato tries to refute Parmenides' claim that we cannot think about what is not. The *Philebus* is famous for its discussion of pleasure. The *Timeaus*, which has been included in this volume, gives a beautiful, semimythical account of the creation of the universe.

EUTHYPHRO

This dialogue takes place shortly before Socrates' trial and subsequent execution in 399 B.C. Euthyphro is a young religious man who believes that piety requires him to prosecute his own father. The father, a rich landowner, accidentally caused the death of a slave who had murdered another slave. Euthyphro's father left the murderer tied up in a ditch while he went to call the authorities, and the slave died. As a consequence, Euthyphro thinks that he is required to accuse his father of manslaughter. This is how the dialogue begins.

If we take his words at face value, Socrates is impressed by Euthyphro's commitment to moral justice and piety. Socrates asks Euthyphro to teach him the true meaning of piety, so that he can better defend himself against the impending charge of impiety. However, none of Euthyphro's answers satisfy the persistent Socrates.

First, Euthyphro gives an example of piety, that is, his own actions: prosecuting someone for some wrongdoing. Socrates points out that an example is not a definition. A definition is a general statement that can then be used to determine whether some particular action is pious or not. To understand a general concept, such as piety, requires more than citing examples because the meaning of the concept is itself necessary for classifying the examples.

Euthyphro tries to rectify his mistake by giving a definition. Pious actions, he says, are those that please the gods, whereas impious actions are those that displease the gods. Instead of agreeing with this definition, Socrates asks another question. Do the gods sometimes disagree? Euthyphro says that they do. Socrates then points out that an action that pleases some gods will anger others, so that, on Euthyphro's definition, a particular action can be both pious and impious, which is contradictory.

Euthyphro replies that, on some things, all the gods agree. Instead of raising objections about how we might know this, Socrates asks one of the most famous and penetrating questions: Is an action pious because it pleases the gods, or does it please the gods because it is holy? In other words, is some action, X, right because God says so, or does God say so because X is right?

This question forces Euthyphro into a dilemma. On the one hand, if being pious is right only because it pleases the gods, then it is not the merits of piety itself that makes it right or wrong. This makes the difference between right and wrong arbitrary. On the other hand, if it is the nature of the pious act that makes the gods love it, then this makes the approval of the gods absolutely irrelevant to what piety itself is. Socrates' persistent questioning has brought the hidden contradictions of Euthyphro's view to the surface.

2a EUTHYPHRO. What is new, Socrates, that you have left the places in Lyceum where you usually spend your time and are now spending time here around the Porch of the King? For surely you don't also happen to have some lawsuit before the King, as I do.

SOCRATES. In fact, Euthyphro, the Athenians don't call it a lawsuit, but an indictment.

EUTHYPHRO. What are you saying? Someone, as

b is likely, has brought an indictment against you. For I won't charge you with doing so against another.

SOCRATES. Certainly not.

EUTHYPHRO. But someone else against you?

SOCRATES. Quite so.

EUTHYPHRO. Who is he?

SOCRATES. I myself don't even recognize the man at all, Euthyphro. He is apparently someone young and unknown. But they say his name is Meletus, as I suppose. He is from the deme Pittheus, if you can think of some Pitthean Meletus with long straight hair, not quite full-bearded, but somewhat hook-nosed.

EUTHYPHRO. I can't think of him, Socrates. But what indictment has he brought against you?

SOCRATES. What indictment? Not an ignoble

c one, it seems to me at least. For it is no paltry thing for one who is so young to have become cognizant of so great a matter. For as he asserts, he knows in what way the young are corrupted and who their corrupters are. And he is probably someone wise, and having discerned my ignorance, he is going before the city, as if before his mother, to accuse me of corrupting those of his own age. And he alone

d of the politicians appears to me to begin correctly. For it is correct to take care of the young first, so that they will be the best possible, just as a good farmer properly takes care of the young plants first, and after this of the

others as well. And so Meletus is perhaps first cleaning us out, the corrupters of the young

3a sprouts, as he asserts. Then, after this, it is clear that when he has taken care of the older ones, he will become the cause of the most and greatest good things for the city. At least that is the likely outcome for someone beginning from such a beginning.

EUTHYPHRO. So I would wish, Socrates, but I am afraid that the opposite will happen. For he seems to me simply to be doing evil to the city, beginning from the hearth, by attempting to do injustice to you. Tell me, what does he assert that you do to corrupt the young?

SOCRATES. Strange things, you wondrous man,

b at least on first hearing. For he asserts that I am a maker of gods, and on this account— that I make novel gods and don't believe in the ancient ones—he has indicted me, as he asserts.

EUTHYPHRO. I understand, Socrates; it's because you assert that the *daimonion* comes to you on occasion. So he has brought this indictment, claiming that you are making innovations concerning the divine things, and he is going into the law court to slander you, knowing that such things are easy to make slander about before the many. And me too—whenever I

c say something in the Assembly concerning the divine things, predicting for them what will be, they laugh at me as if I were mad. And yet, of the things I have foretold, I have spoken nothing that is not true. Nevertheless, they envy us all who are of this sort. But one should not give any thought to them, but should confront them.

SOCRATES. My dear Euthyphro, being laughed at is perhaps no matter. For in fact the Athenians, as it seems to me, do not much care about someone whom they suppose to be clever, unless he is a skillful teacher of his own wisdom. But their spiritedness is aroused against anyone who they suppose makes others like himself, either from envy, as you say, or because of something else.

EUTHYPHRO. That's why I do not at all desire to try out how they are disposed toward me in this regard.

SOCRATES. Perhaps *you* seem to make yourself available only infrequently and not to be willing to teach your own wisdom. But I fear that *I*, because of my philanthropy, seem to them to say profusely whatever I possess to every man, not only without pay, but even paying with pleasure if anyone is willing to listen to me. So if, as I was saying just now, they were going to laugh at me, as you say they do at you, it would not be unpleasant to pass the time in the law court joking and laughing. But if they are going to be serious, then how this will turn out now is unclear except to you diviners.

EUTHYPHRO. Perhaps it will be no matter, Socrates, and your contesting of the lawsuit will proceed as you have a mind for it to do, as I suppose mine will too.

SOCRATES. And your lawsuit, Euthyphro, what is it? Are you defending or prosecuting?

EUTHYPHRO. Prosecuting.

SOCRATES. Whom?

EUTHYPHRO. Someone whom in prosecuting I again seem mad.

SOCRATES. What then? Are you prosecuting someone who flies?

EUTHYPHRO. He is far from flying; in fact, he happens to be quite old.

SOCRATES. Who is he?

EUTHYPHRO. My father.

SOCRATES. Your father, best of men?

EUTHYPHRO. Certainly.

SOCRATES. What is the charge, and what is the lawsuit about?

EUTHYPHRO. Murder, Socrates.

SOCRATES. Heracles! Surely the many, Euthyphro, are ignorant of what way is correct. For I don't suppose that it is the part of just anyone to do this correctly, but of one who is no doubt already far advanced in wisdom.

EUTHYPHRO. Far indeed, by Zeus, Socrates.

SOCRATES. Is the man who was killed by your father one of your family? Or isn't it clear? For surely you wouldn't proceed against him for murder on behalf of an outsider.

EUTHYPHRO. It's laughable, Socrates, that you suppose that it makes any difference whether the dead man is an outsider or of the family, rather than that one should be on guard only for whether the killer killed with justice or not; and if it was with justice, to let it go, but if not, to proceed against him—if, that is, the killer shares your hearth and table. For the pollution turns out to be equal if you knowingly associate with such a man and do not purify yourself, as well as him, by proceeding against him in a lawsuit.

Now the man who died was a laborer of mine, and when we were farming on Naxos, he was serving us there for hire. So in a drunken fit he gets angry with one of the family servants and cuts his throat. So my father, binding his feet and hands together and throwing him into a ditch, sends a man here to ask the exegete what he should do. During this time he paid little attention to the man he had bound and was careless of him, on the ground that he was a murderer and it was no matter even if he should die, which is just what happened to him. For because of hunger and cold and the bonds, he dies before the messenger returns from the exegete.

This, then, is just why my father and the rest of my family are indignant: because on behalf of the murderer I am proceeding against my father for murder, although he didn't kill him, as they assert, and besides, even if he did kill him, since the man who died was a murderer anyway, they say that one needn't give any thought to someone of that sort— for it is impious for a son to proceed against his father for murder—they knowing badly, Socrates, how the divine is disposed concerning the pious and the impious.

SOCRATES. But before Zeus, do you, Euthyphro, suppose you have such precise knowledge about how the divine things are disposed, and the pious and impious things, that, assuming that these things were done just as you say, you don't fear that by pursuing a lawsuit against your father, you in turn may happen to be doing an impious act?

EUTHYPHRO. No, there would be no benefit for me, Socrates, nor would Euthyphro be any different from the many human beings, if I didn't know all such things precisely.

5a

SOCRATES. Then, wondrous Euthyphro, wouldn't it be best for me to become your student and, before Meletus' indictment comes to trial, to challenge him on these very things? I would say that even in time past I regarded it as important to know the divine things, and now, since he asserts that I am doing wrong by acting unadvisedly and making innovations concerning the divine things, I have become your student. "And, Meletus," I would say, "if you agree that Euthyphro is wise in such

b things, then hold that I too believe correctly and drop the lawsuit. But if not, then bring a lawsuit against him, my teacher, instead of me, on the ground that he is corrupting the old, me and his own father, by teaching me and by admonishing and punishing him." And if he isn't persuaded by me and doesn't give up the lawsuit or indict you instead of me, shouldn't I say in the law court these very things on which I challenged him?

EUTHYPHRO. Yes, by Zeus, Socrates, if he should then attempt to indict me, I would discover, as

c I suppose, where he is rotten, and our speech in the law court would turn out to be much more about him than about me.

SOCRATES. And since I am cognizant of these things, my dear comrade, I do desire to become your student, knowing that neither this Meletus nor, no doubt, anyone else even seems to see you; but me he discerns so sharply and easily that he has indicted me for impiety. So tell me now, before Zeus, what you just now strongly affirmed that you know plainly: what sort of things do you say the pious and the

d impious are, concerning murder and concerning other things? Or isn't the pious itself the same as itself in every action, and again, isn't the impious opposite to everything pious, while it itself is similar to itself and has one

certain *idea* in accordance with impiety—everything, that is, that is going to be impious?

EUTHYPHRO. Entirely so, doubtless, Socrates.

SOCRATES. Speak, then, what do you say the pious is, and what the impious?

EUTHYPHRO. I say, then, that the pious is just what I am doing now: to proceed against whoever does injustice regarding murders or thefts of sacred things, or is doing wrong in any other such thing, whether he happens to be a

c father or mother or anyone else at all; and not to proceed against him is impious. Now contemplate, Socrates, how great a proof I will tell you that the law is so disposed—a proof, which I have already told to others as well, that these things would be correctly done if they take place in this way—that one is not to give way to the impious one, whoever he happens to be. Human beings themselves believe that Zeus is the best and most just of the gods, at the same time that they agree that he bound his own father because he gulped down

6a his sons without justice, and that the latter, in turn, castrated his own father because of other such things. Yet they are angry at me because I am proceeding against my father when he has done injustice, and so they contradict themselves both concerning the gods and concerning me.

SOCRATES. Is this, Euthyphro, why I am a defendant against the indictment: that whenever someone says such things about the gods, I receive them somehow with annoyance? Because of this, as is likely, someone will assert that I am a wrongdoer. So now, if these things seem so to you too, who know well

b about such things, it is certainly necessary, as is likely, for us to concede them as well. For what else shall we say, since we ourselves also agree that we know nothing about them? But tell me, before the god of friendship, do you truly hold that these things have happened in this way?

EUTHYPHRO. Yes, and things even more wondrous than these, Socrates, which the many do not know.

SOCRATES. And do you hold that there really is war among the gods against one another, and terrible enmities and battles, and many other such things, as are spoken of by the poets and with which our sacred things have been adorned by the good painters, particularly the robe filled with such adornments which is brought up to the Acropolis in the Great Panathenaea? Shall we assert that these things are true, Euthyphro?

EUTHYPHRO. Not only these, Socrates, but as I said just now, I will also explain many other things to you, if you wish, about the divine things; and when you hear them, I know well that you will be astounded.

SOCRATES. I shouldn't wonder. But you will explain these things to me some other time, at leisure. Now, however, try to say more plainly what I was asking you just now. For you did not teach me sufficiently earlier, comrade, when I asked what ever the pious is. Instead, you told me that what you are now doing, proceeding against your father for murder, happens to be pious.

EUTHYPHRO. Yes, and what I was saying is true, Socrates.

SOCRATES. Perhaps. But in fact, Euthyphro, you also say that many other things are pious.

EUTHYPHRO. Yes, and so they are.

SOCRATES. Do you remember that I didn't bid you to teach me some one or two of the many pious things, but that *eidos* itself by which all the pious things are pious? For surely you were saying that it is by one *idea* that the impious things are impious and the pious things pious. Or don't you remember?

EUTHYPHRO. I do.

SOCRATES. Then teach me what ever this *idea* itself is, so that by gazing at it and using it as a pattern, I may declare that whatever is like it, among the things you or anyone else may do, is pious, and that whatever is not like it is not.

EUTHYPHRO. If this is the way that you wish, Socrates, I'll tell you in this way too.

SOCRATES. Yes, that's just what I wish.

EUTHYPHRO. Then what is dear to the gods is pious, and what is not dear is impious.

SOCRATES. Altogether noble, Euthyphro. You have now answered just as I was seeking for you to answer. Whether it is true, however, I don't yet know. But clearly you will go on to teach me that what you say is true.

EUTHYPHRO. Certainly.

SOCRATES. Come then, let us consider what we are saying. The thing dear-to-the-gods and human being dear-to-the-gods are pious, while the thing hateful-to-the-gods and he who is hateful-to-the-gods are impious. The pious is not the same as the impious, but most opposite. Isn't this so?

EUTHYPHRO. This is so.

SOCRATES. And it appears to have been well said?

EUTHYPHRO. It seems so to me, Socrates, for that is what was said.

SOCRATES. But wasn't it also said that the gods quarrel, Euthyphro, and differ with each other, and that there are enmities among them toward each other?

EUTHYPHRO. Yes, that is what was said.

SOCRATES. What is the difference *about*, best of men, that makes for enmity and anger? Let's consider as follows. If you and I should differ about number—which of two groups of things is greater—would our difference about these things make us enemies and angry at each other? Or would we go to calculation and quickly settle it, at least about such things as these?

EUTHYPHRO. Quite so.

SOCRATES. And if we should differ about the greater and less, wouldn't we go to measuring and quickly put a stop to our difference?

EUTHYPHRO. That is so.

SOCRATES. And would we go to weighing, as I suppose, to come to a decision about the heavier and lighter?

EUTHYPHRO. Of course.

SOCRATES. Then what would we differ about and what decision would we be unable to reach, that we would be enemies and angry at each other? Perhaps you have nothing ready to hand, but consider while I speak whether it is these things: the just and the unjust, and noble and shameful, and good and bad. Isn't it because we differ about these things and can't come to a sufficient decision about them that we become enemies to each other, whenever we do, both I and you and all other human beings?

EUTHYPHRO. Yes, this is the difference, Socrates, and about these things.

SOCRATES. What about the gods, Euthyphro? If they do differ at all, wouldn't they differ because of these same things?

EUTHYPHRO. Most necessarily.

SOCRATES. Then among the gods too, well-born Euthyphro, some believe some things just, others believe others, according to your argument, and noble and shameful and good and bad. For surely they wouldn't quarrel with each other unless they differed about these things, would they?

EUTHYPHRO. What you say is correct.

SOCRATES. And don't they each also love whatever they believe noble and good and just, and hate the opposites of these?

EUTHYPHRO. Quite so.

SOCRATES. But the same things, as you assert, some believe just, and others unjust; and in disputing about these things they quarrel and war with each other. Isn't this so?

EUTHYPHRO. It is so.

SOCRATES. Then the same things, as is likely, are both hated and loved by the gods, and the same things would be hateful-to-the-gods as well as dear-to-the-gods.

EUTHYPHRO. It's likely.

SOCRATES. Then the same things would be both pious and impious, Euthyphro, by this argument.

EUTHYPHRO. Probably.

SOCRATES. Then you didn't answer what I asked, you wondrous man. For I wasn't asking what same thing is at once both pious and impious: whatever is dear-to-the-gods is also hateful-to-the-gods, as is likely. Consequently, Euthyphro, in doing what you are now doing, punishing your father, it is nothing wondrous if you are doing something dear to Zeus but hateful to Kronos and Ouranos, and dear to Hephaestus but hateful to Hera. And if there are other gods who differ with one another about it, it is so with them in the same way.

EUTHYPHRO. But I suppose, Socrates, that none of the gods differs one with another about this, at least: that whoever kills someone unjustly must pay the penalty.

SOCRATES. What, then? Have you ever heard any human being claim in a dispute that one who kills unjustly, or does anything else at all unjustly, need not pay the penalty?

EUTHYPHRO. Certainly. They don't stop disputing in this way, especially in the law courts. For although they have done very many injustices, they will do and say anything at all to escape the penalty.

SOCRATES. Do they in fact agree, Euthyphro, that they have done injustice, and having agreed, do they nevertheless **assert** that they need not pay the penalty?

EUTHYPHRO. In no way, not this at least.

SOCRATES. Then they will not do and say anything at all. For I suppose they don't dare to dispute by saying that even if they have done injustice they need not pay the penalty. Instead, I suppose they assert that they haven't done injustice, don't they?

EUTHYPHRO. What you say is true.

SOCRATES. Then they don't dispute by claiming that the doer of injustice need not pay the penalty; instead, they perhaps dispute who the doer of injustice is, and what he did, and when.

EUTHYPHRO. What you say is true.

SOCRATES. Aren't the gods also affected in the same way, if they do in fact quarrel about the just and unjust things, as your argument says? Don't some of them assert that others do injustice while the others deny it? For surely, you wondrous man, no god or human being dares to say that the doer of injustice ought not to pay the penalty.

EUTHYPHRO. Yes, in this, Socrates, what you say is true, at least in the main.

SOCRATES. But I suppose, Euthyphro, that the disputants dispute about each of the particular things done, both human beings and gods, if gods do dispute. They differ about a certain action, some asserting that it was done justly, others unjustly. Isn't this so?

EUTHYPHRO. Quite so.

SOCRATES. Come then, my dear Euthyphro, teach me too, so that I may become wiser, what your proof is that all gods believe that

that man died unjustly who while serving for hire became a murderer, and then, bound by the master of the man who died, met his end because of his bonds before the one who bound him found out from the exegetes what he should do about him; and that it is correct for a son to proceed against his father and denounce him for murder on behalf of someone of this sort. Come, try to show me in some way plainly about these things, that all gods
b believe more than anything that this action is correct. And if you show me sufficiently, I will never stop extolling you for wisdom.

EUTHYPHRO. But perhaps it is no small work, Socrates, although I could display it to you quite plainly.

SOCRATES. I understand. It's because I seem to you to be poorer at learning than the judges, since clearly you will show *them* that such things are unjust and that all the gods hate them.

EUTHYPHRO. Quite plainly, Socrates, at least if they do listen to me when I speak.

SOCRATES. They will listen, if you do seem to
c speak well. But while you were speaking, I thought of the following and I am considering it with regard to myself: "Even if Euthyphro should teach me that all the gods believe that such a death is unjust, what more will I have learned from Euthyphro about what ever the pious and the impious are? For although this deed would be hateful-to-the-gods, as is likely, it became apparent just now that the pious and the not pious are not defined by this, for it became apparent that the hateful-to-the-gods is also dear-to-the-gods."

So I will let you off from this, Euthyphro. If you wish, let all the gods believe it unjust
d and let all hate it. But is this the correction that we are now making in the argument: that whatever all the gods hate is impious, and whatever they love is pious, but whatever some love and others hate is neither or both? Is this how you now wish it to be defined by us concerning the pious and the impious?

EUTHYPHRO. Yes, for what prevents it, Socrates?

SOCRATES. Nothing on my part, Euthyphro. But consider on your part whether by positing

this you will most easily teach me what you promised.

EUTHYPHRO. Well, I would say that the pious
e is whatever all the gods love, and that the opposite, whatever all gods hate, is impious:

SOCRATES. So shouldn't we consider again, Euthyphro, whether this is said nobly? Or should we let it go and just accept what we ourselves and others say, conceding that something is so if only someone asserts that it is? Or ought we to consider what the speaker says?

EUTHYPHRO. It ought to be considered. However, I suppose that this is now said nobly.

SOCRATES. Soon, my good man, we will know
10a better. Think about something like the following. Is the pious loved by the gods because it is pious, or is it pious because it is loved?

EUTHYPHRO. I don't know what you are saying, Socrates.

SOCRATES. Then I will try to explain more plainly. We speak of something carried and carrying, and of led and leading, and seen and seeing. And do you understand that all such things are different from each other and how they are different?

EUTHYPHRO. It seems to me that I understand.

SOCRATES. And isn't there also something loved and, different from this, the thing loving?

EUTHYPHRO. Of course.

SOCRATES. Then tell me, is the thing carried
10b something carried because it is carried, or because of something else?

EUTHYPHRO. No, it is because of this.

SOCRATES. And the thing led because it is led, and the thing seen because it is seen?

EUTHYPHRO. Quite so.

SOCRATES. Then it isn't because it is something seen that it is seen, but the opposite: because it is seen, it is something seen. Nor is it because it is something led that it is led; rather, because it is led, it is something led. Nor because it is something carried is it carried; rather, because it is carried, it is something carried. Isn't it quite clear, Euthyphro,
c what I wish to say? I wish to say that if something comes to be something or is affected, it isn't because it is something coming to be that it comes to be, but because it comes to be, it is

something coming to be. Nor because it is something affected, is it affected; rather, because it is affected, it is something affected. Or don't you concede that this is so?

EUTHYPHRO. I do.

SOCRATES. And isn't the thing loved either something coming to be or something affected by something?

EUTHYPHRO. Quite so.

SOCRATES. Then this too is just like the previous ones. Not because it is something loved, is it loved by those by whom it is loved, but because it is loved, it is something loved.

EUTHYPHRO. Necessarily.

SOCRATES. Now what are we saying about the
d   pious, Euthyphro? Isn't it loved by all gods, as your argument says?

EUTHYPHRO. Yes.

SOCRATES. Because it is pious, or because of something else?

EUTHYPHRO. No, it's because of this.

SOCRATES. Then is it loved because it is pious, rather than pious because it is loved?

EUTHYPHRO. It's likely.

SOCRATES. But in fact, just because it is loved by gods, it is something loved and dear-to-the-gods.

EUTHYPHRO. Of course.

SOCRATES. Then the dear-to-the-gods is not pious, Euthyphro, nor is the pious dear-to-the-gods, as you say, but the one is different from the other.

10e EUTHYPHRO. How so, Socrates?

SOCRATES. Because we agree that the pious is loved because it is pious, not that it is pious because it is loved, don't we?

EUTHYPHRO. Yes.

SOCRATES. And further, that the dear-to-the-gods, because it is loved by gods, is dear-to-the-gods by this very fact of being loved, and not that it is loved because it is dear-to-the-gods.

EUTHYPHRO. What you say is true.

SOCRATES. But if the dear-to-the-gods and the pious were the same, my dear Euthyphro, then, on the one hand, if the pious were loved because of being pious, the dear-to-the-gods
11a   would also be loved because of being dear-to-the-gods; and on the other hand, if the dear-

to-the-gods were dear-to-the-gods because of being loved by gods, the pious would also be pious because of being loved. But as it is now, you see that the two are opposite, since they are entirely different from each other. For the one, because it is loved, is the sort of thing to be loved; the other, because it is the sort of thing to be loved, is loved.

And probably, Euthyphro, when you are asked what ever the pious is, you don't wish to make clear to me its substance, but rather to speak of a certain affection concerning it: that the pious is affected in being loved by all gods.
b   But what it is, you haven't yet said. So if you please, don't hide it from me, but say again from the beginning what ever the pious is, whether it is loved by gods or however it is affected—for we won't differ about this—but tell me eagerly, what are the pious and the impious?

EUTHYPHRO. But Socrates, I have no way of telling you what I have in mind. For whatever we put forward somehow always keeps going around for us and isn't willing to stay where we place it.

SOCRATES. The things said by you, Euthyphro, are likely to belong to our ancestor Daedalus.
c   And if I were saying them and setting them down, perhaps you would make fun of me by saying that after all it's because of my kinship with him that my works in speech run away and aren't willing to stay where someone sets them down. But as it is now, the suppositions are yours, and some other gibe is needed. For they aren't willing to stay still for you, as it seems to you yourself as well.

EUTHYPHRO. It seems to me, Socrates, that the things said are in need of nearly the same gibe. For as to their going around and not staying in the same place, I didn't put them up to it. Rather, you seem to me the Daedalus,
d   since, as far as I'm concerned, they would stay as they were.

SOCRATES. Then probably, comrade, I have become more clever at the art than that man, insofar as he made only his own things not stay still, while I, besides my own things, also do this to those of others, as is likely. And in particular, for me the most exquisite part of the art is that I am involuntarily wise. For I would wish rather for the speeches to stay still for me and to be placed unmoved, than, in addition to the wisdom of Daedalus, to get the money of Tantalus.

But enough of this. Since you seem to me to be fastidious, I myself will take an eager part in showing you how you may teach me about the pious. And don't get tired out before the end. See if it doesn't seem necessary to you that all the pious is just.

EUTHYPHRO. To me it does.

SOCRATES. And is all the just pious? Or is the pious all just, while the just is not all pious, but part of it is pious, part something else?

EUTHYPHRO. I don't follow, Socrates, what is being said.

SOCRATES. And yet you are no less younger than I am than you are wiser. But as I say, you are being fastidious because of your wealth of wisdom. Come, you blessed man, exert yourself, for it isn't even hard to understand what I am saying. I am saying the opposite of what the poet composed who said:

> Zeus, the one who enclosed and planted all these things, You are not willing to speak of; for where dread is, there too is awe.

Now I differ with the poet in this. Shall I tell you how?

EUTHYPHRO. Quite.

SOCRATES. It doesn't seem to me that "where dread is, there too is awe." For many seem to me to dread when they dread diseases and poverty and many other such things, but to be in awe of none of these things that they dread. Doesn't it seem so to you too?

EUTHYPHRO. Quite so.

SOCRATES. But that "where awe is, there too is dread." For doesn't anyone who feels awe and shame in some matter also fear and dread a reputation for villainy?

EUTHYPHRO. Of course he dreads it.

SOCRATES. Then it is not correct to say, "where dread is, there too is awe," but rather "where awe is, there too is dread"—not, however, "wherever dread is, everywhere is awe." For I suppose that dread extends further than awe. For awe is part of dread, just as "odd" is part of "number." Hence not "wherever 'number' is, there too is 'odd,'" but "where 'odd' is, there too is 'number.'" Surely you follow me now?

EUTHYPHRO. Quite so.

SOCRATES. Now this is the sort of thing I was asking when I was speaking before: is it "where 'just' is, there too is 'pious'"? Or "where 'pious' is, there too is 'just,'" but "where 'just' is, everywhere is not 'pious'"? Is the pious part of the just? Shall we say so, or does it seem otherwise to you?

EUTHYPHRO. No, but this is so. You appear to me to speak correctly.

SOCRATES. Then see what comes after this. If the pious is part of the just, then we need to discover, as is likely, what part of the just the pious would be. Now if you were asking me about one of the things mentioned just now, such as what part of number is the even and what this number happens to be, I would say "whatever is not scalene but rather isosceles." Doesn't it seem so to you?

EUTHYPHRO. It does to me.

SOCRATES. You too, then, try to teach me what part of the just is pious, so that we may also tell Meletus not to do us injustice any longer and not to indict us for impiety, on the ground that we have already learned sufficiently from you the things both reverent and pious and the things not.

EUTHYPHRO. Then it seems to me, Socrates, that that part of the just is reverent as well as pious which concerns the tendance of the gods, while that which concerns the tendance of human beings is the remaining part of the just.

SOCRATES. And what you say appears noble to me, Euthyphro, but I am still in need of a little something. For I don't yet comprehend which tendance you are naming. Surely you aren't saying that that concerning gods is of the same sort as the tendances concerning other things—for surely we do speak of them? For instance, we say that not everyone has knowledge of tending horses, but rather the one skilled with horses, don't we?

EUTHYPHRO. Quite so.

SOCRATES. For surely skill with horses is a tendance of horses.

EUTHYPHRO. Yes.

SOCRATES. Nor does everyone have knowledge of tending dogs, but rather the huntsman.

EUTHYPHRO. Just so.

SOCRATES. For surely the huntsman's skill is a tendance of dogs.

b EUTHYPHRO. Yes.

SOCRATES. And the herdsman's skill is a tendance of cattle?

EUTHYPHRO. Quite so.

SOCRATES. And piety and reverence are a tendance of gods, Euthyphro? Is this what you are saying?

EUTHYPHRO. I am.

SOCRATES. Doesn't every tendance bring about the same thing? For instance, something like this: Is it for a certain good and benefit of the one tended, just as you see that the horses tended by the skill with horses are benefited and become better? Or don't they seem so to you?

EUTHYPHRO. They do to me.

SOCRATES. And surely the same goes for the dogs tended by the huntsman's skill, and the
c cattle by the herdsman's skill, and all the others likewise? Or do you suppose the tendance is for the harm of the one tended?

EUTHYPHRO. By Zeus, not I!

SOCRATES. But for his benefit?

EUTHYPHRO. Of course.

SOCRATES. So is piety too, being a tendance of gods, a benefit to the gods, and does it make the gods better? And would you concede that whenever you do something pious, you make one of the gods better by your work?

EUTHYPHRO. By Zeus, not I!

SOCRATES. No, and neither do I suppose, Euthyphro, that this is what you are saying. Far from it. Rather, I asked what tendance of the gods you were speaking of because I didn't
d believe that you were saying that it is of this sort.

EUTHYPHRO. And you were correct, Socrates; for I am not saying it is of this sort.

SOCRATES. Well, then. But then what tendance of gods would piety be?

EUTHYPHRO. The one with which slaves tend their masters, Socrates.

SOCRATES. I understand. It would be a certain skillful service to gods, as is likely.

EUTHYPHRO. Certainly.

SOCRATES. So could you tell me this: the skillful service to doctors happens to be a skillful service for producing what work? Don't you suppose it is for producing health?

EUTHYPHRO. I do.

SOCRATES. What about the skillful service to
e shipwrights? It is a skillful service for producing what work?

EUTHYPHRO. Clearly, Socrates, for producing a ship.

SOCRATES. And surely that to housebuilders is for producing a house?

EUTHYPHRO. Yes.

SOCRATES. Then tell me, best of men: the skillful service to gods would be a skillful service for producing what work? It is clear that you know, since you assert that you know at least the divine things most nobly of human beings.

EUTHYPHRO. And what I say is true, Socrates.

SOCRATES. Then tell me, before Zeus, what is that altogether noble work which the gods produce, using us as servants?

EUTHYPHRO. Many noble things, Socrates.

SOCRATES. Yes, and so do the generals, my dear
14a man. Nevertheless, you could easily tell me their main one, that they produce victory in war. Or not?

EUTHYPHRO. Of course.

SOCRATES. The farmers too, I suppose, produce many noble things. Nevertheless their main product is the food from the earth.

EUTHYPHRO. Quite so.

SOCRATES. What about the many noble things that the gods produce? What is their main product?

EUTHYPHRO. I also told you a little while ago, Socrates, that to learn precisely how all these
b things are is a rather lengthy work. However, I tell you simply that if someone has knowledge of how to say and do things gratifying to the gods by praying and sacrificing, these are the pious things. And such things preserve private

families as well as the communities of cities. The opposites of the things gratifying are impious, and they overturn and destroy everything.

SOCRATES. You could have told me much more briefly, Euthyphro, if you wished, the main point of what I was asking. But you are not eager to teach me; that is clear. For you turned away just now, when you were at the very point at which, if you had answered, I would already have learned piety sufficiently from you. But as it is—for it is necessary that the lover follow the beloved wherever he leads—again, what do you say the pious and piety are? Isn't it a certain kind of knowledge of sacrificing and praying?

EUTHYPHRO. Yes, I say so.

SOCRATES. Isn't sacrificing giving gifts to the gods, while praying is making requests of the gods?

EUTHYPHRO. Very much so, Socrates.

SOCRATES. Then piety would be a knowledge of requesting from and giving to gods, from this argument.

EUTHYPHRO. You have comprehended what I said, Socrates, quite nobly.

SOCRATES. Yes, for I am desirous, my dear man, of your wisdom and I am applying my mind to it, so that whatever you say won't fall to the ground in vain. But tell me, what is this service to the gods? Do you say that it requests from and gives to them?

EUTHYPHRO. I do.

SOCRATES. Then wouldn't correct requesting be to request the things we need from them?

EUTHYPHRO. Certainly.

SOCRATES. And again, is correct giving to give them as gifts in return the things they happen to need from us? For surely it wouldn't be artful for a giver to bring someone gifts of which he has no need.

EUTHYPHRO. What you say is true, Socrates.

SOCRATES. Then piety, Euthyphro, would be a certain art of commerce for gods and human beings with each other.

EUTHYPHRO. Yes, commerce, if it's more pleasing to you to give it this name.

SOCRATES. But it's not at all more pleasing to me unless it happens to be true. Tell me, what benefit for the gods does there happen to be

from the gifts that they get from us? As to what they give, it is clear to everyone, for there is no good for us that they do not give. But as to what they get from us, how are they benefited? Or do we have so much of an advantage over them in our commerce, that we get all the good things from them, while they get nothing from us?

EUTHYPHRO. But do you suppose, Socrates, that the gods are benefited from the things they get from us?

SOCRATES. Well, Euthyphro, what ever would these gifts from us to the gods be?

EUTHYPHRO. What else do you suppose but honor and respect, and, as I was just saying, gratitude?

SOCRATES. Is the pious then gratifying, Euthyphro, but not beneficial or dear to the gods?

EUTHYPHRO. I for one suppose it is of all things most dear.

SOCRATES. Then this again, as is likely, is the pious: what is dear to the gods.

EUTHYPHRO. Very much so.

SOCRATES. So in saying this, will you wonder if it is apparent that your arguments don't stay still but walk about? And will you accuse me of being the Daedalus who is responsible for making them walk about, when you yourself, being much more artful than Daedalus, even make them go around in a circle? Or don't you perceive that our argument has gone around and come back to the same place? For surely you remember that it became apparent to us earlier that the pious and the dear-to-the-gods are not the same but different from each other. Or don't you remember?

EUTHYPHRO. I do.

SOCRATES. So aren't you aware now that you are asserting that what is dear to the gods is pious? Does this turn out to be anything else but dear-to-the-gods, or not?

EUTHYPHRO. Quite so.

SOCRATES. Therefore either we weren't agreeing nobly before, or, if we did agree nobly then, we aren't setting it down correctly now.

EUTHYPHRO. It's likely.

SOCRATES. Then we must consider again from the beginning what the pious is, since I will not voluntarily give up out of cowardice until I learn it. Do not dishonor me, but apply your mind in every way as much as possible and tell me the truth now. For if in fact any human being knows, you do, and like Proteus, you must not be let go until you tell. For if you didn't know plainly the pious and the impious, there is no way that you would ever have attempted to prosecute an elderly man, your father, for murder on behalf of a hired man. Rather, as to the gods, you would have dreaded the risk that you would not do it correctly, and as to human beings, you would have been ashamed. But as it is now, I know well that you suppose that you know plainly the pious and the not pious. So tell me, Euthyphro, best of men, and don't hide what you hold it to be.

EUTHYPHRO. Some other time, then, Socrates. For now I am in a hurry to go somewhere, and it is time for me to go away.

SOCRATES. Such things you are doing, comrade! By leaving, you are throwing me down from a great hope I had: that by learning from you the things pious and the things not, I would be released from Meletus' indictment. For I hoped to show him that I have now become wise in the divine things from Euthyphro, and that I am no longer acting unadvisedly because of ignorance or making innovations concerning them, and especially that I would live better for the rest of my life.

STUDY QUESTIONS: PLATO, *EUTHYPHRO*

1. What does Socrates mean by 'piety'?
2. Why is an example not a definition?
3. How does Socrates use the point that where there is awe, then there is also dread?
4. Why was Euthyphro prosecuting his own father? What does Socrates make of this?
5. How does Euthyphro try to define piety, and why does he have such trouble doing so?
6. What is the significance of the supposed disagreement among the gods about piety?
7. Is piety the art of commerce with the gods?
8. How would you describe, in your own words, the method of questioning that Socrates uses against Euthyphro?
9. How does Socrates define piety, and what is his objection to his own definition?
10. Plato's argument against Euthyphro's definition of piety as what pleases the gods is often held to be a very important form of argument. What other definitions might this kind of argument apply to?
11. What are the main purposes of this dialogue for Plato?

APOLOGY

Imagine Socrates on trial for corrupting the youth of Athens. The accused, who is in his seventies, is famous throughout the Hellenic world. Plays had been written about him, and he has attracted groups of young students. The prosecution speaks first, outlining the charges. After the prosecution has spoken, the accused speaks in his defense. The jury consists of 501 representative citizens, who must decide his guilt. If the accused is found guilty, the prosecution must propose a punishment, and the defendant may propose an alternative penalty, after which the jury must decide which punishment to apply.

The *Apology* contains a rendering of the extraordinary speech Socrates gave in his defense at his trial (note that the Greek word for 'apology' means 'defense,' not 'request for forgiveness'). The charges against Socrates were corrupting the minds of the young and impiety. Socrates repeats the charges against him, insults his audience, and ridicules his accusers. Socrates is found guilty by a vote of 281 to 220. Meletus proposes the death penalty. Socrates, who has the right to propose an alternative punishment, suggests a life-long pension! Of course, the jury is almost forced to decide the death penalty and does so with 80 more votes.

These events occurred in 399 B.C., five years after Athens' defeat in the Peloponnesian War. Athens was still in a period of political turbulence. In 404, the Council of Thirty assassinated many democratic Athenians and suppressed freedom of speech. However, in 403, democracy was restored to the city. The indictment against Socrates may have had a political motivation: one of his pupils, Critias, was the notorious leader of the Council of Thirty, and Alcibiades, the leader of the disastrous Sicilian military expedition who defected to the Spartans and later the Persians, was his lover. Despite these speculations, Anytus, Meletus, and Lycon brought the charges against Socrates for impiety and corrupting the youth.

In the dialogue, Socrates claims that he has spent his life trying to understand virtue, but that he has not been able to come to a wise conclusion. The only wisdom he can profess is that of knowing that he does not know. Knowledge of the virtues is probably only possessed by the gods. We humans must recognize the limits of our moral understanding. This skeptical attitude is also reflected in some of the other early Platonic dialogues, such as the *Laches*, the *Charmides*, the *Hippias Major*, and the *Euthyphro*. In these dialogues, Socrates pursues understanding of virtue, and in each case, his quarry eludes him. Although he is able to reject false claims, Socrates is not able to reach a positive conclusion. He is wise because he realizes this.

17a [SOCRATES] How you, men of Athens, have been affected by my accusers, I do not know. For my part, even I nearly forgot myself because of them, so persuasively did they speak. And yet they have said, so to speak, nothing true. I wondered most at one of the many falsehoods they told, when they said that you should beware that you are not deceived by me, since I am a clever speaker.

b They are not ashamed that they will immediately be refuted by me in deed, as soon as it becomes apparent that I am not a clever speaker at all; this seemed to me to be most shameless of them—unless of course they call a clever speaker the one who speaks the truth. For if this is what they are saying, then I too would agree that I am an orator—but not of their sort. So they, as I say, have said little or nothing true, while from me you will hear the whole truth—but by Zeus, men of Athens, not beautifully spoken speeches like theirs, c adorned with phrases and words; rather, what you hear will be spoken at random in the words that I happen upon—for I trust that the things I say are just—and let none of you expect otherwise. For surely it would not be becoming, men, for someone of my age to come before you fabricating speeches like a youth. And, men of Athens, I do very much beg and beseech this of you: if you hear me speaking in my defense with the same speeches I am accustomed to speak both in the marketplace at the money-tables, where many of you have heard me, and elsewhere, do not wonder or make a disturbance because of this. For this is how it is: now is the first time I have come before a law court, at the age of seventy; hence I am simply foreign to the manner of speech here. So just as, if I really did happen to be a foreigner, you would surely sympathize with me if I spoke in the dialect and way in which I was raised, so also I do beg this of you now (and it is just, at least as it seems to me): leave aside the manner of my speech—for perhaps it may be worse, but perhaps better—and instead consider this very thing and apply your mind to this: whether the things I say are just or not. For this is the virtue of a judge, while that of an orator is to speak the truth.

So first, men of Athens, it is just for me to speak in defense against the first false charges against me and the first accusers, and next against the later charges and the later accusers. For many have accused me to you, even long ago, talking now for many years and saying nothing true; and I fear them more than Anytus and those around him, although they too are dangerous. But the others are more dangerous, men. They got hold of the many of you from childhood, and they accused me and persuaded you—although it is no more true than the present charge—that there is a certain Socrates, a wise man, a thinker on the things aloft, who has investigated all things under the earth, and who makes the weaker speech the stronger. Those, men of Athens, who have scattered this report about, are my dangerous accusers. For their listeners hold that investigators of these things also do not believe in gods. Besides, there are many of these accusers, and they have been accusing for a long time now. Moreover, they spoke to you at the age when you were most trusting, when some of you were children and youths, and they accused me in a case that simply went by default, for no one spoke in my defense. And the most unreasonable thing of all is that it is not even possible to know and to say their names, unless a certain one happens to be a comic poet. Those who persuaded you by using envy and slander—and those who persuaded others, after being convinced themselves—all of these are most difficult to get at. For it is also not possible to have any of them come forward here and to refute him, but it is necessary for me simply to speak in my defense as though fighting with shadows and refuting with no one to answer. So you too must deem it to be as I say: that there have been two groups of accusers, the ones accusing me now, and the others long ago of whom I speak: and you must also suppose that I should first speak in defense against the latter, for you heard them accusing me earlier and much more than these later ones here.

Well, then. A defense speech must be made, men of Athens, and an attempt must be made in this short time to take away from you this slander, which you acquired over a long time. Now I would wish that it may turn out like this, if it is in any way better both for you and for me, and that I may accomplish something by making a defense speech. But I suppose this is hard, and I am not at all unaware of what sort of thing it is. Nevertheless, let this proceed in whatever way is dear to the god, but the law must be obeyed and a defense speech must be made.

So let us take up from the beginning what the accusation is, from which has arisen the slander against me—which, in fact, is what Meletus trusted in when he brought this indictment against me. Well, then. What did the slanderers say to slander me? Their sworn statement, just as though they were accusers, must be read: "Socrates does injustice and is meddlesome, by investigating the things under the earth and the heavenly things, and by making the weaker speech the stronger, and by teaching others these same things." It is something like this. For you yourselves also used to see these things in the comedy of Aristophanes: a certain Socrates was carried around there, claiming that he was treading on air and spouting much other drivel about which I have no expertise, either much or little. And I do not say this to dishonor this sort of knowledge, if anyone is wise in such things (may I never be prosecuted with such great lawsuits by Meletus!); but in fact I, men of Athens, have no share in these things. Again, I offer the many of you as witnesses, and I maintain that you should teach and tell each other, those of you who have ever heard me conversing—and there are many such among you—tell each other, then, if any of you ever heard me conversing about such things, either much or little, and from this you will recognize that the same holds also for the other things that the many say about me.

But in fact none of these things is so; and if you have heard from anyone that I attempt to educate human beings and make money from it, that is not true either. Though this too seems to me to be noble, if one should be able to educate human beings, like Gorgias of Leontini, and Prodicus of Ceos, and Hippias of Elis. For each of them, men, is able, going into each of the cities, to persuade the young—who can associate with whomever of their own citizens they wish to for free—they persuade these young men to leave off their associations with the latter, and to associate with themselves instead, and to give them money and acknowledge gratitude besides.

And as for that, there is another man here, from Paros, a wise man, who I perceived was in town; for I happened to meet a man who has paid more money to sophists than all the others, Callias, the son of Hipponicus. So I questioned him (for he has two sons):

"Callias," I said, "If your two sons had been born colts or calves, we would have been able to get and hire an overseer for them who could make the two of them noble and good in their appropriate virtue, and he would have been someone from among those skilled with horses or skilled in farming. But as it is, since they are two human beings, whom do you have in mind to get as an overseer for the two of them? Who is knowledgeable in such virtue, that of human being and citizen? For I suppose you have considered it, since you possess sons. Is there someone," I said, "or not?"

"Quite so," he said.

"Who," I said, "and where is he from, and for how much does he teach?"

"Evenus," he said, "Socrates, from Paros: five minae."

And I regarded Evenus as blessed if he should truly have this art and teaches at such a modest rate. As for myself, I would be pluming and priding myself on it if I had knowledge of these things. But I do not have knowledge of them, men of Athens.

Perhaps, then, one of you might retort, "Well, Socrates, what is *your* affair? Where have these slanders against you come from? For surely if you were in fact practicing nothing more uncommon than others, such a report and account would not then have arisen, unless you were doing something different from the many. So tell us what it is, so that we do not deal unadvisedly with you."

In this, it seems to me, what the speaker says is just, and I will try to demonstrate to you what ever it is that has brought me this name and slander. So listen. Now perhaps I will seem to some of you to be joking. Know well, however, that I will tell you the whole truth. For I, men of Athens, have gotten this name through nothing but a certain wisdom. Just what sort of wisdom is this? That which is perhaps human wisdom; for probably I really am wise in this. But those of whom I just spoke might perhaps be wise in some wisdom greater than human, or else I cannot say what it is. For I, at least, do not have knowledge of it, but whoever asserts that I do lies and speaks in order to slander me.

Now please, men of Athens, do not make a disturbance, not even if I seem to you to be boasting somewhat. For "not mine is the story" that I will tell; rather, I will refer it to a speaker trustworthy to you. Of my wisdom, if indeed it is wisdom of any kind, and what sort of thing it is, I will offer for you as witness the god in Delphi. Now you know Chaerephon, no doubt. He was my comrade from youth as well as a comrade of your multitude, and he shared in your recent exile and returned with you. You do know what sort of man Chaerephon was, how vehement he was in whatever he would set out to do. And in particular he once even went to Delphi and dared to consult the oracle about this—now as I say, do not make disturbances, men—and he asked whether there was anyone wiser than I. The Pythia replied that no one was wiser. And concerning these things his brother here will be a witness for you, since he himself has met his end.

b   Now consider why I say these things: I am going to teach you where the slander against me has come from. When I heard these things, I pondered them like this: "What ever is the god saying, and what riddle is he posing? For I am conscious that I am not at all wise, either much or little. So what ever is he saying when he claims that I am wisest? Surely he is not saying something false, at least; for that is not sanctioned for him." And for a long time I was at a loss about what ever he was saying, but then very reluctantly I turned to something like the following investigation of it.

I went to one of those reputed to be wise, on the ground that there, if anywhere, I would refute the divination and show the oracle, "This man is wiser than I, but you declared that I was wisest." So I considered him thoroughly—I need not speak of him by name, but he was one of the politicians—and when I considered him and conversed with

21c   him, men of Athens, I was affected something like this: it seemed to me that this man seemed to be wise, both to many other human beings and most of all to himself, but that he was not. And then I tried to show him that he supposed he was wise, but was not. So from

d   this I became hateful both to him and to many of those present.

For my part, as I went away, I reasoned with regard to myself: "I am wiser than this human being. For probably neither of us knows anything noble and good, but he supposes he knows something when he does not know, while I, just as I do not know, do not even suppose that I do. I *am* likely to be a little bit wiser than he in this very thing: that what-

ever I do not know, I do not even suppose I know."

From there I went to someone else, to one of those reputed to be wiser than he, and these things seemed to me to be the same.

c   And there I became hateful both to him and to many others.

After this, then, I kept going to one after another, all the while perceiving with pain and fear that I was becoming hated. Nevertheless, it seemed to be necessary to regard the matter of the god as most important. So I had to go, in considering what the oracle was say-

22a   ing, to all those reputed to know something. And by the dog, men of Athens—for it is necessary to speak the truth before you—I swear I was affected something like this: those with the best reputations seemed to me nearly the most deficient, in my investigation in accordance with the god, while others with more paltry reputations seemed to be men more fit in regard to being prudent.

Indeed, I must display my wandering to you as a performing of certain labors so that the divination would turn out to be unrefuted. After the politicians I went to the poets, those of tragedies and dithyrambs, and the others, in

b   order that there I would catch myself in the act of being more ignorant than they. So I would take up those poems of theirs which it seemed to me they had worked on the most, and I would ask them thoroughly what they meant, so that I might also learn something from them at the same time. I am ashamed to tell you the truth, men; nevertheless, it must be said. Almost everyone present, so to speak, would have spoken better than the poets did about the poetry that they themselves had made. So again, also concerning the poets, I soon recog-

c   nized that they do not make what they make by wisdom, but by some sort of nature and while inspired, like the diviners and those who deliver oracles. For they too say many noble things, but they know nothing of what they speak. It was apparent to me that the poets are also affected in the same sort of way. At the same time, I perceived that they supposed, on account of their poetry, that they were the wisest of human beings also in the other things, in which they were not. So I went away from there too supposing that I had turned out to be superior to them in the very same thing in which I was to the politicians.

Finally, then, I went to the manual artisans. For I was conscious that I had knowledge of nothing, so to speak, but I knew that I would discover that they, at least, had knowledge of many noble things. And I was not played false about this: they did have knowledge of things which I did not have knowledge of, and in this way they were wiser than I. But, men of Athens, the good craftsmen also seemed to me to go wrong in the same way as the poets: because he performed his art nobly, each one deemed himself wisest also in the other things, the greatest things—and this discordant note of theirs seemed to hide that wisdom. So I asked myself on behalf of the oracle whether I would prefer to be as I am, being in no way wise in their wisdom or ignorant in their ignorance, or to have both things that they have. I answered myself and the oracle that it profits me to be just as I am.

This is the examination, men of Athens, from which I have incurred many hatreds, the sort that are harshest and gravest, so that many slanders have arisen from them, and I got this name of being "wise." For those present on each occasion suppose that I myself am wise in the things concerning which I refute someone else, whereas it is probable, men, that really the god is wise, and that in this oracle he is saying that human wisdom is worth little or nothing. And he appears to say this of Socrates and to have made use of my name in order to make me a pattern, as if he would say, "That one of you, O human beings, is wisest, who, like Socrates, has become cognizant that in truth he is worth nothing with respect to wisdom."

That is why even now I still go around seeking and investigating in accordance with the god any townsman or foreigner I suppose to be wise. And whenever someone does not seem so to me, I come to the god's aid and show that he is not wise. And because of this occupation, I have had no leisure, either to do any of the things of the city worth speaking of or any of the things of my family. Instead, I am in ten-thousandfold poverty because of my devotion to the god.

In addition to these things, the young who follow me of their own accord—those who have the most leisure, the sons of the wealthiest—enjoy hearing human beings examined. And they themselves often imitate me, and in turn they attempt to examine others. And then, I suppose, they discover a great abundance of human beings who suppose they know something, but know little or nothing. Thereupon, those examined by them are angry at me, not at themselves, and they say that Socrates is someone most disgusting and that he corrupts the young. And whenever someone asks them, "By doing what and teaching what?" they have nothing to say, but are ignorant. So in order not to seem to be at a loss, they say the things that are ready at hand against all who philosophize: "the things aloft and under the earth" and "not believing in gods" and "making the weaker speech the stronger." For I do not suppose they would be willing to speak the truth, that it becomes quite clear that they pretend to know, but know nothing. So since they are, I suppose, ambitious and vehement and many, and since they speak about me in an organized and persuasive way, they have filled up your ears, slandering me vehemently for a long time.

From among these men, Meletus attacked me, and Anytus and Lycon, Meletus being vexed on behalf of the poets, Anytus on behalf of the craftsmen and the politicians, and Lycon on behalf of the orators. Therefore, as I said when I began, it would be a wonder to me if I should be able in this short time to take away from you this slander which has become so great. This is the truth for you, men of Athens; I am hiding nothing from you either great or small in my speech, nor am I holding anything back. And yet I know rather well that I incur hatred by these very things; which is also a proof that I speak the truth, and that this is the slander against me, and b that these are its causes. Whether you investigate these things now or later, you will discover that this is so.

So about the things which the first accusers accused me of, let this be a sufficient defense speech before you. But against Meletus, the "good and patriotic," as he says, and the later accusers, I will try to speak next in my defense. Now again, just as though these were other accusers, let us take up their sworn statement. It is something like this: it asserts that Socrates does injustice by corrupting the young, and by not believing in the gods in whom the city believes, but in other *daimonia*

c that are novel. The charge is of this sort. But let us examine each one of the parts of this charge.

Now he asserts that I do injustice by corrupting the young. But I, men of Athens, assert that Meletus does injustice, in that he jests in a serious matter, easily bringing human beings to trial, pretending to be serious and concerned about things for which he never cared at all. That this is so, I will try to display to you as well.

d Now come here, Meletus, tell me: do you not regard it as most important how the youth will be the best possible?

[MELETUS] I do.

[SOCRATES] Come now, tell these men, who makes them better? For it is clear that you know, since you care, at least. For since you have discovered the one who corrupts them, as you say, namely me, you are bringing me before these men and accusing me. But the one who makes them better—come, tell them and reveal to them who it is.

Do you see, Meletus, that you are silent and have nothing to say? And yet does it not seem to be shameful to you, and a sufficient proof of just what I say, that you have never cared? But tell, my good man, who makes them better?

[MELETUS] The laws.

[SOCRATES] But I am not asking this, best of

e men, but rather what human being is it who knows first of all this very thing, the laws?

[MELETUS] These men, Socrates, the judges.

[SOCRATES] What are you saying, Meletus? Are these men here able to educate the young, and do they make them better?

[MELETUS] Very much so.

[SOCRATES] All of them, or some of them, and some not?

[MELETUS] All of them.

[SOCRATES] Well said, by Hera, and you speak of a great abundance of benefiters. What then? Do the listeners here make them better or not?

25a [MELETUS] These too.

[SOCRATES] And what about the Councilmen?

[MELETUS] The Councilmen too.

[SOCRATES] Well, Meletus, then surely those in the Assembly, the Assemblymen, do not corrupt the youth? Or do all those too make them better?

[MELETUS] Those too.

[SOCRATES] Then all the Athenians, as it appears, make them noble and good except me, and I alone corrupt them. Is this what you are saying?

[MELETUS] I do say this, most vehemently.

[SOCRATES] You have charged me with great misfortune. Now answer me. Does it seem to you to be so also concerning horses? That all human beings make them better, while one

b certain one is the corrupter? Or is it wholly opposite to this, that one certain one is able to make them better—or very few, those skilled with horses—while the many, if they ever associate with horses and use them, corrupt them? Is this not so, Meletus, both concerning horses, and all the other animals?

Of course it is, altogether so, whether you and Anytus deny or affirm it. For it would be a great happiness for the young if one alone corrupts them, while the others benefit them. But

c in fact, Meletus, you have sufficiently displayed that you never yet gave any thought to the young. And you are making your own lack of care plainly apparent, since you have cared nothing about the things for which you bring me in here.

But tell us further, Meletus, before Zeus, whether it is better to dwell among upright citizens or villainous ones?

Sir, answer. For surely I am asking nothing hard. Do not the villainous do something bad to whoever are nearest to them, while the good do something good?

[MELETUS] Quite so.

d [SOCRATES] Is there anyone, then, who wishes to be harmed by those he associates with, rather than to be benefited?

Keep answering, my good man. For the law orders you to answer. Is there anyone who wishes to be harmed?

[MELETUS] Of course not.

[SOCRATES] Come then, do you bring me in here saying that I voluntarily corrupt the young and make them more villainous, or involuntarily?

[MELETUS] Voluntarily, I say.

[SOCRATES] What then, Meletus? Are you so much wiser at your age than I at mine, that you have become cognizant that the bad always do something bad to those who are closest to them, and the good do something good; e whereas I have come into so much ignorance that I am not even cognizant that if I ever do something wretched to any of my associates, I will risk getting back something bad from him? So that I do so much bad voluntarily, as you assert? Of this I am not convinced by you, Meletus, nor, do I suppose, is any other human being. But either I do not corrupt, or if I do corrupt, I do it involuntarily, so in both cases 26a what you say is false.

And if I corrupt involuntarily, the law is not that you bring me in here for such involuntary wrongs, but that you take me aside in private to teach and admonish me. For it is clear that if I learn, I will at least stop doing what I do involuntarily. But you avoided associating with me and teaching me, and you were not willing to, but instead you brought me in here, where the law is to bring in those in need of punishment, not learning.

But in fact, men of Athens, what I was saying is already clear, that Meletus never b cared about these things either much or little. Nevertheless, speak to us, how do you say that I corrupt the youth, Meletus? Or is it clear,

according to the indictment that you brought, that it is by teaching them not to believe in the gods in whom the city believes, but in other *daimonia* that are novel? Do you not say that it is by teaching these things that I corrupt them?

[MELETUS] I certainly do say this, most vehemently!

[SOCRATES] Then before these very gods, Meletus, about whom our speech now is, speak to c me and to these men still more plainly. For I am not able to understand whether you are saying that I teach them to believe that there are gods of some sort—and so I myself do believe that there are gods and am not completely atheistic and do not do injustice in this way—but that I do not believe in those in whom the city believes, but in others, and this is what you charge me with, that I believe in others. Or do you assert that I myself do not believe in gods at all and that I teach this to others?

[MELETUS] This is what I say, that you do not believe in gods at all.

d [SOCRATES] Wondrous Meletus, why do you say this? Do I not even believe, then, that sun and moon are gods, as other human beings do?

[MELETUS] No, by Zeus, judges, since he declares that the sun is stone and the moon is earth.

[SOCRATES] Do you suppose you are accusing Anaxagoras, my dear Meletus? And do you so much despise these men here and suppose that they are so inexperienced in letters that they do not know that the books of Anaxagoras of Clazomenae are full of these speeches? Moreover, do the young learn these things from me, when it is sometimes possible for them to buy them in the orchestra for a drachma, if the price is very high, and then to e laugh at Socrates if he pretends that they are his own, especially since they are so strange? But before Zeus, is this how I seem to you? Do I believe there is no god?

[MELETUS] You certainly do not, by Zeus, not in any way at all!

[SOCRATES] You are unbelievable, Meletus, even, as you seem to me, to yourself. This man seems to me, men of Athens, to be very hubristic and unrestrained, and simply to have brought this indictment with a certain hubris and unrestraint and youthful rashness. He is like someone testing me by putting together a riddle: "Will Socrates the 'wise' recognize that I am jesting and contradicting myself, or will I deceive him and the rest of the listeners?" For he himself appears to me to be contradicting himself in the indictment, as if he were to say, "Socrates does injustice by not believing in gods, but believing in gods." And yet this is the conduct of one who jokes.

Now consider with me, men, how he appears to me to be saying this. And you answer us, Meletus. But you others, as I begged of you from the beginning, please remember not to make disturbances if I make the speeches in my accustomed way.

Is there any human being, Meletus, who believes that there are human matters, but does not believe in human beings?

Let him keep answering, men, and let him not make disturbances again and again. Is there anyone who does not believe in horses, but believes in horse-matters? Or anyone who does not believe in flute-players, but believes in flute-matters?

There is not, best of men. If you do not wish to answer, I say it for you and for these others. But at least answer what comes next. Is there anyone who believes that there are daimonic matters, but does not believe in daimons?

[MELETUS] There is not.

[SOCRATES] How helpful you were by answering reluctantly when compelled by these men! Now then, you say that I believe in and teach *daimonia*; so whether they are novel or ancient, at any rate I do believe in *daimonia* according to your speech, and you also swore to this in the indictment. But if I believe in *daimonia*, then surely there is also a great necessity that I believe in daimons. Is this not so?

Of course it is. I set you down as agreeing, since you do not answer. And do we not believe that daimons are either gods or children of gods? Do you affirm this or not?

[MELETUS] Quite so.

[SOCRATES] Therefore if I do believe in daimons, as you say, and if, on the one hand, daimons are gods of some sort, then this would be what I say you are riddling and jesting about, when you say that I do not believe in gods, and again that I believe in gods, since in fact I do believe in daimons.

On the other hand, if daimons are certain bastard children of gods, whether from nymphs or from certain others of whom it is also said they are born, then what human being would believe that there are children of gods, but not gods? It would be as strange as if someone believed in children of horses or asses—mules—but did not believe that there are horses and asses. But, Meletus, there is no way that you did not bring this indictment either to test us in these things, or else because you were at a loss about what true injustice you might charge me with. There is no device by which you could persuade any human being who is even slightly intelligent, that it is not the part of the same man to believe in both *daimonia* and divine things, and further that this same man believes in neither daimons nor gods nor heroes.

But in fact, men of Athens, that I do not do injustice according to Meletus' indictment, does not seem to me to require much of a defense speech, but even this is sufficient. But what I was saying earlier—that I have incurred much hatred, and among many men—know well that this is true. And this is what will convict me, if it does convict me: not Meletus or Anytus, but the slander and envy of the many. This has convicted many other good men too, and I suppose it will also convict me. And there is no danger that it will stop with me.

Perhaps, then, someone might say, "Then are you not ashamed, Socrates, of having followed the sort of pursuit from which you now run the risk of dying?"

I would respond to him with a just speech: "What you say is ignoble, fellow, if you suppose that a man who is of even a little benefit should take into account the danger of living or dying, but not rather consider this alone whenever he acts: whether his actions are just or unjust, and the deeds of a good man or a bad. For according to your speech, those of the demigods who met their end at Troy would be paltry, especially the son of Thetis. Rather than endure anything shameful, he despised danger so much that when his mother (a goddess) spoke to him as he was eager to kill Hector—something like this, as I suppose: 'Son, if you avenge the murder of your comrade Patroclus and kill Hector, you yourself will die; for straightway,' she says, 'after Hector, your fate is ready at hand'—he, upon hearing this, belittled death and danger, fearing much more to live as a bad man and not to avenge his friends. 'Straightway,' he says, 'may I die, after I inflict a penalty on the doer of injustice, so that I do not stay here ridiculous beside the curved ships, a burden on the land.' Surely you do not suppose that he gave any thought to death and danger?"

This is the way it is, men of Athens, in truth. Wherever someone stations himself, holding that it is best, or wherever he is stationed by a ruler, there he must stay and run the risk, as it seems to me, and not take into account death or anything else compared to what is shameful. So I would have done terrible deeds, men of Athens, if, when the rulers whom you elected to rule me stationed me in Potidaea and Amphipolis and at Delium, I stayed then where they stationed me and ran the risk of dying like anyone else, but when the god stationed me, as I supposed and assumed, ordering me to live philosophizing and examining myself and others, I had then left my station because I feared death or any other matter whatever.

Terrible that *would* be, and truly then someone might justly bring me into a law court, saying that I do not believe that there are gods, since I would be disobeying the divination, and fearing death, and supposing that I am wise when I am not. For to fear death, men, is in fact nothing other than to seem to be wise, but not to be so. For it is to seem to know what one does not know: no one knows whether death does not even happen to be the greatest of all goods for the human being; but people fear it as though they knew well that it is the greatest of evils. And how is this not that reproachable ignorance of supposing that one knows what one does not know? But I, men, am perhaps distinguished from the many human beings also here in this, and if I were to say that I am wiser than anyone in anything, it would be in this: that since I do not know sufficiently about the things in Hades, so also I suppose that I do not know. But I do know that it is bad and shameful to do injustice and to disobey one's better, whether god or human being. So compared to the bad things which I know are bad, I will never fear or flee the things about which I do not know whether they even happen to be good.

So that not even if you let me go now and if you disobey Anytus—who said that either I should not have been brought in here at the beginning, or, since I was brought in, that it is not possible not to kill me (he said before you that if I am acquitted, soon your sons, pursuing what Socrates teaches, will all be completely corrupted)—if you would say to me with regard to this, "Socrates, for now we will not obey Anytus; we will let you go, but on this condition: that you no longer spend time in this investigation or philosophize; and if you are caught still doing this, you will die"— if you would let me go, then, as I said, on these conditions, I would say to you, "I, men of Athens, salute you and love you, but I will obey the god rather than you; and as long as I breathe and am able to, I will certainly not stop philosophizing, and I will exhort you and explain this to whomever of you I happen to meet, and I will speak just the sorts of things I am accustomed to: 'Best of men, you are an Athenian, from the city that is greatest and best reputed for wisdom and strength: are you not ashamed that you care for having as much money as possible, and reputation, and honor, but that you neither care for nor give thought to prudence, and truth, and how your soul will be the best possible?' And if one of you disputes it and asserts that he does care, I will not immediately let him go, nor will I go away, but I will speak to him and examine and test him. And if he does not seem to me to possess virtue, but only says he does, I will reproach 30a him, saying that he regards the things worth the most as the least important, and the paltrier things as more important. I will do this to whomever, younger or older, I happen to meet, both foreigner and townsman, but more so to the townsmen, inasmuch as you are closer to me in kin.

"Know well, then, that the god orders this. And I suppose that until now no greater good has arisen for you in the city than my service to the god. For I go around and do nothing but persuade you, both younger and b older, not to care for bodies and money before, nor as vehemently as, how your soul will be the best possible. I say: 'Not from money does virtue come, but from virtue comes money and all of the other good things for human beings both privately and publicly.' If, then, I corrupt the young by saying these things, they may be harmful. But if someone asserts that what I say is other than this, he speaks nonsense. With a view to these things, men of Athens," I would say, "either obey Anytus or not, and either let me go or not, since I would not do otherwise, not even if I were going to c die many times."

Do not make disturbances, men of Athens, but abide by what I begged of you, not to make disturbances at the things I say, but to listen. For, as I suppose, you will even be helped by listening. For in fact I am going to tell you certain other things at which you will perhaps cry out; but do not do this in any way. For know well that if you kill me, since I am the sort of man that I say I am, you will not harm me more than yourselves. For Meletus or Anytus would not harm me—he would not even be able to—for I do not suppose it is sanctioned that a better man be harmed by a d worse. Perhaps, however, he might kill or banish or dishonor me. But this man no doubt supposes, and others too, that these are great evils, while I do not suppose that these are,

but much rather doing what this man here is now doing: attempting to kill a man unjustly.

So I, men of Athens, am now far from making a defense speech on my own behalf, as someone might suppose. I do it rather on your behalf, so that you do not do something wrong concerning the gift of the god to you by e voting to condemn me. For if you kill me, you will not easily discover another of my sort, who—even if it is rather ridiculous to say— has simply been set upon the city by the god, as though upon a great and well-born horse who is rather sluggish because of his great size and needs to be awakened by some gadfly. Just so, in fact, the god seems to me to have set me upon the city as someone of this sort: I awaken and persuade and reproach each one of you, and I do not stop settling down every- 31a where upon you the whole day. Someone else of this sort will certainly not easily arise for you, men. Well, if you obey me, you will spare me. But perhaps you may be vexed, like the drowsy when they are awakened, and if you obey Anytus and slap me, you would easily kill me. Then you would spend the rest of your lives asleep, unless the god sends you someone else in his concern for you.

That I happen to be someone of this sort, given to the city by the god, you might appre- b hend from this: it does not seem human, on the one hand, that I have been careless of all my own things and that for so many years now I have endured that the things of my family be uncared for; and on the other hand, that I always do your business, going to each of you privately, as a father or an older brother might do, persuading you to care for virtue. If I was getting something out of this, and if I was receiving pay while I exhorted you to these things, it would be somewhat reasonable. But as it is, even you yourselves see that the accusers, who accused me so shamelessly in everything else, in this have not been able to become so utterly shameless as to offer a wit- 31c ness to assert that I ever took any pay or asked for it. For, I suppose, I offer a sufficient witness that I speak the truth: my poverty.

Perhaps, then, it might seem to be strange that I do go around counseling these things and being a busybody in private, but that in public I do not dare to go up before your multitude to counsel the city. The cause of this is what you have heard me speak of many times and in many places, that something divine and daimonic comes to me, a voice—which, of course, is also what Meletus wrote about in the indictment, making a comedy over it. This is something which began for me in childhood: a sort of voice comes, and whenever it comes, it always turns me away from whatever I am about to do, but never turns me forward.

This is what opposes my political activity, and its opposition seems to me altogether noble. For know well, men of Athens, if I had long ago attempted to be politically active, I would long ago have perished, and I would have benefited neither you nor myself. Now do not be vexed with me when I speak the truth. For there is no human being who will preserve his life if he genuinely opposes either you or any other multitude and prevents many unjust and unlawful things from happening in the city. Rather, if someone who really fights for the just is going to preserve himself even for a short time, it is necessary for him to lead a private rather than a public life.

I for my part will offer great proofs of these things for you—not speeches, but what *you* honor, deeds. Do listen to what happened to me, so that you may see that I would not yield even to one man against the just because of a fear of death, even if I were to perish by refusing to yield. I will tell you vulgar things, typical of the law courts, but true. I, men of Athens, never held any office in the city except for being once on the Council. And it happened that our tribe, Antiochis, held the prytany when you wished to judge the ten generals (the ones who did not pick up the men from the naval battle) as a group—unlawfully, as it seemed to all of you in the time afterwards. I alone of the prytanes opposed your doing anything against the laws then, and I voted against it. And although the orators were ready to indict me and arrest me, and you were ordering and shouting, I supposed that I should run the risk with the law and the just rather than side with you because of fear of prison or death when you were counseling unjust things.

Now this was when the city was still under the democracy. But again, when the oligarchy came to be, the Thirty summoned five of us into the Tholos, and they ordered us to arrest Leon the Salaminian and bring him from Salamis to die. They ordered many others to do many things of this sort, wishing that as many as possible would be implicated in the responsibility. Then, however, I showed again, not in speech but in deed, that I do not even care about death in any way at all—if it is not too crude to say so—but that my whole care is to commit no unjust or impious deed. That government, as strong as it was, did not shock me into doing anything unjust. When we came out of the Tholos, the other four went to Salamis and arrested Leon, but I departed and went home. And perhaps I would have died because of this, if that government had not been quickly overthrown. And you will have many witnesses of these things.

Do you suppose, then, that I would have survived so many years if I had been publicly active and had acted in a manner worthy of a good man, coming to the aid of the just things and, as one ought, regarding this as most important? Far from it, men of Athens; nor would any other human being.

But through all my life, if I was ever active in public at all, it is apparent that I was the sort of man (and in private I was the same) who never conceded anything to anyone contrary to the just—neither to anyone else, nor to any of those who my slanderers say are my students. I have never been anyone's teacher; but if anyone, whether younger or older, desired to hear me speaking and doing my own things, I never begrudged it to him. And I do not converse only when I receive money, and not when I do not receive it:

rather, I offer myself to both rich and poor alike for questioning, and if anyone wishes to hear what I say, he may answer me. And whether any of them becomes an upright man or not, I would not justly be held responsible, since I have never promised or taught any instruction to any of them. If someone says that he has ever learned from me or heard privately anything that everyone else did not, know well that he does not speak the truth. But why, then, do some enjoy spending so much time with me? You have heard, men of Athens; I told you the whole truth. It is c because they enjoy hearing men examined who suppose they are wise, but are not. For it is not unpleasant.

I have been ordered to practice this by the god, as I affirm, from divinations, and from dreams, and in every way that any divine allotment ever ordered a human being to practice anything at all. These things, men of Athens, are both true and easy to test.

Now if I for my part *am* corrupting some d of the young, and have already corrupted others, and if any of them, when they became older, had recognized that I ever counseled them badly in anything while they were young, then now, no doubt, they should have come forward to accuse me and take their vengeance. If they themselves were not willing to, then some of their families—fathers and brothers and their other relatives—should now have remembered it and taken their vengeance if their families had suffered anything bad from me.

In any event, there are present here many of them whom I see: first of all Crito here, of e my age and deme, the father of Critobulus here; next, Lysanias the Sphettian, the father of Aeschines here; further, here is Antiphon the Cephisean, the father of Epigenes. Moreover, here are others whose brothers have spent time in this way: Theozotides' son Nicostratus, the brother of Theodotus (and Theodotus has met his end, so that he, at least, would not beg him not to), and Demodocus' son Paralus, whose brother was Theages. And here is Ariston's son Adeimantus, whose

34a brother is Plato here, and Aeantodorus, whose brother is Apollodorus here.

And *I* can tell you of many others, from among whom Meletus should particularly have offered someone as a witness during his own speech. If he forgot then, let him offer one now—I will yield—and let him say if he has anyone of this sort at all. But you will discover that it is wholly opposite to this, men; that everyone is ready to come to aid *me*, the corrupter, the one who does evil to their families, as Meletus and Anytus say. Now the corrupted ones themselves would perhaps have a b reason to come to my aid. But the uncorrupted ones, their relatives, are now older men, so what other reason would they have to come to my aid except the correct and just one, that they are conscious that Meletus speaks falsely, while I am being truthful?

Well then, men. These, and perhaps other such things, are about all *I* would have to say in my defense. Perhaps someone among you may be indignant when he recalls himself, c if, in contesting a trial even smaller than this trial, he begged and supplicated the judges with many tears, bringing forward his own children and many others of his family and friends, so as to be pitied as much as possible, while I will do none of these things, although in this too I am risking, as I might seem, the extreme danger. Perhaps, then, someone thinking about this may be rather stubborn toward me, and, angered by this very thing, he may set down his vote in anger. If there is someone among you like this—for I, at least, d do not deem that there is, but if there is—to me it seems decent for me to say to this man, "I, best of men, surely do have some family; for this is also just what Homer says: not even I have grown up 'from an oak or a rock,' but from human beings." So that I do have a family, and sons too, men of Athens, three of them, one already a youth, and two still children. Nevertheless I will bring none of them forward here in order to beg you to vote to acquit me.

Why, then, will I do none of these things? Not because I am stubborn, men of Athens, e nor because I dishonor you. Whether I am daring with regard to death or not is another story; but at any rate as to reputation, mine and yours and the whole city's, to me it does not seem to be noble for me to do any of these things. For I am old and have this name; and whether it is true or false, it is reputed at least that Socrates is distinguished from the many 35a human beings in some way. If, then, those of you who are reputed to be distinguished, whether in wisdom or courage or any other virtue at all, will act in this way, it would be shameful. I have often seen some who are just like this when they are judged: although they are reputed to be something, they do wondrous deeds, since they suppose that they will suffer something terrible if they die—as though they would be immortal if you did not kill them. They seem to me to attach shame to the city, so that a foreigner might take it that those Athenians who are distinguished b in virtue—the ones whom they pick out from among themselves for their offices and other honors—are not at all distinguished from women. For those of you, men of Athens, who are reputed to be something in any way at all, should not do these things; nor, whenever we do them, should you allow it. Instead, you should show that you would much rather vote to convict the one who brings in these piteous dramas and makes the city ridiculous than the one who keeps quiet.

Apart from reputation, men, to me it also c does not seem to be just to beg the judge, nor to be acquitted by begging, but rather to teach and to persuade. For the judge is not seated to give away the just things as a gratification, but to judge them. For he has not sworn to gratify whoever seems favorable to him, but to give judgment according to the laws. Therefore we should not accustom you to swear falsely, nor should you become accustomed to it. For neither of us would be pious.

So do not deem that I, men of Athens, should practice such things before you which I hold to be neither noble nor just nor pious, and certainly, by Zeus, above all not when I d am being prosecuted for impiety by Meletus

here! For plainly, if I should persuade and force you by begging, after you have sworn an oath, I would be teaching you not to hold that there are gods, and in making my defense speech I would simply be accusing myself of not believing in gods. But that is far from being so. For I believe, men of Athens, as none of my accusers does. And I turn it over to you and to the god to judge me in whatever way it is going to be best both for me and for you.

[The jury votes on Socrates' innocence or guilt, and a majority finds him guilty as charged. Meletus then makes a speech proposing the death penalty, and Socrates must offer a counterproposal.]

Many things contribute to my not be- e ing indignant, men of Athens, at what has happened—that you voted to convict me— 36a and one of them is that what has happened was not unexpected by me. But I wonder much more at the number of the votes on each side. For I at least did not suppose it would be by so little, but by much. But as it is, as is likely, if only thirty of the votes had fallen differently, I would have been acquitted. So as it seems to me, I have even now been acquitted as far as Meletus is concerned; and not only have I been acquitted, but it is clear to everyone that if Anytus and Lycon had not come forward to accuse me, he would have had to pay a fine of a thousand drach- b mae, since he would not have gotten a fifth of the votes.

At any rate, the man proposes death as my desert. Well, then. What counterproposal shall I make to you, men of Athens? Or is it not clear that it should be whatever I am worthy of? What then? What am I worthy to suffer or to pay because I did not keep quiet during my life and did not care for the things that the many do—moneymaking and household management, and generalships, and popular oratory, and the other offices, and conspiracies and factions that come to be in the city—since I held that I myself was really too decent to survive if I went into these c things? I did not go into matters where, if I did go, I was going to be of no benefit either to you or to myself; instead, I went to each of you privately to perform the greatest benefaction, as I affirm, and I attempted to persuade each of you not to care for any of his own things until he cares for himself, how he will be the best and most prudent possible, nor to care for the things of the city until he cares for the city itself, and so to care for the other things in the same way. What, then, am I worthy to suffer, being such as this? Something good, men of Athens, at least if you give me what I deserve according to my worth in truth—and besides, a good of a sort that would be fitting for me. What, then, is fitting for a poor man, a benefactor, who needs to have leisure to exhort you? There is nothing more fitting, men of Athens, than for such a man to be given his meals in the Prytaneum, much more so than if any of you has won a victory at Olympia with a horse or a two- or four-horse chariot. For he makes you seem to be happy, while I make you be so; and he is not in need of sustenance, while I am in need of it. So if I must propose what I am worthy of in accordance with the just, I propose this: to be given my meals in the Prytaneum.

Perhaps, then, when I say this, I seem to you to speak in nearly the same way as when I spoke about lament and supplication—quite stubbornly. It is not like that, men of Athens, but rather like this: I am convinced that I do not do injustice to any human being voluntarily, but I am not persuading you of this. For we have conversed with each other a short time. Since, as I suppose, if you had a law like other human beings, not to judge anyone in a matter of death in one day alone, but over many, you would be persuaded. But as it is, it is not easy in a short time to do away with great slanders.

I, being convinced indeed that I do not do injustice to anyone, am far from doing injustice to myself, and from saying against myself that I myself am worthy of something bad, and from proposing this sort of thing as my desert. What would I fear? That I might suffer what Meletus proposes for me, about which I say that I do not know whether it is good or bad? Or instead of this, should I choose something from among the things that I know well are bad and propose that? Should it be prison? And why should I live in jail, enslaved to the authority that is regularly established there, the Eleven? Or money, and imprisonment until I pay? But for me this is the same as what I was saying just now, for I have no money to pay.

Well, should I propose exile, then? For perhaps you would grant me this as my desert. I would certainly be possessed by much love of soul, men of Athens, if I were so unreasonable that I were not able to reason that you who are my fellow citizens were not able to bear my ways of spending time and my speeches, but that instead they have become quite grave and hateful to you, so that you are now seeking to be released from them: will others, then, bear them easily? Far from it, men of Athens. Noble indeed would life be for me, a human being of my age, to go into exile and to live exchanging one city for another, always being driven out! For I know well that wherever I go, the young will listen to me when I speak, just as they do here. And if I drive them away, they themselves will drive me out by persuading their elders. But if I do not drive them away, their fathers and families will drive me out because of these same ones.

Perhaps, then, someone might say, "By being silent and keeping quiet, Socrates, won't you be able to live in exile for us?" It is hardest of all to persuade some of you about this. For if I say that this is to disobey the god and that because of this it is impossible to keep quiet, you will not be persuaded by me, on the ground that I am being ironic. And on the other hand, if I say that this even happens to be a very great good for a human being—to make speeches every day about virtue and the other things about which you hear me conversing and examining both myself and others—and that the unexamined life is not worth living for a human being, you will be persuaded by me still less when I say these things. This is the way it is, as I affirm, men; but to persuade you is not easy.

And at the same time, I am not accustomed to deem myself worthy of anything bad. For if I had money, I would have proposed as much money as I could pay, for that would not harm me. But as it is, I do not have any—unless, of course, you wish me to propose as much money as I am able to pay. Perhaps I would be able to pay you, say, a mina of silver. So I propose that much.

But Plato here, men of Athens, and Crito and Critobulus and Apollodorus bid me to propose thirty minae, and they will stand as guarantors. So I propose that much, and they will be trustworthy guarantors of the money for you.

[Voting between the penalties proposed by the accuser and the accused, the jury condemns Socrates to death. He has time to make some further remarks before he is taken away to prison to await execution.]

For the sake of a little time, men of Athens, you will get a name and be charged with the responsibility, by those wishing to revile the city, for having killed Socrates, a wise man. For those wishing to reproach you *will* assert that I am wise, even if I am not. At any rate, if you had waited a short time, this would have come about for you of its own accord. For you see that my age is already far advanced in life and close to death. I say this not to all of you, but to those who voted to condemn me to death.

I also say the following to these same ones. Perhaps you suppose, men of Athens, that I have been convicted because I was at a loss for the sort of speeches that would have persuaded you, if I had supposed that I should do and say anything at all to escape the penalty. Far from it. Rather, I have been convicted because I was at a loss, not however for speeches, but for daring and shamelessness and willingness to say the sorts of things to you that you would have been most pleased to hear: me wailing and lamenting, and doing and saying many other things unworthy of me, as *I* affirm—such things as you *have* been accustomed to hear from others. But neither did I then suppose that I should do anything

unsuitable to a free man because of the danger, nor do I now regret that I made my defense speech like this: I much prefer to die having made my defense speech in this way than to live in that way.

For neither in a court case nor in war should I or anyone else devise a way to escape death by doing anything at all. In battles it often becomes clear that one might escape death, at least, by letting go of his arms and turning around to supplicate his pursuers. And there are many other devices to escape death in each of the dangers, if one dares to do and say anything at all. But I suspect it is not hard, men, to escape death, but it is much harder to escape villainy. For it runs faster than death. And now I, since I am slow and old, am caught by the slower, while my accusers, since they are clever and sharp, are caught by the faster, by evil. And now I go away, condemned by you to pay the penalty of death, while they have been convicted by the truth of wretchedness and injustice. And I abide by my penalty, and so do they. Perhaps these things even had to be so, and I suppose there is due measure in them.

After this, I desire to deliver oracles to you, O you who voted to condemn me. For in fact I am now where human beings particularly deliver oracles: when they are about to die. I affirm, you men who condemned me to death, that vengeance will come upon you right after my death, and much harsher, by Zeus, than the sort you give me by killing me. For you have now done this deed supposing that you will be released from giving an account of your life, but it will turn out much the opposite for you, as *I* affirm. There will be more who will refute you, whom I have now been holding back; you did not perceive them. And they will be harsher, inasmuch as they are younger, and you will be more indignant. For if you suppose that by killing human beings you will prevent someone from reproaching you for not living correctly, you do not think nobly. For that kind of release is not at all possible or noble; rather, the kind that is both noblest and easiest is not to restrain others, but to equip oneself to be the best possible. So, having divined these things for you who voted against me, I am released.

But with those who voted for me I would be pleased to converse on behalf of this affair which has happened, while the officials are occupied and I do not yet go to the place where, when I do go, I must die. Please stay with me, men, for this much time; nothing prevents our telling tales to one another as long as it is possible. For I am willing to display to you, as to friends, what ever this thing means which has occurred to me just now. For to me, judges—for by calling you judges I would address you correctly—something wondrous has happened. For my customary divination from the *daimonion* was always very frequent in all former time, opposing me even in quite small matters if I were about to do something incorrectly. Now, you yourselves see what has occurred to me, these very things which someone might suppose to be, and are believed to be, extreme evils. But the sign of the god did not oppose me when I left my house this morning, nor when I came up here to the law court, nor anywhere in the speech when I was about to say anything, although in other speeches it has often stopped me in the middle while I was speaking. But as it is, it has nowhere opposed me either in any deed or speech, concerning this action. What, then, do I take to be the cause of this? I will tell you. Probably what has occurred to me has turned out to be good, and there is no way that those of us take it correctly who suppose that being dead is bad. In my view, a great proof of this has happened. For there is no way that the accustomed sign would not have opposed me unless I were about to do something good.

Let us also think in the following way how great a hope there is that it is good. Now being dead is either of two things. For either it is like being nothing and the dead man has no perception of anything, or else, in accordance with the things that are said, it happens to be a sort of change and migration of the soul from the place here to another place.

And if in fact there is no perception, but it is like a sleep in which the sleeper has no dream at all, death would be a wondrous gain. For I suppose that if someone had to select that night in which he slept so soundly that he did not even dream and had to compare the other nights and days of his own life with that night, and then had to say on consideration how many days and nights in his own life he has lived better and more pleasantly than that night, then I suppose that the Great King himself, not to mention some private man, would discover that they are easy to count in comparison with the other days and nights. So if death is something like this, I at least say it is a gain. For all time appears in this way indeed to be nothing more than one night.

On the other hand, if death is like a journey from here to another place, and if the things that are said are true, that in fact all the dead are there, then what greater good could there be than this, judges? For if one who arrives in Hades, released from those here who claim to be judges, will find those who are judges in truth—the very ones who are said to give judgment there, Minos and Rhadamanthys, and Aeacus, and Triptolemus, and those of the other demigods who turned out to be just in their own lives—would this journey be a paltry one? Or again, to associate with Orpheus and Musaeus and Hesiod and Homer, how much would any of you give? For I am willing to die many times if these things are true, since especially for myself spending time there would be wondrous: whenever I happened to meet Palamedes and Telemonian Ajax, or anyone else of the ancients who died because of an unjust judgment, I would compare my own experiences with theirs. As I suppose, it would not be unpleasant. And certainly the greatest thing is that I would pass my time examining and searching out among those there—just as I do to those here—who among them is wise, and who supposes he is, but is not. How much would one give, judges, to examine him who led the great army against Troy, or Odysseus, or Sisyphus, or the thousand others whom one might mention, both men and women? To converse and to associate with them and to examine them there would be inconceivable happiness. Certainly those there surely do not kill on this account. For those there are happier than those here not only in other things but also in that they are immortal henceforth for the rest of time, at least if the things that are said are in fact true.

But you too, judges, should be of good hope toward death, and you should think this one thing to be true: that there is nothing bad for a good man, whether living or dead, and that the gods are not without care for his troubles. Nor have my present troubles arisen of their own accord, but it is clear to me that it is now better, after all, for me to be dead and to have been released from troubles. This is also why the sign did not turn me away anywhere, and I at least am not at all angry at those who voted to condemn me and at my accusers. And yet it was not with this thought in mind that they voted to condemn me and accused me: rather, they supposed they would harm me. For this they are worthy of blame.

This much, however, I beg of them: when my sons grow up, punish them, men, and pain them in the very same way I pained you, if they seem to you to care for money or anything else before virtue. And if they are reputed to be something when they are nothing, reproach them just as I did you: tell them that they do not care for the things they should, and that they suppose they are something when they are worth nothing. And if you do these things, we will have been treated justly by you, both I myself and my sons.

But now it is time to go away, I to die and you to live. Which of us goes to a better thing is unclear to everyone except to the god.

STUDY QUESTIONS: PLATO, APOLOGY

1. Why is Socrates being prosecuted? With what crimes is he charged? How does he defend himself?
2. How does Socrates explain the cause of the slanders against him?
3. What was Socrates' main goal in life? Why?
4. What is a 'gadfly'? Why does Socrates describe himself as a gadfly?
5. What is the point of Socrates' interrogation of Meletus regarding the corruption of youth?
6. Socrates asks Meletus whether there is anyone who believes in human matters but not in human beings. What was the point of that question? What does Socrates finally conclude?
7. Why does Socrates not apologize in his apology?
8. What does he suggest would be an appropriate punishment for his so-called crimes against Athens?
9. Is Socrates really guilty of impiety?
10. If Socrates were alive today, who do you think would be his targets? If he were lecturing at a university, what might be his favorite topics? What examples might he use on students today to make the sorts of points he made back then?
11. Is Socrates afraid of death? Why?

CRITO

In Athens, a death sentence would usually be carried out immediately after the sentencing. But Socrates' trial took place during an important festival, and, for this reason, he was detained in prison for a month. It was probably expected that, during this time, Socrates would flee from prison and live the remainder of his life in exile. In the Crito, his friends come to plead with him to escape. Socrates refuses, arguing that he is morally obliged to stay. Crito appeals to Socrates' self-interest. Socrates replies on behalf of moral obligation, until Crito can no longer contest the logic of his argument. Socrates' final conversation with his students can be found in the *Phaedo*.

43a SOCRATES. Why have you arrived at this hour, Crito? Or isn't it still early?

CRITO. It certainly is.

SOCRATES. What is the hour?

CRITO. Just before daybreak.

SOCRATES. I wonder how it is that the guard of the prison was willing to let you in.

CRITO. He is accustomed to me by now, Socrates, because of my frequent visits here; and besides, he has been done a certain benefaction by me.

SOCRATES. Have you just come, or have you been here long?

CRITO. Fairly long.

b SOCRATES. Then why didn't you wake me up right away, instead of sitting beside me in silence?

CRITO. No, by Zeus, Socrates, nor would I myself willingly be in such great sleeplessness and pain! But I have long been wondering at you, perceiving how pleasantly you sleep. And I kept from waking you on purpose, so that you would pass the time as pleasantly as possible. And though I have of course often previously regarded you through your whole life as happy in your temperament, I do so especially in the present calamity now, so easily and mildly do you bear it.

SOCRATES. That's because it would be discordant, Crito, for someone of my age to be vexed if he now must meet his end.

CRITO. Others of your age, Socrates, are also

c caught in such calamities, but their age does not release them from being vexed at their present fortune.

SOCRATES. This is so. But why *have* you arrived so early?

CRITO. To bear a message, Socrates, that is hard—not hard for you, as it appears to me, but for me and for all your companions it is a hard and grave one. And I, as it seems to me, would bear it the most gravely of all.

SOCRATES. What is it? Or has the ship arrived

d from Delos, after whose arrival I must die?

CRITO. It hasn't arrived yet, but it does seem to me that it will come today, from the report of some men who have come from Sunium and left it there. So it is clear from these messengers that it will come today, and tomorrow it will be necessary, Socrates, for you to end your life.

SOCRATES. Well, may it be with good fortune, Crito; if such is dear to the gods, such let it be. However, I don't suppose it will come today.

44a CRITO. From what do you infer this?

SOCRATES. I will tell you. Surely I must die on the day after the ship comes.

CRITO. That's at least what those having authority over these things say.

SOCRATES. Then I do not suppose it will come on the day that is upon us, but on the next. I infer it from a certain dream I had a little earlier tonight. And there's probably something opportune in your not having awakened me.

CRITO. But what *was* the dream?

SOCRATES. It seemed that a certain woman

b approached me, beautiful and well formed, dressed in white, and that she called me by name and said: "Socrates, on the third day thou would'st arrive in fertile Phthia."

CRITO. The dream is strange, Socrates.

SOCRATES. No, quite manifest, at least as it seems to me, Crito.

CRITO. Too much so, as is likely. But, daimonic Socrates, even now obey me and save yourself, since if you die, for me it is not just one calamity: apart from being deprived of such a companion as I will never discover again, I will also seem to many, those who don't know you and me plainly, to have been able to save you if I had been willing to spend money, but not to have cared. And yet what reputation would be more shameful than to seem to regard money as more important than friends? For the many will not be persuaded that you yourself were not willing to go away from here although we were eager for it.

SOCRATES. But why do we care in this way, blessed Crito, about the opinion of the many? For the most decent men, whom it is more worthy to give thought to, will hold that these things have been done in just the way they were done.

d CRITO. But surely you see that it is necessary, Socrates, to care also about the opinion of the many. The present situation now makes it clear that the many can produce not the smallest of evils but almost the greatest, if someone is slandered among them.

SOCRATES. Would that the many *could* produce the greatest evils, Crito, so that they could also produce the greatest goods! That would indeed be noble. But as it is, they can do neither. For they aren't capable of making someone either prudent or imprudent, but do whatever they happen to do by chance.

e CRITO. Let these things be so. But, Socrates, tell me this. Surely you aren't worrying, are you, on behalf of me and the rest of your companions, over the prospect that if you leave here, the informers will make trouble for us on the ground that we stole you away from here, and we will be compelled to lose either our whole substance or a lot of money, or even to suffer something else besides this? If you fear some 45a such thing, leave it aside. For surely it is just for us to save you and run this risk, and one still greater than this, if need be. But obey me and do not do otherwise.

SOCRATES. I am worrying over the prospect of these things, Crito, and of many others.

CRITO. Then do not fear these things. For in fact it is not even much money that certain people are willing to take to save you and lead you out of here. Furthermore, don't you see

how easily these informers are bought, and that they wouldn't need much money? My money is available to you, and is, as I suppose, b sufficient. Furthermore, even if out of some concern for me you suppose I shouldn't spend mine, these foreigners who are here are ready to spend theirs. And one of them has brought sufficient money for this very thing, Simmias of Thebes; and Cebes is ready too, and very many others.

So as I say, don't hesitate to save yourself because you fear these things, and don't let it be hard for you to accept, as you were saying in the court, because you wouldn't know what to do with yourself if you left. For there are c many places where they will greet you with affection when you arrive. And if you wish to go to Thessaly, I have guest-friends there who will regard you as important and offer you safety, so that no one throughout Thessaly will cause you pain.

Besides, Socrates, you seem to me to be attempting a thing that isn't even just: you are betraying yourself, although it is possible to be saved. And you are hastening the coming to pass of the very things concerning yourself which your very enemies would hasten on, and did hasten on in their wish to ruin you. In addition to these things, you seem to me at least to be betraying your own sons, too, whom you will leave and abandon, although it d is possible for you to nurture and educate them. As far as it lies in you, they will do whatever they happen to do by chance, and chance will bring them, as is likely, just the sorts of things that usually happen to orphans when they are orphaned. Now one either should not have children or should endure the hardship of nurturing and educating them. But you seem to me to be choosing the most easygoing course.

Instead, one should choose just what a good and manly man would choose, particularly if one has claimed to care for virtue through his whole life. For my part I am e ashamed for you and for us, your companions, that the whole affair concerning you will seem to have been conducted with a certain lack of manliness on our part: the way the lawsuit was introduced into the law court, even though it was possible for it not to be introduced; the way the judicial contest itself took place; and now this, the ridiculous conclusion of the affair, will seem to have escaped us completely because of a certain badness and lack of manliness on our part, since we didn't save you, nor did you save yourself, although it was possible and feasible if we had been of even a slight benefit. So see to it, Socrates, that these things be not shameful as well as bad both for you and for us.

But take counsel—rather, there is no longer time to take counsel, but to have taken counsel. And there is only one counsel. For all these things must be done during the coming night. If we wait any longer, it will be impossible and can no longer be done. But in every way, Socrates, obey me and in no way do otherwise.

SOCRATES. Dear Crito, your eagerness is worth much if some correctness be with it. If not, the greater it is, the harder it is to deal with. So we should consider whether these things are to be done or not, since I, not only now but always, am such as to obey nothing else of what is mine than that argument which appears best to me upon reasoning. The arguments that I spoke in the past I am not able to throw out now that this fortune has come to pass for me. Instead, they appear rather alike to me, and I venerate and honor the same ones I did before. If we have no better argument to say at present, know well that I will certainly not yield to you, not even if the power of the many scares us like children with more hobgoblins than those now present, sending against us imprisonments and executions and confiscations of money.

How then would we consider this with all due measure? By taking up first this argument you are making about opinions. Was it said nobly on each occasion or not, that one should pay mind to some opinions, but not others? Or was it said nobly before I had to die, while now it has become very clear that it was said pointlessly just for the sake of argument, and that in truth it was child's play and drivel? I desire to consider in common with you, Crito, whether the argument appears at all different to me, now that I am in this position, or the same; and whether we shall leave it aside or obey it.

On each occasion, as I suppose, those who supposed that they had something to say somehow used to speak as I was speaking just now: of the opinions which human beings opine, some must be regarded as important, others not. Before the gods, Crito, does this not seem to you to be nobly spoken? For you, humanly speaking, are not about to die tomorrow, and the present calamity wouldn't lead you astray. Consider, then. Doesn't it seem to you adequately spoken, that one should not honor all the opinions of human beings, but some and not others? What do you say? Isn't this nobly spoken?

CRITO. Nobly.

SOCRATES. To honor the upright opinions, but not the villainous?

CRITO. Yes.

SOCRATES. Aren't the upright ones those of the prudent, and the villainous ones those of the imprudent?

CRITO. Of course.

SOCRATES. Come then, again, how were such things spoken of? Does a man who is exercising and practicing gymnastics pay mind to the praise and blame and opinion of every man, or of one only, who happens to be a doctor or trainer?

CRITO. Of one only.

SOCRATES. Therefore he should fear the blame and welcome the praises of the one, but not those of the many.

CRITO. Clearly.

SOCRATES. He is to practice and exercise, then, and to eat and drink as seems fitting to the one—the overseer and expert—rather than to all the others.

CRITO. This is so.

SOCRATES. Well, then. If he disobeys the one and dishonors his opinion and praises, while honoring those of the many who have no expertise, won't he suffer evil?

CRITO. Of course.

SOCRATES. What is this evil? And where and at what does it aim among the things belonging to him who disobeys?

CRITO. Clearly at his body, for this is what it destroys.

SOCRATES. Nobly spoken. Aren't the other things also like this (so that we don't have to go through all of them)? And in particular, concerning the just and unjust and shameful and noble and good and bad things, about which we are now taking counsel, must we follow the opinion of the many and fear it

d rather than that of the one—if there is such an expert—whom we must be ashamed before and fear more than all the others? And if we don't follow him, we will corrupt and maim that thing which, as we used to say, becomes better by the just and is destroyed by the unjust. Or isn't there anything to this?

CRITO. I, at least, suppose that there is, Socrates.

SOCRATES. Come then, if we destroy that which becomes better by the healthful and is corrupted by the diseaseful, because we don't obey the opinion of the experts, is life worth living for us when it has been corrupted?

e Surely this is the body, isn't it?

CRITO. Yes.

SOCRATES. So is life worth living for us with a wretched and corrupted body?

CRITO. In no way.

SOCRATES. But is life worth living for us with that thing corrupted which the unjust maims and the just profits? Or do we hold that thing to be more paltry than the body—whatever it is of the things that belong to us which both

48a injustice and justice concern?

CRITO. In no way.

SOCRATES. But more honorable?

CRITO. Much more so.

SOCRATES. Then we ought not at all, O best of men, to give so much thought to what the many will say of us, but rather to what the expert concerning the just and unjust things— to what the one, and truth itself—will say. So first, it's not correct for you to introduce the claim that we must give thought to the opin-

ion of the many concerning things just and noble and good and their opposites.

"But the fact is," someone might say, "the many are able to kill us."

b CRITO. Yes, clearly this is so. For it might be said, Socrates. What you say is true.

SOCRATES. But, you wondrous man, the argument that we have gone through still seems to me, at least, like it did before. Consider, again, whether the following also still stays so for us or not: not living, but living well, is to be regarded as most important.

CRITO. It does stay so.

SOCRATES. And that living well and nobly and justly are the same. Does it stay so or does it not stay?

CRITO. It stays so.

SOCRATES. Therefore from the things agreed upon, it must be considered whether it is just for me to try to go out of here although the Athenians are not permitting me to go, or not

c just. And if it appears just, let us try, but if not, let's leave it aside. As for the considerations that you speak of concerning spending of money and reputation and nurture of children, I suspect that in truth, Crito, these are considerations of those who easily kill and, if they could, would bring back to life again, acting mindlessly: namely, the many. Since this is how the argument holds, nothing else is to be considered by us except what we were saying just now: whether we will do just things by paying money and gratitude to those who will lead me out of here, or whether in truth we

d will do injustice by doing all these things— those of us who are leading out as well as those of us who are being led out. And if it is apparent that these deeds of ours are unjust, we must take nothing into account compared to the doing of injustice, even if we must die by staying here and keeping quiet or must suffer anything else whatever.

CRITO. You seem to me to speak nobly, Socrates; but see what we are to do.

SOCRATES. Let us consider in common, my good man, and if there is some way you can contra-

e dict my argument, contradict it and I will obey you. But if not, blessed man, then stop telling me the same argument again and again, that I ought to go away from here although the Athenians are unwilling. For I regard it as important to act after persuading you, not while you are unwilling. Now see if this beginning of the consideration is stated adequately for you, and try to answer what is asked in 49a whatever way you most suppose it to be.

CRITO. I will try.

SOCRATES. Do we assert that in no way ought injustice to be done voluntarily, or that in one way injustice ought to be done, but in another way not? Or is doing injustice in no way good or noble, as we have often agreed in the past, and which was also said just now? Or have all those former agreements of ours been poured away in these few days? And although at our age, Crito, we old men have long been seriously conversing with each other, were we unaware, then, that we ourselves are no dif-
b ferent from children? Or is it so for us now more than ever just as it was spoken then? Whether the many say so or not, and whether we must suffer things still harder than these or maybe milder, does doing injustice nevertheless happen to be bad and shameful in every way for the one who does injustice? Do we affirm it or not?

CRITO. We affirm it.

SOCRATES. Then one must in no way do injustice.

CRITO. Of course not.

SOCRATES. And even he who has been done injustice, then, must not do injustice in return, as the many suppose, since one must in no way do injustice.

c CRITO. Apparently not.

SOCRATES. What then? Should one do evil or not, Crito?

CRITO. Doubtless one must not, Socrates.

SOCRATES. What then? Is it just or not just for the one to whom evil is done to do evil in return, as the many say?

CRITO. In no way.

SOCRATES. For surely there is no difference between human beings doing evil and doing injustice.

CRITO. What you say is true.

SOCRATES. Then no human being should do injustice in return or do evil, whatever he suffers from others. And see to it, Crito, that by agreeing to this, you aren't agreeing contrary
d to your opinion. For I know that this seems and will seem so only to a certain few. So there is no common counsel for those who hold this opinion and those who do not: it is necessary that they will have contempt for each other when they see each others' counsels. So you too consider very well whether you share this opinion in common with me and whether we should begin taking counsel from here: that it is never correct to do injustice, or to do injustice in return, or for someone to whom evil is done to defend himself by doing evil in return. Or do you stand aloof and not share this beginning? For to me it has long seemed so and still does now, but if it has
e seemed some other way to you, speak and teach me. But if you abide by the things from before, hear what comes after this.

CRITO. I do abide by them and it does seem so to me as well. But speak.

SOCRATES. Again, I'll say what comes after this, or rather ask. Ought someone to do the things he agrees upon with someone—if they are just—or ought he to evade them by deception?

CRITO. He ought to do them.

SOCRATES. Observe what follows from these things. If we go away from here without per-
50a suading the city, do we do evil to some—indeed to those whom it should least be done to—or not? And do we abide by the things we agreed to—if they are just—or not?

CRITO. I have no answer to what you ask, Socrates. For I don't understand.

SOCRATES. Consider it as follows. What if the laws and the community of the city should come and stand before us who are about to run away (or whatever name we should give it) from here and ask: "Tell me, Socrates, what do you have in mind to do? By this deed that you are attempting, what do you think you're
b doing, if not destroying us laws and the whole city, as far as it lies in you? Or does it seem possible to you for a city to continue to exist, and not to be overturned, in which the judg-

ments that are reached have no strength, but are rendered ineffective and are corrupted by private men?"

What shall we say, Crito, to these and other such things? For someone, especially an orator, would have many things to say on behalf of this law if it were destroyed—the law that orders that the judgments reached in trials be authoritative. Or shall we tell them, "The city was doing us injustice and did not pass judg-

c ment correctly"? Shall we say this, or what?

CRITO. Yes, this, by Zeus, Socrates!

SOCRATES. Then what if the laws should say, "Socrates, has it been agreed to by us and by you to do this, or to abide by whatever judgments the city reaches in trials?"

If, then, we should wonder at their saying this, perhaps they would say, "Socrates, do not wonder at what is said, but answer, since you have been accustomed to make use of questioning and answering. Come now, what charge are you bringing against us and the city that you

d are attempting to destroy us? First, didn't we beget you, and didn't your father take your mother and bring you forth through us? Tell us, then, do you in some way blame those of us laws that concern marriages, for not being noble?"

"I do not blame them," I would say.

"What about those that concern the nurture and education (in which you too were educated) of the one born? Or didn't those laws among us which have been ordered for this end order your father nobly when they passed along the command to him to educate

e you in music and gymnastic?"

"Nobly," I would say.

"Well, then. Since you were born and nurtured, and educated, too, could you say, first, that you are not ours, both our offspring and slave, you yourself as well as your forebears? And if this is so, do you suppose that justice is equal for you and for us? And do you suppose that it is just for you to do in return whatever we attempt to do to you? Now with regard to your father (or a master, if you happened to have one), justice was not equal for you, so that you didn't also do in return what-

ever you suffered: you didn't contradict him when he spoke badly of you, nor did you beat

51a him in return when you were beaten, or do any other such thing. So is it then permitted to you to do so with regard to the fatherland and the laws, so that if we, believing it to be just, attempt to destroy you, then you too, to the extent that you can, will attempt to destroy us laws and the fatherland in return? And will you say that in doing this you are acting justly, you who in truth care for virtue? Or are you so wise that you have been unaware that fatherland is something more honorable than mother and father and all the other fore-bears, and more venerable, and more holy, and more highly esteemed among gods and among

b human beings who are intelligent? And that you must revere and give way to and fawn upon a fatherland more than a father when it is angry with you, and either persuade it or do whatever it bids, and keep quiet and suffer if it orders you to suffer anything, whether to be beaten or to be bound? Or that if it leads you into war to be wounded or killed, this must be done? And that this is just and that you are not to give way or retreat or leave your station, but that in war and in court and everywhere, you must do whatever the city and fatherland bid, or else persuade it what the just is by nature? And that it is not pious to do violence to mother or father, and still less by far to the fatherland than to them?"

What shall we say in reply to these things, Crito? That what the laws say is true or not?

CRITO. It seems so to me, at least.

SOCRATES. "Then consider, Socrates," the laws would perhaps say, "that if what we say is true, the things you are attempting to do to us are not just. For although we begat, nourished, and educated you, and gave you and all the

d other citizens a share in all the noble things we could, nevertheless we proclaim, by making it possible for any Athenian who wishes, once he has been admitted to adulthood and has seen the affairs in the city and us laws, that if we do not satisfy him, he is allowed to take his own things and go away wherever he wishes. And none of us laws is an obstacle or forbids anyone from going wherever he wishes, keeping his own things, whether one of you wishes to go to a colony (if we and the city are not satisfactory) or to go and settle in another home somewhere. But to whoever of you stays here and sees the way that we reach judgments and otherwise manage the city, we say that he has already agreed with us in deed to do whatever we bid. And when he does not obey, we say that he does injustice in three ways: in that he does not obey us who begat him; nor us who nurtured him; and in that although he agreed to obey us, he neither obeys nor persuades us if we do something ignobly, although we put forward an alternative to him and do not order him crudely to do whatever we bid, but permit either of two things—either to persuade us or to do it—but he does neither of these.

"To these charges, Socrates, we say that you too will be liable if you do what you have in mind, and you not least of the Athenians, but more than anyone among them."

If then I should say, "Because of what?" perhaps they would accost me justly and say that more than anyone among the Athenians I happen to have agreed to this agreement. They would say, "Socrates, we have great proofs that both we and the city were satisfactory to you. For you would never have exceeded all the other Athenians in staying at home in it unless it had satisfied you exceedingly. You never went out of the city to see the sights except once to the Isthmus, nor did you ever go anywhere else except when you were with the army on campaign somewhere. Nor did you ever make any other journey, as other human beings do, nor did a desire ever take hold of you to know another city or other laws: we and our city were sufficient for you. So vehemently were you choosing us and agreeing to be governed in accordance with us that among other things you also had children in it, as though the city was satisfactory to you. Furthermore, in the trial itself you could have proposed exile as your penalty if you had wished, and what you are attempting now when the city is unwilling, you could have done then when it was willing. But you were then pluming yourself on not being vexed if you should have to die, and you chose death, as you said, before exile; while now you are not ashamed of those speeches, nor do you heed us laws, since you are attempting to corrupt us. And you are doing just what the paltriest slave would do: attempting to run away contrary to the contracts and agreements according to which you contracted with us to be governed.

"So first, answer us this very thing: whether what we say is true or not true when we claim that you have agreed in deed, but not in speech, to be governed in accordance with us?"

What are we to say in reply to this Crito? Shall we not agree?

CRITO. Necessarily, Socrates.

SOCRATES. "So are you not transgressing," they would say, "your contracts and agreements with us, although you did not agree to them under necessity and were not deceived? Nor were you compelled to take counsel in a short time, but during seventy years in which you could have gone away if we were not satisfactory or if the agreements did not appear to be just to you. But you chose instead neither Lacedaemon nor Crete—and you yourself on occasion say that *they* have good laws—nor any other of the Greek cities or the barbarian ones. Rather, you took fewer journeys away from the city than the lame and blind and the other cripples, so exceedingly did it and we laws satisfy you more than the other Athenians, clearly. For whom would a city satisfy without laws? But will you in fact not abide now by what you have agreed to? You will, if you obey us, Socrates; and you will not become ridiculous by going out from the city.

"For consider, if you transgress these things and commit any of these wrongs, what good will you produce for yourself or your own companions? For it is rather clear that your companions will themselves risk being exiled and being deprived of their city or losing their substance. And as for yourself, first, if you go to one of the nearest cities, to Thebes or Megara (for both have good laws), you will come as an enemy, Socrates, to their political regime, and those very ones among them who are concerned for their own cities will look askance at you, believing that you are a corrupter of the laws. And you will confirm the judges in their opinion, so that they will seem to have judged

c the lawsuit correctly. For whoever is a corrupter of laws would surely seem very much to be a corrupter of young and mindless human beings. So will you flee the cities with good laws and the most decorous men? And if you do this, will life be worth living for you? Or will you consort with these men and shamelessly converse with them? With what speeches, Socrates? The ones that you speak here, that virtue and justice are of the most worth to human beings, and customs and laws?

d And do you not suppose the affair of Socrates will appear unseemly? One must suppose so.

"But will you depart from these places and come to the guest-friends of Crito in Thessaly? There, of course, is very much disorder and lack of restraint, and perhaps they would be pleased to hear from you how laughably you ran away from the prison by covering yourself with some disguise—putting on either a leather skin or other disguises such as those who run away usually use—and by altering your own figure. Is there no one who will say that you, an old man with only a little time left in his life, as is likely, dared so greedily to desire to live by transgressing the great-

e est laws? Perhaps not, if you don't cause pain to anyone. Otherwise, Socrates, you will hear many things unworthy of yourself. You will live by fawning upon all human beings and being their slave. And what else will you be doing but feasting well in Thessaly, as though you had journeyed to Thessaly for dinner? Where will those speeches concerning justice

54a and the rest of virtue be for us then?

"Is it rather that you wish to live for your children's sake, so that you may nurture and educate them? What then? Will you take them to Thessaly to nurture and educate them, mak-

ing them foreigners, so that they will have this advantage too? Or if not this, if they are nurtured here, will they be better nurtured and educated because you are alive when you won't be with them? No, for your companions will take care of them for you. Will they take care of them if you journey to Thessaly but not take care of them if you journey to Hades? If in fact those who claim to you to be your companions are of any benefit at all, one must suppose, at

b least, that they will.

"But, Socrates, obey us, your nurturers, and do not regard children or living or anything else as more important than justice, so that when you go to Hades you will have all these things to say in your defense before those who rule there. For if you do these things, it does not appear to be better or more just or more pious here, either for you or for anyone else of those who are yours, nor will it be better for you when you arrive there. If you depart now, you will depart having been done injustice

c not by us laws, but by human beings. But if you go away so shamefully doing injustice in return and doing evil in return, transgressing your own agreements and contracts with us and doing evil deeds to those to whom they should least be done—yourself and friends and fatherland and us—then we will be angry with you while you live, and our brothers, the laws in Hades, will not receive you favorably there, knowing that you even attempted to destroy us as far as it lay in you. But let not

d Crito persuade you to do what he says rather than what we say."

Know well, my dear comrade Crito, that these things are what I seem to hear, just as the Corybantes seem to hear the flutes, and this echo of these speeches is booming within me and makes me unable to hear the others. Know that insofar as these things seem so to me now, if you speak against them, you will speak in vain. Nevertheless, if you suppose that you will accomplish anything, speak.

CRITO. But, Socrates, I have nothing to say.

e SOCRATES. Then let it go, Crito, and let us act in this way, since in this way the god is leading.

STUDY QUESTIONS: PLATO, CRITO

1. Why shouldn't one worry about what most people think of one, according to Socrates?
2. How does Crito argue to Socrates that he should escape? How does Socrates reply to those arguments?
3. According to Socrates, what is most important? (48b)
4. What does Socrates say one should do to a person who causes one injustice? How does he argue for his answer?
5. Why does Socrates compare escaping from prison to retaliation?
6. What sort of benefits does the city-state provide to the individual?
7. Why does Socrates compare the individual's relationship with the state to a contract?
8. Should Socrates have escaped the prison? Was he right to remain?

PROTAGORAS

This dialogue is probably one of the later dialogues from the early period. In other words, it reflects Socrates' views rather than Plato's own theories. Protagoras, one of the great Sophist philosophers, explains his understanding of virtue, arguing that virtue can be taught. Socrates expresses doubt concerning this claim. However, the discussion soon turns to the idea that the virtues are one. Socrates argues that a person who has any one of the five virtues (temperance, courage, wisdom, piety, and justice) must have the others. Against this, Protagoras claims that a person can have courage without the other virtues. Socrates replies with a long argument spanning from 358D to 360D, concluding that courage is knowledge of fearful and nonfearful things. In other words, courage is a form of wisdom. Despite this positive conclusion, the dialogue appears to end with uncertainty regarding the original question, that is, whether virtue is teachable.

328d So Protagoras concluded this lengthy exhibition 5 of his skill as a speaker. I stayed gazing at him, quite spellbound, for a long time, thinking that he was going to say something more, and anxious to hear it; but when I saw that he had really finished, I collected myself with an effort, so to speak, and looked at Hippocrates. 'Son of Apollodorus,' I said, 'I am most grateful to you for suggesting that I should come here; for what I've e learnt from Protagoras is something of great importance. Previously I used to think that there was no technique available to men for making people good; but now I am persuaded that there is. I've just one small difficulty, and it's obvious

5 that Protagoras will explain it too without any trouble, since he has explained so much already. 329a Now if you went to any of the orators about this question, you would perhaps get a similar speech from Pericles, or from some other able speaker; but if you ask them any question, they are no more capable of answering or asking anything themselves than a book is. Ask them anything 5 about what they've said, no matter how small a point, and just as bronze, once struck, goes on sounding for a long time until you take hold of it, b so these orators spin out an answer a mile long to any little question. But Protagoras can not only give splendid long speeches, as he has shown

here, but he can also answer questions briefly, and when he asks one himself he waits and listens to the answer, which is a gift that few possess. Now, 5 Protagoras, I've very nearly got the whole thing, if you would just answer me this. You say that excellence can be taught, and I should accept your view rather than anyone else's; just satisfy me on c something which surprised me when you said it. You said that Zeus bestowed justice and conscience on mankind, and then many times in your discourse you spoke of justice and soundness of 5 mind and holiness and all the rest as all summed up as the one thing, excellence. Will you then explain precisely whether excellence is one thing, and justice and soundness of mind and holiness parts of it, or whether all of these that I've just mentioned are different names of one and the d same thing. This is what I still want to know.'

That's an easy question to answer, Socrates,' he said. 'Excellence is a single thing, and the things you ask about are parts of it.'

'Do you mean in the way that the parts of a 5 face, mouth, nose, eyes, and ears, are parts of the whole,' I asked, 'or like parts of gold, none of which differs from any of the others or from the whole, except in size?'

'The former, I take it, Socrates; the way the e parts of the face are related to the whole face.'

'So do some men possess one of these parts of excellence and some another,' I asked, 'or if someone has one, must he have them all?'

'Not at all,' he said. 'There are many coura- 5 geous men who are unjust, or just men who are not wise.'

'So are wisdom and courage parts of excel- 330a lence as well?' I said.

'Most certainly,' he replied. 'Wisdom is the most important part.'

'But each of them is something different from any of the others?'

'Yes.'

'And does each of them have its own sepa- rate power? When we consider the face, the eye 5 is not like the ear, nor is its power the same, nor is any other part like another in power or in other ways. Is it the same with the parts of excel- b lence, that none is like any other, either in itself

or in its power? Surely it must be, if corresponds to our example.'

'It is so, Socrates.'

'So then,' I said, 'none of the other parts of excellence is like knowledge, none is like justice, 5 none like courage, none like soundness of mind, and none like holiness.'

'No.'

'Well now,' I said, 'let's consider together what sort of thing each one is. Here's the first c question: is justice something, or not a thing at all? It seems to me that it is something; what do you think?'

'I think so too.' . . .

357b5 "Now *which* art, and *what* knowledge, we shall inquire later. But this suffices to show *that* it is knowledge, and to provide the demonstra- tion that Protagoras and I were required to give c in reply to your question. You raised it, if you remember, when we were in agreement that nothing is more powerful than knowledge, and that no matter where it is it always conquers pleasure and everything else. You then said that pleasure often conquers even the man who is in 5 possession of knowledge, and when we didn't agree, it was then that you asked us, 'Well, if this experience isn't being overcome by pleasure, what is it then? What do you call it? Tell us.' If d we had then straight away said 'Error' you have laughed at us; but now, if you laugh at us you will be laughing at yourselves. For you have agreed that those who go wrong in their choice of 5 pleasures and pains—which is to say, of good and bad things—go wrong from lack of knowl- edge, and not merely of knowledge, but, as you have already further conceded, of measurement. And you surely know yourselves that wrong action done without knowledge is done in error. e So this is what being weaker than pleasure is, the greatest of all errors, for which Protagoras here and Hippias and Prodicus claim to have the cure. But because you think that it is some- 5 thing other than error you neither consult these sophists yourselves nor send your sons to them to have them taught this; you don't believe that it can be taught, so you hang on to your money instead of giving it to them, and as a result you do badly both as private individuals and in public affairs."

358a That's what we should have said in reply to the majority. And now, on behalf of Protagoras and myself, I ask you, Hippias and Prodicus (for you can answer jointly), whether you think that what I am saying is true or false.'

5 They were all completely satisfied that it was true.

'You agree, then,' I said, 'that what is pleasant is good, and what is painful bad. I leave aside our friend Prodicus' distinction of names; for whether you call it 'pleasant' or 'delightful' or 'enjoyable',
b or however you care to apply such names, my dear Prodicus, give your answer according to the sense of my question.'

Prodicus laughed, and indicated his agreement, and so did the rest.

'Well, gentlemen,' I said, 'what about this?
5 Aren't all actions praiseworthy which lead to a painless and pleasant life? And isn't praiseworthy activity good and beneficial?'

They agreed.

'So if what is pleasant is good,' I said, 'no one who either knows or believes that something else
c is better than what he is doing, and is in his power to do, subsequently does the other, when he can do what is better. Nor is giving in to oneself anything other than error, nor controlling oneself anything other than wisdom.'

They all agreed.

'Well now. Is this what you mean by error, having false opinions and being mistaken about
5 matters of importance?'

They all agreed to that as well.

'Now surely,' I said, 'no one freely goes for bad things or things he believes to be bad; it's
d not, it seems to me, in human nature to be prepared to go for what you think to be bad in preference to what is good. And when you are forced to choose one of two evils, nobody will choose the greater when he can have the lesser. Isn't that so?'

All of us agreed to all of that.

5 'Well, then,' I said, 'is there something that you call fear or apprehension? And is it the same thing as I mean? (This is a question for you, Prodicus.) I mean by this an expectation of evil, whether you call it fear or apprehension.'

Protagoras and Hippias thought that that's what fear and apprehension are, while Prodicus
e thought it was apprehension, but not fear.

'Well it doesn't make any difference, Prodicus,' I said. 'The point is this. If what has just been said is true, will any man be willing to go for what he fears, when he can go for what he doesn't fear? Or is that impossible, according to what we have agreed? For if anyone fears something, it was
5 agreed that he thinks it bad; and no one who thinks anything bad goes for it or takes it of his own free will.'

359a That too was agreed by everyone.

'On that basis, then, Prodicus and Hippias,' I said, 'let Protagoras defend the correctness of his first answer to me. I don't mean what he said right at the beginning; for at that point he said
5 that while there are five parts of excellence none is like any other, but each has its own separate power. I don't mean that, but what he said later. For later he said that four of the five resemble one another fairly closely, but one is altogether
b different from the others, namely courage. His evidence was the following: "You will find, Socrates, men who are totally irreligious, unjust, wanton, and ignorant, but very courageous; that's how you will see that courage is very different from the other parts of excellence." I was very surprised at his answer at the time, and even more now that I have gone into the question together with you. So I asked him if he called courageous men daring. "Yes, and ready," he said.
c Do you recall that answer, Protagoras?' I said.

'I do.'

'Well, now,' I said, 'tell us, what are courageous men ready for? The same things as cowards?'

'No.'

'Different things, then.'

'Yes,' he said.

'Do cowards go for things which they are
5 confident about, and courageous men for fearful things?'

'So it's generally said, Socrates.'

d 'True,' I said, 'but that isn't what I'm asking. What do *you* say the courageous are ready for?

Fearful things, in the belief that they are fearful, or not?'

'But it's just been shown by what you've said,' he replied, 'that that's impossible.'

'That's true as well,' I said. 'So if that demonstration was correct, no one goes for things that he regards as fearful, since giving in to oneself turned out to be error.'

He agreed.

'But now everyone, coward and courageous alike, goes for what he is confident about, and therefore cowards and courageous go for the same things.'

'But, Socrates,' he said, 'the things that cowards go for are exactly the opposite of those that the courageous go for. For instance, courageous men are willing to go to war, but cowards aren't.'

'Is it praiseworthy to go,' I said, 'or disgraceful?'

'Praiseworthy.'

'So if it's praiseworthy, we agreed previously that it is good; for we agreed that all praiseworthy actions are good.'

'That's true; I remain of that opinion.'

'You are right,' I said. 'But which of them is it you say are not willing to go to war, though that is something praiseworthy and good?'

'Cowards,' he said.

'Well, now,' I said, 'if it's praiseworthy and good, is it also pleasant?'

'Well, that's what was agreed,' he said.

'So cowards are unwilling, in full knowledge of the facts, to go for what is more praiseworthy and better and pleasanter?'

'But if we agree to that,' he said, 'we shall contradict our previously agreed conclusions.'

'And what about the courageous man? Does he not go for what is more praiseworthy and better and pleasanter?'

'I have to agree,' he said.

'So in general, when a courageous man is afraid, his fear is not something disgraceful, nor his confidence when he is confident?'

'That's right,' he said.

'And if not disgraceful, are they not praiseworthy?'

He agreed.

'And if praiseworthy, good as well?'

'Yes.'

'Now by contrast the fear and the confidence of cowards, madmen, and the foolhardy are disgraceful?'

He agreed.

'And is their confidence disgraceful and bad for any other reason than ignorance and error?'

'It's as you say,' he said.

'Well, now, do you call what makes a man a coward, cowardice or courage?'

'I call it cowardice,' he said.

'And didn't it turn out that they are cowards as a result of their error about what is to be feared?'

'Certainly,' he said.

'So it's in consequence of that error that they are cowards?'

He agreed.

'And you agree that what makes them cowards is cowardice?'

He assented.

'So cowardice proves to be error about what is to be feared and what isn't?'

He nodded.

'But now,' I said, 'the opposite of cowardice is courage.'

'Yes.'

'Now wisdom about what is to be feared and what isn't is the opposite of error about that.'

At that he nodded once again.

'And error about that is cowardice?'

With great reluctance he nodded at that.

'So wisdom about what is to be feared and what isn't is courage, since it is the opposite of error about that?'

At this he wasn't even willing to nod agreement, but remained silent. And I said, 'What's this, Protagoras? Won't you even answer yes or no?'

'Carry on yourself,' he said.

'I've only one more question to ask you,' I said. 'Do you still think, as you did at the beginning, that some men are altogether ignorant, but very courageous?'

'I see that you insist, Socrates,' he said, 'that I must answer. So I'll oblige you; I declare that from what we have agreed it seems to me impossible.'

'Indeed I've no other object', I said, 'in asking all these questions than to try to find out the truth about excellence, and especially what it is itself. For I know that once that were apparent we should become perfectly clear on the question about which each of us has had so much to say, I maintaining that excellence can't be taught, and you that it can. And it seems to me that the conclusion we have just reached is jeering at us like an accuser. And if it could speak, it would say "How absurd you are, both of you. You, Socrates, began by saying that excellence can't be taught, and now you are insisting on the opposite, trying to show that all things are knowledge, justice, soundness of mind, even courage, from which it would follow that excellence most certainly could be taught. For if excellence is anything other than knowledge, as Protagoras was trying to make out, it would obviously not be teachable. But now, if it turns out to consist wholly in knowledge, as you insist, Socrates, it will be astonishing if it can't be taught. Protagoras, on the other hand, first assumed that it can be taught, but now seems to be taking the opposite view and insisting that it turns out to be practically anything rather than knowledge; and so it most certainly couldn't be taught." For my part, Protagoras, when I see all this in such terrible confusion, I am desperately anxious to have it all cleared up, and I should like to follow up our discussion by considering the nature of excellence, and then returning to the question of whether or not it can be taught. I shouldn't like that Epimetheus (Afterthought) of yours to fool us with his tricks in our discussion, the way he neglected us in distributing his gifts, as you said. I preferred Prometheus (Forethought) to Epimetheus in the story; it's because I have forethought for my life as a whole that I go into all these questions. And as I said at the beginning, if you were willing I should be most happy to examine them with you.'

'For my part, Socrates,' said Protagoras, 'I applaud your enthusiasm and the way you pursue your arguments. I don't think I'm an inferior person in any respect, but in particular I'm the last man to bear a grudge; for I've said to many people that of all those I've met I like you far the best, especially of those of your age. And I declare that I should not be surprised if you became famous for your wisdom. As to these questions, we shall pursue them some other time, whenever you wish; but now it's time to turn to something else.'

'Indeed that's what we should do,' I said, 'if you prefer. In fact, quite a while ago it was time for me to go where I said, but I stayed to oblige our friend Callias.'

With that we left.

STUDY QUESTIONS: PLATO, *PROTAGORAS*

1. What is the view about excellence (i.e., virtue) that Socrates and Protagoras share?
2. According to Socrates, what are the different ways in which virtue might be said to be one?
3. According to Protagoras, what is the greatest part of virtue?
4. Why does Socrates compare virtue to a face?
5. According to Socrates, when people choose badly with regard to pleasures and pains, what is the reason for this?
6. How does Socrates argue for the conclusion that no one chooses the bad willingly?
7. Socrates uses the above thesis as a premise in another argument. What is he trying to prove with this new argument?
8. How does Socrates define 'fear'? Why is this definition important?
9. How does Socrates finally define 'courage'?
10. According to Socrates, can a person be ignorant and brave? Why?

GORGIAS

This dialogue contains Plato's argument against Sophism. Socrates disputes with three interlocutors, Gorgias, Polus, and Callicles, in turn. The basic conclusion of the dialogue is that the Sophists must be more explicit in their rejection of justice in order to avoid contradictions. Against Gorgias, Socrates argues that rhetoric is not really a craft because its aim is not a real good as such. Furthermore, it does not really benefit the practitioner because the powers that it intends to produce are not directed toward the good. To support these claims, Socrates has to give an analysis of what a real good consists in. Against Polus, Socrates argues that it is better to be just than to acquire the kinds of powers offered by rhetoric.

Callicles rejects Socrates' analysis, arguing that rhetoric gives him the power to pursue his own pleasure and that this is the ultimate good. Socrates tries to refute this hedonistic argument in order to sustain his own criticisms of rhetoric. He argues that the real good is justice rather than pleasure. To refute Callicles' hedonism, Socrates argues that some pleasures are better than others. Once Callicles concedes this point, Socrates uses it to argue against hedonism and hence sophistry.

The *Gorgias* is probably the last of the early dialogues. Its style is slightly different from that of the other early dialogues because Socrates seems more willing to set out his own views in a more systematic way than earlier.

C. What, Chaerephon? Does Socrates desire to 447b5 hear Gorgias?

CH. Yes; that's the very thing we have come for.

C. Then visit me at home whenever you want to; for Gorgias is staying with me, and he'll give you a display.

c **S.** A good idea, Callicles. But would he be willing to have a dialogue with us? For I want to learn from him what the power of the man's craft is, and what it is that he advertises and teaches; the rest of the display he can put on another time, as you suggest.

5 **C.** There's nothing like asking the man himself, Socrates. For indeed, that was one part of his display; just now in fact he was inviting anyone in the house to ask whatever question he liked, and said he would reply to them all.

CH. . . . Tell me, Gorgias, is what Callicles here says true, that you advertise that you answer whatever anyone asks you? . . .

448a **G.** Quite true, Chaerephon. In fact I was advertising this very thing just now; and I tell you

that no one has asked me anything new for many years now.

CH. Then no doubt you'll find it easy to answer, Gorgias.

S. . . . Gorgias, what we ought to call you, as someone with knowledge of what craft?

5 **G.** The rhetorical craft, Socrates.

S. Then you ought to be called a rhetor?

G. Yes, and a good one, Socrates, if you really want to call me 'what I boast I am', as Homer said.

b **S.** And aren't we to say that you are capable (*dunaton*) of making other people rhetors too?

G. Yes indeed. That is what I advertise, not only here, but elsewhere too.

449c **S.** Come, then. You say you have knowledge of
d the rhetorical craft, and that you can make someone else a rhetor. Which of the things that are is rhetoric really about? For instance, weaving is about the production of clothes, isn't it?

G. Yes.

S. And isn't music about the production of melodies?

G. Yes.

5 S. By Hera, Gorgias, I do admire your answers; you answer as briefly as anyone could.

G. Yes, Socrates; I think I do it reasonably well.

S. You're right. Come, then answer me in the same way about rhetoric too. It is knowledge about which of the things that are?

e G. About speech (*logos*).

S. What kind of speech, Gorgias? The kind that explains the treatment to make sick people well?

G. No.

S. Then rhetoric is not about all speech.

G. No, true enough.

S. But still it makes men powerful (*dunatos*) at 5 speaking.

G. Yes.

S. And at understanding the things they speak about?

G. Certainly.

450a S. Now does the medical craft we've just mentioned make people powerful at understanding and speaking about the sick?

G. It must.

S. Then apparently medicine as well is about speech.

G. Yes.

S. Speech about diseases, that is.

G. Certainly.

5 S. And isn't gymnastics too about speech, about the good and bad condition of bodies?

G. Yes, quite.

b S. And indeed the other crafts too are this way, Gorgias; each of them is about the speech which is about the thing which each craft is the craft of.

G. Apparently.

S. Then why ever don't you call the other crafts 450b5 rhetorical, when they are about speech, since you call whatever craft is about speech rhetorical?

G. Because, Socrates, practically all the knowledge of the other crafts is about manual working and suchlike activities, but there is not such manual work in rhetoric; all its activity and its achievement is through speech. That is why I claim that the rhetoric cal craft is about speech, and claim it rightly, so I say.

S. Now do I understand what you want to say it is like? But I'll soon know more clearly. 5 Answer me now—we have crafts haven't we?

G. Yes.

S. Out of all the crafts, I suppose, some are mostly work, and need little speech, and some need none at all, but the task of the craft might be accomplished even in silence, as in painting, sculpture, and many others. I think you speak d of crafts like these when you say that rhetoric is not about them. Is that right?

G. Your assumption is quite right, Socrates.

S. But now there are other crafts which carry on 5 everything through speech, and need practically no work, or only a very little, such as arithmetic, calculating, geometry, and indeed draughts-playing and many other crafts; in some of these the speech is equal to the activities, but in most it is predominant, and altogether the whole of their activity and c achievement is through speech. I think you are saying that rhetoric is one of the crafts of this kind.

G. What you say is true.

S. And yet I don't think you want to call any of those I've mentioned rhetoric—though 5 indeed your actual words were that the craft which achieves its results through speech is rhetoric, and if someone wanted to be quarrelsome in argument (*logos*) he might assume, 'So, Gorgias, you're calling arithmetic rhetoric?' But in fact I don't think you call either arithmetic or geometry rhetoric.

451a G. Yes, what you think is correct, Socrates, and your assumption is just.

453a S. Now I think you have very nearly shown what craft you think rhetoric is, Gorgias, and if I understand you at all, you are saying that rhetoric is a craftsman of persuasion, and that its whole business and the sum of it results in this; or can you mention any broader power for rhetoric than to produce persuasion in the 5 soul of hearers?

G. Not at all, Socrates, but I think you are defining it adequately; for that is the sum of it.

ᵇ **S.** Now listen, Gorgias—for be sure I am persuaded that if anyone ever has a dialogue with
anyone else from a desire to know the thing
which the discussion is about, I too am one of
these people; and I'm sure you are too.

G. Well, Socrates, so what?

S. . . . Do you think only rhetoric produces persuasion, or do other crafts as well? I'm talking
10 about this sort of thing; whoever teaches anything, does he persuade about what he teaches,
or not?

G. He most certainly does persuade, Socrates. . . .

453c **S.** Now let's talk again about the same crafts as
just now. Doesn't arithmetic, and the arithmetician, teach us how many are the things
belonging to number?

G. Quite.

S. And doesn't it also persuade?

G. Yes.

₅ **S.** Then arithmetic too is a craftsman of
persuasion?

G. Apparently.

S. If someone asks us what sort of persuasion this
is, and about what, won't we answer that it is
454a persuasion which teaches about how many the
odd and the even are? And we will be able to
show that the other crafts we just now mentioned are all craftsmen of persuasion, and of
what persuasion, and about what, won't we?

G. Yes.

₅ **S.** Then not only rhetoric is a craftsman of
persuasion.

G. You're right.

S. Then since it is not the only craft which produces this work, but others also do it, wouldn't
it be just for us to ask the previous speaker
over again after this, as about the figure-
painter, 'Rhetoric is the craft of what sort of
persuasion, and about what?'? Or don't you
ᵇ think it would be just to ask over again?

G. Yes, I do.

S. Then answer, Gorgias, since you think so too.

G. Well then, Socrates, I say it is the craft of
₅ persuasion in jury-courts, and in other mobs,
as I was saying just now indeed, and about the
things which are just and unjust.

S. Come then, and let's examine this as well. Do
you call something having learnt?

454c **G.** I do.

S. And do you call something being convinced?

ᵈ **G.** I do.

S. Then do you think having learnt and being
convinced or learning and conviction are the
same, or different?

G. Myself, Socrates, I think they're different.

S. Yes, you're right in thinking so; and you'll
realize it from this:—If someone asked you,
'Gorgias, is there any true and false convic-
₅ tion?', you would say there is, I think.

G. Yes.

S. Now then, is there true and false knowledge?

G. Not at all.

S. Then it's clear that it's not the same.

G. What you say is true.

S. And yet, both those who have learnt and
ᵉ those who have reached conviction are
persuaded.

G. That's so.

S. Then do you want us to lay down two forms
of persuasion, one yielding conviction without knowing, the other yielding knowledge?

G. Quite.

₅ **S.** Then which persuasion does rhetoric produce
in jury-courts and the other mobs, about just
and unjust things? The persuasion from which
conviction comes without knowing, or that
from which knowing comes?

G. Presumably it's clear, Socrates, that it's the
kind from which conviction comes.

455a **S.** Then it seems rhetoric is the craftsman of persuasion which yields conviction but does not
teach about the just and the unjust.

G. Yes.

S. Then neither does the rhetor teach juries and
the other mobs about just and unjust things,
₅ but only produces conviction. For presumably
he couldn't teach such great matters to such a
large mob in a short time.

G. No indeed.

456 But now, Socrates, rhetoric should be used
the same way as any other competitive craft.
ᵈ For indeed someone should not use other competitive crafts against everyone, just because
he has learnt to box and to do mixed fighting
and to fight in armour so as to beat friends and
enemies alike—he shouldn't, just because of

this, strike, wound or kill his friends. Nor yet, by Zeus, if someone has his body in good condition and has become a boxer after going to the training-school, and then strikes his father and mother, or some other relative or friend, we shouldn't, just because of that, detest the trainers and teachers of armed combat, and expel them from the cities. For they transmitted these crafts to be used justly, against enemies and those who do injustice, in defence, not in aggression; but these pupils pervert their strength and craft, and use it wrongly. And so it is not the teachers who are base (*ponēros*), nor is the craft responsible or base because of this, but, I take it, those who don't use it rightly. And the same account (*logos*) applies to rhetoric too. For the rhetor is powerful at speaking against anyone about anything, so as to be more persuasive among masses of people about, in short, whatever he wants; but that is no more reason why he should steal their reputation either from the doctors, just because he has the power to do that, or from the other craftsmen, but he should use rhetoric justly as well, as any competitive craft should be used. But I think that if someone acquires the rhetorical craft and then does injustice with this power and craft, we should not detest his teacher and expel him from the city. For he transmitted his craft for a just man to use, but the pupil is using it the opposite way; and so it is just to detest, expel, and kill the one who used it wrongly, but not his teacher.

S. I think that you as well as I, Gorgias, have had experience of many discussions (*logos*), and have noticed this sort of thing in them:— People can't easily define for each other whatever things they undertake to have a dialogue about, and then learn from each other, teach each other, and so conclude the meeting. No; if they dispute about anything, and one says that the other is speaking wrongly or obscurely, they are annoyed, and think he is speaking from jealousy towards them, competing for victory, not inquiring into what is proposed in the discussion; and some end up by

parting in the most shameful way, covered in insults, when they have said and heard such abuse of each other that the people present are annoyed for themselves that they have seen fit to give a hearing to characters like these.

Now why do I say this? It's because I think now you're saying things which don't quite follow from or harmonize with the things you said at first about rhetoric. And so I'm afraid to complete my examination (*dielenchein*) of you, for fear you will suppose I am not competing to make clear the matter we are discussing, but to defeat you. And so, if you are the same kind of man as I am, I would be pleased to continue the questions; if not, I would rather let it go. And what kind of man am I? One of those who would be pleased to be refuted (*elenchein*) if I say something untrue, and pleased to refute if someone were to say something untrue, yet not at all less pleased to be refuted than to refute. For I think that being refuted is a greater good, in so far as it is a greater good for a man to get rid of the greatest evil himself than to rid someone else of it—for I think there is no evil for a man as great as a false belief about the things which our discussion is about now. And so, if you also say that you are that kind of man, let us continue the dialogue; but if in fact you think we ought to let it go, let us let it go, and finish the discussion.

G. Not at all; I do say that I am also the kind of man you suggest, Socrates. But perhaps we ought to have thought of these people here too. For look, I presented many displays to them for a good while before you people came as well, and now perhaps we'll prolong it too far if we have a dialogue. So we ought to consider them too, in case we keep some of them back when they want to do something else as well. . . .

S. Now it was being said in the opening discussions (*logos*), Gorgias, that rhetoric is about speech (*logos*), not speech about the odd and even, but speech about the just and unjust. Isn't that so?

G. Yes.

S. Well, when you were saying that, I supposed that rhetoric would never be an unjust thing, when it always produces its speech about justice; and when you were saying a little later that the rhetor might actually use rhetoric

461a unjustly, that was why I was surprised, and thought that the things being said did not harmonize; and so I made those remarks (logos), that if you thought it a gain to be refuted, as I think, the dialogue would be worth while, but otherwise we should let it go. But now when we examine the question, you

5 see for yourself that it's agreed on the contrary that the rhetor is powerless to use his rhetoric unjustly and to be willing to do injustice. And so how exactly these things stand—by the

b dog, Gorgias, it will take quite a long meeting to investigate adequately.

POLUS. What, Socrates? Do you really believe what you're saying now about rhetoric? Do you really suppose—just because Gorgias was ashamed not to agree further with you that

5 the rhetor would also know the just, the fine, and the good things, and that if he didn't know them when he came to Gorgias, Gorgias himself would teach him, and then perhaps from that agreement some opposition came about in his statements (logos)—the thing

c that you're so satisfied about, when you yourself led him into those questions—for who do you suppose would deny that he himself knew the just things and would teach others? It's simply the height of bad breeding to lead the discussion (logos) to such things.

5 S. Finest Polus, that's exactly why we acquire companions and sons, so that when we get old and stumble, you younger people will come and set our lives straight, both in our actions and in our speech. And so now, if Gorgias and

d I are stumbling at all in our speech, you must come and set us straight—that is the just thing—and I'm willing to withdraw anything you like of what has been agreed, if you think it was wrongly agreed. For I take it you also

462a5 say you know what Gorgias says he knows, don't you?

P. I do indeed.

S. And don't you also tell people to ask you whatever they want to any time, claiming that you know how to answer?

10 P. Quite.

S. Well then, do whichever of these you want to
b now; ask questions or answer them.

P. All right, I'll do that. Now answer me, Socrates:—Since you think Gorgias is at a loss
5 about rhetoric, which do you say it is?

S. Are you asking me which craft I say it is?

P. I am indeed.

S. Well, I think it's no craft, Polus, to tell you the truth.

10 P. Then what do you think rhetoric is?

S. A thing which you say has produced craft, in
c the work I've recently read.

P. What's this you're talking about?

S. I say it's certain knack.

P. Then you think rhetoric is a knack?

5 S. I do—unless you say something else.

P. A knack of what?

S. Of the production of a certain gratification and pleasure. . . .

P. Then don't you think rhetoric is a fine thing,
462c the ability to gratify people?

S. What's that, Polus? Have you already found out from me what I say it is, so that you ask
d the next question, if I don't it's fine?

P. Yes; haven't I found out that you say it's certain knack?

S. I'm afraid it may be a bit ill-bred to say what's true. For I shrink from saying it, because of Gorgias, for fear he may think I'm ridiculing his own practice. But anyhow, whether the rhetoric Gorgias practices is like this, I don't
463a know—for in fact nothing was made clear for us in our recent discussion about just what he thinks—but anyhow what I call rhetoric is a part of something not at all fine.

5 G. A part of what, Socrates? Tell us; don't be embarrassed for my sake.

S. Well. Gorgias, I think it is a practice, not of a craftsman, but of a guessing, brave soul, naturally clever at approaching people; and I call the sum of it flattery. I think this practice has
b many other parts too, and cookery is also one of them; it seems to be a craft, but on my

account (*logos*) it isn't a craft, but a knack and
procedure. I call rhetoric a part of this too,
and also cosmetics and sophistry—these four
parts set our four things. And so if Polus wants
to find out, he should find out; for he hasn't
yet found out what sort of part of flattery I say
rhetoric is; he hasn't noticed that I haven't
yet answered, but goes on to ask if I don't
think it is fine. But I won't answer him
whether I think rhetoric is fine or shameful
until I first answer what it is—that would not
be just, Polus. But if you want to find out, ask
me what sort of part of flattery I say rhetoric is.

P. All right, I'm asking you. Answer what part it
is.

S. Then would you understand if I answered?
Well, on my account rhetoric is an image of a
part of politics.

P. All right, then; do you say it is fine or shameful?

S. I say it is shameful, since I call evil things
shameful—for I must (*dein*) reply to you as
though you already knew what I am saying.

G. By Zeus, Socrates, I don't understand what
you're saying either. . . .

S. Come then, I'll try to display more clearly to
you what I'm saying, if I can. For these two
things I say there are two crafts; the one set
over the soul I call the political craft; I can't
off-hand find a single name for the single craft
set over the body, but still body-care is one
craft, and I say there are two parts of it, the
gymnastic and the medical crafts. The part of
politics corresponding to gymnastics is legislation, and the part corresponding to medicine is
justice. Each member of these pairs—medicine
and gymnastics, justice and legislation, shares
with the other, in so far as they are both about
the same thing; but still they differ to some
extent from each other. Here are four crafts,
taking care of either body or soul, aiming at
the best. Flattery noticed them—I don't say it
knew, but it guessed—and divided itself into
four impersonating each of these parts, and
pretends to be what it impersonates; it does
not care a bit for the best, but lures and
deceives foolishness with what is pleasantest
at the moment, making itself seem to be
worth most. Cookery impersonates medicine,

then, and pretends to know the best foods for
the body; and so if a doctor and a cook had to
(*dean*) compete among children, or among
men as foolish as children, to decide which
of them understands more about worthy and
base food, the doctor or the cook, then the
doctor would die of starvation.

Well then, I call it flattery, and I say this
sort of thing is shameful, Polus—since I'm
saying this to you—because it guesses at the
pleasant without the best. And I say it is not a
craft, but a knack, because it has no rational
account (*logos*) by which it applies the things it
applies, to say what they are by nature, so that
it cannot say what is the explanation of each
thing; and I don't call anything a craft which is
unreasoning (*alogon*). If you dispute any of
this, I am ready to undergo a discussion (*logos*).

As I say, then, cookery is the flattery disguised as medicine; and cosmetics is disguised
as gymnastics in the same way—crooked,
deceptive, mean, slavish, deceiving by shap-
ing, colouring, smoothing, dressing, making
people assume a beauty (*kallos*) which is not
their own, and neglecting the beauty of their
own which would come through gymnastics.
To avoid going on at length, I want to tell you,
as the geometricians would—for now perhaps
you might follow me—as cosmetics is to gymnastics, so is sophistry to legislation, and as
cookery is to medicine, so is rhetoric to justice.
But as I say, this is how they differ by nature,
but since they are so close to each other,
sophists and rhetors are mixed up in the same
area and about the same thing, so that they
don't know what to make of themselves, and
other people don't know what to make of
them. Indeed, if the soul did not control the
body, but the body controlled itself, and if the
soul did not examine and distinguish cookery
and medicine, but the body by itself discrimi-
nated by guesswork from the gratifications to
it, then the Anaxagorean condition would be
everywhere, Polus my friend—you're familiar
with that; 'all things together' would be mixed
up in the same area, with no distinction
between matters of medicine and health and of
cookery.

What I say rhetoric is, then—you've heard it. It corresponds to cookery, doing in the soul what cookery does in the body. Now

e perhaps I've done something absurd. I didn't allow you to make long speeches, but I've drawn out my own speech to this length.

5 Well, it's fair for you to excuse me; for when I was speaking briefly, you weren't understanding, and you couldn't do anything at all with the answer I gave you, but you needed an

466a explanation. And so if I can't do anything with your answer either, then draw out your speeches; but if I can, let me do it; for that's only just. And now if you can do anything with this answer, do it

10 **P.** Then do you think that good rhetors count as worthless in the cities, as flatterers?

S. I think they don't count at all.

P. What do you mean, they don't count? Don't

5 they have the greatest power in the cities?

S. No—not if you say that having power is a good to the man with the power.

P. Well, I do say so.

S. Then I think the rhetors have the least power of anyone in the city.

c **P.** What? Aren't they like tyrants? Don't they kill whoever they want to, and expropriate and expel from the cities whoever they think fit (*dokein*)? And isn't this having great power?

S. No—at least Polus doesn't agree.

5 **P.** I don't agree? Of course I agree.

S. No, by the. . . . Indeed you don't. For you said that having great power is a good to the man who has it.

P. Yes. I still say so.

S. Then do you think it is a good if someone does whatever seems best to him, when he has

10 no intelligence? Do you call even this having great power?

P. No, I don't.

S. Then won't you show that the rhetors have intelligence and that rhetoric is a craft, not

467a flattery, by refuting me? If you leave me unrefuted, the rhetors who do what they think fit in the cities and the tyrants will have gained no good by it; but power, you say is a good, and you also agree that doing what we think

5 fit without intelligence is an evil, don't you?

P. Yes. I do.

S. Then how are the rhetors or the tyrants to have great power in the cities, unless Socrates is refuted by Polus and convinced that they do

10 what they want to?

474c **P.** Certainly; for I'm anxious to know what on earth you'll say.

S. Well then, so that you'll know, tell me this, as though I were asking you from the

5 beginning:—Which do you think is worse, Polus—doing injustice or suffering it?

P. I think suffering it is worse.

S. Now then—do you think it's more shameful to do injustice or to suffer it? Answer.

P. To do it.

S. Then isn't it also worse, if it's more shameful?

P. Not at all.

d **S.** I understand. Apparently you don't think that the same thing is fine and good or evil and shameful.

P. Certainly not.

S. Then if doing injustice is more shameful than

475b suffering it, then isn't it either more distressing, and more shameful by exceeding in distress, or by exceeding in evil, or in both?

P. Of course.

c **S.** Then first of all, let's see if doing injustice exceeds suffering it in distress, and whether those who do injustice are more in pain than those who suffer it.

P. That's certainly not right, Socrates.

S. Then it doesn't exceed in distress.

P. No indeed.

S. Then by exceeding in evil doing injustice is worse than suffering it.

P. Yes. It's clear that it is.

d **S.** Now didn't the mass of men and you agree with us earlier that doing injustice is more shameful than suffering it?

P. Yes.

S. And now it has turned out worse.

P. It looks like it.

5 **S.** Then would you choose the more evil and shameful over the less? Don't shrink from answering, Polus—you won't be harmed at all; but present yourself nobly to the argument (*logos*) as to a doctor; answer, and say either

e yes or no to what I'm asking you.

P. Well, no; I wouldn't choose it, Socrates.

S. And would any other man?

P. I don't think so—by this argument anyway.

S. Then I was saying what was true, that neither I nor you nor any other man would choose doing injustice over suffering it; for it's actually worse.

P. Apparently.

S. I'm saying this:—Always the most shameful is most shameful by producing the greatest distress or harm or both, from what was agreed in the previous discussion.

P. Certainly.

S. And isn't it just now agreed by us that injustice and all baseness of soul is most shameful?

d P. Yes. It's agreed.

S. Then isn't it either the most painful, and the most shameful of them by exceeding in pain, or by exceeding in harm, or in both ways?

P. It must be.

S. Then is it more painful than being poor and sick to be unjust and intemperate (*akolastos*) and cowardly and stupid?

P. I don't think so, from what we've said, Socrates.

S. Then it is by exceeding the other things in some remarkably serious harm and amazing evil that baseness of soul is the most shameful of all, since it doesn't exceed in pain, on your account.

P. Apparently.

478a S. And which craft rids us of baseness and injustice? If you don't find this easy, consider it this way:—Where and to whom do we take people sick in body?

P. To the doctors, Socrates.

S. And where do we take those who do unjust and intemperate (*akolastainontes*) actions?

5 P. To the court of justice, are you saying?

S. And don't we take them to pay justice?

P. I agree.

S. Then don't those who punish (*kolazein*) rightly practise some kind of justice when they punish?

P. It's clear they do.

b S. Then money-making rids us of poverty, medicine of sickness, and the administration of jus-

tice rids us of intemperance (*akolasia*) and injustice?

P. Apparently.

478d S. Well then, which is the more wretched of two people who have an evil either in body or in soul, the one who is treated and gets rid of the evil, or the one who isn't treated and still has it?

P. The one who isn't treated, I think.

S. Now isn't paying justice getting rid of the greatest evil, baseness?

P. Yes, it is.

S. Yes, for presumably administration of justice makes people temperate and more just, and is in fact the medical craft to cure baseness.

P. Yes.

S. Then the man with no evil in his soul is happiest, since this appeared the greatest of evils.

P. Yes. That's clear.

S. And presumably second to him is the man who gets rid of the evil.

P. It looks like it.

S. And this is the man who is corrected and reprimanded and pays justice.

P. Yes.

S. Then the man who has the evil in his soul and does not get rid of it lives worst.

P. Apparently.

S. And isn't this man in fact whoever does the greatest injustices and exercises the greatest

479a injustice and manages not to be corrected or punished (*kolazesthai*) and not to pay justice— as you say Archelaus and the other tyrants and rhetors and dynasts managed to do?

P. It looks like it. . . .

480a S. All right. If these things are true, then what is the great use of rhetoric, Polus? For in fact from what has been agreed now a man should most of all take care for himself so that he doesn't do injustice, knowing that he will have a great enough evil if he does. Isn't that right?

5 P. Quite.

S. And if he or whoever else he cares about does do injustice, he should go voluntarily wherever he will pay justice as quickly as possible, to the court of justice as to the doctor, eager to prevent the disease of injustice from being b chronic and making his soul festering and incurable—or what else are we saying, Polus, if our previous agreements remain firm? Mustn't what we say now agree with what we said then

5 only this way, and otherwise not?

P. Yes indeed. What else are we to say, Socrates?

S. And then, turning it around the opposite way,

5 if we really should harm anyone—an enemy or anyone at all—as long as we don't ourselves suffer any injustice from the enemy—for we must be careful about that—but if our enemy treats someone else unjustly, we should take

481a every precaution, in speaking and in action, to prevent him from paying justice and appearing before the court of justice. And if he appears, we must arrange it so that he escapes and doesn't pay justice, but if he has stolen a lot of money, we must see he doesn't pay it back, but keeps it and spends it on himself and his relatives, unjustly and godlessly;

5 and if he has done injustice deserving death, we must see he does not suffer death—best of all never, to be immortal in his baseness, but

b otherwise to live the longest possible life in this condition. For these sorts of things I think rhetoric is useful, Polus, since for someone who isn't about to act unjustly, its use doesn't seem to me to be all that great—if indeed it has any use at all, for it wasn't evident any-

5 where in what was said previously.

CALLICLES. Tell me Chaerephon, is Socrates in earnest about all this, or is he joking?

CHAEREPHON. Well, to me he seems remarkably in earnest, Callicles. But there's nothing like asking him.

C. I'm certainly anxious to do that, by the gods. Tell me, Socrates, are we to suppose you're in

c earnest now, or joking? For if you're in earnest, and all these things you say are really true, then wouldn't the life of us men be upside down? And don't we apparently do everything that's the opposite of what we should do?

e S. ... In the Assembly, if you're saying something and the Athenian demos says it's not so, you change and say what it wants. And with this fine young man the son of Pyrilampes you're affected in other similar ways. For

5 you're incapable of opposing the proposals and speeches of your beloved; and if someone were amazed whenever you say the things you say because of your beloveds, at how absurd these things are, then no doubt you'd tell him, if you wanted to tell him what's true, that unless

482a someone stops your beloved from saying these things, you'll never stop saying them either.

And so you must suppose that you're bound to (chrēnai) hear the same sorts of things from me. Don't be amazed that I say these things, but stop my beloved, philosophy,

5 saying them. For she says what you hear from me now, my friend; and she's much less impulsive than my other beloved. For this son of Cleinias here says now this, now that; but phi-

b losophy says always the same. She says what amazes you now, and you were present yourself when it was said. And so either refute her, as I was saying just now, and show that doing injustice and doing injustice without paying

5 justice are not the worst of evils. . . .

C. Socrates, I think you swagger in your

c speeches, as if you were really a mob-orator. And now you're making this speech when you've done the same thing to Polus that Polus was denouncing Gorgias for letting you do to him. For remember he said that you asked Gorgias whether, if anyone wanting to

d learn rhetoric came to him without knowing just things, he would teach him. Then Gorgias was ashamed, said Polus, and said he would teach him, because of men's habit, since they would be offended if someone said he couldn't teach about just things. Because of this agreement, said Polus, Gorgias was forced

5 to contradict himself, and this is exactly what you like. And then Polus laughed at you, rightly, I think. But now you have done the same thing over again to him. And for just this I can't admire Polus myself, for his concession to you that doing injustice is more shameful than suffering it; for from this agree-

e ment he himself in turn was bound up by you in the argument, and was muzzled, after being ashamed to say what he thought. For indeed, Socrates, you lead things to these vulgarities and stock themes of mob-orators, though you claim to pursue the truth—things which are not fine bynature, but only by rule (*nomos*). For mostly these are opposed to each other, nature and rule; and so if someone is ashamed and dare not say what he thinks, he is compelled to contradict himself. And this is the clever device you've thought of and use to make mischief in discussion; if someone speaks according to rule, you craftily question him according to nature, and if he speaks of what belongs to nature, you ask him about what belongs to rule—just as lately about these things—doing injustice and suffering it—Polus was speaking of the fine according to rule, but you pursued the argument according to nature.

For by nature everything is more shameful which is also worse, suffering injustice, but by rule doing injustice is more shameful. For this isn't what happens to a man, to suffer injustice; it's what happens to some slave for whom it's better to die than to live—for if he suffers injustice and abuse, he can't defend himself or anyone else he cares about. But in my view those who lay down the rules are the weak men, the many. And so they lay down the rules and assign their praise and blame with their eye on themselves and their own advantage. They terrorize the stronger men capable of having more; and to prevent these men from having more than themselves they say that taking more is shameful and unjust, and that doing injustice is this, seeking to have more than other people; they are satisfied, I take it, if they themselves have an equal share when they're inferior. That's why by rule this is said to be unjust and shameful, to seek to have more than the many, and they call that doing injustice.

But I think nature itself shows this, that it is just for the better man to have more than the worse, and the more powerful than the less powerful. Nature shows that this is so in many areas—among other animals, and in whole cities and races of men, that the just stands decided in this way—the superior rules over the weaker and has more. For what sort of justice did Xerxes rely on when he marched against Greece, or his father against the Scythians? And you could mention innumerable other such things. But I think these men do these things according to nature—the nature of the just; yes, by Zeus, by the rule of nature, though no doubt not by the rule we lay down—we mould the best and strongest among us, taking them from youth up, like lions, and tame them by spells and incantations over them, until we enslave them, telling them they ought to have equal shares, and that this is the fine and the just.

But I think that if a man is born with a strong enough nature, he will shake off and smash and escape all this. He will trample on all our writings, charms, incantations, all the rules contrary to nature. He rises up and shows himself master, this slave of ours, and there the justice of nature suddenly bursts into light. And I think Pindar too indicates what I say, in the song where he says, 'Rule, the king of all, mortals and immortals. . . .' This, he says, 'leads and makes just what is most violent, with overpowering hand; I judge this by the works of Heracles, since without paying the price. . . .' He says something like this—for I don't know the song—but he says that without payment and without receiving them as a gift from Geryon Heracles drove off the cattle, assuming that this was the just by nature, that the better and superior man possesses the cattle and other goods of the worse and inferior men.

Well then, that's how the truth is. And you'll find it out if you move on to greater things and finally leave philosophy behind. For I tell you, Socrates, philosophy is a delightful thing, if someone touches it in moderation at the right time of life; but if he persists in it longer than he should, it's the ruin of men. For even if someone has an altogether good nature, but philosophizes beyond the right age, he is bound to end up inexperienced in all these things in which anyone who is to be a fine and good and respected man ought to have experience. For indeed they turn out inexperienced in the laws (*nomos*) of the city, and in the speech they should use in meeting men in public and private transactions, and in human pleasures and desires; and altogether they turn out entirely ignorant of the ways of men. And so whenever they come to some private or political business, they prove themselves ridiculous, just as politicians, no doubt, whenever they in turn come to your discourses and discussions, are ridiculous. For it happens as Euripides says; 'Each man shines in that and strives for it, devoting the greatest part of the day to it—where he finds himself best', and wherever he is inferior, he avoids it and abuses it, praising the other thing, from good will to himself, supposing that this way he is praising himself.

But I think that the most correct thing is to have a share in both. It is fine to have a share in philosophy far enough for education, and it is not shameful for someone to philosophize when he is a boy. But whenever a man who's now older still philosophizes, the thing becomes ridiculous, Socrates. I'm struck by the philosophizers most nearly the way I'm struck by those who mumble and act childishly. I mean—whenever I see a child, when that kind of dialogue is still fitting for him, mumbling and being childish, I enjoy it; I find it charming, suitable for a free citizen, suiting the age of a child. And whenever I hear a child speaking a clear dialogue, I find it unpleasing; it annoys my ears; and I find it fit for a slave instead. But whenever someone hears a man mumbling, or sees him act childishly, he finds it ridiculous, unmanly, deserving a beating.

Well, philosophizers strike me the same way too. For when I see philosophy in a young boy, I admire it, I find it suitable, and I regard him as a free man, and a non-philosophizer as un-free, someone who will never expect anything fine or noble from himself. But when I see an older man still philosophizing and not giving it up, I think this man needs a beating, Socrates. For, as I was saying just now, this person is bound to end up being unmanly, even if he has an altogether good nature; for he shuns the city centre and the public squares where the poet says men win good reputations. He is sunk away out of sight for the rest of his life, and lives whispering with three or four boys in a corner, and never gives voice to anything fit for a free man, great and powerful.

Now, Socrates, I'm quite friendly towards you. And so I find you strike me now as Amphion struck Zethus in Euripides, whom I recalled just now. For indeed, the sorts of things come to me to say to you that Zethus said to his brother; 'Socrates, you are careless of what you should care for; you twist this noble nature of your soul in a childish shape; you could not make a speech correctly to the council of justice, nor seize anything likely and persuasive, nor propose any daring resolution to help another.' And look, my dear Socrates—and don't be annoyed with me at all, when I'll be saying it out of goodwill to you—don't you find it shameful to be the way I think you are, along with all those who go further and further into philosophy?

For as it is, suppose someone arrested you, or some other philosopher, and threw you into goal, claiming you were doing injustice when you were doing none; you know you'd have no idea what to do with yourself; you'd be dizzy, you'd gape, not knowing what to say; you'd go into court, to face some inferior wretch of an accuser, and you'd be put to death if he wanted the death penalty for you. Now how can this be wise, Socrates?—'this craft which takes a man of good nature and makes him worse'—with no power to defend himself or save himself or anyone else from the greatest dangers, with only the power to be despoiled of all his property by his enemies, and to live altogether dishonoured in the city. With someone like this, to put it crudely, anyone is at liberty to push his face in and get off scot-free.

S. If I had a soul made of gold, Callicles, don't you think I'd be delighted to find one of those stones on which they test gold—the best one, so that if I brought my soul to it, and it agreed that my soul was well cared for, I would be sure I was in good condition and needed no other touchstone?

e **C.** And what's your point in asking that, Socrates?

S. I'll tell you. I think I've stumbled on that kind of lucky find now, by stumbling on you.

487e   Clearly, then, this is how it is now with these questions: if you agree with me about anything in the discussion, then this will have been adequately tested by me and you, and it will no longer need to be brought to another touchstone. . . . In reality, then, agreement between you and me will finally possess the goal of truth. . . .

488b   But now repeat for me again from the beginning—how do you say the just is, you and Pindar—the just by nature? Is it for the superior man to remove by force what belongs to the inferior men, and for the better man to

5   rule worse men, and for the nobler man to have more than the baser man? You aren't saying that the just is anything else, are you? Or do I remember correctly?

C. Yes. That's what I was saying then, and say now. . . .

488d5 **S.** And do you call the same man better and superior? . . . Define this very thing for me clearly; are the superior and the better and the stronger the same thing, or something different?

C. Yes. I'm telling you clearly that they're the same. . . .

489d **S.** . . . I repeat my question from eagerness to know clearly what you're saying. For presumably you don't think that two men are better than one, or that your slaves are better than

5   you, just because they're stronger than you. But now say again from the beginning what do you say the better men are, since you say they're not the stronger?

C. I say they're the worthier men.

5 **S.** Now do you see that you're just saying names, making nothing clear? Won't you tell me—do you say that the better and the superior men are the wiser men, or some others?

C. Yes indeed. I say they are, very much so.

490a **S.** Then often one wise man is superior to thousands with no wisdom, on your account, and he should rule them, and they should be ruled, and the ruler should have more than the

ruled. I think that's what you want to say—

5   and I'm not trying to catch you with a word—if the one is superior to the thousands.

C. Yes, that's what I'm saying. For this is what I think the just by nature is—that the man who is better and wiser should rule over the lower

491a   men, and have more than them. . . .

5 **S.** Won't you say what the superior and wiser man has more of when he justly takes more? . . .

491b **C.** But I've been saying for a long time. First of all I say who the superior men are—I don't say shoemakers or cooks; they're whoever are wise in the city's affairs, about how to govern it well, and not only wise, but also brave, and capable of fulfilling what they intend—and who don't slacken because of softness of soul.

5 **S.** Do you see, excellent Callicles, that you and I don't accuse each other of the same thing? For you say I'm always saying the same thing, and you blame me for it, but on the contrary I accuse you of never saying the

c   same about the same things. Previously you were defining the better and superior men as the stronger, then as the wiser, now again you've come bringing something else. Some kind of braver men are what you call the superior and the better men. Come on, my friend, tell me once and for all, just who do you call the better and superior—better and

5   superior in what?

C. But I've told you—those who are wise in the city's affairs, and brave. For it is fitting for

d   these to rule cities, and the just is this, for them to have more than the rest—for the rulers to have more than the ruled.

5 **S.** But what about themselves, my friend? Rulers or ruled in what way?

C. What are you talking about?

S. I'm talking about each one of them ruling himself. Or shouldn't he do this at all, rule himself, but only rule the others?

C. What are you talking about, 'ruling himself'?

10 **S.** Nothing complicated, but just as the many say—temperate, master of himself, ruling the

e   pleasures and appetites within him.

C. How funny you are. You're calling the fools the temperate people.

S. What? Anyone would realize that's not what I'm saying.

5 C. But it certainly is, Socrates. For how could a man become happy who's enslaved to anything at all? No. The fine and just according to nature is this, what I'm speaking freely of to you now—the man who is to live rightly should let his appetites grow as large as possible and not restrain (*kolazein*) them, and when these are as large as possible, he must have the power to serve them, because of his bravery and wisdom, and to fill them with whatever he has an appetite for at any time. But I think this isn't in the power of the many. And so they blame these people out of shame, concealing their own powerlessness, and say that intemperance (*akolasia*) is actually shameful, as I was saying previously, enslaving the men with the best natures; and when they haven't the power to find fulfillment for their pleasures, they praise temperance and justice because of their own unmanliness. . . .

492a

b

d S. You're carrying through your speech nobly, Callicles, and speaking freely. For now you're saying clearly what the others think but aren't willing to say. And so I'm asking you not to slacken at all, so that it will really become clear how we should live. And tell me this:—Do you say that a man must not restrain (*kolazein*) his appetites, if he's to be as he should be, but should let them grow as great as possible, and find fulfillment for them from anywhere at all, and that virtue is this?

5

e

C. That's what I say.

S. Then it's wrong to say that those who need (*dein*) nothing are happy.

5 C. Of course. Otherwise stones and corpses would be happiest.

S. But the life you speak of is a strange one too. For I tell you, I wouldn't be surprised if Euripides speaks the truth in those verses where he says, 'Who knows if being alive is really being dead, and being dead being alive?' And perhaps we too are really dead. For once I heard from some wise man that we are dead now, our body is our tomb; and that of our soul with appetites in it is liable to be persuaded and to sway back and forth. And a subtle man,

10

493a

5 perhaps some Sicilian or Italian, who told this story, played on the name, and because it was persuadable (*pithanon*) and impressionable called it a jar (*pithon*), and called the foolish (*anoētous*) the uninitiated (*amuētous*), and said that in the foolish men that of the soul with appetites, the foolish, intemperate, and insatiable in it, was a leaking jar, because it couldn't be filled. This man indicates—contrary to you, Callicles—that of all those in Hades—speaking of the unseen (*aides*) this way—these are the most wretched, the uninitiated, and that they carry water to this leaky jar with another leaky thing, a sieve. And so he's saying—so the man who told me said—that the sieve is the soul; and he likened the soul of the foolish to a sieve because it was leaky, since it could hold nothing, from its unreliability and forgetfulness.

b

5

c

Now this is all fairly strange. But he shows what I'd like to indicate to you, so that I persuade you, if I can, to change your mind, and instead of the insatiable and unrestrained life to choose the orderly life adequately supplied and satisfied with whatever it has at any time. But now do I persuade you at all to change your mind, and agree that the orderly are happier than the intemperate? Or even if I tell you many more stories like this one, won't you change your mind any the more?

5

d

C. You're nearer the truth there, Socrates.

5 S. Come on then, I'll tell you another comparison, from the same school as that one. See now if you're saying something like this about the life of each of the two men, the temperate and the intemperate:—Suppose for instance that each of two men has a lot of jars, and one has sound and full jars, one full of wine, another of honey, another of milk, and many others full of many things. And suppose the sources for each of these things are scarce and hard to find, provided only with much severe effort. Now when one man has filled up, he brings in no more, and doesn't care about them, but is at rest as far as they are concerned. The other man has sources like the first man's that can be drawn on, though with difficulty. But his vessels are leaky and rotten, and he is forced to be always

e

5

494a filling them day and night, or else he suffers the most extreme distresses. Now if this is how each man's life is, do you say that the intemperate man's life is happier than the orderly man's? When I tell you this, do I persuade you at all to

5 concede that the orderly life is better than the intemperate, or don't I persuade you?

C. No, you don't, Socrates. For that one who has filled up has no pleasure at all any more. It's what I was saying just now—living like a stone

b once he has filled up, with no more enjoyment or distress. No; living pleasantly is in this—in having as much as possible flowing in.

S. But if the inflow is large, mustn't the outflow be large too, and mustn't there be big holes for the outflow?

5 C. Of course.

S. Then you're speaking of some kind of torrent-bird's life, not a corpse's or a stone's. Tell me now; are you talking about something like being hungry and eating when you're hungry?

C. I am.

c S. And being thirsty and drinking when you're thirsty?

C. That's what I'm talking about—and about having all the other appetites and having the power to fill them and enjoy it, and so living happily. . . .

495a But tell me even now; do you say that the same thing is pleasant and good, or that there is something of pleasant things which is not good?

5 C. Well, so that I don't leave my argument (logos) inconsistent, if I say that they're different, I say they're the same. . . .

495c5 S. Then return to what has been agreed before. In speaking of hunger, were you saying that it is pleasant or painful? I'm talking about hunger itself.

C. I say it's painful. But I say that eating when you're hungry is pleasant.

S. Then do you see what follows, that you say

496e5 someone is distressed and enjoying at the same time, when you say he is thirsty and drinks? Or doesn't this come about at the same time and in the same place, in soul or body—for I think

e it makes no difference? Is that so or not?

C. It is.

S. But now you say it's impossible for someone

497a doing well to do badly at the same time.

C. Yes, I do.

S. While you are agreed that it's possible to be in pain and enjoyment at the same time.

C. Apparently.

S. Then enjoying is not doing well, nor is being in pain doing badly; and so the pleasant turns

5 out to be different from the good.

C. I don't know what sort of sophistry you're at, Socrates.

S. You know, but you're acting soft, Callicles. Go further on, and see how wise you are when

b you take me to task. Isn't each of us finished with his pleasure from drinking at the same time as he is finished being thirsty?

C. I agree.

S. And don't we cease from hunger and all the other appetites and from pleasures at the same time?

C. That's right.

d S. But now, we don't cease from goods and evils at the same time, as you were agreeing then; don't you agree now?

C. Yes, I do. So what?

5 S. Then goods turn out not to be the same as pleasant things, my friend, and evils not to be the same as painful things. For we cease from pleasant and painful things at the same time, but not from good and evil things, since they're different from pleasant and painful. Then how can pleasant things be the same as goods, or painful things the same as evils? . . .

499b5 C. I've been listening to you for a long time and agreeing, Socrates, thinking that even if someone concedes something to you as a joke, you fasten on it gleefully like young boys. As though you really suppose that I or any other man don't think some pleasures are better and others worse.

S. Ah Callicles, what a scoundrel you are. You

499c treat me like a child, telling me now that the same things are this way, and again that they're some other way, and deceiving me. And I didn't think at the start that you'd voluntarily deceive me, because I thought you were a friend. But it turns out I was misled; and it seems I must 'make the best of what I have', as the old saying goes, and accept what you're offering me. And that is, you're saying now, that there are pleasures, some good and some bad. Isn't that right?

d C. Yes.

S. Then are the beneficial ones good, and the harmful ones evil?

C. Quite.

S. And those which produce some good are beneficial, and those which produce some evil are evil?

C. I agree.

S. Are you speaking of these kinds of pleasures— in the body, for instance, among the pleasures found in eating and drinking that we were speaking of just now—those which produce health in the body, or strength or some other excellence (aretē) of the body, are these good,

e and the ones which produce the opposites of these things evil?

C. Certainly.

S. And similarly among distresses, aren't some worthy, others base?

C. Of course.

S. Then mustn't we choose and do the worthy ones, both pleasures and distresses?

5 C. Certainly.

S. But not the base ones?

C. Clearly not.

S. Yes; for I take it we agreed that we must do everything for the sake of goods, if you remember— Polus and I. Do you agree with us too, that the good is the end of all actions, and that for the sake of it we should do all the other things,

500a not do it for the sake of the other things? Do you cast a third vote with ours?

C. I do.

S. Then for the sake of goods we should do other things, including pleasant things, not good things for the sake of pleasant things?

C. Quite.

5 S. Now is it for anyone to select which kinds of pleasant things are good and which evil? Or does it need a craftsman for each thing?

C. It needs a craftsman.

S. Then let's recall another thing I was saying to Polus and Gorgias. I was saying, if you

b remember, that there are practices, some limited to pleasure, only that one thing, ignorant of the better and the worse, and other practices which know what is good and what is bad. And I was assigning to the practices concerned with pleasures the knack—no

5 craft—of confectionery, and to those concerned with the good the medical craft. And for the sake of the god of friendship, Callicles, don't think you should make jokes at me, and don't answer capriciously, contrary

c to what you think, nor again take what I say that way, as making jokes. For you see that our discussion is about this—and what would anyone with the slightest intelligence be more seriously concerned about than this? I mean— what way ought we to live? The way to which you encourage me, doing what a real man

5 does, speaking in the people's Assembly, practising rhetoric, conducting politics the way you conduct it now—or the life spent in philosophy? And how does the one life differ from the other? Perhaps it's best, then, to

d divide these lives as I set about it lately; when we've divided them, and agreed with each other, if there are these two distinct lives, we should consider how they differ from each other, and which of them is to be lived. Perhaps you don't yet know what I'm saying.

5 C. No. Indeed I don't.

S. Well, I'll tell you more clearly. Since you and I are agreed that something is good and something is pleasant, that the pleasant is different from the good, and that there is a training and practice for the gaining of each, one a pursuit

10 of the pleasant, the other of the good—then accept or deny this point first of all. Do you

e accept it?

C. Yes, I do.

S. Come then, and accept what I was saying to these people too, if you really thought I was saying what was true then. I think I was saying that cookery doesn't seem to me to be a

5 craft, but a knack, while medicine is a craft. I

501a said that medicine has considered the nature

of what it cares for and the explanation of what it does, and can give a rational account (*logos*) of each of these things. But the knack concerned with pleasure, which all its care aims at, goes after this entirely without a craft, not at all considering the nature or the explanation of the pleasure, and altogether without reason, making practically no distinctions. By habit and experience it keeps only memory of what usually happens, by which it produces its pleasures. And so consider first whether you think this is adequately stated and whether there are also other such practices associated with the soul, some of them with craft-knowledge, with forethought for what is best about the soul, and others which despise the best, and have considered, as we said about cookery, only how the pleasure of the soul might come about, but neither consider what pleasure is better or worse nor care about anything else than giving gratification, better or worse. I think there are these practices, Callicles, and I say that this kind of thing is flattery, for the body, for the soul, and for anything else whose pleasure anyone cultivates, when he fails to consider the better and the worse. Do you deposit the same opinion about this as ours, or do you speak against it?

C. No I don't. I'm going along with you, to let the discussion progress for you, and to gratify Gorgias here.

S. Is this so for one soul, but not for two or for many?

C. No. It's so for two and for many as well.

S. And isn't it also possible to gratify souls all in a crowd at the same time, not considering the best at all?

C. Yes, I think so.

S. Then can you tell me which are the practices that produce this? Or rather, if you like, I'll ask the questions; agree with what you think is right, and deny what you think is wrong. And first of all, let's consider flute-playing. Don't you think it is the kind of practice we mentioned, Callicles, pursuing only our pleasure, and concerned with nothing else?

C. I think so.

S. And aren't all of this kind similar—such as lyre-playing before large audiences?

C. Yes.

S. And what about the teaching of choruses, and the making of dithyrambs? Isn't it apparently something of the same kind? Or do you think Cinesias the son of Meles cares at all about saying the kind of thing to make the audience better? Or does he care about what will gratify the mob of spectators?

C. That's clear, Socrates, about Cinesias anyway.

S. And what about his father Meles? Did you think he was looking to what is best when he sang on the lyre? Or didn't he even consider what was pleasantest? For he used to torture the spectators when he sang. But consider— don't you think that all singing to the lyre and composition of dithyrambs has been discovered for the sake of pleasure?

C. I do.

S. Then what about this august and wonderful pursuit, the composition of tragedy, and its concern? Is its undertaking and concern, in your opinion, just to gratify the spectators? Or does it also struggle, if anything is pleasant and gratifying to them, but base, to avoid saying it, and if something is without pleasure but beneficial, to say and sing this, whether they enjoy it or not? Which way do you think the composition of tragedies is equipped?

C. This much is clear, Socrates, that it concentrates on pleasure and on gratifying spectators.

S. And didn't we say just now that this sort of thing is flattery, Callicles?

C. Quite.

S. Well now, if someone took away from all poetic composition the melody, the rhythm, and the metre, doesn't what is left turn out to be speech (*logos*)?

C. It must be.

S. And isn't this speech addressed to a large mob of the people?

C. I agree.

S. Then poetic composition is a kind of public oratory.

C. Apparently.

S. And surely public oratory is rhetoric. Or don't you think the poets practise rhetoric in the theatres?

C. Yes, I think so.

5 S. And so we've found a kind of rhetoric addressed to the people, including children and women and men all together, and slaves and free. And we can't altogether admire it; for we say it's flattering.

502d C. Quite.

S. All right. What about rhetoric addressed to the Athenian people and the other peoples
10 of the cities, the peoples composed of free men, exactly what do we find this is? Do you
e think that rhetors always speak with an eye on what is best, and aim to make the citizens as good as possible by their speeches? Or do
5 they too concentrate on gratifying the citizens, despising the common interest for the sake of their own private interest? Do they
503a approach the people in cities as children, trying only to gratify them, with no concern about whether they will be better or worse from it?

C. That's not just one question you're asking any more. There are some who care about the citizens when they say what they say, and others who are as you claim.

5 S. That's all right. For if there are really two types here, I presume one type is flattery, and shameful public oratory, while the other is fine—trying to make the souls of the citizens as good as possible, and working hard in saying what is best, whether it is pleasant or unpleasant to the audience. But you've never
b yet seen this kind of rhetoric; or if you can mention a rhetor of this type, why haven't you told me as well who he is?

5 C. Well, by Zeus, I can't mention any of the present rhetors to you.

S. Well then, can you mention someone of earlier times who's reputed to have made the Athenians better, after he began his public speaking, when they had previously been worse? For I don't know who this is.

c C. Well, don't you hear it said that Themistocles proved himself a good man, and Cimon and

Miltiades, and Pericles?—he's lately died and you've heard him speak yourself.

S. Yes, Callicles; if real virtue is what you were saying before—filling up appetites, our own
5 or other people's. But if it's not that, but it's what we were forced to agree to in the later discussion—that we should fulfill those appetites which make a man better when they are fulfilled, and not fulfill those which make him
d worse, and that this is some kind of craft—then I can't say that any of these men had that kind of virtue.

C. Well, if you look properly, you'll find one.

S. Then let's see, considering calmly this way,
503d5 whether any of these men proved to be virtuous. Come now, the good man who speaks with a view to the best, surely he won't speak
e at random, but will look to something? He will be like all other craftsmen; each of them selects and applies his efforts with a view to his own work, not at random, but so that what he produces will acquire some form. Look for instance if you like at painters, builders, ship-
5 wrights, all other craftsmen—whichever one you like; see how each of them arranges in a structure whatever he arranges, and compels one thing to be fitting and suitable to
504a another, until he composes the whole thing arranged in a structure and order. All craftsmen, including those we were talking of just now, gymnastic-trainers, and doctors, form the body into order and structure, don't they?
5 Do we agree that this is so, or not?

C. Let's say this is so.

S. Then when a house gets structure and order, it will be worthy, and when it lacks structure, wretched?

C. I agree.

10 S. And surely a boat the same way?

b C. Yes.

S. And don't we say the same about our bodies?

C. Quite.

S. And what about the soul? Will it be worthy if it lacks structure, or if it gains some kind of
5 structure and order?

C. From what's been said before, we must agree on this too.

S. Then what's the name for what comes to be in the body from structure and order?

C. I suppose you're talking about health and strength.

c S. I am. And what's the name for what comes to be in the soul from structure and order? Try to find and say the name for this as for the body.

C. And why don't you say it yourself, Socrates?

5 S. Well, if it pleases you more, I'll say it myself. But you, if you think I speak well, agree, and if you don't, examine me, and don't give in to me. I think that the name for the structures of the body is 'healthy' from which health and the rest of bodily excellence (*aretē*) come to be in the body. Is that so, or isn't it?

504c10 C. It is.

d S. And for the structures and orderings of the soul the name is 'lawful' and 'law', from which people become lawful and orderly; and these are justice and temperance. Do you say so, or not?

C. Let it be so.

5 S. Then won't that rhetor, the craftsman, the good one, look to these things when he applies whatever speeches he makes to souls, and when he applies all his actions to them, and when he gives whatever he gives, and when he takes away whatever he takes away? He'll always have his mind on this; to see that the souls of the citizens acquire justice and get rid of injustice, and that they acquire temperance and get rid of intemperance (*akolasia*) and that they acquire the rest of virtue and get rid of vice. Do you agree or not?

5 C. I agree.

S. Yes, for what's the benefit, Callicles, of giving lots of the most pleasant food or drink or anything else to a sick body in wretched condition, which won't help it one bit more than the opposite method, on the right account, and will help even less? Is that so?

505a C. Let it be so.

S. Yes; for I suppose it's no profit for a man to live with bodily wretchedness; in that condition you must live wretchedly too. Isn't that so?

5 C. Yes.

S. And don't the doctors mostly allow a healthy man to fulfill his appetites, for instance to eat and drink as much as he wants when he's hungry or thirsty? And don't they practically never allow a sick man to fill himself with 10 what he has an appetite for? Don't you also agree with this much?

C. I do.

b S. And isn't it the same way, my excellent man, about the soul? As long as it's corrupt, senseless, intemperate, unjust, and impious, we should restrain it from its appetites, and not allow it to do anything else except what will 5 make it better. Do you say so, or not?

C. I do.

S. For, I take it, that way it's better for the soul itself.

C. Quite.

505b S. And isn't restraining it from what it has an appetite for tempering it?

10 C. Yes.

S. Then being tempered is better for the soul than intemperance, which you just now thought was better.

c C. I don't know what you're saying, Socrates. Ask someone else.

S. This man won't abide being helped and tempered, and himself undergoing the very thing our discussion is about—being tempered.

C. No; I don't care about anything you say; I've 5 answered these questions of yours for Gorgias' sake.

S. Well, what will we do, then? Are we breaking off the discussion in the middle?

C. That's up to you.

10 S. Well, they say it's not right to break stories off in the middle either; we should put a head on d it, so that it won't go around headless. So answer the rest of the questions too, so that our discussion will get its head on.

C. You're so insistent, Socrates. Listen to me, 5 and let this discussion go, or have a dialogue with someone else as well.

S. Then who else is willing? Surely we mustn't leave the discussion incomplete.

C. And couldn't you finish the discussion yourself? Say it all in your own person, or answer your own questions.

ₑ S. Then Epicharmus' words will be true for me; I'll be enough, all alone, for what 'two men were saying before'. It seems that this will be absolutely necessary. But if we do it, I believe we all ought to compete to know what's true

5 and false in the things we're speaking of. For it's a common benefit to all when this becomes clear. Well, I'll go through the dis-

506a cussion myself the way I think it is; and if one of you thinks that what I'm agreeing on with myself isn't what's true, you ought to seize on it, and examine me. For remember I don't have knowledge any more than you have when I say what I say. I search in common

5 with you; and so if my opponent is clearly saying something, I will be the first to concede it. Now I'm saying this in case you think the discussion ought to be completed; but if you don't want that, let's let it go now and leave.

b *Gorgias.* Well, I don't think we ought to leave yet, Socrates. Youshould go through the discussion; and I think the rest agree. For myself, I'd like to hear you go through the rest on your own.

S. Well, Gorgias, for myself I'd be pleased to continue the dialogue with Callicles here,

5 until I've paid him the discourse of Amphion in return for the discourse of Zethus. But since you aren't willing to finish the discussion, Callicles, none the less listen to me, and pull me up if you think I say anything wrongly. And if

c you refute me, I won't be annoyed with you the way you were with me, but I'll keep you inscribed as my greatest benefactor.

C. Say it yourself, my good man, and finish it.

5 S. Then listen to me while I take up the discussion again from the beginning. Are the pleasant and the good the same?

— Not the same, as Callicles and I agreed.

— Then is the pleasant to be done for the sake of the good, or the good for the sake of the pleasant?

— The pleasant for the sake of the good.

d — And the pleasant is that which, if it has come to be present, we take pleasure, and the good that which, if it has come to be present, we are good?

— Quite.

— Now we are good, and so is anything else which is good, when some virtue has come to be present.

— I think it's necessary, Callicles.

5 — But now, the virtue of each thing, a tool, a body, and, further, a soul and a whole animal, doesn't come to be present in the best way just at random, but by some structure and correctness and craft, the one assigned to each of them. Is this so?

— I say so.

ₑ — Then the virtue of each thing is something structured and ordered by a structure?

— I would say so myself.

— Then it is some order—the proper order for each of the things that are—which makes the thing good by coming to be present in it.

— I myself think so.

5 — Then a soul with its own proper order is better than a disordered soul?

— It must be.

506e — But now the soul which has order is orderly?

— Of course it is.

507a — And the orderly soul is temperate?

— It certainly must be.

— Then the temperate soul is good.

— For myself I can say nothing else besides this, my dear Callicles. If you can say anything else, instruct me.

C. Go on, my good man.

5 S. Well, I say that if the temperate soul is good, the soul affected the opposite way to the temperate soul is bad; and this was agreed to be the senseless and intemperate (*akolastos*) soul.

— Quite.

— And now the temperate man would do fitting things towards both gods and men. For surely he wouldn't be acting temperately if he did unfitting things?

b — This must be so.

— Now by doing fitting things towards men he would do just things, and by doing them towards gods, he would do pious things. And someone who does just and pious things must be just and pious.

— That's so.

— And further he must be brave too. For it's not what a temperate man does to avoid or pursue unfitting things; he will avoid or pursue the things and people, pleasures and pains he should, and will resist and endure where he should. And so, Callicles, since the temperate man is just and brave and pious, as we described him, he definitely must be a completely good man; and the good man must do whatever he does well and finely; and the man who does well must be blessed and happy, and the base man who does badly must be wretched—and this would be the man who is the opposite way to the temperate man—the intemperate (*akolastos*) man whom you were praising.

And so I set things down this way, and say that these things are true. And if they are true, then apparently the man who wants to be happy must pursue and practise temperance, and flee intemperance as fast as each of us can run. He must manage, best of all, to have no need of tempering (*kolazesthai*); but if he or any of his own, an individual or a city, needs tempering, justice and tempering must be imposed, if he is to be happy. I believe this is the goal a man should look to in living, on which he should concentrate everything of his own and the city's—to see that justice and temperance are present in everyone who is to be blessed—this is the way he should act. He should not allow his appetites to be intemperate and try to fulfill them—an endless evil—while he lives the life of a brigand.

For no other man would be a friend to such a man; nor would god. For he is incapable of community; and when there is no community with a man, there can be no friendship with him. Now the wise men say, Callicles, that heaven and earth, gods and men are bound by community and friendship and order and temperance and justice; and that is why they call this whole universe the 'world-order', not 'disorder' or 'intemperance', my friend. But I think you don't heed them, though you're wise yourself. You haven't noticed that geometrical equality has great power among gods and men; you think you should practise taking more, because you are heedless of geometry.

Well then; either we must refute this argument and show that it is not by possession of justice and temperance that the happy are happy, and that the wretched are not wretched by the possession of vice; or else if this argument is true, we must examine what are the results that follow. All those previous things follow, Callicles—you asked me if I was serious when I said them, when I said that a man should denounce himself and his son and his companion if he does any unjust action, and should use rhetoric for this. And those things you thought Polus conceded to me out of shame were after all true, that doing injustice is as much worse than suffering it as it is more shameful; and after all someone who is going to be a rhetor in the right way should be a just man, one who knows about just things—which again Polus said Gorgias had conceded out of shame.

Since that is so, let's consider what you're abusing me for, whether it's well said or not. You say indeed that I'm unable to help myself or any of my friends or relatives, or save them from the most serious dangers, but I'm in the power of whoever wishes, just as the dishonoured are at the mercy of whoever feels like it—whether he wants to push my face in, in your vigorous expression, or to confiscate my money, or to expel me from the city, or finally to kill me—and this condition is the most shameful of all, on your account. Now what my argument is has often enough been said already, but nothing prevents it being said over again. I say, Callicles, that having my face pushed in unjustly is not the most shameful thing—nor is having my body or my purse cut. But to strike and cut me and mine unjustly is more shameful and evil, and likewise robbing, enslaving, house-breaking, and in short, any injustice against me and mine is both worse and more shameful for the man who does the injustice than for me who suffer it.

These things which appeared true to us earlier in the previous arguments (*logos*) are

509a held firm and bound down, so I say—even if it is a bit impolite to say so—by iron and adamantine arguments; so at least it appears so far. And if you, or someone more vigorous than you, doesn't untie them, no one who says anything besides what I say now can be right. For my argument (*logos*) is always the same, that I myself don't know how these

5 things are, but no one I've ever met, just as now, is able to speak otherwise without being ridiculous.

b   Well then, again I lay it down that this is so. Now if it's so, and if injustice is the greatest of evils for the man who does injustice, and an even greater evil than the greatest, if that is possible, is doing injustice and not paying justice—then what lack of power to defend himself would make a man really ridiculous? Won't it be the lack of power to defend himself against the greatest of harms

5 to us? Surely this defence definitely must be the most shameful for us to lack power to provide, for ourselves and for friends and family. And the second most shameful will be the

c lack of defence against the second most serious evil, and the third most shameful against the third most serious evil, and so on in the same way—the greater each evil is, the finer it is to have the power to defend ourselves against it, and the more shameful it is to lack the power. Is that how it is, or some other way, Callicles?

5 C. No other way.

S. Then of these two things, doing injustice and suffering it, we say that doing injustice is the greater evil, and suffering it the lesser. Then how should a man equip himself for self-

d defence, so as to gain both of these benefits, from not doing injustice and from not suffering it? Does he need power or wish? I'm saying this:—Is it by not wishing to suffer injustice that a man will avoid suffering it, or by equipping himself with some power for not suffer-

509d5 ing it?

C. It's clear that this is the way, by having a power.

S. And what about doing injustice? If a man doesn't want to do injustice, will that be

enough, because he won't do injustice? Or for this too should he equip himself with some

e power and craft, since if he doesn't learn and practise them he'll do injustice? Why haven't

5 you answered me that, Callicles, whether you think Polus and I were right or not when we were forced to agree in the previous discussion, when we agreed that no one wants to do injustice, but all those who do it do it involuntarily?

510a C. You can say that that's so, Socrates, so that you can complete the argument.

520e S. But in this activity, how to be as good as possible and how best to govern one's own house or the city, it's counted (*nomizein*) shameful to say you won't give advice unless you're paid.

5 Isn't that right?

C. Yes.

S. For it's clear that this is the explanation; this is the only benefit which makes its beneficiary anxious to confer benefits in return for bene-

10 fits received. That's why you think it's a fine sign of having conferred this kind of benefit, that you benefit in return, and if you haven't, you don't. Is this so?

521a C. It is.

S. Then define for me what kind of care for the city you're urging on me. Do you want me to struggle, as a doctor would, to make the Athenians as good as possible, or to serve them and

5 approach them aiming at their gratification? Tell me the truth, Callicles. Since you began by speaking freely to me, it's only just that you should go on saying what you think. Tell me now as well as before, well and nobly.

C. Well, I'm telling you you should serve them.

b S. Then it's flattery you're urging on me, my most noble friend.

C. Yes, if it pleases you more to call a Mysian a Mysian, Socrates. For if you don't do that. . . .

S. Don't tell me what you've often told me, that

5 anyone who wants to will kill me. Save me the trouble of telling you in reply, 'He'll be base, and I'll be a good man.' And don't tell me he'll take away anything I have, or I'll reply, 'But when he takes it, he'll have no good use for it. He took it from me unjustly, and in the same way when he's taken it, he'll

c use it unjustly, if unjustly then shamefully, and if shamefully then badly.'

C. How confident you seem that none of these things will ever happen to you, Socrates. You think you live out of harm's way, and that you'll never be dragged into court, perhaps by some wretched scoundrel.

S. Then I'm really senseless, Callicles, if I don't think that anything might happen to anyone in this city. But here's something I know full well. If I'm brought to court and face one of these penalties, as you say, my prosecutor will be a base man—for no worthy man would ever prosecute someone who wasn't doing injustice—and it wouldn't be at all extraordinary if I were put to death. Do you want me to say why I expect this?

C. Certainly.

S. I think I am one of a few Athenians—not to say the only one—who undertake the real political craft and practise politics—the only one among people now. I don't aim at gratification with each of the speeches I make, but aim at the best, not the pleasantest, and I'm not willing to do 'these subtle things' that you advise me. That's why I won't know what to say in court. But the same account applies to me that I was telling to Polus. For I will be judged as a doctor might be judged by a jury of children with a cook as prosecutor. For consider how such a man would defend himself if he found himself before such a jury, if someone accused him and said 'Children, this man has inflicted many evils on you. He ruins the youngest of you by cutting and burning. He leaves you confused, slimming and choking you, giving you those terribly bitter potions, and compelling you to go hungry and thirsty. He's not like me. I used to feast you on many pleasant things of all kinds.' What do you think a doctor caught in this evil would be able to say? Or suppose he told the truth, and said, 'It was healthy, children, all that I was

doing.' What sorts of protests would he hear from such jurymen? Wouldn't they be loud?

C. Perhaps. We ought to suppose so.

S. Don't you think he'd be caught at a complete loss about what he ought to say?

C. Quite.

S. And yet I know that the same thing would happen to me too if I came before a jury-court. For I won't be able to tell them the pleasures I have provided—which they think are benefits and advantages, while I envy neither the providers nor those provided with them. And suppose someone says that I ruin the younger men by confusing them, or that I speak evil of the older people by harsh remarks in private or in public. Then I'll be able to say neither what's true—'All this that I say and do is just, gentlemen of the jury' (as you rhetors say)— nor anything else. And so perhaps whatever it turns out to be will happen to me.

C. Then do you think, Socrates, that it's a fine condition for a man in the city when he's like this, and without power to defend himself?

S. Yes—if he had this one thing which you have often agreed on, Callicles; if he had secured his own defence, by saying and doing nothing unjust towards men or gods. For we have often agreed that this is the supreme form of self-defence. And so if someone refuted me and showed that I have no power to defend myself or anyone else with this defence, then I would be ashamed if I were refuted before many people or before few, or with the two of us by ourselves; and if I were put to death because I lacked this power, I would be annoyed. But if I died because I lacked flattering rhetoric, I know for sure that you would see me bearing death easily. For being put to death itself—no one fears that unless he's altogether unreasoning and unmanly; it is doing injustice that he fears. For if the soul is full of many injustices when it arrives in Hades, that is the ultimate of all evils.

STUDY QUESTIONS: PLATO, GORGIAS

1. How does Socrates first define 'rhetoric'? How does the definition change during the course of the dialogue, and why?

2. Socrates distinguishes learning and conviction. What is the difference? Why is this distinction important?

3. Why is rhetoric, defined as the knack of gratifying people, something shameful, according to Socrates?

4. Why does Socrates call it a knack as opposed to a craft?

5. Socrates asks, 'Which do you think is worse, Polus—doing injustice or suffering it?' Why does Socrates ask this question? How does Socrates' own answer to this question relate to his views on rhetoric?

6. In his speech, how does Callicles define justice by nature?

7. How does Callicles characterize the person who lives rightly?

8. What is the point of Socrates' leaky jar analogy?

9. Why does Socrates try to show that some pleasures are better than others? How does this pertain to the nature of rhetoric?

10. Why does Socrates ask Callicles whether the good and the pleasant are the same? How does Callicles answer, and how does Socrates use this answer to establish the nature of virtue?

11. How does Socrates try to establish the conclusion that it is worse to do an injustice than to suffer one toward the end of the dialogue?

12. How does Plato's view in the *Gorgias* of committing an injustice compare to what he says about it in the *Crito*?

13. What are the overall aims of this dialogue?

MENO

The *Meno* is probably the first dialogue in which Plato expresses more of his own views rather than those of Socrates. It is a transitional dialogue, a bridge from Plato's early Socratic works to his own mature reflections. It was written probably around 386 B.C., when Plato was in his early forties. It shows Plato's deep interest in mathematics, something not present in the earlier Socratic dialogues and that reveals a Pythagorean influence.

In the first part of the dialogue (up to 81a), Plato outlines Socrates' philosophical method in order to evaluate it critically. For example, Meno claims that Socratic argument actually numbs perplexity rather than stimulating it (79e). Meno also raises the famous paradox of inquiry, namely, that a person cannot discover what he knows or what he does not know. If one does not know what an F is, then one cannot know anything about F's, and thus, one cannot know what one seeks to discover (80d–e).

The main concern of the second half of the *Meno* is whether knowledge is innate or acquired. Plato wants to prove that the knowledge of certain basic principles is innate and that what we call learning is really a recollection of what the soul knew before birth. To demonstrate this, he shows how an ignorant slave boy can display significant knowledge of geometry by answering suitable questions. Plato claims that this result is evidence that the slave is recollecting propositions he already knew, rather than learning them for the first time.

The dialogue introduces the important distinction between knowledge and true belief. True belief becomes knowledge by being 'tied down,' which is a process of 'working out the reason,' which requires recollection (98a). In other words, knowledge requires knowing why a true belief is true, and this involves knowing the basic principles that lie innate in the soul and that can be recollected.

CHARACTERS OF THE DIALOGUE

Meno	A Slave of Meno
Socrates	Anytus

70 **MENO.** Can you tell me, Socrates, whether virtue is acquired by teaching or by practice; or if neither by teaching nor practice, then whether it comes to man by nature, or in what other way?

SOCRATES. O Meno, there was a time when the Thessalians were famous among the other Hellenes only for their riches and their riding; but now, if I am not mistaken, they are equally famous for their wisdom, especially at Larissa, which is the native city of your friend Aristippus. And this is Gorgias' doing; for when he came there, the flower of the Aleuadae, among them your admirer Aristippus, and the other chiefs of the Thessalians, fell in love with his wisdom. And he has taught you the habit of answering questions in a grand and bold style, which becomes those who know, and is the style in which he himself answers all comers; and any Hellene who likes may ask him anything. How different is our lot! my dear Meno. Here at Athens, there is a dearth of the commodity, and all wisdom seems to

71 have emigrated from us to you. I am certain that if you were to ask any Athenian whether virtue was natural or acquired, he would laugh in your face and say: "Stranger, you have far too good an opinion of me if you think that I can answer your question. For I literally do not know what virtue is, and much less whether it is acquired by teaching or not." And I myself, Meno, living as I do in this region of poverty, am as poor as the rest of the world, and I confess with shame that I know literally nothing about virtue; and when I do not know the *"quid"* of anything, how can I know the *"quale"*? How, if I knew nothing at all of Meno, could I tell if he was fair or the opposite of fair; rich and noble, or the reverse of rich and noble? Do you think that I could?

MEN. No, indeed. But are you in earnest, Socrates, in saying that you do not know what virtue is? And am I to carry back this report of you to Thessaly?

SOC. Not only that, my dear boy, but you may say further that I have never known of any one else who did, in my judgment.

MEN. Then you have never met Gorgias when he was at Athens?

SOC. Yes I have.

MEN. And did you not think that he knew?

SOC. I have not a good memory, Meno, and therefore I cannot now tell what I thought of him at the time. And I dare say that he did know, and that you know what he said: please, therefore, do remind me of what he said; or, if you would rather, tell me your own view; for I suspect that you and he think much alike.

MEN. Very true.

SOC. Then as he is not here, never mind him, and do you tell me: By the gods, Meno, be generous and tell me what you say that virtue is; for I shall be truly delighted to find that I have been mistaken, and that you and Gorgias do really have this knowledge, although I have been just saying that I have never found anybody who had.

MEN. There will be no difficulty, Socrates, in answering your question. Let us take first the virtue of a man—he should know how to administer the state, and in the administration of it to benefit his friends and harm his enemies; and he must also be careful not to suffer harm himself. A woman's virtue, if you wish to know about that, may also be easily described: her duty is to order her house and keep what is indoors, and obey her husband. Every age, every condition of life, young or old, male or female, bond or free, has a differ-

72 ent virtue: there are virtues numberless, and no lack of definitions of them; for virtue is relative to the actions and ages of each of us in all that we do. And the same may be said of vice, Socrates.

Soc. How fortunate I am, Meno! When I ask you for one virtue, you present me with a swarm of them, which are in your keeping. Suppose that I carry on the figure of the swarm, and ask of you, What is the nature of the bee? and you answer that there are many kinds of bees, and I reply: But do bees differ as bees because there are many and different kinds of them; or are they not rather to be distinguished by some other quality, as, for example, beauty, size, or shape? How would you answer me?

Men. I should answer that bees do not differ from one another, as bees.

Soc. And if I went on to say: That is what I desire to know, Meno; tell me what is the quality in which they do not differ, but are all alike—would you be able to answer?

Men. I should.

Soc. And so of the virtues, however many and different they may be, they have all a common nature which makes them virtues; and on this he who would answer the question, "What is virtue?" would do well to have his eye fixed; do you understand?

Men. I am beginning to understand; but I do not as yet take hold of the question as I could wish.

Soc. When you say, Meno, that there is one virtue of a man, another of a woman, another of a child, and so on, does this apply only to virtue, or would you say the same of health, and size, and strength? Or is the nature of health always the same, whether in man or woman?

Men. I should say that health is the same, both in man and woman.

Soc. And is not this true of size and strength? If a woman is strong, she will be strong by reason of the same form and of the same strength subsisting in her which there is in the man—I mean to say that strength, as strength, whether of man or woman, is the same. Is there any difference?

Men. I think not.

73 Soc. And will not virtue, as virtue, be the same, whether in a child or in a grown-up person, in a woman or in a man?

Men. I cannot help feeling, Socrates, that this case is different from the others.

Soc. But why? Were you not saying that the virtue of a man was to order a state, and the virtue of a woman was to order a house?

Men. I did say so.

Soc. And can either house or state or anything be well ordered without temperance and without justice?

Men. Certainly not.

Soc. Then they who order a state or a house temperately or justly order them with temperance and justice?

Men. Certainly.

Soc. Then both men and women, if they are to be good men and women, must have the same virtues of temperance and justice?

Men. True.

Soc. And can either a young man or an elder one be good if they are intemperate and unjust?

Men. They cannot.

Soc. They must be temperate and just?

Men. Yes.

Soc. Then all men are good in the same way, and by participation in the same virtues?

Men. Such is the inference.

Soc. And they surely would not have been good in the same way unless their virtue had been the same?

Men. They would not.

Soc. Then now that the sameness of all virtue has been proven, try and remember what you and Gorgias say that virtue is.

Men. Will you have one definition of them all?

Soc. That is what I am seeking.

Men. If you want to have one definition of them all, I know not what to say but that virtue is the power of governing mankind.

Soc. And does this definition of virtue include all virtue? Is virtue the same in a child and in a slave, Meno? Can the child govern his father, or the slave his master; and would he who governed be any longer a slave?

Men. I think not, Socrates.

Soc. No, indeed; there would be small reason in that. Yet once more, fair friend; according to you, virtue is "the power of governing"; but do you not add "justly and not unjustly"?

Men. Yes, Socrates; I agree there; for justice is virtue.

Soc. Would you say "virtue," Meno, or "a virtue"?

Men. What do you mean?

Soc. I mean as I might say about anything; that a round, for example, is "a figure" and not simply "figure," and I should adopt this mode of speaking, because there are other figures.

Men. Quite right; and that is just what I am saying about virtue—that there are other virtues as well as justice.

74 Soc. What are they? Tell me the names of them, as I would tell you the names of the other figures if you asked me.

Men. Courage and temperance and wisdom and magnanimity are virtues; and there are many others.

Soc. Yes, Meno; and again we are in the same case: in searching after one virtue we have found many, though not in the same way as before; but we have been unable to find the common virtue which runs through them all.

Men. Why, Socrates, even now I am not able to follow you in the attempt to get at one common notion of virtue as of other things.

Soc. No wonder; but I will try to get nearer if I can, for you know that all things have a common notion. Suppose now that someone asked you the question which I asked before: Meno, he would say, what is figure? And if you answered "roundness," he would reply to you, in my way of speaking, by asking whether you would say that roundness is "figure" or "a figure"; and you would answer "a figure."

Men. Certainly.

Soc. And for this reason—that there are other figures?

Men. Yes.

Soc. And if he proceeded to ask, What other figures are there? you would have told him.

Men. I should.

Soc. And if he similarly asked what color is, and you answered whiteness, and the questioner rejoined, Would you say that whiteness is color or a color? you would reply, A color, because there are other colors as well.

Men. I should.

Soc. And if he had said, Tell me what they are?—you would have told him of other colors which are colors just as much as whiteness.

Men. Yes.

Soc. And suppose that he were to pursue the matter in my way, he would say: Ever and anon we are landed in particulars, but this is not what I want; tell me then, since you call them by a common name and say that they are all figures, even when opposed to one another, what is that common nature which you designate as figure—which contains straight as well as round, and is no more one than the other—that would be your mode of speaking?

Men. Yes.

Soc. And in speaking thus, you do not mean to say that the round is round any more than straight, or the straight any more straight than round?

Men. Certainly not.

Soc. You only assert that the round figure is not more a figure than the straight, or the straight than the round?

Men. Very true.

75 Soc. To what then do we give the name of figure? Try and answer. Suppose that when a person asked you this question either about figure or color, you were to reply, Man, I do not understand what you want, or know what you are saying; he would look rather astonished and say: Do you not understand that I am looking for the *simile in multis*? And then he might put the question in another form: Meno, he might say, what is that *simile in multis* which you call "figure," and which includes not only round and straight figures, but all? Could you not answer that question, Meno? I wish that you would try; the attempt will be good practice with a view to the answer about virtue.

Men. I would rather that you answer, Socrates.

Soc. Shall I indulge you?

Men. By all means.

Soc. And then you will tell me about virtue?

Men. I will.

Soc. Then I must do my best, for there is a prize to be won.

Men. Certainly.

Soc. Well, I will try and explain to you what figure is. What do you say to this answer?—Figure is the only thing which always follows color. Will you be satisfied with it, as I am sure that I should be if you would let me have a similar definition of virtue?

MEN. But, Socrates, it is such a simple answer.

SOC. Why simple?

MEN. Because, according to you, figure is that which always follows color.

(SOC. Granted.)

MEN. But if a person were to say that he does not know what color is, any more than what figure is—what sort of answer would you have given him?

SOC. I should have told him the truth. And if he were a philosopher of the eristic and antagonistic sort, I should say to him: You have my answer, and if I am wrong, your business is to take up the argument and refute me. But if we were friends, and were talking as you and I are now, I should reply in a milder strain and more in the dialectician's vein; that is to say, I should not only speak the truth, but I should make use of premises which the person interrogated would be willing to admit. And this is the way in which I shall endeavor to approach you. You will acknowledge, will you not, that there is such a thing as an end, or termination, or extremity?—all which words I use in the same sense, although I am aware that Prodicus might draw distinctions about them; but still you, I am sure, would speak of a thing as ended or terminated—that is all which I am saying—not anything very difficult.

MEN. Yes, I should; and I believe that I understand your meaning.

76 SOC. And you would speak of a surface and also of a solid, as for example in geometry.

MEN. Yes.

SOC. Well then, you are now in a condition to understand my definition of figure. I define figure to be that in which the solid ends; or, more concisely, the limit of solid.

MEN. And now, Socrates, what is color?

SOC. You are outrageous, Meno, in thus plaguing a poor old man to give you an answer, when you will not take the trouble of remembering what is Gorgias' definition of virtue.

MEN. When you have told me what I ask, I will tell you, Socrates.

SOC. A man who was blindfolded has only to hear you talking, and he would know that you are a fair creature and have still many lovers.

MEN. Why do you think so?

SOC. Why, because you always speak in imperatives; like all beauties when they are in their prime, you are tyrannical; and also, as I suspect, you have found out that I have a weakness for the fair, and therefore to humor you I must answer.

MEN. Please do.

SOC. Would you like me to answer you after the manner of Gorgias, which is familiar to you?

MEN. I should like nothing better.

SOC. Do not he and you and Empedocles say that there are certain effluences of existence?

MEN. Certainly.

SOC. And passages into which and through which the effluences pass?

MEN. Exactly.

SOC. And some of the effluences fit into the passages, and some of them are too small or too large?

MEN. True.

SOC. And there is such a thing as sight?

MEN. Yes.

SOC. And now, as Pindar says, "read my meaning": color is an effluence of form, commensurate with sight, and palpable to sense.

MEN. That, Socrates, appears to me to be an admirable answer.

SOC. Why, yes, because it happens to be one which you have been in the habit of hearing: and your wit will have discovered, I suspect, that you may explain in the same way the nature of sound and smell, and of many other similar phenomena.

MEN. Quite true.

SOC. The answer, Meno, was in the orthodox solemn vein, and therefore was more acceptable to you than the other answer about figure.

MEN. Yes.

SOC. And yet, O son of Alexidemus, I cannot help thinking that the other was the better; and I am sure that you would be of the same opinion if you would only stay and be initiated, and were not compelled, as you said yesterday, to go away before the mysteries.

77 MEN. But I will stay, Socrates, if you will give me many such answers.

SOC. Well then, for my own sake as well as for yours, I will do my very best; but I am afraid that I shall not be able to give you very many as good; and now, in your turn, you are to fulfill your promise, and tell me what virtue is in the universal; and do not make a singular into a plural, as the facetious say of those who break a thing, but deliver virtue to me whole and sound, and not broken into a number of pieces; I have given you the pattern.

MEN. Well then, Socrates, virtue, as I take it, is when he, who desires the honorable, is able to provide it for himself; so the poet says, and I say, too—

Virtue is the desire of things honorable and the power of attaining them.

SOC. And does he who desires the honorable also desire the good?

MEN. Certainly.

SOC. Then are there some who desire the evil and others who desire the good? Do not all men, my dear sir, desire good?

MEN. I think not.

SOC. There are some who desire evil?

MEN. Yes.

SOC. Do you mean that they think the evils which they desire to be good; or do they know that they are evil and yet desire them?

MEN. Both, I think.

SOC. And do you really imagine, Meno, that a man knows evils to be evils and desires them not withstanding?

MEN. Certainly I do.

SOC. And desire is of possession?

MEN. Yes, of possession.

SOC. And does he think that the evils will do good to him who possesses them, or does he know that they will do him harm?

MEN. There are some who think that the evils will do them good, and others who know that they will do them harm.

SOC. And, in your opinion, do those who think that they will do them good know that they are evils?

MEN. Certainly not.

SOC. Is it not obvious that those who are ignorant of their nature do not desire them; but they desire what they suppose to be goods although they are really evils; and if they are mistaken and suppose the evils to be goods, they really desire goods?

MEN. Yes, in that case.

SOC. Well, and do those who, as you say, desire evils, and think that evils are hurtful to the possessor of them, know that they will be hurt by them?

MEN. They must know it.

SOC. And must they not suppose that those who are hurt are miserable in proportion to the hurt which is inflicted upon them?

MEN. How can it be otherwise?

78 SOC. But are not the miserable ill fated?

MEN. Yes, indeed.

SOC. And does anyone desire to be miserable and ill fated?

MEN. I should say not, Socrates.

SOC. But if there is no one who desires to be miserable, there is no one, Meno, who desires evil; for what is misery but the desire and possession of evil?

MEN. That appears to be the truth, Socrates, and I admit that nobody desires evil.

SOC. And yet, were you not saying just now that virtue is the desire and power of attaining good?

MEN. Yes, I did say so.

SOC. But if this be affirmed, then the desire of good is common to all, and one man is no better than another in that respect?

MEN. True.

SOC. And if one man is not better than another in desiring good, he must be better in the power of attaining it?

MEN. Exactly.

SOC. Then, according to your definition, virtue would appear to be the power of attaining good?

MEN. I entirely approve, Socrates, of the manner in which you now view this matter.

SOC. Then let us see whether what you say is true from another point of view; for very likely you may be right—you affirm virtue to be the power of attaining goods?

MEN. Yes.

SOC. And the goods which you mean are such as health and wealth and the possession of gold and silver, and having office and honor in the state—those are what you would call goods?

MEN. Yes, I should include all those.

SOC. Then, according to Meno, who is the hereditary friend of the great king, virtue is the power of getting silver and gold; and would you add that they must be gained piously, justly, or do you deem this to be of no consequence? And is any mode of acquisition, even if unjust and dishonest, equally to be deemed virtue?

MEN. Not virtue, Socrates, but vice.

SOC. Then justice or temperance or holiness, or some other part of virtue, as would appear, must accompany the acquisition, and without them the mere acquisition of good will not be virtue.

MEN. Why, how can there be virtue without these?

SOC. And the non-acquisition of gold and silver in a dishonest manner for oneself or another; or, in other words, the want of them may be equally virtue?

MEN. True.

79 SOC. Then the acquisition of such goods is no more virtue than the non-acquisition and want of them, but whatever is accompanied by justice or honesty is virtue, and whatever is devoid of justice is vice.

MEN. It cannot be otherwise, in my judgment.

SOC. And were we not saying just now that justice, temperance, and the like, were each of them a part of virtue?

MEN. Yes.

SOC. And so, Meno, this is the way in which you mock me.

MEN. Why do you say that, Socrates?

SOC. Why, because I asked you to deliver virtue into my hands whole and unbroken, and I gave you a pattern according to which you were to frame your answer; and you have forgotten already and tell me that virtue is the power of attaining good justly, or with justice; and justice you acknowledge to be a part of virtue.

MEN. Yes.

SOC. Then it follows from your own admissions that virtue is doing what you do with a part of virtue; for justice and the like are said by you to be parts of virtue.

MEN. What of that?

SOC. What of that! Why, did not I ask you to tell me the nature of virtue as a whole? And you are very far from telling me this, but declare every action to be virtue which is done with a part of virtue, as though you had told me and I must already know the whole of virtue, and this, too, when frittered away into little pieces. And, therefore, my dear Meno, I fear that I must begin again and repeat the same question: What is virtue? for otherwise I can only say that every action done with a part of virtue is virtue; what else is the meaning of saying that every action done with justice is virtue? Ought I not to ask the question over again; for can anyone who does not know virtue know a part of virtue?

MEN. No; I do not say that he can.

SOC. Do you remember how, in the example of figure, we rejected any answer given in terms which were as yet unexplained or unadmitted?

MEN. Yes, Socrates; and we were quite right in doing so.

SOC. But then, my friend, do not suppose that we can explain to anyone the nature of virtue as a whole through some unexplained portion of virtue, or anything at all in that fashion; we should only have to ask over again the old question, What is virtue? Am I not right?

MEN. I believe that you are.

SOC. Then begin again, and answer me. What, according to you and your friend Gorgias, is the definition of virtue?

80 MEN. O Socrates, I used to be told, before I knew you, that you were always doubting yourself and making others doubt; and now you are casting your spells over me, and I am simply getting bewitched and enchanted, and am at my wits' end. And if I may venture to make a jest upon you, you seem to me both in your appearance and in your power over others to be very like the flat torpedo fish, who torpifies those who come near him and touch him, as you have now torpified me, I think.

For my soul and my tongue are really torpid, and I do not know how to answer you; and though I have been delivered of an infinite variety of speeches about virtue before now, and to many persons—and very good ones they were, as I thought—at this moment I cannot even say what virtue is. And I think that you are very wise in not voyaging and going away from home, for if you did in other places as you do in Athens, you would be cast into prison as a magician.

Soc. You are a rogue, Meno, and had all but caught me.

Men. What do you mean, Socrates?

Soc. I can tell why you made a simile about me.

Men. Why?

Soc. In order that I might make another simile about you. For I know that all pretty young gentlemen like to have pretty similes made about them—as well they may—but I shall not return the compliment. As to my being a torpedo, if the torpedo is torpid as well as the cause of torpidity in others, then indeed I am a torpedo, but not otherwise; for I perplex others, not because I am clear, but because I am utterly perplexed myself. And now I know not what virtue is, and you seem to be in the same case, although you did once perhaps know, before you touched me. However, I have no objection to join with you in the inquiry.

Men. And how will you inquire, Socrates, into that which you do not know? What will you put forth as the subject of inquiry? And if you find what you want, how will you ever know that this is the thing which you did not know?

Soc. I know, Meno, what you mean; but just see what a tiresome dispute you are introducing. You argue that a man cannot inquire either about that which he knows, or about that which he does not know; for if he knows, he has no need to inquire; and if not, he cannot; for he does not know the very subject about which he is to inquire.

Men. Well, Socrates, and is not the argument sound?

81 Soc. I think not.

Men. Why not?

Soc. I will tell you why: I have heard from certain wise men and women who spoke of things divine that—

Men. What did they say?

Soc. They spoke of a glorious truth, as I conceive.

Men. What was it and who were they?

Soc. Some of them were priests and priestesses who had studied how they might be able to give a reason of their profession; there have been poets also who spoke of these things by inspiration, like Pindar and many others who were inspired. And they say—mark now and see whether their words are true—they say that the soul of man is immortal, and at one time has an end, which is termed dying, and at another time is born again, but is never destroyed. And the moral is that a man ought to live always in perfect holiness. "*For in the ninth year Persephone sends the souls of those from whom she has received the penalty of ancient crime back again from beneath into the light of the sun above, and these are they who become noble kings and mighty men and great in wisdom and are called saintly heroes in afterages.*" The soul, then, as being immortal, and having been born again many times, and having seen all things that exist, whether in this world or in the world below, has knowledge of them all; and it is no wonder that she should be able to call to remembrance all that she ever knew about virtue and about everything; for as all nature is akin, and the soul has learned all things, there is no difficulty in her eliciting, or as men say "learning," out of a single recollection, all the rest, if a man is strenuous and does not faint; for all inquiry and all learning is but recollection. And therefore we ought not to listen to this sophistical argument about the impossibility of inquiry; for it will make us idle, and is sweet only to the sluggard; but the other saying will make us active and inquisitive. In that confiding, I will gladly inquire with you into the nature of virtue.

Men. Yes, Socrates; but what do you mean by saying that we do not learn, and that what we call learning is only a process of recollection? Can you teach me how this is?

82 Soc. I told you, Meno, just now that you were a rogue, and now you ask whether I can teach you, when I am saying that there is no teaching, but only recollection; and thus you imagine that you will involve me in a contradiction.

Men. Indeed, Socrates, I protest that I had no such intention. I only asked the question from habit; but if you can prove to me that what you say is true, I wish that you would.

Soc. It will be no easy matter, but I will try to please you to the utmost of my power. Suppose that you call one of your numerous attendants, that I may demonstrate on him.

Men. Certainly. Come hither, boy.

Soc. He is Greek, and speaks Greek, does he not?

Men. Yes, indeed; he was born in the house.

Soc. Attend now to the questions which I ask him, and observe whether he learns of me or only remembers.

Men. I will.

Soc. Tell me, boy, do you know that a figure like this is a square?

Boy. I do.

Soc. And you know that a square figure has these four lines equal?

Boy. Certainly.

Soc. And these lines which I have drawn through the middle of the square are also equal?

Boy. Yes.

Soc. A square may be of any size?

Boy. Certainly.

Soc. And if one side of the figure be of two feet, and the other side be of two feet, how much will the whole be? Let me explain: if in one direction the space was of two feet, and in the other direction of one foot, the whole would be of two feet taken once?

Boy. Yes.

Soc. But since this side is also of two feet, there are twice two feet?

Boy. There are.

Soc. Then the square is of twice two feet?

Boy. Yes.

Soc. And how many are twice two feet? Count and tell me.

Boy. Four, Socrates.

Soc. And might there not be another square twice as large as this, and having like this the lines equal?

Boy. Yes.

Soc. And of how many feet will that be?

Boy. Of eight feet.

Soc. And now try and tell the length of the line which forms the side of that double square: this is two feet—what will that be?

Boy. Clearly, Socrates, it will be double.

Soc. Do you observe, Meno, that I am not teaching the boy anything, but only asking him questions; and now he fancies that he knows how long a line is necessary in order to produce a figure of eight square feet; does he not?

Men. Yes.

Soc. And does he really know?

Men. Certainly not.

Soc. He only guesses that because the square is double, the line is double.

Men. True.

83 Soc. Observe him while he recalls the steps in regular order. (*To the Boy.*) Tell me, boy, do you assert that a double space comes from a double line? Remember that I am not speaking of an oblong, but of a figure equal every way, and twice the size of this—that is to say of eight feet; and I want to know whether you still say that a double square comes from a double line?

Boy. Yes.

Soc. But does not this line become doubled if we add another such line here?

Boy. Certainly.

Soc. And four such lines will make a space containing eight feet?

Boy. Yes.

Soc. Let us describe such a figure: Would you not say that this is the figure of eight feet?

Boy. Yes.

Soc. And are there not these four divisions in the figure, each of which is equal to the figure of four feet?

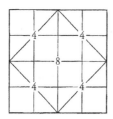

BOY. True.

SOC. And is not that four times four?

BOY. Certainly.

SOC. And four times is not double?

BOY. No, indeed.

SOC. But how much?

BOY. Four times as much.

SOC. Therefore, the double line, boy, has given a space, not twice, but four times as much.

BOY. True.

SOC. Four times four are sixteen—are they not?

BOY. Yes.

SOC. What line would give you a space of eight feet, as this gives one of sixteen feet—do you see?

BOY. Yes.

SOC. And the space of four feet is made from this half line?

BOY. Yes.

SOC. Good; and is not a space of eight feet twice the size of this, and half the size of the other?

BOY. Certainly.

SOC. Such a space, then, will be made out of a line greater than this one, and less than that one?

BOY. Yes, I think so.

SOC. Very good; I like to hear you say what you think. And now tell me, is not this a line of two feet and that of four?

BOY. Yes.

SOC. Then the line which forms the side of eight feet ought to be more than this line of two feet, and less than the other of four feet?

BOY. It ought.

SOC. Try and see if you can tell me how much it will be.

BOY. Three feet.

SOC. Then if we add a half to this line of two, that will be the line of three. Here are two and there is one; and on the other side, here

are two also and there is one: and that makes the figure of which you speak?

BOY. Yes.

SOC. But if there are three feet this way and three feet that way, the whole space will be three times three feet?

BOY. That is evident.

SOC. And how much are three times three feet?

BOY. Nine.

SOC. and how much is the double of four?

BOY. Eight.

SOC. Then the figure of eight is not made out of a line of three?

BOY. No.

84 SOC. But from what line?—tell me exactly; and if you would rather not reckon, try and show me the line.

BOY. Indeed, Socrates, I do not know.

SOC. Do you see, Meno, what advances he has made in his power of recollection? He did not know at first, and he does not know now, what is the side of a figure of eight feet; but then he thought that he knew, and answered confidently as if he knew, and had no difficulty; now he has a difficulty, and neither knows nor fancies that he knows.

MEN. True.

SOC. Is he not better off in knowing his ignorance?

MEN. I think that he is.

SOC. If we have made him doubt, and given him the "torpedo's shock," have we done him any harm?

MEN. I think not.

SOC. We have certainly, as would seem, assisted him in some degree to the discovery of the truth; and now he will wish to remedy his ignorance, but then he would have been ready to tell all the world again and again that the double space should have a double side.

MEN. True.

SOC. But do you suppose that he would ever have inquired into or learned what he fancied that he knew, though he was really ignorant of it, until he had fallen into perplexity under the idea that he did not know, and had desired to know?

MEN. I think not, Socrates.

Soc. Then he was the better for the torpedo's touch?

Men. I think so.

Soc. Mark now the further development. I shall only ask him, and not teach him, and he shall share the inquiry with me; and do you watch and see if you find me telling or explaining anything to him, instead of eliciting his opinion. Tell me, boy, is not this a square of four feet which I have drawn?

Boy. Yes.

Soc. And now I add another square equal to the former one?

Boy. Yes.

Soc. And a third, which is equal to either of them?

Boy. Yes.

Soc. Suppose that we fill up the vacant corner?

Boy. Very good.

Soc. Here, then, there are four equal spaces?

Boy. Yes.

Soc. And how many times larger is this space than this other?

Boy. Four times.

Soc. But it ought to have been twice only, as you will remember.

Boy. True.

85 Soc. And does not this line, reaching from corner to corner, bisect each of these spaces?

Boy. Yes.

Soc. And are there not here four equal lines which contain this space?

Boy. There are.

Soc. Look and see how much this space is.

Boy. I do not understand.

Soc. Has not each interior line cut off half of the four spaces?

Boy. Yes.

Soc. And how many spaces are there in this section?

Boy. Four.

Soc. And how many in this?

Boy. Two.

Soc. And four is how many times two?

Boy. Twice.

Soc. And this space is of how many feet?

Boy. Of eight feet.

Soc. And from what line do you get this figure?

Boy. From this.

Soc. That is, from the line which extends from corner to corner of the figure of four feet?

Boy. Yes.

Soc. And this is the line which the learned call the diagonal. And if this is the proper name, then you, Meno's slave, are prepared to affirm that the double space is the square of the diagonal?

Boy. Certainly, Socrates.

Soc. What do you say of him, Meno? Were not all these answers given out of his own head?

Men. Yes, they were all his own.

Soc. And yet, as we were just now saying, he did not know?

Men. True.

Soc. But still he had in him those notions of his—had he not?

Men. Yes.

Soc. Then he who does not know may still have true notions of that which he does not know?

Men. He has.

Soc. And at present these notions have just been stirred up in him, as in a dream; but if he were frequently asked the same questions, in different forms, he would know as well as anyone at last?

Men. I dare say.

Soc. Without anyone teaching him he will recover his knowledge for himself, if he is only asked questions?

Men. Yes.

Soc. And this spontaneous recovery of knowledge of him is recollection?

Men. True.

Soc. And this knowledge which he now has must he not either have acquired or always possessed?

Men. Yes.

Soc. But if he always possessed this knowledge he would always have known; or if he has acquired the knowledge he could not have acquired it in this life unless he has been taught geometry; for he may be made to do the same with all geometry and every other branch of knowledge. Now, has any one ever taught him all this? You must know about him if, as you say, he was born and bred in your house.

MEN. And I am certain that no one ever did teach him.

SOC. And yet he has the knowledge?

MEN. The fact, Socrates, is undeniable.

86 SOC. But if he did not acquire the knowledge in this life, then he must have had and learned it at some other time?

MEN. Clearly he must.

SOC. Which must have been the time when he was not a man?

MEN. Yes.

SOC. And if there have been always true thoughts in him, both at the time when he was and was not a man, which only need to be awakened into knowledge by putting questions to him, his soul must have always possessed this knowledge, for he always either was or was not a man?

MEN. Obviously.

SOC. And if the truth of all things always existed in the soul, then the soul is immortal. Wherefore be of good cheer and try to recollect what you do not know, or rather what you do not remember.

MEN. I feel, somehow, that I like what you are saying.

SOC. And I, Meno, like what I am saying. Some things I have said of which I am not altogether confident. But that we shall be better and braver and less helpless if we think that we ought to inquire than we should have been if we indulged in the idle fancy that there was no knowing and no use in seeking to know what we do not know—that is a theme upon which I am ready to fight, in word and deed, to the utmost of my power.

MEN. There again, Socrates, your words seem to me excellent.

SOC. Then, as we are agreed that a man should in-quire about that which he does not know, shall you and I make an effort to inquire together into the nature of virtue?

MEN. By all means, Socrates. And yet I would much rather return to my original question, Whether in seeking to acquire virtue we should regard it as a thing to be taught, or as a gift of nature, or as coming to men in some other way?

SOC. Had I the command of you as well as of myself, Meno, I would not have inquired whether virtue is given by instruction or not, until we had first ascertained "what it is." But as you think only of controlling me who am your slave, and never of controlling yourself—such being your notion of freedom—I must yield to you, for you are irresistible. And therefore I have now to inquire into the qualities of a thing of which I do not as yet know the nature. At any rate, will you condescend a little and allow the question "Whether virtue is given by instruction, or in any other way," to be argued upon hypothesis? As the geometrician, when he is asked whether a certain triangle is capable of being inscribed in a certain 87 circle, will reply: "I cannot tell you as yet, but I will offer a hypothesis which may assist us in forming a conclusion. If the figure be such that when you have produced a given side of it, the given area of the triangle falls short by an area corresponding to the part produced, then one consequence follows, and if this is impossible, then some other; and therefore I wish to assume a hypothesis before I tell you whether this triangle is capable of being inscribed in the circle"—that is a geometrical hypothesis. And we too, as we know not the nature and qualities of virtue, must ask whether virtue is or is not taught, under a hypothesis: as thus, if virtue is of such a class of mental goods, will it be taught or not? Let the first hypothesis be that virtue is or is not knowledge—in that case will it be taught or not, or, as we were just now saying, "remembered"? For there is no use in disputing about the name. But is virtue taught or not, or rather, does not everyone see that knowledge alone is taught?

MEN. I agree.

SOC. Then if virtue is knowledge, virtue will be taught?

MEN. Certainly.

SOC. Then now we have made a quick end of this question: if virtue is of such a nature, it will be taught; and if not, not?

MEN. Certainly.

SOC. The next question is whether virtue is knowledge or of another species?

MEN. Yes, that appears to be the question which comes next in order.

SOC. Do we not say that virtue is a good?—This is a hypothesis which is not set aside.

MEN. Certainly.

SOC. Now, if there be any sort of good which is distinct from knowledge, virtue may be that good; but if knowledge embraces all good, then we shall be right in thinking that virtue is knowledge?

MEN. True.

SOC. And virtue makes us good?

MEN. Yes.

SOC. And if we are good, then we are profitable; for all good things are profitable?

MEN. Yes.

SOC. Then virtue is profitable?

MEN. That is the only inference.

SOC. Then now let us see what are the things which severally profit us. Health and strength, and beauty and wealth—these, and the like of these, we call profitable?

MEN. True.

88 SOC. And yet these things may also sometimes do us harm, would you not think so?

MEN. Yes.

SOC. And what is the guiding principle which makes them profitable or the reverse? Are they not profitable when they are rightly used, and harmful when they are not rightly used?

MEN. Certainly.

SOC. Next, let us consider the goods of the soul: they are temperance, justice, courage, quickness of apprehension, memory, magnanimity, and the like?

MEN. Surely.

SOC. And such of these as are not knowledge, but of another sort, are sometimes profitable and sometimes hurtful; as, for example, courage wanting prudence, which is only a sort of confidence? When a man has no sense he is harmed by courage, but when he has sense he is profited?

MEN. True.

SOC. And the same may be said of temperance and quickness of apprehension; whatever things are learned or done with sense are prof-

itable, but when done without sense they are hurtful?

MEN. Very true.

SOC. And in general, all that the soul attempts or endures, when under the guidance of wisdom, ends in happiness; but when she is under the guidance of folly, in the opposite?

MEN. That appears to be true.

SOC. If then virtue is a quality of the soul, and is admitted to be profitable, it must be wisdom or prudence, since none of the things of the soul are either profitable or hurtful in themselves, but they are all made profitable or hurtful by the addition of wisdom or of folly; and therefore, if virtue is profitable, virtue must be a sort of wisdom or prudence?

MEN. I quite agree.

SOC. And the other goods, such as wealth and the like, of which we were just now saying that they are sometimes good and sometime evil, do not they also become profitable or hurtful, accordingly as the soul guides and uses them rightly or wrongly; just as the things of the soul herself are benefited when under the guidance of wisdom, and harmed by folly?

MEN. True.

SOC. And the wise soul guides them rightly, and the foolish soul wrongly?

MEN. Yes.

89 SOC. And is not this universally true of human nature? All other things hang upon the soul, and the things of the soul herself hang upon wisdom, if they are to be good; and so wisdom is inferred to be that which profits—and virtue, as we say, is profitable?

MEN. Certainly.

SOC. And thus we arrive at the conclusion that virtue is either wholly or partly wisdom?

MEN. I think that what you are saying, Socrates, is very true.

SOC. But if this is true, then the good are not by nature good?

MEN. I think not.

SOC. If they had been, there would assuredly have been discerners of characters among us who would have known our future great men; and on their showing we should have adopted them, and when we had got them, we should have kept them in the citadel out of the way of harm, and set a stamp upon them far rather than upon a piece of gold, in order that no one might tamper with them; and when they grew up they would have been useful to the state?

MEN. Yes, Socrates, that would have been the right way.

SOC. But if the good are not by nature good, are they made good by instruction?

MEN. There appears to be no other alternative, Socrates. On the supposition that virtue is knowledge, there can be no doubt that virtue is taught.

SOC. Yes, indeed; but what if the supposition is erroneous?

MEN. I certainly thought just now that we were right.

SOC. Yes, Meno; but a principle which has any soundness should stand firm not only just now, but always.

MEN. Well; and why are you so slow of heart to believe that knowledge is virtue?

SOC. I will try and tell you why, Meno. I do not retract the assertion that if virtue is knowledge it may be taught; but I fear that I have some reason in doubting whether virtue is knowledge; for consider now and say whether virtue, and not only virtue but anything that is taught, must not have teachers and disciples?

MEN. Surely.

SOC. And conversely, may not the art of which neither teachers nor disciples exist be assumed to be incapable of being taught?

MEN. True; but do you think that there are no teachers of virtue?

SOC. I have certainly often inquired whether there were any, and taken great pains to find them, and have never succeeded; and many have assisted me in the search, and they were the persons whom I thought the most likely to know. Here at the moment when he is wanted we fortunately have sitting by us Anytus, the very person of whom we should make inquiry; 90 to him then let us repair. In the first place, he is the son of a wealthy and wise father, Anthemion, who acquired his wealth, not by accident or gift, like Ismenias the Theban (who has recently made himself as rich as Polycrates), but by his own skill and industry, and who is a well-conditioned, modest man, not insolent, or overbearing, or annoying; moreover, this son of his has received a good education, as the Athenian people certainly appear to think, for they choose him to fill the highest offices. And these are the sort of men from whom you are likely to learn whether there are any teachers of virtue, and who they are. Please, Anytus, to help me and your friend Meno in answering our question, Who are the teachers? Consider the matter thus: If we wanted Meno to be a good physician, to whom should we send him? Should we not send him to the physicians?

ANYTUS. Certainly.

SOC. Or if we wanted him to be a good cobbler, should we not send him to the cobblers?

ANY. Yes.

SOC. And so forth?

ANY. Yes.

SOC. Let me trouble you with one more question. When we say that we should be right in sending him to the physicians if we wanted him to be a physician, do we mean that we should be right in sending him to those who profess the art rather than to those who do not, and to those who demand payment for teaching the art and profess to teach it to anyone who will come and learn? And if these were our reasons, should we not be right in sending him?

ANY. Yes.

SOC. And might not the same be said of flute-playing and of the other arts? Would a man who wanted to make another a flute-player refuse to send him to those who profess to teach the art for money, and be plaguing other persons to give him instruction, who are not professed teachers and who never had a single disciple in that branch of knowledge which he wishes to acquire—would not such conduct be the height of folly?

ANY. Yes, by Zeus, and of ignorance, too.

91 SOC. Very good. And now you are in a position to advise with me about my friend Meno. He has been telling me, Anytus, that he desires to

attain that kind of wisdom and virtue by which men order the state or the house, and honor their parents, and know when to receive and when to send away citizens and strangers, as a good man should. Now, to whom should he go in order that he may learn this virtue? Does not the previous argument imply clearly that we should send him to those who profess and avouch that they are the common teachers of all Hellas, and are ready to impart instruction to anyone who likes, at a fixed price?

ANY. Whom do you mean, Socrates?

SOC. You surely know, do you not, Anytus, that these are the people whom mankind call Sophists?

ANY. By Heracles, Socrates, forebear! I only hope that no friend or kinsman or acquaintance of mine, whether citizen or stranger, will ever be so mad as to allow himself to be corrupted by them; for they are a manifest pest and corrupting influence to those who have to do with them.

SOC. What, Anytus? Of all the people who profess that they know how to do men good, do you mean to say that these are the only ones who not only do them no good, but positively corrupt those who are entrusted to them, and in return for this disservice have the face to demand money? Indeed, I cannot believe you; for I know of a single man, Protagoras, who made more out of his craft than the illustrious Phidias, who created such noble works, or any ten other statuaries. How could that be? A mender of old shoes, or patcher-up of clothes, who made the shoes or clothes worse than he received them, could not have remained thirty days undetected, and would very soon have starved; whereas, during more than forty years, Protagoras was corrupting all Hellas and sending his disciples from him worse than he received them, and he was never found out. For, if I am not mistaken, he was about seventy years old at his death, forty of which were spent in the practice of his profession; and during all that time he had a good reputation, which to this day he retains: and not only Protagoras, but many others are well spoken of;

92 some who lived before him, and others who are still living. Now, when you say that they deceived and corrupted the youth, are they to be supposed to have corrupted them consciously or unconsciously? Can those who were deemed by many to be the wisest men of Hellas have been out of their minds?

ANY. Out of their minds! No, Socrates, the young men who gave their money to them were out of their minds; and their relations and guardians who entrusted their youth to the care of these men were still more out of their minds, and most of all, the cities who allowed them to come in, and did not drive them out, citizen and stranger alike.

SOC. Has any of the Sophists wronged you, Anytus? What makes you so angry with them?

ANY. No, indeed, neither I nor any of my belongings has ever had, nor would I suffer them to have, anything to do with them.

SOC. Then you are entirely unacquainted with them?

ANY. And I have no wish to be acquainted.

SOC. Then, my dear friend, how can you know whether a thing is good or bad of which you are wholly ignorant?

ANY. Quite well; I am sure that I know what manner of men these are, whether I am acquainted with them or not.

SOC. You must be a diviner, Anytus, for I really cannot make out, judging from your own words, how, if you are not acquainted with them, you know about them. But I am not inquiring of you who are the teachers who will corrupt Meno (let them be, if you please, the Sophists); I only ask you to tell him who there is in this great city who will teach him how to become eminent in the virtues which I was just now describing. He is the friend of your family, and you will oblige him.

ANY. Why do you not tell him yourself?

SOC. I have told him whom I supposed to be the teachers of these things; but I learn from you that I am utterly at fault, and I dare say that you are right. And now I wish that you, on your part, would tell me to whom among the Athenians he should go. Whom would you name?

ANY. Why single out individuals? Any Athenian gentleman, taken at random, if he will mind him, will do far more good to him than the Sophists.

SOC. And did those gentlemen grow of themselves; and without having been taught by anyone, were they nevertheless able to teach others that which they had never learned themselves?

93

ANY. I imagine that they learned of the previous generation of gentlemen. Have there not been many good men in this city?

SOC. Yes, certainly, Anytus; and many good statesmen also there always have been, and there are still, in the city of Athens. But the question is whether they were also good teachers of their own virtue—not whether there are, or have been, good men in this part of the world, but whether virtue can be taught, is the question which we have been discussing. Now, do we mean to say that the good men of our own and of other times knew how to impart to others that virtue which they had themselves; or is virtue a thing incapable of being communicated or imparted by one man to another? That is the question which I and Meno have been arguing. Look at the matter in your own way: Would you not admit that Themistocles was a good man?

ANY. Certainly; no man better.

SOC. And must not he then have been a good teacher, if any man ever was a good teacher, of his own virtue?

ANY. Yes, certainly—if he wanted to be so.

SOC. But would he not have wanted? He would, at any rate, have desired to make his own son a good man and a gentleman; he could not have been jealous of him, or have intentionally abstained from imparting to him his own virtue. Did you never hear that he made his son Cleophantus a famous horseman; and had him taught to stand upright on horseback and hurl a javelin, and to do many other marvelous things; and in anything which could be learned from a master he was well trained? Have you not heard from our elders of him?

ANY. I have.

SOC. Then no one could say that his son showed any want of capacity?

ANY. Very likely not.

SOC. But did anyone, old or young, ever say in your hearing that Cleophantus, son of Themistocles, was a wise or good man, as his father was?

ANY. I have certainly never heard anyone say so.

SOC. And if virtue could have been taught, would his father Themistocles have sought to train him in these minor accomplishments, and allowed him who, as you must remember, was his own son, to be no better than his neighbors in those qualities in which he himself excelled?

ANY. Indeed, indeed, I think not.

SOC. Here was a teacher of virtue whom you admit to be among the best men of the past.

94

Let us take another—Aristides, the son of Lysimachus; would you not acknowledge that he was a good man?

ANY. To be sure I should.

SOC. And did not he train his son Lysimachus better than any other Athenian in all that could be done for him by the help of masters? But what has been the result? Is he a bit better than any other mortal? He is an acquaintance of yours, and you see what he is like. There is Pericles, again, magnificent in his wisdom; and he, as you are aware, had two sons, Paralus and Xanthippus.

ANY. I know.

SOC. And you know, also, that he taught them to be unrivaled horsemen, and had them trained in music and gymnastics and all sorts of arts—in these respects they were on a level with the best—and had he no wish to make good men of them? Nay, he must have wished it. But virtue, as I suspect, could not be taught. And that you may not suppose the incompetent teachers to be only the meaner sort of Athenians and few in number, remember again that Thucydides had two sons, Melesias and Stephanus, whom, besides giving them a good education in other things, he trained in wrestling, and they were the best wrestlers in Athens: one of them he committed to the care of Xanthias, and the other to Eudorus, who had the reputation of being the most celebrated wrestlers of that day. Do you remember them?

ANY. I have heard of them.

Soc. Now, can there be a doubt that Thucydides, whose children were taught things for which he had to spend money, would have taught them to be good men, which would have cost him nothing, if virtue could have been taught? Will you reply that he was a mean man, and had not many friends among the Athenians and allies? Nay, but he was of a great family, and a man of influence at Athens and in all Hellas, and, if virtue could have been taught, he would have found out some Athenian or foreigner who would have made good men of his sons if he could not himself spare the time from cares of state. Once more, I suspect, friend Anytus, that virtue is not a thing which can be taught.

ANY. Socrates, I think that you are too ready to speak evil of men: and, if you will take my advice, I would recommend you to be careful. Perhaps there is no city in which it is not easier to do men harm than to do them good, and this is certainly the case at Athens, as I believe that you know.

95

Soc. O Meno, I think that Anytus is in a rage. And he may well be in a rage, for he thinks, in the first place, that I am defaming these gentlemen; and in the second place, he is of opinion that he is one of them himself. But some day he will know what is the meaning of defamation, and if he ever does, he will forgive me. Meanwhile I will return to you, Meno; for I suppose that there are gentlemen in your region, too?

MEN. Certainly there are.

Soc. And are they willing to teach the young, and do they profess to be teachers, and do they agree that virtue is taught?

MEN. No, indeed, Socrates, they are anything but agreed; you may hear them saying at one time that virtue can be taught, and then again the reverse.

Soc. Can we call those "teachers" who do not acknowledge the possibility of their own vocation?

MEN. I think not, Socrates.

Soc. And what do you think of these Sophists, who are the only professors? Do they seem to you to be teachers of virtue?

MEN. I often wonder, Socrates, that Gorgias is never heard promising to teach virtue; and when he hears others promising he only laughs at them, but he thinks that men should be taught to speak.

Soc. Then do you not think that the Sophists are teachers?

MEN. I cannot tell you, Socrates; like the rest of the world, I am in doubt, and sometimes I think that they are teachers, and sometimes not.

Soc. And are you aware that not you only and other politicians have doubts whether virtue can be taught or not, but that Theognis the poet says the very same thing?

MEN. Where does he say so?

Soc. In these elegiac verses:

> Eat and drink and sit with the mighty, and make yourself agreeable to them; for from the good you will learn what is good, but if you mix with the bad, you will lose the intelligence which you already have.

Do you observe that here he seems to imply that virtue can be taught?

MEN. Clearly.

Soc. But in some other verses he shifts about and says:

> If understanding could be created and put into a man, then they [who were able to perform this feat] would have obtained great rewards.

And again:

96

> Never would a bad son have sprung from a good sire, for he would have heard the voice of instruction; but not by teaching will you ever make a bad man into a good one.

And this, as you may remark, is a contradiction of the other.

MEN. Clearly.

Soc. And is there anything else of which the professors are affirmed not only not to be teachers of others, but to be ignorant themselves, and bad at the knowledge of that which they are professing to teach; or is there anything about which even the acknowledged "gentlemen" are sometimes saying that "this thing can be taught," and sometimes the opposite? Can you say that they are teachers in any true sense whose ideas are in such confusion?

MEN. I should say, certainly not.

SOC. But if neither the Sophists nor the gentlemen are teachers, clearly there can be no other teachers?

MEN. No.

SOC. And if there are no teachers, neither are there disciples?

MEN. Agreed.

SOC. And we have admitted that a thing cannot be taught of which there are neither teachers nor disciples?

MEN. We have.

SOC. And there are no teachers of virtue to be found anywhere?

MEN. There are not.

SOC. And if there are not teachers, neither are there scholars?

MEN. That, I think, is true.

SOC. Then virtue cannot be taught?

MEN. Not if we are right in our view. But I cannot believe, Socrates, that there are no good men; and if there are, how did they come into existence?

SOC. I am afraid, Meno, that you and I are not good for much, and that Gorgias has been as poor an educator of you as Prodicus has been of me. Certainly we shall have to look to ourselves, and try to find someone who will help in some way or other to improve us. This I say, because I observe that in the previous discussion none of us remarked that right and good action is possible to man under other guidance than that of knowledge (ἐπιστήμη)—and indeed if this be denied, there is no seeing how there can be any good men at all.

MEN. How do you mean, Socrates?

97 SOC. I mean that good men are necessarily useful or profitable. Were we not right in admitting this? It must be so.

MEN. Yes.

SOC. And in supposing that they will be useful only if they are true guides to us of action—there we were also right?

MEN. Yes.

SOC. But when we said that a man cannot be a good guide unless he has knowledge (φρόνησις), in this we were wrong.

MEN. What do you mean by the word "right"?

SOC. I will explain. If a man knew the way to Larisa, or anywhere else, and went to the place and led others thither, would he not be a right and good guide?

MEN. Certainly.

SOC. And a person who had a right opinion about the way, but had never been and did not know, might be a good guide also, might he not?

MEN. Certainly.

SOC. And while he has true opinion about that which the other knows, he will be just as good a guide if he thinks the truth, as he who knows the truth?

MEN. Exactly.

SOC. Then true opinion is as good a guide to correct action as knowledge; and that was the point which we omitted in our speculation about the nature of virtue, when we said that knowledge only is the guide of right action; whereas there is also right opinion.

MEN. True.

SOC. Then right opinion is not less useful than knowledge?

MEN. The difference, Socrates, is only that he who has knowledge will always be right; but he who has right opinion will sometimes be right, and sometimes not.

SOC. What do you mean? Can he be wrong who has right opinion, so long as he has right opinion?

MEN. I admit the cogency of your argument, and therefore, Socrates, I wonder that knowledge should be preferred to right opinion—or why they should ever differ.

SOC. And shall I explain this wonder to you?

MEN. Do tell me.

SOC. You would not wonder if you had ever observed the images of Daedalus; but perhaps you have not got them in your country?

MEN. What have they to do with the question?

SOC. Because they require to be fastened in order to keep them, and if they are not fastened, they will play truant and run away.

MEN. Well, what of that?

SOC. I mean to say that they are not very valuable possessions if they are at liberty, for they will walk off like runaway slaves; but when fastened, they are of great value, for they are really beautiful works of art. Now this is an illustration of the nature of true opinions: while they abide with us they are beautiful and fruitful, but they run away out of the human soul, and do not remain long, and therefore they are not of much value until they are fastened by the tie of the cause; and this fastening of them, friend Meno, is recollection, as you and I have agreed to call it. But when they are bound, in the first place, they have the nature of knowledge; and, in the second place, they are abiding. And this is why knowledge is more honorable and excellent than true opinion, because fastened by a chain.

MEN. What you are saying, Socrates, seems to be very like the truth.

SOC. I, too, speak rather in ignorance; I only conjecture. And yet that knowledge differs from true opinion is no matter of conjecture with me. There are not many things which I profess to know, but this is most certainly one of them.

MEN. Yes, Socrates; and you are quite right in saying so.

SOC. And am I not also right in saying that true opinion leading the way perfects action quite as well as knowledge?

MEN. There again, Socrates, I think you are right.

SOC. Then right opinion is not a whit inferior to knowledge, or less useful in action; nor is the man who has right opinion inferior to him who has knowledge?

MEN. True.

SOC. And surely the good man has been acknowledged by us to be useful?

MEN. Yes.

SOC. Seeing then that men become good and useful to states, not only because they have knowledge, but because they have right opinion, and that neither knowledge nor right opinion is given to man by nature or acquired by him—(do you imagine either of them to be given by nature?

MEN. Not I.)

SOC. Then if they are not given by nature, neither are the good by nature good?

MEN. Certainly not.

SOC. And nature being excluded, then came the question whether virtue is acquired by teaching?

MEN. Yes.

SOC. If virtue was widom [or knowledge], then, as we thought, it was taught?

MEN. Yes.

SOC. And if it was taught, it was wisdom?

MEN. Certainly.

SOC. And if there were teachers, it might be taught; and if there were no teachers, not?

MEN. True.

SOC. But surely we acknowledged that there were no teachers of virtue?

MEN. Yes.

SOC. Then we acknowledged that it was not taught, and was not wisdom.

MEN. Certainly.

SOC. And yet we admitted that it was a good?

MEN. Yes.

SOC. And the right guide is useful and good?

MEN. Certainly.

SOC. And the only right guides are knowledge and true opinion—these are the guides of man; for things which happen by chance are not under the guidance of man; but the guides of man are true opinion and knowledge.

MEN. I think so, too.

SOC. But if virtue is not taught, neither is virtue knowledge.

MEN. Clearly not.

SOC. Then of two good and useful things, one, which is knowledge, has been set aside and cannot be supposed to be our guide in political life.

MEN. I think not.

SOC. And therefore not by any wisdom, and not because they were wise, did Themistocles and those others of whom Anytus spoke govern states. This was the reason why they were unable to make others like themselves—because their virtue was not grounded on knowledge.

MEN. That is probably true, Socrates.

SOC. But if not by knowledge, the only alternative which remains is that statesmen must have guided states by right opinion, which is in politics what divination is in religion; for diviners and also prophets say many things truly, but they know not what they say.

MEN. So I believe.

SOC. And may we not, Meno, truly call those men "divine" who, having no understanding, yet succeed in many a grand deed and word?

MEN. Certainly.

SOC. Then we shall also be right in calling divine those whom we were just now speaking of as diviners and prophets, including the whole tribe of poets. Yes, and statesmen above all may be said to be divine and illumined, being inspired and possessed of the god, in which condition they say many grand things, not knowing what they say.

MEN. Yes.

SOC. And the women, too, Meno, call good men divine—do they not? And the Spartans, when they praise a good man, say "that he is a divine man."

MEN. And I think, Socrates, that they are right, although very likely our friend Anytus may take offense at the word.

SOC. I do not care; as for Anytus, there will be another opportunity of talking with him. To sum up our inquiry—the result seems to be, if we are at all right in our view, that virtue is neither natural nor acquired, but an instinct given by God to the virtuous. Nor is the instinct accompanied by reason, unless there may be supposed to be among statesmen someone who is capable of educating statesmen. And if there be such a one, he may be said to be among the living what Homer says that Tiresias was among the dead, "he alone has understanding; but the rest are flitting shades"; and he and his virtue in like manner will be a reality among shadows.

MEN. That is excellent, Socrates.

SOC. Then, Meno, the conclusion is that virtue comes to the virtuous by divine dispensation. But we shall never know the certain truth until, before asking how virtue is given, we inquire into the actual nature of virtue. I fear that I must go away, but do you, now that you are persuaded yourself, persuade our friend Anytus. And do not let him be so exasperated; if you can conciliate him, you will have done good service to the Athenian people.

STUDY QUESTIONS: PLATO, *MENO*

1. Why does Socrates compare virtue to bees?
2. How does Socrates argue that nobody desires something that is evil or bad?
3. What is the paradox of inquiry or knowledge? How does Socrates propose to solve it?
4. What is the slave boy able to prove? What does this show about the nature of knowledge, according to Socrates?
5. Why does Plato seek to establish that knowledge has an innate nature in this dialogue? How exactly does Plato express the relevant claim about the innate nature of knowledge?
6. What is Socrates' argument for the claim that virtue is some sort of wisdom?
7. Socrates says that if virtue is knowledge, then it must be teachable. But soon afterward, he raises a doubt concerning the claim that virtue is knowledge. What is that doubt?
8. Is Socrates right to think that people cannot desire knowingly what is bad?
9. Is Socrates' claim about the nature of knowledge plausible? What are the main objections to it, and how would Plato respond to those objections?

PHAEDO

This dialogue portrays the last conversation and the death of Socrates. It forms the last of a series consisting in the *Euthyphro* (which portrays Socrates on his way to the court), the *Apology* (the trial), and the *Crito* (Socrates refusing to escape from prison). Contemplating his own death, Socrates argues for the separation of the soul and the body. After death, the philosopher will be able to attain the wisdom he or she sought in this life, but was not able to gain because of the confusion created by the body and its desires.

This dialogue was written after the *Meno*, but before the *Republic*. For the first time, Plato explicitly gives arguments for the existence of changeless and eternal Forms, known only through thought. Plato argues that equality itself cannot be identical to equally sized sticks or any such observable object. We could be mistaken about the equality of two sticks, but we could not think that Equality itself was unequal. Plato affirms the existence of the Forms of Justice, Beauty, Goodness, Health, and Strength (65d).

Plato provides three main arguments for the existence of a soul that can survive bodily death. First, he combines his new theory of Forms with his theory of recollection to demonstrate the existence of the soul (72e–78b). The Forms can only be understood through thought, although we are reminded of them in sensory perception. For example, seeing two equal sticks reminds us of the Form of Equality. Without that prior knowledge, we could not see the sticks as equal. Consequently, we must have known the Forms prior to birth. This constitutes an argument in favor of the existence of a soul that is distinct from the body.

Second, Plato also argues that there is a certain affinity between the soul and the Forms (78b–84b). The Forms are eternal, indivisible, and unchanging, distinct from the destructible things of the perceptible world. Plato suggests that, because these Forms are perceived by the soul, the two must be similar. Therefore, the soul too must be eternal and distinct from the transitory world presented to the senses.

The third and final argument for the immortality of the soul is based on the claim that the soul (anima) is the principle of life (102b–107b). The soul necessarily always brings life (it animates). Since life is the opposite of death, the soul cannot die.

57 **ECHECRATES.** Were you there with Socrates yourself, Phaedo, on the day he drank the poison in the prison, or did you hear of it from someone else?

PHAEDO. I was there myself, Echecrates.

5 **ECHECRATES.** Then what was it that he said before his death? And how did he meet his end? I'd like to hear about it. You see, hardly anyone from Phlius goes to stay at Athens nowadays, and no visitor has come from there

b for a long time who could give us any definite report of those events, beyond the fact that he died by drinking poison; there was nothing more they could tell us.

58 **PHAEDO.** Didn't you even learn, then, about how the trial went?

ECHECRATES. Yes, someone did report that to us, and we were surprised that it was evidently long after it was over that he died. Why was

5 that, Phaedo?

PHAEDO. It was chance in his case, Echecrates: it just chanced that on the day before the trial the stern of the ship that Athenians send to Delos had been wreathed.

ECHECRATES. What ship is that?

10 PHAEDO. According to Athenian legend, it's the ship inwhich Theseus once sailed to Crete, taking the famous 'seven pairs', when he saved

b their lives and his own as well. It is said that at that time the Athenians had made a vow to Apollo that if they were saved, they would, in return, dispatch a mission to Delos every year; and this they have sent annually ever since,

5 down to this day, in honour of the god. Once they've started the mission, it is their law that the city shall be pure during that period, which means that the state shall put no one to death, till the ship has reached Delos and returned; and that sometimes takes a long

c time, when winds happen to hold them back. The mission starts as soon as the priest of Apollo has wreathed the stern of the ship; and, as I say, that chanced to have taken place on the day before the trial. That's why Socrates spent a long time in prison between

5 his trial and death.

ECHECRATES. And what about the circumstances of the death itself, Phaedo? What was it that was said and done, and which of his intimates were there with him? Or would the authorities allow no one to be present, so that he met his end isolated from his friends?

d PHAEDO. By no means: some were present, in fact quite a number.

ECHECRATES. Please do try, then, to give us as definite a report as you can of the whole thing, unless you happen to be otherwise engaged.

PHAEDO. No, I am free, and I'll try to describe it

5 for you; indeed it's always the greatest of pleasures for me to recall Socrates, whether speaking myself or listening to someone else.

ECHECRATES. Well, Phaedo, you certainly have an audience of the same mind; so try to recount everything as minutely as you can.

e PHAEDO. Very well then. I myself was curiously affected while I was there: it wasn't pity that visited me, as might have been expected for someone present at the death of an intimate friend; because the man seemed to me happy, Echecrates, both in his manner and his words,

5 so fearlessly and nobly was he meeting his end; and so I felt assured that even while on his

way to Hades he would not go without divine providence, and that when he arrived there he would

59 fare well, if ever anyone did. That's why I wasn't visited at all by the pity that would seem natural for someone present at a scene of sorrow, nor again by the pleasure from our being occupied, as usual, with philosophy—

5 because the discussion was, in fact, of that sort—but a simply extraordinary feeling was upon me, a sort of strange mixture of pleasure and pain combined, as I reflected that Socrates was shortly going to die. All of us there were affected in much the same way, now laughing, now in tears, one of us quite

b exceptionally so, Apollodorus—I think you know the man and his manner.

ECHECRATES. Of course.

PHAEDO. Well, he was completely overcome by that state; and I myself was much upset, as were the others.

5 ECHECRATES. And just who were there, Phaedo?

PHAEDO. Of the local people there was this Apollodorus, and Critobulus and his father, and then there were Hermogenes, Epigenes, Aeschines, and Antisthenes; Ctesippus of the Paeanian deme was there too, and Menexenus

10 and some other local people. Plato, I believe, was unwell.

ECHECRATES. Were there any visitors there?

c PHAEDO. Yes: Simmias of Thebes, and Cebes and Phaedondes; and Euclides and Terpsion from Megara.

ECHECRATES. What about Aristippus and Cleombrotus? Were they there?

PHAEDO. No, they weren't; they were said to be in Aegina.

5 ECHECRATES. Was anyone else there?

PHAEDO. I think those were about all.

ECHECRATES. Well then, what discussion do you say took place?

PHAEDO. I'll try to describe everything for you from the beginning. Regularly, you see, and

d especially on the preceding days, I myself and Socrates' other companions had been in the habit of visiting him; we would meet at daybreak at the court-house, where the trial was held, as it was close to the prison. We used to

5 wait each day till the prison opened, talking

with one another, as it didn't open very early. When it did, we would go in to Socrates and generally spend the day with him. On that particular day we'd met earlier still; because when we left the prison the evening before, we learnt that the ship had arrived from Delos. So we passed the word to one another to come to our usual place as early as possible. When we arrived, the door-keeper who usually admitted us came out and told us to wait, and not to go in till he gave the word; 'because', he said, 'the Eleven are releasing Socrates, and giving orders that he's to die today.' But after a short interval he came back and told us to go in. On entering we found Socrates, just released, and Xanthippe—you know her—holding his little boy and sitting beside him. When she saw us, Xanthippe broke out and said just the kinds of thing that women are given to saying: 'So this is the very last time, Socrates, that your good friends will speak to you and you to them.' At which Socrates looked at Crito and said: 'Crito, someone had better take her home.'

So she was taken away by some of Crito's people, calling out and lamenting; Socrates, meanwhile, sat up on the bed, bent his leg, and rubbed it down with his hand. As he rubbed it, he said: 'What an odd thing it seems, friends, this state that people call "pleasant"; and how curiously it's related to its supposed opposite, "painful": to think that the pair of them refuse to visit a person together, yet if anybody pursues one of them and catches it, he's always pretty well bound to catch the other as well, as if the two of them were attached to a single head. I do believe that if Aesop had thought of them, he'd have made up a story telling how God wanted to reconcile them in their quarrelling, but when he couldn't he fastened their heads together, and that's why anybody visited by one of them is later attended by the other as well. That is just what seems to be happening in my own case: there was discomfort in my leg because of the fetter, and now the pleasant seems to have come to succeed it.'

'What you both say is fair,' he said; 'as I take you to mean that I should defend myself against these charges as if in a court of law.'

'Yes, exactly,' said Simmias.

'Very well then,' he said; 'let me try to defend myself more convincingly before you than I did before the jury. Because if I didn't believe, Simmias and Cebes, that I shall enter the presence, first, of other gods both wise and good, and next of dead people better than those in this world, then I should be wrong not to be resentful at death; but as it is, be assured that I expect to join the company of good men—although that point I shouldn't affirm with absolute conviction; but I shall enter the presence of gods who are very good masters, be assured that if there's anything I should affirm on such matters, it is that. So that's why I am not so resentful, but rather am hopeful that there is something in store for those who've died—in fact, as we've long been told, something far better for the good than for the wicked.'

'Well then, Socrates,' said Simmias, 'do you mean to go off keeping this thought to yourself, or would you share it with us too? We have a common claim on this benefit as well, I think; and at the same time your defence will be made, if you persuade us of what you say.'

'All right, I'll try,' he said. 'But first let's find out what it is that Crito here has been wanting to say, for some time past, I think.'

'Why Socrates,' said Crito, 'it's simply that the man who's going to give you the poison has been telling me for some time that you must be warned to talk as little as possible: he says people get heated through talking too much, and one must bring nothing of that sort in contact with the poison; people doing that sort of thing are sometimes obliged, otherwise, to drink twice or even three times.'

'Never mind him,' said Socrates. 'Just let him prepare his stuff so as to give two doses, or even three if need be.'

'Yes, I pretty well knew it,' said Crito; 'but he's been giving me trouble for some while.'

'Let him be,' he said. 'Now then, with you for my jury I want to give my defence, and show with what good reason, as it seems to me, a man who has truly spent his life in philosophy feels confident when about to die, and is hopeful that, when he has died, he will win very great benefits in the other world. So I'll try, Simmias and Cebes, to explain how this could be.

'Other people may well be unaware that all who actually engage in philosophy aright are practising nothing other than dying and being dead. Now if this is true, it would be odd indeed for them to be eager in their whole life for nothing but that, and yet to be resentful when it comes, the very thing they'd long been eager for and practised.'

Simmias laughed at this and said: 'Goodness, Socrates, you've made me laugh, even though I wasn't much inclined to laugh just now. I imagine that most people, on hearing that, would think it very well said of philosophers—and our own countrymen would quite agree—that they are, indeed, longing for death, and that they, at any rate, are well aware that that is what philosophers deserve to undergo.'

'Yes, and what they say would be true, Simmias, except for their claim to be aware of it themselves; because they aren't aware in what sense genuine philosophers are longing for death and deserving of it, and what kind of death they deserve. Anyway, let's discuss it among ourselves, disregarding them: do we suppose that death is a reality?'

'Certainly,' rejoined Simmias.

'And that it is nothing but the separation of the soul from the body? And that being dead is this: the body's having come to be apart, separated from the soul, alone by itself, and the soul's being apart, alone by itself, separated from the body? Death can't be anything else but that, can it?'

'No, it's just that.'

'Now look, my friend, and see if maybe you agree with me on these points; because through them I think we'll improve our knowledge of what we're examining. Do you think

it befits a philosophical man to be keen about the so-called pleasures of, for example, food and drink?'

'Not in the least, Socrates,' said Simmias.

'And what about those of sex?'

'Not at all.'

'And what about the other services to the body? Do you think such a person regards them as of any value? For instance, the possession of smart clothes and shoes, and the other bodily adornments—do you think he values them highly, or does he disdain them, except in so far as he's absolutely compelled to share in them?'

'I think the genuine philosopher disdains them.'

'Do you think in general, then, that such a person's concern is not for the body, but so far as he can stand aside from it, is directed towards the soul?'

'I do.'

'Then is it clear that, first, in such matters as those the philosopher differs from other people in releasing his soul, as far as possible, from its communion with the body?'

'It appears so.'

'And presumably, Simmias, it does seem to most people that someone who finds nothing of that sort pleasant, and takes no part in those things, doesn't deserve to live; rather, one who cares nothing for the pleasures that come by way of the body runs pretty close to being dead.'

'Yes, what you say is quite true.'

'And now, what about the actual gaining of wisdom? Is the body a hindrance or not, if one enlists it as a partner in the quest? This is the sort of thing I mean: do sight and hearing afford mankind any truth, or aren't even the poets always harping on such themes, telling us that we neither hear nor see anything accurately? And yet if those of all the bodily senses are neither accurate nor clear, the others will hardly be so; because they are, surely, all inferior to those. Don't you think so?'

'Certainly.'

'So when does the soul attain the truth? Because plainly, whenever it sets about examining anything in company with the body, it is completely taken in by it.'

'That's true.'

c 'So isn't it in reasoning, if anywhere at all, that any realities become manifest to it?'

'Yes.'

5 'And it reasons best, presumably, whenever none of these things bothers it, neither hearing nor sight nor pain, nor any pleasure either, but whenever it comes to be alone by itself as far as possible, disregarding the body, and whenever, having the least possible communion and contact with it, it strives for reality.'

10 'That is so.'

'So there again the soul of the philosopher utterly disdains the body and flees from d it, seeking rather to come to be alone by itself?'

'It seems so.'

'Well now, what about things of this sort, Simmias? Do we say that a just itself is a real-5 ity or not?'

'Yes, we most certainly do!'

'And likewise, a beautiful and a good?'

'Of course.'

'Now did you ever yet see any such things with your eyes?'

10 'Certainly not.'

'Well did you grasp them with any other bodily sense-perception? And I'm talking about them all—about largeness, health, and strength, for example—and, in short, about the being of all other such things, what each e one actually is; is it through the body that the truest view of them is gained, or isn't it rather thus: whoever of us is prepared to think most fully and minutely of each object of his inquiry, in itself, will come closest to the 5 knowledge of each?'

'Yes, certainly.'

'Then would that be achieved most purely by one who approached each object with his intellect alone as far as possible, neither applying sight in his thinking, nor dragging in any other sense to accompany his 66 reasoning; rather, using his intellect alone by itself and unsullied, he would undertake the hunt for each reality alone by itself and unsul-

lied; he would be separated as far as possible from his eyes and ears, and virtually from his 5 whole body, on the ground that it confuses the soul, and doesn't allow it to gain truth and wisdom when in partnership with it: isn't this the one, Simmias, who will attain reality, if anyone will?'

10 'What you say is abundantly true, Socrates,' said Simmias.

b 'For all those reasons, then, some such view as this must present itself to genuine philosophers, so that they say such things to one another as these: "There now, it looks as if some sort of track is leading us, together with our reason, astray in our inquiry: as long as we 5 possess the body, and our soul is contaminated by such an evil, we'll surely never adequately gain what we desire—and that, we say, is truth. Because the body affords us countless distractions, owing to the nurture it must c have; and again, if any illnesses befall it, they hamper our pursuit of reality. Besides, it fills us up with lusts and desires, with fears and fantasies of every kind, and with any amount of trash, so that really and truly we are, as the 5 saying goes, never able to think of anything at all because of it. Thus, it's nothing but the body and its desires that brings wars and factions and fighting; because it's over the gaind ing of wealth that all wars take place, and we're compelled to gain wealth because of the body, enslaved as we are to its service; so far all those reasons it leaves us no leisure for philosophy. And the worst of it all is that if we 5 do get any leisure from it, and turn to some inquiry, once again it intrudes everywhere in our researches, setting up a clamour and disturbance, and striking terror, so that the truth can't be discerned because of it. Well now, it really has been shown us that if we're ever going to know anything purely, we must be rid e of it, and must view the objects themselves with the soul by itself; it's then, apparently, that the thing we desire and whose lovers we claim to be, wisdom, will be ours—when we have died, as the argument indicates, though not while we live. Because, if we can know 5 nothing purely in the body's company, then one of two things must be true: either knowledge is nowhere to be gained, or else it is for the dead; since then, but no sooner, will the soul be alone by itself apart from the body. And therefore while we live, it would seem that we shall be closest to knowledge in this way—if we consort with the body as little as possible, and do not commune with it, except in so far as we must, and do not infect ourselves with its nature, but remain pure from it, until God himself shall release us; and being thus pure, through separation from the body's folly, we shall probably be in like company, and shall know through our own selves all that is unsullied—and that, I dare say, is what the truth is; because never will it be permissible for impure to touch pure." Such are the things, I think, Simmias, that all who are rightly called lovers of knowledge must say to one another, and must believe. Don't you agree?'

'Emphatically, Socrates.'

'Well then, if that's true, my friend,' said Socrates, 'there's plenty of hope for one who arrives where I'm going, that there, if anywhere, he will adequately possess the object that's been our great concern in life gone by; and thus the journey now appointed for me may also be made with good hope by any other man who regards his intellect as prepared, by having been, in a manner, purified.'

'Yes indeed,' said Simmias.

'Then doesn't purification turn out to be just what's been mentioned for some while in our discussion—the parting of the soul from the body as far as possible, and the habituating of it to assemble and gather itself together, away from every part of the body, alone by itself, and to live, so far as it can, both in the present and in the hereafter, released from the body, as from fetters?'

'Yes indeed.'

'And is it just this that is named "death"—a release and parting of soul from body?'

'Indeed it is.'

'And it's especially those who practise philosophy aright, or rather they alone, who are always eager to release it, as we say, and the occupation of philosophers is just this, isn't it—a release and parting of soul from body?'

'It seems so.'

'Then wouldn't it be absurd, as I said at the start, for a man to prepare himself in his life to live as close as he can to being dead, and then to be resentful when that comes to him?'

'It would be absurd, of course.'

'Truly then, Simmias, those who practise philosophy aright are cultivating dying, and for them, least of all men, does being dead hold any terror. Look at it like this: if they've set themselves at odds with the body at every point, and desire to possess their soul alone by itself, wouldn't it be quite illogical if they were afraid and resentful when that came about—if, that is, they didn't go gladly to the place where, on arrival, they may hope to attain what they longed for throughout life, namely wisdom—and to be rid of the company of that with which they'd set themselves at odds? Or again, many have been willing to enter Hades of their own accord, in quest of human loves, of wives and sons who have died, led by this hope, that there they would see and be united with those they desired; will anyone, then, who truly longs for wisdom, and who firmly holds this same hope, that nowhere but in Hades will he attain it in any way worth mentioning, be resentful at dying; and will he not go there gladly? One must suppose so, my friend, if he's truly a lover of wisdom; since this will be his firm belief, that nowhere else but there will he attain wisdom purely. Yet if that is so, wouldn't it, as I said just now, be quite illogical if such a person were afraid of death?'

'Yes, quite illogical!'

'Then if you see a man resentful that he is going to die, isn't that proof enough for you that he's no lover of wisdom after all, but what we may call a lover of the body? . . .

When Socrates had said that, Cebes rejoined: 'The other things you say, Socrates, I find excellent; but what you say about the soul is the subject of much disbelief: people fear that when it's been separated from the body, it may no longer exist anywhere, but that on the very day a person dies, it may be destroyed and perish, as soon as it's separated from the body; and that as it goes out, it may be dispersed like breath or smoke, go flying off, and exist no longer anywhere at all. True, if it did exist somewhere, gathered together alone by itself, and separated from those evils you were recounting just now, there'd be plenty of hope, Socrates, and a fine hope it would be, that what you say is true; but on just this point, perhaps, one needs no little reassuring and convincing, that when the person has died, his soul exists, and that it possesses some power and wisdom.'

'That's true, Cebes,' said Socrates; 'but then what are we to do? Would you like us to speculate on those very questions, and see whether that is likely to be the case or not?'

'For my part anyway,' said Cebes, 'I'd gladly hear whatever opinion you have about them.'

'Well,' said Socrates, 'I really don't think anyone listening now, even if he were a comic poet, would say that I'm talking idly, and arguing about things that don't concern me. If you agree, then, we should look into the matter.

'Let's consider it, perhaps, in this way: do the souls of human beings exist in Hades when they have died, or do they not? Now there's an ancient doctrine, which we've recalled, that they do exist in that world, entering it from this one, and that they re-enter this world and are born again from the dead; yet if that is so, if living people are born again from those who have died, surely our souls would have to exist in that world? Because they could hardly be born again, if they didn't exist; so it would be sufficient evidence for the truth of those claims, if it really became plain that living people are born from the dead and from nowhere else; but if that isn't so, some other argument would be needed.'

'Certainly,' said Cebes.

'Well now, consider the matter, if you want to understand more readily, in connection not only with mankind, but with all animals and plants; and, in general, for all things subject to coming-to-be, let's see whether everything comes to be in this way: opposites come to be only from their opposites—in the case of all things that actually have an opposite—as, for example, the beautiful is opposite, of course, to the ugly, just to unjust, and so on in countless other cases. So let's consider this: is it necessary that whatever has an opposite comes to be only from its opposite? For example, when a thing comes to be larger, it must, surely, come to be larger from being smaller before?'

'Yes.'

'And again, if it comes to be smaller, it will come to be smaller later from being larger before?'

'That's so.'

'And that which is weaker comes to be, presumably, from a stronger, and that which is faster from a slower?'

'Certainly.'

'And again, if a thing comes to be worse, it's from a better, and if more just, from a more unjust?'

'Of course.'

'Are we satisfied, then, that all things come to be in this way, opposite things from opposites?'

'Certainly.'

'Now again, do those things have a further feature of this sort: between the members of every pair of opposites, since they are two, aren't there two processes of coming-to-be, from one to the other, and back again from the latter to the former? Thus, between a larger thing and a smaller, isn't there increase and decrease, so that in the one case we speak of "increasing" and in the other of "decreasing"?'

'Yes.'

'And similarly with separating and combining, cooling and heating, and all such; even if in some cases we don't use the names, still in actual fact mustn't the same principle everywhere hold good: they come to be from each other, and there's a process of coming-to-be of each into the other?'

'Certainly.'

'Well then, is there an opposite to living,
c   as sleeping is opposite to being awake?'

'Certainly.'

'What is it?'

5   'Being dead.'

'Then those come to be from each other,
if they are opposites; and between the pair of
them, since they are two, the processes of
coming-to-be are two?'

'Of course.'

'Now then,' said Socrates, 'I'll tell you
one of the couples I was just mentioning, the
10   couple itself and its processes; and you tell me
the other. My couple is sleeping and being
awake: being awake comes to be from sleep-
d   ing, and sleeping from being awake, and their
processes are going to sleep and waking up. Is
that sufficient for you or not?'

'Certainly.'

'Now it's for you to tell me in the same
5   way about life and death. You say, don't you,
that being dead is opposite to living?'

'I do.'

'And that they come to be from each
other?'

'Yes.'

'Then what is it that comes to be from
10   that which is living?'

'That which is dead.'

'And what comes to be from that which
is dead?'

'I must admit that it's that which is living.'

'Then it's from those that are dead, Cebes,
15   that living things and living people are born?'

e   'Apparently.'

'Then our souls do exist in Hades.'

'So it seems.'

'Now one of the relevant processes here
is obvious, isn't it? For dying is obvious
5   enough, surely?'

'It certainly is.'

'What shall we do then? Shan't we assign
the opposite process to balance it? Will nature
be lame in this respect? Or must we supply
10   some process opposite to dying?'

'We surely must.'

'What will this be?'

'Coming to life again.'

'Then if there is such a thing as coming to
life again, wouldn't this, coming to life again,
72   be a process from dead to living people?'

'Certainly.'

'In that way too, then, we're agreed that
living people are born from the dead no less
5   than dead people from the living; and we
thought that, if that were the case, it would
be sufficient evidence that the souls of the
dead must exist somewhere, whence they are
born again.'

'I think, Socrates, that that must follow
10   from our admissions.'

'Where did we get the knowledge of it [i.e.,
74b equality]? Wasn't it from the things we were
5   just mentioning: on seeing logs or stones or
other equal things, wasn't it from those that
we thought of that object, it being different
from them? Or doesn't it seem different to
you? Look at it this way: aren't equal stones
and logs, the very same ones, sometimes evidently equal to one, but not to another?'

10   'Yes, certainly.'

c   'But now, were the equals themselves
ever, in your view, evidently unequal, or
equality inequality?'

'Never yet, Socrates.'

5   'Then those equals, and the equal itself,
are not the same.'

'By no means, Socrates, in my view.'

'But still, it is from those equals, different
as they are from that equal, that you have
thought of and got the knowledge of it?'

10   'That's perfectly true.'

'It being either similar to them or
dissimilar?'

'Certainly.'

'Anyway, it makes no difference; so long
as on seeing one thing, one does, from that
d   sight, think of another, whether it be similar
or dissimilar, that must be recollection.'

'Certainly.'

'Well now, with regard to the instances in
the logs, and, in general, the equals we men-
5   tioned just now, are we affected in some way
as this: do they seem to us to be equal in the

same way as is the thing itself, that which it is? Do they fall short of it at all in being like the equal, or not?'

'Very far short of it.'

'Then whenever anyone, on seeing a thing, thinks to himself, "this thing that I now see seeks to be like another reality, but falls short, and cannot be like that object: it is inferior", do we agree that the man who thinks that must previously have known the object he says it resembles but falls short of?'

'He must.'

'Now then, have we ourselves been affected in just that way, or not, with regard to the equals and the equal itself?'

'Indeed we have.'

'Then we must previously have known the equal, before that time when we first, on seeing the equals, thought that all of them were striving to be like the equal but fell short of it.'

'That is so.'

'Yet we also agree on this: we haven't derived the thought of it, nor could we do so, from anywhere but seeing or touching or some other of the senses—I'm counting all those as the same.'

'Yes, they are the same, Socrates, for what the argument seeks to show.'

'But of course it is from one's sense-perceptions that one must think that all sensible items are striving for that thing which equal is, yet are inferior to it; or how shall we put it?'

'Like that.'

'Then it must, surely, have been before we began to see and hear and use the other senses that we got knowledge of the equal itself, of what it is, if we were going to refer the equals from our sense-perceptions to it, supposing that all things are doing their best to be like it, but are inferior to it.'

'That must follow from what's been said before, Socrates.'

'Now we were seeing and hearing, and were possessed of our other senses, weren't we, just as soon as we were born?'

'Certainly.'

'But we must, we're saying, have got our knowledge of the equal before those?'

'Yes.'

'Then it seems that we must have got it before we were born.'

'It seems so.'

'Now if, having got it before birth, we were born in possession of it, did we know, both before birth and as soon as we were born, not only the equal, the larger and the smaller, but everything of that sort? Because our present argument concerns the beautiful itself, and the good itself, and just and holy, no less than the equal; in fact, as I say, it concerns everything on which we set this seal, "that which it is", in the questions we ask and in the answers we give. And so we must have got pieces of knowledge of all those things before birth.'

'Then let's go back to those entities to which we turned in our earlier argument. Is the reality itself, whose being we give an account of in asking and answering questions, unvarying and constant, or does it vary? Does the equal itself, the beautiful itself, that which each thing itself is, the real, ever admit of any change whatever? Or does that which each of them is, being uniform alone by itself, remain unvarying and constant, and never admit of any kind of alteration in any way or respect whatever?'

'It must be unvarying and constant, Socrates,' said Cebes.

'But what about the many beautiful things, such as human beings or horses or cloaks or anything else at all of that kind? Or equals, or all things that bear the same name as those objects? Are they constant, or are they just the opposite of those others, and practically never constant at all, either in relation to themselves or to one another?'

'That is their condition,' said Cebes; 'they are never unvarying.'

'Now these things you could actually touch and see and sense with the other senses, couldn't you, whereas those that are constant you could lay hold of only by reasoning of the intellect; aren't such things, rather, invisible and not seen?'

'What you say is perfectly true.'

'Then would you like us to posit two kinds of beings, the one kind seen, the other invisible?'

'Let's posit them.'

'And the invisible is always constant, whereas the seen is never constant?'

'Let's posit that too.'

'Well, but we ourselves are part body and part soul, aren't we?'

'We are.'

'Then to which kind do we say that the body will be more similar and more akin?'

'That's clear to anyone: obviously to the seen.'

'And what about the soul? Is it seen or invisible?'

'It's not seen by human beings, at any rate, Socrates.'

'But we meant, surely, things seen and not seen with reference to human nature; or do you think we meant any other?'

'We meant human nature.'

'What do we say about soul, then? Is it seen or unseen?'

'It's not seen.'

'Then it's invisible?'

'Yes.'

'Then soul is more similar than body to the invisible, whereas body is more similar to that which is seen.'

'That must be so, Socrates.'

'Now weren't we saying a while ago that whenever the soul uses the body as a means to study anything, either by seeing or hearing or any other sense—because to use the body as a means is to study a thing through sense-perception—then it is dragged by the body towards objects that are never constant; and it wanders about itself, and is confused and dizzy, as if drunk, by virtue of contact with things of a similar kind?'

'Certainly.'

'Whereas whenever it studies alone by itself, it departs yonder towards that which is pure and always existent and immortal and unvarying, and by virtue of its kinship with it, enters always into its company, whenever it has come to be alone by itself, and whenever it may do so; then it has ceased from its wandering and, when it is about those objects, it is always constant and unvarying, because of its contact with things of a similar kind; and this condition of it is called "wisdom", is it not?'

'That's very well said and perfectly true, Socrates.'

'Once again, then, in the light of our earlier and present arguments, to which kind do you think that soul is more similar and more akin?'

'Everyone, I think, Socrates, even the slowest learner, following this line of inquiry, would agree that soul is totally and altogether more similar to what is unvarying than to what is not.'

'And what about the body?'

'That is more like the latter.'

'Now look at it this way too: when soul and body are present in the same thing, nature ordains that the one shall serve and be ruled, whereas the other shall rule and be master; here again, which do you think is similar to the divine and which to the mortal? Don't you think the divine is naturally adapted for ruling and domination, whereas the mortal is adapted for being ruled and for service?'

'I do.'

'Which kind, then, does the soul resemble?'

'Obviously, Socrates, the soul resembles the divine, and the body the mortal.'

'So what I was saying we were to define, the kind of things which, while not opposite to a given thing, nevertheless don't admit it, the opposite in question—as we've just seen that threeness, while not opposite to the even, nevertheless doesn't admit it, since it always brings up its opposite, just as twoness brings up the opposite of the odd, and the fire brings up the opposite of the cold, and so on in a great many other cases—well, see whether you would define them thus: it is not only the opposite that doesn't admit its opposite; there is also that which brings up an opposite into whatever it enters itself; and that thing, the very thing that brings it up, never admits the quality opposed to the one that's brought up. Recall it once more: there's no harm in hearing it several times. Five won't admit the form of the even, nor will ten, its double, admit that of the odd. That, of course, is itself also the opposite of something else; nevertheless, it won't admit the form of the odd. Nor again will one-and-a-half, and the rest of that series, the halves, admit the form of the whole; and the same applies to a third, and all that series. Do you follow and agree that that is so?'

'I agree most emphatically, and I do follow.'

'Then please repeat it from the start; and don't answer in the exact terms of my question, but in imitation of my example. I say this, because from what's now being said I see a different kind of safety beyond the answer I gave initially, the old safe one. Thus, if you were to ask me what it is, by whose presence in a body, that body will be hot, I shan't give you the old safe, ignorant answer, that it's heat, but a subtler answer now available, that it's fire. And again, if you ask what it is, by whose presence in a body, that body will ail, I shan't say that it's illness, but fever. And again, if asked what it is, by whose presence in a number, that number will be odd, I shan't say oddness, but oneness, and so on. See whether by now you have an adequate understanding of what I want.'

'Yes, quite adequate.'

'Answer then, and tell me what it is, by whose presence in a body, that body will be living.'

'Soul.'

'And is that always so?'

'Of course.'

'Then soul, whatever it occupies, always comes to that thing bringing life?'

'It comes indeed.'

'And is there an opposite to life, or is there none?'

'There is.'

'What is it?'

'Death.'

'Now soul will absolutely never admit the opposite of what it brings up, as has been agreed earlier?'

'Most emphatically,' said Cebes.

'Well now, what name did we give just now to what doesn't admit the form of the even?'

'Uneven.'

'And to that which doesn't admit the just, and to whatever doesn't admit the musical?'

'Unmusical, and unjust.'

'Well then, what do we call whatever doesn't admit death?'

'Immortal.'

'But soul doesn't admit death?'

'No.'

'Then soul is immortal.'

'It's immortal.'

'Very well. May we say that that much has been proved? Or how does it seem to you?'

'Yes, and very adequately proved, Socrates.'

'Now what about this, Cebes? If it were necessary for the uneven to be imperishable, three would be imperishable, wouldn't it?'

'Of course.'

'Or again, if the non-hot were necessarily imperishable likewise, then whenever anyone brought hot against snow, the snow would get out of the way, remaining intact and unmelted? Because it couldn't perish, nor again could it abide and admit the heat.'

'True.'

'And in the same way, I imagine, if the non-coolable were imperishable, then whenever something cold attacked the fire, it could never be put out nor could it perish, but it would depart and go away intact.'

'It would have to.'

'Then aren't we compelled to say the same thing about the immortal? If the immortal is also imperishable, it's impossible for soul, whenever death attacks it, to perish. Because it follows from what's been said before that it won't admit death, nor will it be dead, just as we said that three will not be even, any more than the odd will be; and again that fire will not be cold, any more than the heat in the fire will be. "But", someone might say, "what's to prevent the odd, instead of coming to be even, as we granted it didn't, when the even attacks, from perishing, and there coming to be even in its place?" Against one who said that, we could not contend that it doesn't perish; because the uneven is not imperishable. If that had been granted us, we could easily have contended that when the even attacks, the odd and three depart and go away. And we could have contended similarly about fire and hot and the rest, couldn't we?'

'Certainly we could.'

'So now, about the immortal likewise: if it's granted us that it must also be imperishable, then soul, besides being immortal, would also be imperishable; but if not, another argument would be needed.'

'But there's no need of one, on that score at least. Because it could hardly be that anything else wouldn't admit destruction if the immortal, being everlasting, is going to admit destruction.'

'Well God anyway,' said Socrates, 'and the form of life itself, and anything else immortal there may be, never perish, as would, I think, be agreed by everyone.'

'Why yes, to be sure; by all human beings and still more, I imagine, by gods.'

'Then, given that the immortal is also indestructible, wouldn't soul, if it proves to be immortal, be imperishable as well?'

'It absolutely must be imperishable.'

'Then when death attacks a person, the mortal part, it seems, dies; whereas the immortal part gets out of the way of death, departs, and goes away intact and undestroyed.'

'It appears so.'

'Beyond all doubt then, Cebes, soul is immortal and imperishable, and our souls really will exist in Hades.'

'Well, Socrates, for my part I've no further objection, nor can I doubt the arguments at any point. But if Simmias here or anyone else has anything to say, he'd better not keep silent; as I know of no future occasion to which anyone wanting to speak or hear about such things could put it off.'

'Well no,' said Simmias; 'nor have I any further ground for doubt myself, as far as the arguments go; though in view of the size of the subject under discussion, and having a low regard for human weakness, I'm bound to retain some doubt in my mind about what's been said.'

'Not only that, Simmias,' said Socrates; 'what you say is right, so the initial hypotheses, even if they're acceptable to you people, should still be examined more clearly: if you analyse them adequately, you will, I believe, follow the argument to the furthest point to which a human being can follow it up; and if you get that clear, you'll seek nothing further.'

'What you say is true.'

'Now to insist that those things are just as I've related them would not be fitting for a man of intelligence; but that either that or something like it is true about our souls and their dwellings, given that the soul evidently is immortal, that, I think, is fitting and worth risking, for one who believes that it is so—for a noble risk it is—so one should repeat such things to oneself like a spell; which is just why I've so prolonged the tale. For those reasons, then, any man should have confidence for his own soul, who during his life has rejected the pleasures of the body and its adornments as alien, thinking they do more harm than good, but has devoted himself to the pleasures of learning, and has decked his soul with no alien adornment, but with its own, with temperance and justice, bravery, liberality, and truth, thus awaiting the journey he will make to Hades, whenever destiny shall summon him. Now as for you, Simmias and Cebes and the rest, you will make your several journeys at some future time, but for myself, "e'en now", as a tragic hero might say, "destiny doth summon me"; and it's just about time I made for the bath: it really seems better to take a bath before drinking the poison, and not to give the women the trouble of washing a dead body.'

b When he'd spoken, Crito said: 'Very well, Socrates: what instructions have you for these others or for me, about your children or about anything else? What could we do, that would be of most service to you?'

'What I'm always telling you, Crito,' said he, 'and nothing very new: if you take care for yourselves, your actions will be of service to me and mine, and to yourselves too, whatever they may be, even if you make no promises now; but if you take no care for yourselves, and are unwilling to pursue your lives along the tracks, as it were, marked by our present and earlier discussions, then even if you make many firm promises at this time, you'll do no good at all.'

'Then we'll strive to do as you say,' he said; 'but in what fashion are we to bury you?'

'However you wish,' said he; 'provided you catch me, that is, and I don't get away from you.' And with this he laughed quietly, looked towards us and said: 'Friends, I can't persuade Crito that I am Socrates here, the one who is now conversing and arranging each of the things being discussed; but he imagines I'm that dead body he'll see in a little while, so he goes and asks how he's to bury me! But as for the great case I've been arguing all this time, that when I drink the poison, I shall no longer remain with you, but shall go off and depart for some happy state of the blessed, this, I think, I'm putting to him in vain, while comforting you and myself alike. So please stand surety for me with Crito, the opposite surety to that which he stood for me with the judges: his guarantee was that I would stay behind, whereas you must guarantee that, when I die, I shall not stay behind, but shall go off and depart; then Crito will bear it more easily, and when he sees the burning or interment of my body, he won't be distressed for me, as if I were suffering dreadful things, and won't say at the funeral that it is Socrates they are laying out or bearing to the grave or interring. Because you can be sure, my dear Crito, that misuse of words is not only troublesome in itself, but actually has a bad effect on the soul. Rather, you should be of good cheer, and say you are burying my body; and bury it however you please, and think most proper.'

After saying this, he rose and went into a room to take a bath, and Crito followed him but told us to wait. So we waited, talking among ourselves about what had been said and reviewing it, and then again dwelling on how great a misfortune had befallen us, simply thinking of it as if we were deprived of a father and would lead the rest of our life as orphans. After he'd bathed and his children had been brought to him—he had two little sons and one big one—and those women of his household had come, he talked with them in Crito's presence, and gave certain directions as to his wishes; he then told the women and children to leave, and himself returned to us.

By now it was close to sunset, as he'd spent a long time inside. So he came and sat down, fresh from his bath, and there wasn't much talk after that. Then the prison official came in, stepped up to him and said, 'Socrates, I shan't reproach you as I reproach others for being angry with me and cursing, whenever by order of the rulers I direct them to drink the poison. In your time here I've known you for the most generous and gentlest and best of men who have ever come to this place; and now especially, I feel sure it isn't with me that you're angry, but with others, because you know who are responsible. Well now, you know the message I've come to bring: goodbye, then, and try to bear the inevitable as easily as you can.' And with this he turned away in tears, and went off.

Socrates looked up at him and said: 'Goodbye to you too, and we'll do as you say.' And to us he added: 'What a civil man he is! Throughout my time here he's been to see me, and sometimes talked with me, and been the best of fellows; and now how generous of him to weep for me! But come on, Crito, let's obey him: let someone bring in the poison, if it has been prepared; if not, let the man prepare it.'

Crito said: 'But Socrates, I think the sun is still on the mountains and hasn't yet gone down. And besides, I know of others who've taken the draught long after the order had been given them, and after dining well and drinking plenty, and even in some cases enjoying themselves with those they fancied. Be in no hurry, then: there's still time left.'

Socrates said: 'It's reasonable for those you speak of to do those things—because they think they gain by doing them; for myself, it's reasonable not to do them; because I think I'll gain nothing by taking the draught a little later: I'll only earn my own ridicule by clinging to life, and being sparing when there's nothing more left. Go on now; do as I ask, and nothing else.'

Hearing this, Crito nodded to the boy who was standing nearby. The boy went out, and after spending a long time away he returned, bringing the man who was going to administer the poison, and was carrying it ready-pounded in a cup. When he saw the man, Socrates said: 'Well, my friend, you're an expert in these things: what must one do?'

'Simply drink it,' he said, 'and walk about till a heaviness comes over your legs; then lie down, and it will act of itself.' And with this he held out the cup to Socrates.

He took it perfectly calmly, Echecrates, without a tremor, or any change of colour or countenance; but looking up at the man, and fixing him with his customary stare, he said: 'What do you say to pouring someone a libation from this drink? Is it allowed or not?'

'We only prepare as much as we judge the proper dose, Socrates,' he said.

'I understand,' he said; 'but at least one may pray to the gods, and so one should, that the removal from this world to the next will be a happy one; that is my own prayer: so may it be.' With these words he pressed the cup to his lips, and drank it off with good humour and without the least distaste.

Till then most of us had been fairly well able to restrain our tears; but when we saw he was drinking, that he'd actually drunk it, we could do so no longer. In my own case, the tears came pouring out in spite of myself, so that I covered my face and wept for myself—

not for him, no, but for my own misfortune in being deprived of such a man for a companion. Even before me, Crito had moved away, when he was unable to restrain his tears. And Apollodorus, who even earlier had been continuously in tears, now burst forth into such a storm of weeping and grieving, that he made everyone present break down except Socrates himself.

But Socrates said: 'What a way to behave, my strange friends! Why, it was mainly for that reason that I sent the women away, so that they shouldn't make this sort of trouble; in fact, I've heard one should die in silence. Come now, calm yourselves and have strength.'

When we heard this, we were ashamed and checked our tears. He walked about, and when he said that his legs felt heavy he lay down on his back—as the man told him—and then the man, this one who'd given him the poison, felt him, and after an interval examined his feet and legs; he then pinched his foot hard and asked if he could feel it, and Socrates said not. After that he felt his shins once more; and moving upwards in this way, he showed us that he was becoming cold and numb. He went on feeling him, and said that when the coldness reached his heart, he would be gone.

By this time the coldness was somewhere in the region of his abdomen, when he uncovered his face—it had been covered over—and spoke; and this was in fact his last utterance: 'Crito,' he said 'we owe a cock to Asclepius: please pay the debt, and don't neglect it.'

'It shall be done,' said Crito; 'have you anything else to say?'

To this question he made no answer, but after a short interval he stirred, and when the man uncovered him his eyes were fixed; when he saw this, Crito closed his mouth and his eyes.

And that, Echecrates, was the end of our companion, a man who, among those of his time we knew, was—so we should say—the best, the wisest too, and the most just.

STUDY QUESTIONS: PLATO, *PHAEDO*

1. As Socrates rubs his leg, he comments what an odd thing pleasure is. What does he say about it?
2. Why, according to Socrates, should a person who has spent his life in philosophy feel confident when about to die?
3. How does Socrates define 'death'? Why is this definition important?
4. Why does Socrates think that after death the soul shall know the truth?
5. Why is practicing philosophy the cultivation of dying?
6. Socrates says that whatever has an opposite comes to be only from its opposite. How does he support this thesis? How does he use this thesis?
7. What is Plato's argument concerning equality in favor of the existence of Forms?
8. What is required to be able to perceive two sticks as equal? How does that demonstrate the existence of the soul?
9. What affinities does Plato point to between the Forms and the soul? For what purpose does he draw our attention to those affinities?
10. Why does Plato define the soul as the principle of life?
11. What argumentative purpose does that definition serve?
12. According to the view expressed in the *Phaedo*, if there were no immortal soul, what would the implications be for morality?

SYMPOSIUM

The *Symposium* consists in an account of a dinner party, held in 416 B.C., at which the distinguished guests discussed the nature of love. Apollodorus reports to an unnamed friend about the conversations as heard by Aristodemus, who was present at the party.

At the party, Eryximachus proposes that each of the guests should give a speech in praise of love. The speeches were delivered by Phaedrus, Pausanias, Eryximachus, Aristophanes, Agathon, and, finally, Socrates. At the end of Socrates' speech, Alcibiades enters with some drunken friends, and he is also invited to give a speech. He replies that he will speak in favor of Socrates, and he praises his friend in laudatory terms. Finally, more drunken people arrive at the party, and, after a while, Aristodemus falls asleep. When he awakes in the morning, he finds Agathon, Aristophanes, and Socrates still drinking and talking. The heart of the dialogue is Socrates' speech, which we have reproduced here, together with the speech of Alcibiades. The dialogue was probably written around 385 B.C.

After a rhetorical speech by the poet Agathon, Socrates declares that he will not engage in a contest of rhetorical skill but that he will make a plain statement about love. After quizzing Agathon, Socrates delivers his speech, which consists in a report of a dialogue between him and a woman, called Diotima. Diotima describes love as an intermediary or bridge between the world of the Forms and that of sensible objects. The object of love is always beauty, and beautiful things in the sensible world lead the lover to seek the Form of Beauty itself, which is identical to the Form of the Good. The contemplation of the Beautiful is a mystical experience, which Plato describes toward the end of the speech. Love itself cannot be identified with the Beautiful or the Good, because when love has attained its true

Plato, from *Symposium* (1994), edited by Robin Waterfield (Translator).

goal, it lies halfway between the Beautiful and the Ugly, in much the same way that true opinion is halfway between wisdom and ignorance.

The significance of Alcibiades' speech is a little contentious. Is the main point that the speech reveals Socrates' indifference to interpersonal love, a detachment that is necessary to attain higher love of the Form of Beauty? Or, perhaps, is Plato showing us through Alcibiades that real love must be first of an individual person rather than primarily of a Form?

201d 'Anyway, I'll leave you in peace now. But there's an account of Love which I heard from a woman called Diotima, who came from Mantinea and was an expert in love, as well as in a large number of other areas too. For instance, on one occasion when the Athenians performed their sacrificial rites to ward off the plague, she delayed the onset of the disease for ten years. She also taught me the ways of love, and I'll try to repeat for you what she told me. I'll base myself on the conclusions Agathon and I reached, but I'll see if I can manage on my own now.

'As you explained, Agathon, it's important to start with a description of Love's nature and e characteristics, before turning to what he does. I think the easiest way for me to do this is to repeat the account the woman from Mantinea once gave me in the course of a question-and-answer session we were having. I'd been saying to her, in my own words, almost exactly what Agathon was just saying to me—that Love is an important god and must be accounted attractive. She used the same arguments I used on him to prove that it actually followed from my own ideas that Love *wasn't* attractive or good.

'"What?" I exclaimed. "Do you mean to tell me, Diotima, that Love is repulsive and bad?"

'"You should be careful what you say," she replied. "Do you think that anything which isn't attractive has to be repulsive?"

202a '"Yes, I certainly do."

'"Do you also think that lack of knowledge is the same as ignorance? Haven't you noticed that there's middle ground between knowledge and ignorance?"

'"What middle ground?"

'"True belief," she replied. "Don't you realize that, as long as it isn't supported by a justification, true belief isn't knowledge (because you

must be able to explain what you know), but isn't ignorance either (because ignorance can't have *any* involvement with the truth of things)? In fact, of course, true belief is what I said it was, an intermediate area between knowledge and ignorance."

'"You're right," I said.

b '"Stop insisting, then, that 'not attractive' is the same as 'repulsive', or that 'not good' is the same as 'bad'. And the you'll also stop thinking that, just because—as you yourself have conceded—Love isn't good or attractive, he therefore has to be repulsive and bad. He might fall between these extremes."

'"Still, everyone agrees that he's an important god," I said.

'"Do you mean every expert, or are you counting non-experts too?" she asked.

'"Absolutely everyone."

'Diotima smiled and said, "But how could people who deny that he's even a god admit that c he's an important god, Socrates?"

'"Who are you talking about?" I asked.

'"You for one," she said, "and I'm another."

'"How can you say that?" I demanded.

'"Easily," she said, "as you'll see if you answer this question. Don't you think that good fortune and beauty are attributes which belong to every single god? Can you really see yourself claiming that any god fails to be attractive and to have an enviable life?"

'"No, of course I wouldn't," I said.

'"And isn't it when someone has good and attractive attributes that you call him enviable?"

'"Yes."

'"You've admitted, however, that it's pre-d cisely because Love lacks the qualities of goodness and attractiveness that he desires them."

'"Yes, I have."

"'But it's inconceivable that a *god* could fail to be attractive and good in any respect, isn't it?'

"'I suppose so.'

"'Can you see now that you're one of those who don't regard Love as a god?' she asked.

"'What is Love, then?' I asked. 'Mortal?'

"'Of course not.'

"'What, then?'

"'He occupies middle ground,' she replied, 'like those cases we looked at earlier; he lies between mortality and immortality.'

"'And what does that make him, Diotima?'

"'An important spirit, Socrates. All spirits occupy the middle ground between humans and e gods.'

"'And what's their function?' I asked.

"'They translate and carry messages from men to gods and from gods to men. They convey men's prayers and the gods' instructions, and men's offerings and the gods' returns on these offerings. As mediators between the two, they fill the remaining space, and so make the universe an interconnected whole. They enable divination to take place and priests to perform sacrifices and rit-
203a uals, cast spells, and do all kinds of prophecy and sorcery. Divinity and humanity cannot meet directly; the gods only ever communicate and converse with men (in their sleep or when conscious) by means of spirits. Skill in this area is what makes a person spiritual, whereas skill in any other art or craft ties a person to the material world. There are a great many different kinds of spirits, then, and one of them is Love.'

"'But who are his parents?' I asked.

b   "'That's rather a long story'' she replied, 'but I'll tell you it all the same. Once upon a time, the gods were celebrating the birth of Aphrodite, and among them was Plenty, whose mother was Cunning. After the feast, as you'd expect at a festive occasion, Poverty turned up to beg, so there she was by the gate. Now, Plenty had got drunk on nectar (this was before the discovery of wine) and he'd gone into Zeus' garden, collapsed, and fallen asleep. Prompted by her lack of means, Poverty came up with the idea of having a child by Plenty, so she lay with him and became preg-
c nant with Love. The reason Love became Aphrodite's follower and attendant, then, is that he was conceived during her birthday party; also, he is innately attracted towards beauty and Aphrodite is beautiful.

"'Now, because his parents are Plenty and Poverty, Love's situation is as follows. In the first place, he never has any money, and the usual notion that he's sensitive and attractive is quite wrong: he's a vagrant, with tough, dry skin and
d no shoes on his feet. He never has a bed to sleep on, but stretches out on the ground and sleeps in the open in doorways and by the roadside. He takes after his mother in having need as a constant companion. From his father, however, he gets his ingenuity in going after things of beauty and value, his courage, impetuosity, and energy, his skill at hunting (he's constantly thinking up captivating stratagems), his desire for knowledge, his resourcefulness, his lifelong pursuit of education, and his skills with magic, herbs, and words.

e   "'He isn't essentially either immortal or mortal. Sometimes within a single day he starts by being full of life in abundance, when things are going his way, but then he dies away . . . only to take after his father and come back of life again. He has an income, but it is constantly trickling away, and consequently Love isn't ever destitute, but isn't ever well off either. He also falls between knowledge and ignorance, and the reason for this is as follows. No *god* loves knowl-
204a edge or desires wisdom, because gods are already wise; by the same token, no one else who is wise loves knowledge. On the other hand, ignorant people don't love knowledge or desire wisdom either, because the trouble with ignorance is precisely that if a person lacks virtue and knowledge, he's perfectly satisfied with the way he is. If a person isn't aware of a lack, he can't desire the thing which he isn't aware of lacking.'

"'But Diotima,' I said, 'if it isn't either wise people or ignorant people who love wisdom, then who is it?'

b   "'Even a child would have realized by now that it is those who fall between wisdom and ignorance,' Diotima said, 'a category which includes Love, because knowledge is one of the most attractive things there is, and attractive things are Love's province. Love is bound, therefore, to love knowledge, and anyone who loves knowledge is bound to fall between knowledge and ignorance. Again, it's the circumstances of his birth which are responsible for this feature of his, given that his father is clever and resourceful and his mother has neither quality.

c "'There you are, then, my dear Socrates: that's what Love is like. Your conception of Love didn't surprise me at all, though. In so far as I can judge by your words, you saw Love as an object of love, rather than as a lover; that would explain why you imagined that Love was so attractive. I mean, it's true that a lovable object has to be blessed with beauty, charm, perfection and so on, but a lover comes from a different mould, whose characteristics I've described.'

"'Well, Diotima,' I remarked, 'I like what you're saying, but if that's what Love is like, what do we humans gain from him?'

d "'That's the next point for me to try to explain, then, Socrates,' she said. 'I mean, we've covered Love's nature and parentage, but there's also the fact that, according to you, he loves beauty. Suppose we were to be asked, "Can you two tell me in what sense Love loves attractive things?" or, more clearly, "A lover loves attractive things—but why?"

"'Because he wants them to be his,' I suggested.

"'But your answer begs another question,' she pointed out. 'What will a person gain if he gets these attractive things?'

'I confessed that I didn't find that a particularly easy question to answer and she went on, e 'Well, suppose the questioner changed tack and phrased his question in terms of goodness instead of attractiveness. Suppose he asked, "Now then, Socrates, a lover loves good things—but why?"'

"'He wants them to be his,' I replied.

"'And what will a person gain if he gets these good things?'

"'That's a question I think I can cope with better,' I said. 'He'll be happy.'

205a "'The point being that it's the possession of good things that makes people happy,' she said, 'and there's no need for a further question about a person's reasons for wanting to be happy. Your answer seems conclusive.'

"'That's right,' I said.

"'Now, do you think this desire, this love, is common to all of us? Do you think everyone wants good things to be his for ever, or do you have a different view?'

"'No,' I said. 'I think it's common to everyone.'

"'But if everyone loves the same thing, and always does so, Socrates,' she said, 'why don't we describe everyone as a lover, instead of using b the term selectively, for some people but not for others?'

"'Yes, that *is* odd, isn't it?' I said.

"'Not really,' she replied. 'What we do, in fact, is single out a particular kind of love and apply to it the term which properly belongs to the whole range. We call *it* "love" and use other terms for other kinds of love.'

"'Can you give me an analogy?' I asked.

"'Yes, here's one. As you know, there are all kinds of creativity. It's always creativity, after all, which is responsible for something coming into existence when it didn't exist before. And it fol- c lows that all artefacts are actually creations or poems and that all artisans are creators or poets.'

"'Right.'

"'As you also know, however,' she went on, 'artisans are referred to in all sorts of ways, not exclusively as poets. Just one part of the whole range of creativity, the part whose domain is music and metre, has been singled out and has gained the name of the whole range. The term "poetry" is reserved for it alone, and it's only those with cre- ativity in this sense who are called "poets".'

"'You're right,' I said.

"'The same goes for love. Basically, it's d always the case that the desire for good and for happiness is everyone's "dominant, deceitful love". But there are a wide variety of ways of expressing this love, and those who follow other routes—for instance, business, sport, or philosophy—aren't said to be in love or to be lovers. The terminology which properly applies to the whole range is used only of those who dedicate themselves to one particular manifestation—which is called "love" and "being in love", while they're called "lovers".'

"'I suppose you're right,' I said.

"'Now,' she continued, 'what of the idea one hears that people in love are looking for

their other halves? What I'm suggesting, by con-
e trast, my friend, is that love isn't a search for a
half or even a whole unless the half or the
whole happens to be good. I mean, we're even
prepared to amputate our arms and legs if we
think they're in a bad state. It's only when a person describes what he's got as good and what he
hasn't got as bad that he's capable of being content with what belongs to him. In other words,
the sole object of people's love is goodness. Do
206a you agree?"

'"Definitely," I said.

'"So," she said, "the simple truth of the matter is that people love goodness. Yes?"

'"Yes," I answered.

'"But hadn't we better add that they want to
get goodness for themselves?" she asked.

'"Yes."

'"And that's not all: there's also the fact that
they want goodness to be their *for ever*," she said.

'"Yes, we'd better add that too."

'"To sum up, then," she said, "the object of
love is the permanent possession of goodness for
oneself."

'"You're absolutely right," I agreed.

b '"Now since this is Love's purpose in *all* his
manifestations," she said, "we need to ask under
what conditions and in what sphere of activity
the determination and energy of people with this
purpose may be called love. What does love actually do? Can you tell me?"

'"Of course not, Diotima," I said. "If I could, I
wouldn't be so impressed by your knowledge. This
is exactly what I come to *you* to learn about."

'"All right," she said. "I'll tell you. Love's
purpose is physical and mental procreation in an
attractive medium."

'"I don't understand what you mean," I said.
"I need a diviner to interpret it for me."

c '"All right," she said. "I'll speak more
plainly. The point is, Socrates, that every human
being is both physically and mentally pregnant.
Once we reach a certain point in the prime of
our lives, we instinctively desire to give birth, but
we find it possible only in an attractive medium,
not a repulsive one—and yes, sex between a man
and a woman is a kind of birth. It's a divine business; it is immortality in a mortal creature, this

matter of pregnancy and birth. But it can't take
place where there's incompatibility, and whereas
repulsiveness is incompatible with anything
d divine, beauty is compatible with it. So Beauty
plays the parts of both Fate and Eileithyia at
childbirth. That's why proximity to beauty makes
a pregnant person obliging, happy, and relaxed,
and so we procreate and give birth. Proximity to
repulsiveness, however, makes us frown, shrink
in pain, back off, and withdraw; no birth takes
place, but we retain our children unborn and suffer badly. So the reason why, when pregnant and
swollen, ready to burst, we get so excited in the
presence of beauty is that the bearer of beauty
e releases us from our agony. You see, Socrates,"
she concluded, "the object of love is not beauty,
as you imagine."

'"What is it, then?"

'"It is birth and procreation in a beautiful
medium."

'"All right," I said.

'"It certainly is," she said. "Why procreation? Because procreation is as close as a mortal
can get to being immortal and undying. Given
our agreement that the aim of love is the
207a *permanent* possession of goodness for oneself, it
necessarily follows that we desire immortality
along with goodness, and consequently the aim
of love has to be immortality as well."

'You can see how much I learned from what
she said about the ways of love. Moreover, she
once asked me, "Socrates, what do you think
causes this love and desire? I mean, you can see
what a terrible state animals of all kinds—beasts
and birds—get into when they're seized by the
desire for procreation. Their behaviour becomes
b manic under the influence of love. First, all they
want is sex with one another, then all they want
is to nurture their offspring. The weakest creatures are ready to fight even the strongest ones to
the death and to sacrifice themselves for their
young; they'll go to any lengths, including
extreme starvation, if that's what it takes to nurture their young. If it were only human beings "
she pointed out, "you might think this be⌐
was based on reason; but what causes ⸏
behave this way under the influence of l⸏
c you explain it?"

'When I said that I had no idea, she asked, "How do you expect to become an expert in the ways of love if you don't understand this?"

'"But that's exactly why I come to you, Diotima, as I've told you before, because I'm aware of my need for teachers. So will you explain it to me, please—and also anything else I need to know about the ways of love?"

'"Well," she said, "provided you're confident about the view we've expressed time and again about what love aims for, you shouldn't be surprised to hear that the same argument applies to animals as to humans: mortal nature does all it can to achieve immortality and live for ever. Its sole resource for this is the ability of reproduction constantly to replace the past generation with a new one. I mean, even during the period when any living creature is said to be a living creature and not to change . . . you know how we say that someone is the same person from childhood all the way up to old age. Although we say this, a person in fact never possesses the same attributes, but is constantly being renewed and constantly losing other qualities; this goes for his hair, flesh, bones, blood, and body in general. But it's not just restricted to the body: no one's mental characteristics, traits, beliefs, desires, delights, troubles, or fears ever remain the same: they come and go. But what is far more extraordinary even than this is the fact that our knowledge comes and goes as well: we gain some pieces of information and lose others. The implication of this is not just that *we* don't remain the same for ever as far as our knowledge is concerned either, but that exactly the same thing happens to every single item of information. What we call 'practice', for instance, exists because knowledge leaks away. Forgetfulness is the leakage of information, and practice is the repeated renewal of vanishing information in one's memory, which preserves the knowledge. This is what makes the knowledge *appear* to be the same as before.

'"The point is that the continued existence of any mortal creature does not involve its remaining absolutely unchanging for all time—only gods do that. Instead, as its attributes pass away and age, they leave behind a new generation of attributes which resemble the old ones.

This process is what enables mortal life—a body or whatever—to share in immortality, Socrates, but immortal beings do things differently. So you shouldn't be surprised if everything instinctively values its own offspring: it is immortality which makes this devotion, which is love, a universal feature."

'In fact, I did find what she'd said surprising, so I said, "Well, you're the expert, Diotima, but is what you've been telling me really so?"

'She answered like a true sophist and said, "You can be sure of it, Socrates. I mean, you can see the same principle at work in men's lives too, if you take a look at their status-seeking. You'll be surprised at your stupidity if you fail to appreciate the point of what I've been saying once you've considered how horribly people behave when they're under the influence of love of prestige and they long to 'store up fame immortal for ever'. Look how they're even more willing to face danger for the sake of fame than they are for their children; look how they spend money, endure any kind of hardship, sacrifice their lives. Do you really think that Alcestis would have died for Admetus, that Achilles would have joined Patroclus in death, or that your Athenian hero Codrus would have died in defence of his sons' kingdom, if they didn't think their courage would be remembered for ever, as in fact it is by us? No, they certainly wouldn't," she said. "I'm not sure that the prospect of undying virtue and fame of this kind isn't what motivates people to do anything, and that the better they are, the more this is their motivation. The point is, they're in love with immortality.

'"Now, when men are *physically* pregnant," she continued, "they're more likely to be attracted to women; their love manifests in trying to gain immortality, renown, and what they take to be happiness by producing children. Those who are *mentally* pregnant, however . . . I mean, there are people whose minds are far more pregnant than their bodies; they're filled with the offspring you might expect a mind to bear and produce. What offspring? Virtue, and especially wisdom. For instance, there are the creations brought into the world by the poets and any craftsmen who count as having done original work, and then there's the most important and attractive kind of wisdom by far, the kind which enables people to manage political and domestic affairs—in other words, self-discipline and justice. And here's another case: when someone's b mind has been pregnant with virtue from an early age and he's never had a partner, then once he reaches adulthood, he longs to procreate and give birth, and so he's another one, in my opinion, who goes around searching for beauty, so that he can give birth there, since he'll never do it in an unattractive medium. Since he's pregnant, he prefers physical beauty to ugliness, and he's particularly pleased if he comes across a mind which is attractive, upright, and gifted at the same time. This is a person he immediately finds he can talk fluently to about virtue and about what qualities and practices it takes for a man to be good. In short, he takes on this per-c son's education.

'"What I'm saying, in other words, is that once he's come into contact with an attractive person and become intimate with him, he produces and gives birth to the offspring he's been pregnant with for so long. He thinks of his partner all the time, whether or not he's there, and together they share in raising their offspring. Consequently, this kind of relationship involves a far stronger bond and far more constant affection than is experienced by people who are united by ordinary children, because the offspring of this relationship are particularly attractive and are closer to immortality than ordinary children. We'd all prefer to have children of this sort rather than the human kind, and we cast envious glances at good poets like Homer and d Hesiod because the kind of children they leave behind are those which earn their parents renown and 'fame immortal', since the children themselves are immortal. Or what about the children Lycurgus left in Sparta who maintain the integrity of Sparta and, it's hardly going too far to say, of Greece as a whole? Then there's Solon, whom you Athenians hold in high regard as the father of your constitution. All over the e world, in fact, in Greece and abroad, various men in various places have on a number of occasions engendered virtue in some form or other by cre-

ating works of beauty for public display. Quite a few of these men have even been awarded cults before now because of the immortality of their children, whereas no human child has ever yet earned his father a cult.

'"Now, it's not impossible, Socrates, that you too could be initiated into the ways of love 210a I've spoken of so far. But I don't know whether you're ready for the final grade of Watcher, which is where even the mysteries I've spoken of lead if you go about them properly. All I can do", she said, "is tell you about them, which I'm perfectly willing to do; you must try to follow as best you can.

'"The proper way to go about this business", she said, "is for someone to start as a young man by focusing on physical beauty and initially—this depends on whether his guide is giving him proper guidance—to love just one person's body and to give birth in that medium to beautiful reasoning. He should realize next that the beauty b of any one body hardly differs from that of any other body, and that if it's physical beauty he's after, it's very foolish of him not to regard the beauty of all bodies as absolutely identical. Once he's realized this and so become capable of loving every single beautiful body in the world, his obsession with just one body grows less intense and strikes him as ridiculous and petty. The next stage is for him to value mental beauty so much more than physical beauty that even if someone is almost entirely lacking the bloom of youth, but still has an attractive mind, that's enough to kindle his love and affection, and that's all he needs c to give birth to and enquire after the kinds of reasoning which help young men's moral progress. And this in turn leaves him no choice but to look at what makes people's activities and institutions attractive and to see that here too any form of beauty is much the same as any other, so that he comes to regard physical beauty as unimportant. Then, after activities, he must press on towards the things people know, until he can see the beauty there too. Now he has beauty before his eyes in abundance, no longer a d single instance of it; now the slavish love of isolated cases of youthful beauty or human beauty of any kind is a thing of the past, as is his love of some single activity. No longer a paltry and small-minded slave, he faces instead the vast sea of beauty, and in gazing upon it his boundless love of knowledge becomes the medium in which he gives birth to plenty of beautiful, expansive reasoning and thinking, until he gains enough energy and bulk there to catch sight of a unique kind of knowledge whose natural object is the kind of beauty I will now describe.

e   '"Try as hard as you can to pay attention now," she said, "because anyone who has been guided and trained in the ways of love up to this point, who has viewed things of beauty in the proper order and manner, will now approach the culmination of love's ways and will suddenly catch sight of something of unbelievable beauty—something, Socrates, which in fact gives meaning to all his previous efforts. What he'll see is, in the first place, eternal; it doesn't come to be
211a or cease to be, and it doesn't increase or diminish. In the second place, it isn't attractive in one respect and repulsive in another, or attractive at one time but not at another, or attractive in one setting but repulsive in another, or attractive here and repulsive elsewhere, depending on how people find it. Then again, he won't perceive beauty as a face or hands or any other physical feature, or as a piece of reasoning or knowledge, and he won't perceive it as being anywhere else either—in something like a creature or the earth or the heavens. No, he'll perceive it in itself and
b by itself, constant and eternal, and he'll see that every other beautiful object somehow partakes of it, but in such a way that their coming to be and ceasing to be don't increase or diminish it at all, and it remains entirely unaffected.

'"So the right kind of love for a boy can help you ascend from the things of this world until you being to catch sight of *that* beauty, and then you're almost within striking distance of the goal. The proper way to go about or be
c guided through the ways of love is to start with beautiful things in this world and always make the beauty I've been talking about the reason for your ascent. You should use the things of this world as rungs in a ladder. You start by loving one attractive body and step up to two; from

there you move on to physical beauty in general, from there to the beauty of people's activities, from there to the beauty of intellectual endeavours, and from there you ascend to that final intellectual endeavour, which is no more and no less than the study of *that* beauty, so that you finally recognize true beauty.

d   '"What else could make life worth living, my dear Socrates," the woman from Mantinea said, "than seeing true beauty? If you ever do catch sight of it, gold and clothing and good-looking boys and youths will pale into insignificance beside it. At the moment, however, you get so excited by seeing an attractive boy that you want to keep him in your sight and by your side for ever, and you'd be ready—you're far from being the only one, of course—to go without food and drink, if that were possible, and to try to survive only on the sight and presence of your beloved. How do you think someone would react, then, to the sight of beauty itself, in its perfect, immacu-
e late purity—not beauty tainted by human flesh and colouring and all that mortal rubbish, but absolute beauty, divine and constant? Do you think someone with his gaze fixed there has a miserable life? Is that what you think about
212a someone who uses the appropriate faculty to see beauty and enjoy its presence? I mean, don't you appreciate that there's no other medium in which someone who uses the appropriate faculty to see beauty can give birth to true goodness instead of phantom goodness, because it is truth rather than illusion whose company he is in? And don't you realize that the gods smile on a person who bears and nurtures true goodness and that, to the extent that any human being does, it is he who has the potential for immortality?"

b   'So there you are, Phaedrus—not forgetting the rest of you. That's what Diotima told me, and I believe her. As a believer, I try to win others as well round to the view that, in the business of acquiring immortality, it would be hard for human nature to find a better partner than Love. That's the basis of *my* claim that everyone should treat Love with reverence, and that's why I for one consider the ways of love to be very impor-tant. So I follow them exceptionally carefully myself and recommend others to do the same. It's also why, today and every day, I do all I can to praise Love's power and courage.

c 'That's my contribution, then, Phaedrus. You can think of it as a eulogy of Love if you want, or you can call it whatever you like. It's up to you.'

That was Socrates' speech. During the applause, Aristophanes was trying to get a word in, because at one point Socrates had referred to his speech, when suddenly there was a loud knocking at the front door. It sounded like people from a street-party, and they could hear a pipe-girl's voice. Agathon called over his slaves and said, 'Go and d see who it is. If it's one of my friends, invite him in, but otherwise tell them the party's over and we're off to bed.'

A short while later, they heard the sound of Alcibiades, extremely drunk, in the courtyard. He was bellowing, 'Where's Agathon? Take me to Agathon.' In he came, supported by the pipe-girl and some of the other people who were with him. He stood at the door wearing a chaplet of e leafy ivy entwined with violets, and with ribbons galore trailing over his head, and said, 'Greetings, gentlemen. Will you let someone who's drunk—very drunk, actually—join your party? If not, we'll just put a chaplet on Agathon, which is why we came, and then we'll be on our way. I couldn't come yesterday, you see, but here I am now, and I've got these ribbons on my head so that I can take them off *my* head and put them on the cleverest and most attractive man in the world, along with a public announcement to that effect. I suppose you'll laugh at me, because I'm drunk, but even if you do, it doesn't make any difference: *I* know perfectly well I'm right. 213a Come on, hurry up and tell me. Do you agree to my terms? Can I come in and join you for a drink or not?'

Everyone shouted out for him to come in and find a place on a couch, and Agathon called him over. So his friends brought him in. On the way, he started to untie the ribbons, with the intention of putting them on Agathon, and they fell over his eyes. So he didn't see Socrates, but sat next to Agathon, between him and Socrates,

b who'd moved over when he saw him coming. As soon as he was seated, he embraced Agathon and put the chaplet on him.

Agathon told his slaves to undo Alcibiades' shoes, so that he could lie on the couch. 'There's room here for three,' he said.

'Fine,' said Alcibiades. 'But who's this third person? Who have we here at the party with us?' Even while speaking, he was turning around to look. As soon as he saw Socrates, he leapt up and said, 'God, what's this? Socrates? You've been lurking there waiting for me—and this isn't the c first time: you're always suddenly popping up where I least expect to find you. What are you doing here this time? And why here, on this couch? I know: you didn't want to be next to Aristophanes and his jokes, or anyone else who might fancy himself a comedian, so you found a way to share a couch with the handsomest man at the party.'

'I need your protection, Agathon, please,' said Socrates. 'You can't imagine what a nuisance my love for this man has become. Ever since the start of our affair, I've never been able to look at d or talk to anyone attractive without him getting so jealous and resentful that he goes crazy and calls me names and comes close to beating me up. So please make sure that he doesn't get up to anything tonight. Perhaps you can calm things down between us, but if not, and if he starts to get violent, please protect me from him, because he gets insanely attached to his lovers, and it terrifies me.'

'There's no chance of peace between us,' Alcibiades said. 'Anyway, I'll pay *you* back later e for what you've been saying, but for now can you give me back some of the ribbons, please, Agathon, so that I can make a chaplet for his head too? And what a wonderful head! Otherwise, he'll tell me off for making one for you, but not for him, despite the fact that he beats all comers every day in battles of words, not just yesterday like you.'

With these words, he took back some of the ribbons and made a chaplet for Socrates. Then he lay down on the couch, and once he'd settled down, he said, 'Well now, gentlemen, you look sober to me, and that's not allowed. You have to drink, because that was part of our agreement. We need somebody to take charge of your drinking and decide when you've had enough, and I elect—me! Have a big goblet brought in, won't you, Agathon, if you've got one? Oh no, don't bother. Hey you, slave, bring over that cooler.'

He'd spotted a cooler with a capacity of 214a more than eight *kotylai*, and once it had been filled up, he first drained it himself and then told the slave to fill it for Socrates, while commenting, 'Not that this ploy of mine will do any good as far as Socrates is concerned. It doesn't matter how much you tell him to drink, he drinks it all down without ever getting drunk.'

When the slave had filled it up, and while Socrates was drinking, Eryximachus said, 'What's going on here, Alcibiades? Are we just going to gulp drinks down like this, as if we had thirsts to b quench? We could at least make conversation or sing some songs as we drink.'

'Hello there, Eryximachus,' said Alcibiades, 'most noble son of a noble—and temperate—sire.'

'And hello to you too,' Eryximachus replied. 'But what would you have us do?'

'Whatever you suggest,' said Alcibiades. 'We ought to do as you say, "for a healer's worth is that of many men". So we're yours to command.'

'All right,' said Eryximachus. 'Here's what I suggest. Before you arrived, we'd decided that each of us should take turns, going around from c left to right, to speak as well as he could in praise of Love. Now, all the rest of us have already spoken, so it's only fair, since you haven't had a turn (except at drinking), that you should deliver a speech. Then, when you've finished, you can choose a task to set Socrates, then he can do the same for the person on his right, and so on.'

'What a good idea, Eryximachus!' Alcibiades said. 'But I don't think it's fair to pit someone who's drunk against speeches delivered by sober men. Also, you don't believe a word of what Socrates was saying a moment ago, do you? I d mean, the truth is exactly the opposite of what he said, you know. It's *he* who'll beat me up if I praise anyone except him—even a god, let alone another human being—when he's around.'

'Be careful what you say,' Socrates said.

'No, I won't have you trying to talk me out of it,' said Alcibiades. 'I swear I'm not going to deliver a eulogy to anyone else while you're around.'

'All right, then,' Eryximachus said, 'Go ahead, if you want. Let's hear your eulogy of Socrates!'

'What?' Alcibiades exclaimed. 'Do you think e I should, Eryximachus? Shall I lay into him and pay him back in front of all of you?'

'Hang on,' Socrates said. 'What are you planning to do—deliver a kind of mock eulogy of me, or what?'

'I'll tell the truth—if you'll let me do that.'

'Of course I'll let you tell the truth,' Socrates said. 'In fact, I insist that you do.'

'Here I go, then,' said Alcibiades. 'I'll tell you what you can do, Socrates. If anything I say isn't true, you can interrupt, if you want, and show that what I'm saying is wrong. Not that I intend any of what I'm going to say to be untrue. But don't be 215a surprised if I don't remember things in the right order: it isn't easy for someone in my condition to list all the aspects of your extraordinary nature and fluently tick them off, one after another.

'I'm going to use some imagery to help me praise Socrates, gentlemen. *He* might think I'm going for comic effect, but actually the point of the imagery will be the truth, not mockery. It's my considered opinion, you see, that he's just like those Sileni you find sitting in sculptors' shops, b the ones they make holding wind-pipes or reed-pipes, which when opened up are found to contain effigies of gods inside. Alternatively, I could compare his to Marsyas, the Satyr. Now, even you can't deny that you *look* like these figures, Socrates, but what you're about to hear is how you resemble them in other respects as well.

'You treat people brutally—now, don't try to deny it. If you do, I'll call up witnesses. But you don't play the pipes? No, because you're far more extraordinary than Marsyas. He had to use an c instrument to charm people with his oral abilities, and even now anyone who plays his pipes—I'm counting Olympus' pipe-playing as really attributable to Marsyas, because Marsyas was

Olympus' teacher. . . . Anyway, whether his pipes are played by an expert player or a worthless pipe-girl, there's no other instrument which is so divine that it's capable of casting a spell over people and of showing who is reaching for the gods and is ready for initiation. The only difference between you and Marsyas is that *you* don't need any instrument: you produce the same effect with plain words! What I mean is this. If d we're listening to even a first-rate speech from someone else, it's hardly an exaggeration to say that none of us takes the slightest bit of notice of him; but when we hear you speaking, or listen to even a second-rate report of one of your arguments, then it doesn't matter who we are— woman, man or child—we're all overwhelmed and spellbound.

'If it weren't for the fact that you would put it down to the drink, gentlemen, I'd call on the gods to witness the truth of my account of what I personally have experienced when listening to him speak in the past—which is not to say that he doesn't still have the same effect on me even c now. Whenever I listen to him speak, I get more ecstatic then the Corybantes! My heart pounds and tears flood from my eyes under the spell of his words. I've seen him have the same effect on plenty of others too. I've heard some great speakers, including Pericles, and while I thought they did a good job, they never had that kind of effect on me, and they never disturbed my mental composure or made me dissatisfied with the slavishness of my life. This Marsyas here, however, has often changed my outlook and made me think 216a that the life I lead isn't worth living. You can't deny the truth of this, Socrates. In fact, I know perfectly well that if I allowed myself to listen to him, I wouldn't be able to resist even now, and I'd go through it all over again. You see, he forces me to admit that I busy myself with Athenian politics when I'm far from perfect and should be doing something about myself instead. So I make myself block my ears and run away, as if I were escaping the Sirens; otherwise I'd spend the rest of my life sitting there at his feet.

'He's the only person in the world in whose company I've felt something which people b wouldn't think I was capable of feeling—shame:

I feel shame before him and him alone. What happens is that although I'm perfectly well aware of the inescapable force of his recommendations as to what I should do, yet as soon as I'm away from him, I get seduced by the adulation of the masses. So I act like a runaway slave and keep away from him, and whenever I do see him, I feel ashamed because of the promises I made him. In fact, there've been quite a few occasions when I'd gladly have seen him removed from the face c of the earth, but I also know that my predominant reaction by far to that happening would be sadness, and so I just don't know how to cope with the man.

'So that's the kind of effect this Satyr here has on me, and on lots of other people too, with his piping. But I haven't finished with the ways in which he resembles the figures I compared him to, and I can give you further examples of his incredible abilities. You have to appreciate that none of you really knows him. Now that I've d started, I'll show you what he's like. The Socrates of your experience has a habit of falling in love with good-looking people, and he's constantly hanging around them in a stupor; secondly, he's completely ignorant and has no knowledge at all. Do you see how Silenus-like he looks? The resemblance is striking. The point is, this is just an outer coating, like the outside shell of those carved Sileni. But if he were opened up, my friends, you'd find him chock-full of self-control inside. I tell you, the fact that someone is attractive doesn't matter to him at all; he has an e unbelievably low opinion of that, and the same goes for wealth and any of the other advantages which are commonly regarded as enviable. None of these possessions have the slightest value, according to him, and we amount to nothing. You must appreciate that he spends his whole life pretending and playing with people.

'I don't know if any of you has seen the genuine Socrates, opened up to reveal the effigies he has inside, but I saw them once, and they struck 217a me as so divine, so glorious, so gorgeous and wonderful that—to cut a long story short—I felt I should obey him in everything. I thought he'd genuinely fallen for my charms and that this was a godsend, an amazing piece of good luck, because now, as his boyfriend, I'd be in a position to hear everything he knew. I was incredibly proud of my good looks, you see. Now, I'd never been alone with him: there was usually a slave in attendance as well. But once I'd got this idea in my mind, I dismissed the attendant and there I b was, alone with him—yes, I know, but I'm committed to telling you the whole truth, so please just listen. And Socrates, you're welcome to point out any time I stray from the truth.

'Anyway, there we were, gentlemen, the two of us together on our own. I thought he'd launch straight into the kind of conversation lovers make when they've got their boyfriends on their own, and this made me happy. But nothing like that happened at all. He talked to me in the way he always had, and at the end of the day off he went. Next, I invited him to join me in the gymnasium and we exercised together—I thought c *that* would get me somewhere! Anyway, we exercised together and wrestled together, often with no one else around . . . and do I have to spell it out? I got precisely nowhere.

'Since these tactics weren't advancing my cause at all, I decided on a direct assault, and I determined to persevere with what I'd started and to find out what was going on. So I invited him to have dinner with me—for all the world as if I were the lover and he were the boy I had designs on. He didn't rush to accept this invitation either, but he did eventually say he'd come. d The first time he came, he wanted to leave after the meal, and I let him on that occasion because I was feeling ashamed of myself. But I continued with my plan, and the next time I kept him talking far into the night after we'd finished eating, and when he felt it was time to go, I pointed out how late it was and made him stay. So he settled down to sleep on the same couch he'd used at dinner, which was next to mine. And we were the only people sleeping in the house.

'Now, it would have been all right for anyone e to have heard everything I've told you so far, but from now on you'll hear things I wouldn't have told you except that, firstly, truth comes from wine (as the saying goes), whether or not I take the slaves into consideration, and secondly, I think it would be wrong of me to pass over

Socrates' awe-inspiring behaviour when I'm supposed to be delivering a eulogy of him. Besides, I feel rather like someone who's been bitten by a snake, in the sense that people who've had this experience, are, I'm told, reluctant to talk about what it was like except to someone who has also been bitten, on the grounds that he's the only one who'll know what they went through and 218a will make allowances for any shocking actions or remarks of theirs, as having been prompted by the pain. In fact, I've been bitten by something with a far more excruciating bite than a snake, and it couldn't have attacked a more vulnerable part of me. My heart or mind—I don't know what the proper term is—has been struck and bitten by philosophy, and when philosophy seizes on the mind of a young man of calibre, it clings more fiercely than any snake and makes him do and say all sorts of things. Besides, when I look around at b people like Phaedrus, Agathon, Eryximachus, Pausanias, Aristodemus, and Aristophanes—and then there's Socrates himself and all the rest of you . . . You've *all* experienced the madness and ecstasy of philosophy, and that's why I can talk in front of you, because you'll make allowances for what I did then and what I'm going to say now. But you slaves had better batten sizeable hatches down on your ears, and the same goes for any other coarse non-initiates here.

'So anyway, gentlemen, when the lamp had c been extinguished and the slaves had left the room, I decided to cut out the frills and come right out with my thoughts. I nudged him and said, "Socrates, are you asleep?"

'"No, far from it," he answered.

'"Do you know what I've been thinking?"

'"What's that, then?"

'"I think you're in love with me," I said, "and that you're the only lover I've got who's good enough for me. You're too shy to bring it up in my company, so I'll tell you what *I* feel. I think it would be stupid of me not to gratify you in this and in anything else you want—anything that is mine to give or that I can get from my friends. d You see, there's nothing more important to me than becoming as good a person as I can, and I think no one offers more effective assistance in this than you. I'd be far more ashamed, then, of what people of intelligence would think of me if I didn't gratify someone who has so much to offer than of what the ignorant masses would think of me it I did."

'His response to my words was absolutely typical—full of mock modesty, as you'd expect. "My dear Alcibiades," he said, "it looks as though you really are no ordinary person. Suppose your opinion of me is actually true and I do somehow e have the ability to make you a better person. You must find me remarkably attractive, then, with a beauty that is infinitely superior to your own good looks. Now, if this is what you see in me, and you then try to make a deal with me which involves us trading our respective beauties, then you're planning to do quite a bit better than me out of it; you're trying to give the semblance of beauty and get truth in return. In other words, 219a this is a real 'gold for bronze' exchange you're planning. But anyway, I think you'd better have a closer look, otherwise you might make the mistake of thinking I've got something to offer. I tell you, it's only when your eyesight goes into decline that your mental vision begins to see clearly, and you've got a long way to go yet."

'"As far as I'm concerned," I replied, "my plans are no more and no less than what I've said. That leaves it up to you to decide what's best, in your opinion, for you and for me."

'"Now, *that* is a good idea," he said. "Yes, from now on we'll put our heads together and do whatever seems best. This goes for everything, not just b the issue currently facing us."

'After this conversation, I thought the shots I'd fired, so to speak, had wounded him, so I got up from my couch, and before he had time to say anything else, I put my thick cloak over him (it was winter) and lay down under his short cloak. I put my arms around this remarkable, wonderful c man—he is, you know—and lay there with him all night long. No, you can't deny the truth of this either, Socrates. And after all that, he spurned and disdained and scorned my charms so thoroughly, and treated me so brutally—and remember, gentlemen of the jury, this was something I prided myself on . . . I might as well call you "gentlemen of the jury", because you're listening to evidence of Socrates' high-handed

treatment of me. Anyway, the point is—and I call on all the gods and goddesses in heaven to witness the truth of this—that I got up the next morning, after having spent the night with d Socrates, and for all the naughtiness we'd got up to, I might as well have been sleeping with my father or an elder brother.

'What do you think my state of mind was after that? Although I felt I'd been insulted, I was full of admiration for his character, self-control, and courage. I'd never have believed such a man could exist—that I could come across such intelligence and resolve. So although I couldn't possibly feel cross with him and keep away from him, I couldn't find a way to make him mine either. I e mean, I was well aware that you'd be more likely to get a weapon through Ajax's guard than you would money through Socrates', and now he'd escaped the only trap I thought stood a chance of ensnaring him. So I didn't know what to do, and there I was: no slave has ever been more utterly in the power of any master than I was in his.

'This was the situation I was already in when we saw active service together at Potidaea and shared a mess there. Now, the first thing to point out is that there was no one better than him in the whole army at enduring hardship: it wasn't just me he showed up. Once, when we were cut off (as happens during a campaign), we had to do 220a without food and no one else could cope at all. At the same time, when there *were* plenty of provisions, he was better than the rest of us at making the most of them, and especially when it came to drinking: he was reluctant to drink, but when pushed he proved more than a match for everyone. And the most remarkable thing of all is that no one has ever seen Socrates drunk.

'Anyway, I expect he'll be tested on this point a little later tonight. Meanwhile, back to Potidaea, where the winters are terrible, but Socrates' endurance of them was miraculous. Once—and this was the most astonishing thing b he did—the cold was so terribly bitter that everyone was either staying inside or, if they did venture out, they wore an incredible amount of clothing, put shoes on, and then wrapped pieces of felt and sheepskin around their feet. Socrates, however, went out in this weather wearing only the outdoor cloak he'd usually worn earlier in the campaign as well, and without anything on his feet; but he still made his way through the ice more easily than the rest of us with our covered feet. His fellow soldiers thought he was setting himself up as superior to them, and they gave c him suspicious looks.

'So much for that episode, "but here's another exploit the indomitable man performed" once during the campaign there, and it's well worth hearing. One morning, a puzzling problem occurred to him and he stayed standing where he was thinking about it. Even when it proved intractable, he didn't give up: he just stood there exploring it. By the time it was midday, people were beginning to notice him and were telling one another in amazement that Socrates had been standing there from early in the morning deep in thought. Eventually, after their evening meal, some men from the Ionian contingent d took their pallets outside—it was summer at the time—so that they could simultaneously sleep outside where it was cool and watch out for whether he'd stand there all night as well. In fact, he stood there until after sunrise the following morning, and then he greeted the sun with a prayer and went on his way.

'Then there's his behaviour in combat; I owe him an account of this, to cover my debt. You see, during the battle which led to my being awarded the prize for valour by the commanding officers, my life was saved by one man and one man alone—Socrates. He refused to leave me e when I was wounded, and he kept my weapons and armour safe, as well as my life. I *told* the commanding officers at the time that it was you who should be awarded the prize for valour, Socrates: you won't find anything to tell me off for here, or any reason to claim I'm lying either. But the commanding officers had an eye on my status and wanted to award it to me, and you were actually more insistent than them that it should go to me rather than you.

'And that's not all, gentlemen. You should have seen Socrates during the army's hasty with-221a drawal from Delium. I was serving in the cavalry there, in fact, while Socrates was a hoplite. The army had scattered into small units, and I hap-

pened to come across Socrates trying to make his way back with Laches. As soon as I saw them, I told them not to lose heart and promised to stay with them. Now, I was even better placed to observe Socrates there than I was at Potidaea, because being on horseback I didn't have to worry so much for my own safety. The main thing I noticed was how much more self-possessed he was then Laches; secondly, it struck me how even in that situation he was walking b along just as he does here in Athens—as you put it, Aristophanes, "with head held high and eyes alert", calmly looking out for friends and enemies. Anyone could tell, even from a distance, that here was a man who would resist an attack with considerable determination. And that's why he and Laches got out of there safely, because the enemy generally don't take on someone who can remain calm during combat; they prefer to go c after people who are in headlong flight.

'There are many other remarkable things about Socrates which could feature in a eulogy, but most of the things he does could perhaps be paralleled in some other person's life. However, what's absolutely astonishing about the man is his uniqueness: there's no human being, from times past or present, who can match him. For example, you can compare Achilles to Brasidas and others, or Pericles to Nestor and Antenor (to name only two), and you can find the same kinds d of correspondences for other people. But this man here is so out of the ordinary that however hard you look you'll never find anyone from any period who remotely resembles him, and the way he speaks is just as unique as well. All you can do, in fact, is what I did, and compare him and his arguments not to any human being, but to Sileni and Satyrs.

'The point is, you see, that I forgot to mention at the beginning that his conversations too are just like those Sileni you can open up. The first time a person lets himself listen to one of e Socrates' arguments, it sounds really ridiculous. Trivial-sounding words and phrases form his arguments' outer coating, the brutal Satyr's skin. He talks of pack-asses, metal-workers, shoemakers, tanners; he seems to go on and on using the same arguments to make the same points, with

the result that ignoramuses and fools are bound to find his arguments ridiculous. But if you could
222a see them opened up, if you can get through to what's under the surface, what you'll find inside is that his arguments are the only ones in the world which make sense. And that's not all: under the surface, his arguments abound with divinity and effigies of goodness. They turn out to be extremely far-reaching, or rather they cover absolutely everything which needs to be taken into consideration on the path to true goodness.

'That's what I have to say in praise of Socrates, gentlemen—though I've included some critical comments as well, and told you how brutally he treated me. I'm not the only one, in fact, to have received this treatment from him: there's Charmides the son of Glau-
b con, Euthydemus the son of Diocles, and a great many others too. He takes people in by pretending to be their lover, and then he swaps roles and becomes their beloved instead. So I'm warning you, Agathon: don't be duped by him like this. Learn from *our* experiences and take care. You don't have to behave like the proverbial fool and experience something yourself before understanding it.'

c So that was Alcibiades' speech. People found his candour amusing, because he was evidently still in love with Socrates. And Socrates said, 'It's you who are sober, I think, Alcibiades. Otherwise, the elegance with which you surrounded and tried to conceal the underlying motive of your whole speech would have been beyond you. You just added it on at the end, as if it were an aside—as if the whole point of your speech hadn't been to
d make me and Agathon fall out with each other, because you think that I ought to love you and nobody else, and Agathon ought to be loved by you and nobody else. Well, you didn't get away with it: we saw through this Satyrical, Silenus-like play-acting of yours. My dear Agathon, he mustn't succeed: please make sure that no one comes between us.'

'I think you're probably right, Socrates,' Agathon replied. 'Did you notice how he lay
e down on the couch with you and me to either side of him? He *has* come between us, literally!

But that's the limit of his success: I'll come and lie next to you.'

'Please do,' said Socrates. 'Lie down here on the other side of me.'

'Oh God!' groaned Alcibiades. 'Look at what he puts me through! He thinks he always has to go one better than me. Come on, Socrates, you could at least let Agathon lie between us.'

'No, that's not on,' Socrates replied. 'I mean, *you*'ve delivered a eulogy of *me*, and now *I* have to deliver a eulogy of the person on my right. If Agathon moves between us, then surely he'll have to eulogize me all over again, won't he, before I've had time to eulogize him instead? No,
223a forget it, Alcibiades. Don't deprive him of the chance of having me sing his praises; I'm really looking forward to doing it.'

'Oh!' cried Agathon. 'Alcibiades, I can't possibly stay here! I really must change places, so that I can be the subject of a eulogy from Socrates!'

'This is typical,' said Alcibiades. 'When Socrates is around, nobody else gets a look-in at any attractive man. Do you see how glibly he's found a plausible reason why this handsome man should lie down next to him?'

Agathon had stood up to go and lie next to
b Socrates, when a large number of people from a street-party suddenly arrived at the front door. They found it open, because someone was just leaving, so they barged straight in to where the others were and settled themselves down on couches. Everything went utterly out of control; all there was left to do was to drink a great deal, and even that was completely unsystematic.

Aristodemus said that a few people, including Eryximachus and Phaedrus, left at this point, while he fell asleep and slept for a long time, since
c the nights were long. When he woke up, it was almost light and cocks were already crowing. Once his eyes were open, he could see that although by and large people were asleep or had gone home, Agathon, Aristophanes, and Socrates were still awake, all by themselves, and were drinking from a large bowl which they were passing round from left to right. Socrates was carrying on a conversation with them. Aristodemus said he couldn't remember most of the discussion,
d because he'd missed the start of it and anyway he

was sleepy, but the nub of it, he said, was that Socrates was trying to get them to agree that knowing how to compose comedies and knowing how to compose tragedies must combine in a single person and that a professional tragic playwright was also a professional comic playwright. They were coming round to his point of view, but they were too sleepy to follow the argument very well; Aristophanes fell asleep first and Agathon joined him after daybreak.

Now that he'd put them to sleep, Socrates got up and left. Aristodemus went with him, as usual. Socrates went to the Lyceum for a wash, spent the day as he would any other, and then went home to sleep in the evening.

STUDY QUESTIONS: PLATO, *SYMPOSIUM*

1. According to Diotima, why does Love not possess good and beautiful things? What conclusion does she draw about Love from this point?
2. Why does she say that Love is a spirit? What conclusions about the nature of Love follow from that?
3. Love is the son of Poverty and Plenty. What does that mean?
4. What is the only object of people's love?
5. Diotima asks Socrates to explain why some people are called lovers and others are not. Why does he need to explain that? How does she explain it?
6. According to Diotima, what is the function of love?
7. How does the love of immortality express itself in the life of mortals?
8. Diotima describes the correct approach to love and finally the ultimate objective of this process. What is the process toward this ultimate vision? How does Diotima describe this ultimate objective?
9. Alcibiades characterizes his speech as telling the truth. Why does Plato have him say that? What is the point of Alcibiades' speech?
10. Why does Alcibiades assert that Socrates spends his whole life pretending and playing with people?
11. What does Socrates characterize as the exchange of gold for bronze?

REPUBLIC

This is the most important dialogue of the middle period and is perhaps Plato's greatest work. The dialogue gives us an overview of Plato's grand theory from epistemology to metaphysics, and from ethics to politics and art. Plato's thought reaches its maturity in the *Republic*. He tries to resolve the fundamental ethical problems raised by Socrates without appealing to the afterlife as he had done in the *Phaedo*.

The *Republic* consists of ten books. The main unifying theme is that it is better, or more advantageous, to be just than unjust, but many other illuminating ideas revolve around this central theme. To present the overall structure of the book, here is a brief synopsis of the work as a whole, even though we provide selections from Books II–VII only.

In Book I, Plato's character Socrates tries to define justice, and fails. Some scholars think that Book I is a Socratic dialogue from the early period, later added to the other nine books of the *Republic*. Against Socrates, Thrasymachus, a Sophist, affirms that justice is not necessarily beneficial to the person who performs just actions. He defines justice as 'the advantage of the stronger' and 'the good of another.' Socrates now has a challenge to meet: to argue that justice is beneficial.

Book II defines this challenge. Glaucon and Adeimantus add to Socrates' task by arguing that one should act unjustly if one can get away with it by using the imaginary example of the ring of Gyges, which makes a person invisible. In reply, Socrates affirms that, to understand justice, we must examine it first in the case of the state (386c–369a). In other words, Plato proposes to answer the challenges concerning the just individual by examining justice and the state. He describes a model of the perfectly just city-state.

In the remainder of Book II and in Book III and IV, Plato portrays a society consisting of three groups: artisans and merchants, soldiers, and the rulers. Plato's main thesis in this part of the book is that the society he describes would be just because the three elements would be working harmoniously, each fulfilling its proper role according to its nature. The reader should beware because, at first, Plato calls the military class 'the guardians,' but later he reserves the term for the ruling class only and calls the military class 'auxilaries.' Part of Plato's discussion (376c–403c) concerns the role of poetry and myths in the education of the guardians.

In Book IV, Plato introduces the idea of a tripartite division of the soul. He argues for the principle that the same thing will not be able to undergo opposites in the same part of itself at the same time (436b). He employs this principle to conclude that the soul must have three parts: desire, emotion, and reason. He then compares the divisions of the soul with the three parts of the state, and he argues that justice for the individual also consists in the three elements of the soul working harmoniously, each fulfilling its role according to its nature (423b–436b and 441c–445e).

In Plato's political philosophy, a good political community is one that promotes the well-being of all the citizens. The basis of political power is not the consent of the governed, because people may not understand well what is in their best interests and may accept a system that is not beneficial to them. In contrast, the leaders must have such understanding, and it is their duty to educate the people. In Plato's republic, the leaders have great power, but this does not mean that they should abuse it. For this reason, Plato recommends abolishing private property and the family for the ruling class. The city-state should be designed for the happiness of all the citizens and not for just one group.

Book V begins with a controversial discussion of the status of women within the society. Around section 472, Plato begins to argue that the rulers of the society should be philosophers, or lovers of wisdom.

In Book VI, to show what a true philosopher is, Plato distinguishes between opinion and knowledge, arguing that the latter requires acquaintance with the Forms. Around section 507, he introduces his famous simile that compares the Form of the Good to the sun. The Form of the Good makes the Forms knowable, just as the sun makes physical things visible. Around 510, he uses the Divided Line analogy to describe four types of access to reality in order to clarify his distinction between knowledge and opinion.

In Book VII, Plato draws the famous analogy of the cave. He compares the situation of most people to that of prisoners in a cave who can only see things as shadows cast by torchlight. Like these prisoners, we are subject to a systematic illusion, believing that transitory ordinary objects are real, while in fact these are only the shadows of the Forms. Plato's analogy implies that the world of ordinary everyday objects is less real than that of the Forms. This shows the real importance of virtue. By coming to know the Forms, we can acquire virtue and thereby escape from the cave or from illusions.

Book VIII considers different imperfect societies and compares them to the imperfections of an individual person. For example, Plato compares the problems of an oligarchic society to the nature of an oligarchic personality or character. Book IX contains the argument that the just person would be happier than an unjust person.

In Book X, Plato discusses art. He distinguishes three uses of the word 'bed.' It can apply to the painting or image of a bed, to a physical bed, and to the Form. Plato suggests that the relation between the image and the physical bed is similar to the relation of the physical bed to the Form: in both cases, the former is less real than the latter. Only the Form is completely real. The physical bed is less real than the Form because it depends on the latter in a manner similar to the dependency of the image on the bed. Plato uses this comparison to argue that poetry and art do give us real knowledge and can corrupt the soul.

BOOK I

327a Yesterday I went down to the Piraeus with Glaucon the son of Ariston to worship the goddess and also because I wanted to see how they would conduct the festival on this, its first performance.

One our worshipping and watching were b over, we were starting to make out way back to town, when Polemarchus the son of Cephalus spotted us from a distance setting off home, and he told his slave to run over to us and tell us to wait for him.

Polemarchus soon caught up with us, and so c did Galucon's brother Adeimanuts, Niceratus the son of Nicias, and some others; they had all apparently been at the procession.

'Socrates,' Polemrchus said, 'it looks to me as though the two of you are setting off back to town.'

'That's right,' I replied.

'Well,' he said, 'do you see how many of us there are?'

'Of course.'

'You'd better choose, then,' he said, 'between overpowering us and staying here.'

It looks as though we'd better stay,' said Gloucon.

'Well, if you think so,' I said, 'then that's what we should do.'

So we went to Polemarchus' house, and there we found his brother Lysias and Euthydemus, and also Thrasymachus of Chalcedon, Charmantides of Paeania, and Cleitophon the son of Aristony-

mus. Polemarchus' father Cephalus was in the house too; I through he looked very old, but then c I hadn't seen him for quite a while.

As son as Cephalus saw me, he said hello and then went on, 'Socrates, unfortunately for us, you're not in the habit of coming down to the Piraeus.

328d   So please do as I ask: by all means spend time with these young men who are your companions, but treat us too as your friends—as your very close friends—and come here to visit us.'

'I certainly will, Cephalus,' I replied. 'I do in fact enjoy taking with very old people, because I e think we ought to learn from them. They've gone on ahead of us, as it were, on a road which we too will probably have to travel, and we ought to find out from them what the road is like—whether it is rough and hard, to easy and smooth. And I'd be especially glad to ask you your opinion about it, since you've reached the time of life the poets describe as being "on the threshold of old age". Is it a difficult period of one's life, would you say, or what?'

329a   'Of course I'll tell you my opinion, Socrates,' he said. 'You see, it's not uncommon for some of us old men of approximately the same age to get together (and so vindicate the ancient proverb!). These gatherings are invariably used for grumbling, by those who miss the pleasures of youth. They remind themselves of their love lives, drinking, feasting, and the like, and consequently complain of having been robbed of

(Pending) *Plato: Republic*, translated by Robin Waterfield, Oxford University Press, 1993.

things that are important and claim that in those days they used to live well, whereas nowadays they aren't even alive.

But in the past I, at any rate, have met others like myself who do not feel this way. In particular, I was once with Sophocles the poet c when someone asked him, "How do you feel about sex, Sophocles? Are you still capable of having sex with a woman?" He replied, "Be quiet, man! To my great delight, I have broken free of that, like a slave who has got away from a rabid and savage master." I thought at the time that this was a good response, and I haven't changed my mind. I mean, there's no doubt that in old age you get a great deal of peace and freedom from things like sex. When the desires lose their intensity and ease up, then what happens is absolutely as Sophocles described—freedom d from a great many demented masters. However, the one thing responsible for this, and for one's relationship with relatives as well, is not a person's old age, Socrates, but his character. If someone is self-disciplined and good-tempered, old age isn't too much of a burden; otherwise, it's not just a question of old age, Socrates—such a person will find life difficult when he's young as well.'

I was filled with admiration for him and his e words, and because I wanted him to continue, I tried to provoke him by saying, 'Cephalus, I think that most people would react to what you're saying with scepticism; they'd think that you're finding old age easy to bear not because of your character, but because of your great wealth. The rich have many consolations, they say.'

'You're right,' he said, 'they are sceptical. And they do have a point, though not as important a point as they imagine.

It's true that a good man wouldn't find old age particularly easy to bear if he were poor, but it's also true that a bad man would never be content with himself even if he were wealthy.'

d 'Yes,' I said. 'But there's another question I wanted to ask you. What do you think is the greatest benefit you've gained from being rich?'

'Something which many people might find implausible,' he answered. 'You see, Socrates, when thoughts of death start to impinge on a person's mind, he entertains fears and worries about things which never occurred to him before.

Anyone who discovers that during his life he has committed a lot of crimes wakes up constantly in terror from his dreams, as children do, and also lives in dread; on the other hand, any-331a one who is aware of no wrong in himself faces the future with confidence and optimism which, as Pindar says as well, "comforts him in old age". To my mind, Socrates, he expresses it beautifully when he says that anyone who has spent his life behaving morally and justly has "Sweet hope as a companion, joyfully fostering his heart, comforting him in old age—hope which steers, more than anything else does, men's fickle intention." This is incredibly well put. And this is the context in which I value the possession of money so highly—at least for a decent, orderly person. I b mean, the possession of money has a major role to play if one is to avoid cheating or lying against one's better judgement, and also avoid the fear of leaving this life still owing some ritual offerings to a god or some money to someone.

c 'A thoroughly commendable sentiment, Cephalus,' I said. 'But what about this thing you mentioned, doing right? Shall we say that it is, without any qualification, truthfulness and giving back anything one has borrowed from someone? Or might the performance of precisely these actions sometimes be right, but sometimes wrong? This is the kind of thing I mean. I'm sure everyone would agree that if you'd borrowed weapons from a friend who was perfectly sane, but he went insane and then asked for the weapons back, you shouldn't give them back, and if you were to give them back you wouldn't be doing right, and neither would someone who was ready to tell the whole truth to a person like that.'

d 'You're right,' he agreed.

'It follows that this isn't the definition of morality, to tell the truth and to give back whatever one has borrowed.'

'Yes, it is, Socrates,' Polemarchus interjected. 'At least, it is if we're to believe Simonides.' Thrasymachus bellowed out for all to 336c hear, 'What a lot of drivel, Socrates! Why are you deferentially bowing and scraping to each other like simpletons? If you really want to know what morality is, then don't just ask questions and look for applause by refuting any and every answer you get, because you've realized that it's easier to ask questions than it is to answer them. No, state an opinion yourself: say what you think morality is. And make sure you state your view d clearly and precisely, without saying that it is duty or benefit or profit or gain or advantage; I won't let you get away with any rubbish like that.'

I was scared stiff at his words, and I looked at him in fear. I think that if I hadn't seen him before he saw me, I'd have been unable to speak. But in fact I had got in the first look, when he originally began to get furious at the discussion, c and so I was able to respond to him. 'Thrasymachus,' I said, trembling with fear, 'please don't be cross with us.

Believe me, Thrasymachus, we're doing all we can. If we lack competence—which I suppose is the case—then pity is a far more reason-337a able feeling for you experts to have for us than impatience.'

He erupted into highly sarcastic laughter at my words and said, 'God, there goes Socrates again, pretending to be an ignoramus! I knew this would happen;

'That's because you're clever, Thrasymachus,' I said, 'You were well aware of the fact that if you were to ask someone what twelve is, and were to add as a rider to the question, "And b just make sure you avoid saying that twelve is two times six, or three times four, or six times two, or four times three. I won't let you get away with any nonsense like that"—well, I'well sure it was obvious to you that no one would answer a question phrased like that.

'That's what you're going to do as well, is it?' he asked. 'Respond with one of the answers I ruled out?'

'I wouldn't be surprised if I decided to do that, once I'd looked into the matter,' I said.

d 'What if I were to demonstrate that there's another answer you can give about morality,' he asked, 'which isn't any of those answers and is better than any of them? What penalty would you expect?'

'The penalty which is appropriate for ignorance, of course,' I said, 'which is learning from an expert. That's the penalty I expect.'

'Don't be naïve,' he said. 'You can't just learn: you must pay for it too.'

'If I ever have the money, I will,' I said.

'He has it,' said Glaucon. 'We'll all help Socrates out financially, so as far as the money is concerned, Thrasymachus, go ahead and speak.'

e 'Oh yes, sure!' he said. 'So that Socrates can get his way and not make any claims himself, while he attacks and criticizes someone else's claims.'

'That's because I have no choice, Thrasymachus,' I explained. 'How can anyone express a view when he's not only ignorant, but also admits his ignorance? Moreover, when he's been forbidden to mention any opinion he might happen to hold by a man of considerable caliber? No, 338a it's you who ought to speak, really, since you do claim to have knowledge and to be able to express it. So please do what I'm asking: if you state your view, you'll be doing me a favour, and also generously teaching Glaucon here and all the others too.'

c 'All right, then, listen to this,' he said. 'My claim is that morality is nothing other than the advantage of the stronger party . . . Well, why aren't you applauding? No, you won't let yourself do that.'

'First I need to understand your meaning,' I told him. 'I don't yet. You say that right is the advantage of the stronger party, but what on earth do you mean by this, Thrasymachus? Surely you're not claiming, in effect, that if Poulydamas the pancratiast is stronger than us and it's to his advantage, for the sake of his physique, to eat beef, then this food is advantageous, and there-d fore right, for us too, who are weaker than him?'

'Foul tactics, Socrates,' he said, 'to interpret what I say in the way which allows you unscrupulously to distort it most.'

'No, you've got me wrong, Thrasymachus,' I said. 'I just want you to explain yourself better.'

'Don't you know, then,' he said, 'that some countries are dictatorships, some are democracies, and some are aristocracies?'

'Of course I do.'

'And that what has power in any given country is the government?'

'Yes.'

c 'Now, each government passes laws with a view to its own advantage: a democracy makes democratic laws, a dictatorship makes dictatorial laws, and so on and so forth. In so doing, each government makes it clear that what is right and moral for its subjects is what is to its own advantage; and each government punishes anyone who deviates from what is advantageous to itself as if he were a criminal and a wrongdoer. So, Socrates, this is what I claim morality is: it is the same in every country, and it is what is to the

339a advantage of the current government. Now, of course, it's the current government which has power, and the consequence of this, as anyone who thinks about the matter correctly can work out, is that morality is every where the same— the advantage of the stronger party.'

'Now I see what you mean,' I said. 'And I'll try to see whether or not your claim is true. Your position too, Thrasymachus, is that morality is advantage—despite the fact that you ruled this answer our for me—except that you immediately add "of the stronger party".'

b 'Hardly a trivial addition,' he said.

'Whether or not it is important isn't yet clear. What is clear is that we must try to find out whether your claim is true. The points is that I agree that morality is some kind of advantage, but you are qualifying this and claiming that it is the advantage of the stronger party; since I haven't made up my mind about this qualified version, we must look into the matter.'

'Go ahead,' he said.

'All right,' I said. 'Here's a question for you: you're also claiming, I assume, that obedience to the government is right?'

'Yes, I am.'

c 'And is the government in every country infallible, or are they also capable of error?'

'They are certainly capable of error,' he said.

'So when they turn to legislation, they sometimes get it right, and sometimes wrong?'

'Yes, I suppose so.'

'When they get it right, the laws they make will be to their advantage, but when they get it wrong, the laws will be to their disadvantage. Is that what you're saying?'

'Yes.'

'And you're also saying that their subjects must act in accordance with any law that is passed, and that this constitutes doing right?'

'Of course.'

d 'Then it follows from your line of argument that it is no more right to act to the advantage of the stronger party than it is to do the opposite, to act to their disadvantage.'

'What are you saying?' he asked.

'Exactly the same as you, I think; but let's have a closer look. We're agreed that sometimes, when a government orders its subjects to do things, it is utterly mistaken about its own best interest, but that it's right for the subjects to act in accordance with any order issued by the government. Isn't that what we agreed?'

'Yes, I suppose so.'

e 'Then you must also suppose', I continued, 'that you have agreed that it is right to do things which are not to the advantage of the government and the stronger party. When the rulers mistakenly issue orders which are bad for themselves, and since you claim that it is right for people to act in conformity with all the government's orders, then, my dear Thrasymachus, doesn't it necessarily follow that it is right to do the opposite of what your position affirmed? I mean, the weaker party is being ordered to do what is disadvantageous to the stronger party, obviously.'

340a 'Yes, Socrates,' said Polemarchus, 'that's perfectly clear.'

'Of course,' Cleitophon interrupted, 'if you're going to act as a witness for Socrates.'

'There's no need for a witness,' Polemarchus replied. 'Thrasymachus himself admits that rulers sometimes issue orders which are bad for themselves, and that it's right for people to carry out these orders.'

340c I said,

But do please tell me, Thrasymachus: *did* you mean to define morality as what appears to the stronger party to be to its advantage, whether or not it really is to its advantage? Is that how we are to understand your meaning?'

'Absolutely not!' he protested. 'Do you suppose I would describe someone who makes mistakes as the stronger party when he is making a mistake?'

'Yes,' I replied, 'I did think you were saying this, when you agreed that rulers are not infallible, but also make mistakes.'

'That's because you're a bully in discussions, d Socrates,' he said.

'Well, Thrasymachus,' I said, 'so you think I'm a bully, do you?'

'Yes, I do,' he said.

c 'Do you think I'm crazy enough to try to shave a lion and bully Thrasymachus?' I asked.

'Well, you tried just now,' he said, 'even though you're a nonentity at that too.'

'That's enough of that sort of remark,' I said. 'But let's take this doctor you were talking about a short while ago—the one who's a doctor in the strict sense of the term. Is he a businessman, or someone who attends to sick people? Think about the genuine doctor, please.'

'He attends to sick people,' the replied.

'What about a ship's captain? Is the true captain in charge of sailors or a sailor?'

'In charge of sailors.'

d 'In other words, we shouldn't take any account of the fact that he is on board a ship and describe him as a sailor. I mean, it isn't because he's on a ship that he's called a captain, but because of his expertise and because he has authority over the sailors.'

'True,' he said.

'And isn't it the case,' I went on, 'that the *raison d'être* of a branch of expertise is to consider the welfare and interest of each party and then procure it?'

'Yes, that is what expertise is for,' he answered.

'Is there anything which is in the interest of any branch of expertise except being as perfect as possible?'

e 'I don't understand the question.'

'For instance,' I said, ' suppose you were to ask me whether it's enough for the body just to

be the body, to whether it needs anything else. I'd reply, "There's no doubt at all that it needs something else. That's why the art of medicine has been invented, because the body is flawed and it isn't enough for it to be like that. The branch of expertise has been developed precisely for the purpose of procuring the body's welfare." Would this reply of mine be correct, do you think, or not?' I asked.

'Yes, it would,' he said.

342a 'Well now, is medicine itself flawed? Are all branches of expertise imperfect? For instance, eyes need sight and ears need hearing, and that's why they need a branch of expertise to consider their welfare in precisely these respects and to procure it. Is expertise itself somehow inherently flawed as well, so that each branch of expertise needs a further branch to consider its welfare, and this supervisory branch needs yet another one, and so on ad infinitum? Or does every art b consider its own interest and welfare? Or is the whole question of it, or another art, being needed to consider its welfare in view of its flaws irrelevant, in the sense that no branch of expertise is flawed or faulty in the slightest, and it's inappropriate for any branch of expertise to investigate the welfare of anything other than its own area of expertise? In other words, any branch of expertise is flawless and perfect, provided it's a genuine branch of expertise—that is, as long as it wholly is what it is, nothing more and nothing less. Please consider this issue with the same strict use of langue we were using before, and tell me: am I right or not?'

'I think you're right,' he said.

c 'It follows, then,' I said, 'that medicine does not consider the welfare of medicine, but the welfare of the body.'

'Yes,' he said.

'And horsemanship considers the welfare of horses, not of horsemanship. In short, no branch of expertise considers its own advantage, since it isn't deficient in any respect: it considers the welfare of its area of expertise.'

'So it seems,' he said.

'But surely, Thrasymachus, the branches of expertise have authority and power over their particular areas of expertise.'

He gave his assent to this with extreme reluctance.

'So no branch of knowledge considers or enjoins the advantage of the stronger party, but d the advantage of the weaker party, which is subject to it.'

Eventually, he agreed to this too, although he tried to argue against it. Once he'd agreed, however, I said, 'Surely, then, no doctor, in this capacity as doctor, considers or enjoins what is advantageous to the doctor, but what is advantageous to the patient? I mean, we've agreed that a doctor, in the strict sense of the term, is in charge of bodies, not a businessman. Isn't that what we agreed?'

He concurred.

'And a ship's captain too is, strictly speaking, in charge of sailors, not a sailor?'

e   He agreed.

'So since captains are like this and wield authority in this way, they won't consider and enjoin the interest of the captain, but what is advantageous to the sailor, the subject.'

He reluctantly agreed.

'Therefore, Thrasymachus,' I said, 'no one in any other kind of authority either, in his capacity as ruler, considers or enjoins his own advantage, but the advantage of his subject, the person for whom the practises his expertise. Everything he says and everything he does is said and done with this aim in mind and with regard to what is advantageous to and appropriate for this person.'

343a   Once we'd reached this point in the discussion, it was perfectly clear to everyone that the definition of morality had been turned upside down.

BOOK II

357a At this point, I through I'd be exempt from further talking, but apparently that was only the preamble. You see, it's not in Glaucon's nature to cut and run from anything, and on this occasion he refused to accept Thrasymachus' capitulation, but said, 'Socrates, do you want us *really* to be con-b vinced that in all circumstances morality is better than immorality or merely to pretend to be?'

"If it were up to me,' I replied, 'I'd prefer your conviction to be genuine.'

'Well,' he remarked, 'your behaviour is at odds with your wishes, then. I mean, here's a question for you. Don't you describe as good something which is welcomed for its own sake, rather than because its consequences are desired? Enjoyment, for instance, and all those pleasures which are harmless and whose future consequences are only enjoyable?'

'Yes,' I agreed, '"good" seems to me the right description for that situation.'

c   'And what about things which are welcome not just for their own sakes, but also for their consequences? Intelligence, sight, and health, for instance, are evidently welcomed for both reasons.'

'Yes,' I said.

'And isn't there, in your experience,' he asked, 'a third category of good things—the category in which we find exercise, medical treatment, and any moneymaking job like being a doctor? All these things are regarded as nuisances, but beneficial, and are not welcomed for d their own sakes, but for their financial rewards and other consequences.'

'Yes,' I agreed, 'there is this third category as well. What of it?'

'To which category do you think morality belongs?' he asked.

358a   'In my opinion,' I replied, 'it belongs in the best category—the category which anyone who expects to be happy should welcome both for its own sake and for its consequences.'

'That's not the usual view,' he said, 'which consigns morality to the nuisance category of things which have to be done for the sake of financial reward and for the prospect of making a good impression, but which, taken in isolation, are so trying that one should avoid them.'

'I'm aware of this view,' I said, 'and it's the reason why Thrasymachus has been running morality down all this time, and praising immorality. But I'm slow on the uptake, apparently.'

b   'All right, then,' he said, 'listen to what I have to say too, and see if you agree with me. The point is that Thrasymachus gave up too soon, in my opinion: you charmed him into docility as if he were a snake. The arguments that have been offered about both morality and immorality leave *me* unsatisfied, however, in the sense that I still want to hear a definition of them both, and to be told what the effect is of the occurrence of each of them in the mind—each of them in isolation, without taking into consideration financial reward or any other consequence they might have.

'So if it's right with you, what I'll do is revive Thrasymachus' position. First, I'll explain the
c usual view of the nature and origin of morality; second, I'll claim that it is only ever practised reluctantly, as something necessary, but not good; third, I'll claim that this behaviour is reasonable, because people are right to think that an immoral person's life is much better than a moral person's life.

'Now, I don't agree with any of this, Socrates, but I don't know what to think. My ears are ringing from listening to Thrasymachus and countless others, but I've never yet heard the kind of support for morality, as being preferable
d to immorality, that I'd like to hear, which is a hymn to the virtues it possesses in and of itself. If I can get this from anyone, it'll be you, I think. That is why I'll speak at some length in praise of the immoral life; by doing so, I'll be showing you the kind of rejoinder I want you to develop when you criticize immorality and commend morality. What do you think of this plan?'

'I thoroughly approve,' I replied. 'I mean, I can't think of another topic which any thinking person would more gladly see cropping up again and again in his conversations.'

e 'That's wonderful,' he said. 'Well, I promised I'd talk first about the nature and origin of morality, so here goes. The idea is that although it's a fact of nature that doing wrong is good and having wrong done to one is bad, nevertheless the disadvantages of having it done to one outweigh the benefits of doing it. Consequently, once people have experienced both committing wrong and being at the receiving end of it, they see that the disadvantages are unavoidable and the bene-
359a fits are unattainable; so they decide that the most profitable course is for them to enter into a contract with one another, guraranteeing that no

wrong will be committed or received. They then set about making laws and decrees, and from then on they use the terms "legal" and "right" to describe anything which is enjoined by their code. So that's the origin and nature of morality, on this view: it is a compromise between the ideal of doing wrong without having to pay for it, and the worst situation, which is having wrong done to one while lacking the means of exacting compensation. Since morality is a compromise, it is endorsed because, while it may not be good, it does gain value by preventing people from doing
b wrong. The point is that any real man with the ability to do wrong would never enter into a contract to avoid both wronging and being wronged: he wouldn't be so crazy. Anyway, Socrates, that is what this view has to say about the nature and origin of morality and so on.

'As for the fact that morality is only ever practised reluctantly, by people who lack the ability to do wrong—this would become particularly obvious if we performed the following
c thought-experiment. Suppose we grant both types of people— moral and immoral—the scope to do whatever they want, and we then keep an eye on them to see where their wishes lead them. We'll catch our moral person red-handed: his desire for superiority will point him in the same direction as the immoral person, towards a destination which every creature naturally regards as good and aims for, except that people are compelled by convention to deviate from this path and respect equality.

'They'd have the scope I'm talking about especially if they acquired the kind of power which, we hear, an ancestor of Gyges of Lydia
d once acquired. He was a shepherd in the service of the Lydian ruler of the time, when a heavy rainstorm occurred and an earthquake cracked open the land to a certain extent, and a chasm appeared in the region where he was pasturing his flocks. He was fascinated by the sight, and went down into the chasm and saw there, as the story goes, among other artefacts, a bronze horse, which was hollow and had windows set in it; he stooped and looked in through the windows and saw a corpse inside, which seemed to be that of a

giant. The corpse was naked, but had a golden ring on one finger; he took the ring off the finger and left. Now, the shepherds used to meet once a month to keep the king informed about his flocks, and our protagonist came to the meeting wearing the ring. He was sitting down among the others, and happened to twist the ring's bezel in the direction of his body, towards the inner part of his hand. When he did this, he became invisible to his neighbours, and to his astonishment they talked about him as if he'd left. While he was fiddling about with the ring again, he turned the bezel outwards, and became visible. He thought about this and experimented to see if it was the ring which had this power; in this way he eventually found that turning the bezel inwards made him invisible and turning it outwards made him visible. As soon as he realized this, he arranged to be one of the delegates to the king; once he was inside the palace, he seduced the king's wife and with her help assaulted and killed the king, and so took possession of the throne.

'Suppose there were two such rings, then— one worn by our moral person, the other by the immoral person. There is no one, on this view, who is iron-willed enough to maintain his morality and find the strength of purpose to keep his hands off what doesn't belong to him, when he is able to take whatever he wants from the market-stalls without fear of being discovered, to enter houses and sleep with whomever he chooses, to kill and to release from prison anyone he wants, and generally to act like a god among men. His behaviour would be identical to that of the other person: both of them would be heading in the same direction.

'Now this is substantial evidence, it would be claimed, that morality is never freely chosen. People do wrong whenever they think they can, so they act morally only if they're forced to, because they regard morality as something which isn't good for one personally. The point is that everyone thinks the rewards of immorality far outweigh those of morality—and they're right, according to the proponent of this view. The sight of someone with that kind of scope refusing all those opportunities for wrongdoing and never

laying a finger on things that didn't belong to him would lead people to think that he was in an extremely bad way, and was a first-class fool as well—even though their fear of being wronged might make them attempt to mislead others by singing his praises to them in public.

'That's all I have to say on this. As for actually assessing the lives of the people we're talking about, we'll be able to do that correctly if we make the gap between a moral person and an immoral person as wide as possible. That's the only way to make a proper assessment. And we should set them apart from each other by leaving their respective immorality and morality absolutely intact, so that we make each of them a consummate professional. In other words, our immoral person must be a true expert. A top-notch ship's captain, for instance, or doctor, recognizes the limits of his branch of expertise and undertakes what is possible while ignoring what is impossible; moreover, if he makes a mistake, he has the competence to correct it. Equally, our immoral person must get away with any crimes he undertakes in the proper fashion, if he is to be outstandingly immoral; getting caught must be taken to be a sign of incompetence, since the acme of immorality is to give an impression of morality while actually being immoral. So we must attribute consummate immorality to our consummate criminal, and if we are to leave it intact, we should have him equipped with a colossal reputation for morality even though he is a colossal criminal. He should be capable of correcting any mistakes he makes. He must have the ability to argue plausibly, in case any of his crimes are ever found out, and to use force wherever necessary, by making use of his courage and strength and by drawing on his fund of friends and his financial resources.

'Now that we've come up with this sketch of an immoral person, we must conceive of a moral person to stand beside him—someone who is straightforward and principled, and who, as Aeschylus says, wants genuine goodness rather than merely an aura of goodness. So we must deprive him of any such aura, since if others think him moral, this reputation will gain him privileges and rewards, and it will become unclear whether it is morality or the rewards and privileges which might be motivating him to be what he is. We should strip him of everything except morality, then, and our portrait should be of someone in the opposite situation to the one we imagined before. I mean, even though he does no wrong at all, he must have a colossal reputation for immorality, so that his morality can be tested by seeing whether or not he is impervious to a bad reputation and its consequences; he must unswervingly follow his path until he dies—a saint with a lifelong reputation as a sinner. When they can both go no further in morality and immorality respectively, we can decide which of them is the happier.'

'My dear Glaucon,' I said, 'I'm very impressed at how industriously you're ridding each of them of defects and getting them ready for assessment. It's as if you were working on statues.'

'I'm doing the best I can,' he replied. 'And now that we've established what the two of them are like, I'm sure we won't find it difficult to specify what sort of life is in store for either of them. That's what I must do, then—and if my words are rather coarse, Socrates, please remember that the argument is not mine, but stems from those who prefer immorality to morality.

'Here's what they'll say: for a moral person in the situation I've described, the future holds flogging, torture on the rack, imprisonment in chains, having his eyes burnt out, and every ordeal in the book, up to and including being impaled on a stake. Then at last he'll realize that one's goal should be not actual morality, but the appearance of morality. In fact, that phrase of Aeschylus' has far more relevance for an immoral person, in the sense that, as they will claim, it is really an immoral person who wants genuine immorality rather than merely an aura of immorality, because his occupation takes account of the way things are and his life is not concerned with appearances. He is the one who "reaps the harvest of wise plans which grow in his mind's deep furrow"—and what he plans is first to use his reputation for morality to gain control over his country, and then to marry a woman from any family he wants, to have his children marry whomever he wants, to deal and do business with whomever he wants, and, over and above all this, to secure his own benefit by ensuring that his lack of distaste for crime makes him a financial profit. If he's challenged privately or publicly, he wins the day and comes off better than his enemies; because he gains the upper hand, he gets rich; he therefore does good to his friends and harm to his enemies, and the religious rites he performs and the offerings he makes to the gods are not just adequate but magnificent; his service to the gods and to the men he favours is far better than a moral person's; and consequently it is more appropriate for the gods to smile on him rather than on a moral person, and more likely that they will. And this, Socrates, is why both gods and men provide a better life for an immoral person than for a moral person, according to this view.'

Now, I've always admired Glaucon's and Adeimantus' temperaments, but I was particularly delighted with them on this occasion, once I'd heard what they had to say. 'Like father, like sons,' I remarked. 'The first line of the elegiac poem which Glaucon's lover composed when you distinguished yourselves at the battle of Megara wasn't wrong in addressing you as "sons of Ariston, godlike offspring of an eminent sire". I think this is quite right: "godlike" is certainly the word for your state, if you can speak like that in support of immorality, and yet remain unconvinced that it is better than morality. I *do* think that you really are unconvinced; my evidence is what I know of your characters from other occasions. If I'd had to judge from your words alone, I would have doubted it. But it's precisely because I don't doubt it that I'm in a quandary. On the one hand, I can't come to the assistance of morality, since I am incompetent—as is proven by the fact that although I thought the points I'd made to Thrasymachus had shown that morality was better than immorality, you weren't satisfied. On the other hand, I can't not come to morality's assistance, since I'm afraid that it might actually be sacrilegious to stand idly by while morality is being denigrated and not try to assist as long as one has breath in one's body and a voice to protest with. Anyway, the best thing is for me to offer it whatever help I can.'

Glaucon and the others begged me to do everything I could to help; they implored me not to abandon the discussion, but to make a thorough enquiry into the nature of both morality and immorality, and to search out the truth about their expediency. I told them what occurred to me: 'We're undertaking an investigation which, in my opinion, requires care and sharp eyesight. d Now, we're not experts,' I pointed out, 'so I suggest we conduct the investigation as follows. Suppose we were rather short-sighted and had been told to read small writing from a long way off, and then one of us noticed the same letters written elsewhere in a larger size and on a larger surface: I'm sure we'd regard this as a godsend and would read them there before examining the smaller ones, to see if they were really identical.'

'Of course we would,' said Adeimantus. 'But how is this analogous to our investigation into e morality, Socrates, in your view?'

'I'll tell you,' I replied. 'Wouldn't we say that morality can be a property of whole communities as well as of individuals?'

'Yes,' he said.

'And a community is larger than a single person?'

'Yes,' he said.

'It's not impossible, then, that morality might exist on a larger scale in the larger entity and be easier to discern. So, if you have no objection, why don't we start by trying to see 369a what morality is like in communities? And then we can examine individuals too, to see if the larger entity is reflected in the features of the smaller entity.'

'I think that's an excellent idea,' he said.

'Well,' I said, 'the theoretical observation of a community in the process of formation would enable us to see its morality and immorality forming too, wouldn't it?'

'I should think so,' he said.

'And once the process is complete, we could expect to see more easily what we're looking for?'

b 'Yes, much more easily.'

'Are we agreed, then, on the necessity of trying to see this plan through? I'm asking because I think it'll take a lot of work. So are you sure?'

'Yes, we are,' said Adeimantus. 'Please do what you're proposing.'

'Well,' I said, 'a community starts to be formed, I suppose, when individual human beings find that they aren't self-sufficient, but that each of them has plenty of requirements which he can't fulfil on his own. Do you have an alternative suggestion as to why communities are founded?'

'No,' he said.

c 'So people become involved with various other people to fulfil various needs, and we have lots of needs, so we gather lots of people together and get them to live in a single district as our associates and assistants. And then we call this living together a community. Is that right?'

'Yes.'

'And people trade goods with one another, because they think they'll be better off if each gives or receives something in exchange, don't they?'

'Yes.'

'All right, then,' I said. 'Let's construct our theoretical community from scratch. Apparently, its cause is our neediness.'

'Of course.'

d 'And the most basic and most important of our needs is that we are provided with enough food for existence and for life.'

'Absolutely.'

'The second most important is our need for somewhere to live, and the third is our need for clothing and so on.'

'True.'

'All right,' I said. 'How will our community cope with all this provisioning? Mustn't one member of it be a farmer, another a builder, and another a weaver? Is that all the people we need to look after our bodily needs? Shall we add a shoemaker to it as well?'

'Yes.'

'And there we'd have our community. Reduced to its bare essentials, it would consist of four or five people.'

e 'So it seems.'

'Well now, should each of them make what he produces publicly available for everyone? For instance, although the farmer is only one person, should he supply all four people with food? Should he spend four times as long and work four times as hard on supplying food and share it out, or should he ignore everyone else and spend a quarter of his time producing only a quarter of this amount of food for himself, and divide the 370a other three-quarters between getting a house and clothes and shoes for himself, and not have all the bother of associating with other people, but look after his own affairs on his own?'

Adeimantus said, 'It looks as though the first alternative is simpler, Socrates.'

'That's not surprising, of course,' I said. 'I mean, it occurred to me while you were speaking that, in the first place, different people are inherently suitable for different activities, since people b are not particularly similar to one another, but have a wide variety of natures. Don't you agree?'

'I do.'

'And is success a more likely consequence of an individual working at several jobs or specializing in only one?'

'Of his specializing in only one,' he said.

'Now, here's another obvious point, I'm sure—that missing the critical opportunity has a deleterious effect.'

'Yes, obviously.'

'The reason being that the work isn't prepared to wait for the worker to make time for it. No, it's crucial for the worker to fall in with the c work and not try to fit it into his spare time.'

'Yes, that's crucial.'

'So it follows that productivity is increased, the quality of the products is improved, and the process is simplified when an individual sets aside his other pursuits, does the one thing for which he is naturally suited, and does it at the opportune moment.'

'Absolutely.'

'We need more than four citizens, then, Adeimantus, to supply the needs we mentioned. I mean, if the farmer's going to have a good plough, he will apparently not be making it him- d self, and the same goes for his hoe and all the rest

of his farming implements. Moreover, the builder won't be making his own tools either, and he too needs plenty of them; nor, by the same token, will the weaver and the shoemaker. True?'

'True.'

'So plenty of other craftsmen—joiners, metalworkers, and so on—will join our little settlement and swell its population.'

'Yes.'

'All right,' I said. 'I see. We're not just investigating the origins of a community, apparently, but of an indulgent community. Well, that may not be wrong: if we extend our enquiry like that, we might perhaps see how morality and immorality take root in communities. Now, I think that the true community—the one in a healthy condition, as it were—is the one we've described; but if you want us to inspect an inflamed community as well, so be it. There's no reason not to. I 373a mean, some people apparently won't be satisfied with the provisions and the lifestyle we've described, but will have all sorts of furniture like couches and tables, and a wide selection of savouries, perfumes, incense, prostitutes, and pastries. Moreover, the essential requirements can no longer be restricted to the houses and clothing and shoes we originally mentioned; no, we have to invent painting and ornamentation, and get hold of gold and ivory and so on. Don't you agree?'

b   'Yes,' he said.

'So we have to increase the size of our community once again. That healthy community will no longer do; it must become bloated and distended with occupations which leave the essential requirements of a community behind—for instance, with all kinds of hunters and imitators. Among the latter will be hordes of people concerned with shapes and colours, and further hordes concerned with music (poets and their dependants—rhapsodes, actors, dancers, producers), and manufacturers of all kinds of contraptions and all sorts of things, especially women's c cosmetics. Furthermore, we'll need a larger number of workers—don't you think?—such as children's attendants, nurses, nannies, hairdressers, barbers, and savoury-cooks and meat-cooks too.

And that's not the end of it: we'll need pig-farmers as well—a job which didn't exist in our previous community, since there was no need of it, but which will be needed in the present one—and huge numbers of cows and sheep, if they are to be eaten, won't we?'

'Of course.'

d 'And with this lifestyle won't we be in far greater need of doctors than we were before?'

'Yes.'

'And, of course, although the inhabitants of our former community could live off the produce of the land, the land will be too small now, don't you think?'

'I agree.'

'So we'll have to take a chunk of our neighbours' land, if we're going to have enough for our herds and our crops, won't we? And suppose they too have stopped limiting themselves to necessities and have gone in for the uncontrolled acquisition of innumerable possessions: then they'll have to take a chunk of our land too, won't they?'

e 'That's more or less inevitable, Socrates,' he replied.

'And the next step will be war, Glaucon, don't you think?'

'I agree,' he said.

'Now, let's not commit ourselves yet to a view on whether the effects of war are good or bad,' I said. 'All we're saying at the moment is that we've now discovered the origin of war. It is caused by those factors whose occurrence is the major cause of a community's troubles, whether it's the community as a whole which is afflicted or any individual member of it.'

'Yes.'

'We need another sizeable increase in our community, then, Glaucon—an army-sized 374a increase. We need an army to go out and defend all the community's property and all the people we were talking about a moment ago against invaders.'

'But can't the inhabitants do this themselves?' he asked.

'No,' I replied. 'At any rate, they can't if the proposition we all—including you—agreed to when we were forming our community was cor-

rect. The proposition was, if you remember, that it is impossible for one person to work properly at more than one area of expertise.'

'You're right.'

b 'Well,' I said, 'don't you think that warfare requires expertise?'

'I certainly do,' he answered.

'So should we take more trouble over our shoemakers than we do over our soldiers?'

'Not at all.'

'Well now, we prohibited a shoemaker from simultaneously undertaking farming or weaving or building, but had him concentrating exclusively on shoemaking, to ensure quality achievements in shoemaking; and we similarly allotted every single person just one job—the one for which he was naturally suited, and which he was to work at all his life, setting aside his other pur-
c suits, so as not to miss the opportunities which are critical for quality achievement. Isn't it crucial, however, that the achievements of warfare are of a high standard? Or is soldiering so easy that someone can be expert at it while carrying on with his farming or shoemaking or whatever his profession might be, despite the fact that no one could even become a competent backgammon-player or dice-player if he took it up only in his spare time and didn't concentrate on it for years, starting when he was a young man? Does some-
d one just have to pick up a shield (or whatever military implement or instrument it may be) and he instantaneously becomes a competent fighter in a heavy infantry engagement (or in whatever form of armed conflict it may be)? This would be unique, since no other implement makes person a craftsman or an athlete if he just holds it, and no other implement is the slightest good to anyone unless he's acquired the knowledge of how to use it and has devoted sufficient attention to it.'

'Yes,' he said, 'if tools could do that, they'd be highly prized.'

'Now,' I said, 'the amount of time allotted just to it, and also the degree of professionalism
e and training, should reflect the supreme importance of the guardians' work'.

'I certainly think so,' he said.

'And a natural talent for the job would help too, Wouldn't it?'

'Of course.'

'Our job then, if we're up to it, would seem to be to select which people and what types of person have a natural gift for protecting our community,'

'Yes, it is.'

'We've certainly taken an awesome task, then,' I said. 'Still, we mustn't be intimidated; we must do the best we can.'

375a   'I agree.'

'All right, then, let's devise a theoretical education for these people, as if we were making up a story and weren't worried about time.'

c   'Yes, that's a good idea.'

'How shall we educate them, then? Or is it hard to improve on the educational system which has evolved over a long period of time? This, as you know, consists of exercise for the body and cultural studies for the mind.'

'Yes.'

'And shall we begin the cultural programme before the physical one?'

'Of course.'

'Cultural studies include literature, don't you think?' I asked.

'I do.'

'Aren't there two kinds of literature, true and false?'

'Yes.'

377a   'Should we include both kinds in our educational system, and start with the untrue kind?'

'I don't understand what you're getting at,' he said.

'Don't you realize,' I asked, 'that we start by telling children stories which are, by and large, untrue, though they contain elements of truth? And stories precede physical exercise in our education of children.'

'True.'

'Which is why I suggested that cultural studies should be taken up before physical exercise.'

'It was a good suggestion,' he said.

'Now, do you appreciate that the most important stage of any enterprise is the beginning, especially when something young and sen-

b sitive is involved? You see, that's when most of its formation takes place, and it absorbs every impression that anyone wants to stamp upon it.'

'You're absolutely right.'

'Shall we, then, casually allow our children to listen to any old stories, made up by just anyone, and to take into their minds views which, on the whole, contradict those we'll want them to have as adults?'

'No, we won't allow that at all.'

'So our first job, apparently, is to oversee the c work of the story-writers, and to accept any good story they write, but reject the others. We'll let nurses and mothers tell their children the acceptable ones, and we'll have them devote themselves far more to using these stories to form their children's minds than they do to using their hands to form their bodies. However, we'll have to disallow most of the stories they currently tell.'

'Which stories?' he asked.

'If we examine the grander kind of story,' I said, 'that will give us insights into the more lightweight kind as well, because the same principle must be involved and both kinds are bound d to have the same effect, don't you think?'

'That sounds fine to me,' he replied, 'but I don't even understand which stories you're describing as grander.'

'The ones which Hesiod, Homer, and their fellow poets tell us. In the past, it's always been the poets who've composed untrue stories to tell people, and it's no different nowadays.'

'Which stories?' he asked. 'And what's their defect, in your view?'

'There is no defect which one ought to condemn more quickly and more thoroughly,' I replied, 'especially if the lies have no redeeming feature.'

'Yes, but what is this defect?'

e   'Using the written word to give a distorted image of the nature of the gods and heroes, just as a painter might produce a portrait which completely fails to capture the likeness of the original.'

'Yes,' he said, 'it's quite right to find fault with that sort of things. But how do they do that? What kinds of things do they say?'

'First and most important, since the subject is so important,' I said, 'there is no redeeming feature to the lies which Hesiod repeats, about 378a Uranus' deeds and Cronus' revenge on Uranus. Then there are Cronus' deeds and what his son did to him. Now, I think that even if these stories are true, they oughtn't to be told so casually to young people and people who lack discrimination; it's better to keep silent, and if one absolutely has to speak, to make them esoteric secrets told to as few people as possible, who are to have sacrificed no mere piglet, but something so large and rare that the smallest conceivable number of people get to hear them.'

'Yes,' he said, 'these stories are definitely dangerous.'

b 'And we must censor them in our community, Adeimantus,' I said, 'No young person is to hear stories which suggest that were he to commit the vilest of crimes, and were he to do his utmost to punish his father's crimes, he wouldn't be doing anything out of the ordinary, but would simply be behaving like the first and the greatest gods.'

'No, I absolutely agree,' he said, 'I share your view that these stories are unsuitable and shouldn't be repeated.'

'And that's not all,' I said. 'The stories which c have gods fighting and scheming and battling against one another are utterly unsuitable too, because they're just as untrue. If the prospective guardians of our community are to loathe casual quarrels with one another, we must take good care that battles between gods and giants and all the other various tales of gods and heroes coming to blows with their relatives and friends don't occur in the stories they hear and the pictures they see. No, if we're somehow to convince them that fellow citizens never fall out with one another, that this is wrong, then that is the kind of story they must hear, from childhood onwards, d from the community's elders of both sexes; and the poets they'll hear when they're older must be forced to tell equivalent stories in their poetry.

But we'd better not admit into our community the story of any of the battles between the gods which Homer has in his poetry, whether or not their intention is allegorical. The point is that a young person can't tell when something is allegorical and when it isn't, and any idea admitted by a person of that age tends to become e almost ineradicable and permanent. All things considered, then, that is why a very great deal of importance should be placed upon ensuring that the first stories they hear are best adapted for their moral improvement.'

'Yes, that makes sense,' he said. 'But suppose we were once again to be asked, in this context as well, what stories we meant, how would we respond?'

'Adeimantus,' I said, 'you and I are not making up stories at the moment; we're founding a 379a community. Founders ought to know the broad outlines within which their poets are to compose stories, so that they can exclude any compositions which do not conform to those outlines; but they shouldn't themselves make stories up.'

'You're right,' he said. 'But that's precisely the point: what are these guidelines for talking about the gods?'

'They'd be something like this,' I said. 'Whatever the type of poetry—epic, lyric, or tragic—God must of course always be portrayed as he really is.'

'Yes, he must.'

b 'Well, isn't God good, in fact, and shouldn't he be described as such?'

'Of course.'

'And nothing good is harmful, is it?'

'I don't think so.'

'Now, can anything harmless cause damage?'

'No, of course not.'

'Can anything incapable of causing damage do anything bad?'

'Again, no.'

'And something which never does bad couldn't be responsible for bad, could it?'

'Of course not.'

'Well now, is goodness beneficial?'

'Yes.'

'And it's responsible for doing good, then?'

'Yes.'

'So goodness is not responsible for everything: it's responsible for things that are in a good state, but bad things cannot be attributed to it.'

c 'Exactly,' he said.

'The same goes of God too, then,' I said. 'Since he is good, he cannot be responsible for everything, as is commonly said. He is responsible only for a small part of human life, and many things cannot be attributed to him—I mean, there's far more bad than good in the world. He and he alone must be held responsible for the good things, but responsibility for bad things must be looked for elsewhere and not attributed to God.'

'I think you're absolutely right,' he said.

'So,' I said, 'we shouldn't connive at Homer d or any other poet making the stupid mistake of saying about the gods, "Two jars sit on Zeus' threshold: one is full of good destinies, but the other is full of wretched destines", and that if Zeus mixes the two up together and doles them out to someone, that person "sometimes meets with bad, sometimes with good" whereas if he doesn't mix them up, but allots the pernicious ones to someone in an unadulterated from, that person "is driven over the glorious earth by the evil of poverty". Nor will we connive at them claiming that "Zeus is the dispenser of both good e and evil".

'I approve of this law,' he said. 'I'll be right behind you when you cast your vote for it.'

'So now we have the first of the laws and guidelines which pertain to the gods,' I said. 'Any spoken words or composed works will have to conform to the principle that God is not responsible for evening, but only for good.'

'Well, I'm certainly happy with it,' he said.

BOOK III

'All right,' I said. 'What do we have to decide about next? Shouldn't we decide which members of this particular class will be the rulers and which will be the subjects?'

412c 'Of course.'

'It's obvious that the older ones should be the rulers and the younger ones the subjects, isn't it?'

d 'Yes.'

'And only the best of the older ones?'

'Yes, that's obvious too.'

'Now, the best farmers are the most accomplished farmers, aren't they?'

'Yes.'

'And in the present case since we're after the best guardians, they must be those who are particularly good at safeguarding the community, mustn't they?'

'Yes.'

'They not only have to have the intelligence and the competence for the job, but they also have to care for the community, wouldn't you say?'

'Yes.'

'Now, you care most for things that happen to be dear to you.'

'Inevitably.'

'And something is particularly dear to you if you regard your interests and its interests as identical, and if you think that your success and failure follow from its success and failure.'

'Yes,' he said.

'It follows that we should select from among the guardians men who particularly strike us, on investigation, as being the type to devote their e whole lives to wholeheartedly doing what they regard as advantageous to the community, and to completely refusing to do anything they regard as disadvantageous to it.'

'Yes, they would make suitable rulers,' he said.

'I think we'll have to watch them at every stage of their lives, then, to make sure that they're good at safeguarding this idea and aren't magically or forcibly induced to shed and forget the notion that it's essential to do what's best for the community.'

'What do you mean by this shedding?' he asked.

'I'll explain,' I said. 'It seems to me that the departure of an idea from a person's mind can be either intentional or unintentional. It's intentional if the idea is false and the person learns bet- 413a ter, and unintentional whenever the idea is true.'

'I understand intentional loss,' he said, 'but I still don't understand unintentional loss.'

'But don't you think that the loss of good things is unintentional, while the loss of bad things is intentional?' I asked. 'And don't you think that being deceived about the truth is a bad thing, while having a grasp of the truth is good? And don't you think that having a grasp of the truth is having a belief that matches the way things are?'

'Yes, you're right,' he said. 'I agree that the loss of a true belief is unintentional.'

b 'So when this happens, it's the result of robbery, magic, or brute force, wouldn't you say?'

'I don't understand again,' he said.

'I suppose I am talking pompously,' I said. 'When I talk of a person being robbed of a belief, I mean that he's persuaded by an argument to change his mind, or time causes him to forget it: in either case, he doesn't notice the departure of the belief. I should think you understand now, don't you?'

'Yes.'

'And when I talk of a person being forced out of a belief, I mean that pain or suffering makes him change his mind.'

'Yes, I understand that too,' he said, 'and you're right.'

c 'And I'm sure you'd agree that anyone who changes his mind because he's been beguiled by pleasure or terrified by threats has had magic used on him.'

'Yes,' he said, 'any deception is a form of magic, I suppose.'

'As I was starting to say a moment ago, then, we must try to discover which of our guardians are particularly good at safe-guarding within themselves the belief that they should only ever pursue courses of action which they think are in the community's best interests. We must watch them from childhood onwards, and set them tasks which maximize the possibility of their forgetting a belief like this and being misled; those who bear the belief in mild and prove hard to mislead are the ones we should select, while d excluding the others. Do you agree?'

'Yes.'

'And we should also set them tough and painful assignments and ordeals, and watch for exactly the same things.'

'Right,' he said.

'Now, we'll have to invent a selection procedure for our third category, magic, as well,' I

said, 'and observe how they perform. People test a foal's nervousness by introducing it to noise and commotion, and in the same way we must bring our guardians, while they're young, face to face with fear and then shift them into facing e pleasure. People use fire to test gold, but our test must be far more thorough, and must show us how well they resist magic and whether they remain graceful whatever the situation, keep themselves and their cultural education intact, and display rhythm and harmony throughout; if they're capable of doing this, their value to themselves and to the community will be very high. Anyone who emerges without impurities from every single test—as a child, as a young 414a man, and as an adult—should be made a ruler and guardian of our community, and should be honoured in life and in death, in the sense of being awarded the most privileged of funerals and tombs. Anyone who gets corrupted, however, should be excluded. So, Glaucon,' I concluded, 'I think that this is how we should select and appoint our rulers and guardians. These are just guidelines, though: I haven't gone into details.'

'I agree,' he said. 'It must be something like this.'

b 'And we really and truly could hardly go wrong if we reserved and term "guardian" in its fullest sense of these people, who ensure that neither the desire nor the capacity for harming the community arises, whether from external enemies or from internal friends. As for the young men we've been calling guardians up to now, we should strictly call them auxiliaries and assistants of the guardians and their decision-making, don't you think?'

'Yes, I do,' he said.

'I wonder if they'd turn out as we want if their lifestyle and living-quarters were somewhat as follows,' I said. 'See what you think. In the first place, none of them is to have any private property, except what is absolutely indispensable. In the second place, none of them is to have living-quarters and storerooms which are not able to be entered by anyone who wants to. Their provisions (which should be suitable in quantity e for self-controlled and courageous warriors) are to be their stipend, paid by their fellow citizens for their guarding, the amount being fixed so that, at the end of a year, there is no excess or shortfall. There will be shared mess-halls for them to go to, and their lives will be communal, as if they were on campaign. We'll tell them that the permanent presence in their minds of divine gold and silver, which they were granted by the gods, means that they have no need of earthly gold and silver as well; and we'll add that it is sacrilegious for them to adulterate and contaminate that heavenly possession by owning the earthly variety, because in the past this earthly variety, which is accepted as

417a currency by the masses, has provoked many acts of desecration, whereas theirs is untainted. So, unlike any of their fellow citizens, they are not permitted to have any contact or involvement with gold and silver: they are not to come under the same roof as gold and silver, or wear them on their bodies, or drink from gold and silver cups. These precepts will guarantee not only their own integrity, but also the integrity of the community which is in their safe keeping. If they do come to own land and homes and money, they will be estate-managers and farmers instead of guardians; they will become despots, and enemies rather

b than allies of the inhabitants of the community; they will spend their lives hating and being hated, plotting and being plotted against; they will have internal enemies to fear more, and more intensely, than their external enemies. With private property, they will be racing ever closer to the ruin of themselves and the whole community. All this confirms the importance of our stated arrangements for the guardians' living-quarters and so on,' I concluded, 'so shall we enshrine them in law, or not?'

'We certainly must,' said Glaucon.

BOOK IV

419a Adeimantus came in with an objection: 'Tell me, Socrates,' he said. 'How are you going to reply to the accusation that you're not making these men at all happy, and moreover you're making it their own fault? In a real sense, the community belongs to them, but they don't derive any bene-

fit from the community. Others own estates, build beautiful mansions and stock them with suitable furniture, perform their own special religious rites, entertain, and of course own the items you were just talking about, gold and silver, and everything else without which happiness is, on the usual view, impossible. Instead of all this, a critic might say, their role in our community really is just like that of auxiliary troops—mercenaries—with nothing to do except main-

420a tain a garrison.'

'Yes,' I agreed. 'And they don't even get paid like other auxiliary troops: they get no more than their provisions. Consequently, they can't even take a trip for personal reasons out of town if they want to, or give presents to mistresses, or spend money on anything else they might want to, as so-called happy people can. You're leaving all this out of your accusation, and plenty of other things too.'

'All right,' he said. 'Please assume that the accusation includes them.'

b 'So you're asking how we'll defend ourselves, are you?'

'Yes.'

'I don't think we need to change direction at all to come across a suitable defence,' I said. 'We'll reply that although it wouldn't surprise us in the slightest if in fact there were no people happier than these men, all the same we're not constructing our community with the intention of making one group within it especially happy, but to maximize the happiness of the community as a whole. We thought we'd be most likely to find morality in a community like ours and also immorality in a community with the worst pos-

c sible management, and that once we'd examined them we'd reach the decision which is the original purpose of our investigation. What we're doing at the moment, we think, is forming a community which is happy as a whole, without hiving off a few of its members and making them the happy ones; and before long we'll be looking at a community in the opposite condition.

'Suppose we were painting a statue and someone came up and criticized us for not using the most beautiful paint for the creature's most beautiful features, because the eyes are the most beautiful part and they hadn't been painted purple but black. It would be perfectly reasonable, in d our opinion, for us to reply to this critic by saying, "My dear chap, you can't expect us to paint beautiful eyes in a way which stops them looking like eyes, or to do that to the other parts of the body either. Don't you think that if we treat every single part in an appropriate fashion, we're making the creature as a whole beautiful? Likewise, in the present case, please don't force us to graft the sort of happiness on to the guardians which will make them anything but guardians. e You see, we know we could dress our farmers in soft clothes and golden jewellery and tell them to work the land only when they have a mind to, and we know we could have our potters lie basking in their kiln-fire's warmth on a formal arrangement of couches, drinking and feasting with their wheel beside them as a table, and doing pottery only as much as they feel like, and we know we could make everyone else happy in this sort of way, and so have a community which was happy overall; but please don't advise us to do so, because if we follow your recommendation, then our farmers won't be farmers and our 421a potters won't be potters and no one else will retain that aspect of himself which is a constituent of a community. Now, this isn't so important where the rest of the community is concerned. I mean, if cobblers go to the bad and degenerate and pretend to be other than what they are, it's not catastrophic for a community; but if the people who guard a community and its laws ignore their essence and start to pose, then obviously they're utterly destroying the community, despite the fact that its good management and happiness are crucially in their hands and their hands alone."

'Now, if we're creating genuine guardians, who can hardly harm their community, and the b originator of that other idea is talking about a certain kind of farmer and people who are, as it were, happy to fill their stomachs on holiday, but aren't members of a community, then he's not talking about a community, but something else. What we have to consider is whether our inten-

tion in putting the guardians in place is to maximize their happiness, or whether we ought to make the happiness of the community as a whole our goal and should, by fair means and foul, convince these auxiliaries and guardians that their c task is to ensure that they, and everyone else as well, are the best at their own jobs. Then, when the community as a whole is flourishing and rests on a fine foundation, we can take it for granted that every group within it will find happiness according to its nature.'

'I'm sure you're right,' he said.

'So there you are, Adeimantus,' I said. 'Your community seems to have been founded. The 427d next thing for you to do is to get hold of a bright enough light and explore the community—you should invite your brother and Polemarchus and the rest of us to join you—to see if we can locate morality and immorality within it, discover how they differ from each other, and find out which of them is a prerequisite for happiness, whether or not its possession is hidden from the eyes of gods and men.'

'Rubbish,' said Glaucon. 'You promised you'd do the investigating, on the grounds that it was sacrilegious for you not to do everything you e could to assist morality.'

'You're right,' I said. 'Thanks for the reminder. But you should still help me while I do so.'

'We will,' he said.

'I think I know how we'd better conduct the search,' I said. 'I assume that if the community has been founded properly, it has everything it takes to be good.'

'Necessarily,' he replied.

'Obviously, then, it has wisdom, courage, self-discipline, and morality.'

'Obviously.'

'And clearly, as we go about our search, we'll discover some of these elements and there'll be some we have yet to discover.'

428a 'Of course.'

'Now, imagine any set of four things, and imagine we're exploring something for one of the four. Either we'd recognize it straight away and that would do the job, or we would recognize the one we're looking for by first recognizing the other three, in the sense that whatever is left is bound to be the one we're looking for.'

'Right,' he said.

'Well, we're faced with a set of four things here, so the principles of exploration are the same. Yes?'

'Obviously.'

'Now, the first thing which I think is visible here is wisdom. And there's a peculiarity in its b case.'

'What?' he asked.

'Well, I do think that the community we've described really is wise. I mean, it's resourceful, isn't it?'

'Yes.'

'And this thing, resourcefulness, is obviously a king of knowledge. I mean, it's not ignorance which makes people resourceful; it's knowledge.'

'Obviously.'

'Now, there are many branches of knowledge in our community, of all different kinds.'

'Naturally.'

'So is it the knowledge its carpenters have which makes the community deserve to be described as wise and resourceful?'

'No, that only entitles us to call it good at c carpentry,' he replied.

'It shouldn't be called wise, then, because of its knowledge of carpentry and because it is resourceful at ensuring the excellence of its furniture.'

'Certainly not.'

'Because it knows how to make metal implements, then, or anything like that?'

'Definitely not that either,' he said.

'And the fact that it knows how to grow crops only entitles us to describe it as good at agriculture.'

'That's what I think.'

'All right,' I said. 'Is there a branch of d knowledge which some of the inhabitants of the community we've just founded have, which enables it to think resourcefully about the whole community, not just some element of it, and about enhancing the whole community's domestic and foreign policies?'

'There certainly is.'

'What is it?' I asked. 'And which of the citizens have it?'

'It is guardianship,' he replied, 'and the people who have it are those rulers—the ones we not long ago called guardians in the strict sense of the world.'

'And what description does this branch of knowledge earn the community, in your opinion?'

'Resourceful and genuinely wise,' he answered.

'Now, do you think that in our community metalworkers will outnumber these true guard-e ians, or the other way round?' I asked.

'There'll be far more metalworkers,' he said.

'And wouldn't these guardians be outnumbered by any of the other acknowledged categories of experts?' I asked.

'Yes, by a long way.'

'So when a community is founded on natural principles, the wisdom it has as a whole is due to the smallest grouping and section within it and to the knowledge possessed by this group, which is the authoritative and ruling section of the community. And we also find that this category, which is naturally the least numerous, is the one 429a which inherently possesses the only branch of knowledge which deserves to be called wisdom.'

'You're absolutely right,' he said.

'So we've somehow stumbled across one of the four qualities we were looking for and found whereabouts in the community it is located.'

'I think it's clear enough, anyway,' he said.

'Now, it's not too hard to spot courage and to see which section of the community possesses it and enables the community to be described as courageous.'

'Why?'

'The only feature of a community which b might justify describing it as either cowardly or courageous', I answered, 'is its defensive and military arm.'

'Yes, that's the only one,' he agreed.

'The point is', I went on, 'that whether the rest of its inhabitants are cowardly or brave wouldn't affect the nature of the community either way, I imagine.'

'No, it wouldn't.'

'Again, then, it is a section of a community that earns it the right to be called courageous. This section possesses the ability to retain under all circumstances the notion that the things and c kinds of things to be feared are precisely those things and kinds of things which during their education the legislator pronounced fearful. Isn't this what you call courage?'

'I haven't understood your point,' he said. 'Please could you repeat it.'

'I'm saying that courage is a sort of retention,' I explained.

'What do you mean, retention?'

'I mean the retention of the notion, which has been inculcated by law through the agency of education, about what things and what kinds of things are to be feared. And by its retention "under all circumstances" I meant keeping it d intact and not losing it whether one is under the influence of pain or pleasure, desire or aversion. I can tell you what strikes me as analogous, if you like.'

'Yes, please.'

'Well,' I said, 'you know how when dyers want to dye wool purple, they first select something which is naturally white, rather than any other colour; then they subject it to a lengthy preparatory treatment designed to ensure that the colour will take as well as possible; and when e it's in the required condition, they dye it. Anything dyed in this way holds its colour, and the colour can't be washed out, whether or not one uses solvent. But you know what happens to anything which isn't dyed in this way, when something of another colour is dyed, or when something white is dyed without having been treated first.'

'Yes,' he said. 'The dye washes out and they look ridiculous.'

'So I want you to imagine', I said, 'that we too were doing our best to achieve something similar, when we selected our militia and put them through their cultural and physical educa-430a tion. You should assume that the educational programme was designed for one purpose only: to indoctrinate them so thoroughly that the laws take in them like a dye, so that their notions about what is to be feared and about everything else hold fast (which requires a suitable character as well as a suitable upbringing), with the dye being incapable of being washed out by those solvents which are so frighteningly good at scouring—pleasure, which is a more efficient cleanser than any soda and lye, and pain and b aversion and desire, which outclass any solvent. So this ability to retain under all circumstances a true and lawful notion about what is and is not to be feared is what I'm calling courage. That's how I'll use the term, unless you have an alternative suggestion.'

'No, I don't,' he said. 'I mean, I think your idea is that any true notion about these matters which is formed in an animal or a slave without the benefit of education is not really lawful, and I suppose you'd find some other name for it, not courage.'

c 'You're quite right,' I said.

'I accept your definition of courage, then.'

'Accept it by all means,' I said, 'but as a definition of the kind of courage a community has; then your acceptance will be all right. We'll go into the subject more thoroughly later, if you want; you see, at the moment our quarry is morality, not courage, which I think we've explored enough.'

'That's fine by me,' he said.

'Well, we've still got two qualities to detect in the community,' I said, 'self-discipline and the d purpose of the whole enquiry, morality.'

'Quite so.'

'Can we somehow locate morality and not bother any more about self-discipline?'

'I don't know if we can,' he said, 'and anyway I wouldn't like morality to be discovered first if that entails dropping the search for self-discipline. I'd be grateful if you'd look for self-discipline before morality.'

e 'Then it's my duty to do so, of course,' I said.

'Go on, then,' he said.

'All right,' I said. 'From my point of view, we're faced here with a closer similarity to some kind of harmony and attunement than we were before.'

'Why?'

'To be self-disciplined', I replied, 'is somehow to order and control the pleasures and desires. Hence the opaque expression "self-mastery"; and there are other expressions which hint at its nature. Yes?'

'Absolutely,' he said.

'Isn't the phrase "self-mastery" absurd? I mean, anyone who is his own master is also his own slave, of course, and vice versa, since it's the 431a same person who is the subject in all these expressions.'

'Of course.'

'What this expression means, I think,' I continued, 'is that there are better and worse elements in a person's mind, and when the part which is naturally better is in control of the worse part, then we use this phrase "self-mastery" (which is, after all, complimentary). But when, as a result of bad upbringing or bad company, the smaller better part is defeated by the superior numbers of the worse part, then b we use critical and deprecatory language and describe someone in this state as lacking self-mastery and discipline.'

'That sounds plausible,' he said.

'Have a look at our new community, then,' I said, 'and you'll find that the first of these alternatives is attributable to it. I mean, you must admit the justice of describing it as having self-mastery, since anything whose better part rules its worse part should be described as having self-discipline and self-mastery.'

'Yes, I can see the truth of what you're saying,' he said.

'Now, children, women, slaves, and (among c so-called free men) the rabble who constitute the majority of the population are the ones who evidently experience the greatest quantity and variety of forms of desire, pleasure, and pain.'

'Yes.'

'Whereas simple and moderate forms, which are guided by the rational mind with is intelligence and true beliefs, are encountered only in those few people who have been endowed with excellence by their nature and their education.'

'True,' he said.

'And is it clear to you that this is a property of your community, where the desires of the d common majority are controlled by the desires and the intelligence of the minority of better men?'

'It is,' he said.

'So if any community deserves to be described as having mastered pleasure and desire, and as having self-mastery, it is this one.'

'Without the slightest doubt,' he said.

'So it also deserves to be called self-disciplined, doesn't it?'

'Yes, indeed,' he said.

'Moreover, it is in this community, more than in any other conceivable community, that e the rulers and their subjects agree on who the rulers should be, don't you think?'

'Definitely,' he said.

'In a situation like this, then, is it the rulers or the subjects of the community who, in your opinion, possess self-discipline?'

'Both,' he replied.

'Is it clear to you, then,' I asked, 'that our recent conjecture that self-discipline resembles a kind of attunement wasn't bad?'

'Why?'

'Because unlike courage and wisdom, both of which imbued the community with their 432a respective qualities while being properties of only a part of the community, self-discipline literally spans the whole octaval spread of the community, and makes the weakest, the strongest, and the ones in between all sing in unison, whatever criterion you choose in order to assess their relative strengths—intelligence, physical strength, numerical quantity, wealth, and so on. And the upshot is that we couldn't go wrong if we claimed that self-discipline was this unanimity, a harmony between the naturally worse and naturally better elements of society as to which of them should rule both in a community and in every individual.'

b 'I certainly agree,' he said.

'All right,' I said. 'We've detected three of the qualities in our community, as far as we can tell. But there's one final way in which a community achieves goodness. What precisely is morality? I mean, morality is this missing type of goodness, clearly.'

'Clearly.'

'We must now imitate hunters surrounding a thicket, Glaucon, and make sure that morality doesn't somehow elude us and disappear into obscurity. I mean, we know it's somewhere round here. Keep your eyes peeled and try to
c spot it. If you see it before I do, let me know where it is.'

'I wish I could,' he said. 'But in fact it would be more realistic of you to regard me as someone who follows in your footsteps and can see things only when they're pointed out to him.'

'Follow me, then,' I said, 'and pray for success.'

'I will,' he said. 'You have only to lead on.'

'Now, we're in a rather rugged and overcast spot, it seems,' I said. 'At any rate, it's gloomy and hunting won't be easy. Still, we must carry on.'
d 'Yes, we must,' he said.

I caught a glimpse of something and shouted, 'Hurray! Glaucon, I believe we're on its trail! I don't think it will get clean away from us.'

'That's good news,' he said.

'What a stupid state to find ourselves in!' I exclaimed.

'What do you mean?'

'It looks as though it's been curled up at our feet all the time, right from the beginning, my friend, and we didn't see it, but just made absolute fools of ourselves. You know how people some-times go in search of something they're holding in
e their hands all the time? That's what we've been like. We've been looking off into the distance somewhere, instead of at our quarry, and that was why we didn't notice it, I suppose.'

'What do you mean?'

'I'll tell you,' I said. 'I think it's been the subject of our discussion all along and we just didn't appreciate that we were in a sense talking about it.'

'What a long preamble,' he said, 'when I'm so keen to hear what you're getting at!'

433a 'All right,' I said. 'See if you think there's anything in what I say. From the outset, when we first started to found the community, there's a principle we established as a universal requirement—and this, or some version of it, is in my opinion morality. The principle we established, and ten repeated time and again, as you'll remember, is that every individual has to

do just one of the jobs relevant to the community, the one for which his nature has best equipped him.'

'Yes, that's what we said.'

'Furthermore, the idea that morality is doing one's own job and not intruding elsewhere is commonly voiced, and we ourselves have often
b said it.'

'Yes, we have.'

'So, Glaucon,' I said, 'it seems likely that this is in a sense what morality is—doing one's own job. Do you know what makes me think so?'

'No,' he answered. 'Please tell me.'

'We've examined self-discipline, courage, and wisdom,' I said, 'and it occurs to me that this principle is what is left in the community, because it is the principle which makes it possible for all those other qualities to arise in the community, and its continued presence allows them to flourish in safety once they have arisen.
c And we did in fact say that if we found the other three, then whatever was left would be morality.'

'Yes, that's necessarily so,' he said.

'But if we had to decide which of these qualities it was whose presence is chiefly responsible for the goodness of the community,' I said, 'it would be hard to decide whether it's the unanimity between rulers and subjects, or the militia's retention of the lawful notion about what is and is not to be feared, or the wise guardianship
d which is an attribute of the rulers, or the fact that it is an attribute of every child, woman, slave, free person, artisan, ruler, and subject that each individual does his own job without intruding elsewhere, that is chiefly responsible for making it good.'

'Yes, of course that would be a difficult decision,' he said.

'When it comes to contributing to a community's goodness, then, there's apparently a close contest between the ability of everyone in a community to do their own jobs and its wisdom, self-discipline, and courage.'

'There certainly is,' he said.

'And wouldn't you say that anything which rivals these qualities in contributing towards a
e community's goodness must be morality?'

'Absolutely.'

'See if you also agree when you look at it from this point of view. Won't you be requiring the rulers to adjudicate when lawsuits occur in the community?'

'Of course.'

'And won't their most important aim in doing so be to ensure that people don't get hold of other people's property and aren't deprived of their own?'

'Yes.'

'Because this is right?'

'Yes.'

'So from this point of view too we are agreed that morality is keeping one's own property and 434a keeping to one's own occupation.'

'True.'

'See if you agree with me on this as well: if a joiner tried to do a shoemaker's job, or a shoemaker a carpenter's, or if they swapped tools or status, or even if the same person tried to do both jobs, with all the tools and so on of both jobs switched around, do you think that much harm would come to the community?'

'Not really,' he said.

'On the other hand, when someone whom nature has equipped to be an artisan or to work for money in some capacity or other gets so b puffed up by his wealth or popularity or strength or some such factor that he tries to enter the military class, or when a member of the militia tries to enter the class of policy-makers and guardians when he's not qualified to do so, and they swap tools and status, or when a single person tries to do all these jobs simultaneously, then I'm sure you'll agree that these interchanges and intrusions are disastrous for the community.'

'Absolutely.'

'There's nothing more disastrous for the community, then, than the intrusion of any of the three classes into either of the other two, and c the interchange of roles among them, and there could be no more correct context for using the term "criminal".'

'Indubitably.'

'And when someone commits the worst crimes against his own community, wouldn't you describe this as immorality?'

'Of course.'

'Then this is what immorality is. Here's an alternative way of putting it. Isn't it the case (to put it the other way round) that when each of the three classes—the one that works for a living, the auxiliaries, and the guardians—performs its proper function and does its own job in the community, then this is morality and makes the community a moral one?'

d 'Yes, I think that's exactly right,' he said.

'Let's not be too inflexible about it yet,' I warned. 'If we also conclude that this type of thing constitutes morality in the case of individual human beings as well, then we'll have no reservations. I mean, how could we under those circumstances? However, if we find that it doesn't apply to humans as well, then we'll have to take the enquiry into new areas. So let's now wind up that aspect of the enquiry which is based on the idea we had that it would be easier to detect the nature of morality in an individual human being if we first tried to observe it in something larger and to watch its operation there. We decided that the larger thing was a community, and so we e founded as good a community as we could, because we were well aware that it would have to be a good community for morality to exist in it. What we have to do now is apply the results we found in the case of the community to an individual. If there's a match, that will be fine; but if we find something different in the case of an individual, then we'll return to the community to test the new result. With luck, the friction of 435a comparing the two cases will enable morality to flare up from these fire-sticks, so to speak, and once it's become visible we'll make it more of a force in our own lives.'

'That's a viable notion,' he said. 'We should do as you suggest.'

'Well,' I said, 'if a single property is predicated of two things of different sizes, then in so far as it's the same predicate, is it in fact dissimilar or similar in the two instances?'

'Similar,' he said.

'So in respect of the actual type of thing b morality is, a moral person will be no different from a moral community, but will resemble it.'

'Yes,' he said.

'Now, we decided that a community was moral when each of the three natural classes that exist within it did its own job, and also that certain other states and conditions of the same three classes made it self-disciplined and courageous and wise.'

'True.'

'It follows, my friend, that we should expect c an individual to have the same three classes in himself, and that the same conditions make him liable to the same predicates as the community receives.'

'That's absolutely inevitable,' he said.

'Glaucon,' I said, 'now we're faced with another simple enquiry, to see whether or not the mind contains these three features.'

'It hardly seems to me to be a simple one,' he remarked. 'But then it's probably a true saying, Socrates, that anything fine is difficult.'

'I think that's right,' I said. 'In fact, I have to d tell you, Glaucon, that in my opinion we'll never completely understand this issue by relying on the kinds of methods we've employed so far in our discussion: a longer and fuller approach is needed. Still, we can hope to come up with something which is in keeping with what we've already said in the earlier stages of our enquiry.'

'Shouldn't we be content with that?' he asked. 'I for one would be satisfied with that for the time being.'

'And it'll do perfectly well for me too,' I said.

'No flagging, then,' he said. 'On with the enquiry.'

'Well, here's something we're bound to agree e on, aren't we?' I asked. 'That we do contain the same kinds of features and characteristics as the community. I mean, where else could it have got them from? When the general population of a community consists of people who are reputedly passionate—Thracians and Scythians, for example, and almost any northerner—it would be absurd to think that passion arises in this community from any other source. And the same goes for love of knowledge, for which our country 436a has a strong reputation; and being mercenary might be claimed to be a particular characteristic of Phoenicians and Egyptians.'

'Certainly.'

'This is a matter of fact, then,' I said, 'and it wasn't hard to discover.'

'No.'

'But here's a hard one: is there just a single thing which we use for doing everything, or are there three and we use different things for different tasks? Do we learn with one of our aspects, get worked up with another, and with a third desire the pleasures of eating, sex, and so on, or do we use the whole of our mind for every task b we actually get going on? These questions won't be easy to answer satisfactorily.'

'I agree,' he said.

'Well, let's approach an answer by trying to see whether these aspects are the same as one another or are different.'

'How?'

'It's clear that the same one thing cannot simultaneously either act or be acted on in opposite ways in the same respect and in the same context. And consequently, if we find this happening in the case of these aspects of ourselves, c we'll know that there are more than one of them.'

'All right.'

'What about this, then?'

'What?'

'Is it possible for the same thing to be simultaneously at rest and in motion in the same respect?' I asked.

'Of course not.'

'Let's take a closer look before agreeing, otherwise we'll start arguing later. My assumption is that if someone claims that a person who is standing still, but moving his hands and head, is the same person simultaneously being still and moving, we won't approve of this way of putting it, as opposed to saying that one part of him is d still, and another part of him is moving. Yes?'

'Yes.'

'So even if the advocate of the claim were to get even more subtle and ingeniously maintain that when a top is spinning round with its peg fixed in place, then this is definitely a case of something simultaneously being still and moving as a whole, or that the same goes for anything else which spins round on one spot, we wouldn't accept this assertion. We'll say that in this situation these objects are not still and moving in the e same respects. We'll point out that they include an axis and a circumference, and that they may be still in respect of their axes (in the sense that they're not tipping over at all), but they have circular motion in respect of their circumferences; and we'll add that when one of these objects tips its upright to the right or left or front or back while simultaneously spinning round, then it has no stillness in any respect.'

'Yes, that's right,' he said.

'No assertion of this kind will put us off, then, or make us in the slightest inclined to believe that the same thing could ever simul-
437a taneously be acted on or exist or act in opposite ways in the same respect and in the same context.'

'I won't be put off, anyway,' he said.

'That's as may be,' I said. 'But let's not feel compelled to have all the bother of going through every single one of these arguments and proving them false. Let's assume that we're right and carry on, with the understanding that if we ever turn out to have been mistaken, all the conclusions we draw on the basis of this assumption will be invalidated.'

'Yes, that's what we'd better do,' he said.

b 'Wouldn't you count assent and dissent,' I asked, 'seeking and avoidance, and liking and disliking, as all pairs of opposites? It'll make no difference whether you think of them as ways of acting or of being acted on.'

'Yes, they're opposites,' he answered.

'What about thirst and hunger and the desires generally,' I went on, 'and what about wishing and wanting? Wouldn't you say that all these things belong somewhere among the sets we've just mentioned? For example, won't you
c describe the mind of anyone who is in a state of desire as seeking to fulfil his desires, or as liking whatever the desired object is? Or again, to the extent that it wants to get hold of something, don't you think it is internally assenting to this thing, as if in response to a question, and is longing for it to happen?'

'Yes, I do.'

'And what about the states of antipathy, reluctance, or unwillingness? Won't we put these states in the opposite category, which includes dislike and aversion?'

d 'Of course.'

'Under these circumstances, then, won't we say that there is a category which consists of the desires, and that the most conspicuous desires are the ones called thirst and hunger?'

'Yes,' he said.

'And the one is desire for drink, the other desire for food?'

'Yes.'

'Now, is thirst, in itself, the mental desire for anything more than the object we mentioned? For example, is thirst thirst for a hot drink or a cold one, a lot of drink or a little, or in short for any particular kind of drink at all? Doesn't it take heat in addition to thirst to give it the extra fea-
e ture of being desire for something cold, and cold to make it desire for something hot? Doesn't it take a thirst which has been aggravated into becoming strong to produce the desire for a lot of drink, and doesn't it take a weak thirst to produce the desire for a little drink? The actual state of being thirsty, however, cannot possibly be desire for anything other than its natural object, which is just drink; and the same goes for hunger and food.'

'Yes,' he said. 'Each desire is for its natural object only, and the desire for an object of this or that type is a result of some addition.'

438a 'It should be quite impossible, then,' I said, 'for anyone to catch us unawares and rattle us with the claim that no one desires drink, but a good drink, and no one desires food, but good food. Everyone desires good, they say, so if thirst is a desire, it must be desire for a good drink or whatever; and so on for the other desires.'

'There might seem to be some plausibility to the claim,' he remarked.

'But there are only two categories of things whose nature it is to be relative,' I said. 'The first category consists, in my opinion, of things which have particular qualities and whose correlates have particular qualities; the second category
b consists of things which are just what they are and whose correlates are just what they are.'

'I don't understand,' he said.

'Don't you realize', I said, 'that anything which is greater is greater than something?'

'Yes.'

'Than something smaller?'

'Yes.'

'Whereas anything which is a lot greater is relative to something which is a lot smaller. Agreed?'

'Yes.'

'And anything which was once greater (or will be) is relative to something which was once smaller (or will be), isn't it?'

'Of course,' he said.

c   'And the same goes for more in relation to less, and double in relation to half (and all similar numerical relations); also for heavier in relation to lighter, quicker in relation to slower, and moreover hot in relation to cold, and so on and so forth, don't you think?'

'Yes.'

'And what about the branches of knowledge? Isn't it the same story? Knowledge in itself is knowledge of information in itself (or whatever you choose to call the object of knowledge), but a particular branch of knowledge, knowledge d qualified, is knowledge of a particular qualified kind of thing. Here's an example: when the knowledge of making houses was developed, didn't it differ from the rest of the branches of knowledge and consequently gain its own name, building?'

'Of course.'

'And didn't it do so by virtue of the fact that it is a particular kind of knowledge, a kind which none of the other branches of knowledge is?'

'Yes.'

'And wasn't it when its object came into being as a particular kind of thing that it too came into being as a particular kind of knowledge? And doesn't the same go for all the other branches of expertise and knowledge?'

'Yes, it does.'

'I wonder if you've grasped my meaning now,' I said. 'You should think of this as the point I was trying to make before, when I said that there are two categories of things whose nature it is to be relative: some are only themselves and are related to objects which are only themselves; others have particular qualities and are related to objects with particular qualities. I don't mean to e imply that their quality is the same as the quality of their objects—that knowledge of health and illness is itself healthy and ill, and knowledge of evil and good is itself evil and good. I mean that when knowledge occurs whose object is not the unqualified object of knowledge, but an object with a particular quality (say, health and illness), then the consequence is that the knowledge itself also acquires a particular quality, and this is why it is no longer called just plain knowledge: the qualification is added, and it is called medical knowledge.'

'I do understand,' he said,' and I agree as well.'

'As for thirst, then,' I said, 'don't you think it 439a finds its essential place among relative things? And what it essentially is, of course, is thirst . . . '

' . . . for drink,' he said. 'Yes, I agree.'

'So for drink of a particular kind there is also thirst of a particular kind; but thirst in itself is not thirst for a lot of drink or a little drink, or a beneficial drink or a harmful drink, or in short for drink of any particular kind. Thirst in itself is essentially just thirst for drink in itself.'

'Absolutely.'

'When someone is thirsty, then, the only thing—in so far as he is thirsty—that his mind wants is to drink. This is what it longs for and b strives for.'

'Clearly.'

'So imagine an occasion when something is making it resist the pull of its thirst: isn't this bound to be a different part of it from the thirsty part, which is impelling it towards drink as if it were an animal? I mean, we've already agreed that the same one thing cannot thanks to the same part of itself simultaneously have opposite effects in the same context.'

'No, it can't.'

'As an analogy, it isn't in my opinion right to say that an archer's hands are simultaneously pushing the bow away and pulling it closer. Strictly, one hand is pushing it away and the other is pulling it close.'

c 'I quite agree,' he said.

'Now, do we know of cases where thirsty people are unwilling to drink?'

'Certainly,' he said. 'It's a common occurrence.'

'What could be the explanation for these cases?' I asked. 'Don't we have to say that their mind contains a part which is telling them to drink, and a part which is telling them not to drink, and that this is a different part and overcomes the part which is telling them to drink?'

'I think so,' he said.

'And those occasions when thirst and so on are countermanded occur thanks to rationality, whereas the pulls and impulses occur thanks to d afflictions and diseased states, don't they?'

'I suppose so.'

'So it wouldn't be irrational of us to expect that these are two separate parts,' I said, 'one of which we can describe as rational, and the other as irrational and desirous. The first is responsible for the mind's capacity to think rationally, and the second—which is an ally of certain satisfactions and pleasures—for its capacity to fell lust, hunger, and thirst, and in general to be stirred by desire.'

e 'No, it wouldn't be irrational,' he said. 'This would be a perfectly reasonable view for us to hold.'

'Let's have these, then,' I said, 'as two distinct aspects of our minds. What about the passionate part, however, which is responsible for the mind's capacity for passion? Is it a third part or might it be interchangeable with one of the other two?'

'I suppose it might be the same as the desirous part,' he said.

'But there's a story I once heard which seems to me to be reliable,' I said, 'about how Leontius the son of Aglaeon was coming up from the Piraeus, outside the North Wall but close to it, when he saw some corpses with the public executioner standing near by. On the one hand, he experienced the desire to see them, but at the same time he felt disgust and averted his gaze. For a while, he struggled and kept his 440a hands over his eyes, but finally he was overcome by the desire; he opened his eyes wide, ran up to the corpses, and said, "There you are, you

wretches! What a lovely sight! I hope you feel satisfied!"'

'Yes, I've heard the story too,' he said.

'Now, what it suggests', I said, 'is that it's possible for anger to be at odds with the desires, as if they were different things.'

'Yes, it does,' he agreed.

'And that's far from being an isolated case, isn't it?' I asked. 'It's not at all uncommon to find a b person's desires compelling him to go against his reason, and to see him cursing himself and venting his passion on the source of the compulsion within him. It's as if there were two warring factions, with passion fighting on the side of reason. But I'm sure you wouldn't claim that you had ever, in yourself or in anyone else, met a case of passion siding with the desires against the rational mind, when the rational mind prohibits resistance.'

'No, I certainly haven't,' he said.

c 'And what about when you feel you're in the wrong?' I asked. 'If someone who in your opinion has a right to do so retaliates by inflicting on you hunger and cold and so on, then isn't it the case that, in proportion to your goodness of character, you are incapable of getting angry at this treatment and your passion, as I say, has no inclination to get worked up against him?'

'True,' he said.

'But suppose you feel you're being wronged. Under these circumstances, your passion boils and rages, and fights for what you regard as right. Then hunger, cold, and other sufferings make you stand firm and conquer them, and only success or death can stop it fighting the good fight, d unless it is recalled by your rational mind and calmed down, as a dog is by a shepherd.'

'That's a very good simile,' he said. 'And in fact the part we've got the auxiliaries to play in our community is just like that of dogs, with their masters being the rulers, who are, as it were, the shepherds of the community.'

'Yes, you've got it,' I said. 'That's exactly what I mean. . . .

441c 'It's not been easy,' I said, 'but we've made it to the other shore: we've reached the reasonable conclusion that the constituent categories of a community and of any individual's mind are identical in nature and number.'

'Yes, they are.'

'Isn't it bound to follow that the manner and cause of a community's and an individual's wisdom are identical?'

'Naturally.'

'And that the manner and cause of a com-
d munity's and an individual's courage are identical, and that the same goes for every other factor which contributes in both cases towards goodness?'

'Inevitably.'

'So no doubt, Glaucon, we'll also be claming that human morality is the same in kind as a community's morality.'

'Yes, that's absolutely inevitable too.'

'We can't have forgotten, however, that a community's mortality consists in each of its three constituent classes doing its own job.'

'No, I'm sure we haven't,' he said.

'So we should impress upon our minds the idea that the same goes for human beings as well. Where each of the constituent parts of an indi-
e vidual does its own job, the individual will be moral and will do *his* own job.'

'Yes, we certainly should do that,' he said.

'Since the rational part is wise and looks out for the whole of the mind, isn't it right for it to rule, and for the passionate part to be its subordinate and its ally?'

'Yes.'

'Now—to repeat—isn't it the combination of culture and exercise which will make them attuned to each other? The two combined provide fine discussions and studies to stretch and educate the rational part, and music and rhythm
442a to relax, calm, and soothe the passionate part.'

'Absolutely.'

'And once these two parts have received this education and have been trained and conditioned in their true work, then they are to be put in charge of the desirous part, which is the major constituent of an individual's mind and is naturally insatiably greedy for things. So they have to watch over it and make sure that it doesn't get so saturated with physical pleasures (as they are called) that in its bloated and strengthened state it stops doing its own job, and tries to dominate
b and rule over things which it is not equipped by its

hereditary status to rule over, and so plunges the whole of everyone's life into chaos.'

'Yes, indeed,' he said.

'Moreover, these two are perfect for guarding the entire mind and the body against external enemies, aren't they?' I asked. 'The rational part will do the planning, and the passionate part the fighting. The passionate part will obey the ruling part and employ its courage to carry out the plans.'

'True.'

'I imagine, then, that it is the passionate part of a person which we are taking into considera-
c tion when we describe him as courageous: we're saying that neither pain nor pleasure stops his passionate part retaining the pronouncements of reason about what is and is not to be feared.'

'That's right,' he agreed.

'And the part we take into consideration when we call him wise is that little part—his internal ruler, which made these pronouncements—which knows what is advantageous for each of the three parts and for their joint unity.'

'Yes.'

'And don't we call him self-disciplined when there's concord and attunement between these same parts—that is, when the ruler and its two subjects unanimously agree on the necessity of the rational part being the ruler and when they
d don't rebel against it?'

'Yes, that's exactly what self-discipline is, in both a community and an individual,' he said.

'And we're not changing our minds about the manner and cause of morality.'

'Absolutely not.'

'Well,' I said, 'have we blunted the edge of our notion of mortality in any way? Do we have any grounds for thinking that our conclusions about its nature in a community don't apply in this context?'

'I don't think so,' he replied.

BOOK V

'I get the impression, though, Socrates, that this is the kind of topic where, if no one interrupts you, you'll forget that it is all a digression from a previous topic—that is, whether this political system is viable, and if so, how. I accept that all

these practices, if realized, would be good for any community they were practiced in, and I can supplement your account: they are highly likely
471d to fight well against enemy forces, in so far as they are highly unlikely to abandon one another, since they regard one another as brothers, fathers, sons, and call one another by these names; if women joined them on a campaign (whether their task was to fight alongside the men or to support them in the rear), they'd have the effect of terrifying the enemy and could come up as reinforcements in an emergency, and I'm sure this would make our militia completely invincible; and I can see all the domestic benefits they'd bring which you haven't mentioned. You
e can take for granted my agreement that the realization of the constitution would result in all these advantages and innumerable others as well; so you don't have to talk about the actual constitution any more. Let's just try now to convince ourselves that it is viable and to find out how it is viable, and let's not bother with anything else.'

472a 'I wasn't expecting you to ambush my argument like this,' I said. 'Can't you sympathize with my procrastination? Perhaps you don't realize that it was hard enough for me to escape from the first two waves, and not now you're invoking the largest and most problematic of the set of three waves. When you see it and hear it, then you'll sympathize with me and see that it was perfectly realistic of me to have misgivings and qualms about proposing such a paradoxical idea for investigation.'

'The more you say this kind of thing,' he said, 'the less likely we are to let you off dis-
b cussing how this political system might be realized. Please don't waste any more time: just get on with it.'

'Well, the first thing we have to do,' I said, 'is remember that it's our search for the nature of morality and immorality that has brought us here.'

'All right,' he said. 'So what?'

'Nothing really. It's just that if we do discover what morality is, will we expect a moral man to be indistinguishable from it, and to be a perfect image of morality? Or will we be satisfied
c if he resembles it as closely as possible and participates in it more thoroughly than anyone else?'

'Yes, we'll be happy with that,' he said.

'Therefore,' I said, 'it's because we need a paradigm that we're trying to find out what morality is, and are asking whether a perfectly moral man could exist and, if so, what he would be like (and likewise for immorality and an immoral man). We want to be able to look at these men, to see how they stand as regards happiness and misery, and to face the inevitable conclusion about ourselves, that the more we resemble these exemplars, the more our condi-
d tion will resemble their condition. In other words, the purpose of our enquiry is not to try to prove that perfect morality or immorality could ever actually exist.'

'True,' he said.

'Do you doubt an artist's competence if he paints a paradigmatically good-looking human being, and portrays everything perfectly well in the painting, but can't prove that a person like that could actually exist?'

'I certainly do not,' he protested.

'Well, aren't we saying that we're trying to construct a theoretical paradigm of a good community?'
e 'Yes.'

'Then do you doubt our competence as theoreticians in this context if we can't prove that a community with our theoretical constitution could actually exist?'

'Of course not,' he said.

'So that's how matters really stand,' I said. 'However, if for your sake I also have to apply myself to proving how and under what circumstances it might get as close as possible to viability, then although this is a different kind of argument, I must ask you to make the same concession as before.'

'What concession?'

473a 'Is it possible for anything actual to match a theory? Isn't any actual thing bound to have less contact with truth than a theory, however much people deny it? Do you agree or not?'

'I do,' he said.

'So please don't force me to point to an actual case in the material world which conforms in all respects to our theoretical construct. If we can discover how a community's administration could come very close to our theory, then let's say that we've fulfilled your demands and discovered how it's all viable. I mean, won't you be satisfied b if we get that close? I would.'

'I would too,' said.

'Next, then, I suppose we should try to discover and show what the flaw is in current political systems which stops communities being governed as well as we've described, and what the smallest change is which could enable a community to achieve this type of constitution. By the smallest change, I mean preferably a single change, but if that's impossible, then two changes, or at any rate as few as possible and the least drastic ones possible.'

c 'Absolutely,' he said.

'Well,' I said, 'I think there is a single change which can be shown to bring about the transformation. It's not a small change, however, or easy to achieve, but it is feasible.'

'What is it?' he asked.

'I'm now about to confront the difficulty which, in our image, is the largest wave,' I said. 'Still, it must be voiced, even if it's going to swamp us, exactly like a wave, with scornful and contemptuous laughter. Are you ready for me to speak?'

'Go ahead,' he said.

'Unless communities have philosophers as kings,' I said, 'or the people who are currently d called kings and rulers practise philosophy with enough integrity—in other words, unless political power and philosophy coincide, and all the people with their diversity of talents who currently head in different directions towards either government or philosophy have those doors shut firmly in their faces—there can be no end to political troubles, my dear Glaucon, or even to human troubles in general, I'd say, and our theo-e retical constitution will be stillborn and will never see the light of day. Now you can appreciate what made me hesitate to speak before: I saw how very paradoxical it would sound, since it is difficult to realize that there is no other way for an individual or a community to achieve happiness.'

'What a thing to say, Socrates!' Glaucon said in response. 'This is quite an idea! Now that it's out in the open, you'd better expect hordes of

people—and not second-rate people either—to 474a fling off their clothes (so to speak), pick up the nearest weapon, and rush naked at you with enough energy to achieve heroic feats. And if you don't come up with an argument to keep them at bay while you make your escape, then your punishment will be to discover what scorn really is.'

'And it'll all be your fault, won't it?' I said.

'I've no regrets,' he replied. 'But that doesn't mean I'll desert you: I'll defend you to the best of my ability. Goodwill and encouragement are my arsenal, and my answers probably suit you more b than someone else's might. You can count on this assistance, so please try to win the sceptics round to your point of view.'

'You're providing such major support that I must make the effort,' I said. 'Now, in my opinion, we'll never escape from the people you mentioned unless we offer them a definition of a philosopher so that it is clear what we mean by our rash claim that philosophers should have political power. When there's no doubt about what it is to be a philosopher, then a defence becomes possible, if we can show that some peo-c ple are made to practise philosophy and to be political leaders, while others shouldn't engage in philosophy and should follow a leader.'

'The definition would be timely,' he remarked.

'All right. I wonder if this route leads to any kind of adequate clarification. Why don't you join me, and we'll see?'

'Lead on,' he said.

'I'm sure you're aware, without me having to remind you,' I said, 'that if the claim that someone loves something is to be accurate, he must undeniably love that thing as a whole, not just some aspects of it.'

d 'You've got to remind me, apparently,' he said, 'because I don't quite understand.'

'I'd have expected someone else to say that, Glaucon, not you,' I said. 'It's unlike an expert in love to forget that an amorous lover finds some pretext for being smitten and unhinged by every single alluring boy. They all seem to deserve his attention and devotion. I mean, isn't this how you and others like you behave towards good-looking young men? Don't you compliment a snub nose by calling it "pert", describe a hooked nose as "regal", and call one which falls between these two e extremes "perfectly proportioned"? Don't you call swarthy young men "virile" and pallid ones "children of the gods"? And who do you think invented the term "honey-coloured"? It could only have been some lover glossing over and making light of a sallow complexion, because its possessor was in the alluring period of adolescence. In short, you come up with every conceivable excuse and all kinds of terms to 475a ensure that you can give your approval to every alluring lad.'

'If you insist on trying out your ideas of how lovers behave on me,' he said, 'you can have my assent, because I don't want to jeopardize the argument.'

'And haven't you seen people who are fond of drinking behave in exactly the same way?' I went on. 'They make all kinds of excuses for their devotion to wine of every kind.'

'Yes.'

'And I'm sure you've noticed that if ambitious people can't get the command of a whole army, they take a company; and if they can't win b the respect of important and high-powered people, they're happy to be respected by lesser people. It's status in general which they desire.'

'Absolutely.'

'So tell me where you stand on this question. If in our opinion someone desires something, are we to say that he desires that type of thing as a whole, or only some aspects of it?'

'The whole of it,' he replied.

'So the same goes for a philosopher too: we're to say that what he desires is the whole of knowledge, not just some aspects of it. True?'

'True.'

'If someone fusses about his lessons, then, especially when he's still young and without c rational understanding of what is and isn't good for him, we can't describe him as a lover of knowledge, a philosopher, just as we can't describe someone who is fussing about his food as hungry, as desiring food, and don't call him a gourmand, but a poor eater.'

'Yes, it would be wrong to call him anything else.'

'On the other hand, if someone is glad to sample every subject and eagerly sets about his lessons with an insatiable appetite, then we'd be perfectly justified in calling him a philosopher, don't you think?'

d 'Then a motley crowd of people will be philosophers,' Glaucon said. 'For instance, sightseers all do what they do because they enjoy learning, I suppose; and it would be very odd to count theatre-goers as philosophers, when they'd never go of their own accord to hear a lecture or spend time over anything like that, but they rush around the festivals of Dionysus to hear every theatrical troupe, as if they were getting paid for the use of their ears, and never miss a single festival, whether it's being held in town or out of town. Are we to describe all these people and the disciples of other amusements as philosophers? And what e about students of trivial branches of expertise?'

'No,' I replied, 'they're not philosophers, but they resemble philosophers.'

'Who are the true philosophers you have in mind?' he asked.

'Sightseers of the truth,' I answered.

'That must be right, but what exactly does it mean?' he asked.

'It wouldn't be easy to explain to anyone else,' I said. 'But you'll grant me this, surely.'

'What?'

'Since beautiful is the opposite of ugly, they are two things.'

476a 'Of course.'

'In so far as they are two, each of them is single?'

'Yes.'

'And the same principle applies to moral and immoral, good and bad, and everything of any type: in itself, each of them is single, but each of them has a plurality of manifestations because they appear all over the place, as they become associated with actions and bodies and one another.'

'You're right,' he said.

'Well,' I continued, 'this is what enables me to distinguish the sightseers (to borrow your

term) and the ones who want to acquire some expertise or other and the men of action from the people in question, the ones who are philoso-
b phers in the true sense of the term.'

'What do you mean?' he asked.

'Theatre-goers and sightseers are devoted to beautiful sounds and colours and shapes, and to works of art which consist of these elements, but their minds are constitutionally incapable of seeing and devoting themselves to beauty itself.'

'Yes, that's certainly right,' he said.

'However, people with the ability to approach beauty itself and see beauty as it actually is are bound to be few and far between, aren't they?'

'Definitely.'

c 'So does someone whose horizon is limited to beautiful things, with no conception of beauty itself, and who is incapable of following guidance as to how to gain knowledge of beauty itself, strike you as living in a dream-world or in the real world? Look at it this way. Isn't dreaming precisely the state, whether one is asleep or awake, of taking something to be the real thing, when it is actually only a likeness?'

'Yes, that's what I'd say dreaming is,' he said.

'And what about someone who does the opposite—who does think that there is such a thing as beauty itself, and has the ability to see it
d as well as the things which partake in it, and never gets them muddled up? Do you think he's living in the real world or in a dream-world?'

'Definitely in the real world,' he said.

'So wouldn't we be right to describe the difference between their mental states by saying that while this person has knowledge, the other one has beliefs?'

'Yes.'

'Now, suppose this other person—the one we're saying has beliefs, not knowledge—were to get cross with us and query the truth of our assertions. Will we be able to calm him down and gently convince him of our point of view, while keeping him in the dark about the poor state of
e his health?'

'We really ought to,' he said.

'All right, but what shall we say to him, do you think? Perhaps this is what we should ask him. We'll tell him that we don't resent any knowledge he might have—indeed, we'd be delighted to see that he does know something—and then we'll say, "But can you tell us, please, whether someone with knowledge knows something or nothing?" You'd better answer my questions for him.'

'My answer will be that he knows something,' he said.

'Something real or something unreal?'

'Real. How could something unreal be known?'

477a 'We could look at the matter from more angles, but we're happy enough with the idea that something completely real is completely accessible to knowledge, and something utterly unreal is entirely inaccessible to knowledge. Yes?'

'Perfectly happy.'

'All right. But if something is in a state of both reality and unreality, then it falls between that which is perfectly real and that which is utterly unreal, doesn't it?'

'Yes.'

'So since the field of knowledge is reality, and since it must be incomprehension whose field is unreality, then we need to find out if there is in fact something which falls between incomprehension and knowledge, whose field is this intermediate, don't we?'

'Yes.'

b 'Now, we acknowledge the existence of belief, don't we?'

'Of course.'

'Is it a different faculty from knowledge, or is it the same?'

'Different.'

'Every faculty has its own distinctive abilities, so belief and knowledge must have different domains.'

'Yes.'

'Now, since the natural field of knowledge is reality—its function is to know reality as reality . . . Actually, I think there's something else we need to get clear about first.'

'What?'

'Shall we count as a distinct class of things the faculties which give human beings and all c other creatures their abilities? By "faculties" I mean things like sight and hearing. Do you understand the type of thing I have in mind?'

'Yes, I do,' he said.

'Let me tell you something that strikes me about them. I can't distinguish one faculty from another the way I commonly distinguish other things, by looking at their colours or shapes or anything like that, because faculties don't have any of those sorts of qualities for me to look at. The only aspect of a faculty I can look at is its field, its effect. This is what enables me to iden- d tify each of them as a particular faculty. Where I find a single domain and a single effect, I say there is a single faculty; and I distinguish faculties which have different fields and different effects. What about you? What do you do?'

'The same as you,' he said.

'Let's go back to where we were before, then, Glaucon,' I said. 'Do you think that knowledge is a faculty, or does it belong in your opinion to some other class?'

'I think it belongs to that class,' he said, 'and is the most powerful of all the faculties."

'And shall we classify belief as a faculty, or what?'

e   'As a faculty,' he said. 'Belief is precisely that which enables us to entertain beliefs.'

'Not long ago, however, you agreed that knowledge and belief were different.'

'Of course,' he said. 'One is infallible and the other is fallible, so anyone with any sense would keep them separate.'

'Good,' I said. 'There can be no doubt of our position: knowledge and belief are different.'

'Yes.'

'Since they're different faculties, then, they 478a have different natural fields, don't they?'

'Necessarily.'

'The field of knowledge is reality, isn't it? Its function is to know the reality of anything real?'

'Yes.'

'And the function of belief, we're saying, is to entertain beliefs?'

'Yes.'

'Does it entertain beliefs about the same thing which knowledge knows? Will what is accessible to knowledge and what is accessible to belief be identical? Or is that out of the question?'

'It ruled out by what we've already agreed,' he said. 'If different faculties naturally have different fields, and if both knowledge and belief are faculties, and different faculties too, as we said, then it follows that it is impossible for what is b accessible to knowledge and what is accessible to belief to be identical.'

'So if it is reality that is accessible to knowledge, then it is something else, not reality, that is accessible to belief, isn't it?'

'Yes.'

'Does it entertain beliefs about what is unreal? Or is it also impossible for that to happen? Think about this: isn't it the case that someone who is entertaining a belief is bringing his believing mind to bear on something? I mean, is it possible to have a belief, and to be believing nothing?'

'That's impossible.'

'In fact, someone who has a belief has some single thing in mind, doesn't he?'

'Yes.'

'But the most accurate way to refer to something unreal would be to say that it is nothing, not that it is a single thing, wouldn't it?'

'Yes.'

c   'Didn't we find ourselves forced to relate incomprehension to unreality and knowledge to reality?'

'That's right,' he said.

'So the field of belief is neither reality nor unreality?'

'No.'

'Belief can't be incomprehension or knowledge, then?'

'So it seems.'

'Well, does it lie beyond their limits? Does it shed more light than knowledge or spread more obscurity than incomprehension?'

'It does neither.'

'Alternatively, does belief strike you as more opaque than knowledge and more lucid than incomprehension?'

'Considerably more,' he said.

'It lies within their limits?'

'Yes.'

d   'Then belief must fall between them.'

'Absolutely.'

'Now, didn't we say earlier that something which is simultaneously real and unreal (were such a thing to be shown to exist) would fall between the perfectly real and the wholly unreal, and wouldn't be the field of either knowledge or incomprehension, but of an intermediate (again, if such a thing were shown to exist) between incomprehension and knowledge?'

'Right.'

'And now we've found that what we call belief is such an intermediate, haven't we?'

'We have.'

'So the only thing left for us to discover, apparently, is whether there's anything which e partakes of both reality and unreality, and cannot be said to be perfectly real or perfectly unreal. If we were to come across such a thing, we'd be fully justified in describing it as the field of belief, on the principle that extremes belong together, and so do intermediates. Do you agree?'

'Yes.'

'Let's return, on this basis, to the give and take of conversation with that fine fellow who doesn't acknowledge the existence of beauty 479a itself or think that beauty itself has any permanent and unvarying character, but takes the plurality of beautiful things as his norm—that sightseer who can't under any circumstances abide the notion that beauty, morality, and so on are each a single entity. What we'll say to him is, "My friend, is there one beautiful thing, in this welter of beautiful things, which won't turn out to be ugly? Is there one moral deed which won't turn out to be immoral? Is there one just act which won't turn out to be unjust?"'

'No, there isn't,' he said. 'It's inevitable for these things to turn out to be both beautiful and b ugly, in a sense, and the same goes for all the other qualities you mentioned in your question.'

'And there are doubles galore—but they turn out to be halves just as much as doubles, don't they?'

'Yes.'

'And do things which are large, small, light, and heavy deserve these attributes any more than they deserve the opposite attributes?'

'No, each of them is bound to have both qualities,' he said.

'So isn't it the case, then, that any member of a plurality no more *is* whatever it is said to be than it *is not* whatever it is said to be?'

'This is like those *double entendres* one hears at parties,' he said, 'or the riddle children tell about the eunuch and his hitting a bat—they c make a riddle by asking what he hit it with and what it was on—in the sense that the members of the plurality are also ambiguous: it is impossible to form a stable conception of any of them as either being what it is, or not being what it is, or being both, or being neither.'

'How are you going to cope with them, then?' I asked. 'Can you find a better place to locate them than between real being and unreality? I mean, they can't turn out to be more opaque and unreal than unreality, or more lucid and real than reality.'

d   'True,' he said.

'So there we are. We've discovered that the welter of things which the masses conventionally regard as beautiful and so on mill around somewhere between unreality and perfect reality.'

'Yes, we have.'

'But we have a prior agreement that were such a thing to turn up, we'd have to call it the field of belief, not of knowledge, since the realm which occupies some uncertain intermediate point must be accessible to the intermediate faculty.'

'Yes, we do.'

'What shall we say about those spectators, e then, who can see a plurality of beautiful things, but not beauty itself, and who are incapable of following if someone else tries to lead them to it, and who can see many moral actions, but not morality itself, and so on? That they only ever entertain beliefs, and do not *know* any of the things they believe?'

'That's what we have to say,' he said.

'As for those who can see each of these things in itself, in its permanent and unvarying nature, we'll say they have knowledge and are not merely entertaining beliefs, won't we?'

'Again, we have to.'

'And won't our position be that they're devoted to and love the domain of knowledge, as 480a opposed to the others, who are devoted to and love the domain of belief? I mean, surely we haven't forgotten our claim that these others love and are spectators of beautiful sounds and colours and so on, but can't abide the idea that there is such a thing as beauty itself?'

'No, we haven't forgotten.'

'They won't think us nasty if we refer to them as "lovers of belief" rather than as philosophers, who love knowledge, will they? Are they going to get very cross with us if we say that now?'

'Not if they listen to me,' he replied. 'It's not right to get angry at the truth.'

'But the term "believers" is inappropriate for those who are devoted to everything that is real: they should be called philosophers, shouldn't they?'

'Absolutely.'

BOOK VI

484a 'It's taken a long and thorough discussion, Glaucon,' I said, 'and it's not been easy, but we've now demonstrated the difference between philosophers and non-philosophers.'

'A short discussion probably wouldn't have been enough,' he replied.

'I suppose you're right,' I said. 'Anyway, I think the conclusion would have been clearer if that had been the only subject we'd had to discuss, and there weren't plenty of topics left for us to cover if we're to see the difference between a b moral and an immoral life.'

'What's the next issue for us to look into?' he asked.

'The next one's the one that follows, of course,' I replied. 'Given that philosophers are those who are capable of apprehending that which is permanent and unvarying, while those who can't, those who wander erratically in the midst of plurality and variety, are not lovers of knowledge, which set of people ought to be rulers of a community?'

'What would be a sensible answer for us to give?' he asked.

'That the position of guardianship should be given to whichever set we find capable of guard- c ing the laws and customs of a community,' I said.

'Right,' he said.

'I assume it's clear whether someone who's going to guard something should be blind or have good eyesight?' I said.

'Of course it is,' he answered.

'Well, imagine someone who really lacks the ability to recognize any and every real thing and has no paradigm to shed light for his mind's eye. He has nothing absolutely authentic to contemplate, as painters do, and use as a reference-point whenever he needs to, and gain a completely d accurate picture of, before establishing human norms of right, morality, and goodness (if establishing is what is required), and before guarding and protecting the norms that have already been established. Do you think there's any difference between his condition and blindness?'

'No, there's hardly any difference at all,' he said.

'Is this the type of person you'd prefer us to appoint as guardians? Or shall we appoint those who can recognize every reality, and who not only have just as much practical experience as the others, but are also at least as good as them in every other respect?'

'If they really are at least equal in every other sphere,' he said, 'and since they are pre-eminent in the sphere you've mentioned, which is just about the most important one there is, then it would be ridiculous to choose anyone else.'

485a 'So what we'd better explain is how a single person can combine both sets of qualities, hadn't we?'

'Yes.'

'Well, right at the beginning of this argument we said that the first thing we had to grasp was what it is to be a philosopher. I'm sure that if we reached a satisfactory agreement on that point, we'd also agree that despite being a single person, he can combine both sets of qualities, and that philosophers are the only ones who should rule over communities.'

'Why?'

'Let's start by agreeing that it's natural for philosophers to love every field of study which
b reveals to them something of that reality which is eternal and is not subject to the vicissitudes of generation and destruction.'

'All right.'

'Moreover,' I said, 'we can agree that they're in love with reality as a whole, and that therefore their behaviour is just like that of ambitious people and lovers, as we explained before, in that they won't willingly give up even minor or worthless parts of it.'

'You're right,' he said.

'The next thing for you to think about is
c whether there's a further feature they must have, if they're going to live up to our description of them.'

'What feature?'

'Honesty—the inability consciously to tolerate falsehood, rather than loathing it, and loving truth.'

'It makes sense that they should,' he said.

'It doesn't only make sense, my friend: a lover is absolutely bound to love everything which is related and belongs to his beloved.'

'Right,' he said.

'Well, can you conceive of anything more closely related to knowledge than truth?'

'Of course not,' he replied.

'Is it possible, then, for love of knowledge
d and love of falsehood to be found in the same nature?'

'Definitely not.'

'Then a genuine lover of knowledge will from his earliest years find nothing more attractive than truth of every kind.'

'Indisputably.'

'And we know that anyone whose predilection tends strongly in a single direction has correspondingly less desire for other things, like a stream whose flow has been diverted into another channel.'

'Of course.'

'So when a person's desires are channelled towards learning and so on, that person is concerned with the pleasure the mind feels of its own accord, and has nothing to do with the pleasures which reach the mind through the agency of the body, if the person is a genuine
e philosopher, not a fake one.'

'Inevitably.'

'He'll be self-disciplined, then, and not mercenary, since he's constitutionally incapable of taking seriously the things which money can buy—at considerable cost—and which cause others to take money seriously.'

'Yes.'

486a 'And here's another point you'd better take into consideration, to help you distinguish a philosophical from a non-philosophical character.'

'What?'

'You must watch out for the presence of small-mindedness. Nothing stops a mind constantly striving for an overview of the totality of things human and divine more effectively than involvement in petty details.'

'Very true,' he said.

'When a mind has broadness of vision and contemplates all time and all existence, do you think it can place much importance on human life?'

'Impossible,' he said.

b 'So it won't find death terrifying either, will it?'

'Not at all.'

'Then a cowardly and small-minded person is excluded from true philosophy, it seems.'

'I agree.'

'Well now, take a person who's restrained and uninterested in money, and who isn't small-minded or specious or cowardly. Could he possibly drive hard bargains or act immorally?'

'No.'

'So when you're trying to see whether or not someone has a philosophical mind, you'll watch out for whether, from his earliest years, he shows himself to be moral and well mannered, or antisocial and uncouth.'

'Yes.'

c 'And there's something else you won't forget to look out for as well, I imagine.'

'What?'

'Whether he's quick or slow at learning. I mean, you wouldn't expect someone to be particularly fond of something it hurt him to do and where slight gains were hard to win, would you?'

'I'd never do that.'

'What about if he's incapable of retaining anything he's learnt? Is there any way he can have room for knowledge, when he's full of forgetfulness?'

'Of course not.'

'In the end, don't you think, after all his thankless toil, he's bound to loathe both himself and intellectual activity?'

'Yes.'

'So we'd better count forgetfulness as a fac-
d tor which precludes a mind from being good enough at philosophy. We'd better make a good memory a prerequisite.'

'Absolutely.'

'Now, isn't it the case that lack of culture and grace in someone can only lead him to lack a sense of proportion?'

'Of course.'

'And do you think that truth is closely related to proportion or to its opposite?'

'To proportion.'

'So we need to look for a mind which, in addition to the qualities we've already mentioned, has an inherent sense of proportion and elegance, and which makes a person instinctively inclined towards anything's essential character.'

'Of course we do.'

e   'All right. Surely you don't think that any of the interconnected qualities we've mentioned are at all inessential for a competent and complete mental grasp of reality?'

487a   'No, they're absolutely essential,' he said.

'Can you find any flaw, then, in an occupation like this, which in order to be competently practiced requires the following inherent qualities in a person: a good memory, quickness at learning, broadness of vision, elegance, and love of and affiliation to truth, morality, courage, and self-discipline?'

'Not even Momus could criticize this occupation,' he replied.

'Now, aren't people who, thanks to their education and their age, have these qualities in

full the only ones to whom you would entrust your community?'

b   Adeimantus spoke up. 'Socrates,' he said, 'no one's going to take you up on this point; but that may be due to the fact that there's a particular experience which people who hear you speak on any occasion always have. They get the impression that, because they lack expertise at the give and take of discussion, they're led a little bit astray by each question, and then when all the little bits are put together at the end of the discussion, they find that they were way off the mark and that they've contradicted their original position. They're like unskilled backgammon players, who end up being shut out by skilled ones and incapable of making a move:
c they too end up being shut out and incapable of making an argumentative move in this alternative version of backgammon, which uses words rather than counters, since they feel that this is not necessarily a certain route to the truth. From my point of view, what I'm saying is relevant to our current situation. You see, someone might object that his inability to find the words to challenge you doesn't alter the evident fact that the majority of the people who take up philoso-
d phy and spend more than just their youth on it—who don't get involved in it just for educational purposes and then drop it—turn out to be pretty weird (not to say rotten to the core), and that the effect of this pursuit you're praising even on those of its practitioners who are supposed to be particularly good is that they become incapable of performing any service to their communities.'

I responded by asking, 'Do you think this view is right?'

'I don't know,' he replied. 'But I'd be happy to hear what you have to say on the matter.'

'What you'd hear from me is that I think they're telling the truth.'

e   'Then how can it be right', he said, 'to say that there'll be no end to political troubles until philosophers have power in their communities, when we agree that philosophers are no use to them?'

'It'll take an analogy to answer your question,' I said.

'And you never use analogies, of course,' he said.

'What?' I exclaimed. 'It's hard enough to prove my point without you making fun of me as well as forcing me to try. Anyway, here's my anal-
488a ogy: now you'll be in a better position to see how inadequate it is. I mean, what society does to the best practitioners of philosophy is so complex that there's no other single phenomenon like it: in order to defend them from criticism, one has to compile an analogy out of lots of different elements, like the goat-stags and other compound creatures painters come up with.

'Imagine the following situation on a fleet of ship, or on a single ship. The owner has the edge over everyone else on board by virtue of his size
b and strength, but he's rather deaf and short-sighted, and his knowledge of naval matters is just as limited. The sailors are wrangling with one another because each of them thinks that he ought to be the captain, despite the fact that he's never learnt how, and can't name his teacher or specify the period of his apprenticeship. In any case, they all maintain that it isn't something that can be taught, and are ready to butcher any-one who says it is. They're for ever crowding
c closely around the owner, pleading with him and stopping at nothing to get him to entrust the rud-der to them. Sometimes, if their pleas are unsuc-cessful, but others get the job, they kill those others or throw them off the ship, subdue their worthy owner by drugging him or getting him drunk or something, take control of the ship, help themselves to its cargo, and have the kind of drunken and indulgent voyage you'd expect from people like that. And that's not all: they think highly of anyone who contributes towards their gaining power by showing skill at winning over or subduing the owner, and describe him as
d an accomplished seaman, a true captain, a naval expert; but they criticize anyone different as use-less. They completely fail to understand that any genuine sea-captain has to study the yearly cycle, the seasons, the heavens, the stars and winds, and everything relevant to the job, if he's to be properly equipped to hold a position of authority in a ship. In fact, they think it's impossible to study and acquire expertise at how to steer a ship

(leaving aside the question of whether or not
e people want you to) and at the same time be a good captain. When this is what's happening on board ships, don't you think that the crew of ships in this state would think of any true captain as nothing but a windbag with his head in the
489a clouds, of no use to them at all?'

'They definitely would,' Adeimantus replied.

'I'm sure you don't need an analysis of the analogy to see that it's a metaphor for the atti-tude of society towards true philosophers,' I said. 'I'm sure you take my point.'

'I certainly do,' he said.

'You'd better use it, then, in the first in-stance, to clarify things for that person who expressed surprise at the disrespect shown to philosophers by society, and try to show him how much more astonishing it would be if they were
b respected.'

'All right, I will,' he said.

'And that you're right to say that the best practitioners of philosophy are incapable of per-forming any public service. But you'd better tell him to blame their uselessness on the others' fail-ure to make use of them, rather than on the fact that they are accomplished philosophers. I mean, it's unnatural for the captain to ask the sailors to accept his authority and it's unnatural for wise men to dance attendance on rich men; this story is misleading. The truth of the matter is that it makes no difference whether you're rich or poor: if you feel ill, you're bound to dance attendance
c on a doctor, and if you need to accept author-
489c ity, you must dance attendance on someone in authority who is capable of providing it. If he is really to serve any useful purpose, it's not up to him to ask those under him to accept his author-ity. And you won't be mistaken if you compare present-day political leaders to the sailors in our recent tale, and the ones they call useless air-heads to the genuine captain.'

'You're absolutely right,' he said.

'Under these conditions and circumstances, it's not easy for the best of occupations to gain a good reputation, when reputations are in the hands of people whose occupations are incom-
d patible with it. But by far the worst and most influential condemnation of philosophy comes

about as a result of the people who claim to practise it—the ones the critic of philosophy was talking about, in your report, when he described the majority of the people who take up philosophy as rotten to the core (although the best of them are merely useless). And I agreed that you were telling the truth, didn't I?'

'Yes.'

'I was too scared to make the reckless assertions that have now been expressed,' I said, 'but now the presumptuous statement that if we are to have absolutely authentic guardians, then we must appoint philosophers, is out in the open.'

'Yes, it is,' he said.

'Do you realize how few they'll be, in all likelihood? Consider the nature which, in our account, they have to have and how rare it is for its various parts to coalesce into a single entity: it usually ends up in bits and pieces.'

'What do you mean?' he asked.

'People who are quick at learning, have good memories, and are astute and smart and so on, tend—as you know—not to combine both energy and broadness of mental vision with the ability to live an orderly, peaceful, and stable life. Instead, their quickness carries them this way and that, and stability plays no part at all in their lives.'

'You're right,' he said.

'On the other hand, a sound and stable character, which makes people more dependable and slow to respond to frightening situations in battle, also makes them approach their studies in the same way. There're as slow to respond and to learn as if they'd been drugged, and they're constantly dozing off and yawning when they're asked to do anything intellectually arduous.'

'True,' he said.

'But our claim is that a good and sufficient helping of both sets of qualities is a prerequisite for anyone to be allowed to take part in an authentic educational programme or to be awarded political office and power.'

'Right,' he said.

'So it'll be a rare phenomenon, don't you think?'

'Of course it will.'

'It's not just a matter of testing someone in the ways we've already mentioned, then—by means of ordeals and fear and pleasure. There's a further point we omitted before, but are including now: we must give him plenty of intellectual exercise as well, so that we can see whether he is capable of enduring fundamental intellectual work, or whether he'll cut and run as cowards do in other spheres.'

'Yes, we certainly ought to try to find that out,' he said. 'But what do you mean by fundamental intellectual work?'

'I'm sure you remember when, as a result of distinguishing three aspects within the mind, we defined morality, self-discipline, courage, and wisdom,' I said.

'If I didn't,' he said, 'then we might as well stop right now.'

'Do you also remember how we prefaced our discussion of those qualities?'

'How?'

'We said that it would take a different route, a longer one, to reach the best possible vantagepoint and that they would be plainly visible to anyone who went that way, but that it was possible to come up with arguments which were in keeping with the kinds of discussions we'd already been having. You said that would do, and we proceeded at the time on that basis. I think the argument was defective, in terms of precision, but it's up to you to say whether you were happy with it.'

'Yes, I was happy enough with it,' he said, 'and so was everyone else.'

'But in these sorts of matters, my friend,' I said, 'anything which misses the truth by even a tiny amount is nowhere near "enough". Anything less than perfect is not up to the mark at all, though people occasionally think it's adequate and that they don't need to look any further.'

'Yes, a great many people feel this,' he said, 'because they're lazy.'

'But it's a completely inappropriate feeling for a guardian of a community and its laws to have,' I said.

'I suppose so,' he said.

'Then a guardian had better take the longer route, Adeimantus,' I said, 'and put just as much effort into his intellectual work as his physical exercise. Otherwise, as we said a moment ago, he'll never see that fundamental field of study through to the end—and it's not just fundamental, but particularly appropriate for him.'

'Are you implying that morality and the other qualities we discussed are not the most important things there are—that there's something even more fundamental than them?' he asked.

'It's not only more fundamental,' I said, 'but it's exactly the kind of thing which requires viewing as a completely finished product, without skimping and looking merely at an outline, as we did just now. I mean, wouldn't it be absurd to devote extremes of energy and effort to getting as precise and clear a picture as possible of insignificant matters, and then not to think that the most important matters deserve the utmost precision too?'

'An excellent sentiment,' he said. 'But surely you don't expect to get away without being asked what this fundamental field of study of yours is, and what it is concerned with?'

'No, I don't,' I answered. 'Go ahead and ask your questions. In actual fact, you've not infrequently been told what it is, but it's either slipped your mind for the moment, or you're intending to make trouble for me by attacking my position. I incline towards the latter alternative, since you've often been told that the most important thing to try to understand is the character of goodness, because this is where anything which is moral (or whatever) gets its value and advantages from. It can hardly have escaped your notice that this is my position, and you must know what I'm going to add: that our knowledge of goodness is inadequate. And you appreciate, I'm sure, that there's absolutely no point in having expert knowledge of everything else, but lacking knowledge of goodness, just as there isn't in having anything else either, unless goodness comes with it. I mean, do you think there's any advantage in owning everything in the world except good things, or in understanding everything else except goodness, and therefore failing to understand anything worth while and good?'

'I certainly don't,' he said.

'Now, it can't have escaped your notice either that the usual view of goodness is that it's pleasure, while there's also a more ingenious view around, that it's knowledge.'

'Of course it hasn't.'

'As you also know, however, my friend, the people who hold the latter view are incapable of explaining exactly *what* knowledge constitutes goodness, but are forced ultimately to say that it is knowledge of goodness.'

'And so to make complete fools of themselves,' he remarked.

'Of course they do,' I said. 'First they tell us off for not knowing what goodness is, then they talk to us as if we did know what it is. I mean, to say it's knowledge of goodness is to assume that we understand what they're saying when they use the term "goodness".'

'You're absolutely right,' he said.

'What about the definition of goodness as pleasure? Aren't its proponents just as thoroughly misguided as the others? I mean, they too are forced to make a concession, in this case that there are bad pleasures, aren't they?'

'Certainly.'

'So their position ends up being that it is possible for a single thing to be both good and bad, doesn't it?'

'Naturally.'

'It's clear, therefore, that there's plenty of scope for serious disagreement where goodness is concerned. Yes?'

'Of course.'

'Well, isn't it also clear that whereas (whether it's a matter of doing something, or owning something, or having a certain reputation) people usually prefer the appearance of morality and right, even if there's no reality involved, yet no one is content with any possession that is only apparently good? It's the reality of goodness they want; no one thinks at all highly of mere appearance in this sphere.'

'Yes, that's perfectly clear,' he said.

'So here we have something which everyone, whatever their temperament, is after, and which is the goal of all their activities. They have an inkling of its existence, but they're confused about it and can't adequately grasp its nature or be as certain and as confident about it as they can about other things, and consequently they fail to derive any benefit even from those other activities. When something of this kind and this importance is involved, can we allow the best members of our community, the ones to whom we're going to entrust everything, to be equally in the dark?'

'Certainly not,' he protested.

'Anyway,' I said, 'I imagine that anyone who is ignorant about the goodness of moral and right conduct would make a second-rate guardian of morality and right, and I suspect that no one will fully understand them until he knows about their relation to goodness.'

'Your suspicion is right,' he said.

'So the constitution and organization of our community will be perfect only if they are overseen by the kind of guardian who has this knowledge, won't they?'

'Necessarily,' he said. 'But Socrates, do *you* identify goodness with knowledge or pleasure, or with something else?'

'Just listen to him!' I exclaimed. 'It's been perfectly obvious all along that other people's views on the matter weren't going to be enough for you.'

'That's because I don't think it's right, Socrates,' he said, 'for someone who's devoted so much time to the matter to be in a position to state others' beliefs, but not his own.'

'But do you think it's right', I responded, 'for someone to talk as if he knew what he doesn't know?'

'Of course not,' he said. 'Not as if he knew, but as if he'd formed opinions—he should be prepared to say what he thinks.'

'But aren't ideas which aren't based on knowledge always defective, in your experience?' I asked. 'The best of them are blind. I mean, don't people who have a correct belief, but no knowledge, strike you as exactly like blind people who happen to be taking the right road?'

'Yes,' he said.

'Well, do you want to see things which are defective, blind, and deformed,' I asked, 'when you could be getting lucid, correct views from elsewhere?'

'Socrates,' said Glaucon, 'please don't back away from the finishing-line, so to speak. We'd be happy with the kind of description of goodness that you gave of morality, self-discipline, and so on.'

'So would I, Glaucon,' I said, 'very happy. But I'm afraid it'll be more than I can manage, and that my malformed efforts will make me ridiculous. What I suggest, my friends, is that we forget about trying to define goodness itself for the time being. You see, I don't at the moment think that our current impulse is enough to take us to where I'd like to see us go. However, I am prepared to talk about something which seems to me to be the child of goodness and to bear a very strong resemblance to it. Would you like me to do that? If not, we can just forget it.'

'Please do,' he said. 'You can settle your account by discussing the father another time.'

'I hope I can make the repayment,' I said, 'and you can recover the debt, rather than just the interest, as you are now. Anyway, as interest on your account, here's an account of the child of goodness. But please be careful that I don't cheat you—not that I intend to—by giving you a counterfeit description of the child.'

'We'll watch out for that as best we can,' he replied. 'Just go ahead, please.'

'First I want to make sure that we're not at cross purposes,' I said, 'and to remind you of something that came up earlier, though you've often heard it on other occasions as well.'

'What?' he asked.

'As we talk,' I said, 'we mention and differentiate between a lot of beautiful things and a lot of good things and so on.'

'Yes, we do.'

'And we also talk about beauty itself, goodness itself and so on. All the things we refer to as a plurality on those occasions we also conversely count as belonging to a single class by virtue of the fact that they have a single particular character, and we say that the *x* itself is "what really is".'

'True.'

'And we say that the first lot is visible rather than intelligible, whereas characters are intelligible rather than visible.'

'Absolutely.'

'With what aspect of ourselves do we see the c things we see?'

'With our sight,' he replied.

'And we use hearing for the things we hear, and so on for all the other senses and the things we perceive. Yes?'

'Of course.'

'Well, have you ever stopped to consider', I asked, 'how generous the creator of the sense was when he created the domain of seeing and being seen?'

'No, not really,' he said.

'Look at it this way. Are hearing and sound deficient? Do they need an extra something to make the one hear and the other be heard— d some third thing without which hearing won't hear and sound won't be heard?'

'No,' he answered.

'And in my opinion', I went on, 'the same goes for many other domains, if not all: they don't need anything like this. Or can you point to one that does?'

'I can't,' he said.

'But do you realize that sight and the visible realm *are* deficient?'

'How?'

'Even if a person's eyes are capable of sight, and he's trying to use it, and what he's trying to look at is coloured, the sight will see nothing and the colours will remain unseen, surely, unless there is also present an extra third thing which is e made specifically for this purpose.'

'What is this thing you're getting at?' he asked.

'It's what we call light,' I said.

'You're right,' he said.

'So if light has value, then because it links the sense of sight and the ability to be seen, it is 508a far and away the most valuable link there is.'

'Well, it certainly does have value,' he said.

'Which of the heavenly gods would you say is responsible for this? Whose light makes it possible for our sight to see and for the things we see to be seen?'

'My reply will be no different from what yours or anyone else's would be,' he said. 'I mean you're obviously expecting the answer, "the sun".'

'Now, there are certain conclusions to be drawn from comparing sight to this god.'

'What?'

'Sight and the sun aren't to be identified: neither the sense itself nor its location—which b we call the eye—is the same as the sun.'

'True.'

'Nevertheless, there's no sense-organ which more closely resembles the sun, in my opinion, than the eye.'

'The resemblance is striking.'

'Moreover, the eye's ability to see has been bestowed upon it and channelled into it, as it were, by the sun.'

'Yes.'

'So the sun is not to be identified with sight, but is responsible for sight and is itself within the visible realm. Right?'

'Yes,' he said.

'The sun is the child of goodness I was talking about, then,' I said. 'It is a counterpart to its father, goodness. As goodness stands in the intelc ligible realm to intelligence and the things we know, so in the visible realm the sun stands to sight and the things we see.'

'I don't understand,' he said. 'I need more detail, please.'

'As you know,' I explained, 'when our eyes are directed towards things whose colours are no longer bathed in daylight, but in artificial light instead, then they're less effective and seem to be virtually blind, as if they didn't even have the potential for seeing clearly.'

'Certainly,' he said.

'But when they're directed towards things d which are lit up by the sun, then they see clearly and obviously do have that potential.'

'Of course.'

'Well, here's how you can think about the mind as well. When its object is something which is lit up by truth and reality, then it has— and obviously has—intelligent awareness and knowledge. However, when its object is permeated with darkness (that is, when its object is something which is subject to generation and decay), then it has beliefs and is less effective, because its beliefs chop and change, and under these circumstances it comes across as devoid of intelligence.'

'Yes, it does.'

e   'Well, what I'm saying is that it's goodness which gives the things we know their truth and makes it possible for people to have knowledge. It is responsible for knowledge and truth, and you should think of it as being within the intelligible realm, but you shouldn't identify it with knowledge and truth, otherwise you'll be wrong: for all their value, it is even more valuable. In the other 509a realm, it is right to regard light and sight as resembling the sun, but not to identify either of them with the sun; so in this realm it is right to regard knowledge and truth as resembling goodness, but not to identify either of them with goodness, which should be rated even more highly.'

'You're talking about something of inestimable value,' he said, 'if it's not only the source of knowledge and truth, but is also more valuable than them. I mean, you certainly don't seem to be identifying it with pleasure!'

'How could you even think it?' I exclaimed. 'But we can take our analogy even further.'

b   'How?'

'I think you'll agree that the ability to be seen is not the only gift the sun gives to the things we see. It is also the source of their generation, growth, and nourishment, although it isn't actually the process of generation.'

'Of course it isn't.'

'And it isn't only the known-ness of the things we know which is conferred upon them by goodness, but also their reality and their being, although goodness isn't actually the state of being, but surpasses being in majesty and might.'

c   'It's way beyond human comprehension, all right,' was Glaucon's quite amusing comment.

'It's your fault for forcing me to express my views on the subject,' I replied.

'Yes, and please don't stop,' he said. 'If you've left anything out of your explanation of the simile of the sun, then the least you could do is continue with it.'

'There are plenty of omissions, in fact,' I said.

'Don't leave any gaps,' he said, 'however small.'

'I think I'll have to leave a lot out,' I said, 'but I'll try to make it as complete as I can at the moment.'

'All right,' he said.

d   'So bear in mind the two things we've been talking about,' I said, 'one of which rules over the intelligible realm and its inhabitants, while the other rules over the visible realm—I won't say over the heavens in case you think I'm playing clever word-games. Anyway, do you understand this distinction between visible things and intelligible things?'

'Yes.'

'Well, picture them as a line cut into two unequal sections and, following the same proportion, subdivide both the section of the visible realm and that of the intelligible realm. Now you can compare the sections in terms of clarity and unclarity. The first section in the visible realm e consists of likenesses, by which I mean a number 510a of things: shadows, reflections (on the surface of water or on anything else which is inherently compact, smooth, and bright), and so on. Do you see what I'm getting at?'

'I do.'

'And you should count the other section of the visible realm as consisting of the things whose likenesses are found in the first section: all the flora and fauna there are in the world, and every kind of artefact too.'

'All right.'

'I wonder whether you'd agree,' I said, 'that truth and lack of truth have been the criteria for distinguishing these sections, and that the image stands to the original as the realm of beliefs stands to the realm of knowledge?'

b   'Yes,' he said, 'I certainly agree.'

'Now have a look at how to subdivide the section which belongs to the intelligible realm.'

'How?'

'Like this. If the mind wants to explore the first subdivision, it can do so only by using those former originals as likenesses and by taking things for granted on its journey, which leads it to an end-point, rather than to a starting-point. If it wants to explore the second subdivision, however, it takes things for granted in order to travel to a starting-point where nothing needs to be taken for granted, and it has no involvement with likenesses, as before, but makes its approach by means of types alone, in and of themselves.'

'I don't quite understand what you're saying,' he said.

c   'You will if I repeat it,' I said, 'because this preamble will make it easier to understand. I'm sure you're aware that practitioners of geometry, arithmetic, and so on take for granted things like numerical oddness and evenness, the geometrical figures, the three kinds of angle, and any other things of that sort which are relevant to a given subject. They act as if they know about these things, treat them as basic, and don't feel any further need to explain them either to themselves or to anyone else, on the grounds that there is d nothing unclear about them. They make them the starting-points for their subsequent investigations, which end after a coherent chain of reasoning at the point they'd set out to reach in their research.'

'Yes, I'm certainly well aware of this,' he said.

'So you must also be aware that in the course of their discussions they make use of visible forms, despite the fact that they're not interested in visible forms as such, but in the things of which the visible forms are likenesses: that is, their discussions are concerned with what it is to be a square, and with what it is to be a diagonal (and so on), rather than with the diagonal (and e so on) which occurs in their diagrams. They treat their models and diagrams as likenesses, when these things have likenesses themselves, in fact (that is, shadows and reflections on water); but they're actually trying to see squares and so on in 511a themselves, which only thought can see.'

'You're right,' he said.

'So it was objects of this type that I was describing as belonging to the intelligible realm, with the rider that the mind can explore them only by taking things for granted, and that its goal is not a starting-point, because it is inca-pable of changing direction and rising above the things it is taking for granted. And I went on to say that it used as likenesses those very things which are themselves the originals of a lower order of likenesses, and that relative to the likenesses, the originals command respect and admiration for their distinctness.'

b   'I see,' he said. 'You're talking about the objects of geometry and related occupations.'

'Now, can you see what I mean by the second subdivision of the intelligible realm? It is what reason grasps by itself, thanks to its ability to practise dialectic. When it takes things for granted, it doesn't treat them as starting-points, but as basic in the strict sense—as platforms and rungs, for example. These serve it until it reaches a point where nothing needs to be taken for granted, and which is the starting-point for everything. Once it has grasped this starting-point, it turns around and by a process of depending on the things which depend from the starting-point, it descends to an end-point. It makes absolutely no use of anything perceptible c by the senses: it aims for types by means of types alone, in and of themselves, and it ends its journey with types.'

'I don't quite understand,' he said. 'I mean, you're talking about crucial matters here, I think. I do understand, however, that you want to mark off that part of the real and intelligible realm which is before the eyes of anyone who knows how to practise dialectic as more clear than the other part, which is before the eyes of practitioners of the various branches of expertise, as we call them. The latter make the things they take for granted their starting-points, and although they inevitably use thought, not the senses, to observe what they observe, yet because of their failure d to ascend to a starting-point—because their enquiries rely on taking things for granted—you're saying that they don't understand these things, even though they are intelligible, when related to a starting-point. I take you to be describing what geometers and so on do as thinking rather than knowing, on the grounds that thinking is the intermediate state between believing and knowing.'

'There's nothing wrong with your understanding,' I said. 'And you should appreciate that there are four states of mind, one for each of the four sections. There's knowledge for the highest section and thought for the second one; and

e you'd better assign confidence to the third one and conjecture to the final one. You can make an orderly progression out of them, and you should regard them as possessing as much clarity as their objects possess truth.'

'I see,' he said. 'That's fine with me: I'll order them in the way you suggest.'

BOOK VII

514a 'Next,' I said, 'here's a situation which you can use as an analogy for the human condition—for our education or lack of it. Imagine people living in a cavernous cell down under the ground; at the far end of the cave, a long way off, there's an entrance open to the outside world. They've been there since childhood, with their legs and

b necks tied up in a way which keeps them in one place and allows them to look only straight ahead, but not to turn their heads. There's firelight burning a long way further up the cave behind them, and up the slope between the fire and the prisoners there's a road, beside which you should imagine a low wall has been built—like the partition which conjurors place between themselves and their audience and above which they show their tricks.'

'All right,' he said.

'Imagine also that there are people on the other side of this wall who are carrying all sorts of artefacts. These artefacts, human statuettes, and

c animal models carved in stone and wood and all kinds of materials stick out over the wall; and as

515a you'd expect, some of the people talk as they carry these objects along, while others are silent.'

'This is a strange picture you're painting,' he said, 'with strange prisoners.'

'They're no different from us,' I said. 'I mean, in the first place, do you think they'd see anything of themselves and one another except the shadows cast by the fire on to the cave wall directly opposite them?'

'Of course not,' he said. 'They're forced to

b spend their lives without moving their heads.'

'And what about the objects which were being carried along? Won't they only see their shadows as well?'

'Naturally.'

'Now, suppose they were able to talk to one another: don't you think they'd assume that their words applied to what they saw passing by in front of them?'

'They couldn't think otherwise.'

'And what if sound echoed off the prison wall opposite them? When any of the passers-by spoke, don't you think they'd be bound to assume that the sound came from a passing shadow?'

'I'm absolutely certain of it,' he said.

'All in all, then,' I said, 'the shadows of arte-

c facts would constitute the only reality people in this situation would recognize.'

'That's absolutely inevitable,' he agreed.

'What do you think would happen, then,' I asked, 'if they were set free from their bonds and cured of their inanity? What would it be like if they found that happening to them? Imagine that one of them has been set free and is suddenly made to stand up, to turn his head and walk, and to look towards the firelight. It hurts him to do all this and he's too dazzled to be capable of making out the objects whose shadows he'd formerly been looking at. And suppose

d someone tells him that what he's been seeing all this time has no substance, and that he's now closer to reality and is seeing more accurately, because of the greater reality of the things in front of his eyes—what do you imagine his reaction would be? And what do you think he'd say if he were shown any of the passing objects and had to respond to being asked what it was? Don't you think he'd be bewildered and would think that there was more reality in what he'd been seeing before than in what he was being shown now?'

'Far more,' he said.

e 'And if he were forced to look at the actual firelight, don't you think it would hurt his eyes? Don't you think he'd turn away and run back to the things he could make out, and would take the truth of the matter to be that these things are clearer than what he was being shown?'

'Yes,' he agreed.

'And imagine him being dragged forcibly away from there up the rough, steep slope,' I went on, 'without being released until he's been pulled out into the sunlight. Wouldn't this treatment 516a cause him pain and distress? And once he's reached the sunlight, he wouldn't able to see a single one of the things which are currently taken to be real, would he, because his eyes would be overwhelmed by the sun's beams?'

'No, he wouldn't,' he answered, 'not straight away.'

'He wouldn't be able to see things up on the surface of the earth, I suppose, until he'd got used to his situation. At first, it would be shadows that he could most easily make out, then he'd move on to the reflections of people and so on in water, and later he'd be able to see the actual things themselves. Next, he'd feast his eyes on the heavenly bodies and the heavens themselves, which would be easier at night: he'd look at the b light of the stars and the moon, rather than at the sun and sunlight during the daytime.'

'Of course.'

'And at last, I imagine, he'd be able to discern and feast his eyes on the sun—not the displaced image of the sun in water or elsewhere, but the sun on its own, in its proper place.'

'Yes, he'd inevitably come to that,' he said.

'After that, he'd start to think about the sun and he'd deduce that it is the source of the seasons and the yearly cycle, that the whole of the visible realm is its domain, and that in a sense everything which he and his peers used to see is c its responsibility.'

'Yes, that would obviously be the next point he'd come to,' he agreed.

'Now, if he recalled the cell where he'd originally lived and what passed for knowledge there and his former fellow prisoners, don't you think he'd feel happy about his own altered circumstances, and sorry for them?'

'Definitely.'

'Suppose that the prisoners used to assign prestige and credit to one another, in the sense that they rewarded speed at recognizing the shadows as they passed, and the ability to remember which ones normally come earlier and later and at the same time as which other ones, and

d expertise at using this as a basis for guessing which ones would arrive next. Do you think our former prisoner would covet these honours and would envy the people who has status and power there, or would he much prefer, as Homer describes it, "being a slave labouring for someone else—someone without property", and would put up with anything at all, in fact, rather than share their beliefs and their life?'

e   'Yes, I think he'd go through anything rather than live that way,' he said.

'Here's something else I'd like your opinion about,' I said. 'If he went back underground and sat down again in the same spot, wouldn't the sudden transition from the sunlight mean that his eyes would be overwhelmed by darkness?'

'Certainly,' he replied.

'Now, the process of adjustment would be quire long this time, and suppose that before his eyes had settled down and while he wasn't seeing 517a well, he had once again to compete against those same old prisoners at identifying those shadows. Wouldn't he make a fool of himself? Wouldn't they say that he'd come back from his upward journey with his eyes ruined, and that it wasn't even worth trying to go up there? And wouldn't they—if they could—grab hold of anyone who tried to set them free and take them up there and kill him?'

'They certainly would,' he said.

'Well, my dear Glaucon,' I said, 'you should apply this allegory, as a whole, to what we were b talking about before. The region which is accessible to sight should be equated with the prison cell, and the firelight there with the light of the sun. And if you think of the upward journey and the sight of things up on the surface of the earth as the mind's ascent to the intelligible realm, you won't be wrong—at least, *I* don't think you'd be wrong, and it's my impression that you want to hear. Only God knows if it's actually true, however. Anyway, it's my opinion that the last thing to be seen—and it isn't easy to see either—in the realm of knowledge is goodness; and the c sight of the character of goodness leads one to deduce that it is responsible for everything that is right and fine, whatever the circumstances, and that in the visible realm it is the progenitor of light and of the source of light, and in the intelligible realm it is the source and provider of truth and knowledge. And I also think that the sight of it is a prerequisite for intelligent conduct either of one's own private affairs or of public business.'

'I couldn't agree more,' he said.

'All right, then,' I said, 'I wonder if you also agree with me in not finding it strange that people who've travelled there don't want to engage in human business: there's nowhere else their minds would ever rather be than in the upper d region—which is hardly surprising, if our allegory has got this aspect right as well.'

'No, it's not surprising,' he agreed.

'Well, what about this?' I asked. 'Imagine someone returning to the human world and all its misery after contemplating the divine realm. Do you think it's surprising if he seems awkward and ridiculous while he's still not seeing well, before he's had time to adjust to the darkness of his situation, and he's forced into a contest (in a lawcourt or wherever) about the shadows of morality or the statuettes which cast the shadows, and into a competition whose terms are the e conceptions of morality held by people who have never seen morality itself?'

'No, that's not surprising in the slightest,' he said.

518a   'In fact anyone with any sense,' I said, 'would remember that the eyes can become confused in two different ways, as a result of two different sets of circumstances: it can happen in the transition from light to darkness, and also in the transition from darkness to light. If he took the same facts into consideration when he also noticed someone's mind in such a state of confusion that it was incapable of making anything out, his reaction wouldn't be unthinking ridicule. Instead, he'd try to find out whether this person's mind was returning from a mode of existence which involves greater lucidity and had been blinded by the unfamiliar darkness, or whether it was moving from relative ignorance to relative lucidity and had been overwhelmed and dazzled by the increased brightness. Once he'd distinguished between the two conditions and modes of exis-

tence, he'd congratulate anyone he found in the second state, and feel sorry for anyone in the first b state. If he did choose to laugh at someone in the second state, his amusement would be less absurd than when laughter is directed at someone returning from the light above.'

'Yes,' he said, 'you're making a lot of sense.'

'Now, if this true,' I said, 'we must bear in mind that education is not capable of doing what some people promise. They claim to introduce knowledge into a mind which doesn't have it, as if they were introducing sight into eyes which c are blind.'

'Yes, they do,' he said.

'An implication of what we're saying at the moment, however,' I pointed out, 'is that the capacity for knowledge is present in everyone's mind. If you can imagine an eye that can turn from darkness to brightness only if the body as a whole turns, then our organ of understanding is like that. Its orientation has to be accompanied by turning the mind as a whole away from the world of becoming, until it becomes capable of bearing the sight of real being and reality at its most bright, which we're saying is goodness. d Yes?'

'Yes.'

'That's what education should be,' I said, 'the art of orientation. Educators should devise the simplest and most effective methods of turning minds around. It shouldn't be the art of implanting sight in the organ, but should proceed on the understanding that the organ already has the capacity, but is improperly aligned and isn't facing the right way.'

'I suppose you're right,' he said.

'So although the mental states which are described as good generally seem to resemble good physical states, in the sense that habitua- e tion and training do in fact implant them where they didn't use to be, yet understanding (as it turns out) is undoubtedly a property of something which is more divine: it never loses its 519a power, and it is useful and beneficial, or useless and harmful, depending on its orientation. For example, surely you've noticed how the petty minds of those who are acknowledged to be bad, but clever, are sharp-eyed and perceptive enough to gain insights into matters they direct their attention towards. It's not as if they weren't sharp-sighted, but their minds are forced to serve evil, and consequently the keener their vision is, the greater the evil they accomplish.'

'Yes, I've noticed this,' he said.

'However,' I went on, 'if this aspect of that b kind of person is hammered at from an early age, until the inevitable consequences of incarnation have been knocked off it—the leaden weights, so to speak, which are grafted on to it as a result of eating and similar pleasures and indulgences and which turn the sight of the mind downwards—if it sheds these weights and is reoriented towards the truth, then (and we're talking about the same organ and the same people) it would see the truth just as clearly as it sees the objects it faces at the moment.'

'Yes, that makes sense,' he said.

'Well, doesn't this make sense as well?' I asked. 'Or rather, isn't it an inevitable conse-c quence of what we've been saying that uneducated people, who have no experience of truth, would make incompetent administrators of a community, and that the same goes for people who are allowed to spend their whole lives educating themselves? The first group would be no good because their lives lack direction: they've got no single point of reference to guide them in all their affairs, whether private or public. The second group would be no good because their hearts wouldn't be in the business: they think they've been transported to the Isles of the Blessed even while they're still alive.'

'True,' he said.

'Our job as founders, then,' I said, 'is to make sure that the best people come to that fundamental field of study (as we called it earlier): we must have them make the ascent we've been talking d about and see goodness. And afterwards, once they've been up there and had a good look, we mustn't let them get away with what they do at the moment.'

'Which is what?'

'Staying there,' I replied, 'and refusing to come back down again to those prisoners, to share their work and their rewards, no matter whether those rewards are trivial or significant.'

e   'But in that case,' he protested, 'we'll be wronging them: we'll be making the quality of their lives worse and denying them the better life they could be living, won't we?'

'You're again forgetting, my friend,' I said, 'that the point of legislation is not to make one section of a community better off than the rest, 520a but to engineer this for the community as a whole. Legislators should persuade or compel the members of a community to mesh together, should make every individual share with his fellows the benefit which he is capable of contributing to the common welfare, and should ensure that the community does contain people with this capacity; and the purpose of all this is not for legislators to leave people to choose their own directions, but for them to use people to bind the community together.'

'Yes, you're right,' he said. 'I was forgetting.'

'I think you'll also find, Glaucon,' I said, 'that we won't be wronging any philosophers who b arise in our community. Our remarks, as we force them to take care of their fellow citizens and be their guardians, will be perfectly fair. We'll tell them that it's reasonable for philosophers who happen to occur in other communities not to share the work of those communities, since their occurrence was spontaneous, rather than planned by the political system of any of the communities in question, and it's fair for anything which arises spontaneously and doesn't owe its nurture to anyone or anything to have no interest in repaying anyone for having provided its nourishment. "We've bred *you*, however," we'll say, "to act, as it were, as the hive's leaders and kings, for c your own good as well as that of the rest of the community. You've received a better and more thorough education than those other philosophers, and you're more capable of playing a part in both spheres. So each of you must, when your time comes, descend to where the rest of the community lives, and get used to looking at things in the dark. The point is that once you become acclimatized, you'll see infinitely better than the others there; your experience of genuine right, morality, and goodness will enable you to identify every one of the images and recognize what it is an image of. And then the administration of our community—ours as well as yours— will be in the hands of people who are awake, as distinct from the norm nowadays of communities being governed by people who shadow-box and fall out with one another in their dreams over who should rule, as if that were a highly desirable d thing to do. No, the truth of the matter is this: the less keen the would-be rulers of a community are to rule, the better and less divided the administration of that community is bound to be, but where the rulers feel the opposite, the administration is bound to be the opposite.'''

'Yes,' he said.

'And do you think our wards will greet these views of ours with scepticism and will refuse to join in the work of government when their time comes, when they can still spend most of their time living with one another in the untainted realm?'

e 'No, they couldn't,' he answered. 'They're fair-minded people, and the instructions we're giving them are fair. However, they'll undoubtedly approach rulership as an inescapable duty— an attitude which is the opposite of the one held by the people who have power in communities at the moment.'

'You're right, Glaucon,' I said. 'You'll only 521a have a well-governed community if you can come up with a way of life for your prospective rulers that is preferable to ruling! The point is that this is the only kind of community where the rulers will be genuinely well off (not in material terms, but they'll possess the wealth which is a prerequisite of happiness—a life of virtue and intelligence), whereas if government falls into the hands of people who are impoverished and starved of any good things of their own, and who expect to wrest some good for themselves form political office, a well-governed community is an impossibility. I mean, when rulership becomes something to fight for, a domestic and internal war like this destroys not only the perpetrators, but also the rest of the community.'

'You're absolutely right,' he said.

b 'Apart from the philosophical life,' I said, 'is there any way of life, in your opinion, which looks down on political office?'

'No, definitely not,' he answered.

'In fact, political power should be in the hands of people who aren't enamoured of it. Otherwise their rivals in love will fight them for it.'

'Of course.'

'There's no one you'd rather force to undertake the guarding of your community, then, than those who are experts in the factors which contribute towards the good government of a community, who don't look to politics for their rewards, and whose life is better than the political life. Agreed?'

'Yes,' he said.

'What I'd say', I continued, 'is that engaging in d all the subjects we've been discussing has some relevance to our purposes, and all that effort isn't wasted, if the work takes one to the common ground of affinity between the subjects, and enables one to work out how they are all related to one another; otherwise it's a waste of time.'

'I suspect you're right,' he said. 'But you're talking about an awful lot of hard work, Socrates.'

'What?' I asked. 'The prelude is hard, you say? Don't you realize that this is all just the prelude to the main theme, which is the important subject? I mean, you surely don't think that being accomplished in these subjects makes one good e at dialectic.'

'No, certainly not,' he answered, 'although it does happen sometimes—very occasionally—in my experience.'

'But don't you think the inability to explain anything, and to understand explanations, rules out the possibility of knowing any of the things we're saying are important?' I asked.

'Yes, I agree with you on this too,' he replied.

532a 'And isn't this exactly the theme which dialectic develops, Glaucon?' I asked. 'It may be an intelligible theme, but sight can be said to reflect it, when, as we were saying, it sets about looking at actual creatures, at the heavenly bodies themselves, and finally at the sun itself. Just as, in this case, a person ends up at the supreme point of the visible realm, so the summit of the intelligible realm is reached when, by means of dialectic and without relying on anything perceptible, a person perseveres in using rational b argument to approach the true reality of things until he has grasped with his intellect the reality of goodness itself.'

'Absolutely,' he said.

'And this is the journey a practitioner of dialectic makes, wouldn't you say?'

'Of course.'

'And the prisoners' release from their bonds,' I went on, 'their reorientation away from shadows and towards figurines and firelight, their ascent out from under the ground into sunlight, their lingering inability to look in the upper world at creatures and plants and the light of the sun, rather than gazing at reflections in water and at c shadows (shadows, that is, of real things, not the shadows of figurines cast by a light which, relative to the sun, is of the same order as the figurines)— just as, in this case, the most lucid part of the body is taken up to see the most lucid part of the material, visible realm, so the whole business of studying the areas of expertise we've been discussing has the ability to guide the best part of the d mind upwards until it sees the best part of reality.'

'I'm happy with that,' he said, 'despite the fact that acceptance and rejection both seem to me to be problematic, from different points of view. However, we shouldn't let this be just a one-off discussion today, but should often return to the issue. So let's assume that our ideas are correct, and get on with discussing the actual main theme in as much detail as we did the prelude. So please tell us the ins and outs of the ability to do dialectic, and how many different types e of it there are, and what methods it employs, since they'd presumably be the means of approaching that place which, once reached, is travellers' rest and journey's end.'

533a 'You won't be able to follow me there, my dear Glaucon,' I said, 'which is a pity, because there'd be no shortage of determination from me, and what you'd see there wouldn't be an image of what we're talking about: you'd see the truth itself—or that's what I think, anyway. I may be

right, and I may be wrong—that's not for us to insist on at the moment; but we can state with confidence that there'd be something of the kind to be seen, don't you think?'

'Of course.'

'And what about the idea that dialectic alone can elucidate these matters, to someone with experience in the subjects we've discussed, and that otherwise it's impossible?'

'Yes, we should state that confidently too,' he said.

b 'Anyway, what is indisputable in what we're saying', I said, 'is that dialectic is the only field of enquiry which sets out methodically to grasp the reality of any and every thing. All the other areas of expertise, on the other hand, are either concerned with fulfilling people's beliefs and desires, or are directed towards generation and manufacture or looking after things while they're being generated and manufactured. Even any that are left— geometry and so on, which we were saying do grasp reality to some extent—are evidently dreaming c about reality. There's no chance of their having a conscious glimpse of reality as long as they refuse to disturb the things they take for granted and remain incapable of explaining them. For if your starting-point is unknown, and your end-point and intermediate stages are woven together out of unknown material, there may be coherence, but knowledge is completely out of the question.'

'Yes, it is,' he agreed.

'So dialectic is the only field of enquiry', I went on, 'whose quest for certainty causes it to uproot the things it takes for granted in the course of its journey, which takes it towards an d actual starting-point. When the mind's eye is literally buried deep in mud, far from home, dialectic gently extracts it and guides it upwards, and for this reorientation it draws on the assistance of those areas of expertise we discussed. It's true that we've often called them branches of *knowledge* in the past, but that's only a habit and they really need a different word, which implies a higher degree of clarity than belief has, and a higher degree of opacity than knowledge has. Earlier, we used the term "thought". But I don't suppose we'll quarrel about terminology when we're faced with matters as important as the ones we're looking into at the moment.'

'No, we won't,' he said, 'just so long as whatever term is used expresses the state of mental clarity.'

'So the terms we used earlier will do,' I said, 'We'll call the first section knowledge, the second thought, the third confidence, and the fourth conjecture; and the first pair constitute intellect (which is concerned with real being), the second pair belief (which is concerned with becoming). As being stands to becoming, so intellect stands to belief; and as intellect stands to belief, so knowledge stands to confidence and thought to conjecture. However, we'd better pass over the proportionate relations between the objects of intellect and belief, Glaucon, and the twofold division of each of the two realms—the domain of belief and the domain of intellect—if we want to avoid getting entangled in an argument which would be many times as long as the ones our discussion has already thrown up.'

'Well, I agree with everything else you've said, in so far as I can follow it,' he said.

'And don't you think that the ability to understand what it is to be any given thing, when someone else explains it, is indicative of a dialectician? And wouldn't you say that, in so far as anyone who lacks this ability is incapable of explaining anything to himself or to anyone else either, then he doesn't know anything?'

'Of course I would,' he answered.

'The same principle applies to goodness, then, as well. If someone is incapable of arguing for the separation and distinction of the character of goodness from everything else, and can-

not, so to speak, fight all the objections one by one and refute them (responding to them resolutely by referring to the reality of things, rather than to people's beliefs), and can't see it all through to the end without his position suffering a fall—if you find someone to be in this state, you'll deny that he has knowledge of goodness itself or, in general, of anything good at all. Instead, if he does somehow manage to make contact with a reflection of goodness, you'll claim that the contact is due to belief, not knowledge. He dreams his current life away in a state of semi-consciousness, you'll say, and he'll never wake up here: he'll go to Hades, the place of total sleep, first. Agreed?'

'Yes, definitely,' he said. 'I'll certainly be making all of these claims.'

'Now, suppose your theoretical upbringing and education of your younger generation were to become a reality. I imagine you'd deny them power and crucial responsibility in the community if they were as irrational as surds.'

'Yes, I would.' he said.

'Will you include in your legislation, then, the ruling that a major part of the education they engage in must be the subject which will enable them to acquire particular expertise at the give and take of discussion?'

'I will,' he replied, 'if you join me.'

'Don't you think', I asked, 'that dialectic occupies the highest position and forms, as it were, the copestone of the curriculum? And that, if so, there's no subject which ought to occupy a higher position, and therefore it completes our educational programme?'

'Yes, I agree,' he answered.

STUDY QUESTIONS: PLATO, *REPUBLIC*

1. What is the ring of Gyges? What purpose does it serve as an example?
2. For what theoretical purposes does Plato construct the ideal city-state?
3. What are the three functional groupings of Plato's ideal community? What are the corresponding virtues?
4. How does Plato define justice in a city-state?
5. How does Plato divide the soul of a person? What is the principle that he uses to make this division?
6. How does Plato define justice in the individual person?

7. How does Plato distinguish between knowledge and belief in the *Republic?*
8. What is intermediate between reality and unreality?
9. According to Plato, why is there a norm of beauty that exists unvarying and permanent?
10. What is a philosopher?
11. What object is the eye like? What sense organ is the soul like?
12. What is the good in the intellectual world in relation to the mind and its objects?
13. How does Plato distinguish between the intelligible and the visible realms? Which is the most real?
14. What is the practice of dialectic?
15. How does the soul ascend above the hypotheses to the idea of the good?
16. What is the purpose of the allegory of the cave? What do the prisoners look at? What do they see? What do they think they see?
17. What would Plato say about the 2004 U.S. election? What are the fundamental principles involved?

PHAEDRUS

The *Phaedrus* is one of Plato's most beautiful works, the central part of which returns to the natures of beauty and love. Socrates is alone with Phaedrus in an attractive spot outside the city. Phaedrus reads him a speech on love by Lysias, and this inspires Socrates to make his own speech. Socrates' first speech, like that of Lysias, is critical of love, which he characterizes as fickle and self-seeking. Soon afterward, however, Socrates has a change of heart, and, in his second speech, he praises love. Even mad feelings of love point to some good, the vision of the Beautiful itself. The sight of a lover will reawaken the memory of the Beautiful.

To further this understanding of love, Socrates presents the implications of a tripartite division of the soul for the nature of love. He compares love to a winged chariot with two horses. The charioteer represents reason that seeks knowledge of the Forms, and loves wisdom and truth. The white horse represents the love of honor, and the dark horse, the wish to have one's own way. We have selected the central part of Socrates' second speech.

The *Phaedrus* can be divided into two parts. The first part finishes at the end of Socrates' second speech. After this speech, Socrates praises the merits of the spoken as opposed to the written word. He also warns against the power of rhetoric, which is inferior to the true method of inquiry, dialectic. Socrates uses his two speeches to illustrate these points, in effect arguing that only a combination of the content of both speeches would be adequate, reflecting the difference between two kinds of love. In the early part of the dialogue, he had been seduced by the beauty of Lysias' written word, and this led him to give his first speech, which he later repudiates and replaces with his second speech. But now, Socrates suggests that even his second speech should not be taken too seriously, just because it is a speech rather than a dialectic or philosophical conversation. In other words, Plato points to the inherent limitation of all written philosophical works, including his own, namely, that they cannot answer questions and defend themselves.

From *Plato: Phaedrus, Aris, and Phillips*, 1986. Edited with an introduction, translation and commentary by C. J. Rowe. Reprinted by permission of Oxbow Books.

'All soul is immortal. For that which is always in movement is immortal; that which moves something else and is moved by something else, in ceasing from movement, ceases from living. Only that which moves itself, because it does not abandon itself, never stops moving. It is also d source and first principle of movement for the other things which move. A first principle is something which does not come into being. For all that comes into being must come into being from a first principle, but a first principle itself cannot come into being from anything at all; for if a first principle came into being from anything, it would not do so from a first principle. Since it does not come into being, it must also be something which does not perish. For if a first princi- 5 ple is destroyed, neither will it ever come into being from anything nor anything else from it, given that all things must come into being from a first principle. It is in this way, then, that that which moves itself is first principle of movement. It is not possible for this either to be destroyed or e to come into being, or else the whole universe and the whole of that which comes to be might collapse together and come to a halt, and never again have a source from which things will come to be moved. And since that which is moved by itself has been shown to be immortal, it will incur no shame to say that this is the essence and the definition of soul. For all body which has its 5 source of motion outside itself is soulless, whereas that which has it within itself and from itself is ensouled, this being the nature of soul; and if this is so —that that which moves itself is nothing other than soul, soul will be necessarily some- 246 thing which neither comes into being nor dies.

'About its immortality, then, enough has been said; about its form we must say the following. To say what kind of thing it is would require 5 a long exposition, and one calling for utterly superhuman powers; to say what it resembles requires a shorter one, and one within human capacities. So let us speak in the latter way. Let it then resemble the combined power of a winged team of horses and their charioteer. Now in the case of gods, horses and charioteers are all both good and of good stock; whereas in the case b of the rest there is a mixture. In the first place our

driver has charge of a pair; secondly one of them he finds noble and good, and of similar stock, while the other is of the opposite stock, and opposite in its nature; so that the driving in our 5 case is necessarily difficult and troublesome. How then it is that some living creatures are called mortal and some immortal, we must now try to say. All soul has the care of all that is soulless, and ranges about the whole universe, coming to be now in one form, now in another. Now when c it is perfectly winged, it travels above the earth and governs the whole cosmos; but the one that has lost its wings is swept along until it lays hold of something solid, where it settles down, taking on an earthy body, which seems to move itself because of the power of soul, and the 5 whole is called a living creature, soul and body fixed together, and acquires the name "mortal"; immortal it is not, on the basis of any argument which has been reasoned through, but because we have not seen or adequately conceived of a d god we imagine a kind of immortal living creature which has both a soul and a body, combined for all time. But let this, and our account of it, be as is pleasing to god; let us grasp the reason for the loss of wings—why they fall from a soul. It is 5 something like this.

'The natural property of a wing is to carry what is heavy upwards, lifting it aloft to the region where the race of the gods resides, and in a way, of all the things belonging to the sphere of the body, it has the greatest share in the divine, the divine being noble, good, and everything e which is of that kind; so it is by these things that the plumage of the soul is most nourished and increased, while the shameful, the bad and in general the opposites of the other things make it waste away and perish. First in the heavens travels Zeus, the great leader, driving a winged char- 5 iot, putting all things in order and caring for all; after him there follows an army of gods and 247 divinities, ordered in eleven companies. For Hestia remains in the house of the gods alone; of the rest, all those who have their place among the number of the twelve take the lead as commanders in the station given to each. Many, then, and 5 blessed are the paths to be seen along which the happy race of gods turn within the heavens, each

of them performing what belongs to him; and after them follows anyone who wishes and is able to do so, for jealousy is excluded from the divine chorus. But when they go to their feasting and to
b banquet, then they travel to the summit of the arch of heaven, and the climb is steep: the chariots of the gods travel easily, being well-balanced and easily controlled, while the rest do so with difficulty; for the horse which is partly bad weighs them down, inclining them towards the
5 earth through its weight, if any of the charioteers has not trained him well. Here the harshest toil and struggle awaits a soul. When those souls that are called immortal are at the top, they travel
c outside and take their stand upon the outer part of the heavens, and positioned like this they are carried round by its revolution, and gaze on the things outside the heavens.

'The region above the heavens has never yet been celebrated as it deserves by any earthly poet, nor will it ever be. But it is like this—for
5 one must be bold enough to say what is true, especially when speaking about truth. This region is occupied by being which really is, which is without colour or shape, intangible, observable by the steersman of the soul alone, by intellect, and to which the class of true knowl-
d edge relates. Thus because the mind of a god is nourished by insight and knowledge unmixed, and so too that of every soul which is concerned to receive what is appropriate to it, it is glad at last to see what is and is nourished and made happy by gazing on what is true, until the revolu-
5 tion brings it around in a circle to the same point. In its circuit it catches sight of justice itself, of self-control, of knowledge—not that knowledge to which coming into being attaches,
e or that which seems to be different in each different one of the things that we now say are, but that which is in what really is and which is really knowledge; and having gazed and feasted in the same way on the other things which really are, it descends back into the region within the heav-
5 ens and goes home. When it is there, the charioteer stations his horses at their manger, throwing them ambrosia and giving them nectar to drink.
248   'This is the life of gods; of the other souls, the one which follows a god best and has come to

resemble him most raises the head of its charioteer into the region outside, and is carried round with the revolution, disturbed by its horses and
5 scarcely catching sight of the things that are; while another now rises, now sinks, and because of the force exerted by its horses sees some things but not others. The remaining souls follow after them, all of them eager to rise up, but unable to do so, and are carried round together under the
b surface, trampling and jostling one another, each trying to overtake the next. So there ensues the greatest confusion, competition and sweated exertion, in which through incompetent driving many souls are maimed, and many have their wings all broken; and all of them having had
5 much trouble depart without achieving a sight of what is, and afterwards feed on what only appears to nourish them. The cause of their great eagerness to see the plain of truth where it lies is that the pasturage which is fitting for the best part of the soul comes from the meadow there,
c and that the nature of the wing which lifts up the soul is nourished by this. And this is the ordinance of Necessity: that whichever soul follows
5 in the train of a god and catches sight of part of what is true shall remain free from sorrow until the next circuit, and if it is always able to do this, it shall always remain free from harm; but whenever through inability to follow it fails to see, and through some mischance is weighed down by being filled with forgetfulness and incompetence, and because of the weight loses its wings and falls
d to the earth, then it is the law that this soul shall not be planted in any wild creature at its first birth; rather the one which saw most shall be planted in a seed from which will grow a man who will become a lover of wisdom or of beauty, or devoted to the Muses and to love; the second in the seed of a law-abiding king, or someone fit
5 for generalship and ruling; the third in that of a man who devotes himself to the affairs of a city, or perhaps to those of a household or to business; the fourth, in that of an exercise-loving trainer in the gymnasium, or of someone who will be concerned with healing the body; the fifth will
e have the life of a seer or of an expert in some mystic rites; for the sixth, the fitting life will be that of a poet or some other life from among

those concerned with imitation; for the seventh that of a craftsman or farmer; for the eighth that of sophist or demagogue; for the ninth that of a tyrant. Among all these kinds of life, the man who lives justly receives a better portion, while the man who lives unjustly receives a worse. For each soul only returns to the place from which it 249 has come after ten thousand years; for it does not become winged before then, except for that of the man who has lived the philosophical life without guile or who has united his love for his boy with philosophy; and these souls, with the third circuit of a thousand years, if they choose this life three times in succession, on that condition become winged and depart, in the three-thousandth year. But the rest, when they finish their first life, undergo judgement, and after judgement some of them go to the places of correction under the earth and pay full penalty, while others are lifted up by Justice into some region of the heavens and live a life of a kind b merited by their life in human form. In the thousandth year, both sorts come to the allotment and choice of their second life, and each chooses whichever it wishes: then a human soul may pass into the life of a wild animal, and what was once a man back into a man from an animal. For a soul which has never seen the truth will not enter this shape. A man must comprehend what is said uni-c versally, arising from many sensations and being collected together into one through reasoning; and this is a recollection of those things which our soul once saw when it travelled in company with a god and treated with contempt the things we now say are, and when it rose up into what really is. Hence it is with justice that only the mind of the philosopher becomes winged: for so far as it can it is close, through memory, to those things his closeness to which gives a god his divinity. Thus if a man uses such reminders rightly, being continually initiated in perfect mysteries, he alone through that initiation d achieves real perfection; and standing aside from human concerns, and coming close to the divine, he is admonished by the many for being disturbed, when his real state is one of possession, which goes unrecognized by the many.

'Well then, the result of my whole account of the fourth kind of madness is clear—the madness of the man who, on seeing beauty here on earth, and being reminded of true beauty, becomes winged, and fluttering with eagerness to fly upwards, but unable to leave the ground, looking upwards like a bird, and taking no heed of the e things below, causes him to be regarded as mad: my conclusion is that this then reveals itself as the best of all the kinds of divine possession and from the best of sources for the man who is subject to it and shares in it, and that it is when he partakes in this madness that the man who loves the beautiful is called a lover. For as has been said, every human soul has by the law of its nature observed the things that are, or else it 250 would not have entered this creature, man; but it is not easy for every soul to gain from things here a recollection of those other things, either for those which only briefly saw the things there at that earlier time, or for those which fall to earth and have the misfortune to be turned to injustice by keeping certain kinds of company, and to forget the holy things they saw then. Few souls are left who have sufficient memory; and these, when they see some likeness of the things there, are driven out of their wits with amazement and lose control of themselves, though they do not know b what has happened to them for lack of clear perception. Now in the earthly likenesses of justice and self-control and the other things which are of value to souls, there is no illumination, but through dulled organs just a few approach their images and with difficulty observe the nature of what is imaged in them; but before it was possible to see beauty blazing out, when with a happy company they saw a blessed sight before them—ourselves following with Zeus, others with differ-c ent gods—and were initiated into what it is right to call most blessed of mysteries, which we celebrated, whole in ourselves, and untouched by the evils which awaited us in a later time, with our gaze turned in our final initiation towards whole, simple, unchanging and blissful revelations, in a pure light, pure ourselves and not entombed in this thing which we now carry round with us and call body, imprisoned like oysters.

'Let this be our concession to memory, which has made me speak now at some length d out of longing for what was before; but on the subject of beauty—as we said, it shone out in company with those other things, and now that we have come to earth we have found it gleaming most clearly through the clearest of our senses. For of all the sensations coming to us through the 5 body, sight is the keenest: wisdom we do not see—the feelings of love it would cause in us would be terrible, if it allowed some such clear image of itself to reach our sight, and so too with e the other objects of love; as it is, beauty alone has acquired this privilege, of being most evident and most loved. Thus the man whose initiation was not recent, or who has been corrupted, does not move keenly from here to there, to beauty itself, when he observes its namesake here, so that he does not revere it when he looks at it, but surren- 5 dering himself to pleasure does his best to go on four feet like an animal and father offspring, and 251 keeping close company with excess has no fear or shame in pursuing pleasure contrary to nature; while the newly initiated, the man who observed much of what was visible to him before, on seeing a godlike face or some form of body which imi- tates beauty well, first shudders and experiences 5 something of the fears he had before, and then reveres it like a god as he looks at it, and if he were not afraid of appearing thoroughly mad would sacrifice to his beloved as if to a statue of a god. After he has seen him, the expected change b comes over him following the shuddering— sweating and a high fever; for he is warmed by the reception of the effluence of beauty through his eyes, which is the natural nourishment of his plumage, and with that warmth there is a melting of the parts around its base, which have long since become hard and closed up, so preventing it 5 from sprouting, and with the incoming stream of nourishment the quills of the feathers swell and set to growing from their roots under the whole c form of the soul; for formerly the whole of it was winged. Meanwhile, then, all of it throbs and palpitates, and the experience is like that of cut- ting teeth, the itching and the aching that occur around the gums when the teeth are just coming

through: such is the state affecting the soul of the man who is beginning to sprout wings—it throbs 5 and aches and tickles as it grows its feathers. So when it gazes at the boy's beauty, and is nourished and warmed by receiving particles (*merē*) which come to it (*epionta*) in a flood (*rheonta*) from there—hence, of course, the name we give them, "desire" (*himeros*)—it experiences relief from its d anguish and is filled with joy; but when it is apart and becomes parched, the openings of the pas- sages through which the feathers push their way out are dried up and closed, so shutting off their shoots, and these, shut in with the desire, throb like pulsing arteries, each of them pricking at the 5 outlet corresponding to it, so that the entire soul, stung all over, goes mad with pain; but then, remembering the boy with his beauty, it rejoices again. The mixture of both these states makes it despair at the strangeness of its condition, raging in its perplexity, and in its madness it can neither e sleep at night nor keep still where it is by day, but runs wherever it thinks it will see the possessor of the beauty it longs for; and when it has seen him and channelled desire in to itself it releases what 5 was pent up before, and finding a breathing space it ceases from its stinging birth-pains, once more 252 enjoying this for the moment as the sweetest pleasure. This it does not willingly give up, nor does it value anyone above the one with beauty, but quite forgets mother, brothers, friends, all (252) together, not caring about the loss of his wealth 5 through neglect, and with contempt for all the accepted standards of propriety and good taste in which it previously prided itself it is ready to act the part of a slave and sleep wherever it is allowed to do so, provided it is as close as possible to the object of its longing; for in addition to its b reverence for the possessor of beauty, it has found him the sole healer of its greatest sufferings. This experience, my beautiful boy, the one to whom my speech is addressed, men term love; but when you hear what the gods call it I expect you will laugh because of your youth. I think some Home- 5 ric experts cite two verses from the less well- known poems, the second of which is quite outrageous and not very metrical: they celebrate him like this—

"We mortals call him Mighty Love, a wingèd
power of great renown,
Immortals call him Fledgeling Dove—since Eros'
wings lack down."

c You may believe this or not; but at any rate the cause of the lover's experience and this experience itself are as I have described.

'If the man who is taken by Love belongs among the followers of Zeus, he is able to bear the burden of the feathery one with some sedate- 5 ness; but those who were attendants of Ares and made the circuit with him, when they are captured by Love and think that they are being wronged in some way by the one they love, become murderous and ready to sacrifice both d themselves and their beloved. Just so each man lives after the pattern of the god in whose chorus he was, honouring him by imitating him so far as he can, so long as he is uncorrupted and living out the first of the lives which he enters here; and he behaves in this way in his associations 5 both with those he loves and with everyone else. So each selects his love from the ranks of the beautiful according to his own disposition, and fashions and adorns him like a statue, as if he were himself his god, in order to honour him and e celebrate his mystic rites. And so those who belong to Zeus seek that the one they love should be someone like Zeus in respect of his soul; so they look to see whether he is naturally disposed towards philosophy and towards leadership, and when they have found him and fall in 5 love they do everything to make him of such a kind. So if they have not previously set foot on this way, they undertake it now, both learning from wherever they can and finding out for themselves; and as they follow the scent from 253 within themselves to the discovery of the nature of their own god, they find the means to it through the compulsion on them to gaze intensely on the god, and grasping him through memory, and possessed by him, they take their habits and ways from him, to the extent that it is possible for man to share in god; and because 5 they count their beloved responsible for these very things they love him still more, and if it is from Zeus that they draw, like Bacchants, they

b pour the draught over the soul of their loved one and make him as like their god as possible. Those in their turn who followed with Hera seek someone regal in nature, and when they have found him they do all the same things in respect of him. Those who belong to Apollo and each of the other gods proceed in the same way in accordance with their god and seek that their boy 5 should be of the same nature, and when they acquire him, imitating the god themselves and persuading and disciplining their beloved they draw him into the way of life and pattern of the god, to the extent that each is able, without showing jealousy or mean ill-will towards their beloved; rather they act as they do because they c are trying as much as they can, in every way, to draw him into complete resemblance to themselves and to whichever god they honour. The eagerness of those who are truly in love, then, and its issue, if, that is, they achieve what they eagerly desire in the way I have said, thus 5 acquires nobility and brings happiness from the friend who is maddened through love to the object of his affection, if he is caught; and one who is caught is captured in the following way.

'Just as at the beginning of this tale we divided each soul into three forms, two like horses and the third with the role of charioteer, d so now let this still stand. Of the horses, one, we say, is good, the other not; but we did not describe what the excellence of the good horse was, or the badness of the bad horse, and that is what we must now say. Well then, the first of the two, which is on the nobler side, is erect in form 5 and clean-limbed, high-necked, nose somewhat hooked, white in colour, with black eyes, a lover of honour when joined with restraint and a sense of shame, and a companion of true glory, needing e no whip, responding to the spoken command alone; the other is crooked in shape, gross, a random collection of parts, with a short, powerful neck, flat-nosed, black-skinned, grey-eyed, bloodshot, companion of excess and boastfulness, shaggy around the ears, deaf, hardly yielding to 5 whip and goad together. So when the charioteer first catches sight of the light of his love, warming the whole soul through the medium of perception, and begins to be filled with tickling and

254 pricks of longing, the horse which is obedient to the charioteer, constrained then as always by shame, holds itself back from leaping on the loved one; while the other no longer takes notice of goading or the whip from the charioteer, but

5 springs powerfully forward, and causing all kinds of trouble to his companion and the charioteer forces them to move towards the beloved and mention to him the delights of sex. At the start

b the two of them resist, indignant at being forced to do terrible and improper things; but finally, when there is no limit to their plight, they follow its lead, giving in and agreeing to do what it tells them. Now they come close to the beloved and

5 see the flashing of his face. As the charioteer sees it, his memory is carried back to the nature of beauty, and again sees it standing together with self-control on a holy pedestal; at the sight he becomes frightened, and in sudden reverence

c falls on his back, and is forced at the same time to pull back the reins so violently as to bring both horses down on their haunches, the one willingly, because of its lack of resistance to him, but the unruly horse much against its will. When they are a little way off, the first horse drenches

5 the whole soul with sweat from shame and alarm, while the other, when it has recovered from the pain caused to it by the bit and its fall, scarcely gets its breath back before it breaks into angry abuse, repeatedly reviling the charioteer and its companion for cowardly and unmanly desertion of their agreed position; and again it tries to com-

d pel them to approach, unwilling as they are, and barely concedes when they beg him to postpone it until a later time. When the agreed time comes, and they pretend not to remember, it reminds them; struggling, neighing, pulling, it

5 forces them to approach the beloved again to make the same proposition, and when they are nearby, head down and tail outstretched, teeth clamped on its bit, it pulls shamelessly; but the

e same happens to the charioteer as before, only still more violently, as he falls back as if from a *husplex*; still more violently he wrenches the bit back, and forces it from the teeth of the unruly horse, spattering its evil-speaking tongue and its jaws with blood, and thrusting its legs and

5 haunches to the ground delivers it over to pains.

When the same thing happens to the evil horse many times, and it ceases from its excesses, now humbled it allows the charioteer with his foresight to lead, and when it sees the boy in his beauty, it nearly dies with fright; and the result is that now the soul of the lover follows the beloved in reverence and awe. So because he

255 receives every kind of service, as if equal to the gods, from a lover who is not pretending but genuinely in love, and because he naturally feels affection for a man who renders him service, even if perhaps in the past he has been preju-

5 diced against him by hearing his schoolfellows or others say that it is shameful to associate with a lover, and repulses the lover for that reason, as time goes on he is led both by his age, and by necessity, to admit him to his company; for it is

b fated that evil shall never be friend to evil, nor good fail to be friend to good. Once he has admitted him and accepted his conversation and his company, the goodwill that he experiences at close quarters from his lover amazes the beloved,

5 as he clearly sees that not even all his other friends and his relations together have anything to offer by way of affection in comparison with the friend who is divinely possessed. And when he continues doing this and association is combined with physical contact in the gymnasium and on the other occasions when

c people come together, then it is that the springs of that stream which Zeus as lover of Ganymede named 'desire' flow in abundance upon the lover, some sinking within him, and some flowing off outside him as he brims over; and as a breath of

5 wind or an echo rebounds from smooth hard surfaces and returns to the source from which it issued, so the stream of beauty passes back into its possessor through his eyes, which is its natural

d route to the soul; arriving there and setting him all of a flutter, it waters the passages of the feathers and causes the wings to grow, and fills the soul of the loved one in his turn with love. So he is in love, but with what, he does not know; and he

5 neither knows what has happened to him, nor can he even say what it is, but like a man who has caught an eye-disease from someone he can give no account of it, and is unaware that he is seeing himself in his lover as if in a mirror. And

when his lover is with him, like him he ceases from his anguish; when he is absent, again like him he longs and is longed for, because his return of love is a reflection of love, though he calls what he has and thinks of it as friendly affection rather than love. His desires are similar to his lover's, but weaker: to see, touch, kiss and lie down with him; and indeed, as one might expect, soon afterwards he does just that. So as they lie together, the lover's licentious horse has something to suggest to the charioteer, and claims a little enjoyment as recompense for much hardship; while its counterpart in the beloved has nothing to say, but swelling with confused passion it embraces the lover and kisses him, welcoming him as someone full of good-will, and whenever they lie down together, it is ready not to refuse to do its own part in granting favours to the lover, should he beg to receive them; but its companion, for its part, together with the charioteer, resists this with a reasoned sense of shame. Well then, if the better elements of their minds get the upper hand by drawing them to a well-ordered life, and to philosophy, they pass their life here in blessedness and harmony, masters of themselves and orderly in their behaviour, having enslaved that part through which evil attempted to enter the soul, and freed that part through which goodness enters it; and when they die they become winged and light, and have won the first of their three submissions in these, the true Olympic games—and neither

human sanity nor divine madness has any greater good to offer a man than this. But if they turn to a coarser way of life, devoted not to wisdom but to honour, then perhaps, I suppose, when they are drinking or in some other moment of care-lessness the licentious horses in the two of them catch them off their guard, and bringing them together take that choice which is called blessed by the many, and carry it through; and once hav-ing done so, they continue with it, but sparingly, because what they are doing has not been approved by their whole mind. So these too spend their lives as friends, though not to the same degree as the other pair, both during their love and when they have passed beyond it, believing that they have given and received the most binding pledges, which it would be wrong to break by ever becoming enemies. On their death they leave the body without wings but with the impulse to gain them, so that they carry off no small reward for their lovers' madness; for it is ordained that those who have already begun on the journey under the heavens shall no longer pass into the darkness of the journey under the earth, but rather live in the light and be happy as they travel with each other, and acquire match-ing plumage, when they acquire it, because of their love.

'These are the blessings, my boy, so great as to be counted divine, which will come to you from the friendship of a lover, in the way I have described.'

STUDY QUESTIONS: PLATO, PHAEDRUS

1. For what reasons does Socrates say that it is impossible for a first principle to come into being? How does Socrates use this claim?
2. What is Plato's definition of 'the soul'? How does Plato prove its immortality?
3. What is the nature of the human soul?
4. Why is it right and appropriate that the soul of a philosopher alone should recover her wings? What do the wings represent?
5. What is a lover? How does this definition relate to the immortality of the soul and Beauty?
6. What do the two horses stand for?
7. What are the blessings of the friendship of a lover?
8. Compare and contrast what Plato has to say about love in the *Symposium* with what he affirms in this dialogue.

PARMENIDES
Zeno, Socrates, Parmenides

The *Parmenides* is probably Plato's most intriguing dialogue. The first part (126a to 136e) consists of a conversation between Parmenides, Zeno, and Socrates as a youth, in which the older Parmenides grills Socrates. The dialogue is usually understood as a criticism by Plato of his own theory of Forms, which he later amends in light of this self-criticism. However, the interpretations of this dialogue are contentious.

After stating the theory of Forms (128e–130a), Socrates tries to answer the question of what kinds of things have Forms, but apparently without success. Later, Parmenides asks another difficult question: when individual things participate in the Forms, does each individual thing participate in the whole of the Form or only part of it? Can we even think of the Forms being divided or shared? Once again, it seems that Plato is noting a lack of clarity in his own theory. Neither of these two lines of questioning, however, amounts to a refutation. But, following these passages, Plato seems to give an argument against his own theory of Forms (131e–132b). One interpretation of this argument is as follows.

1. *If several objects have the property of being F, then there is a Form of F-ness (in virtue of participating in which, they are F).*
2. *Several objects (i.e., a, b, and c) are large.*
3. *Therefore, there is a Form of Largeness (call it L1).*
4. *The Form of Largeness is itself large (this is called the assumption of self-predication).*
5. *Therefore, there exists a set of things, a, b, c, and L1 itself, which are all large.*
6. *Therefore, by (1) above, there exists a second form of Largeness (i.e., L2).*
7. *The same steps (1–6) can be repeated infinitely for L2 and for any Form Ln, thus generating an infinity of Forms.*

Although Plato's argument concerns largeness, it is known as the third man argument, following a similar argument advanced by Aristotle. Note that the argument requires the self-predication assumption, namely, that any Form itself has the property that it names. For example, in earlier dialogues, Plato claims that the Form of the Good is itself good or that the Form of Beauty is itself beautiful. They serve as paradigms or models. Such statements require self-predication regarding the Forms.

The above interpretation probably reflects the text of Plato's argument. The problem is, what does he do with it? Some scholars argue that Plato's aim is to criticize his own theory of Forms insofar as it involves self-predication. They also assert that, having made this criticism, Plato abandons this version of the theory. This view is made problematic by the apparent fact that Plato seems to accept a self-predicated view of the Forms in the later dialogue, the *Timaeus*. At least, he says that sensible objects resemble the relevant Forms.

Plato, from *Parmenides' Lesson: Translation and Explication of Plato's Parmenides*, translated by Kenneth M. Sayre. University of Notre Dame Press, 1996.

127 Having heard his [treatise], Socrates then asked
E [Zeno] to read the first hypothesis of the first
argument again. This having been read, he said,
Zeno, how do you mean this? If things are many,
[you say], then they must be both like and
unlike; but this is impossible. For what is unlike
cannot be like, nor what is like unlike?—is that
not your meaning?

It is, said Zeno.

And if it is impossible for what is unlike to
be like and what is like unlike, it is impossible
that there be many? For if there were many,
impossibilities would be attached. Then is this
the purport of your arguments—nothing other
than to contend that there is no plurality, contrary to everything people say? And you regard
each of your arguments as a proof of just that, so
that you maintain you have presented just as
many proofs that there is no plurality as there are
128A arguments in your treatise? Is that what you
mean, or have I not understood you rightly?

Not at all, said Zeno, you have grasped the
intent of the whole treatise admirably.

I notice, Parmenides, said Socrates, that
Zeno here wishes to be associated with you not
only by friendship of other sorts but by this writing as well. He has written very much in the
same manner as you, but by changing tactics has
tried to deceive us [into thinking] that he is saying something different. You say in your poem
B that all is one, and for this you offer an abundance of admirable proofs. He, on the other
hand, says it is not many, and himself offers a
large number of really great proofs. You say one,
he says not many. Each of you speaks so that you
appear not to have said at all the same thing,
while saying something to just the same effect.
That is why your respective sayings seem to speak
above the heads of the rest of us.

Yes, Socrates, said Zeno; but you have not
fully perceived the truth about my treatise.
C Although you pick up and track the argument as
well as a young Spartan hound, this has escaped
you from the outset—my book is not so thoroughly pretentious as to have been written with
the intent you allege, disguising itself from people as some great accomplishment. What you

mention rather is something incidental. In truth,
these writings are a bolster of sorts for Par-
D menides' argument against those who try to
ridicule it [by showing] that many absurd consequences afflict his supposition 'if there is one'
and contradict it. This book argues against those
who maintain plurality, and pays them back in
kind with interest. Its intent is to make clear that
their own hypothesis, 'if things are many', gone
through in sufficient detail, would be afflicted by
even more ridiculous consequences then the
hypothesis of there being one. It was written
in the contentiousness that marked my youth
and someone copied it secretly—so I was not
given the freedom of determining whether or not
E it should be brought to light. That, Socrates, is
what you have failed to notice. You imagine that
it was written by an older man out of ambition
rather than by a young man out of controversy.
Though otherwise, as I said, you did not describe
it badly.

Oh I grant that, said Socrates, and believe
things are as you say. But tell me this. Do you not
acknowledge that there exists, itself by itself, a
129A certain Form of Likeness, and again another such
as this but opposite, the really unlike; and that I
and you and other things we call 'many' take on a
share of these two things? And that things that
come to share in likeness become like so far as and
only insofar as they come to share in it; while
things [that come to share in] unlikeness [become]
unlike; and things [that come to share in] both
[come to be] both? So if all things come to share in
both, contrary as they are, and by partaking of
B both [become] like and unlike themselves, what
is surprising about that? To be sure, if someone
were to declare that Likeness itself becomes
unlike, or what is [itself] Unlike [becomes] like, I
would consider that foreboding. But if things that
partake of both are shown to receive both [charac-
ters], Zeno, it would not strike me as odd at all;
nor if someone shows that all things are one by
partaking of the One, and that the same things
again are many by partaking of the Myriad. But if
C someone shows that the really One itself is many,
or again that the really Many is one, I would
regard that with immediate wonder. The same

goes for all the other cases. If someone were to show that the Kinds or Forms themselves receive these contrary features in themselves, then wonder is due. But if someone shows me to be one and many, what's the wonder[?]—saying, when he wants to show [that I am] many, that my right side is one thing and my left side another, that there is my front on one hand and my back on the other, and my upper and lower portions likewise—for no doubt I partake of numerous things—and D when [he wants to show that I am] one, he will say that since I partake of the One I am one person among the seven of us here. So both declarations are true. At any rate, if someone should attempt to show that such multiple things as sticks and stones, and the like, are also one, we shall say that he is showing the thing to be both many and one, but not [showing] that the One is many or that the Many is one; he is not saying anything extraordinary, but what all of us should admit. But as I said just now, if someone first were to distinguish the Forms separately, themselves by E themselves—such as Likeness and Unlikeness, Myriad and One, Rest and Motion, and all such like—and then shows that these can be compounded and partitioned among themselves, then Zeno, I said, I should be most astonished. I am sure that you have dealt with this matter in a most vigorous fashion. But as I say, my admiration would certainly be many times greater if someone were to show the same perplexity bound up so 130A variously in the Forms themselves as you [and Parmenides] have detailed in the things we see—[if this perplexity] thus should show up in the things we grasp by reason.

While Socrates was speaking in this way, said Pythodorus, he expected Parmenides and Zeno to be annoyed at his every [remark]. Yet they attended to him carefully, and frequently exchanged glances and smiled as if in admiration of Socrates. When he finally stopped, Parmenides expressed this [feeling]. Socrates, he said, how fitting for you to take this delight at the B onrush of argument. Now tell me: do you yourself make this distinction, as you say, between certain Forms [existing] separately by themselves on the one hand, and on the other the things that sepa-

rately partake of them? And do you think that Likeness itself is separate from the likeness we possess, and so on with One and Plurality, and however many [other characters] you have heard Zeno [mention] just now?

I do indeed, said Socrates.

And also in such cases, said Parmenides—a Form of Justice, itself by itself, and of Beauty and of Good, and all such things as well?

Yes, he said.

C   And again, a Form of Man separate from us and all such as we are—a Form of Man as something by itself, or [a Form of] Fire, or even Water?

I have often been puzzled about those things, Parmenides, whether one ought to speak [about these] as about the former or otherwise.

And what about these, Socrates—which might seem to be ridiculous—such as hair and mud and dirt, or some other thing utterly base and worthless. Are you puzzled whether we ought to say there are separate Forms of these, of a sort again D different from such things as we deal with, or not?

Not at all, said Socrates. These things, on the other hand, are just as we see them; it would be rather too absurd to believe that there is a Form of any of these. Nevertheless I am worried from time to time whether it is not the same for all cases as for a given one. But when I take that position I beat a retreat, fearing I might be corrupted by falling in with some kind of deep nonsense. So when I come to deal with those things we were saying just now possess Forms, I spend my time occupied with them [exclusively].

E   That is because you are still young, Socrates, said Parmenides, and philosophy still has not yet taken hold of you as I believe it yet will. You will disdain none of these things when [that happens]. But at the present, because of your youth, you still regard what people think as authoritative. Now tell me this. You believe, so you say, that there are certain Forms in which these other things come to share and thereby to be invested 131A with their names—as things that come to share in Likeness, for instance, become alike, [those in] Largeness become large, and [those in] Beauty and Justice become beautiful and just?

Certainly, said Socrates.

So then does each thing that shares come to share in the whole Form or in part? Or could there be some other [manner of] sharing apart from these?

How could there be? said Socrates.

Does it seem to you, then, that the whole Form, being one, is in each of the many, or what?

What prevents if from being in [each], Parmenides? said Socrates.

B   Just that while being one and the same, the whole [Form] will be in many separate things at once, and thus it would be separate from itself.

No it would not, he replied, at least if it were like one and the same day, which is many places at the same time and not at all separate from itself. In that way each of the Forms, [while] one and the same, could be in all [of these many separate things] simultaneously.

Nicely done, Socrates, he said. You make one and the same thing be in many places at once, just as if you were to spread a sail over many people and say that one thing as a whole is over many. Or isn't that the sort of thing you mean to say?

C   Perhaps, he said.

Now would the whole sail be over each [person], or part over one and another [part] over another?

Part.

Thus, he said, the Forms themselves are divisible, Socrates, and things that partake of them would partake of their parts; the whole no longer would be in each thing, but rather a part of each [Form] would be [in each].

So it appears.

Well, Socrates, are you willing to say that the single Form actually divides for us, but will still be one?

Not at all, he said.

[No], he said, for consider: if you divide Largeness itself, and each of the many big things is to be big by a part of Largeness smaller than Large-
D ness itself, would that not seem unreasonable?

Certainly, he said.

And what of this? For something that has a part of the Equal, thus being the recipient of a particular smallness, will the possessor be equal to any one thing by reason of what is smaller than the Equal itself?

Impossible.

[Suppose] rather that one of us has a part of the Small; the Small will be larger than this part itself, inasmuch as [the latter is] part of it, and then in truth the Small itself will be larger. Yet
E that to which the portion taken away is added will be smaller, but not larger, than before.

That could not happen, he said, in any event.

Then in what way, Socrates, [Parmenides] demanded, will the others for you come to share in the Forms, if they can come to share in them neither in part nor as wholes?

Nay by Zeus, he said, it doesn't seem to me that such a thing is at all easy to determine.

Then what of this? How do you manage this?

What?

132A   I imagine you believe there is a single Form in each case for some reason such as this: when some number of things seems to you to be large, there perhaps seems to be some one character that is the same when you look at them all, wherefore you suppose the Large to be one thing.

What you say is true, he said.

But what of the Large itself and the other large things; if you look at all these in your mind in the same fashion, will not some single Large again appear by which these all necessarily appear large?

So it seems.

Thus another Form of Largeness will have made an appearance, alongside the former Largeness itself and the things partaking of it; and over and above all these again a different [Largeness] by which these all will be large. And each of
B these Forms no longer will be one for you, but indefinitely multitudinous.

But Parmenides, Socrates said, might it not be that each of these Forms is a thought, which properly can occur nowhere else than in minds? For in this way each [of them] could be unique, and no longer encounter [the difficulties] that were spoken of just now.

Well, he said, is each of these thoughts one, but a thought of nothing?

Impossible, he said.

Then of something?

Yes.

c   [Of something] that is, or is not?

That is.

[A thought of] some one thing, is it not, which that thought thinks as covering all the cases and as being a certain single character?

Yes.

Then will not this thing that is thought to be one, being always the same over all the cases, be a Form?

It seems again that it must.

Then what of this? said Parmenides. Given the necessity by which you say the other things partake of the Forms, does it not seem to you that each of these things consists of thoughts and all of them think, or else [despite] being thoughts they are unthought?

That's not reasonable either, he said. But still, Paramenides, what seems clearest of all to

D   me is this—that these Forms are paradigms fixed in nature, as it were, and that the other things resemble them and are likenesses of them; and that this sharing that the other things come to have in the Forms is nothing other than being made like them.

Then if something resembles a Form, he replied, must not that Form be like the thing that is made like [it], just insofar as it has been made like [it]? Or is there any way in which what is like is not like what is like it?

There is not.

On the other hand, it is not entirely neces-sary that what is like partake of one and the same

E   [Form] with what is like it?

It is necessary.

And will not that of which like things par-take in order to be alike be that Form itself?

Altogether so.

Then it is not the case that anything can be like the Form, or the Form [like] another thing. Otherwise another Form will always appear

133A beside the [first] Form. And if that [second Form] is like anything, yet a different [Form will appear]. And there will be no end to this contin-ual generation of new Forms, if the Form is to be like the thing that partakes of it.

What you say is most true.

Therefore the other things do not come to share in the Forms by being like them. It is nec-essary to seek some other way in which they come to share.

So it seems.

Then you see, Socrates, he said, how great is the difficulty [that ensues] if one distinguishes as Forms things that exist themselves by themselves?

Very much so.

Be well aware, nonetheless, Socrates, that you cannot yet say how great the difficulty is, so

B to speak, if you are always going to institute a single Form for each determination you make among things.

How is that? he said.

There are many other [perplexities], he said, but the greatest is this. Suppose someone were to declare the Forms not available for discernment, if such as we say they ought to be; one could not show a person to be mistaken in that assertion, unless the person happened to be much experi-enced in controversy and not naturally without

C talent, fully willing to follow many remote and laborious demonstrations. Otherwise the one who constrains them by argument to be unknowable would not be convinced.

Why so, Parmenides? said Socrates.

Because, Socrates, I should think that you, and anyone else who maintains that each of these [Forms] has a certain being itself by itself, would admit first of all that none of them is among us.

For how [otherwise] could it still be itself by itself? replied Socrates.

Well said, he answered. And furthermore, such characters as are what they are relative to each other, [among Forms] they have their being in

D relation to themselves, but not in relation to things among us—whether one takes them as likenesses or in some other way—which we have as our share and [so] are named case by case. And things among us, although they have the same names as those, are relative themselves to themselves in turn, but not relative to the Forms; and whatever designa-tions of this sort they have are with reference to one another and not to those [Forms].

How do you mean? said Socrates.

For instance, said Parmenides, if one of us is master or slave of someone, that person of whom he is slave is not Master itself, the real Master, of course, nor is the master a master of Slave itself, the real Slave. Being rather a man, it is of a man that he is either of these two. But Mastership itself is what it is in comparison with Slavehood itself, and Slavehood itself in like manner with Mastership itself. Things in our domain do not have force in relation to those things, nor do those things in relation to us. As I say, rather, those things are of themselves and in relation to themselves [only], and in like manner things in our 134A domain are in relation to themselves. Or don't you see what I mean?

I understand entirely, said Socrates.

So then Knowledge, he said—what is Knowledge itself—would be knowledge of that domain, of the really True itself?

Certainly.

And each particular case of knowledge that exists, in turn, would be knowledge of some being that exists specifically. Not so?

Yes.

And would not knowledge among us be B knowledge of what is true among us; and would it not follow in turn that each particular case of knowledge among us is knowledge of some specific thing that happens among us?

Necessarily.

As you admit, however, we do not entertain the Forms themselves, nor is this possible among us.

Certainly not.

But each Kind that itself exists, I take it, is known through Knowledge, the Form itself?

Yes.

Which we do not entertain.

Indeed not.

Then none of the Forms is known by us, since we do not share in Knowledge itself.

Apparently not.

So the really Beautiful itself is unknowable c by us, along with the Good, and indeed all things we accept as being Ideas themselves.

That may be.

Now consider this [consequence] which is yet more wondrous.

What is it?

You would say, I take it, that if there is such a Kind as Knowledge itself, it is far more exact than knowledge among us; and so with Beauty and all the rest.

Yes.

And if anything partakes of Knowledge itself, would you not say that none other than god possesses this most exact Knowledge?

Necessarily.

D Then will it be possible for the god, once more, possessing Knowledge itself, to perceive things among us?

Why not?

Because, Socrates, said Parmenides, we agreed that those Forms do not have the force they have in relation to things among us, nor things among us [have force] in relation to those [Forms]. Each rather [has force] in relation to itself.

Indeed, we agreed.

Then if the most exact Mastership in itself E exists with the god, and also the most exact Knowledge in itself, mastership of things there would never be master of us, nor would knowledge [there] discern us or anything among us. But just as we do not govern those things by sovereignty among us, nor discern things pertaining to god by means of our knowledge, so they again, being gods, by just the same reasoning, are not our masters nor have discernment of human deeds.

But that it surely an exceedingly amazing argument, he said, particularly if it were to deprive the god of knowing.

Yet these [difficulties], Socrates, said Parmenides, and many, many others beside them, 135A are still necessarily bound up with the Forms, if these Ideas of things exist and one is to define each Form as something [existing] just by itself. As a result the hearer is perplexed, and contends that they do not exist—or if it should be the case perforce [that they do exist, contends] that they most necessarily are unknowable by human nature. In saying these things, that person seems to be saying something [meaningful] and, as we said just now, is extraordinarily hard to convince [otherwise]. [It would take] a man of great natural gifts to be able to understand that for each particular thing there is a certain Kind or nature

B itself by itself. [And it would take] someone more remarkable still to discover [these Forms] and to be able to instruct someone else who has analyzed all these [difficulties] with adequate thoroughness.

I yield to you, Parmenides, said Socrates. What you say accords fully with my thought.

But as a matter of fact, Socrates, said Parmenides, if in view of all the present [difficulties], and others like them, one will not allow that Forms of things exist, nor that some single Form is fixed for each individual thing, then one will have nothing toward which to direct one's thought, not allowing that there is a character for each thing which is always the same—and C thus will completely destroy the power of discourse. You are only too well aware of such a thing, it seems to me.

What you say is true, he said.

What will you do about philosophy, then? Not knowing these things, what way will you turn?

At least for the moment, I don't seem to see at all.

Because, Socrates, he said, you undertake prematurely—before being trained—to mark off D Beauty, Justice, and Good, and each of the single Forms. I noticed that when I heard you conversing earlier with Aristoteles here. The impulse that spurs [you] on toward argument, be assured, is god-sent and noble. But draw yourself up while you are still young, and exercise yourself thoroughly by means of what is commonly regarded to be useless, and what the multitude cite as idle talk. Otherwise, the truth will escape you.

STUDY QUESTIONS: PLATO, *PARMENIDES*

1. What was the purpose of Zeno's book?
2. What question does Parmenides ask of Socrates concerning trivial objects such as hair and mud? How does Socrates reply? How would have Socrates replied in earlier dialogues such as the *Phaedo* and the *Republic*?
3. Do the Forms have parts? How does Parmenides use this question?
4. Why would Plato need to postulate a second form of Largeness that was over and above largeness itself and all things that share in largeness?
5. What is the problem with having to make such a postulation? How does Plato employ this point in his overall argument in the dialogue?
6. Why does Parmenides rather than Socrates take the lead in most of this dialogue? What is Parmenides' role? Why did Plato choose specifically Parmenides to play this role?
7. What are the main aims of Plato in the selection from this dialogue?
8. In general, what is Plato's theory of Forms? What are the main criticisms one might have of it? What aspects of it can be defended?

THEAETETUS

The *Theaetetus* was probably written after the *Parmenides*. It contains Plato's analysis of knowledge. It is often considered to be his most intricate and sophisticated dialogue. Plato offers us three definitions of knowledge. In the end he rejects all three, but the third is the most reasonable, and it became the basis of the accepted definition of knowledge for 2,400 years, until the later half of the twentieth century.

First, Socrates rejects Theaetetus' definition of knowledge as perception (151d–186e). The main argument is that to know something requires the judgment that something is so and so. Judging is different from perceiving because it involves the soul rather than the senses. After this argument, Plato offers a refutation of Protagoras' thesis that man is the measure of all things, and of Heraclitus' assertion that everything is always changing.

Second, Plato argues against the definition of knowledge as true belief or judgment: a judgment can be true by sheer luck, in which case, it does not count as knowledge. Plato uses the contentious example of a jury that makes a true judgment, but without knowing the truth. This section of the dialogue also contains a discussion of the problem of false judgment (from 187c to 200d). How is it possible to make a false judgment, given that to judge something one must first know it, and that to know it requires some infallible beliefs about it?

Third, Plato discusses the claim that knowledge is true belief with an account, or *logos* (from 201c to 210a). This probably means that knowledge requires knowing why the relevant belief is true. This section of the dialogue has two main parts. In the first part, Socrates recounts a dream that he had, which contains an explanation of knowledge. He dreamt that all things are either primary elements or complexes (compounds), and that accounts can be given only for the complexes but for not the simples. Afterward, Plato provides two objections to the theory given in Socrates' dream. The first objection is that a whole is identical to its parts, and the second is the claim that the elements of a complex are indeed knowable.

In the second section of this part of the dialogue, Plato tries to understand what 'giving an account' (or *logos*) means (from 206c). He considers three alternatives, of which the third is the most favorable. The first says that giving an account is making one's thoughts vocal. The second alternative, which probably refers back to the theory given in Socrates' dream, is that providing an account consists in enumerating the elements out of which a complex is composed. The third analysis claims that providing an account of X consists in being able to distinguish X from everything else. According to this third explanation, to know P is to believe P when P is true and to be able to explain how P is different from anything else. Again, this suggestion was the basis of the standard definition of knowledge as justified true belief, which was accepted by most philosophers until the last half of the twentieth century.

Despite this promising analysis, the dialogue seems to have an inconclusive ending. Plato argues that his third definition is circular because one would have to *know* that one's account of what distinguishes the thing from all other things was a correct account.

151 So start again from the beginning, Theaetetus, and try to say what, exactly, knowledge is.

5 Don't ever say you can't; because if God is willing, and you keep your courage up, you'll be able.

THEAETETUS. Well, Socrates, with you encouraging one like that, it would be disgraceful not to do one's best, in every way, to say what one

e can. Very well, then: it seems to me that a person who knows something is perceiving the thing he knows. The way it looks to me at

the moment is that knowledge is nothing but perception.

5 SOCRATES. Well done: you're right to come out with it like that. But now let's look into it together, to see if it really is genuine or the result of a false pregnancy. You say knowledge is perception?

THEAETETUS. Yes.

SOCRATES. Well, it looks as though what you've

151e said about knowledge is no ordinary theory,

152 but the one that Protagoras, too, used to state.

But he put that same point in a different way. Because he says, you remember, that a man is the measure of all things: of those which are, that they are, and of those which are not, that they are not. You've read that, I take it?

5 THEAETETUS. Yes, often.

SOCRATES. And he means something on these lines: everything is, for me, the way it appears to me, and is, for you, the way it appears to you; and you and I are, each of us, a man?

THEAETETUS. Yes, that's what he means.

b SOCRATES. Well, it's plausible that a wise man wouldn't be saying something silly; so let's follow him up. It sometimes happens, doesn't it, that when the same wind is blowing one of us feels cold and the other not? Or that one feels slightly cold and the other very?

THEAETETUS. Certainly.

SOCRATES. Now on those occasions, shall we say
5 that the wind itself, taken by itself, is cold or not cold? Or shall we accept it from Protagoras that it's cold for the one who feels cold, and not for the one who doesn't?

THEAETETUS. That seems plausible.

SOCRATES. Now it appears that way to each of us?

10 THEAETETUS. Yes.

SOCRATES. And this 'appears' is perceiving?

THEAETETUS. Yes.

c SOCRATES. So appearing and perception are the same, in the case of that which is hot and everything of that sort. So it looks as though things are, for each person, the way he perceives them.

THEAETETUS. That seems plausible.

184 SOCRATES. Well then, Theaetetus, take your consideration of what has been said a bit fur-
5 ther. You answered that knowledge is perception, didn't you?

THEAETETUS. Yes.

SOCRATES. Now suppose someone put this question to you: 'With what does a man see things which are white and black, and with what does he hear things which are high and low in pitch?'
10 I suppose you'd say 'With eyes and ears'.

THEAETETUS. Yes.

c SOCRATES. It isn't usually a sign of ill breeding to be easy-going with words and expressions, and not subject them to a strict scrutiny: in fact it's the opposite of that, rather, that's ungentlemanly. But sometimes it's necessary: as, for instance, now, it's necessary for me to take exception to a point in your answer on
5 which it isn't correct. Because look here, which answer is more correct: that eyes are what we see with, or what we see by means of? and that ears are what we hear with, or what we hear by means of?

THEAETETUS. It seems to me, Socrates, that they're what we perceive each set of things by means of, rather than what we perceive them with.

d SOCRATES. Yes, because it would surely be strange if we had several senses sitting in us, as if in wooden horses, and it wasn't the case that all those things converged on some one kind of thing, a mind or whatever one ought to call it: something with which we perceive all the perceived things by means of the senses, as if by means of instruments.

5 THEAETETUS. Yes, I think the second alternative is better than the first.

SOCRATES. Well now, here's why I'm subjecting you to such strictness about it: I want to know if there's something in us with which we get at not only white and black things, by means of
e the eyes, but also other things, by means of the other sense organs—doing it with the same thing in each case. If the question is put to you, will you be able to refer everything of that sort to the body? But perhaps it would be better that you should state the point by answering questions, rather than that I should interfere on your behalf. Tell me this. Take
5 the things by means of which you perceive things which are hot, hard, light, and sweet. You classify each of them as belonging to the body, don't you? Or do you think they belong to something else?

THEAETETUS. No, they belong to the body.

SOCRATES. And will you also be willing to agree
185 that if you perceive something by means of one power, it's impossible to perceive that same thing by means of another? For instance, you can't perceive by means of sight what you
185a perceive by means of hearing, or perceive by

means of hearing what you perceive by means of sight?

THEAETETUS. Of course.

SOCRATES. So if there's something which you think about both of them, it can't be some-
5 thing which you're perceiving about both, either by means of one of the two instruments or by means of the other.

THEAETETUS. No.

SOCRATES. Now take a sound and a colour. First of all, you think just this about them: that they both are?

10 THEAETETUS. Yes.

SOCRATES. And that each is different from the other and the same as itself?

b THEAETETUS. Of course.

SOCRATES. And that both together are two and each is one?

THEAETETUS. Yes, that too.

SOCRATES. And you're able to raise the question whether they're like or unlike each other?

5 THEAETETUS. I suppose so.

SOCRATES. Well now, by means of what do you think all those things about them? Because it's impossible to get hold of what they have in common either by means of hearing or by means of sight. Besides, here's another proof of the point we're talking about. If it were possi-
10 ble to raise the question whether both are salty
c or not, of course you'll be able to say what you'd investigate it with: it would clearly be neither sight nor hearing, but something else.

THEAETETUS. Yes, of course: the power that's exercised by means of the tongue.

SOCRATES. Good. But what about the power which makes clear to you that which is com-
5 mon to everything, including these things: that to which you apply the words 'is', 'is not', and the others we used in our questions about them just now? What is that power exercised by means of? What sort of instruments are you going to assign to all those things, by means of which the perceiving element in us perceives each of them?

THEAETETUS. You mean being and not being, likeness and unlikeness, the same and differ-
10 ent, and also one and any other number applied to them. And it's clear that your ques-
d tion is also about odd and even, and every-thing else that goes with those. What you're asking is by means of what part of the body we perceive them with our minds.

5 SOCRATES. You follow me perfectly, Theaetetus. That's exactly what I'm asking.

THEAETETUS. Well, good heavens, Socrates, I couldn't say; except that I think there simply isn't any instrument of that kind peculiar to those things, as there is in the case of those
e others. On the contrary, it seems to me that the mind itself, by means of itself, considers the things which apply in common to everything.

SOCRATES. Theaetetus, you're handsome, not ugly, as Theodorus was saying; because some-one who speaks handsomely, is handsome,
5 and a fine person too. And besides being handsome, you've done me a favour: you've let me off a very long argument, if you think there are some things which the mind itself considers, by means of itself, and some which it considers by means of the capacities of the body. That was what I thought myself, but I wanted you to think so too.

186 THEAETETUS. Well, I do think so.

SOCRATES. Well now, in which class do you put being? Because that's pre-eminently some-thing that goes with everything.

THEAETETUS. I put it in the class of things which the mind itself tries to get hold of, by means of itself.

5 SOCRATES. And similarly with like and unlike, the same and different?

THEAETETUS. Yes.

SOCRATES. What about beautiful and ugly, good and bad?

THEAETETUS. They, too, seem to me to be pre-
10 eminently things whose being the mind con-
b siders in relation to one another, calculating in itself things past and present in relation to things in the future.

SOCRATES. Hold on. It'll perceive the hardness of what's hard by means of touch, won't it, and the softness of what's soft in the same way?

5 THEAETETUS. Yes.

SOCRATES. But their being, and what they both are, and their oppositeness to each other, and the being, in its turn, of this oppositeness, are things which the mind itself tries to decide for us, by reviewing them and comparing them with one another.

10 THEAETETUS. That's quite right.

SOCRATES. So there are some things which both men and animals are able by nature to per-

c ceive from the moment they're born: namely, all the things which direct experiences to the mind by means of the body. But as for calculations about those things, with respect to being and usefulness, they're acquired, by those who do acquire them, with difficulty and over a long time, by means of a great deal of troublesome education.

5 THEAETETUS. Definitely.

SOCRATES. Well now, is it possible that someone should attain truth if he doesn't even attain being?

THEAETETUS. No.

SOCRATES. And will someone ever have knowledge of something whose truth he doesn't attain?

d THEAETETUS. Of course not, Socrates.

SOCRATES. So knowledge is located, not in our experiences, but in our reasoning about those things we mentioned; because it's possible, apparently, to grasp being and truth in the latter, but impossible in the former.

5 THEAETETUS. Evidently.

SOCRATES. Well now, are you going to call them by the same name, when they have such great differences?

THEAETETUS. No, that wouldn't be right.

SOCRATES. Then what name do you give the

10 first: seeing, hearing, smelling, feeling cold, feeling hot?

e THEAETETUS. Perceiving, of course.

SOCRATES. So you call all of that, taken together, perception?

186e THEAETETUS. Yes, one must.

SOCRATES. And we say it has no share in the grasping of truth; because it has no share in

5 the grasping of being either.

THEAETETUS. No.

SOCRATES. So it has no share of knowledge, either?

THEAETETUS. No.

SOCRATES. So knowledge and perception could never be the same thing, Theaetetus.

10 THEAETETUS. Evidently not, Socrates. It has now become absolutely clear that knowledge is something other than perception.

SOCRATES. But our aim in starting this discussion

187 was to find out what knowledge is, not what it isn't. All the same, we've made enough progress to stop looking for it in perception altogether,

5 and look for it in whatever one calls what the mind is doing when it's busying itself, by itself, about the things which are.

THEAETETUS. I think that's called judging, Socrates.

SOCRATES. Yes, you're right.

So start again from the beginning: wipe out

b everything that has gone before, and see if you can get a better view, now that you've come on this far. Tell me, once again, what, exactly, knowledge is.

THEAETETUS. I can't say it's judgement in general, Socrates, because there's false judgement

5 as well; but perhaps true judgement is knowledge. Let that be my answer. If it turns out, as we go along, that it isn't as good as it seems now, we'll try to find something else to say.

SOCRATES. You're right to speak willingly like that, Theaetetus, rather than hesitate to answer, as you did at first. If we go on like this,

c one of two things will happen: either we'll find what we're after, or we'll be less inclined to think we know what we don't in fact know at all; and such a reward wouldn't be anything to complain about. Well, what is it that you're saying now? Is it that, whereas there are two kinds of judgement, one true and the other

5 false, you're defining knowledge as the true kind of judgement?

THEAETETUS. Yes; because that's how I see things at the moment.

200d5 SOCRATES. Well then, let's start again from the beginning: what should one say knowledge is? Because we're presumably not going to give up yet.

THEAETETUS. No, not unless you do.

SOCRATES. Tell me, then, what can we say it is with the least risk of contradicting ourselves?

ₑ THEAETETUS. What we were trying before, Socrates; because I haven't got anything else to suggest.

200ₑ SOCRATES. And what was that?

THEAETETUS. That true judgement is knowledge. Making a true judgement is, at any rate, something free of mistakes, and everything that results from it is admirable and good.

SOCRATES. Well, Theaetetus, the man who was leading the way across the river said, apparently, 'It will show for itself'. The same goes for this: if we go on and search into it, perhaps the very thing we're looking for will come to 201 light at our feet, but if we stay put, nothing will come clear to us.

THEAETETUS. Yes, you're right; let's go on and look into it.

SOCRATES. Well, this point doesn't take much looking: because there's a whole art which shows you that that isn't what knowledge is.

THEAETETUS. How do you mean? What art?

SOCRATES. The art of those who are greatest of all in point of wisdom: people call them speech-makers and litigants. Because those people, you see, persuade others by means of their art, not teaching them, but making them judge whatever they want them to judge. Or do 10 you think there are people who are so clever as ᵇ teachers that, in the short time allowed by the clock, they can teach the truth, about what happened, to people who weren't there when some others were being robbed of money or otherwise violently treated?

THEAETETUS. No, I don't think so at all. What they can do is persuade.

₅ SOCRATES. And you say persuading is making someone judge something?

THEAETETUS. Of course.

SOCRATES. So when jurymen have been persuaded, in accordance with justice, about things which it's possible to know only if one has seen them and not otherwise, then, in deciding those matters by hearsay, and getting hold of a true judgement, they have decided without knowledge; though what they have been persuaded of is correct, given

that they have reached a good verdict. Is that right?

201c THEAETETUS. Absolutely.

SOCRATES. But if true judgement and knowledge were the same thing, then even the best of jurymen would never make correct judgements without knowledge; and, as things are, it seems that the two are different.

THEAETETUS. Yes, Socrates, there's something I once heard someone saying, which I'd forgotten, but it's coming back to me now. He said that true judgement with an account is knowledge, and the kind without an account d falls outside the sphere of knowledge. Things of which there's no account are not knowable, he said—he actually called them that— whereas things which have an account are knowable. . . .

208c We said that there were three kinds of thing, one of which would be what our man meant by 'account'—I mean, the man who defines knowledge as being correct judgement with an account. Now perhaps someone will define it, not in the way we've just discussed, but as the last of the three.

THEAETETUS. You're right to remind us, because there's still one left. One was a sort of image of ₅ thought in speech, and one, which we've just discussed, was the way to go through the thing, element by element, till one has gone through the whole. Now what do you say the third is?

SOCRATES. What most people would say: being able to state some mark by which the thing one is asked for differs from everything else.

THEAETETUS. Can you give me an account of something as an example?

SOCRATES. Well, about the sun, if you like to d take that as an example, I imagine you'll accept as adequate that it's the brightest of the heavenly bodies that go round the earth.

THEAETETUS. Certainly.

₅ SOCRATES. Well, let me tell you why I said that. It was to bring out what we were saying just now: that if you get hold of the differentiation of anything, by which it differs from everything else, then some people say you'll have got hold of an account; whereas as long as you grasp something common, your account will be about those things to which the common quality belongs.

e THEAETETUS. I understand; and it seems to me that it's right to call something of that sort an account.

SOCRATES. And anyone who, along with a correct judgement about any of the things which are, gets hold of its differentiation from everything else as well, will have come to have

5 knowledge of that thing, of which he previously had a judgement.

THEAETETUS. Yes, that's what we're saying.

SOCRATES. But now that I've got close to what we're saying, Theaetetus, as if it were a picture with shading, I simply can't understand it, not even a little; whereas, as long as I was standing some distance away, it seemed to me that there was something in it.

10 THEAETETUS. How do you mean?

209 SOCRATES. I'll tell you, if I can. Suppose I have a correct judgement about you; then if I get hold of your account as well, I know you, and if not, I merely have you in my judgement.

THEAETETUS. Yes.

5 SOCRATES. And an account was to be what gives expression to your differentness.

THEAETETUS. Yes.

SOCRATES. Well then, when I was merely judging, wasn't it the case that I had no grasp in my thought of any of the things by which you're different from everything else?

THEAETETUS. Apparently not.

209a10 SOCRATES. So I had in my thought one of the common things, none of which you have to any greater extent than anyone else does.

b THEAETETUS. Yes, that must be so.

SOCRATES. But, for heaven's sake, in such conditions how on earth could it be you that I had in my judgement any more than anyone else? Suppose my thought was that Theaetetus is

5 the one who is a man, and has a nose, eyes, a mouth, and so on with each part of the body. Now, could that thought make it Theaetetus that I have in my thought, any more than Theodorus, or, as one might say, the remotest peasant in Asia?

THEAETETUS. No, how could it?

10 SOCRATES. And if I have in my thought not
c merely the one who has a nose and eyes, but the one with a snub nose and prominent eyes, it still won't be you that I have in my judgement any more than myself or anyone else who is like that, will it?

THEAETETUS. No.

SOCRATES. In fact it won't, I think, be Theaetetus who figures in a judgement in me until

5 precisely that snubness has imprinted and deposited in me a memory trace different from those of the other snubnesses I've seen, and similarly with the other things you're composed of. Then if I meet you tomorrow, that snubness will remind me and make me judge correctly about you.

10 THEAETETUS. Yes, that's quite true.

d SOCRATES. So correct judgement about anything, too, would seem to be about its differentness.

THEAETETUS. Evidently.

SOCRATES. Well then, what about getting hold of an account in addition to one's correct judgement: what's left for it to be? Because if, on the

5 one hand, it means adding a judgement as to how the thing differs from everything else, the instructions turn out to be quite absurd.

THEAETETUS. In what way?

SOCRATES. When we already have a correct judgement as to how something differs from everything else, those instructions tell us to add a correct judgement as to how that same thing differs from everything else. On those

10 lines, 'the turning of a treadmill' would be
e nowhere near right as a description of them; they might more justly be called a case of a blind man telling one the way. Because telling us to add something we already have in order to get to know what we have in our judgements looks like the behaviour of someone who is well and truly in darkness.

THEAETETUS. And if, on the other hand . . . ?

5 You put forward a hypothesis just now as if you were going to state another: what was it going to be?

SOCRATES. If, when it tells us to add an account, it's telling us to get to know, rather than judge,

210 the differentness, then we'll have an amusing thing in this most admirable of our accounts of knowledge. Because to get to know is surely to get hold of knowledge, isn't it?

THEAETETUS. Yes.

SOCRATES. So when it's asked what knowledge is, this account will apparently answer that it's

5 correct judgement together with knowledge of differentness. Because that's what adding an account would be, according to it.

THEAETETUS. Apparently.

SOCRATES. And when we're investigating know-ledge, it's absolutely silly to say it's correct judgement together with knowledge, whether of differentness or of anything else.

So it would seem, Theaetetus, that knowledge is neither perception, not true

b judgement, nor an account added to true judgement.

THEAETETUS. Apparently not.

SOCRATES. Well now, are we still pregnant and

5 in labour with anything about knowledge, or have we given birth to everything?

210b THEAETETUS. Yes, indeed, Socrates; actually you've got me to say more than I had in me.

SOCRATES. And my art of midwifery tells us that they're all the results of false pregnancies and not worth bringing up?

10 THEAETETUS. Yes, definitely.

SOCRATES. Well then, if you try, later on, to con-ceive anything else, and do so, what you're

c pregnant with will be the better for our pres-ent investigation. And if you stay barren, you'll be less burdensome to those who associ-ate with you, and gentler, because you'll have the sense not to think you know things which in fact you don't know. That much my art can

5 do, but no more, and I don't know any of the things which others know, all the great and admirable men there are and have been; but this gift of midwifery my mother and I received

d from God, she with women, and I with young and noble men and all who are beautiful.

Well, now I must go to the King's Porch to face the charge Meletus has brought against me. But let's meet here again, Theodorus, in the morning.

STUDY QUESTIONS: PLATO, *THEAETETUS*

1. How does Theaetetus first define 'knowledge'?
2. What is Socrates' objection to this definition?
3. What is Theaetetus' second definition of 'knowledge'?
4. How does Socrates use the example of jurymen to argue against this second definition?
5. What is Theaetetus' third definition of 'knowledge'?
6. What does Socrates mean by 'account'? What example does Socrates give of an account?
7. What is the problem that Socrates raises against the third definition of knowledge?
8. Is Plato's view of knowledge reasonable?

TIMAEUS

The *Timaeus* is one of the last of Plato's dialogues. When he was almost 70, Plato con-ceived an ambitious project consisting of three dialogues: the *Timaeus, Critias,* and *Herm-ocrates.* He never wrote the last of these, and the second breaks off in the middle of a

Plato, from *Plato's Cosmology: The Timeus of Plato,* translated by Francis MacDonald Cornford. Routledge & Kegan Paul, 1937. Reprinted by permission of the publisher.

sentence. Only the *Timeaus* is complete. His plan was to replace or supplement the *Republic* with the vision of an ideal, mythical state that existed in the remote past. The introduction to the trilogy is the myth of creation given in the *Timaeus*. Probably Plato's idea was to give a metaphysical grounding for his theories of ethics and politics. The order in the universe is reflected in the harmony of the soul, and so human morality must accord with the cosmic order.

In the *Timaeus*, Plato claims that the eternal is grasped by reason alone; the changing, or that which comes to be, is sensible or perceived by the senses. Anything that changes must have a cause. Thus, the world must have a cause, or a maker. However, a maker needs a model, and the only good model of this world is something eternal. Consequently, this world of becoming is a changing image or likeness of an eternal world of being upon which it is modeled.

Plato presents his account of creation in the form of a myth in order to analyze the rational order in the universe without imputing literal truth for his claims. In the act of creation, the demiurge (or demigod) employs divine reason and goodness to create the most perfect and beautiful copies possible of the pure Forms or Ideas. Nevertheless, this created world is not absolutely perfect; the copies are limited because, to be real, they must exist in space. Next, the demiurge creates a world soul, which imbues the cosmos with reason and intelligence. This world soul is the living principle of everything and the intermediary between the indivisible, eternal Being (the Idea) and the divisible, ephemeral realm of Becoming (Space), and, as such, it possesses the opposite qualities of sameness and change. The world soul contains all numbers and all dimensions, and is itself the mathematical form of the cosmos. Next, the demiurge distributes the world soul throughout the universe according to various harmonious and disharmonious relations, thereby setting the entire cosmos into motion. This motion consists in the world soul permeating the whole cosmos and then returning to itself, and, through this motion, it creates within itself individual consciousness, perception, and thought.

29D. **TIM.** Let us, then, state for what reason becom-
E. ing and this universe were framed by him who framed them. He was good; and in the good no jealousy in any matter can ever arise. So, being without jealously, he desired that all things should come as near as possible to being like himself. That this is the supremely valid principle of becoming and of the order of the world, we shall most surely be right to accept from men of understanding. Desiring,
30. then, that all things should be good and, so far as might be, nothing imperfect, the god took over all that is visible—not at rest, but in discordant and unordered motion—and brought it from disorder into order, since he judged that order was in every way the better.

Now it was not, nor can it ever be, permitted that the work of the supremely good should be anything but that which is best.
B. Taking thought, therefore, he found that, among things that are by nature visible, no work that is without intelligence will ever be better than one that has intelligence, when each is taken as a whole, and moreover that intelligence cannot be present in anything apart from soul. In virtue of this reasoning, when he framed the universe, he fashioned reason within soul and soul within body, to the end that the work he accomplished might be by nature as excellent and perfect as possible. This, then, is how we must say, according to the likely account, that this world came to be, by the god's providence, in very truth a
C. living creature with soul and reason.

This being premised, we have now to state what follows next: What was the living creature in whose likeness he framed the world? We must not suppose that it was any creature that ranks only as a species; for no copy of that which is incomplete can ever be good. Let us rather say that the world is like, above all things, to that Living Creature of which all other living creatures, severally and in their families, are parts. For that embraces

D. and contains within itself all the intelligible living creatures, just as this world contains ourselves and all other creatures that have been formed as things visible. For the god, wishing to make this world most nearly like that intelligible thing which is best and in every way complete, fashioned it as a single visible living creature, containing within itself all living things whose nature is of the

31. same order.

Have we, then, been right to call it one Heaven, or would it have been true rather to speak of many and indeed of an indefinite number? One we must call it, if we are to hold that it was made according to its pattern. For that which embraces all the intelligible living creatures that there are, cannot be one of a pair; for then there would have to be yet another Living Creature embracing those two, and they would be parts of it; and thus our world would be more truly described as a likeness, not of them, but of that other which

B. would embrace them. Accordingly, to the end that this world may be like the complete Living Creature in respect of its uniqueness, for that reason its maker did not make two worlds nor yet an indefinite number; but this Heaven has come to be and is and shall be hereafter one and unique.

Now that which comes to be must be bodily, and so visible and tangible; and nothing can be visible without fire, or tangible without something solid, and nothing is solid without earth. Hence the god, when he began to put together the body of the universe, set about making it of fire and earth. But two things alone cannot be satisfactorily united without a third; for there must be some bond

C. between them drawing them together. And of all bonds the best is that which makes itself and the terms it connects a unity in the fullest sense; and it is of the nature of a continued geometrical proportion to effect this most perfectly. For whenever, of three num-

32. bers, the middle one between any two that are either solids (cubes?) or squares is such that, as the first is to it, so is it to the last, and conversely as the last is to the middle, so is the middle to the first, then since the middle becomes first and last, and again the last and first become middle, in that way all will necessarily come to play the same part towards one another, and by so doing they will all make a unity.

Now if it had been required that the body of the universe should be a plane surface with no depth, a single mean would have been

B. enough to connect its companions and itself; but in fact the world was to be solid in form, and solids are always conjoined, not by one mean, but by two. Accordingly the god set water and air between fire and earth, and made them, so far as was possible, proportional to one another, so that as fire is to air, so is air to water, and as air is to water, so is water to earth, and thus he bound together the frame of a world visible and tangible.

For these reasons and from such con-

C. stituents, four in number, the body of the universe was brought into being, coming into concord by means of proportion, and from these it acquired Amity, so that coming into unity with itself it became indissoluble by any other save him who bound it together.

35C. Next, he went on to fill up both the double

36. and the triple intervals, cutting off yet more parts from the original mixture and placing them between the terms, so that within each interval there were two means, the one (harmonic) exceeding the one extreme and being exceeded by the other by the same fraction of the extremes, the other (arithmetic) exceeding the one extreme by the same number whereby it was exceeded by the other.

These links gave rise to intervals of $\frac{3}{2}$ and $\frac{4}{3}$ and $\frac{9}{8}$ within the original intervals.

When the father who had begotten it saw it set in motion and alive, a shrine brought into being for the everlasting gods, he rejoiced and being well pleased he took thought to make it yet more like its pattern. So as that pattern is the Living Being that is for ever existent, he sought to make this universe also like it, so far as might be, in that respect. Now the nature of that Living Being was eternal, and this character it was impossible to confer in full completeness on the generated thing. But he took thought to make, as it were, a moving likeness of eternity; and, at the same time that he ordered the Heaven, he made, of eternity that abides in unity, an everlasting likeness moving according to number—that to which we have given the name Time.

For there were no days and nights, months and years, before the Heaven came into being; but he planned that they should now come to be at the same time that the Heaven was framed. All these are parts of Time, and 'was' and 'shall be' are forms of time that have come to be; we are wrong to transfer them unthinkingly to eternal being. We say that it was and is and shall be; but 'is' alone really belongs to it and describes it truly; 'was'

and 'shall be' are properly used of becoming which proceeds in time, for they are motions. But that which is for ever in the same state immovably cannot be becoming older or younger by lapse of time, nor can it ever become so; neither can it now have been, nor will it be in the future; and in general nothing belongs to it of all that Becoming attaches to the moving things of sense; but these have come into being as forms of time, which images eternity and revolves according to number. And besides we make statements like these: that what is past *is* past, what happens now *is* happening now, and again that what will happen *is* what will happen, and that the non-existent *is* non-existent: no one of these expressions is exact. But this, perhaps, may not be the right moment for a precise discussion of these matters.

Be that as it may, Time came into being together with the Heaven, in order that, as they were brought into being together, so they may be dissolved together, if ever their dissolution should come to pass; and it is made after the pattern of the ever-enduring nature, in order that it may be as like that pattern as possible; for the pattern is a thing that has being for all eternity, whereas the Heaven has been and is and shall be perpetually throughout all time.

STUDY QUESTIONS: PLATO, *TIMAEUS*

1. Why did the god bring order into all that is visible?
2. Why did he create only one single living being?
3. What is necessary to unite or combine two things?
4. Why does the one living being have the shape of a sphere?
5. What does Plato say about the creation of time?
6. Why does Plato use myth? How did Plato use myths in the *Republic*? Is the use of myths here in the *Timaeus* comparable to that of the *Republic*?

LETTER VII

Plato wrote this letter in 353 B.C., six years before his death. The letter is important for two reasons. First, much of the letter is biographical, and it contains Plato's views on his own shadow career as a politician. Plato explains that after the defeat of Athens in 404 B.C. and the collapse of democracy, during the period of the oligarchy of the Council of Thirty, a public career in Athens was nearly impossible for him. Afterward, the trial and death of Socrates confirmed his belief that the politics of Athens was corrupt. Therefore, Plato viewed philosophy as a way to continue his concern for politics. Governance requires and aims at moral wisdom.

Second, in the passage selected, Plato outlines his reasons for claiming that philosophical understanding transcends language. It is debatable to what extent this later apparently more mystical claim conflicts with the views expressed by Plato in his dialogues. Nevertheless, it is clear that Plato thinks that philosophy requires more than secondhand knowledge of the appropriate words. Wisdom requires more than being a wordsmith.

323e *To the friends and companions of Dion, Prosperity*

In your letter you urged me to believe that your political convictions are the same as Dion's were, and in this connection you exhorted me 324 to lend your cause such aid as I can by action or by speech. My reply is that I will aid your cause if your views and your aims really are the same as Dion's; if they differ from his, I will take time to think about it. But what was Dion's policy, and what were his aims? To that question I think I could give an answer based not on conjecture but on sure knowledge. For when I first came to Syracuse—I was about forty years old—Dion's age was the same as that of Hipparinus b now, and he at that time arrived at a conclusion that he never departed from. He believed in liberty for the Syracusans under the guidance of the best system of laws. . . .

Now when I was thus urgently sent for—when my friends in Sicily and Italy were pulling me, while those at Athens were, you might say, by their entreaties actually shoving me out of e Athens—once more came the same message, that I ought not to betray either Dion or my friends and companions in Tarentum. Besides, I knew anyway without being told that no one need be surprised if a young man on hearing a really great enterprise suggested, quick to grasp the idea, had yielded to the spell of the ideal life. It seemed accordingly my duty to make the experiment so as to arrive at a definite conclusion one way or the other, for I must not be guilty of betraying that very ideal and of exposing my beliefs to the reproach they would deserve if 340 there were any truth in the reports I had received.

So I did set out under cover of these arguments, full of fears, as you might expect, and foreboding no very good result. At any rate in going I found that here at least it was really a case of the third to the savior, for I was fortunately brought safely home again. For this I have to thank Dionysius next to God, because, when many wished to put me out of the way, he interfered and gave some place to conscience in his dealings with me.

b When I had arrived, I thought I ought first to put it to the proof whether Dionysius was really all on fire with philosophy or whether the frequent reports that had come to Athens to that

---

Plato, from *Thirteen Epistles of Plato*, translated by L. A. Post. Clarendon Press, 1925. Reprinted by permission of Oxford University Press.

effect amounted to nothing. Now there is an experimental method for determining the truth in such cases that, far from being vulgar, is truly appropriate to despots, especially those stuffed with secondhand opinions, which I perceived, as soon as I arrived, was very much the case with Dionysius. One must point out to such men that e the whole plan is possible and explain what preliminary steps and how much hard work it will require, for the hearer, if he is genuinely devoted to philosophy and is a man of God with a natural affinity and fitness for the work, sees in the course marked out a path of enchantment, which he must at once strain every nerve to follow, or die in the attempt. Thereupon he braces himself and his guide to the task and does not relax his efforts until he either crowns them with final accomplishment or acquires the faculty of tracing his own way no longer accompanied by the d pathfinder. When this conviction has taken possession of him, such a man passes his life in whatever occupations he may engage in, but through it all never ceases to practice philosophy and such habits of daily life as will be most effective in making him an intelligent and retentive student, able to reason soberly by himself. Other practices than these he shuns to the end.

As for those, however, who are not genuine converts to philosophy, but have only a superficial tinge of doctrine—like the coat of tan that people get in the sun—as soon as they see how many subjects there are to study, how much hard work they involve, and how indispensable it is e for the project to adopt a well-ordered scheme of living, they decide that the plan is difficult if not 341 impossible for them, and so they really do not prove capable of practicing philosophy. Some of them too persuade themselves that they are well enough informed already on the whole subject and have no need of further application. This test then proves to be the surest and safest in dealing with those who are self-indulgent and incapable of continued hard work, since they throw the blame not on their guide but on their own inability to follow out in detail the course of training subsidiary to the project.

The instruction that I gave to Dionysius was accordingly given with this object in view. I certainly did not set forth to him all my doctrines, b nor did Dionysius ask me to, for he pretended to know many of the most important points already and to be adequately grounded in them by means of the secondhand interpretations he had got from the others.

I hear too that he has since written on the subjects in which I instructed him at that time, as if he were composing a handbook of his own which differed entirely from the instruction he received. Of this I know nothing. I do know, however, that some others have written on these same subjects, but who they are they know not themselves. One statement at any rate I can make in regard to all who have written or who c may write with a claim to knowledge of the subjects to which I devote myself—no matter how they pretend to have acquired it, whether from my instruction or from others or by their own discovery. Such writers can in my opinion have no real acquaintance with the subject. I certainly have composed no work in regard to it, nor shall I ever do so in future, for there is no way of putting it in words like other studies. Acquaintance with it must come rather after a long period of attendance on instruction in the subject itself and of close companionship, when, suddenly, like a blaze kindled by a leaping spark, d it is generated in the soul and at once becomes self-sustaining.

Besides, this at any rate I know, that if there were to be a treatise or a lecture on this subject, I could do it best. I am also sure for that matter that I should be very sorry to see such a treatise poorly written. If I thought it possible to deal adequately with the subject in a treatise or a lecture for the general public, what finer achievement would there have been in my life than to write a work of great benefit to mankind and to bring the nature of things to light for all men? I do not, however, think the attempt to tell mankind of e these matters a good thing, except in the case of some few who are capable of discovering the truth for themselves with a little guidance. In the case of the rest to do so would excite in some an unjustified contempt in a thoroughly offensive 342 fashion, in others certain lofty and vain hopes, as if they had acquired some awesome lore.

It has occurred to me to speak on the subject at greater length, for possibly the matter I am discussing would be clearer if I were to do so. There is a true doctrine, which I have often stated before, that stands in the way of the man who would dare to write even the least thing on such matters, and which it seems I am now called upon to repeat.

For everything that exists there are three classes of objects through which knowledge about it must come; the knowledge itself is a fourth, b and we must put as a fifth entity the actual object of knowledge which is the true reality. We have then, first, a name, second, a description, third, an image, and fourth, a knowledge of the object. Take a particular case if you want to understand the meaning of what I have just said; then apply the theory to every object in the same way. There is something for instance called a circle, the name of which is the very word I just now uttered. In the second place there is a description of it which is composed of nouns and verbal expressions. For example the description of that which is named round and circumference and circle would run as follows: the thing which has c everywhere equal distances between its extremities and its center. In the third place there is the class of object which is drawn and erased and turned on the lathe and destroyed—processes which do not affect the real circle to which these other circles are all related, because it is different from them. In the fourth place there are knowledge and understanding and correct opinion concerning them, all of which we must set down as one thing more that is found not in sounds nor in shapes of bodies, but in minds, whereby it evidently differs in its nature from the real circle and from the aforementioned three. Of all these four, d understanding approaches nearest in affinity and likeness to the fifth entity, while the others are more remote from it.

The same doctrine holds good in regard to shapes and surfaces, both straight and curved, in regard to the good and the beautiful and the just, in regard to all bodies artificial and natural, in regard to fire and water and the like, and in regard to every animal, and in regard to every quality of character, and in respect to all states

active and passive. For if in the case of any of e these a man does not somehow or other get hold of the first four, he will never gain a complete understanding of the fifth. Furthermore these four [names, descriptions, bodily forms, concepts] do as much to illustrate the particular quality of any object as they do to illustrate its essential reality because of the inadequacy of 343 language. Hence no intelligent man will ever be so bold as to put into language those things which his reason has contemplated, especially not into a form that is unalterable—which must be the case with what is expressed in written symbols.

Again, however, the meaning of what has just been said must be explained. Every circle that is drawn or turned on a lathe in actual operations abounds in the opposite of the fifth entity, for it everywhere touches the straight, while the real circle, I maintain, contains in itself neither much nor little of the opposite character. Names, I maintain, are in no case stable. Nothing pre- b vents the things that are now called round from being called straight and the straight round, and those who have transposed the names and use them in the opposite way will find them no less stable than they are now. The same thing for that matter is true of a description, since it consists of nouns and of verbal expressions, so that in a description there is nowhere any sure ground that is sure enough. One might, however, speak forever about the inaccurate character of each of the four! The important thing is that, as I said a little earlier, there are two things, the essential reality and the particular quality, and when the mind is in quest of knowledge not of the particu- c lar but of the essential, each of the four confronts the mind with the unsought particular, whether in verbal or in bodily form. Each of the four makes the reality that is expressed in words or illustrated in objects liable to easy refutation by the evidence of the senses. The result of this is to make practically every man a prey to complete perplexity and uncertainty.

Now in cases where as a result of bad training we are not even accustomed to look for the real essence of anything but are satisfied to accept what confronts us in the phenomenal presentations, we are not rendered ridiculous by each other—the examined by the examiners, who have the ability to handle the four with dexterity and to subject them to examination. In those cases, however, where we demand answers and proofs in regard to the fifth entity, anyone who pleases among those who have skill in confutation gains the victory and makes most of the audience think that the man who was first to speak or write or answer has no acquaintance with the matters of which he attempts to write or speak. Sometimes they are unaware that it is not the mind of the writer or speaker that fails in the test, but rather the character of the four—since that is naturally defective. Consideration of all of the four in turn—moving up and down from one to another—barely begets knowledge of a naturally flawless object in a naturally flawless man. If a man is naturally defective—and this is the natural state of most people's minds with regard to intelligence and to what are called morals—while the objects he inspects are tainted with imperfection, not even Lynceus could make such a one see.

To sum it all up in one word, natural intelligence and a good memory are equally powerless to aid the man who has not an inborn affinity with the subject. Without such endowments there is of course not the slightest possibility. Hence all who have no natural aptitude for and affinity with justice and all the other noble ideals, though in the study of other matters they may be both intelligent and retentive—all those too who have affinity but are stupid and unretentive—such will never any of them attain to an understanding of the most complete truth in regard to moral concepts. The study of virtue and vice must be accompanied by an inquiry into what is false and true of existence in general and must be carried on by constant practice throughout a long period, as I said in the beginning. Hardly after practicing detailed comparisons of names and definitions and visual and other sense perceptions, after scrutinizing them in benevolent disputation by the use of question and answer without jealousy, at last in a flash understanding of each blazes up, and the mind, as it exerts all its powers to the limit of human capacity, is flooded with light.

For this reason no serious man will ever think of writing about serious realities for the general public so as to make them a prey to envy and perplexity. In a word, it is an inevitable conclusion from this that when anyone sees anywhere the written work of anyone, whether that of a lawgiver in his laws or whatever it may be in some other form, the subject treated cannot have been his most serious concern—that is, if he is himself a serious man. His most serious interests have their abode somewhere in the noblest region of the field of his activity. If, however, he really was seriously concerned with these matters and put them in writing, 'then surely' not the gods, but mortals 'have utterly blasted his wits.'

STUDY QUESTIONS: PLATO, LETTER VII

1. What is the test that Plato gave to Dionysius to see whether or not he was enthusiastic about philosophy?
2. What is Plato's view of the idea that the method to attain philosophical understanding can be given in a manual?
3. Plato distinguishes five entities. What are these? For what purpose does he make this distinction?
4. According to Plato, why is it impossible to express in writing what reason has contemplated? Why would the attempt to do that result in confusion?
5. According to Plato, what can one do to attain the state where the understanding is flooded with light?

Philosophical Bridges: The Platonic Influence

It is difficult to overestimate the influence of Plato on the history of thought, especially his views concerning the reality of the Forms and the nature of the soul and knowledge. Additionally, we have mentioned already how the ideas of Pythagoras and Parmenides entered western thought largely through Plato. His influence came in three major waves: the first, around 380, in wedlock with Christianity; the second, around 1450, in opposition to the doctrine of the Church; and the third in the form of seventeenth-century Rationalism.

The first wave began with Plotinus (205–270 A.D.), who argued in favor of Platonism and against Stoicism and Epicureanism. Broadly speaking, Plotinus identified Plato's form of the Good with God, with which the inner part of the soul has direct contact. In brief, Plotinus' influential neo-Platonism highlighted certain affinities between Plato's thought and the emerging Christianity. Augustine (354–430), who studied Plotinus and Plato before converting to Christianity, made those affinities more explicit by trying to reconcile Platonism and Christianity. In the process, he produced a theology that dominated Christian and, hence, western thought until Thomas Aquinas, around 1260. Because of Aquinas, Plato's influence was eclipsed by that of Aristotle, when the latter's works, which had been largely unknown in Europe, were reintroduced into the continent by Arab thinkers through the Moors in Spain.

However, 200 years later, a second wave of Platonism broke upon western thought. During the Renaissance, Europeans scholars rediscovered their forgotten ancient pagan heritage, including much of Plato's philosophy, which, as a consequence, had, for the second time, a major impact on the history of thought. In 1441, Cosimo Medici established a Platonic Academy in Florence, which was attended by the artist Michelangelo and the thinker Pico della Mirandola, who wrote *On the Dignity of Man*. Cosimo also funded Marsilio Ficino to devote himself to the translation of Plato's works. This revival of Plato helped to establish the humanism of the fifteenth century, and end the supremacy of Scholastic philosophy based on Aquinas' interpretation of Aristotle. The humanism of the Renaissance focused attention away from God and toward the individual. Consequently, it drew inspiration less from Plato's otherworldly theory of Forms but more from his theory of the soul, which emphasizes the noble nature of a person, as well as from the breadth and literary quality of Plato's dialogues.

In turn, humanism enabled the scientific revolution that marked the transition from medieval to modern philosophy in the later half of the sixteenth century. At this stage in the development of thought, Plato's writings became influential for another reason: like the thought of Pythagoras, they stressed the mathematical order of the universe, which inspired scientists such as Galileo and Kepler to formulate their scientific theories in precise mathematical terms.

The third surge of Platonic thinking occurred in the seventeenth and eighteenth centuries. Rationalists such as Spinoza and Leibniz opposed Empiricist thinkers, such as John Locke, who argued that all knowledge and concepts must be derived from sense-experience. In opposition to this, the Rationalists were impressed by the Platonic arguments for the conclusion that sense-experience is illusory. Moreover, according to these Rationalists, sense-experience never provides knowledge of real causes, which requires appeal to general principles, such as the principle of sufficient reason, which can be known through reason alone.

There are at least two major aspects to Plato's philosophy: his mathematical rationalism and his more mystical conception of the good. Both aspects are reflected in contemporary thinking.

Contemporary versions of Plato's theory of Forms are popular in some areas of philosophy. For instance, mathematical Platonism, the claim that there exist abstract entities such as numbers and sets, is an important view in recent philosophy of mathematics, advanced by the great logician Kurt Gödel and the contemporary mathematician Roger Penrose, among many others. Penrose's book *The Emperor's New Clothes* contains a popular exposition of his philosophy of mathematics.

Furthermore, philosophers today still question the nature of properties and universals. In what sense are properties real? The idea that they can exist apart from particulars (for example, that there exists the property of being a dodo, even though no such birds have survived) seems to provide support for a quasi-Platonist position regarding properties or universals. Some contemporary thinkers, such as David Armstrong and Michael Tooley, argue that a realist position regarding universals is required for understanding causal laws. Such laws express a relationship of necessity between universals that exist independently of physical objects.

A central thesis of Plato's philosophy is that a proper understanding of morality requires knowledge of the supreme form of goodness. According to Plato, this thesis is required to refute the ethical subjectivism inherent in Sophism. While many contemporary philosophers agree with Plato in rejecting ethical subjectivism, few have followed Plato's thesis regarding the Form of Goodness. One of the notable exceptions is the British/Irish philosopher and novelist Iris Murdoch (1919–1999), whose famous works *The Sovereignty of the Good* and *Metaphysics as a Guide for Morals* are explicitly Platonic in parts.

This brief account fails to give justice to the extent and scope of Plato's historical importance. He has influenced greatly many specific areas of philosophy. For example, he defined knowledge as justified true belief, and this definition was accepted widely until the 1970s, when causal and other theories of knowledge also became popular. His claim that sense perception cannot yield understanding of the reasons why things are as they are expresses a dissatisfaction with a purely Empiricist account of knowledge that has been felt by some thinkers over the generations. This dissatisfaction is expressed at times in terms of the need for innate concepts or abilities, and sometimes as the need for universal principles. More generally, Plato's discussion of, for instance, democracy, the soul, the virtues, love, the nature of pleasure, and the meaning of art form part of the culture of western philosophy.

BIBLIOGRAPHY

Primary

Collected Dialogues, ed. E. Hamilton and H. Cairns, Princeton University Press, 1961

Euthyphro, Apology, and *Crito,* trans. Thomas and Gale West, Cornell University Press, 1986

Gorgias, trans. T.H. Irwin, Clarendon Press, 1979

Meno, trans. J. M. Day, London, 1994

Parmenides, trans. Kenneth Sayre, University of Notre Dame Press, 1996

Phaedo, trans. David Gallup, Clarendon Press, 1975

Phaedrus, trans. J. C. Rowe, Aris and Philips, 1986

Protagoras, trans. C. C. W. Taylor, Clarendon Press, 1991

Republic, trans. R. Waterfield, Oxford University Press, 1993

Symposium, trans. R. Waterfield, Oxford University Press, 1994

Theaetetus, trans. John McDowell, Oxford University Press, 1977

Timaeus, trans. F. M. Cornford, Routledge, 1937

Secondary

Annas, Julia, *An Introduction to Plato's Republic*, Clarendon Press, 1981

Brickhouse, T., and Smith, N., *Plato's Socrates*, Clarendon Press, 1994

Gosling, J. C. B., *Plato*, Arguments of the Philosophers, Routledge, 1973

Grube, G. M. A, *Plato's Thought*, Hackett, 1980

Hare, R. M., *Plato*, Past Master Series, Oxford University Press, 1982

Irwin, T. H., *Plato's Ethics*, Clarendon Press, 1995

Kahn, C. H., *Plato and the Socratic Dialogue*, Cambridge University Press, 1996

Kraut, Richard, *The Cambridge Companion to Plato*, Cambridge University Press, 1992

Santas, Gerasimos, *Socrates*, Arguments of the Philosophers, Routledge, 1979

Vlastos, Gregory, *Plato's Universe*, University of Washington Press, 1975

SECTION III

◆ ARISTOTLE ◆

PROLOGUE

Aristotle's work achieved a greatness that perhaps surpasses even that of Plato's. During the medieval period, thinkers would refer to him as '*the* Philosopher.' Aristotle's thought had a deep influence on the development of Christian theology and ethics. He systematized the whole of knowledge, dividing it into different subject matters in a way that is still generally accepted today. In many areas of study, we still rely on concepts that Aristotle first developed. Moreover, Aristotle emphasized the role of systematic empirical investigation, which is one of the basic foundations of science.

ARISTOTLE (384–322 B.C.)

Biographical History

Aristotle's father, who was personal physician to the king of Macedonia in northern Greece, sent the 17-year-old Aristotle to the Academy. About 20 years later, in 347 B.C., Plato died. Plato's nephew, Speusippus, became head of the Academy, and Aristotle left Athens to embark on a new independent life of intellectual exploration. He moved to Assos, and later to the island of Lesbos, in eastern Greece. During this period, Aristotle made many biological observations. He collected information regarding about 500 animal species.

In 343 B.C., he was invited by Philip of Macedonia to return to his homeland to tutor his son, Alexander the Great, then aged 14. Aristotle remained in this post for some seven years, until 336 B.C., when Alexander himself became the king of Macedonia and began his conquest of the ancient world. In 334 B.C., at the age of 50, Aristotle returned to Athens to establish his own school, the Lyceum, in a grove in the north of Athens. The return to Athens marks the mature period of Aristotle's intellectual life, during which he composed most of his famous works. The Lyceum was a center of teaching, learning, and investigation. Aristotle gathered around him fellow students of nature and coordinated a systematic investigation covering almost all areas of human knowledge, which continued after his death. Aristotle also collected hundreds of manuscripts, maps, and natural specimens, and the Lyceum became one of the first libraries and museums.

Although he was a prolific writer, only fragments of his published writings remain. However, his unpublished writings have survived in the form of lecture notes or texts used by his students. He produced groundbreaking texts not just in metaphysics and logic, but on virtually every subject: physics, astronomy, meteorology, taxonomy, psychology, biology, ethics, politics, and aesthetics. Given his incredible powers of observation, classification, and deduction, it is not surprising that later generations thought of him as a superman. When Alexander died in 323 B.C., Athens became a center of anti-Macedonian feelings, and Aristotle decided to leave the city. A year later he died. He was 62.

Philosophical Overview

It is important to compare the thinking of Plato and Aristotle because the contrast between their works produces a fork in the development of philosophy. As a broad generalization, Plato was more analytic, humanistic, and religious, with an eye cast toward mathematics. Aristotle was more synthetic, scientific, and secular in his epistemology, with an eye directed toward logic. These very general differences of approach foreshadow the later splits between the humanities and the sciences, and also between Rationalism and Empiricism.

In brief, there are three major differences between the two great philosophers. First, Aristotle rejects the Platonic realm of Forms or Ideas. For Aristotle, the forms exist as the essence or properties of material things in the natural world. Aristotle replaced Plato's distinction between the eternal Forms and the transient world of appearances with his own form/matter distinction. According to Aristotle, the form and the matter of a natural object are simply two aspects of its existence.

Second, Aristotle developed a method of investigation very different from Plato's, for whom the world of sensory perception is ultimately an illusion and for whom true knowledge is confined to the Ideas or Forms and can only be attained by pure reason. Plato's work is often mystical and otherworldly; in contrast, Aristotle displays detailed knowledge of animals, physics, and many other natural phenomena. Aristotle developed the idea of the systematic scientific investigation of nature. With others in the Lyceum, he carried out such research, but Aristotle also made this methodology part of his investigations. In other words, he practiced science, but he also developed a philosophy of science.

Much of Aristotle's scientific work is dedicated to biology, in which he employs the notions of essence, natural development, and natural purposes. The world primarily consists of natural things that belong to certain kinds, which define their essence. Biological classification must reflect these natural essences, thereby placing animals on a natural scale according to their development at birth, with humans at the top and bloodless mollusks near the bottom. Higher life forms are more perfect than the lower ones. Additionally, Aristotle looks for natural purposes to explain physiological processes and organs. For example, higher animals are naturally hotter. Because breathing cools, they need to breathe a lot, and for this reason, they have lungs.

Aristotle extends the biological notions of natural hierarchies and purposes or ends into physics. The universe consists of two realms. From the moon upward, there is the heavenly world, consisting of the stars and planets, which are in a constant circular motion but are otherwise unchanging. In contrast, below the moon, everything changes and decays and is composed of the four elements: earth, water, air, and fire. These last three lie in concentric layers around the stationary spherical earth, each according to its proper place or natural end. Without intervention, earth will fall downward, in a straight line toward the center of the universe. Likewise, fire will rise naturally upward, away from the center of the universe. Each element has its own natural end. Aristotelian physics did not have the modern notion of inanimate matter. Aristotle's cosmology was based on the (alleged) observation that the celestial bodies move in constant circles. But the four elements (earth, water, fire, and air) always move naturally in a straight line. Therefore, the stars cannot be made of the four elements.

Aristotle's scientific methodology is presented in six works, later compiled as the *Organon*, which together served as a definitive text until the sixteenth century. *The Categories* concerns the basic types of words, which are the parts of complete statements. *On Interpretation* is about these whole statements, which form part of syllogisms. The *Prior Analytics* is a work in the logic of syllogisms. The *Posterior Analytics* explains the use of these syllogisms in scientific investigation. Finally, the *Topics* and the *Sophistical Refutations* systematize the use of arguments in dialectics and identify some informal fallacies.

The third characteristic of Aristotle's work is his interest in classification, which extends from his work in biology to philosophy, language, and politics. For example, he classifies different categories, logical inferences, types of explanation, and political systems. This is a more empirical approach than Plato's. Furthermore, Aristotle examines and classifies the way language is employed, such as the different uses of philosophically key terms such as 'being' and 'is,' and this forms the basis of his metaphysics.

Form and matter are not two independently existing things. They are two aspects of any substance or thing, which are separable only in thought. This distinction distances Aristotle from Plato, who conceived of the Forms as independently existing universals. Provisionally, we can conceive of Aristotelian form as the structure or organization of a natural thing. For example, the form of an animal is the way the matter of its body is organized such that it has the power to grow, perceive, and move in the way it does. This is the essence of the animal, and this nature defines its power of movement. The matter is the material out of which the substance or object in question is composed. Matter cannot exist without form, and form requires matter. They are two aspects of any particular thing. The form/matter distinction can be drawn at different levels. The body is the matter of a person. Flesh is the matter of the body. The matter of any compound will be one or more of the four elements, fire, air, earth, and water, and the form/matter distinction can be applied to the elements themselves.

The form/matter distinction allows Aristotle to advance a view that transcends the metaphysics of both the pre-Socratics and Plato. According to Aristotle, the pre-Socratics describe the matter, or the stuff of the universe, but not what reality consists in, that is, individual substances or particulars, such as plants and animals. Against the pre-Socratics, Aristotle argues that these substances are not reducible to the matter out of which they are composed. On the other hand, Plato claims that reality consists ultimately of eternal Ideas or Forms, such as Beauty, Justice, and Goodness. According to Aristotle, Plato's theory misunderstands form. It treats universals as if they were substances. This does not mean that Aristotle denies the existence of Forms. Rather, he denies that universals or forms are substances, or primary existents. According to Aristotle, they exist, but Plato is mistaken about the type of existence they have. Aristotle is able to transcend the pre-Socratics and Plato because he classifies types of existence. He recognizes that there are different ways in which things can be said to exist. This classification of 'exists' or 'be' is the ontological reflection of the categories.

CATEGORIES

The *Categories* is probably an early work. It is the basis of Aristotle's metaphysics and of his arguments against both Parmenides' claim that change is an illusion and Plato's theory of Forms. Aristotle argues that both theories are based on a misunderstanding of the word 'is.' This word has different uses, which are reflected in the categories. The first four chapters of the *Categories* explain the general concept of a category, and the remaining chapters discuss each particular category in turn. The fifth chapter concentrates on the primary category of substance.

Aristotle explains that the terms 'exists,' 'is,' and 'be' are paronymous. Two things are named paronymously when the two names do not pick out the same thing and do not have the same definition, but the one term is derived from the other. For example, sports, athletes, complexions, and diets are all said to be healthy, but they are so in different, but connected, ways. They are all healthy in a secondary or a derivative way. The primary way of being healthy is to have a body in excellent functioning shape. The secondary ways of being healthy derive from this primary way. Aristotle uses this analysis of 'healthy' to better understand existence or 'to be.' The term 'exists' has a primary use and also secondary uses. The categories are like a catalogue of the paronymous uses of 'exists.' Aristotle lists ten categories. These are as follows:

1. *Substance, or what is it?* (e.g., 'horse')
2. *Quantity, or how much?* (e.g., 'is four foot tall')
3. *Quality, or what kind?* (e.g., 'is white')
4. *Relations, or in relation to what?* (e.g., 'is larger than')
5. *Where?* (e.g., 'is in the market-place')
6. *When?* (e.g., 'yesterday')
7. *Position?* (e.g., 'is upright')
8. *Having?* (e.g., 'has-shoes-on')
9. *Doing?* (e.g., 'is running')
10. *Being affected by?* (e.g., 'is being ridden')

The most fundamental category is the first, substance (*ousia*). Aristotle argues that substances are the basic or primary constituents of reality, and this point is central to all his metaphysics. This means that all the other categories indicate dependent existents. This is why substance is always included in all lists of the categories, in addition to quality and quantity. From this point, we can also see that, although Aristotle's list is of basic types of predicate terms (i.e., it is a linguistic classification), it is also a list of the different ways in which things can exist (i.e., it is also ontological). For this reason, Aristotle employs the categories in his metaphysics by arguing that 'exists' is paronymous. The linguistic list has ontological implications.

The reasoning that led Aristotle to conclude that the list of basic predicates is the same as that of basic type of existents is possibly as follows. If we ask what blue is, the answer is 'a color.' If we ask what color is, the answer is 'a quality.' However, we cannot ask for a higher classification for quality itself. For this reason, it is a category, an ultimate classification. The basic predicates indicate the fundamental classes into which all things fall. Therefore, they indicate fundamental types of things.

¹ᵃ¹ **1.** When things have only a name in common and the definition of being which corresponds to the name is different, they are called *homonymous*. Thus, for example, both a man and a picture are animals. These have only a name in common and the definition of being which corresponds to the name is different; for if one is to say what being an animal is for each of them, one ⁵ will give two distinct definitions.

When things have the name in common and the definition of being which corresponds to the name is the same, they are called *synonymous*. Thus, for example, both a man and an ox are animals. Each of these is called, by a common name, an animal, and the definition of being is ₁₀ also the same; for if one is to give the definition of each—what being an animal is for each of them—one will give the same definition.

When things get their name from something, with a difference of ending, they are called *paronymous*. Thus, for example, the grammarian gets his name from grammar, the brave get theirs ₁₅ from bravery.

2. Of things that are said, some involve combination while others are said without combination. Examples of those involving combination are: man runs, man wins; and of those without combination: man, ox, runs, wins.

Of things there are: (*a*) some are *said of* a sub-₂₀ject but are not *in* any subject. For example, man is said of a subject, the individual man, but is not in any subject. (*b*) Some are in a subject but are not said of any subject. (By 'in a subject' I mean what is in something, not as a part, and cannot ₂₅ exist separately from what it is in.) For example, the individual knowledge-of-grammar is in a subject, the soul, but is not said of any subject; and the individual white is in a subject, the body (for all colour is in a body), but is not said of any subject. (*c*) Some are both said of a subject and in a subject. For example, knowledge is in a subject, ¹ᵇ¹ the soul, and is also said of a subject, knowledge-of-grammar. (*d*) Some are neither in a subject nor said of a subject, for example, the individual man or the individual horse—for nothing of this sort ⁵ is either in a subject or said of a subject. Things that are individual and numerically one are, without exception, not said of any subject, but there is nothing to prevent some of them from being in a subject—the individual knowledge-of-grammar is one of the things in a subject.

3. Whenever one thing is predicated of another as of a subject, all things said of what is predicated will be said of the subject also. For example, man is predicated of the individual man, and animal of man; so animal will be predicated of the individual man also—for the individual man is both a man and an animal.

The differentiae of genera which are different and not subordinate one to the other are themselves different in kind. For example, animal and knowledge: footed, winged, aquatic, two-footed, are differentiae of animal, but none of these is a differentia of knowledge; one sort of knowledge does not differ from another by being two-footed. However, there is nothing to prevent genera subordinate one to the other from having the same differentiae. For the higher are predicated of the genera below them, so that all differentiae of the predicated genus will be differentiae of the subject also.

4. Of things said without any combination, each signifies either substance or quantity or qualification or a relative or where or when or being-in-a-position or having or doing or being-affected. To give a rough idea, examples of substance are man, horse; of quantity: four-foot, five-foot; of qualification: white, grammatical; of a relative: double, half, larger; of where: in the

Aristotle, from *Aristotle: Categories and De Interpretatione*, translated by J. L. Ackrill. Clarendon Aristotle Series, 1963. Reprinted by permission of Oxford University Press.

Lyceum, in the market-place; of when: yester-day, last-year; of being-in-a-position: is-lying, is-sitting; of having: has-shoes-on, has-armour-on; of doing: cutting, burning; of being-affected: being-cut, being-burned.

None of the above is said just by itself in any affirmation, but by the combination of these with one another an affirmation is produced. For every affirmation, it seems, is either true or false; but of things said without any combination none is either true or false (e.g. man, white, runs, wins).

5. A *substance*—that which is called a sub-stance most strictly, primarily, and most of all—is that which is neither said of a subject nor in a subject, e.g. the individual man or the individual horse. The species in which the things primarily called substances are, are called *secondary sub-stances*, as also are the genera of these species. For example, the individual man belongs in a species, man, and animal is a genus of the species; so these—both man and animal—are called sec-ondary substances.

It is clear from what has been said that if something is said of a subject both its name and its definition are necessarily predicated of the subject. For example, man is said of a subject, the individual man, and the name is of course predi-cated (since you will be predicating man of the individual man), and also the definition of man will be predicated of the individual man (since the individual man is also a man). Thus both the name and the definition will be predicated of the subject. But as for things which are in a subject, in most cases neither the name nor the definition is predicated of the subject. In some cases there is nothing to prevent the name from being predi-cated of the subject, but it is impossible for the definition to be predicated. For example, white, which is in a subject (the body), is predicated of the subject; for a body is called white. But the definition of white will never be predicated of the body.

35 All the other things are either said of the primary substances as subjects or in them as sub-jects. This is clear from an examination of cases. For example, animal is predicated of man and therefore also of the individual man; for were it predicated of none of the individual men it would not be predicated of man at all. Again, 2ᵇ1 colour is in body and therefore also in an individ-ual body; for were it not in some individual body it would not be in body at all. Thus all the other things are either said of the primary substances as subjects or in them as subjects. So if the primary 5 substances did not exist it would be impossible for any of the other things to exist.

Of the secondary substances the species is more a substance than the genus, since it is nearer to the primary substance. For if one is to say of the primary substance what it is, it will be more informative and apt to give the species 10 than the genus. For example, it would be more informative to say of the individual man that he is a man than that he is an animal (since the one is more distinctive of the individual man while the other is more general); and more informative to say of the individual tree that it is a tree than 15 that it is a plant. Further, it is because the pri-mary substances are subjects for all the other things and all the other things are predicated of them or are in them, that they are called sub-stances most of all. But as the primary substances stand to the other things, so the species stands to the genus: the species is a subject for the genus 20 (for the genera are predicated of the species but the species are not predicated reciprocally of the genera). Hence for this reason too the species is more a substance than the genus.

But of the species themselves—those which are not genera—one is no more a substance than another: it is no more apt to say of the individual man that he is a man than to say of the individ-25 ual horse that it is a horse. And similarly of the primary substances one is no more a substance than another: the individual man is no more a substance than the individual ox.

It is reasonable that, after the primary sub-stances, their species and genera should be the only other things called secondary substances. 30 For only they, of things predicated, reveal the primary substance. For if one is to say of the indi-vidual man what he is, it will be in place to give the species or the genus (though more informa-tive to give man than animal); but to give any of the other things would be out of place—for

example, to say white or runs or anything like
35 that. So it is reasonable that these should be the
only other things called substances. Further, it is
because the primary substances are subjects for
everything else that they are called substances
most strictly. But as the primary substances stand
3ᵃ1 to everything else, so the species and genera of
the primary substances stand to all the rest: all
the rest are predicated of these. For if you will
call the individual man grammatical, then you
will call both a man and an animal grammatical;
5 and similarly in other cases.

It is a characteristic common to every substance not to be in a subject. For a primary substance is neither said of a subject nor in a subject.
10 And as for secondary substances, it is obvious at
once that they are not in a subject. For man is
said of the individual man as subject but is not
in a subject: man is not *in* the individual man.
Similarly, animal also is said of the individual
15 man as subject, but animal is not *in* the individual man. Further, while there is nothing to prevent the name of what is in a subject from being
sometimes predicated of the subject, it is impossible for the definition to be predicated. But the
definition of the secondary substances, as well as
the name, is predicated of the subject: you will
predicate the definition of man of the individual
man, and also that of animal. No substance,
20 therefore, is in a subject.

This is not, however, peculiar to substance,
since the differentia also is not in a subject. For
footed and two-footed are said of man as subject
but are not in a subject; neither two-footed nor
25 footed is *in* man. Moreover, the definition of the
differentia is predicated of that of which the differentia is said. For example, if footed is said of
man the definition of footed will also be predicated of man; for man is footed.

30   We need not be disturbed by any fear that
we may be forced to say that the parts of a substance, being in a subject (the whole substance),
are not substances. For when we spoke of things
in a subject we did not mean things belonging in
something as *parts*.

It is a characteristic of substances and differentiae that all things called from them are so
called synonymously. For all the predicates from

35 them are predicated either of the individuals or
of the species. (For from a primary substance
there is no predicate, since it is said of no subject; and as for secondary substances, the species
is predicated of the individual, the genus both of
the species and of the individual. Similarly, differentiae too are predicated both of the species
3ᵇ1 and of the individuals.) And the primary substances admit the definition of the species and of
the genera, and the species admits that of the
genus; for everything said of what is predicated
will be said of the subject also. Similarly, both
5 the species and the individuals admit the definition of the differentiae. But synonymous things
were precisely those with both the name in common and the same definition. Hence all the
things called from substances and differentiae are
so called synonymously.

Every substance seems to signify a certain
10 'this'. As regards the primary substances, it is
indisputably true that each of them signifies a
certain 'this'; for the thing revealed is individual
and numerically one. But as regards the secondary substances, though it appears from the form of
the name—when one speaks of man or animal—
that a secondary substance likewise signifies a
15 certain 'this', this is not really true; rather, it signifies a certain qualification—for the subject is
not, as the primary substance is, one, but man
and animal are said of many things. However, it
does not signify simply a certain qualification, as
white does. White signifies nothing but a qualification, whereas the species and the genus mark
20 off the qualification of substance—they signify
substance of a certain qualification. (One draws a
wider boundary with the genus than with the
species, for in speaking of animal one takes in
more than in speaking of man.)

Another characteristic of substances is that
there is nothing contrary to them. For what
would be contrary to a primary substance? For
25 example, there is nothing contrary to an individual man, nor yet is there anything contrary to
man or to animal. This, however, is not peculiar
to substance but holds of many other things also,
for example, of quantity. For there is nothing
contrary to four-foot or to ten or to anything of
this kind—unless someone were to say that many

30 is contrary to few or large to small; but still there is nothing contrary to any *definite* quantity.

Substance, it seems, does not admit of a more and a less. I do not mean that one substance is not more a substance than another (we have said that it is), but that any given substance is not called more, or less, that which it is. For example, if this substance is a man, it will not be more a man or less a man either than itself or than another man. For one man is not more a man than another, as 4ᵇ1 one pale thing is more pale than another and one beautiful thing more beautiful than another. Again, a thing is called more, or less, such-and-such than itself; for example, the body that is pale is called more pale now than before, and the one that is hot is called more, or less, hot. Substance, however, is not spoken of thus. For a man is not 5 called more a man now than before, nor is anything else that is a substance. Thus substance does not admit of a more and a less.

10　It seems most distinctive of substance that what is numerically one and the same is able to receive contraries. In no other case could one bring forward anything, numerically one, which is able to receive contraries. For example, a colour which is numerically one and the same will not be black and white, nor will numerically one and the same action be bad and good; and 15 similarly with everything else that is not substance. A substance, however, numerically one and the same, is able to receive contraries. For example, an individual man—one and the same—becomes pale at one time and dark at 20 another, and hot and cold, and bad and good.

Nothing like this is to be seen in any other case, unless perhaps someone might object and say that statements and beliefs are like this. For the same statement seems to the both true and false. Suppose, for example, that the statement that somebody is sitting is true; after he has got up 25 this same statement will be false. Similarly with beliefs. Suppose you believe truly that somebody is sitting; after he has got up you will believe falsely if you hold the same belief about him. However, even if we were to grant this, there is still a difference in the *way* contraries are received. For in the case of substances it is by them- 30 selves changing that they are able to receive contraries. For what has become cold instead of hot, or dark instead of pale, or good instead of bad, has changed (has altered); similarly in other cases too it is by itself undergoing change that each thing is able to receive contraries. Statements and beliefs, on the other hand, themselves 35 remain completely unchangeable in every way; it is because the *actual thing* changes that the contrary comes to belong to them. For the statement that somebody is sitting remains the same; it is because of a change in the actual thing that it 4ᵇ1 comes to be true at one time and false at another. Similarly with beliefs. Hence at least the *way* in which it is able to receive contraries—through a change in itself—would be distinctive of substance, even if we were to grant that beliefs and 5 statements are able to receive contraries. However, this is not true. For it is not because they themselves receive anything that statements and beliefs are said to be able to receive contraries, but because of what has happened to something else. For it is because the actual thing exists or does not exist that the statement is said to be true or false, 10 not because it is able itself to receive contraries. No statement, in fact, or belief is changed at all by anything. So, since nothing happens in them, they are not able to receive contraries. A substance, on the other hand, is said to be able to receive contraries because it itself receives con- 15 traries. For it receives sickness and health, and paleness and darkness; and because it itself receives the various things of this kind it is said to be able to receive contraries. It is, therefore, distinctive of substance that what is numerically one and the same is able to receive contraries. This brings to an end our discussion of substance.

STUDY QUESTIONS: ARISTOTLE, *CATEGORIES*

1. What is it when two things have the same name paronymously?
2. What is a subject?
3. What is the difference between the primary and secondary uses of 'substance'? Why does Aristotle draw this distinction?

4. What does he mean by saying that 'as for secondary substances, it is obvious . . . that they are not in a subject?'
5. What is the difference between 'white' and species and genus?
6. What is the most distinctive feature of 'substance'?
7. What is a category? How many categories are there? What is the most basic category, and why is it basic?
8. What is the role of language and classification in relation to substance?

ON INTERPRETATION

In *On Interpretation*, Chapter 4, Aristotle distinguishes sentences and statements. A sentence is a significant combination of words. A statement is a sentence that affirms or denies a predicate of a subject. For example, 'Socrates is bald' is a statement. Not all sentences are statements. Prayers, commands, and questions are sentences that are neither true nor false.

Chapter 9 is one of Aristotle's most famous pieces of philosophy. He notes that, apparently, for any statement, either it or its denial must be true. This is called 'the principle of the excluded middle.' Does this principle apply to statements about particular future events? Aristotle thinks not. Suppose I predict that tomorrow there will be a sea battle in the nearby straits. According to Aristotle, the prediction is neither true nor false yet.

His argument for this claim has two parts. In the first part, Aristotle presents a piece of reasoning that concludes that the future is fixed because the law of the excluded middle is true concerning statements about the future. In the second part, Aristotle rejects this reasoning and tries to show that, to avoid the idea of a fixed future, we must abandon the law of the excluded middle with regard to statements about the future.

Regarding the first part, suppose that I predict that there will be a sea battle tomorrow. Is my prediction now true, or is it false? Either way, there is a problem. Necessarily, if the prediction is now true, then there will be a sea battle tomorrow. Given that the statement is true now, there is no alternative; necessarily, the sea battle will take place. On the other hand, suppose that the prediction is already false; assume that it is false now that there will be a sea battle tomorrow. Once again, necessarily, if my prediction is now false, then there will not be a sea battle tomorrow. Given that the prediction is now false, then there is no alternative outcome. Either way, it looks as if the future is fixed or predetermined, or that there is no possibility of chance or contingency, given that the law of the excluded middle applies to particular predictions.

This conclusion does not depend on the fact that we do not know what the future will hold. Today, we are ignorant about what will happen tomorrow. However, this ignorance is irrelevant to the argument. Even if we are ignorant about the future, given that the above piece of reasoning is sound, the future is fixed. To be clear, we can express the argument of the first step as follows:

1. *Necessarily, it is now either true or false that there will be a sea battle tomorrow.*
2. *If (1) is true, then the future is fixed and there is no chance.*

---

3. *Therefore, the future is fixed and there is no chance.*

In the second part of the argument, Aristotle argues that the first premise in the above syllogism is false. In other words, he claims that the principle of the excluded middle is false concerning statements about the future because, since the conclusion (3) is false and the second premise is true, therefore the first premise must be false. In this way, Aristotle concludes that statements about particular future events are not true or false now.

16ᵃ1 **1.** First we must settle what a name is and what a verb is, and then what a negation, an affirmation, a statement and a sentence are.

Now spoken sounds are symbols of affections in the soul, and written marks symbols of spoken sounds. And just as written marks are not the 5 same for all men, neither are spoken sounds. But what these are in the first place signs of—affections of the soul—are the same for all; and what these affections are likenesses of—actual things—are also the same. These matters have been discussed in the work on the soul and do not belong to the present subject.

Just as some thoughts in the soul are neither 10 true nor false while some are necessarily one or the other, so also with spoken sounds. For falsity and truth have to do with combination and separation. Thus names and verbs by themselves—for instance 'man' or 'white' when nothing 15 further is added—are like the thoughts that are without combination and separation; for so far they are neither true nor false. A sign of this is that even 'goat-stag' signifies something but not, as yet, anything true or false—unless 'is' or 'is not' is added (either simply or with reference to time).

2. A *name* is a spoken sound significant by convention, without time, none of whose parts is significant in separation. For in 'Whitfield' the 20 'field' does not signify anything in its own right, as it does in the phrase 'white field'. Not that it is the same with complex names as with simple ones: in the latter the part is in no way significant, in the former it has some force but is not 25 significant of anything in separation, for example the 'boat' in 'pirate-boat'.

I say 'by convention' because no name is a name naturally but only when it has become a symbol. Even inarticulate noises (of beasts, for instance) do indeed reveal something, yet none of them is a name.

30 'Not man' is not a name, nor is there any correct name for it. It is neither a phrase nor a negation. Let us call it an indefinite name.

16ᵇ1 'Philo's', 'to-Philo', and the like are not names but inflexions of names. The same account holds for them as for names except that an inflexion when combined with 'is', 'was', or 'will be' is not true or false whereas a name always is. Take, for example, 'Philo's is' or 'Philo's 5 is not'; so far there is nothing either true or false.

3. A *verb* is what additionally signifies time, no part of it being significant separately; and it is a sign of things said of something else.

It additionally signifies time: 'recovery' is a name, but 'recovers' is a verb, because it additionally signifies something's holding *now*. And 10 it is always a sign of what holds, that is, holds of a subject.

'Does not recover' and 'does not ail' I do not call verbs. For though they additionally signify time and always hold of something, yet there is a difference—for which there is no name. Let us call them indefinite verbs, because they hold 15 indifferently of anything whether existent or nonexistent. Similarly, 'recovered' and 'will-recover' are not verbs but inflexions of verbs. They differ from the verb in that it additionally signifies the present time, they the time outside the present.

When uttered just by itself a verb is a name 20 and signifies something—the speaker arrests his thought and the hearer pauses—but it does not

Aristotle, from *Aristotle: Categories and De Interpretatione*, translated by J. L. Ackrill. Clarendon Aristotle Series, 1963. Reprinted by permission of Oxford University Press.

yet signify whether it is or not. For not even 'to be' or 'not to be' is a sign of the actual thing (nor if you say simply 'that which is'); for by itself it is 25 nothing, but it additionally signifies some combination, which cannot be thought of without the components.

17ᵃ **4.** A *sentence* is a significant spoken sound some part of which is significant in separation—as an expression, not as an affirmation.

I mean that animal, for instance, signifies 30 something, but not that it is or is not (though it will be an affirmation or negation if something is added); the single syllables of 'animal', on the other hand, signify nothing. Nor is the 'ice' in 'mice' significant; here it is simply a spoken sound. In double words, as we said, a part does signify, but not in its own right.

17ᵇ¹ Every sentence is significant (not as a tool but, as we said, by convention), but not every sentence is a statement-making sentence, but only those in which there is truth or falsity. There is not truth or falsity in all sentences: a prayer is a sentence but is neither true or false. The present 5 investigation deals with the statement-making sentence; the others we can dismiss, since consideration of them belongs rather to the study of rhetoric or poetry.

9. With regard to what is and what has been it is necessary for the affirmation or the negation to be true or false. And with universals taken 30 universally it is always necessary for one to be true and the other false, and with particulars too, as we have said; but with universals not spoken of universally it is not necessary. But with particulars that are going to be it is different.

For if every affirmation or negation is true or 35 false it is necessary for everything either to be the case or not to be the case. For it one person says that something will be and another denies this same thing, it is clearly necessary for one of them to be saying what is true—if every affirmation is true or false; for both will not be the case together under such circumstances. For if it is 18ᵇ¹ true to say that it is white or is not white, it is necessary for it to be white or not white; and if it is white or is not white, then it was true to say or deny this. If it is not the case it is false, if it is false it is not the case. So it is necessary for the affirmation or the negation to be true. It follows that nothing either is or is happening, or will be 5 or will not be, by chance or as chance has it, but everything of necessity and not as chance has it (since either he who says or he who denies is saying what is true). For otherwise it might equally well happen or not happen, since what is as chance has it is no more thus than not thus, nor will it be.

Again, if it is white now it was true to say 10 earlier that it would be white; so that it was always true to say of anything that has happened that it would be so. But if it was always true to say that it was so, or would be so, it could not not be so, or not be going to be so. But if something cannot not happen it is impossible for it not to happen; and if it is impossible for something not to happen it is necessary for it to happen. Everything that will be, therefore, happens necessarily. 15 So nothing will come about as chance has it or by chance; for if by chance, not of necessity.

Nor, however, can we say that *neither* is true—that it neither will be nor will not be so. For, firstly, though the affirmation is false the negation is not true, and though the negation is false the affirmation, on this view, is not true. 20 Moreover, if it is true to say that something is white and large, both have to hold of it, and if true that they will hold tomorrow, they will have to hold tomorrow; and if it neither will be nor will not be the case tomorrow, then there is no 'as chance has it'. Take a sea-battle: it would *have* 25 neither to happen nor not to happen.

These and others like them are the absurdities that follow if it is necessary for every affirmation and negation either about universals spoken of universally or about particulars, that one of the opposites be true and the other false, and that nothing of what happens is as chance has it, 30 but everything is and happens of necessity. So there would be no need to deliberate or to take trouble (thinking that if we do this, this will happen, but if we do not, it will not). For there is nothing to prevent someone's having said ten thousand years beforehand that this would be the case, and another's having denied it; so that whichever of the two was true to say then, will be the case of necessity. Nor, of course, does it make any difference whether any people made the contradictory statements or not. For clearly this is how the actual things are even if someone did not affirm it and another deny it. For it is not because of the affirming or denying that it will be or will not be the case, nor is it a question of ten thousand years beforehand rather than any other time. Hence, if in the whole of time the state of things was such that one or the other was true, it was necessary for this to happen, and for the state of things always to be such that everything that happens happens of necessity. For what anyone has truly said would be the case cannot not happen; and of what happens it was always true to say that it would be the case.

But what if this is impossible? For we see that what will be has an origin both in deliberation and in action, and that, in general, in things that are not always actual there is the possibility of being and of not being; here both possibilities are open, both being and not being, and consequently, both coming to be and not coming to be. Many things are obviously like this. For example, it is possible for this cloak to be cut up, and yet it will not be cut up but will wear out first. But equally, its not being cut up is also possible, for it would not be the case that it wore out first unless its not being cut up were possible. So it is the same with all other events that are spoken of in terms of this kind of possibility. Clearly, therefore, not everything is or happens of necessity: some things happen as chance has it, and of

the affirmation and the negation neither is true rather than the other; with other things it is one rather than the other and as a rule, but still it is possible for the other to happen instead.

What is, necessarily is, when it is; and what is not, necessarily is not, when it is not. But not everything that is, necessarily is; and not everything that is not, necessarily is not. For to say that everything that is, is of necessity, when it is, is not the same as saying unconditionally that it is of necessity. Similarly with what is not. And the same account holds for contradictories: everything necessarily is or is not, and will be or will not be; but one cannot divide and say that one or the other is necessary. I mean, for example: it is necessary for there to be or not to be a sea-battle tomorrow; but it is not necessary for a sea-battle to take place tomorrow, nor for one not to take place—though it is necessary for one to take place or not to take place. So, since statements are true according to how the actual things are, it is clear that wherever these are such as to allow of contraries as chance has it, the same necessarily holds for the contradictories also. This happens with things that are not always so or are not always not so. With these it is necessary for one or the other of the contradictories to be true or false—not, however, this one or that one, but as chance has it; or for one to be true *rather* than the other, yet not *already* true or false.

Clearly, then, it is not necessary that of every affirmation and opposite negation one should be true and the other false. For what holds for things that are does not hold for things that are not but may possibly be or not be; with these it is as we have said.

STUDY QUESTIONS: ARISTOTLE, *ON INTERPRETATION*

1. What was the point of Aristotle comparing 'Whitfield' and 'pirate-boat'?
2. What does Aristotle mean by convention?
3. What needs to happen to a name and a verb for them to become a sentence?
4. What is the difference between a sentence and a name?
5. How does Aristotle distinguish between a sentence and a statement? Why does Aristotle draw this distinction? What is Aristotle's example of a sentence that is not a statement?
6. What is the difference between a statement and an affirmation?
7. What are the absurdities that follow if it is necessary for every affirmation and its negation that one should be true and the other false?

8. Aristotle argues that for these absurdities to follow, it is not necessary for someone to have actually affirmed the relevant statements. What reason does he give for claiming that?
9. 'If it is white now it was true to say earlier that it would be white.' What would be the consequence of asserting this sentence? How does this relate to the sea battle?
10. How does Aristotle state the law of the excluded middle?

PRIOR ANALYTICS

In the *Prior Analytics*, Aristotle develops his theory of the syllogism. His aims are to determine which syllogisms are logically valid and which are not, and to explain why. He achieves these by classifying the different types of syllogisms in order to explain what their validity consists in. He attains these aims with five steps.

The first step is presented in the first chapter of the book. Aristotle classifies all propositions, which can form the premises of any syllogism. He assumes that all statements are of the subject-predicate form. He classifies them according to quantity, quality, and modality. Any statement is either universal or particular (its quantity) and either affirmative or negative (its quality). (For the sake of simplicity, let us ignore modality.) This means that there are four basic combinations. For example, 'All animals are mortal' is a universal affirmative proposition, and 'Some animals are not mortal' is a particular negative.

The second step consists in the classification of different syllogistic forms or structures based on the position of the middle term, which is the word the two premises have in common (shown in bold below). For example,

Major premise: All **animals** are mortal.
Minor premise: All humans are **animals.**
Conclusion: All humans are mortal.

Here the middle term is 'animal.' It appears in both premises but not in the conclusion. The major term is the predicate in the conclusion (i.e., 'mortal'), and the minor term is the subject in the conclusion (i.e., 'human'). The premises are named major and minor accordingly. Aristotle uses the concept of the middle term as a basis to classify the general types of syllogisms based on the structural relations between their premises. There are three forms of combination, which Aristotle calls the three figures. For instance, the first figure consists of a major premise in which something is predicated of the middle term and a minor premise in which the middle term is predicated of something else. The argument given above is an example of a syllogism of the first figure.

Aristotle's third step is to combine the two classifications. The three structures mentioned in the second step must be filled by the different kinds of statements mentioned in step 1. There are three possible syllogistic figures or forms. In each of these three figures, each of the two premises could be a statement of one of the four forms mentioned above in the first step. Therefore, each of the three figures has 16 possible combinations. For example, argument 1 is a syllogism of the first figure with two universal affirmative premises.

In the fourth step, Aristotle shows which syllogistic forms are valid and which are not. He works methodically through all 16 combinations for each one of the three figures. He claims that some deductions are obvious; these he calls complete or perfect syllogisms. He employs certain rules to deduce which of the other syllogisms are valid from these perfect syllogisms. Aristotle derives 10 other valid syllogistic forms, giving a total of 14 types of valid syllogism. The perfect syllogistic forms and the rules are given below.

In the fifth step, for the sake of completeness, Aristotle also shows that these 14 forms are the only valid syllogisms. He does this by argument from counterexamples, showing that other syllogistic forms are not valid because they can have true premises and a false conclusion.

Aristotle's logical theory is remarkably systematic. He was the first person to use symbols to stand for words in an argument. This is a simple but very deep insight because it amounts to seeing that the validity of an argument depends on its logical form and not on its content.

The elements of steps 1, 2, and 4 are as follows.

Step 1: The four types of statements (the filling)

A:	Universal affirmative	All humans are mortal.
E:	Universal negative	No humans are mortal.
I:	Particular affirmative	Some humans are mortal.
O:	Particular negative	Some humans are not mortal.

Step 2: The three figures (the structure)

FIRST FIGURE	SECOND FIGURE	THIRD FIGURE
Subject-Predicate	Subject-Predicate	Subject-Predicate
. . . M's are A.	. . . A's are M.	. . . M's are A.
. . . C's are M.	. . . C's are M.	. . . M's are C.

Step 4: Deriving the valid syllogistic forms

A. The four complete or perfect syllogisms are as follows:

BARBARA	CELARENT	DARII	FERIO
All M's are A.	No B's are A.	All B's are A.	No B is A.
All B's are M.	All C's are B.	Some C is B.	Some C is B.
All B's are A.	No C's are A.	Some C's are A.	Some C is not A.

B. The rules are as follows:
If every S is P, then some S is P.
If some S is P, then some P is S.
If no S is P, then no P is S.

BOOK I

1. First we must state the subject of the enquiry 24ª10 and what it is about: the subject is demonstration, and it is about demonstrative understanding. Next we must determine what a proposition is, what a term is, and what a deduction is (and what sort of deduction is perfect and what imper-fect); and after that, what it is for one thing to be or not be in another as a whole, and what we 15 mean by being predicated of every or of no.

A proposition, then, is a statement affirming or denying something of something; and this is either universal or particular or indefinite. By universal I mean a statement that something belongs to all or none of something; by particular that it belongs to some or not to some or not to all; by indefinite that it does or does not belong, without any mark of being universal or particu-20 lar, e.g. 'contraries are subjects of the same science', or 'pleasure is not good'. A demonstrative proposition differs from a dialectical one, because a demonstrative proposition is the assumption of one of two contradictory statements (the demonstrator does not ask for his premiss, but lays it down), whereas a dialectical proposition choice between two contradictories. But this will make 25 no difference to the production of a deduction in either case; for both the demonstrator and the dialectician argue deductively after assuming that something does or does not belong to something. Therefore a deductive proposition without qualification will be an affirmation or denial of something concerning something in the way we have described: it will be demonstrative, if it is true and assumed on the basis of the first principles of its science; it will be dialectical if it asks for a choice between two contradictories (if one 24ᵇ10 is enquiring) or if it assumes what is apparent and reputable, as we said in the *Topics* (if one is deducing). Thus as to what a proposition is and how deductive, demonstrative and dialectical propositions differ, we have now said enough for our present purposes—we shall discuss the matter 15 with precision later on.

I call a term that into which the proposition is resolved, i.e. both the predicate and that of which it is predicated, 'is' or 'is not' being added.

A deduction is a discourse in which, certain 20 things being stated, something other than what is stated follows of necessity from their being so. I mean by the last phrase that it follows because of them, and by this, that no further term is required from without in order to make the consequence necessary.

I call perfect a deduction which needs nothing other than what has been stated to make the necessity evident; a deduction is imperfect if it 25 needs either one or more things, which are indeed the necessary consequences of the terms set down, but have not been assumed in the propositions.

That one term should be in another as in a whole is the same as for the other to be predicated of all of the first. And we say that one term is predicated of all of another, whenever nothing can be found of which the other term cannot be asserted; 'to be predicated of none' must be understood in the same way.

25ᵃ1 **2.** Every proposition states that something either belongs or must belong or may belong; of these some are affirmative, others negative, in respect of each of the three modes; again some affirmative and negative propositions are univer-5 sal, others particular, others indefinite. It is necessary then that in universal attribution the terms of the negative proposition should be convertible, e.g. if no pleasure is good, then no good will be pleasure; the terms of the affirmative must be convertible, not however universally, but in part, e.g. if every pleasure is good, some good must be 10 pleasure; the particular affirmative must convert in part (for if some pleasure is good, then some good will be pleasure); but the particular negative need not convert, for if some animal is not man, it does not follow that some man is not animal.

First then take a universal negative with the 15 terms A and B. Now if A belongs to no B, B will not belong to any A; for if it does belong to some B (say to C), it will not be true that A belongs to no B—for C is one of the Bs. And if A belongs to every B, then B will belong to some A; for if it 20 belongs to none, then A will belong to no B—but it was laid down that it belongs to every B. Similarly if the proposition is particular: if A belongs to some B, it is necessary for B to belong to some A; for if it belongs to none, A will belong to no B. But if A does not belong to some B, it is not necessary that B should not belong to 25 some A: e.g., if B is animal and A man; for man does not belong to every animal, but animal belongs to every man.

4. After these distinctions we now state by what means, when, and how every deduction is produced; subsequently we must speak of demonstration. Deduction should be discussed before demonstration, because deduction is the more

general: a demonstration is a sort of deduction,
but not every deduction is a demonstration.

Whenever three terms are so related to one another that the last is in the middle as in a whole, and the middle is either in, or not in, the first as in a whole, the extremes must be related by a perfect deduction. I call that term middle which both is itself in another and contains another in itself: in position also this comes in the middle. By extremes I mean both that term which is itself in another and that in which another in contained. If A is predicated of every B, and B of every C, A must be predicated of every C: we have already explained what we mean by 'predicated of every'. Similarly also, if A is predicated of no B, and B of every C, it is necessary that A will belong to no C.

But if the first term belongs to all the middle, but the middle to none of the last term, there will be no deduction in respect of the extremes; for nothing necessary follows from the terms being so related; for it is possible that the first should belong either to all or to none of the last, so that neither a particular nor a universal conclusion is necessary. But if there is no necessary consequence, there cannot be a deduction by means of these propositions. As an example of a universal affirmative relation between the extremes we may take the terms animal, man, horse; of a universal negative relation, the terms animal, man, stone. Nor again can a deduction be formed when neither the first terms belongs to any of the middle, nor the middle to any of the last. As an example of a positive relation between the extremes take the terms science, line, medicine: of a negative relation science, line, unit.

If then the terms are universally related, it is clear in this figure when a deduction will be possible and when not, and that if a deduction is possible the terms must be related as described, and if they are so related there will be a deduction.

But if one term is related universally, the other in part only, to its subject, there must be a perfect deduction whenever universality is posited with reference to the major term either affirmatively or negatively, and particularity with reference to the minor term affirmatively; but whenever the universality is posited in relation to the minor term, or the terms are related in any other way, a deduction is impossible. I call that term the major in which the middle is contained and that term the minor which comes under the middle. Let A belong to every B and B and to some C. Then if 'predicated of every' means what was said above, it is necessary that A belongs to some C. And if A belongs to no B and B to some C, it is necessary that A does not belong to some C. (Then meaning of 'predicated of none' has also been defined.) So there will be a perfect deduction. This holds good also if deduction BC should be indefinite, provided that it is affirmative; for we shall have the same deduction whether it is indefinite or particular.

But if the universality is posited with respect to the minor term either affirmatively or negatively, a deduction will not be possible, whether the other is affirmative or negative, indefinite or particular: e.g. if A belongs or does not belong to some B, and B belongs to every C. As an example of a positive relation between the extremes take the terms good, state, wisdom; of a negative relation, good, state, ignorance. Again if B belongs to no C, and A belongs or does not belong to some B (or does not belong to every B), there cannot be a deduction. Take the terms white, horse, swan; white, horse, raven. The same terms may be taken also if BA is indefinite.

Nor when the proposition relating to the major extreme is universal, whether affirmative or negative, and that to the minor is negative and particular, can there be a deduction: e.g. if A belongs to every B, and B does not belong to some C or not to every C. For the first term may be predictable both of all and of none of the term to some of which the middle does not belong. Suppose the terms are animal, man, white: next take some of the white things of which man is not predicated—swan and snow: animal is predicated of all of the one, but of none of the other. Consequently there cannot be a deduction. Again let A belong to no B, but let B not belong to some C. Take the terms inanimate, man, white: then take some white things of which man is not predicated—swan and snow: inanimate is predicated of all of the one, of none of the other.

Further since it is indefinite to say that B does not belong to some C, and it is true that it does not belong to some C both if it belongs to none and if it does not belong to every, and since if terms are assumed such that it belongs to none, no deduction follows (this has already been stated), it is clear that this arrangement of terms will not afford a deduction: otherwise one would have been possible in the other case too. A similar proof may also be given if the universal proposition is negative.

Nor can there in any way be a deduction if both the relations are particular, either positively or negatively, or the one positively and the other negatively, or one indefinite and the other definite, or both indefinite. Terms common to all the above are animal, white, horse; animal, white, stone.

It is clear then from what has been said that if there is a deduction in this figure with a particular conclusion, the terms must be related as we have stated: if they are related otherwise, no deduction is possible at all. It is evident also that all the deductions in this figure are perfect (for they are all completed by means of what was originally assumed) and that all conclusions are proved by this figure, viz. universal and particular, affirmative and negative. Such a figure I call the first.

STUDY QUESTIONS: ARISTOTLE, *PRIOR ANALYTICS*

1. What is the subject matter of this work?
2. What is a proposition?
3. Define the three types of proposition: universal, particular, and indefinite.
4. What is the difference between a demonstrative and a dialectical proposition?
5. What is the difference between a perfect and an imperfect deduction?
6. Why and how does Aristotle distinguish between deduction, demonstration, and dialectic?
7. What is the middle term? What is the extreme? Why does Aristotle draw this distinction?
8. What is the first figure? What does it mean to say that all deductions in this first figure are perfect?

POSTERIOR ANALYTICS

Book I of the *Posterior Analytics* shows how syllogistic logic can be employed to gain knowledge by scientific demonstration. Aristotle divides the basic premises of any demonstration into three kinds: axioms, definitions, and hypotheses. Axioms are principles without which reasoning would be impossible, such as the law of the excluded middle. Definitions state the meaning of the relevant terms. A hypothesis is an assumption about what exists. Not all propositions can be demonstrated.

Aristotle defines a scientific demonstration as follows. First, he says that scientific understanding must cite the cause of something. Scientific explanation must take the form of a conclusion explained by various premises, from which it (the conclusion) follows logically. Second, to be scientific, the premises of such an argument must have certain characteristics: they must be true and real explanations of the conclusion. Third, Aristotle claims that the premises themselves must be necessary truths. This claim seems to remove the empirical and contingent elements from scientific demonstration by restricting it to necessary truths. This appears to contradict Aristotle's own method of work, for he was a very keen observer of nature. However, we should not assume that the equivalent Greek word really corresponds to what we mean now by 'science.' Today, we think of the natural sciences as the systematic empirical investigation of nature. Aristotle may have meant something more akin to the pursuit of knowledge that is certain and universal.

In Book II of the *Posterior Analytics*, Aristotle gives his theory of definition. According to Aristotle, reality consists primarily of natural kinds of objects, such as individual plants and animals of different species. The natural kinds have a real essence (without which they would not be what they are). For example, the real essence of a human being is to be rational. Based on these real essences, there are real definitions of each natural kind; for example, by definition, humans are rational animals. These real definitions have an important role in science because explanations must begin with them.

Much of the *Posterior Analytics* is dedicated to elucidating the idea of demonstration based on universal principles. Toward the end of the work (Book II, Chapter 19), Aristotle asks how we know these universal principles. He rejects the claim that such knowledge is innate, and instead argues that we acquire such knowledge through sense perception; we ascend from particular sense experiences to knowledge of universal statements by induction. He contrasts deduction with induction. The deductive syllogistic reasoning of the *Prior Analytics* only yields knowledge of particulars from that of universals. Induction is necessary to obtain knowledge of universals from that of particulars. In other words, Aristotle recognizes that induction is necessary to acquire the knowledge for the hypotheses on which deduction is based.

BOOK I

71ᵃ1 **1.** All teaching and all intellectual learning come about from already existing knowledge. This is evident if we consider it in every case; for the mathematical sciences are acquired in this fash-
5 ion, and so is each of the other arts. And similarly too with arguments—both deductive and inductive arguments proceed in this way; for both produce their teaching through what we are already aware of, the former getting their premisses as from men who grasp them, the latter proving the universal through the particular's being clear.
10 (And rhetorical arguments too persuade in the same way; for they do so either through examples, which is induction, or through enthymemes, which is deduction.)

It is necessary to be already aware of things in two ways: of some things it is necessary to believe already that they are, of some one must grasp what the thing said is, and of others both—e.g. of the fact that everything is either affirmed or denied truly, one must believe that it is; of the
15

triangle, that it signifies *this*; and of the unit both (both what it signifies and that it is). For each of these is not equally clear to us.

But you can become familiar by being familiar earlier with some things but getting knowledge of the others at the very same time—i.e. of whatever happens to be under the universal of which you have knowledge. For that every triangle has angles equal to two right angles was
20 already known; but that there is a triangle in the semicircle here became familiar at the same time as the induction. (For in some cases learning occurs in this way, and the last term does not become familiar through the middle—in cases dealing with what are in fact particulars and not said of any underlying subject.)

Before the induction, or before getting a
25 deduction, you should perhaps be said to understand in a way—but in another way not. For if you did not know if it is *simpliciter*, how did you know that it has two right angles *simpliciter*? But it is clear that you understand it in *this* sense—

Aristotle, from *Aristotle: Posterior Analysis*, translated by Jonathan Barnes. Clarendon Aristotle Series, 1975. Reprinted by permission of Oxford University Press.

that you understand it universally—but you do not understand it *simpliciter*. (Otherwise the puzzle in the *Meno* will result; for you will learn either nothing or what you know.)

For one should not argue in the way in which some people attempt to solve it: Do you or don't you know of every pair that it is even? And when you said Yes, they brought forward some pair of which you did not think that it was, nor therefore that it was even. For they solve it by denying that people know of every pair that it is even, but only of anything of which they know that it is a pair.—Yet they know it of that which they have the demonstration about and which they got their premisses about; and they got them not about everything of which they know that it is a triangle or that it is a number, but of every number and triangle *simpliciter*. For no proposition of such a type is assumed (that *what you know to be a number . . .* or *what you know to be rectilineal . . .*), but they are assumed as holding of every case.

But nothing, I think, prevents one from in a sense understanding and in a sense being ignorant of what one is learning; for what is absurd is not that you should know in some sense what you are learning, but that you should know it in *this* sense. i.e. in the way and sense in the which you are learning it.

2. We think we understand a thing *simpliciter* (and not in the sophistic fashion accidentally) whenever we think we are aware both that the explanation because of which the object is is its explanation, and that it is not possible for this to be otherwise. It is clear then, that to understand is something of this sort; for both those who do not understand and those who do understand—the former think they are themselves in such a state, and those who do understand actually are. Hence that of which there is understanding *simpliciter* cannot be otherwise.

Now whether there is also another type of understanding we shall say later; but we say now that we do know through demonstration. By demonstration I mean a scientific deduction; and by scientific I mean one in virtue of which, by having it, we understand something.

If, then, understanding is as we posited, it is necessary for demonstrative understanding in particular to depend on things which are true and primitive and immediate and more familiar than and prior to and explanatory of the conclusion (for in this way the principles will also be appropriate to what is being proved). For there will be deduction even without these conditions, but there will not be demonstration; for it will not produce understanding.

Now they must be true because one cannot understand what is not the case—e.g. that the diagonal is commensurate. And they must depend on what is primitive and non-demonstrable because otherwise you will not understand if you do not have a demonstration of them; for to understand that of which there is a demonstration non-accidentally is to have a demonstration. They must be both explanatory and more familiar and prior—explanatory because we only understand when we know the explanation; and prior, if they are explanatory, and we are already aware of them not only in the sense of grasping them but also of knowing that they are.

Things are prior and more familiar in two ways; for it is not the same to be prior by nature and prior in relation to us, nor to be more familiar and more familiar to us. I call prior and more familiar in relation to us what is nearer to perception, prior and more familiar *simpliciter* what is further away. What is most universal is furthest away, and the particulars are nearest; and these are opposite to each other.

Depending on things that are primitive is depending on appropriate principles; for I call the same thing primitive and a principle. A principle of a demonstration is an immediate proposition, and an immediate proposition is one to which there is no other prior. A proposition is the one part of a contradiction, one thing said of one; it is dialectical if it assumes indifferently either part, demonstrative if it determinately assumes the one that is true. [A statement is either part of a contradiction.] A contradiction is an opposition of which of itself excludes any intermediate; and the part of a contradiction saying something *of* something is an affirmation, the one saying something *from* something is a denial.

15 An immediate deductive principle I call a posit if one cannot prove it but it is not necessary for anyone who is to learn anything to grasp it; and one which it is necessary for anyone who is going to learn anything whatever to grasp, I call an axiom (for there are some such things); for we are accustomed to use this name especially of such things. A posit which assumes either of the 20 parts of a contradiction—i.e., I mean, that something is or that something is not—I call a supposition; one without this, a definition. For a definition is a posit (for the arithmetician posits that a unit is what is quantitatively indivisible) but not a supposition (for what a unit is and that a unit is are not the same).

25 Since one should both be convinced of and know the object by having a deduction of the sort we call a demonstration, and since this is the case when *these* things on which the deduction depends are the case, it is necessary not only to be already aware of the primitives (either all or some of them) but actually to be better aware of them. For a thing always belongs bet- 30 ter to that thing because of which it belongs— e.g. that because of which we love is better loved. Hence if we know and are convinced because of the primitives, we both know and are convinced of them better, since it is because of them that we know and are convinced of what is posterior.

It is not possible to be better convinced than one is of what one knows, of what one in fact neither knows nor is more happily disposed toward than if one in fact knew. But this will result if someone who is convinced because of a 35 demonstration is not already aware of the primitives, for it is necessary to be better convinced of the principles (either all or some of them) than of the conclusion.

Anyone who is going to have understanding through demonstration must not only be familiar with the principles and better convinced of them 72b1 than of what is being proved, but also there must be no other thing more convincing to him or more familiar among the opposites of the principles on which a deduction of the contrary error may depend—if anyone who understands *simpliciter* must be unpersuadable.

3. Now some think that because one must 5 understand the primitives there is no understanding at all; others that there is, but that there are demonstrations of everything. Neither of these views is either true or necessary.

For the one party, supposing that one cannot understand in another way, claim that we are led back *ad infinitum* on the grounds that we would not understand what is posterior because of what is prior if there are no primitives; and they argue correctly, for it is impossible to go through infi- 10 nitely many things. And if it comes to a stop and there are principles, they say that these are unknowable since there is no *demonstration* of them, which alone they say is understanding; but if one cannot know the primitives, neither can what depends on them be understood *simpliciter* or properly, but only on the supposition that they are the case.

The other party agrees about understanding; 15 for it, they say, occurs only through demonstration. But they argue that nothing prevents there being demonstration of everything; for it is possible for the demonstration to come about in a circle and reciprocally.

But *we* say that neither is all understanding demonstrative, but in the case of the immediates it is non-demonstrable—and that this is neces- 20 sary is evident; for if it is necessary to understand the things which are prior and on which the demonstration depends, and it comes to a stop at some time, it is necessary for these immediates to be non-demonstrable. So as to that we argue thus; and we also say that there is not only understanding but also some principle of understanding by which we become familiar with the definitions.

And that it is impossible to demonstrate *sim-* 25 *pliciter* in a circle is clear, if demonstration must depend on what is prior and more familiar; for it is impossible for the same things at the same time to be prior and posterior to the same things— unless one is so in another way (i.e. one in relation to us, the other *simpliciter*), which induction makes familiar. But if so, knowing *simpliciter* will 30 not have been properly defined, but will be twofold. Or is the other demonstration not demonstration *simpliciter* in that it comes from about what is more familiar *to us*?

There results for those who say that demonstration is circular not only what has just been described, but also that they say nothing other than that this is the case if this is the case—and it is easy to prove everything in this way. It is 35 clear that this results if we posit three terms. (For it makes no difference to say that it bends back through many terms or through few, or through few or two.) For whenever if A is the case, of necessity B is, and if this then C, then if A is the case C will be the case. Thus given that if A is the case it is necessary that B is, and if this is that A is (for that is what being circular is)—let A be 73ª1 C: so to say that if B is the case A is, is to say that C is, and this implies that if A is the case C is. But C is the same as A. Hence it results that those who assert that demonstration is circular say nothing but that if A is the case A is the case. 5 And it is easy to prove everything in this way.

Moreover, not even this is possible except in the case of things which follow one another, as properties do. Now if a single thing is laid down, it has been proved that it is never necessary that anything else should be the case (by a single 10 thing I mean that neither if one term nor if one posit is posited . . .), but two posits are the first and fewest from which it is possible, if at all, actually to deduce something. Now if A follows B and C, and these follow one another and A, in this way it is possible to prove all the postulates reciprocally in the first figure, as was proved in 15 the account of deduction. (And it was also proved that in the other figures either no deduction comes about or none about what was assumed.) But one cannot in any way prove circularly things which are not counterpredicated; hence, since there are few such things in demonstrations, it is evident that it is both empty and impossible to say that demonstration is reciprocal and that because of this there can be demonstra-20 tion of everything.

4. Since it is impossible for that of which there is understanding *simpliciter* to be otherwise, what is understandable in virtue of demonstrative understanding will be necessary (it is demonstrative if we have it by having a demonstration). Demonstration, therefore, is deduction

25 from what is necessary. We must therefore grasp on what things and what sort of things demonstrations depend. And first let us define what we mean by holding of every case and what by in itself and what by universally.

Now I say that something holds of every case if it does not hold in some cases and not others, nor at some times and not at others; e.g. if animal 30 holds of every man, then if it is true to call this a man, it is true to call him an animal too; and if he is now the one, he is the other too; and the same goes if there is a point in every line. Evidence: when asked if something holds of every case, we bring our objections in this way—either if in some cases it does not hold or if at some time it does not.

One thing belongs to another in itself both if 35 it belongs to it in what it is—e.g. line to triangle and point to line (for their substance depends on these and they belong in the account which says what they are)—and also if the things it belongs to themselves belong in the account which makes clear what it is—e.g. straight belongs to line and so does curved, and odd and even to number, and 73ᵇ1 prime and composite, and equilateral and oblong; and for all these there belongs in the account which says what they are in the one case line, and in the others number. And similarly in other cases too it is such things that I say belong to something 5 in itself; and what belongs in neither way I call accidental, e.g. musical or white to animal.

Again, what is not said of some other underlying subject—as what is walking is something different walking (and white), while a substance, and whatever signifies some 'this,' is just what it is without being something else. Thus things which are not said of an underlying subject I call things in themselves, and those which are said of an underlying subject I call accidentals.

10 Again, in another way what belongs to something because of itself belongs to it in itself, and what does not belong because of itself is accidental—e.g. if it lightened when he was walking, that was accidental; for it was not because of his walking that it lightened, but that, we say, was accidental. But if because of itself, then in itself—e.g. if something died while being 15 sacrificed, it died *in* the sacrifice since it died

because of being sacrificed, and it was not accidental that it died while being sacrificed.

Whatever, therefore, in the case of what is understandable *simpliciter*, is said to belong to things in themselves in the sense of inhering in the predicates or of being inhered in, holds both because of themselves and from necessity. For it is not possible for them not to belong, either *simpliciter* or as regards the opposites—e.g. straight or crooked to line, and odd or even to number. For the contrary is either a privation or a contradiction in the same genus—e.g. even is what is not odd among numbers, in so far as it follows. Hence if it is necessary to affirm or deny, it is necessary too for what belongs in itself to belong.

Now let holding of every case and in itself be defined in this fashion; I call universal whatever belongs to something both of every case and in itself and as such. It is evident, therefore, that whatever is universal belongs from necessity to its objects. (To belong in itself and as such are the same thing—e.g. point and straight belong to line in itself (for they belong to it as line), and two right angles belong to triangle as triangle (for the triangle is in itself equal to two right angles).)

Something holds universally whenever it is proved of a chance case and primitively; e.g. having two right angles neither holds universally of figure (yet one may prove of a figure that it has two right angles—but not of a chance figure, nor does one use a chance figure in proving it; for the quadrangle is a figure but it does not have angles equal to two right angles)—and a chance isosceles does have angles equal to two right angles, but not primitively—the triangle is prior. If, then, a chance case is proved primitively to have two right angles or whatever else, it belongs universally to this primitively, and of this the demonstration holds universally in itself; but of the others it holds in some fashion not in itself, nor does it hold of the isosceles universally, but with a wider extension.

BOOK II

1. The things we seek are equal in number to those we understand. We seek four things: the fact, the reason why, if it is, what it is.

For when we seek whether it is this or this, putting it into a number (e.g. whether the sun is eclipsed or not), we seek the fact. Evidence for this: on finding that it is eclipsed we stop; and if from the start we know that it is eclipsed, we do not seek whether it is. When we know the fact we seek the reason why (e.g. knowing that it is eclipsed and that the earth moves, we seek the reason why it is eclipsed or why it moves).

Now while we seek these things in this way, we seek some things in another fashion—e.g. if a centaur or a god is or is not (I mean if one is or not *simpliciter* and not if one is white or not). And knowing that it is, we seek what it is (e.g. so what is a god? or what is a man?).

2. Now what we seek and what on finding we know are these and thus many. We seek, whenever we seek the fact or if it is *simpliciter*, whether there is or is not a middle term for it; and whenever we become aware of either the fact or if it is—either partially or *simpliciter*—and again seek the reason why or what it is, then we seek what the middle term is. (I mean by the fact that it is partially and *simpliciter*—partially: Is the moon eclipsed? or is it increasing? (for in such cases we seek if it is something or is not something); *simpliciter*: if the moon or night is or is not.) It results, therefore, that in all our searches we seek either if there is a middle term or what the middle term is.

For the middle term is the explanation, and in all cases that is sought. Is it eclipsed?—Is there some explanation or not? After that, aware that there is one, we seek what this is. For the explanation of a substance being not this or that but *simpliciter*, or of its being not *simpliciter* but one of the things which belong to it in itself or accidentally—that is the middle term. I mean by *simpliciter* the underlying subject (e.g. moon or earth or sun or triangle) and by one of the things eclipse, equality, inequality, whether it is in the middle or not.

For in all these cases it is evident that what it is and why it is are the same. What is an eclipse? Privation of light from the moon by the earth's screening. Why is there an eclipse? or Why is the moon eclipsed? Because the light leaves it when the earth screens it. What is a harmony? An 20 arithmetical ratio between high and low. Why does the high harmonize with the low? Because an arithmetical ratio holds between the high and the low. Can the high and the low harmonize?— Is there an arithmetical ratio between them? Assuming that there is, what then is the ratio?

That the search is for the middle term is 25 made clear by the cases in which the middle is perceptible. For if we have not perceived it, we seek, e.g. for the eclipse, if there is one or not. But if we were on the moon we would seek neither if it comes about nor why, but it would be clear at the same time. For from perceiving, it would come about that we knew the universal 30 too. For perception tells us that it is now screening it (for it is clear that it is now eclipsed); and from this the universal would come about.

So, as we say, to know what it is is the same as to know why it is—and that either *simpliciter* and not one of the things that belong to it, or one of the things that belong to it, e.g. that it has two right angles, or that it is greater or less.

35   **3.** Now, that everything we seek is a search for a middle term is clear; let us now say how one proves what a thing is, and what is the fashion of the reduction, and what definition is and of what, first going through the puzzles about them. 90ᵇ1 Let the start of what we are about to say be whatever is most appropriate to the neighbouring arguments.

A man might puzzle over whether one can know the same thing in the same respect by definition and by demonstration, or whether that is impossible.

For definition seems to be of what a thing is, 5 and what a thing is is in every case universal and affirmative, but deductions are some of them negative and some not universal—e.g. those in the second figure are all negative and those in the third not universal.

Next, there is not definition even of all the affirmatives in the first figure—e.g. that every triangle has angles equal to two right angles. The argument for this is that to understand what is demonstrable is to have a demonstration; so that 10 since there is demonstration of such things,

clearly there will not also be definition of them— for someone might understand them in virtue of the definition without having the demonstration; for nothing prevents him from not having them together.

An induction, too, is sufficiently convincing; for we have never yet become aware of anything by giving a definition—neither of anything 15 belonging in itself nor of any accidental.

Again, if definition is becoming familiar with some substance, it is evident that *such* things are not substances.

So it is clear that there is not definition of everything of which there is demonstration.

Well then, is there demonstration of everything of which there is definition, or not?

Well, one argument is the same in this case 20 too. For of one thing, as one, there is one mode of understanding. Hence, if to understand what is demonstrable is to have a demonstration, something impossible will result; for anyone who has the definition without the demonstration will understand.

Again, the principles of demonstrations are 25 definitions, and it has been proved earlier that there will not be demonstrations of these—either the principles will be demonstrable and there will be principles of the principles, and this will go on *ad infinitum*, or the primitives will be nondemonstrable definitions.

But if the objects of definition and demonstration are not all the same, are some of them the same? or is this impossible? For there is no demonstration of that of which there is definition. For definition is of what a thing is and of 30 substance; but all demonstrations evidently suppose and assume what a thing is—e.g. mathematical demonstrations assume what a unit is and what odd, and the others similarly.

Again, every demonstration proves something of something, i.e. that it is or is not; but in a definition one thing is not predicated of another—e.g. neither animal of two-footed nor 35 this of animal, nor indeed figure of plane (for plane is not figure nor is figure plane).

Again, proving what a thing is and that it is are different. So the definition makes clear what it is, and the demonstration that this is or is not

91ᵃ1 true of that. And of different things there are different demonstrations—unless they are related as a part to the whole (I mean by this that the isosceles has been proved to have two right angles if every triangle has been proved to be so; for one is a part and the other a whole). But these things—that it is and what it is—are not 5 related to one another in this way; for neither is part of the other.

It is evident, therefore, that neither is there demonstration of everything of which there is definition, nor is there definition of everything of which there is. . . .

8. We must inquire again which of these 93ᵃ1 points is correctly argued and which not correctly; and what a definition is; and whether there is in some way demonstration and definition of what a thing is, or in no way at all.

Since, as we said, to know what something is and to know the explanation of the fact that it is are the same—the argument for this is 5 that there is some explanation, and this is either the same thing or something else, and it is something else it is either demonstrable or non-demonstrable—if, then, it is something else and it is possible to demonstrate it, it is necessary for the explanation to be a middle term and to be proved in the first figure; for what is being proved is both universal and affirmative.

Well, one way would be the one just 10 examined—proving what a thing is through another definition. For in the case of what a thing is, it is necessary for the middle term to state what the thing is (and in the case of what is proper it must be proper). Hence you will prove the one but you will not prove the other instance of what it is to be the same object. Now that this way will not be a demonstration was said earlier (but it is a 15 general deduction of what the thing is).

But let us say in what way a demonstration is possible, speaking again from the beginning. Just as we seek the reason why when we grasp the fact—sometimes they actually become clear together, but it is not possible to become familiar with the reason why *before* the fact—it is clear that similarly we cannot grasp what it is to be something without grasping the fact that it is;

20 for it is impossible to know what a thing is if we are ignorant of whether it is. But as to whether it is, sometimes we grasp this accidentally, and sometimes when grasping something of the object itself—e.g. of thunder, that it is a sort of noise of the clouds; and of eclipse, that it is a sort of privation of light; and of man, that he is a sort of animal; and of soul, that it is something moving itself.

25 Now in cases in which we know accidentally that a thing is, necessarily we have no hold on what it is; for we do not even know that it is, and to seek what it is without grasping that it is, is to seek nothing. But in the cases in which we grasp something, it is easier. Hence in so far as we grasp that it is, to that extent we also have some hold on what it is.

So in cases in which we grasp something of 30 what the thing is, let it be first like this:—eclipse A, moon C, screening by the earth B. So to ask whether it is eclipsed or not is to seek whether B is or not. And this is no different from seeking whether there is an account of it; and if this is, we say that that is too. (Or: of which of the contradictory pair does the account hold—of its having two right angles or of its not having them?)

35 When we discover it, we know at the same time the fact and the reason why, if it is through immediates; if not, we know the fact but not the reason why. Moon, C; eclipse, A; not being able to produce a shadow during full moon though there is nothing evident between us, B. Then if 93ᵇ1 B—not being able to produce a shadow though there is nothing evident between us—belongs to C, and A—being eclipsed—to this, then it is clear *that* it is eclipsed but not yet *why*; and we know *that* an eclipse is but we do not know *what* it is.

When it is clear that A belongs to C, then 5 to seek why it belongs is to seek what B is— whether screening or rotation of the moon or extinction. And this is the account of the one extreme, i.e. in this case of A. For an eclipse is a screening by the earth.

What is thunder? Extinction of fire in cloud. Why does it thunder? Because the fire in the cloud is extinguished. Cloud C, thunder A, 10 extinction of fire B. Thus B belongs to C, the cloud (for the fire is extinguished in it); and A, noise, to this; and B is indeed an account of A, the first extreme. And if again there is another middle term for this, it will be from among the remaining accounts.

15 We have said, then, how what a thing is is grasped and becomes familiar, hence no deduction and no demonstration of what a thing is comes about—yet it is clear through deduction and through demonstration. Hence without a demonstration you cannot become aware of what a thing is (in cases where the explanation is something else), yet there is no demonstration of 20 it (as we said when we went through the puzzles).

9. Of some things there is something else that is their explanation, of others there is not. Hence it is clear that in some cases what a thing is is immediate and a principle; and here one must suppose, or make apparent in some other 25 way, both that they are and what they are (which the arithmetician does; for he supposes both what the unit is and that it is); but in those cases which have a middle term and for which something else is explanatory of their substance, one can, as we said, make them clear through a demonstration, but not by demonstrating what they are.

10. Since a definition is said to be an 30 account of what a thing is, it is evident that one type will be an account of what the name, or a different name-like account, signifies—e.g. what triangle signifies. And when we grasp that this is, we seek why it is; but it is difficult to grasp in this way why a thing is if we do not know that it is. The explanation of the difficulty has been stated already—that we do not even know whether it is or not, except accidentally. (An account is a 35 unity in two ways—either by connection, like the *Iliad,* or by making one thing clear of one thing non-accidentally.)

Thus one definition of definition is the one stated; another definition is an account which makes clear why a thing is. Hence the former type of definition signifies but does not prove, 94ᵃ1 whereas the latter evidently will be a sort of demonstration of what a thing is, differing in position from the demonstration. For there is a

difference between saying why it thunders and what thunder is; for in the one case you will say: Because the fire is extinguished in the clouds. What is thunder?—A noise of fire being extin-5 guished in the clouds. Hence the same account is put in a different way, and in *this* way it is a continuous demonstration, in *this* way a definition.

Again, a definition of thunder is noise in the clouds; and this is a conclusion of the demonstration of what it is.

The definition of immediates is an undemon-10 strable positing of what they are.

One definition, therefore, is an undemonstrable account of what a thing is; one is a deduction of what it is, differing in aspect from the demonstration; a third is a conclusion of the demonstration of what it is.

So it is evident from what has been said, both in what way there is a demonstration of what a thing is, and in what way there is not; 15 and in what cases there is and in what cases there is not; and again in how many ways something is called a definition, and in what way it proves what a thing is and in what way it does not, and in what cases it does and in what cases it does not; and again how it is related to demonstration and in what way it is possible for them to be of the same thing and in what way it is not possible.

19. Now as for deduction and demonstra-15 tion, it is evident both what each is and how it comes about—and at the same time this goes for demonstrative understanding too (for that is the same thing). But as for the principles—how they become familiar and what is the state that becomes familiar with them—that will be clear from what follows, when we have first set down the puzzles.

Now, we have said earlier that it is not possi-20 ble to understand through demonstration if we are not aware of the primitive, immediate, principles. But as to knowledge of the immediates, one might puzzle both whether it is the same or not the same—whether there is understanding of each, or rather understanding of the one and some other kind of thing of the other—and also whether the states are not present in us but come

about in us, or whether they are present in us but
25 escape notice.

Well, if we have them, it is absurd; for it results that we have pieces of knowledge more precise than demonstration and yet this escapes notice. But if we get them without having them earlier, how might we become familiar with them and learn them from no pre-existing knowledge? For that is impossible, as we said in the case of demonstration too. It is evidently impossible,
30 then, both for us to have them and for them to come about in us when we are ignorant and have no such state at all. Necessarily, therefore, we have some capacity, but do not have one of a type which will be more valuable than these in respect of precision.

35 And *this* evidently belongs to all animals; for they have a connate discriminatory capacity, which is called perception. And if perception is present in them, in some animals retention of the percept comes about, but in others it does not comes about. Now for those in which it does not come about, there is no knowledge outside perceiving (either none at all, or none with regard to that of which there is no retention); but for some perceivers, it is possible to grasp it in their minds. And when many such things come about, then a difference comes about, so
100ᵇ1 that some come to have an account from the retention of such things, and others do not.

So from perception there comes memory, as we call it, and from memory (when it occurs often in connection with the same thing), experi-
5 ence; for memories that are many in number from a single experience. And from experience, or from the whole universal that has come to rest in the soul (the one apart from the many, whatever is one and the same in all those things), there comes a principle of skill and of understanding— of skill if it deals with how things come about, of understanding if it deals with what is the case.

10 Thus the states neither belong in us in a determinate form, nor come about from other states that are more cognitive; but they come about from perception—as in a battle when a rout occurs, if one man makes a stand another does and then another, until a position of strength is reached. And the soul is such as to be capable of undergoing this.

15 What we have just said but not said clearly, let us say again: when one of the undifferentiated things makes a stand, there is a primitive universal in the mind (for though one perceives the particular, perception is of the universal—e.g. of man but not of Callias the man); again a stand is
100ᵇ1 made in these, until what has no parts and is universal stands—e.g. *such and such* an animal stands, until animal does, and in this a stand is made in the same way. Thus it is clear that it is necessary for us to become familiar with the primitives by induction; for perception too instils
5 the universal in this way.

Since of the intellectual states by which we grasp truth some are always true and some admit falsehood (e.g. opinion and reasoning—whereas understanding and comprehension are always true), and no kind other than comprehension is more precise than understanding, and the principles of demonstrations are more familiar, and all understanding involves an account—there will
10 not be understanding of the principles; and since it is not possible for anything to be truer than understanding, except comprehension, there will be comprehension of the principles—both if we inquire from these facts and because demonstration is not a principle of demonstration so that understanding is not a principle of understanding either—so if we have no other true kind apart from understanding, comprehension will be the
15 principle of understanding. And the principle will be of the principle, and understanding as a whole will be similarly related to the whole object.

STUDY QUESTIONS: ARISTOTLE, POSTERIOR ANALYTICS

1. What does it mean to understand a thing *simpliciter?*
2. What was Plato's puzzle about knowledge in the *Meno*, and how does Aristotle attempt to solve it?
3. What is a scientific deduction?

4. What does demonstrative understanding depend on?
5. What does Aristotle mean when he says that 'things are prior and more familiar'?
6. What does Aristotle mean by 'an immediate deductive principle'?
7. Why does understanding through demonstration require knowledge of immediate and primitive principles?
8. How does Aristotle contrast deduction with induction? What are their different uses and roles?
9. How is experience related to perception? How can experience lead to understanding?
10. 'All understanding involves an account.' Why does Aristotle say that, and what does it mean?
11. Does Aristotle have a correct view of the relationship between perception and reasoning in scientific knowledge? How does his view compare with that of Plato in the *Meno*?

PHYSICS

The *Physics* is concerned with the fundamental general principles of nature, which consists in those things that change. As such, the work is about the nature of change. In the first book, Aristotle tries to refute the Eleatic monism of Parmenides according to which changes are impossible.

Chapter 1 presents the notion of a first principle, which is the object of scientific enquiry. Understanding nature requires us to grasp the principles of natural change. According to Parmenides' monism, there is only one first principle, and it is unchanging.

After having argued against monism in Chapters 2–4, Aristotle gives an analysis of change, which begins in Chapter 5 of Book 1. Change requires the idea of opposite qualities: something becomes red when it stops being not-red. In the sixth chapter, Aristotle also argues that there must be something underlying any change. All alterations involve three elements: the thing that alters, how it was before, and how it is after the change. Aristotle concludes that change requires the ideas of opposites and of something underlying the alteration.

In Chapter 7 of Book 1, he extends this analysis by arguing that there are two kinds of change. He distinguishes (1) an X comes to be a Y, and (2) Y comes to be from X. The first kind of change is an alteration in an already existing substance. For instance, a person learns music; she becomes musical. The second kind of change, which he calls substantial generation, involves the coming into being of a new substance. This generation of substances requires the form/matter distinction. New substances are generated when a new form is imposed on already existing matter. For example, a statue comes into being when bronze is given a form. This twofold analysis of change allows Aristotle to show how Parmenides' position is mistaken. Both of the two kinds of change involve an underlying permanent that is altered; in the first, this is a substance, such as a person; and in the second, this permanent is matter, such as bronze.

Book 2 of the *Physics* examines how we should explain changes in physics. In Chapter 1, he contrasts the notion of a natural object with that of an artifact. Something with a nature is the source of its own changes; in the case of artifacts, changes are imposed from without.

In Chapter 3, Aristotle lists four types of cause, or *aition*: the material, formal, efficient, and final causes. It is best to think of these causes as different types of explanation. For the most part, Aristotle thinks that any change has all four types of cause or explanation.

This implies that, for Aristotle, natural objects have final causes or ends. This claim seems alien to us who think of nature and its diverse forms as the result only of physical laws, without reference to ends.

In Book II, Chapter 8, of the *Physics*, Aristotle argues against a purely mechanistic view of nature on the grounds that the regularities in nature cannot be due to pure chance, and that what does not happen by chance must happen for a purpose. Aristotle's view is not that stones have desires. It is rather that all natural things have a nature, which is their form, in accordance with which they develop. This natural development is an end.

In Book III, Aristotle argues that there are no actual, but only potential, infinities. Book VIII, Chapters 5 and 6, contains Aristotle's famous argument for an unmoved mover, a theme that he develops also in Book XII of the *Metaphysics*.

BOOK I

184a10 **1.** Since understanding and *knowing* in every *inquiry* concerned with things having principles or causes or elements results from the knowledge of these (for we think that we know each thing when we know the first causes and the first prin-
15 ciples and have reached the elements), clearly, in the science of nature too we should first try to determine what is the case with regard to the principles.

The natural way to proceed is from what is more known and *clearer* to us to what is by nature *clearer* and more known; for what is known to us and what is known without qualification are not
20 the same. So we should proceed in this manner, namely, from what is less *clear* by nature, though *clearer* to us, to what is by its nature *clearer* and more known. Now the things that are at first plain and *clear* to us are rather mingled, and it is later that their elements and principles become known to those who distinguish them. Consequently, in the case of each thing, we should proceed from its entirety to each of its constituents,
25 for it is the whole that is more known by sensa-
184b10 tion; and a thing in its entirety, since it includes many constituents as parts, is a kind of a whole. In a sense, a name is related to its formula in the same way, for a name signifies some whole without distinguishing its parts, as in the case of "a circle"; but its definition analyzes the whole into its constituents. Children, too, at first call every

man "papa" and every woman "mama", but later on they distinguish each of them.

15 **2.** It is necessary that there be either one principle or many; and if one, then either immovable, as Parmenides and Melissus say, or in motion, as the physicists say—some of the latter asserting that the first principle is *Air* and others that it is *Water*, but if many, then either finite or infinite. If finite, but more than one, then they
20 are two or three or four or some other number; but if infinite, then they are either generically one but differ in shape or kind, as Democritus says, or even contrary.

Also those who inquire into the number of things do so in a similar way; for they first inquire whether the constituents of things are one or
25 many, and if many, whether finite or infinite. Thus they inquire whether the principles or elements are one or many.

Now to inquire whether being is one and
185a immovable is not to inquire about nature; for just as the geometer has no arguments at all against one who rejects the principles of geometry, seeing that their discussion belongs to another science or to a science common to all others, so too in the case of principles; for if being is only one and is one in this manner [immovable], no prin-
5 ciple exists at all, seeing that a principle is a principle of some thing or things. Indeed, to inquire whether being is one in this manner is like arguing against any other paradox maintained for the

sake of argument, such as that of Heraclitus or the one which might assert that being is one man, or it is like refuting an eristic argument, such as that of Melissus and that of Parmenides.
10 (The latter two thinkers assume false premises, and the conclusions they draw do not follow from the premises; as for Melissus, his argument is rather crude and presents no problem, for once an absurd premise is granted, the rest follow, and there is no difficulty at all in this.)

We, on the other hand, make the assumption that things existing by nature are in motion,
15 either all or some of them; and this is clear by induction. In addition, we should refute only those conclusions which are falsely drawn from the principles of the science in question, and no others. For example, the task of refuting the squaring of the circle by means of segments belongs to the geometer, but that of refuting the squaring of the circle by Antiphon's method does not belong to the geometer. However, since these thinkers dis-
20 cuss problems in physics even if their subject is not nature, perhaps it is well to go over their views somewhat; for such inquiry has philosophic value.

The most appropriate starting-point is to raise this question: In what sense are all things one? for "being" has many senses. Are all things substances or quantities or qualities; and if sub-
25 stances, are they all one substance, as, for example, one man or one horse or one soul, or are they one quality, as, for example, whiteness or hotness or some other thing of this sort? These alternative answers differ much and cannot all be true. If, on the one hand, [they say that] all things are substances and quantities and qualities, then whether these are detached from each other or not, things will be many. But if [they say that] all
30 things are qualities or are quantities, then whether substances exist or not, their statement is absurd, if one is to call the impossible "absurd"; for none of these can exist separately (except substances), since all of them are said of substances as their subjects.

Now Melissus says that being is the *Infinite*;
185b so, it is a quantity, for the infinite exists in quantity. But a substance or a quality or an affection cannot be infinite except in virtue of another attribute, that is, if each of them were at the same time a quantity; for the formula of the infinite uses "quantity" but not "substance" or "quality". So, if being is both a substance and a quantity, then it is two and not one; but if it is
5 only a substance, then neither will it be infinite nor will it have any magnitude, since to have a magnitude it would have to be a quantity.

Next, since the term "one" itself, like the term "being", also has many senses, we should consider in what sense the totality [of things] is *One*. Now to be one is to be (a) the continuous or (b) the indivisible or (c) things whose formula of their essence is the same and one, like what we call "vintage" and "wine".

10 Accordingly, if (a) the totality is one by being continuous, then the *One* will be many; for the continuous is infinitely divisible. . . .

Moreover, if (b) the totality is one in the sense of being indivisible, no·thing will be a quantity or a quality, and so being will not be infinite, as Melissus says, nor limited, as Parmenides says; for it is the limit that is indivisible and not that which is limited.

20 Further, if (c) all things are one by having the same formula, like a dress and a garment, then what they are saying is what Heraclitus says; for to be good and to be bad will be the same, and to be not good and to be good, likewise, so that the same thing will be good and not good and a man and a horse. Indeed, what they will be say-
25 ing is not that things are one but that they are not even one, and that to be such-and-such will be the same as to be so-much.

Even the later ancient thinkers were troubled lest the same thing should turn out to be both one and many. So some of them, like Lycophron, omitted the "is", and others changed
30 the form of expression and used, for example, "man grayed" and not "man is gray", "walks" and not "is walking", lest by adding the "is" they should find themselves making what is one to be many, as if "one" and "being" had only one meaning. But beings are many, either in formula (for example, to be white is distinct from to be musical, even if the same thing should turn out to be both white and musical; so the one may be

186a many) or by division (like the whole and its parts). And in the latter cases they are even raising *difficulties* and admitting that the one is many, as if the same thing could not be one and also many (that is, one and many but not as opposites); for what is one may be potentially one or actually one.

5. All thinkers posit contraries as princi-
20 ples, e.g., (a) those who say that the universe is one and motionless (even Parmenides posits the *Hot* and the *Cold* as principles and calls them "*Fire*" and "*Earth*") and (b) those who speak of the *Rare* and the *Dense* and (c) Democritus, who posits the *Solid* and the *Void*, calling them "*Being*" and "*Nonbeing*", respectively, and who uses [as differentiae] *Position, Shape,* and *Order* as genera of contraries (for example, in the case of position,
25 these are *up* and *down,* and also *in front* and *behind;* but in the case of shape, they are the *angular* and the *non-angular,* and also the *straight* and the *circular*).

It is clear, then, that in a sense all thinkers posit contraries as principles, and with good reason; for (a) neither must one principle be composed of another principle, (b) nor should they be composed of other things but the other things should be composed of them. Now the primary contraries possess both these attributes: (b) They
30 are not composed of other things because they are primary, and (a) neither of them is composed of the other because they are contraries. However, we should attend to an argument as well in order to see how this turns out to be the case.

First we must grant that no thing by nature acts on, or is acted on by, any other chance thing, nor does any thing come to be from any other [chance] thing, unless one grants that this takes
35 place in virtue of an attribute. For how could the white come to be from the musical unless the musical were an accident of the not-white or the black? But the white does come to be from the
188b nonwhite, not from any nonwhite but from black or some intermediate color; and the musical comes to be from the nonmusical, not from any nonmusical but from the unmusical or something between the musical and the unmusical, if there is such.

Nor again does any thing, when destroyed, change into any chance thing. For example, the
5 white is destroyed not into the musical, unless it be in virtue of an attribute, but into the nonwhite, not into any chance nonwhite but into black or some other intermediate color; and the musical is similarly destroyed into the nonmusical, not into any chance nonmusical but into the unmusical or some intermediate between the two, if there is such.

It is likewise with all other cases, since the
10 same formula applies even to things which are not simple but composite; but we fail to notice this happening because no names have been given to the opposite dispositions. For the harmonious must come to be from the inharmonious, and the inharmonious, from the harmonious; and the harmonious must be destroyed into something which is not harmonious, not into any
15 chance thing but into that which is opposed to the harmonious. It makes no difference whether we speak of harmony or of order or of composition, for evidently it is the same formula which applies to them. Again, the generation of a house and of a statue and of any other thing takes place in a similar way. For a house is generated from objects which exist not in composition but are divided in a certain way, and likewise for a statue
20 or anything that has been shaped from shapelessness; and what results in each of these are order in one case and a composition in the other.

If, then, all this is true, every thing that is generated or destroyed is so from or to a contrary or an intermediate. As for the intermediates, they are composed of contraries; the other colors,
25 for example, are composed of white and black. Thus every thing which is generated by nature is a contrary or composed of contraries.

Up to this point most of the other thinkers were quite close in following this line of thinking, as we said before; for they all said that the elements, also called "principles" by them, are
30 contraries, as if compelled by truth itself even if they gave no reason. However, they differed from each other thus: Some of them used prior contraries, while others used posterior, and some used contraries more known in formula, while others used contraries more known according to

sensation; for some posited as causes of generation the *Hot* and the *Cold*, others the *Moist* and
the *Dry*, while others posited the *Odd* and the
35 *Even*, and still others, *Strife* and *Friendship*; and
these differ from each other in the way stated. So
the principles which they used are in one way the
same but in another distinct. They are distinct in
189a the manner in which most thinkers took them to
be; but they are the same insofar as they are analogous, for they are taken from the same two sets
of contraries, some of them being wider while
others narrower in extent. In this way, then, they
spoke of them in the same and also in a distinct
manner, some in a worse and others in a better
way, and, as we said, some posited them as more
known according to formula while others as more
5 known according to sensation. For the universal
is known according to formula but the individual
according to sensation, since the formula is of
the universal but sensation is of the part; for
example, contrary principles according to formula are the *Great* and the *Small*, those according to sensation are the *Dense* and the *Rare*.

10 It is evident, then, that the principles should
be contraries.

30 **7.** We shall now give our own account by
first going over generation universally, for in proceeding according to nature we should first
investigate what is common and then what is
proper in each case.

We say that something comes to be from
something else or that some one thing is coming
to be from some other thing by speaking either of
simple or of composite things. By this I mean the
following: (a) A man becomes musical or the
35 not-musical becomes musical, and (b) the not-
190a musical man becomes a musical man. In (a), I
call "simple" the man or the not-musical, which
is becoming something else, and also the musical,
which is what the former [the man or the musi-
cal] becomes; and in (b), when we say that the
5 not-musical man becomes a musical man, we call
"composite" both the thing generated and that
which is in the process of becoming.

Now of these, in some cases we say not only
"A becomes B" but also "B comes to be from A",
as in "The musical comes to be from the not-

musical"; but we do not speak likewise in all
cases, for we do not say "the musical came to be
from the man" but "the man became musical".

10 Of simple things that come to be something, some of them persist throughout the generation but others do not. For when a man
becomes musical, he persists during the generation and is still a man [at the end of it], but the
not-musical or the unmusical does not so persist,
whether as a simple thing or when combined
with the subject.

With these distinctions granted, then from
all things which are being generated one may
gather this, if he is to attend carefully to the man-
15 ner of our statement—that there must always be
something which underlies that which is in the
process of becoming and that this, even if numerically one, in kind at least is not one (and by "in
kind" I mean the same thing as by "in formula",
for "to be a man" and "to be unmusical" do not
have the same meaning). And one part of that
which is being generated persists but the other
does not, that is, what is not an opposite persists
(for the man persists) but the musical or the
20 unmusical does not, and neither does the composite persist, i.e., the unmusical man.

We say "B comes to be from A" rather than
"A becomes B" of things which do not persist,
i.e., we say "the musical is generated from the
unmusical" but not "the musical is generated
25 from the man"; but occasionally we do likewise
also of things which persist, for we say "a statue
comes to be from bronze" but not "bronze
becomes a statue". As for the generation from
the opposite which does not persist, it is stated in
both ways: We say both "B comes to be from A"
and "A becomes B"; for we say both "the musical
comes to be from the unmusical" and "the unmusical becomes musical"; and in view of this, we
30 do likewise in the case of the composite, for we
say both "from being an unmusical man he
becomes musical" and "the unmusical man
becomes musical".

Now "becoming" has many senses: (a) In
certain cases a thing is said to become a *this* in a
qualified sense, while (b) a becoming without qualification exists only of substances. And it is evident that in the former cases something underlies

35 that which is in the process of generation; for in the generation of some quantity or some quality or some relation or sometime or somewhere, there is some underlying subject, because only a sub-stance is not said of [predicated of] some other 190b underlying subject whereas all others are said of substances. However, it will become evident on further examination that also substances and all other unqualified beings are generated from some underlying subject, for there is always some under-lying subject from which the thing generated 5 comes to be, e.g., plants and animals from seeds.

Things in the process of generation without specification may be generated by the changing of shape, as a statue from bronze; or by addition, like things which increase; or by the removal of something, like the statue *Hermes* from stone; or by composition, like a house; or by alteration, like things which alter with respect to their mat-10 ter. It is evident that all things which are being generated in this manner are generated from an underlying subject. So it is clear from what has been said that the thing in generation is always a composite, and there is that [say, A] which is generated, and what comes to be that [i.e., A] is something else, and this in two senses, either the subject or the opposite. By "the opposite" I mean, for example, the unmusical; by "the subject" I 15 mean the man; and the shapelessness and the formlessness and the disorder are opposites, while the bronze and the stone and the gold are under-lying subjects.

Thus if, of things by nature, there are causes or principles of which those things are composed primarily and from which they come to be not accidentally, but come to be what each of them is 20 called according to its *substance*, then everything which is generated is generated from a subject and a *form*; for the musical man is composed, in a sense, of a man and the musical, since one would be analyzing the formula [of the musical man] by giving a formula of each of these two. Clearly, then, things in generation come to be from these [causes or principles].

25 Now the subject is in number one but in kind two; for a man or gold or matter in general can be numbered, for it is rather this [the subject] which is a *this*, and it is not as from an attribute

that the thing in generation comes to be from this, but what is an attribute is the privation or the contrary; and the form is one, as in the case of order or music of some other such predicate. 30 So in a sense the principles may be spoken of as being two, but in another sense as being three; and they may also be spoken of as being the con-traries, for example, if one were to say that they are the musical and the unmusical or the hot and the cold or the harmonious and the inharmo-nious; but in another sense they may not be so spoken of, for the contraries cannot be acted upon by each other. And this problem is solved 35 because there is a subject which is distinct [from the contraries], for it is not a contrary. So in some sense the principles are not more than the 191a contraries but are two in number, so to speak; yet on the other hand, they are not entirely two but are three because in each of them there is a dis-tinction in essence; for the essence of a man is distinct from the essence of the unmusical, and the essence of the unshaped is distinct from that of bronze.

We have stated, then, the number of the principles concerning the generation of physical objects and how they are so many, and it is clear 5 that there must be something which underlies the contraries and that the contraries are two. Yet in another sense this is not necessary, for one of the contraries is sufficient to produce the change by its absences or presence.

As for the underlying nature, it is *knowable* by analogy. Thus, as bronze is to the statue or the 10 wood is to the bed or the matter or the *formless* object prior to receiving a *form* is to that which has a *form*, so is this [underlying nature] to a sub-stance or to a *this* or to being. This then is one of the principles, though it is not one nor a being in the manner of a *this*; another [principle] is the formula; then there is the contrary of the latter, and this is the privation.

15 In what sense these [principles] are two and in what sense more than two has been stated above. First is was stated that only the contraries are principles, the it was stated that there must be something else, an underlying subject, and so the principles must be three. From the preceding statements it is evident how the contraries differ,

how the principles are related to each other, and
20 what the underlying subject is. As to whether it
is the form or the underlying subject that is a substance, this is not yet clear. Bu that the principles
are three and how they are three and what their
manner of existence is, this is clear.

Concerning the number of the principles
and what they are, then, let the above be our
investigation.

8. We will now proceed to state that the
difficulty of the early thinkers, too, is solved only
in this manner.

In seeking the truth and the nature of things
25 from the philosophical point of view, the first
thinkers, as if led astray by inexperience, were
misled into another way of thinking by maintaining the following: No thing can be generated or
be destroyed because a thing must be generated
either from being or from nonbeing; but both of
30 these are impossible, for being cannot become
something since it already exists, and a thing
generated cannot come to be from nonbeing
since there must be some underlying subject
[from which it is to be generated]. And exagger-
ating the consequences in this manner, they concluded by saying that there is no plurality of
things, but that only *Being* itself exists. This is
the doctrine they adopted, then, and for the
reasons stated.

Our position, however, is that, in one way,
35 the expressions "to be generated from being or
from nonbeing" or "nonbeing or being acts upon
or is acted upon by something, or becomes a *this,*
191b whatever this may be" do not differ from "a doctor acts upon or is acted upon by something" or
"from a doctor something else is or comes to be";
hence, since each of these expressions has two
senses, it is clear that also each of the expressions
"from being [or nonbeing]" and "being [or nonbe-
ing] acts upon or is acted upon" has two senses.
5 Thus, the doctor builds [a house] not qua a doctor but qua a builder, and he becomes grey-haired
not qua a doctor but qua black-haired; but he
heals or becomes a nondoctor qua a doctor. So
since, in saying "a doctor acts or is acted upon by
something, or from a doctor he becomes something else", we do so mainly when is qua a doctor

that he acts upon or is acted upon by something
or that he becomes something else; it is clear that
10 also "to become something from nonbeing"
means this, namely, to become something qua
not-being.

It is the failure to make this distinction that
led those thinkers astray, and through their ignorance of this they added so much more as to
think that nothing else is generated or exists
[besides *Being*], thus doing away with every [kind
of] generation. Now we too maintain, as they do,
that nothing is generated from unqualified nonbeing, yet we do maintain that generation from
15 nonbeing in a qualified sense exists, namely, with
respect to an attribute; for from the privation,
which in itself is a not-being, something which
did not exist is generated. Such generation from
nonbeing, of course, is surprising and is thought
to be impossible. In the same way, we maintain
that being is not generated from being, except
with respect to an attribute; so this generation
20 too takes place in the same manner, as if an animal were to be generated from an animal, or an
animal of one kind from an animal of another
kind, i.e., if a dog were to come to be from a
horse. For the dog would then come to be not
only from an animal of another kind, but also
from an animal, but not qua an animal since this
is already there. But if an object is to become an
animal not with respect to an attribute, then it
will do so not from an animal, and if it is to
become a being, then it will do so not from
25 being, nor from nonbeing, since we have stated
that "from nonbeing" means qua not-being. And
we may add here that [by this] we do not reflect
the truth of "everything either is or is not".

This then is one way [of solving the diffi-
culty]; but there is another, in view of the fact
that we may speak of things with respect to their
potentiality as well as with respect to their
actuality, and we have settled this elsewhere with
greater accuracy.

30   As we said, then, the difficulties through
which some thinkers are compelled to reject
some of the things which we maintain are now
solved; for it was because of these [*difficulties*] that
earlier thinkers also deviated so much from the
path which leads to the belief in generation,

destruction, and change in general. If they had perceived this [underlying] nature, this would have released them from all their ignorance.

BOOK II

192b 1. Of things, some exist by nature, others 10 through other causes. Animals and their parts exist by nature, and so do plants and the simple bodies, for example, earth, fire, air, and water; for we say that these and other such exist by nature. Now all the things mentioned appear to differ from things which are composed not by nature. All things existing by nature appear to have in themselves a principle of motion and of standstill, 15 whether with respect to place or increase or decrease or alteration. But a bed or a garment or a thing in some other similar genus, insofar as each of them is called by a similar predicate and in virtue of existing by art, has no natural tendency in itself for changing; but insofar as it happens to 20 be made of stone or earth or to be a composite of these, it has such a tendency and only to that extent. So nature is a principle and a cause of being moved or of rest in the thing to which it belongs primarily and in virtue of that thing, but not accidentally. I say "not accidentally" in view of the fact that the same man may cause himself to become healthy by being a doctor; however, it 25 is not in virtue of becoming healthy that he has the medical art, but it is an accident that the same man is both a doctor and becoming healthy, and on account of this, the one is at times separate from the other. Similarly, each of the other things produced has in itself no principle of producing, but in certain cases [in most cases] such a principle is in another thing or is outside of the thing produced, as in the case of a house and other 30 manufactured products, while in the remaining cases it is in the thing itself but not in virtue of that thing, that is, whenever it is an accident in the thing that causes the production in it.

We have stated, then, what nature is. Things which have such a principle are said to have a nature; and they are all substances, for each of them is a subject, and nature exists always in 35 a subject. And they and whatever essentially

belongs to them are said to exist according to nature, as, for example, the upward locomotion of fire; for this [locomotion] is not nature, nor 193a does it have a nature, but it exists by nature or according to nature.

We have stated, then, what nature is and what exists by nature and according to nature. As far as trying to prove that nature exists, this would be ridiculous, for it is evident that there are many such things; and to try to prove what is 5 evident through what is not evident is a mark of a man who cannot *judge* what is known through itself from what is known not through itself. That this can take place is clear; for a man born blind may form syllogisms concerning colors, but such a man must be using mere names without conceiving the corresponding things.

Some think that the nature or *substance* of a 10 thing existing by nature is the first constituent which is in the thing and which in itself is without shape, like wood in the case of a bed or bronze in a bronze statue. (According to Antiphon, a sign of this is the fact that if one plants a bed and the moistened wood acquires the power of sending up a shoot, what will result is not a 15 bed but wood, thus showing that the arrangement of the parts according to custom or art belongs to the object planted by accident, but that the substance is that which persists while it is acted upon continuously.) And if each of these is also related to another object in the same way, say bronze and gold to water, bones and wood to earth, and similarly with any others, then it is 20 that other object which is the nature and the *substance* of those things. It is in view of this that some say that the nature of all things is earth; others, that it is fire; others, air; others, water; others, some of these; and others, all of them. For whatever each thinker believed to be of this sort, whether only one object or more than one, he posited this or these as being all that is substance, 25 but all other things as being affections or possessions or dispositions of substances, and also this or these as being eternal (for they said that there is no change from one of them to something else), but the other things [he posited] as being in generation and destruction a countless number of times.

In one way, then, nature is said to be the first underlying matter in things which have in themselves a principle of motion or of change, but in another it is said to be the *shape* or form according to formula; for just as we call "art" that which exists in virtue of art and is artistic, so we call "nature" that which exists in virtue of nature and is natural. Neither in the former case would we say that a thing has something in virtue of art or that there is art if the thing is only potentially a bed but has not yet the form of a bed, nor is it so in things which are *composites* by nature; for that which is potentially flesh or bone has not yet its nature or does not yet exist by nature until it acquires the form according to the formula by which [form] we state what flesh or bone is when we define it. Thus, in another way, the nature of things which have in themselves a principle of motion would be the *shape* or form, which does not exist separately from the thing except according to formula. As for the *composite* of the two, e.g., a man, this is not nature, but [we say] it exists by nature.

Indeed, the form is a nature to a higher degree than the matter; for each thing receives a name when it exists in actuality rather than when it exists potentially. Moreover, it is from a man that a man is generated, but a bed is not generated from a bed (and in view of this they say that nature is not the shape but the wood, since, if it buds, what is generated is wood and not a bed); so if in the latter case it is the art, in the former too it is the form that should be nature, for it is from a man that a man is generated. Again, when we speak of nature as being a generation, this is a process toward nature [as a form]; for the term "nature" as signifying a process is not like the term "doctoring". The latter term signifies a process toward health, not toward the art of doctoring, for doctoring which begins from the art of doctoring cannot be a process toward the art of doctoring; but nature [as a process] is not related to nature [as a form] in the same way, for from something the growing object proceeds to something or grows into something. Into what does it grow? Not into that from which it begins but into that toward which it proceeds. Thus it is the *form* that is nature. "Form" or "nature", it

may be added, has two senses, for privation, too, is in a way a form; but whether there is a privation or a contrary in an unqualified generation or not must be considered later.

2. Having distinguished the various senses of "nature", we should next investigate how the mathematician and the physicist differ with respect to their objects, for physical bodies have also surfaces and solids and lengths and points, and these are the concern of the mathematician. Moreover, is astronomy a distinct science or a part of physics? For it is absurd that the physicist should understand what the Sun or the Moon is but not what their essential attributes are, not to mention the fact that those who are concerned with nature appear to be discussing the shape of the Moon and of the Sun and to be raising the problem of whether the Earth and the universe are spherical or not.

Now the mathematician, too, is concerned with these, but not insofar as each is a limit of a physical body; nor does he investigate attributes qua existing in such bodies. That is why he separates them, for in thought they are separable from motion; and it makes no difference, nor does any falsity occur in separating them [in thought]. Those who posit Ideas, too, are doing the same but are unaware of it; for they are separating the physical objects [from motion], although these are less separable than the mathematical objects. This becomes clear if one tries to state the definitions in each [science], both of the subjects and of their attributes. For oddness and evenness and straightness and curvature, and also a number and a line and a figure, will each be defined without reference to motion; but not so in the case of flesh and bone and a man, for these are defined like a snub nose and not like curvature. This is also clear in those parts of mathematics which are more physical, such as optics and harmonics and astronomy, for these are related to geometry in a somewhat converse manner. On the one hand, geometry is concerned with physical lines but not qua physical; on the other, optics is concerned with mathematical lines not qua mathematical but qua physical.

Since we speak of nature in two ways, as form as well as matter, we should investigate the whatness [of the objects of physics] as we would the whatness of snubness. Such objects, then, should be investigated neither without matter nor 15 with respect to matter [alone]. With regard to this we might also raise another problem. Since there are two natures, with which of them should the physicist be concerned? Or should he be concerned with that which has both natures? Of course, if with both natures, then also with each of the two natures. So should the same science be concerned with both natures, or one science with one and another with the other?

If we turn our attention to the ancients, physics would seem to be concerned with matter, 20 for even Empedocles and Democritus touched upon form or essence only slightly. But if art imitates nature and the same science should understand the form and the matter to some extent (for example, the doctor should understand health, and also bile and phlegm in which health exists; the builder should likewise understand the form of the house, and also the matter, namely, bricks and 25 wooden materials; and similarly in each of the other arts), it should be the concern of physics, too, to know both natures.

Moreover, it belongs to the same science to be concerned with the final cause or the end and also with whatever is needed for the sake of the final cause or the end. But nature is [also] an end and a final cause; for if, in that which is in contin- 30 uous motion, there is some end of that motion, this [end] is the last and the final cause. And it is in view of this that the poet was carried away when he made the ridiculous statement "he has an end [death], for the sake of which he was born". For not every last thing tends to be an end, but only the best, seeing that in the case of the arts, too, some of them just make the matter but others make it serviceable and that we use things as if 35 they exist all for our own sake (since in a certain sense, we too are an end, for "final cause" has two senses, as we stated in "On Philosophy"). Indeed, 194b there are two arts which rule over matter and have knowledge of it—the art which is concerned with the use of it and the art which directs the production of it. Thus the art which uses matter is also in

a sense directive, but as directive it differs from the other insofar as it knows the form, while the art which directs the production knows the mat- 5 ter; for the steersman knows what kind of form the rudder should have and orders its production, but the engineer knows from what kind of wood it should be produced and how it should move. Now in objects produced according to art, it is we who produce the matter for the sake of some function, but in natural objects it is there all along.

Again, matter is relative to some thing, for distinct forms require distinct matter.

To what extent should the physicist under- 10 stand the form or the what-ness? Up to a point, just as the doctor understands sinews and the smith understands bronze, for each of them [sinews and bronze] is for the sake of something, and the physicist is concerned with what is separable in kind but exists in matter; for both man and the Sun beget man. As for a separate form, how it exists and what it is, this is a task to be 15 settled by first philosophy.

3. Having made these distinctions, we should next examine the causes, their kinds and number. Since our *inquiry* is for the sake of understanding, and we think that we do not understand a thing until we have acquired the *why* of it (and this is to acquire the first cause), 20 clearly we should do this as regards generation and destruction and every physical change so that, with an understanding of their principles, we may try to refer to them each of the things we seek.

In one sense, "a cause" means (1) that from which, as a constituent, something is generated; 25 for example, the bronze is a cause of the statue, and the silver, of the cup, and the genera of these [are also causes].

In another, it means (2) the form or the pattern, this being the formula of the essence, and also the genera of this; for example, in the case of the octave, the ratio 2:1, and, in general, a number and the parts in the formula.

30 In another, it means (3) that from which change or coming to rest first begins; for example, the adviser is a cause, and the father is the cause of the baby, and, in general, that which

acts is a cause of that which is acted upon, and that which brings about a change is a cause of that which is being changed.

Finally, it means (4) the end, and this is the final cause [that for the sake of which]; for example, walking is for the sake of health. Why does he walk? We answer, "In order to be healthy"; and having spoken thus, we think that we have 35 given the cause. And those things which, after that which started the motion, lie between the beginning and the end, such as reducing weight 195a or purging or drugs or instruments in the case of health, all of them are for the sake of the end; and they differ in this, that some of them are operations while others are instruments.

The term "cause", then, has about so many senses. And since they [the causes] are spoken of 5 in many ways, there may be many nonaccidental causes of the same thing; for example, in the case of a statue, not with respect to something else but qua a statue, both the art of sculpture and the bronze are causes of it, though not in the same manner, but the bronze as matter and the art as the source of motion. There may be also causes of each other; for example, exercise is a cause of good physical condition, and good physical condition is a cause of exer- 10 cise, although not in the same manner, but good physical condition as an end, while exercise as a principle of motion. Again, the same thing may be a cause of contraries, for if one thing, when present, is the cause of another, then the first, when absent, is sometimes also said to be the cause of the contrary of the second; for example, we say that the absence of the pilot was the cause of the capsizing, while his presence was the cause of safety.

15 All of the causes just mentioned fall into four most evident types. For, the letters of the syllables, the matter of manufactured articles, fire and all such in the case of bodies, the parts of the whole, the hypotheses of the conclusion—in all of these there are causes in the sense that they are *that of which* the latter consists; and in these, those first mentioned in each case are causes in 20 the sense that they are the underlying subject, as in the case of the parts, but each of the others is a cause in the sense of essence, and this is the whole or the composition or the form. As for the seed and the doctor and the adviser and, in general, that which acts, all these are causes in the sense of the source of change or of standstill or of motion. Finally, each of the rest is a cause as the end or the good of the others; for that for the sake of which the others exist or are done tends 25 to be the best or their end. Let there be no difference here between calling this "the good" or "the apparent good".

These, then, are the causes and their number in kind; but their modes are numerically many, although when summarized they too are fewer. For causes are spoken of in many ways, and even within the same kind one cause may be prior or posterior to another; for example, 30 the cause of health is the doctor or the artist, and the cause of the octave is the ratio 2:1 or a number, and whatever includes each is always a cause. Again, there are accidental causes and their genera; for example, Polyclitus as a cause of a statue is distinct from a sculptor as a cause, since the sculptor is by accident Polyclitus. 35 Also, whatever includes the accident would be a 195b cause; for example, a man, or, in general, an animal, would be a cause of the statue. Even of accidents, some are more remote or more near than others; for example, this would be the case if the white or the musical were to be called "a cause" of the statue.

Of all causes, both those said to be *proper* and those said to be accidental, some are said to be causes in the sense of being in potentiality, others in *actuality;* for example, the cause of the 5 house to be built is the builder and of the house that is being built the builder who is building. Similar remarks will apply to the things caused by the causes already listed; for example, the cause may be a cause of this statue or of a statue or of a portrait in general, and it may be a cause of this bronze or of bronze or of matter in general. Similar remarks may be made in the case of acci- 10 dents. Again, both accidental and *proper* causes and also the objects caused may be spoken of in combination; for example, not Polyclitus, nor the sculptor, but Polyclitus the sculptor.

However, all these are six in number, and each is spoken of in two ways. For as a cause or an object caused each may be stated as a particular or as a genus of a particular; as an accident or as a 15 genus of an accident; in combination or singly taken; and in each of these either in *actuality* or in virtue of its potentiality. And there is this difference, that causes which are in *actuality* and are taken as individuals exist, or do not exist, at the same time as the things of which they are the causes, for example, as in the case of this doctor who is healing and this man who is being healed, 20 and this builder who is building and that building which is being built. But with respect to potentiality this is not always so; for the house is not destroyed at the same time as the builder.

We should always seek the ultimate cause of each thing, as in other cases; for example, a man builds in view of the fact that he is a builder, and a builder builds in virtue of his art of building; accordingly, this latter is the prior cause. It is like- 25 wise with all other cases. Moreover, causes generically given should be stated of effects generically given, and particular causes, of particular effects; for example, a sculptor [in general] of a statue [in general], and this sculptor of this statue. Also potential causes should be stated of potential effects, and causes in *actuality* of effects in *actuality*.

Let this, then, be a sufficient description of the number of causes and the manner in which 30 they are causes.

7. It is clear, then, that there are causes and that there are as many [in kind] as we have 15 stated; for the *why* of things includes just so many [in kind]. For the *why* in referred either (a) ultimately to the whatness in the case of what is immovable, as in mathematics (for it is ultimately referred to the definition of a straight line or of commensurability or of something else), or (b) to the first mover—for example: Why did 20 they declare war? Because they were raided—or (c) to a final cause: [in declaring war] for the sake of ruling the enemy, or (d) to matter, as in things generated. Evidently, then, the causes are those stated and are as many in number.

Since the causes are four, it is the task of the physicist to understand all of them; and as a physicist he should state the *why* by referring it to all of them—the matter, the form, the mover, and the final cause. The last three often amount to 25 one; for both the whatness and the final cause are one, and the first source of motion is the same in kind as these (for man begets man), and, in general, this is so in the case of a movable mover. But a mover that is not movable is not a cause within physics, for it moves without having in itself motion or a principle of motion but is immovable. Accordingly, there are three disciplines: one 30 concerning immovable things, a second concerning things which are in motion but are indestructible, and a third concerning destructible things.

The *why*, then, is given by being referred to matter, to the whatness, and to the first mover, for in generations causes are sought mostly in this manner: "What comes after what?", "What was 35 the first thing that acted or was acted upon?", and at each step always in this way. Now the principles that cause physical motion are two: One of these is not physical, for it has no princi- 198b ple of motion in itself, and such is that which moves another without itself being moved, as in the case of that which is completely immovable and primary among all; and such is also the whatness or the *form*, for this is the end or final cause. So, since nature is a final cause, we should also understand this [cause]. So the *why* must be given in all [four] ways, namely, (1) that this 5 must follow from that (the phrase "this from that" to be taken either without qualification or for the most part); (2) that if this is to be, then that will be (as in the case of premises, from which conclusions follow); (3) that this was the essence; and (4) because it is better in this way (not without qualification, but relative to the *substance* of each thing).

10 **8.** We must discuss first (a) why nature is a cause for the sake of something; then (b) how necessity exists in physical things, for all thinkers make reference to this cause by saying, for example, that since the hot and the cold and each of such things are by nature of such-and-such a kind, certain other things must exist or come to be (for even if they mention some other cause—

15 one of them mentions *Friendship* and *Strife,* another mentions *Intelligence*—they just touch upon it and let it go at that).

The following question arises: What prevents nature from acting, not for the sake of something or for what is better, but by necessity, as in the case of rain, which does not fall in order that wheat may grow. For, one may say, what goes 20 up must be cooled, and the resulting cold water must come down, and when this takes place, the growth of corn just happens; similarly, if a man's wheat is spoiled on the threshing floor, rain did not fall for the sake of spoiling the wheat, but this just happened. So what should prevent the parts in nature, too, from coming to be of necessity in this manner, for example, the front teeth of necessity coming out sharp and so fit for tear-25 ing but the molars broad and useful for grinding food, not however for the sake of this but by coincidence? A similar question arises with the other parts in which final cause seems to exist. If so, then whenever all the parts came together as if generated for the sake of something, the wholes 30 which by *chance* were fitfully composed survived, but those which came together not in this manner, like the man-faced offspring of oxen mentioned by Empedocles, perished and still do so.

This is the argument, then, or any other such, that might cause a *difficulty*. Yet it is impossible for things to come to be in this manner; for the examples cited and all things by nature 35 come to be either always or for the most part, but none of those by luck or *chance* do so likewise. It is not during the winter that frequent rain is 199a thought to occur by luck or by coincidence, but during the summer, nor frequent heat during the summer, but during the winter. So if these be thought to occur either by coincidence or for the sake of something and if they cannot occur by coincidence or by chance, then they occur for 5 the sake of something. Besides, those who use the preceding arguments, too, would admit that all such things exist by nature. There is, then, final cause in things which come to be or exist by nature.

Moreover, in that which has an end, a prior stage and the stages that follow are done for the sake of that end. Accordingly, these are done in the manner in which the nature of the thing dis-10 poses them to be done; and the nature of the thing disposes them to be done in the manner in which they are done at each stage, if nothing obstructs. But they are done for the sake of something; so they are by nature disposed to be done for the sake of something. For example, if a house were a thing generated by nature, it would have been generated in a way similar to that in which it is now generated by art. So if things by nature were to be generated not only by nature but also by art, they would have been generated just as 15 they are by nature disposed to be generated. So one stage is for the sake of the next. In general, in some cases art completes what nature cannot carry out to an end, in others, it imitates nature. Thus, if things done according to art are for the sake of something, clearly also those according to nature are done for the sake of something; for the later stages are similarly related to the earlier stages in those according to art and those according to nature.

This is most evident in those of the other 20 animals which make things neither by art nor by having inquired or deliberated about them; and from this latter fact arise discussions by some thinkers about the problem of whether spiders and ants and other such animals work by intellect or by some other power. If we go a little further in this direction, we observe that in plants, 25 too, parts appear to be generated which contribute to an end, for example, leaves for the sake of protecting the fruit. So if it is both by nature and for the sake of something that the swallow makes its nest and the spider its web and that plants grow leaves for the sake of fruit and send their roots not up but down for the sake of food, it is evident that there exists such a cause in 30 things which come to be or exist by nature. And since nature may be either matter or *form*, and it is the latter that may be an end while all the rest are for the sake of an end, it is *form* that would be a cause in the sense of a final cause.

Now error occurs even with respect to things produced according to art, for example, a grammarian did not write correctly and a doctor did

35 not give the right medicine; so clearly this may occur also in things that come to be according to nature. If then there are (a) things produced 199b according to art in which there is a right final cause and (b) also things done erroneously when the final cause has been aimed at but failed, a similar situation would exist also in natural things, 5 and monstrosities in these would be failures of final causes. So too must have been the case in the original formation of the offspring of oxen, if they could not attain a certain limit or end; for there must have been some corruption in the source from which their generation started, like that in the seed nowadays. We might add, too, that the seed must have come into being first and not the animals all at once, and the expression "first the whole-natured" meant the seed. And final cause exists also in plants, though it is less capable of being articulated. So did olive-headed offspring of 10 vines come into being just as man-faced offspring did from oxen, or not? It would seem absurd; but they must have, if indeed this was also the case in animals. Again, any chance thing might otherwise be generated from a seed.

15 In general, he who asserts this rejects things existing by nature as well as nature itself. For what exists by nature is a thing which, having started from some principle in itself, finally arrives by a continuous motion at a certain end; and neither is the end the same from every principle, nor does any chance end come to be from a given principle, but from the same principle the same end comes to be, if nothing obstructs. As for the final cause or what acts for the sake of the 20 final cause, it might take place by luck. (For example, we say "the stranger came by luck and departed after paying the ransom" if he would have come for the sake of doing this [had he known], not that he came for the sake of this; and this happened by accident, for luck is an 25 accidental cause, as we stated earlier.) But if it takes place always or for the most part, it is not an accident nor does it come to be by luck; and in natural things it takes place always, if nothing obstructs.

It is absurd to think that nothing comes to be for the sake of something if the moving cause

is not observed deliberating (and we may add, even art does not deliberate); and if the ship-building art were in the wood, it would have produced results similar to those produced by nature. 30 So if there is a final cause in art, so also in nature. This is most clearly seen in a doctor who heals himself; nature is like that.

It is evident, then, that nature is a cause and that it is a cause also in this manner, namely, for the sake of something.

BOOK III

1. Since nature is a principle of motion or of change and our *inquiry* is about nature, we should 200b not neglect to inquire what a motion is; for if we are ignorant of what a motion is, we are of neces- 15 sity ignorant of what nature is. When we have explained motion, then we shall try in the same manner to take up what follows.

Now a motion is thought to be one of those things which are continuous, and it is in the continuous that the infinite first appears; and for this reason, it often happens that those who define the continuous use the formula of the infinite, that is, 20 they say that the continuous is that which is infinitely divisible. Again, a motion is thought to be impossible without place and void and time. Clearly, then, because of all this and because of the fact that these are common and belong universally to all the others, we must first undertake 25 to inquire about each of these; for the investigation of what is specific should come after that of what is common.

As we said, then, our first inquiry is about motion. To begin, there is (a) that which exists in actuality only and also (b) that which exists both potentially and in actuality, and this may be a *this* or a *so-much* or a *such* or, likewise, any of the other categories of being. As for that which is relative to something, it may be stated with 30 respect to excess or deficiency or with respect to its being able to act or be acted upon or, in general, with respect to its being able to move or be moved; for that which is able to move is able to move that which can be moved, and that which can be moved can be moved by that which can move.

Now no motion exists apart from things; for that which changes always does so either with respect to substance or with respect to quantity 35 or with respect to quality or with respect to place, and there can be no thing common to these which is not, as is our manner of speaking, 201a a *this* or a quantity or a quality or some one of the other categories. Thus neither a motion nor a change can exist apart from these [categories] if nothing else exists but these.

In all cases, each of these [categories] may exist in two ways; for example, with respect to a *this*, it may be the *form* or the privation of the 5 *form*, with respect to quality it may be whiteness or blackness, and with respect to quantity it may be the complete or the incomplete. Similarly, with respect to locomotion the thing may be up or down or it may be heavy or light. Thus there 10 are as many kinds of motion or of change as there are kinds of being. In view of this distinction between the actual and the potential in each genus, a motion is [defined as] the actuality of the potentially existing qua existing potentially. For example, the actuality of the alterable qua alterable is an alteration, the actuality of what can be increased or (its opposite) what can be decreased [qua such] is an increase or decrease (no name exists which is a common predicate of both), the 15 actuality of the generable or destructible [qua such] is a generation or a destruction, and the actuality of the movable with respect to place [qua such] is a locomotion.

That a motion is what we have stated it to be is clear from the following. When the buildable, insofar as it is said to be such, exists in actuality, it is then [in the process of] being built, and this is [the process of] building; and similarly in the case of learning, healing, rolling, leaping, ripening, and aging.

20 Since, in some cases, the same things exist both potentially and actually, but not at the same time nor with respect to the same thing (as in the case of that which is potentially hot but actually cold), many of them will eventually both act and be acted upon by each other; for each of them has the potentiality both of acting and of being acted upon. Consequently, that which causes a 25 motion physically is also movable, for every such thing which causes a motion is itself moved. There are some who think that every thing that moves another is itself moved; now what the situation is with respect to this will be made clear from other arguments (for there exists also something which causes a motion but is itself immovable), but as for a motion, it is the actuality of that which exists potentially when it is in *actuality* not qua itself but qua movable.

30 By "qua" I mean the following. Bronze is potentially a statue, yet it is not qua bronze that the actuality of bronze is a motion; for to be bronze and to be movable by something are not the same, since if they were the same without qualification or according to formula, the actuality of bronze qua bronze would be a motion. So 35 they are not the same, as stated. This is clear in the case of contraries; for to be capable of being 201b healthy and to be capable of being sick are distinct, for otherwise being sick and being healthy would be the same. It is the underlying subject, be it moisture or blood, which is one and the same, whether in health or in sickness. Since, then, to be bronze and to be potentially some-5 thing else are not the same, just as to be a color and to be visible are not the same, evidently it is the actuality of the potential qua potential that is a motion.

It is clear, then, that this is what a motion is and that an object happens to be in motion just when this actuality exists, and neither before nor after. For each [such] thing may be sometimes in *actuality* and sometimes not, as in the case of the 10 buildable, and it is qua buildable that the *actuality* of the buildable is [the process of] building. For this *actuality* is either [the process of] building or the house. But when the house exists, it is no longer buildable; and it is the buildable that is being built. This *actuality*, then, must be [the process of] building, and [the process of] building is a [kind of] motion. Moreover, the same argu-15 ment applies to the other motions.

Conviction about the existence of the infinite might arise from the following five considerations:

(1) From time, for this is regarded as infinite.

(2) From the division of magnitudes, for the mathematicians also use the infinite.

(3) If generation and destruction are not to
20 come to an end, it will be only if there is an infinite source from which things to be generated can be taken.

(4) From the view that what is finite always has its limits coincide with something [which contains it]; so if the finite is always limited by something, then there can be no ultimate limit.

(5) The greatest and most important point, which gives rise to a *difficulty* affecting everyone,
25 is this: Numbers and mathematical magnitudes and [also] what is outside of the heaven are considered to be infinite because in thought they never come to an end. And if that which is outside of the heaven is infinite, then it seems that there is also an infinite body and an infinity of universes; for why should mass be in one part of the void rather than in another? So if indeed it is in one part, then it should be everywhere. Also,
30 if void or place is infinite, then there must be an infinite body, too; for, in the case of eternal things, that which may be does not differ from that which exists.

Now the investigation of the infinite gives rise to a *difficulty*; for may impossibilities result whether it is posited to exist or not to exist. Moreover, if existing, how does it exist—as a substance or as an essential attribute of some nature? Or does it exist in neither of these ways, but an infinity or an infinite plurality of things nevertheless exist?

204a   Now it belongs most of all to the physicist to inquire whither there exists a sensible magnitude which is infinite. First, then, let us distinguish the various meanings of the term "infinite". The infinite is

(1) That which cannot be gone through, since it does not by nature admit of being gone through, as in the case of a voice, which is invisible.

5   (2) That which admits of being traversed but without end, either (a) almost so [i.e., almost without end] or (b) when by nature it admits of being traversed but it cannot be traversed or it has no limit.

Further, everything considered as infinite may be so either with respect to addition or with respect to division or with respect to both.

5. Now the infinite, being itself just an infinite, cannot exist as something separate from
10 sensible things; for if it is neither a magnitude nor a plurality but is itself a substance and not an attribute, it will be indivisible, for what is divisible is either a magnitude or a plurality; and if it indivisible, it cannot be infinite, except in the sense in which the voice is invisible. However, neither those who assert that the infinite exists speak of it as existing in this manner nor do we inquire about it as such, but only as something which cannot be traversed.

15   But if the infinite exists as an attribute, then just as invisibility is not an element of speech, even if voice is invisible, so the infinite qua infinite would not be an element of things. Moreover, how can the infinite be itself something if it is not also a number or a magnitude, of which that infinite is an essential *attribute*? And besides,
20 the infinite will be of necessity less likely to exist than a number or a magnitude.

It is also evident that the infinite cannot exist as a thing in *actuality* and as a substance and a principle; for, if it can have parts, each part that may be taken would be infinite. . . .

35   However, perhaps this is a more universal
204b inquiry, that is, whether the infinite can be in mathematical objects as well as in those which are intelligible and have no magnitude. We are now examining the sensible objects and those with which our *inquiry* is concerned, and we are asking if there is among them a body which is infinite in the direction of increase.

If we consider the problem logically, it would
5 seem from the following that no such body can exist; for if the formula of a body is "that which is limited by a surface", no infinite body can exist, whether intelligible or sensible. Moreover, also a number cannot exist as something separate and infinite; for a number of that which has a number
10 is numerable, so if the numerable may be numbered, it would also be possible to traverse the infinite.

If we consider the problem rather from the point of view of physics, it would seem from what follows that no infinite body can be either (1) composite or (2) simple.

(1) If the [kinds of] elements are finite in number, an infinite body cannot exist. For it is necessary that the elements be more than one, that the contraries always balance, and that no 15 one of these be infinite; for however much one contrary in one body falls short in power relative to the other contrary in another body (for example, if fire is finite and air is infinite, but, volume for volume, the power of fire is any multiple m relative to that of air, as long as m is a number), still it is evident that the infinite body will over- power and destroy the finite body. Nor is it 20 possible for each element to be infinite; for (a) a body is that which is extended in all directions, (b) what is infinite would be infinitely extended, and so an infinite body would be infinitely extended in all directions.

(2) Nor can there be an infinite body which is one and simple, whether (a) as something which exists apart from the elements and from which the elements are generated (as some thinkers say) or 25 (b) as something without any qualification. For (a) there are some who posit the infinite in the first sense, and not as being air or water, since thus there would be no infinite element which might destroy the other finite elements. For these ele- ments have contrarieties relative to each other (for example, air is cold, water is moist, and fire is hot); so if one of them were infinite, it would have already destroyed the others, and so they say that the infinite from which these elements are gener- 30 ated is distinct from them. However, no such body can exist, not in view of its infiniteness (for, in connection with this, something common should be stated which applies to all alike, whether to air or water or whatever this may be), but in view of the fact that no such sensible body exists besides the so-called "elements". For, in all cases, a body is resolved into that of which it consists; so such a 35 body would have existed besides air and fire and earth and water, but no such body appears to exist. 205a Also, it is not possible for fire or for any of the other elements to be infinite. For, in general, even apart from the problem of whether any of them can be infinite, it is impossible for the universe, even if it were finite, to be or to become one of them, as Heraclitus says that at times all things

5 become fire; and the same argument applies to the one [element], which the physicists posit besides the elements; for all things are changing, from one contrary to another contrary, for example, from hot to cold. . . .

206a   It is evident from what has been said, then, that no infinite body exists in *actuality*.

6. That many impossibilities result if the 10 infinite, taken without qualification, does not exist is clear from what will follow, namely, (a) there will be a beginning and an end for time, (b) magnitudes will not [always] be divisible into magnitudes, and (c) there will not be an infinite number.

If no alternative appears possible when things are stated in this manner, then an arbiter is needed; and clearly there is a way in which the infinite exists and a way in which it does not. 15 Indeed, in one sense, "to be" is used for what exists potentially, and in another, for what exists actually; moreover, the infinite exists by addition and also by removal. That the infinite does not exist in actuality has already been stated, but it exists by division; and it is not hard to reject the hypothesis that *indivisible* lines exists. Accord- ingly, we are left with the alternative that the infinite exists potentially.

However, the potential existence of the infi- 20 nite must not be taken to be like that of a statue; for what is potentially a statue may come to be *actually* a statue, but this is not so for what is potentially infinite. But since "to be" has many sense, the infinite exists in the sense in which the day exists or games exist, namely, by always com- 25 ing into being one after another; for these too exist both potentially and actually, e.g., Olympic games exist both in the sense that they *can* come to be and in the sense that they are *occuring*. However, it is clear that there is a distinction in the way in which the infinite exists in time and in men and in the division of magnitudes. For, although in general the infinite exists in the sense that one thing is always being taken after another, each thing so taken being always finite 30 but always another and another (hence, the infi- nite should not be considered as being a *this*, e.g., a man or a house, but as we speak of a day or a game whose being, even if finite, is always in generation and destruction, not as something which became a *substance*, but always becoming one thing after another), yet in the case of magnitudes 206b the parts taken persist, while in the case of time and of men they are destroyed but not exhausted.

The infinite by addition is in a sense the 5 same as that by division, for in a finite magnitude the infinite by addition occurs in a way inverse to that by division; for as that magnitude is seen to be divided to infinity, the sum of the parts taken appears to tend toward something definite. For if in a finite magnitude one takes a definite part and then from what remains keeps on taking a part, not equal to the first part but always using the same ratio, he will not traverse the original 10 finite magnitude; but if he is to so increase the ratio that the parts taken are always equal, he will traverse it, because every finite magnitude is exhausted by any definite magnitude. Thus it is in this and not in any other way that the infinite exists, namely, potentially and by reduction. And it exists actually in the way in which a day and 15 the games are said to exist, and potentially in the way in which matter exists; and, unlike that which is limited, it exists not by itself.

And the infinite by addition exists potentially in this manner, which as we said is in a sense the same as that by division; for although there is always something outside of it that can 20 be taken, it will not surpass every definite magnitude, unlike the infinite by division, which surpasses in smallness any given definite magnitude and remains smaller thereafter. As to surpassing every magnitude by addition, the infinite cannot do so even potentially if indeed it does not exist actually as an attribute; and this is unlike what the natural philosophers say, namely, that the body which is outside of the world, whose 25 *substance* is air or some other such thing, is infinite. But if no sensible body can be actually infinite in this manner, it is evident that neither can it exist potentially by addition, except in a manner inverse to that by division, as already stated. It is because of this that Plato, too, posited two infinities, namely, in view of the fact that it is thought possible to surpass all magnitudes and proceed to infinity in the direction both of 30 increase and of reduction. Yet though he posits two infinites, he does not make any use of them; for neither in numbers does the infinite exist in the direction of reduction, seeing that the unit is the smallest, nor in the direction of increase, seeing that he posits Numbers up to Ten only.

207a   Now the infinite turns out to be the contrary of what they say it is; for it is not that outside of which there is nothing, but that outside of which there is always something. A sign of this is the following: People say that rings without a bezel are infinite [endless] as there is always something outside [beyond] that may be taken. But they say 5 this in virtue of some similarity and not in the main sense; for both (a) this must be the case and (b) the same thing must not be taken again, while in the circle this is not what happens but [only] (a) the succeeding part is always distinct. Thus the infinite is that outside of which, with respect to taking a quantity, there is always some part [yet] to be taken. On the other hand, that of 10 which there is no part outside is complete or a whole; for this is how we define a whose, namely, that from which no part is absent, as in the case of a whole man or a whole box. And as in the case of each individual, so it is when the term whole" is considered in the main sense, that is, the whole is the outside of which no part exists; but, in every case, that from which there is a part absent (whatever that part may be) is not a whole. The whole and the complete are either entirely the same or 15 quite close in their nature. Nothing is complete which has no end, and the end is a limit.

7. . . . Our account, which rejects the infi-207b nite as existing in *actuality* and as being untraversible in the direction of increase, does not 30 deprive the mathematicians from investigating their objects; for neither do they need it nor do they use it in this way, but only in the way in which, for example, they extend a finite line as far as they wish, and any magnitude may be divided in the same ratio as that in which the greatest magnitude may. Thus, as far as proofs are concerned, an infinite of this sort makes no difference, but as for the existence of an infinite, it is in existing magnitudes.

35 As there are four senses of "cause", it is evi-
208a dent that the infinite is a cause as matter and that
its being is a privation, and the subject in virtue
of which it exists is that which is continuous and
sensible. All the other thinkers who use the infinite appear likewise to use it as matter; and for
this reason, too, it is absurd that they should
posit it as containing and not as being contained.

BOOK VIII

256a **5.** Now this may take place in two ways: Either
5 it is not through itself that the mover moves [the
object] but through some other thing by which
the mover is moved, or it moves the object
through itself; and it [the mover] moves either by
being next to the last [object moved] or through
a number of [intermediate] things, as in the case
of a stick which moves the stone but is moved by
the hand, which is itself moved by the man, who
is not moved by anything else. Now we say that
10 both the last mover and the first mover cause
motion, but that the first does so to a higher
degree; for the first moves the last but the last
does not move the first, and without the first the
last will not cause motion but without the last
the first may do so, as in the case of the stick,
which will not move the object unless the man
causes it to do so. So if in every case a thing in
motion must be moved by a second thing, which
15 either is moved by a third or is not, and if by a
third then there must be a first mover which is
not moved by anything else, while if not by a
third then the second itself is such [a first mover]
and no other mover is necessary (for it is impossible that a mover which is itself moved by another
proceed to infinity since in this infinity there will
be no first mover); if, to repeat, every thing in
20 motion is moved by another thing and the first
mover is also moved but not by another thing,
then the first mover must be moved by itself.

We may arrive at this very same conclusion
also in another way. Every mover moves something, and it moves it with something [as with
an instrument], either with itself or with something else; e.g., a man moves something either
with himself or with a stick, and the wind has
25 knocked down something either with itself or

with a stone which it dislodged. Now it is impossible for a mover to cause a motion [in an object]
unless it causes a motion with itself as with an
instrument; but if it is with itself that a mover
moves [the object], then no other thing is necessary with which to move [that object], whereas if
it is with something else that the mover moves
[that object], then there will be a [first] thing
which it moves not with something else but with
itself, or else there will be an infinite series.
Accordingly, if a thing causes something to be in
motion, the series must stop and not proceed to
30 infinity; for if a stick causes a motion by being
itself moved by the hand, it is the hand that
moves the stick, and if it is something else that
moves this [i.e., the hand], then some other thing
is the mover of this. Thus, whenever that which
causes a motion with something, say A, is something else, say B, there must be a prior mover
which causes a motion with itself. Accordingly, if
256b this [prior mover] is in motion but there is no
other mover which moves it, then it must move
itself. So, according to this argument, too, either
a thing in motion is moved directly by a thing
that moves itself, or it is so moved that through
intermediate steps we come to such a mover. . . .

258b From what has been said, then, it is evident
5 that the first mover is motionless; for (a) whether
the thing which is in motion but is moved by
something leads immediately to that which is
first and motionless or (b) whether it leads to a
thing which moves itself and stops itself, in both
cases the result is that in all things which are in
motion the first mover is motionless.

10 **6.** Since motion must always exist without
interruption, there exists necessarily something
first which causes motion, and this may be one or
many; and a first mover must be immovable. The
problem of whether each immovable mover is
eternal is not relevant to the present argument;
but the fact that there must exist something
15 which is immovable and exempt from all external change, both unqualified and accidental, and
which can move another, is clear from the following considerations.

If one wishes, let it be possible for some
things to exist sometime and then not to exist,

but without being in the process of generation or destruction; for, if any thing without parts exists at one time and does not exist at another, perhaps it is necessary for it to be at one time and
20 not at another without being in the process of changing. And let also this be possible, namely, that some principles which are immovable but can cause motion be now existing and now not existing. Still, not all of them [i.e., the principles] can be so; for clearly there is something that causes things which move themselves to be at one time and not to be at another. For although
25 every thing that moves itself must have a magnitude, that is, if no thing without parts can be moved, still from what has been said this is not necessary for a mover.

Now no one of the things which are immovable but not always existing can be the cause of [all] the things that are continuously being generated and destroyed, nor yet can any of those which always move certain things while others [always] move others. For neither each of them nor all of them can be the cause of a process which
30 exists always and is continuous, for that process is eternal and exists of necessity whereas all those [movers] are infinite and do not exist at the same time. So it is clear that, even if (a) countless
259a times some principle which are immovable movers and man of those which move themselves are being destroyed while others are coming into being and (b) one immovable mover moves one thing while another moves another, nevertheless, there is something which contains and exists apart from each of some of them and the nonexistence of them and which is the cause of the existence of the others and also of the continuous
5 change; and this is a cause of these [movers], while these are the causes of the motion in other things. So if motion is indeed eternal, the primary mover too will be eternal, if it is just one; but if there are many [primary movers], there will be many eternal [movers]. We should regard them to be one rather than many, or finite rather than
10 infinite; for if the consequences are the same, we should always posit a finite number [of causes], since in things existing by nature what is finite and better should exist to a higher degree, if this is possible. It is sufficient even if it [i.e., the mover]

is just one, which, being first among the immovable [movers] and also eternal, would be the principle of motion in all the rest.

It is evident also from the following that
15 there must be some one mover which is eternal. Now we have shown that there must always be a motion, and if always, it must also be continuous; for also that which exists always may also be continuous, but what is in succession is not [necessarily] continuous. Further, if [a motion is] continuous, it is one. And it is one if both the mover is one and the thing in motion is one; for if now one thing causes it to move and now another,
20 the whole motion will be not continuous but in succession.

One might be led to the belief that there exists a first immovable mover, both from the arguments just given and by attending to the principles of movers. Evidently there are some things which are sometimes moved but sometimes at rest, and because of this it was made clear that neither all things are moved or all are
25 at rest, nor that some of them are always at rest and the others are always moved; for this is shown by those things which have the double potentiality of being sometimes moved and sometimes at rest. So since such things are clear to all and since we also wish to show the nature of each of the other two (namely, that there are things which are always immovable and
30 also others which are always in motion), having proceeded in this direction and posited that (a) every thing in motion is moved by something which is either immovable or in motion and (b) a thing in motion is always moved either by itself or by another, we arrived at the position that of things in motion there is a first;
259b and this is (a) a self-mover if [only] things in motion are considered but (b) immovable if all are considered. And evidently we do observe such things which move themselves, for example, living things or the genus of animals. Indeed, these [e.g., animals] even helped create the opinion that in a thing a motion which did not
5 exist at all [before] may arise, because we observe this happening in them; for it seems that at one time they are without motion but later they are moved.

This must be granted, then, that such things do cause in themselves one [kind of] motion, but that they do not cause it independently; for the cause is not from them, but there are other natural motions which animals have but not through 10 themselves, such as increase, decrease, and respiration, and each animal has these motions while it is at rest and is not being moved by itself. The cause of these [motions] is the surrounding objects [e.g., air] and many things which enter the animal, such as food in some [motions]; for while this is being digested, it sleeps, and when the food is distributed, the animal wakes up and moves itself, but the first source [of these motions] 15 comes from the outside. On account of this, animals are not moved by themselves continuously; for what causes the motion is something else, which is itself in motion and is changing in relation to each thing that can move itself.

Now in all these the first mover and the cause of that which moves itself is [also] moved by itself, but accidentally, for it is the body that 20 changes its place; and so what is in the body also moves itself as if by a lever. From these arguments one may be convinced that if there is an immovable mover that is itself in motion but accidentally, then that mover cannot cause a continuous motion. So if indeed a motion must exist continuously, then there should be some first mover 25 which cannot be moved even accidentally, if, as we have said, there is to be in things an unceasing and everlasting motion and if being itself is to *rest* [always] in itself and be in the same [state]; for if the principle stays [always] the same, then the whole too must stay the same and be continuous in its relation to the principle. Now to be moved accidentally by itself is not the same as to be 30 moved accidentally by another; for to be moved by another belongs also to some principles in the

heavens, those which have many locomotions, whereas the former belongs only to destructible things. Further, if there is something which is eternally of this kind, causing something to be 260a moved but being itself immovable and eternal, then the first thing that is moved by it must also be eternal. This is clear also from the fact that there would otherwise be no generation or destruction or change in the other things unless there were something which would cause motion while being in motion. For the immovable [mover] will always cause one and the same 5 motion and in the same manner inasmuch as it itself in no way changes in relation to the thing moved; and as for that which is moved by something whose motion is directly caused by the immovable [mover], because of the fact that it is related to things [which it moves] now in one way and now in another, it is a cause but not of the same motion. And so, because of the fact that it is in contrary places or forms [at different 10 times], it imparts motion to each thing in contrary ways and so makes it be [for example] now at rest and now in motion. From what has been said, then, the problem which was first raised—why it is that not all things are in motion or at rest or why some are not always in motion and the others not always at rest, but some of them are now in motion and now at rest—has now 15 become evident, for the cause of it is now clear: It is the fact that some things are moved by an eternal immovable mover, and so they are always changing; others are moved by an object in motion, which [object] is changing, and so they too much change; and as for the immovable [mover], as already stated, inasmuch as it remains [always] simple and in the same manner and in the same [state], it causes [always] one and a simple motion.

STUDY QUESTIONS: ARISTOTLE, *PHYSICS*

1. How is understanding attained? What is the method we should follow to understand nature?
2. What does Aristotle say that we should take for granted? Why is this reasonable?
3. Why does Aristotle ask, 'In what sense [according to some pre-Socratics] are all things one'? Why is this a significant point?

4. What does it mean to assert that the contraries are principles? How does this relate to change?

5. How does Aristotle distinguish between the simple and the complex at I.7?

6. What comes to be without qualification? What is the main point that Aristotle makes about such coming to be?

7. How does Aristotle identify the aspect or part of a change that survives or remains the same underlying the change?

8. For what purposes does Aristotle analyze change?

9. How does Aristotle distinguish between form and matter in I.7?

10. What is the main conclusion that Aristotle draws from his review of pre-Socratic philosophy?

11. For what purpose does Aristotle make the point that a doctor builds a house but not qua doctor?

12. In how many ways does Aristotle characterize nature?

13. What is the significance of the difference between natural objects and artifacts? How does Aristotle distinguish between them?

14. How does Aristotle characterize mathematics? How is the mathematician different from the physicist?

15. Explain how Aristotle enumerates the different uses of the word 'cause.' What are the different kinds of causation or explanation, according to Aristotle?

16. What role can purposes play in explanation, according to Aristotle? What are the examples of changes in natural objects that need to be explained in terms of ends (Book II, Chapter 8)?

17. At III.1, Aristotle says, 'No motion exists apart from things.' What does this mean?

18. What does Aristotle mean by 'qua'? How does this relate to his definition of motion in terms of fulfillment of potential?

19. What are the five considerations that give rise to the belief in the infinite?

20. What is Aristotle's dialectical argument for the claim that the infinite cannot be an actual thing?

21. Aristotle says that the infinite must exist in some way. Why? How does Aristotle reconcile this with the claim that the infinite is not an actual thing?

22. How is his account of the infinite compatible with mathematics?

23. What is Aristotle's argument for an unmoved mover? How does Aristotle argue for the claim that there must be an eternal first unmoved mover?

METAPHYSICS

The aim of metaphysics is to acquire knowledge that deserves to be called wisdom. It is the study of the most universal and primary of all causes, or 'first principles.' Aristotle's *Metaphysics* is a compilation of shorter pieces written at different times; it has 14 different books, of which we have selected parts of the following:

1. *Book I, or A (Alpha), which introduces the science of metaphysics by arguing against the view of the Pre-Socratics and Plato*

2. *Book IV, or Γ (Gamma), which explains metaphysics as the study of being qua being and shows how the principle of noncontradiction is an assumption of meaning itself*

3. *Book V, or* Δ *(Delta), which is a lexicon of philosophical terms*
4. *Book VI, or* E *(Epsilon), which contains a description of the task of a metaphysics*
5. *Book VII, or* Z *(Zeta), an outline of the relation of substance to the form/matter distinction*
6. *Book VIII, or* H *(Eta), which contains concluding remarks on the nature of substance*
7. *Book XII, or* Λ *(Lambda), concerning the idea of the unmoved mover*

Aristotle defines 'substance' as the primary existent. The existence of other things is dependent on that of substance. The mistake of the pre-Socratics is to think of matter, or the stuff out of which things are composed, as substance. Plato's mistake was to think of the universal Forms as substances. Both of these are dependent existences, and hence not substance.

In Book V (Delta), Aristotle defines 'substance' as a 'this so-and-so,' which is also separable. The phrase 'this so-and-so' or a 'this something' (a *tode ti*) means that a substance is a particular: it is a 'this.' It is also a 'so-and-so,' because the individual thing has general characteristics, which define what it is.

Our brief introductory comments shall be focused on Book VII, which is the central and most difficult part of the *Metaphysics*. Book VII outlines how the fundamental questions of metaphysics require an understanding of the concept of substance because substances are primary. The pursuit of reality becomes the search for substance. So, metaphysics must show us what kinds of things are substances. In Chapter 3 of VII, Aristotle lists three general candidates for the title 'substance': substratum, essence, and universals. (He also mentions genus, but this is treated under universals.)

In Chapter 3 of Book VII, Aristotle also examines the definition of substance as an ultimate subject or pure substratum, something that in itself has no characteristics but that supports all properties. He argues that this substratum is not substance because substratum is not a particular, a 'this,' whereas substance is. Furthermore, substratum does not have an independent existence. Pure substratum cannot exist independently of the things that are putatively made out of it, and, therefore, it is not a substance.

In Chapters 4–6, Aristotle turns to essence as a general candidate for the title 'substance.' Essence is what a thing is in virtue of being itself. By specifying essence, we identify what the subject really is. Aristotle argues that only substances really have essences; all other things have essence in a secondary way. Furthermore, to have an essence, a thing must be strictly definable. Only species meet this criterion of being strictly definable. Therefore, Aristotle concludes that only species have essence and the only substances are species. For example, the species human has a real essence. In contrast, a tailor does not have to be a tailor. A tailor is only a person who happens to make clothes. He could change his occupation without ceasing to be. Being a tailor is not part of a person's essence. Consequently, tailors and philosophers are not substances. Human beings and other species are.

In Chapter 6 of Book VII, Aristotle claims that things are identical with their essence. This seems to indicate that particular individual things in the natural world can have essences. For example, 'Socrates is human' makes an essential attribution to the individual, Socrates. This is part of his essence. This point constitutes a radical difference between the philosophies of Plato and Aristotle. For Plato, essences belong to the separate world of Forms, whereas for Aristotle, essences are in the natural world, and consequently, understanding must be directed toward this world and not to a separate realm of Forms.

Chapter 13 of Book VII argues that universals should not be considered as substances. Having rejected universals as a candidate for substance, Aristotle can also reject genus, since the genus of a thing is a type of universal. (If human is the species, then the relevant genus is animal.)

There are many interpretations of Aristotle's notion of substance. Tentatively, the most generally accepted one is that primary substances are individuals or particulars, but only insofar as they are members of natural kinds. Substances must be a 'this so-and-so.' The 'this' indicates that they be individuals, and the 'so-and-so' specifies that they be natural kinds or species. In other words, we identify a particular individual as a primary substance if and only if we refer to it as a natural kind or species.

Book XII, or Λ (Lambda), seems to argue for a view of metaphysics quite different from the rest of the treatise. It defines a science of theology, a study of God. The unmoved mover must be an eternal and unchanging substance, whose essence is actuality. It consists of pure activity, without any power or potentiality. The activity in question could not be physical and must be purely spiritual activity, because all material things are changeable. The activity must be pure thought or contemplation.

BOOK I

1. All men by nature desire to know. An indication of this is the delight we take in our senses; for even apart from their usefulness they are loved for themselves; and above all others the sense of sight. For not only with a view to action, but even when we are not going to do anything, 980ᵃ25 we prefer sight to almost everything else. The reason is that this, most of all the senses, makes us know and brings to light many differences between things.

By nature animals are born with the faculty of sensation, and from sensation memory is produced in some of them, though not in others. And therefore the former are more intelligent and apt at learning than those which cannot remember; those which are incapable of hearing sounds are intelligent though they cannot be taught, e.g. the bee, and any other race of animals that may be like it; and those which besides memory 980ᵇ25 have this sense of hearing, can be taught.

The animals other than man live by appearances and memories, and have but little of connected experience; but the human race lives also by art and reasonings. And from memory experience is produced in men; for many memories of the same thing produce finally the capacity for a 981ᵃ1 single experience. Experience seems to be very similar to science and art, but really science and art come to men *through* experience; for 'experience made art', as Polus says, 'but inexperience

luck'. And art arises, when from many notions gained by experience one universal judgement about similar objects is produced. For to have a judgment that when Callias was ill of this disease this did him good, and similarly in the case of Socrates and in many individual cases, is a matter of experience; but to judge that it has done 10 good to all persons of a certain constitution, marked off in one class, when they were ill of this disease, e.g. to phlegmatic or bilious people when burning with fever,—this is a matter of art.

With a view to action experience seems in no respect inferior to art, and we even see men of experience succeeding more than those who have theory without experience. The reason is that experience is knowledge of individuals, art 15 of universals, and actions and productions are all concerned with the individual; for the physician does not cure a man, except in an incidental way, but Callias or Socrates or some other called by 20 some such individual name, who happens to be a man. If, then, a man has theory without experience, and knows the universal but does not know the individual included in this, he will often fail to cure; for it is the individual that is to be cured. But yet we think that *knowledge* and *understanding* belong to art rather than to experience, 25 and we suppose artists to be wiser than men of experience (which implies that wisdom depends in all cases rather on knowledge); and this because the former know the cause, but the latter do not. For men of experience know that the thing is so, but do not know why, while the others know the 'why' and the cause. Hence we think that the master-workers in each craft are 30 more honourable and know in a truer sense and are wiser than the manual workers, because they know the causes of the things that are done (we 981ᵇ1 think the manual workers are like certain lifeless things which act indeed, but act without knowing what they do, as fire burns,—but while the lifeless things perform each of their functions by a natural tendency, the labourers perform them through habit); thus we view them as being wiser not in virtue of being able to act, but of hav-5 ing the theory for themselves and knowing the causes. And in general it is a sign of the man who knows, that he can teach, and therefore we think art more truly knowledge than experience is; for artists can teach, and men of mere experience cannot.

10 Again, we do not regard any of the senses as wisdom; yet surely these give the most authoritative knowledge of particulars. But they do not tell us the 'why' of anything—e.g., why fire is hot; they only say that it is hot.

At first he who invented any art that went beyond the common perceptions of man was naturally admired by men, not only because there 15 was something useful in the inventions, but because he was thought wise and superior to the rest. But as more arts were invented, and some were directed to the necessities of life, others to its recreation, the inventors of the latter were always regarded as wiser than the inventors of the former, because their branches of knowledge 20 did not aim at utility. Hence when all such inventions were already established, the sciences which do not aim at giving pleasure or at the necessities of life were discovered, and first in the places where men first began to have leisure. This is why the mathematical arts were founded in Egypt; for there the priestly caste was allowed to be at leisure.

We have said in the *Ethics* what the differ-25 ence is between art and science and the other kindred faculties; but the point of our present discussion is this, that all men suppose what is called wisdom to deal with the first causes and the principles of things. This is why, as has been said 30 before, the man of experience is thought to be wiser than the possessors of any perception whatever, the artist wiser than the men of experience, the master-worker than the mechanic, and the theoretical kinds of knowledge to be more of the nature of wisdom than the productive. Clearly 982ᵃ1 then wisdom is knowledge about certain causes and principles.

2. Since we are seeking this knowledge, we must inquire of what kind are the causes and the principles, the knowledge of which is wisdom. If 5 we were to take the notions we have about the wise man, this might perhaps make the answer more evident. We suppose first, then, that the wise man knows all things, as far as possible, although he has not knowledge of each of them individually; secondly, that he who can learn things that are difficult, and not easy for man to 10 know, is wise (sense-perception is common to all, and therefore easy and no mark of wisdom); again, he who is more exact and more capable of teaching the causes is wiser, in every branch of knowledge; and of the sciences, also, that which is desirable on its own account and for the sake 15 of knowing it is more of the nature of wisdom than that which is desirable on account of its results, and the superior science is more of the nature of wisdom than the ancillary; for the wise man must not be ordered but must order, and he must not obey another, but the less wise must obey *him*.

20 Such and so many are the notions, then, which we have about wisdom and the wise. Now of these characteristics that of knowing all things must belong to him who has in the highest degree universal knowledge; for he knows in a sense all the subordinate objects. And these things, the most universal, are on the whole the hardest for men to know; for they are furthest 25 from the senses. And the most exact of the sciences are those which deal most with first principles; for those which involve fewer principles are more exact than those which involve additional principles, e.g. arithmetic than geometry. But the

science which investigates causes is also more capable of reaching, for the people who teach are those who tell the causes of each thing. And understanding and knowledge pursued for their 30 own sake are found most in the knowledge of that which is most knowable; for he who chooses to know for the sake of knowing will choose most readily that which is most truly knowledge, and such is the knowledge of that which is most 982ᵇ1 knowable; and the first principles and the causes are most knowable; for by reason of these, and from these, all other things are known, but these are not known by means of the things subordinate to them. And the science which knows to 5 what end each thing must be done is the most authoritative of the sciences, and more authoritative than any ancillary science; and this end is the good in each class, and in general the supreme good in the whole of nature. Judged by all the tests we have mentioned, then, the name in question falls to the same science; this must be a science that investigates the first principles and causes; for the good, i.e. that for the sake of 10 which, is one of the causes.

That it is not a science of production is clear even from the history of the earliest philosophers. For it is owing to their wonder that men both now begin and at first began to philosophize; they wondered originally at the obvious difficulties, then advanced little by little and 15 stated difficulties about the greater matters, e.g. about the phenomena of the moon and those of the sun and the stars, and about the genesis of the universe. And a man who is puzzled and wonders thinks himself ignorant (whence even the lover of myth is in a sense a lover of wisdom, for myth is composed of wonders); therefore 20 since they philosophized in order to escape from ignorance, evidently they were pursuing science in order to know, and not for any utilitarian end. And this is confirmed by the facts; for it was when almost all the necessities of life and the things that make for comfort and recreation were present, that such knowledge began to be sought. 25 Evidently then we do not seek it for the sake of any other advantage; but as the man is free, we say, who exists for himself and not for another, so

we pursue this as the only free science, for it alone exists for itself.

Hence the possession of it might be justly regarded as beyond human power: for in many ways human nature is in bondage, so that accord- 30 ing to Simonides 'God alone can have this privilege', and it is unfitting that man should not be content to seek the knowledge that is suited to him. If, then, there is something in what the poets say, and jealousy is natural to the divine 983ᵃ1 power, it would probably occur in this case above all, and all who excelled in this knowledge would be unfortunate. But the divine power cannot be jealous (indeed, according to the proverb, 'bards tell many a lie'), nor should any science be thought more honourable than one of this sort. For the most divine science is also most 5 honourable; and this science alone is, in two ways, most divine. For the science which it would be most meet for God to have is a divine science, and so is any science that deals with divine objects; and this science alone has both these qualities; for God is thought to be among the causes of all things and to be a first principle, and such a science either God alone can have, or God above all others. All the sciences, 10 indeed, are more necessary than this, but none is better.

Yet the acquisition of it must in a sense end in something which is the opposite of our original inquiries. For all men begin, as we said, by wondering that the matter is so (as in the case of automatic marionettes or the solstices or the 15 incommensurability of the diagonal of a square with the side; for it seem wonderful to all men who have not yet perceived the explanation that there is a thing which cannot be measured even by the smallest unit). But we must end in the contrary and, according to the proverb, the better state, as is the case in these instances when men learn the cause; for there is nothing which 20 would surprise a geometer so much as if the diagonal turned out to be commensurable.

We have stated, then, what is the nature of the science we are searching for, and what is the mark which our search and our whole investigation must reach.

3. Evidently we have to acquire knowledge 983ᵃ of the original causes (for we say we know each thing only when we think we recognize its first 25 cause), and causes are spoken of in four senses. In one of these we mean the substance, i.e. the essence (for the 'why' is referred finally to the formula, and the ultimate 'why' is a cause and principle); in another the matter or substratum, in a 30 third the source of the change, and in a fourth the cause opposed to this, that for the sake of which and the good (for this is the end of all generation and change). We have studied these causes sufficiently in our work on nature, but yet 983ᵇ1 let us call to our aid those who have attacked the investigation of being and philosophized about reality before us. For obviously they too speak of certain principles and causes; to go over their views, then, will be of profit to the present inquiry, for we shall either find another kind of cause, or be more convinced of the correctness of 5 those which we now maintain.

Of the first philosophers, most thought the principles which were of the nature of matter were the only principles of all things; that of which all things that are consist, and from which they first come to be, and into which they are finally resolved (the substance remaining, but 10 changing in its modifications), this they say is the element and the principle of things, and therefore they think nothing is either generated or destroyed, since this sort of entity is always conserved, as we say Socrates neither comes to be absolutely when he comes to be beautiful or musical, nor ceases to be when he loses these 15 characteristics, because the substratum, Socrates himself, remains. So they say nothing else comes to be or ceases to be; for there must be some entity—either one or more than one—from which all other things come to be, it being conserved. . . .

Yet they do not all agree as to the number and the nature of these principles. Thales, the founder of this school of philosophy, says the 20 principle is water.

984ᵃ Anaximenes and Diogenes make air prior to 5 water, and the most primary of the simple bodies, while Hippasus of Metapontium and Heraclitus of Ephesus say this of fire, and Empedocles says it of the four elements, adding a fourth—earth—to those which have been named. . . .

From these facts one might think that the only cause is the so-called material cause; but as men thus advanced, the very facts showed them the way and joined in forcing them to investigate the subject. However true it may be that all generation and destruction proceed from some one 20 or more elements, why does this happen and what is the cause? For at least the substratum itself does not make itself change; e.g. neither the wood nor the bronze causes the change of either of them, nor does the wood manufacture a bed and the bronze a statue, but something else is 25 the cause of the change. And to seek this is to seek the second cause, as *we* should say,—that from which comes the beginning of movement. Now those who at the very beginning set themselves to this kind of inquiry, and said the substratum was one, were not at all dissatisfied with themselves; but some at least of those who maintain it to be one—as though defeated by this 30 search for the second cause—say the one and nature as a whole is unchangeable not only in respect of generation and destruction (for this is an ancient belief, and all agreed in it), but also of 984ᵇ1 all other change; and this view is peculiar to them. . . .

When these men and the principles of this kind had had their day, as the latter were found inadequate to generate the nature of things, men were again forced by the truth itself, as we said, to inquire into the next kind of cause. For surely 10 it is not likely either that fire or earth or any such element should be the reason why things manifest goodness and beauty both in their being and in their coming to be, or that those thinkers should have supposed it was. . . .

985a **4.** [I]f we were to follow out the view of Empedocles, and interpret it according to its meaning and not to its lisping expression, we should find that friendship is the cause of good

things, and strife of bad. Therefore, if we said
5 that Empedocles in a sense both mentions, and is
the first to mention, the bad and the good as
principles, we should perhaps be right, since the
10 cause of all goods is the good itself.

These thinkers, as we say, evidently got hold
up to a certain point of two of the causes which
we distinguished in our work on nature—the
matter and the source of the movement,—
vaguely, however, and with no clearness, but as
untrained men behave in fights; for they go round
15 their opponents and often strike fine blows, but
they do not fight on scientific principles, and so
these thinkers do not seem to know what they
say; for it is evident that, as a rule, they make no
use of their causes except to a small extent. For
Anaxagoras uses reason as a *deus ex machina* for
the making of the world, and when he is at a loss
to tell for what cause something necessarily is,
20 then he drags reason in, but in all other cases
ascribes events to anything rather than to reason.
And Empedocles, though he uses the causes to a
greater extent than this, neither does so sufficiently nor attains consistency in their use. At
least, in many cases he makes friendship segregate
things, and strife aggregate them. For when the
25 universe is dissolved into its elements by strife,
fire is aggregated into one, and so is each of the
other elements; but when again under the influence of friendship they come together into one,
the parts must again be segregated out of each
element.

Regarding the two causes, then, as we say,
985ᵃ1 the inquiry seems to have been pushed thus far
by the early philosophers.

6. After the systems we have named came
the philosophy of Plato, which in most respects
followed these thinkers, but had peculiarities
30 that distinguished it from the philosophy of the
Italians. For, having in his youth first become
familiar with Cratylus and with the Heraclitean
doctrines (that all sensible things are ever in a
state of flux and there is no knowledge about
them), these views he held even in later years.
Socrates, however, was busying himself about

987ᵃ1 ethical matters and neglecting the world of
nature as a whole but seeking the universal in
these ethical matters, and fixed thought for the
first time on definitions; Plato accepted his teaching, but held that the problem applied not to any
5 sensible thing but to entities of another kind—
for this reason, that the common definition could
not be a definition of any sensible thing, as they
were always changing. Things of this other sort,
then, he called Ideas, and sensible things, he
said, were apart from these, and were all called
after these; for the multitude of things which
have the same name as the Form exist by participation in it. Only the name 'participation' was
10 new; for the Pythagoreans say that things exist by
imitation of numbers, and Plato says they exist
by participation, changing the name. But what
the participation or the imitation of the Forms
could be they left an open question.

Further, besides sensible things and Forms he
says there are the objects of mathematics, which
occupy an intermediate position, differing from
15 sensible things in being eternal and unchangeable, from Forms in that there are many alike,
while the Form itself is in each case unique.

Since the Forms are the causes of all other
things, he thought their elements were the elements of all things. As matter, the great and the
20 small were principles; as substance, the One; for
from the great and the small, by participation in
the One, come the numbers.

But he agreed with the Pythagoreans in saying that the One is substance and not a predicate
of something else; and in saying that the numbers
are the causes of the substance of other things, he
25 also agreed with them; but positing a dyad and
constructing the infinite out of great and small,
instead of treating the infinite as one, is peculiar
to him; and so is his view that the numbers exist
apart from sensible things, while *they* say that the
things themselves are numbers, and do not place
the objects of mathematics between Forms and
sensible things. His divergence from the Pythagoreans in making the One and the numbers sepa-
30 rate from things, and his introduction of the
Forms, were due to his inquiries in the region of
definitory formulae (for the earlier thinkers had

no tincture of dialectic), and his making the other entity besides the One a dyad was due to the belief that the numbers, except those which were prime, could be neatly produced out of the dyad as out of a plastic material.

988ᵃ1 Yet what happens is the contrary; the theory is not a reasonable one. For they make many things out of the matter, and the form generates only once, but what we observe is that one table is made from one matter, while the man who applies the form, though he is one, makes many tables. 5 And the relation of the male to the female is similar; for the latter is impregnated by one copulation, but the male impregnates many females; yet these are imitations of those first principles.

Plato, then, declared himself thus on the points in question; it is evident from what has been said that he has used only two causes, that of the essence and the material cause (for the Forms are the cause of the essence of all other 10 things, and the One is the cause of the essence of the Forms); and it is evident what the underlying matter is, of which the Forms are predicated in the case of sensible things, and the One in the case of Forms, viz. that this is a dyad, the great and the small. Further, he has assigned the cause of good and that of evil to the elements, one to each of the two, as we say some of his 15 predecessors sought to do, e.g. Empedocles and Anaxagoras.

9. Let us leave the Pythagoreans for the present; for it is enough to have touched on them as much as we have done. But as for those who posit the Ideas as causes, firstly, in seeking 990ᵃ1 to grasp the causes of the things around us, they introduced others equal in number to these, as if a man who wanted to count things thought he could not do it while they were few, but tried to count them when he had added to their number. For the Forms are practically equal to or not fewer than the things, in trying to explain which these thinkers proceeded from them to 5 the Forms: For to each set of substances answers a Form which has the same name and exists apart from the substances, and so also in the case of all other groups in which there is one character common to many things, whether the things are in this changeable world or are eternal.

Further, of the ways in which we prove that the Forms exist, none is convincing; for from some no inference necessarily follows, and from 10 some it follows that there are Forms of things of which we think there are no Forms.

For according to the arguments from the existence of the sciences there will be Forms of all things of which there are sciences, and according to the argument that there is one attribute common to many things there will be Forms even of negations, and according to the argument that there is an object for thought even when the thing has perished, there will be Forms of perishable things; for we can have an image of these. 15 Further, of the more accurate arguments, some lead to Ideas of relations, of which we say there is no independent class, and others involve the difficulty of the 'third man'.

And in general the arguments for the Forms destroy the things for whose existence we are more anxious than for the existence of the Ideas; for it follows that not the dyad but number is first, 20 i.e. that the relative is prior to the absolute— besides all the other points on which certain people by following out the opinions held about the Ideas have come into conflict with the principles of the theory.

Further, according to the assumption on which our belief in the Ideas rests, there will be Forms not only of substances but also of many other things (for the concept is single not only in the case of substances but also in the other 25 cases, and there are sciences not only of substance but also of other things, and a thousand other such conclusions also follow). But according to the necessities of the case and the opinions held about the Forms, if they can be shared there must be Ideas of substances only. For they are not shared incidentally, but a thing must 30 share in its Form as in something not predicated of a subject (e.g. if a thing shares in double itself, it shares also in eternal, but incidentally; for eternal happens to be predicable of the double). Therefore the Forms will be substance; and the same terms indicate substance in this and in the ideal world (or what will be the meaning of 991ᵃ1 saying that there is something apart from the particulars—the one over many?). And if the Ideas and the particulars that share them have the same Form, there will be something common to these; for why should 2 be one and the same in the perishable 2's or in those which are many but eternal, and not the same in the 2 itself as in 5 the particular 2? But if they have not the same Form, they must have only the name in common, and it is as if one were to call both Callias and a wooden image a man, without observing any community between them.

Above all one might discuss the question what on earth the Forms contribute to sensible things, either to those that are eternal or to those 10 that come into being and cease to be. For they cause neither movement nor any change in them. But again they help in no way towards the *knowledge* of the other things (for they are not even the substance of these, else they would have been in them), nor towards their being, if they are not *in* the particulars which share in them; though if they were, they might be thought to be causes, 15 as white causes whiteness in that with which it is mixed. But this argument, which first Anaxagoras and later Eudoxus and certain others used, is too easily upset; for it is not difficult to collect many insuperable objections to such a view.

But further all other things cannot come 20 from the Forms in any of the usual senses of 'from'. And to say that they are patterns and the other things share them is to use empty words and poetical metaphors. For what is it that works, looking to the Ideas? Anything can either be, or become, like another without being copied from it, so that whether Socrates exists or not a man 25 might come to be like Socrates; and evidently this might be so even if Socrates were eternal. And there will be several patterns of the same thing, and therefore several Forms, e.g. animal and two-footed and also man himself will be Forms of man. Again, the Forms are patterns not only of sensible things, but of themselves too, e.g. 30 the Form of genus will be a genus of Forms; therefore the same thing will be pattern and copy.

Again it must be held to be impossible that 991ᵇ1 the substance and that of which it is the substance should exist apart; how, therefore, can the Ideas, being the substances of things, exist apart?

In the *Phaedo* the case is stated in this way— that the Forms are causes both of being and of becoming; yet when the Forms exist, still the things that share in them do not come into being, unless there is some efficient cause; and many 5 other things come into being (e.g. a house or a ring), of which we say there are no Forms. Clearly, therefore, even the other things can both be and come into being owing to such causes as produce the things just mentioned.

10   **10.** It is evident, then, even from what we have said before, that all men seem to seek the causes named in the *Physics*, and that we cannot name any beyond these; but they seek these vaguely; and though in a sense they have all been described before, in a sense they have not been 15 described at all. For the earliest philosophy is, on all subjects, like one who lisps, since in its beginnings it is but a child.

BOOK IV

1. There is a science which investigates being as being and the attributes which belong to this in virtue of its own nature. Now this is not the same as any of the so-called special sciences; for none of these others deals generally with being as being. They cut off a part of being and investi- 25 gate the attributes of this part—this is what the mathematical sciences for instance do. Now since we are seeking the first principles and the highest causes, clearly there must be some thing to which these belong in virtue of its own nature. If then our predecessors who sought the elements of existing things were seeking these same principles, it is necessary that the elements must be elements of being not by accident but just 30 because it *is* being. Therefore it is of being as being that we also must grasp the first causes.

2. There are many senses in which a thing may be said to 'be', but they are related to one central point, one definite kind of thing, and are not homonymous. Everything which is healthy is related to health, one thing in the sense that it preserves health, another in the sense that it produces it, another in the sense that it is a symptom of health, another because it is capable of it. And that which is medical is relative to the medical 1003ᵇ1 art, one thing in the sense that it possesses it, another in the sense that it is naturally adapted to it, another in the sense that it is a function of the medical art. And we shall find other words used similarly to these. So, too, there are many senses in which a thing is said to be, but all refer 5 to one starting-point; some things are said to be because they are substances, others because they are affections of substance, others because they are a process towards substance, or destructions or privations or qualities of substance, or productive or generative of substance, or of things which are relative to substance, or negations of some of these things or of substance itself. It is for 10 this reason that we say even of non-being that it *is* non-being. As, then, there is one science which deals with all healthy things, the same applies in the other cases also. For not only in the case of things which have one common notion does the investigation belong to one science, but also in the case of things which are related to one common nature; for even these in a sense have one common notion. It is clear then 15 that it is the work of one science also to study all things that are, *qua* being.—But everywhere science deals chiefly with that which is primary, and on which the other things depend, and in virtue of which they get their names. If, then, this is substance, it is of substances that the philosopher must grasp the principles and the causes.

Now for every single class of things, as there is one perception, so there is one science, as for instance grammar, being one science, investi-20 gates all articulate sounds. Therefore to investigate all the species of being *qua* being, is the work of a science which is generically one, and to investigate the several species is the work of the specific parts of the science.

If, now, being and unity are the same and are one thing in the sense that they are implied in one another as principle and cause are, not in the sense that they are explained by the same formula (though it makes no difference even if we 25 interpret them similarly—in fact this would strengthen our case); for one man and a man are the same thing and existent man and a man are the same thing, and the doubling of the words in 'one man' and 'one existent man' does not give any new meaning (it is clear that they are not separated either in coming to be or in ceasing to be); and similarly with 'one', so that it is obvious 30 that the addition in these cases means the same thing, and unity is nothing apart from being; and if, further, the essence of each thing is one in no merely accidental way, and similarly is from its very nature something that *is*:—all this being so, there must be exactly as many species of being as of unity. And to investigate the essence of these is the work of a science which is generically one—I mean, for instance, the discussion of the 35 same and the similar and the other concepts of this sort; and nearly all contraries are referred to this source; but let us take them as having been 1004ᵃ1 investigated in the 'Selection of Contraries'.— And there are as many parts of philosophy as there are kinds of substance, so that there must necessarily be among them a first philosophy and one which follows this. For being falls immedi-5 ately into genera; and therefore the sciences too will correspond to these genera. For 'philosopher' is like 'mathematician'; for mathematics also has parts, and there is a first and a second science and other successive ones within the sphere of mathematics.

Now since it is the work of one science to 10 investigate opposites, and plurality is opposite to unity, and it belongs to one science to investigate the negation and the privation because in both cases we are really investigating unity, to which the negation or the privation refers (for we either say simply that unity is not present, or that it is not present in some particular class; in the latter case the characteristic difference of the class modifies the meaning of 'unity', as compared with the meaning conveyed in the bare negation; for the negation means just the 15 absence of unity, while in privation there is also implied an underlying nature of which the privation is predicated),—in view of all these facts, the contraries of the concepts we named above, the other and the dissimilar and the unequal, and everything else which is derived either from these or from plurality and unity, must fall within the province of the science above-named.—And 20 contrariety is one of these concepts, for contrariety is a kind of difference, and difference is a kind of otherness. Therefore, since there are many senses in which a thing is said to be one, these terms also will have many senses, but yet it belongs to one science to consider them all; for a term belongs to different sciences not if it has different senses, but if its definitions neither are identical nor can be referred to one central meaning. And since all things are referred to that which is primary, as for instance all things which are one are referred to the primary one, we must say that this holds good also of the same and the other and of contraries in general; so that after distinguishing the various senses of each, we must then explain by reference to what is primary in each term, saying how they are related to it; some in the sense that they possess it, others in the sense that they produce it, and others in other such ways.

It is evident then that it belongs to one science to be able to give an account of these concepts as well as of substance. This was one of the questions in our book of problems.

And it is the function of the philosopher to be able to investigate all things. For if it is not the function of the philosopher, who is it who will inquire whether Socrates and Socrates seated are the same thing, or whether one thing has one contrary, or what contrariety is, or how many meanings it has? And similarly with all other such questions. Since, then, these are essential modifications of unity *qua* unity and of being *qua* being, not *qua* numbers or lines or fire, it is clear that it belongs to this science to investigate both the essence of these concepts and their properties. And those who study these properties err not by leaving the sphere of philosophy, but by forgetting that substance, of which they have no correct idea, is prior to these other

things. For number *qua* number has peculiar attributes, such as oddness and evenness, commensurability and equality, excess and defect, and these belong to numbers either in themselves or in relation to one another. And similarly the solid and the motionless and that which is in motion and the weightless and that which has weight have other peculiar properties. So too certain properties are peculiar to being as such, and it is about these that the philosopher has to investigate the truth.—An indication of this may be mentioned:—dialecticians and sophists assume the same guise as the philosopher, for sophistic is philosophy which exists only in semblance, and dialecticians embrace all things in their dialectic, and being is common to all things; but evidently their dialectic embraces these subjects because these are proper to philosophy.—For sophistic and dialectic turn on the same class of things as philosophy, but this differs from dialectic in the nature of the faculty required and from sophistic in respect of the purpose of the philosophic life. Dialectic is merely critical where philosophy claims to know, and sophistic is what appears to be philosophy but is not.

Again, in the list of contraries one of the two columns is privative, and all contraries are referred to being and nonbeing, and to unity and plurality, as for instance rest belongs to unity and movement to plurality. And nearly all thinkers agree that being and substance are composed of contraries; at least all name contraries as their first principles—some name odd and even, some hot and cold, some limit and the unlimited, some love and strife. And everything else is evidently referred to unity and plurality (this reference we must take for granted), and the principles stated by other thinkers fall entirely under these as their 1005ª1 genera. It is obvious then from these considerations too that it belongs to one science to examine being *qua* being. For all things are either contraries or composed of contraries, and unity and plurality are the starting-points of all con- 5 traries. And these belong to one science, whether they have or have not one common notion. Probably they have not; yet even if 'one' has several meanings, the other meanings will be related to the primary meaning—and similarly in the case of the contraries.—And if being or unity is not a universal and the same in every instance, or is not separable from the particular instances (as in fact it probably is not; the unity is in some

10 cases that of common reference, in some cases that of serial succession),—just for this reason it does not belong to the geometer to inquire what is contrariety or completeness or being or unity or the same or the other, but only to presuppose these concepts.—Obviously then it is the work of one science to examine being *qua* being, and the attributes which belong to it *qua* being, and

15 the same science will examine not only substances but also their attributes, both those above named and what is prior and posterior, genus and species, whole and part, and the others of this sort.

3. We must state whether it belongs to one or to different sciences to inquire into the truths which are in mathematics called axioms, and

20 into substance. Evidently the inquiry into these also belongs to one science, and that the science of the philosopher; for these truths hold good for everything that is, and not for some special genus apart from others. And all men use them, for they are true of being *qua* being, and each genus has being. But men use them just so far as to sat-

25 isfy their purposes; that is, as far as the genus, whose attributes they are proving, extends. Therefore since these truths clearly hold good for all things *qua* being (for this is what is common to them), he who studies being *qua* being will inquire into them too.—And for this reason no one who is conducting a special inquiry tries to

30 say anything about their truth or falsehood,— neither the geometer nor the arithmetician. Some natural philosophers indeed have done so, and their procedure was intelligible enough; for they thought that they alone were inquiring about the whole of nature and of being. But since there is one kind of thinker who is even above the natural philosopher (for nature is only one particular genus of being), the discussion of these truths also will belong to him whose inquiry is universal and deals with primary sub-

stance. Natural science also is a kind of wisdom,

1005ᵇ1 but it is not the first kind.—And the attempts of some who discuss the terms on which truth should be accepted, are due to a want of training in logic; for they should know these things already when they come to a special study, and

5 not be inquiring into them while they are pursuing it.—Evidently then the philosopher, who is studying the nature of all substance, must inquire also into the principles of deduction.

But he who knows best about each genus must be able to state the most certain principles of his subject, so that he whose subject is being

10 *qua* being must be able to state the most certain principles of all things. This is the philosopher, and the most certain principle of all is that regarding which it is impossible to be mistaken; for such a principle must be both the best known (for all men may be mistaken about things which they do not know), and non-hypothetical. For

15 a principle which every one must have who knows anything about being, is not a hypothesis; and that which every one must know who knows anything, he must already have when he comes to a special study. Evidently then such a principle is the most certain of all; which principle this is, we proceed to say. It is, that the same attribute cannot at the same time belong and not belong to the same subject in the same

20 respect; we must presuppose, in face of dialectical objections, any further qualifications which might be added. This, then, is the most certain of all principles, since it answers to the definition given above. For it is impossible for any one to believe the same thing to be and not to be, as some think Heraclitus says; for what a man says he does not necessarily believe. If it is impossi-

25 ble that contrary attributes should belong at the same time to the same subject (the usual qualifications must be presupposed in this proposition too), and if an opinion which contradicts another is contrary to it, obviously it is impossible for the same man at the same time to believe the same thing to be and not to be; for if a man were mistaken in this point he would have contrary opinions at the same time. It is

1005ᶜ1 for this reason that all who are carrying out a

demonstration refer it to this as an ultimate belief; for this is naturally the starting-point even for all the other axioms.

4. There are some who, as we have said, both themselves assert that it is possible for the same thing to be and not to be, and say that people can judge this to be the case. And among others many writers about nature use this lan-⁵guage. But we have now posited that it is impossible for anything at the same time to be and not to be, and by this means have shown that this is the most indisputable of all principles.—Some indeed demand that even this shall be demonstrated, but this they do through want of education, for not to know of what things one may demand demonstration, and of what one may not, argues simply want of education. For it is impossible that there should be demonstration of absolutely everything; there would be an infinite regress, so that there would still be no demon-¹⁰stration. But if there are things of which one should not demand demonstration, these persons cannot say what principle they regard as more indemonstrable than the present one.

We can, however, demonstrate negatively even that this view is impossible, if our opponent will only say something; and if he says nothing, it is absurd to attempt to reason with one who will not reason about anything, in so far as he ¹⁵refuses to reason. For such a man, as such, is seen already to be no better than a mere plant. Now negative demonstration I distinguish from demonstration proper, because in a demonstration one might be thought to be assuming what is at issue, but if another person is responsible for the assumption we shall have negative proof, not demonstration. The starting-point for all such ²⁰arguments is not the demand that our opponent shall say that something either is or is not (for this one might perhaps take to be assuming what is at issue), but that he shall say something which is significant both for himself and for another; for this is necessary, if he really is to say anything. For, if he means nothing, such a man will not be capable of reasoning, either with himself or with another. But if any one grants this, demonstration will be possible; for we shall

already have something definite. The person ²⁵responsible for the proof, however, is not he who demonstrates but he who listens; for while disowning reason he listens to reason. And again he who admits this has admitted that something is true apart from demonstration [so that not everything will be 'so and not so'.]

First then this at least is obviously true, that the word 'be' or 'not be' has a definite meaning, so that not everything will be so and not ³⁰so.—Again, if 'man' has one meaning, let this be 'two-footed animal'; by having one meaning I understand this; if such and such is a man, then if anything is a man, that will be what being a man is. . . .

¹⁰⁰⁶ᵇ¹ Let it be assumed then, as was said at the beginning, that the name has a meaning and has one meaning; it is impossible, then, that being a man should mean precisely not being a man, if ¹⁵'man' is not only predicable of one subject but also has one meaning (for we do not identify 'having one meaning' with 'being predicable of one subject', since on that assumption even 'musical' and 'white' and 'man' would have had one meaning, so that all things would have been one; for they would all have been synonymous).

And it will not be possible for the same thing to be and not to be, except in virtue of an ambiguity, just as one whom we call 'man,' others ²⁰might call 'not-man'; but the point in question is not this, whether the same thing can at the same time be and not be a man in name, but whether it can in fact. Now if 'man' and 'not-man' mean nothing different, obviously 'not being a man' will mean nothing different from 'being a man'; so that being a man will be not being a man; for ²⁵they will be one. For being one means this—what we find in the case of 'raiment' and 'dress'—viz. that the definitory formula is one. And if 'being a man' and 'not being a man' are to be one, they must mean one thing. But it was shown earlier that they mean different things. Therefore, if it is true to say of anything that it is a man, it must be a two-footed animal; for this was ³⁰what 'man' meant; and if this is necessary, it is impossible that the same thing should not be a two-footed animal; for this is what 'being necessary' means—that it is impossible for the thing not to be. It is, then, impossible that it should be at the same time true to say the same thing is a 1007ᵃ1 man and is not a man. . . .

Again, if all contradictories are true of the 1007ᵇ same subject at the same time, evidently all things will be one. For the same thing will be a 20 trireme, a wall, and a man, if it is equally possible to affirm and to deny anything of anything,— and this premise must be accepted by those who share the views of Protagoras. For if any one thinks that the man is not a trireme, evidently he is not a trireme; so that he also is a trireme, if, as they say, the contradictory is true. . . .

1008ᵃ Further, it follows that all would then be 30 right and all would be in error, and our opponent himself confesses himself to be in error.—And at the same time our discussion with him is evidently about nothing at all; for he says nothing. For he says neither 'yes' nor 'no', but both 'yes' and 'no'; and again he denies both of these and says 'neither yes nor no'; for otherwise there would already be something definite.—Again, if when the assertion is true, the negation is false, and when this is true, the affirmation is false, it will not be possible to assert and deny the same 1008ᵇ1 thing truly at the same time. But perhaps they might say we had assumed the very thing at issue.

BOOK V

10 **8.** We call substances (1) the simple bodies, i.e. earth and fire and water and everything of the sort, and in general bodies and the things composed of them, both animals and divine beings, and the parts of these. All these are called substance because they are not predicated of a subject but everything else is predicated of them.—
15 (2) That which, being present is such things as are not predicated of a subject, is the cause of their being, as the soul is of the being of animals.— (3) The parts which are present in such things, limiting them and marking them as individuals, and by whose destruction the whole is destroyed, as the body is by the destruction of the plane, as some say, and the plane by the destruction of the line; and in general number is thought by some 20 to be of this nature; for if it is destroyed, they say, nothing exists, and it limits all things.—(4) The

essence, the formula of which is a definition, is also called the substance of each thing.

It follows, then, that substance has two senses, (a) the ultimate substratum, which is no longer predicated of anything else, and (b) that which is a 'this' and separable—and of this 25 nature is the shape or form of each thing.

BOOK VI

1. We are seeking the principles and the causes of the things that are, and obviously of things *qua* being. For there is a cause of health and of good condition, and the objects of mathematics 5 have principles and elements and causes, and in general every science which is ratiocinative or at all involves reasoning deals with causes and principles, exact or indeterminate; but all these sciences mark off some particular being—some genus, and inquire into this, but not into being simply nor *qua* being, nor do they offer any dis-10 cussion of the essence of the things of which they treat; but starting from the essence—some making it plain to the senses, others assuming it as a hypothesis—they then demonstrate, more or less cogently, the essential attributes of the genus with which they deal. It is obvious, therefore, from such a review of the sciences, that there is no demonstration of substance or of the essence, but some other way of revealing it. And similarly 15 the sciences omit the question whether the genus with which they deal exists or does not exist, because it belongs to the same line of thought to show what it is and that it is.

And since natural science, like other sciences, confines itself to one class of beings, i.e. to that sort of substance which has the principle of 20 its movement and rest present in itself, evidently it is neither practical nor productive. For the principle of production is in the producer—it is either reason or art or some capacity, while the principle of action is in the doer—viz. choice, for that which is done and that which is chosen are the same. Therefore, if all thought is either prac-25 tical or productive or theoretical, natural science must be theoretical, but it will theorize about such being as admits of being moved, and only about that kind of substance which in respect of its formula is for the most part not separable from matter. Now, we must not fail to notice the nature of the essence and of its formula, for, with-30 out this, inquiry is but idle. Of things defined, i.e., of essences, some are like snub, and some like concave. And these differ because snub is bound up with matter (for what is snub is a concave *nose*), while concavity is independent of 1026ᵃ1 perceptible matter. If then all natural things are analogous to the snub in their nature—e.g. nose, eye, face, flesh, bone, and, in general, animal; leaf, root, bark, and, in general, plant (for none of these can be defined without reference to movement—they always have matter), it is clear how we must seek and define the essence in the 5 case of natural objects, and also why it belongs to the student of nature to study soul to some extent, i.e., so much of it as is not independent of matter.—That nature science, then, is theoretical, is plain from these considerations. Mathematics also is theoretical; but whether its objects are immovable and separable from matter, is not at present clear; it is clear, however, that it considers some mathematical objects *qua* immovable 10 and *qua* separable from matter. But if there is something which is eternal and immovable and separable, clearly the knowledge of it belongs to a theoretical science,—not, however, to natural science (for natural science deals with certain movable things) nor to mathematics, but to a science prior to both. For natural science deals with things which are inseparable from matter but not 15 immovable, and some parts of mathematics deal with things which are immovable, but probably not separable, but embodied in matter; while the first science deals with things which are both separable and immovable. Now all causes must be eternal, but especially these; for they are the causes of so much of the divine as appears to us. There must, then, be three theoretical philosophies, mathematics, natural science, and theol-20 ogy, since it is obvious that if the divine is present anywhere, it is present in things of this sort. And the highest science must deal with the highest genus, so that the theoretical sciences are superior to the other sciences, and this to the other theoretical sciences. One might indeed raise the

question whether first philosophy is universal, or 25 deals with one genus, i.e. some one kind of being; for not even the mathematical sciences are all alike in this respect,—geometry and astronomy deal with a certain particular kind of thing, while universal mathematics applies alike to all. We answer that if there is no substance other than those which are formed by nature, natural science will be the first science; but if there is an 30 immovable substance, the science of this must be prior and must be first philosophy, and universal in this way, because it is first. And it will belong to this to consider being *qua* being—both what it is and the attributes which belong to it *qua* being.

BOOK VII

10 **1.** There are several senses in which a thing may be said to be, as we pointed out previously in our book on the various senses of words; for in one sense it means what a thing is or a 'this', and in another sense it means that a thing is of a certain quality or quantity or has some such predicate asserted of it. While 'being' has all these senses, obviously that which is primarily is the 'what', which indicates the substance of the thing. For when we say of what quality a thing is, we say 15 that it is good or beautiful, but not that it is three cubits long or that it is a man; but when we say *what* it is, we do not say 'white' or 'hot' or 'three cubits long', but 'man' or 'God'. And all other things are said to be because they are, some of them, quantities of that which *is* in this primary sense, others qualities of it, others affections of it, and others some other determination of it. And so one might raise the question whether 'to walk' 20 and 'to be healthy' and 'to sit' signify in each case something that is, and similarly in any other case of this sort; for none of them is either self-subsistent or capable of being separated from substance, but rather, if anything, it is that which walks or is seated or is healthy that is an existent 25 thing. Now these are seen to be more real because there is something definite which underlies them; and this is the substance or individual, which is implied in such a predicate; for 'good' or 'sitting' are not used without this. Clearly then it

is in virtue of this category that each of the others *is*. Therefore that which is primarily and *is* simply (not is something) must be substance.

Now there are several senses in which a thing is said to be primary; but substance is primary in every sense—in formula, in order of knowledge, in time. For of the other categories none can exist independently, but only substance. And in formula also this is primary; for in the formula of each term the formula of its substance must be present. And we think we know each thing most fully, when we know what it is, e.g. what man is or what fire is, rather than when we know its quality, its quantity, or where it is; since we know each of these things also, only when we know *what* the quantity or the quality *is*.

And indeed the question which, both now and of old, has always been raised, and always been the subject of doubt, viz. what being is, is just the question, what is substance? For it is this that some assert to be one, others more than one, and that some assert to be limited in number, others unlimited. And so we also must consider chiefly and primarily and almost exclusively what that is which *is* in this sense.

2. Substance is thought to belong most obviously to bodies; and so we say that both animals and plants and their parts are substances, and so are natural bodies such as fire and water and earth and everything of the sort, and all things that are parts of these or composed of these (either of parts or of the whole bodies), e.g. the heaven and its parts, stars and moon and sun. But whether these alone are substances, or there are also others, or only some of these, or some of these and some other things are substances, or none of these but only some other things, must be considered. Some think the limits of body, i.e. surface, line, point, and unit, are substances, and more so than body or the solid. Further, some do not think there is anything substantial besides sensible things, but others think there are eternal substances which are more in number and more real, e.g. Plato posited two kinds of substance— the Forms and the objects of mathematics—as well as a third kind, viz. the substance of sensible

bodies. And Speusippus made still more kinds of substance, beginning with the One, and making principles for each kind of substance, one for numbers, another for spatial magnitudes, and then another for the soul; and in this way he multiplies the kinds of substance. And some say Forms and numbers have the same nature, and other things come after them, e.g. lines and planes, until we come to the substance of the heavens and to sensible bodies.

Regarding these matters, then, we must inquire which of the common statements are right and which are not right, and what things are substances, and whether there are or are not any besides sensible substances and how sensible substances exist, and whether there is a separable substance (and if so why and how) or there is no substance separable from sensible substances; and we must first sketch the nature of substance.

3. The word 'substance' is applied, if not in more senses, still at least to four main objects; for both the essence and the universal and the genus are thought to be the substance of each thing, and fourthly the substratum. Now the substratum is that of which other things are predicated, while it is itself not predicated of anything else. And so we must first determine the nature of this; for that which underlies a thing primarily is thought to be in the truest sense its substance. And in one sense matter is said to be the nature of substratum, in another, shape, and in a third sense, the compound of these. By the matter I mean, for instance, the bronze, by the shape the plan of its form, and by the compound of these (the concrete thing) the statue. Therefore if the from is prior to the matter and more real, it will be prior to the compound also for the same reason.

We have now outlined the nature of substance, showing that it is that which is not predicated of a subject, but of which all else is predicated. But we must not merely state the matter thus; for this is not enough. The statement itself is obscure, and further, on this view, *matter* becomes substance. For if this is not substance, it is beyond us to say what else is. When all else is taken away evidently nothing but matter remains. For of the other elements some are affections, products, and capacities of bodies, while length, breadth, and depth are quantities and not substances. For a quantity is not a substance; but the substance is rather that to which these belong primarily. But when length and breadth and depth are taken away we see nothing left except that which is bounded by these, whatever it be; so that to those who consider the question thus matter alone must seem to be substance. By matter I mean that which in itself is neither a particular thing nor of a certain quantity nor assigned to any other of the categories by which being is determined. For there is something of which each of these is predicated, so that its being is different from that of each of the predicates; for the predicates other than substance are predicated of substance, while substance is predicated of matter. Therefore the ultimate substratum is of itself neither a particular thing nor of a particular quantity nor otherwise positively characterized; nor yet negatively, for negations also will belong to it only by accident.

For those who adopt this point of view, then, it follows that matter is substance. But this is impossible; for both separability and individuality are thought to belong chiefly to substance. And so form and the compound of form and matter would be thought to be substance, rather than matter. The substance compounded of both, i.e. of matter and shape, may be dismissed; for it is posterior and its nature is obvious. And matter also is in a sense manifest. But we must inquire into the third kind of substance; for this is the most difficult.

It is agreed that there are some substances among sensible things, so that we must look first among these. For it is in an advantage to advance to that which is more intelligible. For learning proceeds for all in this way—through that which is less intelligible by nature to that which is more intelligible; and just as in conduct our work is to start from what is good for each and make what is good in itself good for each, so it is our work to start from what is more intelligible to oneself and make what is intelligible by nature intelligible to oneself. Now what is intelligible and primary for particular sets of people is often intelligible to a very small extent, and has little or nothing of reality. But yet one must start from that which is barely intelligible but intelligible to oneself, and try to understand what is intelligible in itself, passing, as has been said, by way of those very things which one understands.

4. Since at the start we distinguished the various marks by which we determine substance, and one of these was thought to be the essence, we must investigate this. And first let us say something about it in the abstract. The essence of each thing is what it is said to be in virtue of itself. For being you is not being musical; for you are not musical in virtue of yourself. What, then, you are in virtue of yourself is your essence. . . .

But since there are compounds of substance with the other categories (for there is a substrate for each category, e.g. for quality, quantity, time, place, and motion), we must inquire whether there is a formula of the essence of each of them, i.e. whether to these compounds also there belongs an essence, e.g. to white man. Let the compound be denoted by 'cloak'. What is being a cloak? But, it may be said, this also is not said of something in its own right. We reply that there are two ways in which a predicate may fail to be true of a subject in its own right, and one of these results from addition, and the other not. *One* kind of predicate is not said of a thing in its own right because the term that is being defined is added to something else, e.g. if in defining the essence of white one were to state the formula of white *man; another* because something else is added to it, e.g. if 'cloak' meant white man, and one were to define cloak as white; white man is white indeed, but its essence is not to be white. But is being a cloak an essence at all? Probably not. For the essence is what something is; but when one thing is said of another, that is not what a 'this' is, e.g. white man is not what a 'this' is since being a 'this' belongs only to substances. Therefore there is an essence only of those things whose formula is a definition. But we have a definition not where we have a word and a formula identical in meaning (for in that case all formulae would be definitions; for there will be some name for formula whatever, so that even the *Iliad*

10 would be a definition), but where there is a formula of something primary; and primary things are those which do not involve one thing's being said of another. Nothing, then, which is not a species of a genus will have an *essence*— only species will have it, for in these the subject is not thought to participate in the attribute and 15 to have it as an affection, nor to have it by accident; but for everything else as well, if it has a name, there will be a formula of its meaning— viz. that this attribute belongs to this subject; or instead of a simple formula we shall be able to give a more accurate one; but there will be no definition nor essence.

But after all, 'definition', like 'what a thing is', has several meanings; 'what a thing is' in one sense means substance and a 'this', in another 20 one or other of the predicates, quantity, quality, and the like. For as 'is' is predicable of all things, not however in the same sense, but of one sort of thing primarily and of others in a secondary way, so too the 'what' belongs simply to substance, but in a limited sense to the other categories. . . .

1030ᵃ Now we must inquire how we should express 27 ourselves on each point, but still more how the facts actually stand. And so now also since it is evident what language we use, essence will belong, just as the 'what' does, primarily and in the simple sense to substance, and in a secondary way to the other categories also.

1031ᵃ1 **5.** Clearly then only substance is definable. For if the other categories also are definable, it must be by addition, e.g. [the qualitative is defined thus, and so is] the odd, for it cannot be defined apart from number; nor can female be defined apart from animal. (When I say 'by addition' I mean the expressions in which we have to 5 say the same thing twice, as in these instances.) And if this is true, coupled terms also, like 'odd number', will not be definable (but this escapes our notice because our formulae are not accurate). But if these also are definable, either it is in some other way or, as we said, definition and essence must be said to have more than one 10 sense. Therefore in one sense nothing will have a definition and nothing will have an essence, except substances, but in another sense other

things will have them. Clearly, then, definition is the formula of the essence, and essence must belong to substances either alone or chiefly and primarily and in the unqualified sense.

15 **6.** We must inquire whether each thing and its essence are the same or different. This is of some use for the inquiry concerning substance; for each thing is thought to be not different from its substance, and the essence is said to be the substance of each thing.

Now in the case of things with accidental 20 attributes the two would be generally thought to be different, e.g. white man would be thought to be different from the essence of white man. For if they are the same, the essence of man and that of white man are also the same; for a man and a 25 white man are the same, as people say, so that the essence of white man and that of man would be also the same. But probably it is not necessary that things with accidental attributes should be the same.

But in the case of so-called self-subsistent things, is a thing necessarily the same as its essence? E.g. if there are some substances which 30 have no other substances nor entities prior to them—substances such as some assert the Ideas to be? If the essence of good is to be different from the Idea of good, and the essence of animal from the Idea of animal, and the essence of 1031ᵇ1 being from the Idea of being, there will, firstly, be other substances and entities and Ideas besides those which are asserted, and, secondly, these others will be prior substances if the essence is substance. And, if the posterior substances are severed from one another, there will be no knowledge of the ones and the others will have no 5 being. (By 'severed' I mean, if the Idea of good has not the essence of good, and the latter has not the property of being good.) For there is knowledge of each thing only when we know its essence.

And the case is the same for other things as for the good; so that if the essence of good is not good, neither will the essence of being be, nor the essence of unity be one. And all essences alike exist or none of them does; so that if the 10 essence of being is not, neither will any of the others be. Again, that which has not the property of being good is not good. The good, then, must be one with the essence of good, and the beautiful with the essence of beauty, and so with all things which do not depend on something else but are self-subsistent and primary. For it is enough if they are this, even if there are no Forms; and 15 perhaps all the more if there are Forms.—At the same time it is clear that if there are Ideas such as some people say there are, the substratum of them will not be substance; for these must be substances, and not predicable of a substratum; for if they were they would exist only by being participated in.—Each thing then and its essence are one and the same in no merely accidental way, as is evident both from the preceding arguments and because to *know* each thing, at least, is to know its essence, so that even by the exhibition of *know* each thing, at least, is to know its essence, 20 so that even by the exhibition of instances it becomes clear that both must be one. . . .

The absurdity of the separation would appear also if one were to assign a name to each of the essences; for there would be another essence besides the original one, e.g. to the essence of horse there will belong a second essence. Yet why 30 should not some things be their essences from the start, since essence is substance? But not only are a thing and its essence one, but the formula of 1032ᵃ1 them is also the same, as is clear even from what has been said; for it is not by accident that the essence of one, and the one, are one. Further, if they were different, the process would go on to infinity; for we should have the essence of one, and the one, so that in their case also the same infinite regress would be found. Clearly, then, each primary and self-subsistent thing is one and 5 the same as its essence. . . .

30   **7.** It is impossible that anything should be produced if there were nothing before. Obviously then some part of the result will pre-exist of necessity; for the matter is a part; for this is present in the process and it is this that becomes something. But do some also of the elements in 1033ᵃ1 the *formula* pre-exist? Well, we describe in both ways what bronze circles are; we describe both the matter by saying it is bronze, and the form by

saying that it is such and such a figure; and figure is the proximate genus in which it is placed. The 5 bronze circle, then, has its matter *in its formula*.

And as for that out of which as matter they are produced, some things are said, when they have been produced, to be not it but of it, e.g. the statue is not stone but of stone. But though what becomes healthy is a man, a man is not what the healthy product is said to come from. The reason is that though a thing comes both from its privation and from its substratum, which we call its matter (e.g. what becomes healthy is both a man and an invalid), it is said to come 10 rather from its privation (e.g. it is from an invalid rather than from a man that a healthy subject is produced). . . .

And so, as there also a thing is not said to be that from which it comes, here the statue is not said to be wood but is said by a verbal change to be not wood but wooden, not bronze but of bronze, not stone but of stone, and the house is said to be not bricks but of bricks (since we should not say without qualification, if we looked at things carefully, even that a statue is produced 20 from wood or a house from bricks, because its coming to be implies change in that from which it comes, and not permanence). For this reason, then, we use this way of speaking.

8. Since anything which is produced is produced by something (and this I call the starting-point of the production), and from something 25 (and let this be taken to be not the privation but the matter; for the meanings we attach to these have already been distinguished), and since something is produced (and this is either a sphere or a circle or whatever else it may chance to be), just as we do not make the substratum—the bronze, so we do not make the sphere, except incidentally, because the bronze sphere is a sphere and we make the former. For to make a 'this' is to 30 make a 'this' out of the general substratum. I mean that to make the bronze round is not to make the round or the sphere, but something else, i.e. to produce this form in something else. For if we make the form, we must make it out of 1033ᵇ1 something else; for this was assumed. E.g. we make a bronze sphere; and that in the sense that out of this, which is bronze, we make this other, which is a sphere. If, then, we make the sphere itself, clearly we must make it in the same way, and the processes of making will regress to infinity. Obviously then the form also, or whatever we ought to call the shape of the sensible thing, is not produced, nor does production relate to it,—i.e. the essence is not produced; for this is that which is made to be in something else by art or by nature or by some capacity. But that there is a *bronze sphere*, this we make. For we make it out of bronze and the sphere; we bring the form into this particular matter, and the result is a bronze sphere. But if the essence of sphere in general is produced, something must be produced out of something. For the product will always have to be divisible, and one part must be this and another that, I mean the one must be matter and the other form. If then a sphere is the figure whose circumference is at all points equidistant from the centre, part of this will be the medium in which the thing made will be, and part will be in that medium, and the whole will be the thing produced, which corresponds to the bronze sphere. It is obvious then from what has been said that the thing, in the sense of form or substance, is not produced, but the concrete thing which gets its name from this is produced, and that in everything which comes to be matter is present, and one part of the thing is matter and the other form.

Is there then a sphere apart from the individual spheres or a house apart from the bricks? Rather we may say that no 'this' would ever have been coming to be, if this had been so. The 'from' however means the 'such', and is not a 'this'—a definite thing; but the artist makes, or the father generates, a 'such' out of a 'this'; and when it has been generated, it is a 'this such'. And the whole 'this', Callias or Socrates, is analogous to this bronze sphere, but man and animal to bronze sphere in general. Obviously then the cause which consists of the Forms (taken in the sense in which some maintain the existence of the Forms, i.e. if they are something apart from the individuals) is useless with regard both to comings-to-be and to substances; and the Forms need not, for this reason at least, be self-subsistent substances.

9. And it is clear also from what has been said that in a sense everything is produced from another individual which shares its name (natural products are so produced), or a part of itself which shares its name (e.g. the house produced by reason is produced from a house; for the art of building is the form of the house), or something which contains a part of it,—if we exclude things produced by accident. For what directly and of itself causes the production is a part of the product. The heat in the movement causes heat in the body, and this is either health, or a part of health, or is followed by a part of health or by health itself. And so it is said to cause health, because it produces that on which health follows.

Therefore substance is the starting-point of all production, as of deduction. It is from the 'what' that deductions start; and from it also we now find processes of production to start. And things which are formed by nature are in the same case as these products of art. For the seed produces them as the artist produces the works of art; for it has the form potentially, and that from 1034ᵇ1 which the seed comes has *in a* sense the same name as the offspring; only in a sense, for we must not expect *all* cases to have exactly the same name, as in the production of human being from human being (for a women also can be produced by a man—unless there is a deformity: that is why it is not from a mule that a mule is produced). The natural things which (like some artificial objects) can be produced spontaneously are those whose matter can be moved even by itself in the way in which the seed usually moves it; but those things which have not such matter cannot be produced except by parents.

But not only regarding substance does our argument prove that its form does not come to be, but the argument applies to all the primary classes alike, i.e. quantity, quality, and the other categories. For as the bronze sphere comes to be, but not the sphere nor the bronze, and so too in the case of bronze itself, if it comes to be, (for the matter and the form must always exist before), so is it as regards both 'what' and quality and quantity and the other categories likewise; for the quality does not come to be, but the wood of that quality, and the quantity does not come to be, but the wood or the animal of that size. But we may learn from these instances a peculiarity of substance, that there must exist beforehand another actual substance which produces it, e.g. an animal if an animal is produced; but it is not necessary that a quality or quantity should pre-exist otherwise than potentially.

13. Let us again return to the subject of our inquiry, which is substance. As the substrate and the essence and the compound of these are called substance, so also is the universal. About two of these we have spoken; about the essence and about the substrate, of which we have said that it underlies in two senses, either being a 'this'—which is the way in which an animal underlies its attributes—, or as the matter underlies the complete reality. The universal also is thought by some to be in the fullest sense a cause, and a principle; therefore let us attack the discussion of this point also. For it seems impossible that any universal term should be the name of a substance. For primary substance is that kind of substance which is peculiar to an individual, which does not belong to anything else; but the universal is common, since that is called universal which naturally belongs to more than one thing. Of which individual then will this be the substance? Either of all or of none. But it cannot be the substance of all; and if it is to be the substance of one, this one will be the others also; for things whose substance is one and whose essence is one are themselves also one.

Further, substance means that which is not predicable of a subject, but the universal is predicable of some subject always.

But perhaps the universal, while it cannot be substance in the way in which the essence is so, can be present in this, e.g. animal can be present in man and horse. Then clearly there is a formula of the universal. And it makes no difference even if there is not a formula of everything that is in the substance; for none the less the universal will be the substance of something. Man is the substance of the individual man in whom it is present; therefore the same will happen again, for a substance, e.g. animal, must be the substance of that in which it is present as something peculiar

to it. And further it is impossible and absurd that the 'this', i.e. the substance, if it consists of parts, should not consist of substances nor of what is a 'this', but of quality; for that which is not substance, i.e. the quality, will then be prior to substance and to the 'this'. Which is impossible; for neither in formula nor in time nor in coming to be can the affections be prior to the substance; for then they would be separable from it. Further, in Socrates there will be a substance in a substance, so that he will be the substance of two things. And in general it follows, if man and such things are substances, that none of the elements in their formulae is the substance of anything, nor does it exist apart from the species or in anything else; I mean, for instance, that no animal exists apart from the particular animals, nor does any other of the elements present in formulae exist apart.

If, then, we view the matter from these standpoints, it is plain that no universal attribute is a substance, and this is plain also form the fact that no common predicate indicates a 'this', but rather a 'such'. If not, many difficulties follow and especially the 'third man'.

17. We should say what, and what sort of thing, substance is, taking another starting-point; for perhaps from this we shall get a clear view also of that substance which exists apart from sensible substances. Since, then, substance is a principle and a cause, let us attack it from this standpoint. The 'why' is always sought in this form—'why does one thing attach to another?' For to inquire why the musical man is a musical man, is either to inquire—as we have said—why the man is musical, or it is something else. Now 'why a thing is itself' is doubtless a meaningless inquiry; for the fact or the existence of the thing must already be evident (e.g. that the moon is eclipsed), but the fact that a thing is itself is the single formula and the single cause to all such questions as why the man is man, or the musical musical, unless one were to say that each thing is inseparable from itself; and its being one just meant this. This, however, is common to all things and is a short and easy way with the question. But we *can* inquire why man is an animal of

such and such a nature. Here, then, we are evidently not inquiring why he who is a man is a man. We are inquiring, then, why something is predicable of something; that it is predicable must be clear; for if not, the inquiry is an inquiry
25 into nothing. E.g. why does it thunder?—why is sound produced in the clouds? Thus the inquiry is about the predication of one thing of another. And why are certain things, i.e. stones and bricks, a house? Plainly we are seeking the cause. And this is the essence (to speak abstractly), which in some cases is that for the sake of which,
30 e.g. perhaps in the case of a house or a bed, and in some cases is the first mover; for this also is a cause. But while the efficient cause is sought in the case of genesis and destruction, the final cause is sought in the case of being also.

The object of the inquiry is most overlooked
1041ᵇ1 where one term is not expressly predicated of another (e.g. when we inquire why man is), because we do not distinguish and do not say definitely 'why do these parts form this whole'? But we must distinguish the elements before we begin to inquire; if not, it is not clear whether the inquiry is significant or unmeaning. Since we
5 must know the existence of the thing and it must be given, clearly the question is *why* the matter is some individual thing, e.g. why are these materials a house? Because that which was the essence of a house is present. And why is this individual thing, or this body in this state, a man? Therefore what we seek is the cause, i.e. the form, by reason of which the matter is some definite thing; and this is the substance of the thing. Evidently, then, in the case of simple things no inquiry nor
10 teaching is possible; but we must inquire into them in a different way.

As regards that which is compounded out of something so that the whole is one—not like a heap, however, but like a syllable,—the syllable is not its elements, *ba* is not the same as *b* and *a*, nor is flesh fire and earth; for when they are dis-
15 solved the wholes, i.e. the flesh and the syllable, no longer exist, but the elements of the syllable exist, and so do fire and earth. The syllable, then, is something—not only its elements (the vowel and the consonant) but also something else; and the flesh is not only fire and earth or the hot and

the cold, but also something else. Since, then,
20 that something must be either an element or composed of elements, if it is an element the same argument will again apply; for flesh will consist of this and fire and earth and something still further, so that the process will go on to infinity; while if it is a compound, clearly it will be a compound not of one but of many (or else it will itself be that one), so that again in this case
25 we can use the same argument as in the case of flesh or of the syllable. But it would seem that this is something, and not an element, and that it is the cases which makes *this* thing flesh and *that* a syllable. And similarly in all other cases. And this is the substance of each thing; for this is the primary cause of its being; and since, while some
30 things are not substances, as many as are substances are formed naturally and by nature, their substance would seem to be this nature, which is not an element but a principle. An *element* is that into which a thing is divided and which is present in it as matter, e.g. *a* and *b* are the elements of the syllable.

BOOK VIII

1. We must draw our conclusions from what has been said, and sum up our results, and put the finishing touch to our inquiry. We have said that the causes, principles, and elements of sub-
5 stances are the object of our search. And some substances are recognized by all thinkers, but some have been advocated by particular schools. Those generally recognized are the natural substances, i.e. fire, earth, water, air, &c., the simple bodies; secondly, plants and their parts, and animals and the parts of animals; and finally the
10 heavens and the parts of the heavens. Some particular schools say that Forms and the objects of mathematics are substances. And it follows from our arguments that there are other substances, the essence and the substratum. Again, in another way the genus seems more substantial than the species, and the universal than the particulars. And with the universal and the genus the Ideas are connected; it is in virtue of the
15 same argument that they are thought to be substances. And since the essence is substance, and

the definition is a formula of the essence, for this reason we have discussed definition and essential predication. Since the definition is a formula, and a formula has parts, we had to consider with respect to the notion of part, what are parts of 20 the substance and what are not, and whether the same things are also parts of the definition. Further, then, neither the universal nor the genus is a substance; we must inquire later into the Ideas and the objects of mathematics; for some say these exist apart from sensible substances.

But now let us resume the discussion of the generally recognized substances. These are the sensible substances, and sensible substances all 25 have matter. The substratum is substance, and this is in one sense the matter (and by matter I mean that which, not being a 'this' actually, is potentially a 'this'), and in another sense the formula or form (which being a 'this' can be separately formulated), and thirdly the complex of matter and form, which alone is generated and 30 destroyed, and is, without qualification, capable of separate existence; for of substances in the sense of formulae some are separable and some are not.

But clearly matter also is substance; for in all the opposite changes that occur there is something which underlies the changes, e.g. in respect of place that which is now here and again elsewhere, and in respect of increase that which is 35 now of one size and again less or greater, and in respect of alteration that which is now healthy and again diseased; and similarly in respect of 1042ᵇ1 substance there is something that is now being generated and again being destroyed, and now underlies the process as a 'this' and again underlies it as the privation of positive character. In this last change the others are involved. But in either one or two of the others this is not 5 involved; for it is not necessary if a thing has matter for change of place that it should also have matter for generation and destruction.

2. The difference between becoming in the unqualified sense and becoming in a qualified sense has been stated in the *Physics*. Since the substance which exists as substratum and as matter is generally recognized, and this is that which 10 exists potentially, it remains for us to say what is

the substance, in the sense of *actuality*, of sensible things. Democritus seems to think there are three kinds of difference between things; the underlying body, the matter, is one and the same, but they differ either in rhythm, i.e. shape, or in turning, i.e. position, or in inter-contact, i.e. 15 order. But evidently there are many differences; for instance, some things are characterized by the mode of composition of their matter, e.g. the things formed by mixture, such as honey-water; and others by being bound together, e.g. a bundle; and others by being glued together, e.g. a book; and others by being nailed together, e.g. a casket; and others in more than one of these ways; 20 and others by position, e.g. the threshold and the lintel (for these differ by being placed in a certain way); and others by time, e.g. dinner and breakfast; and others by place, e.g. the winds; and others by the affections proper to sensible things, e.g. harness and softness, density and rarity, dryness and wetness; and some things by some of 25 these qualities, others by them all, and in general some by excess and some by defect. Clearly then the word 'is' has just as many meanings; a thing is a threshold because it lies in such and such a position, and its being means its lying in that position, while being ice means having been solidified in such and such a way. And the being of some things will be defined by *all* these qualities, because some parts of them are mixed, others 30 are fused, others are bound together, others are solidified, and others possess the other differentiae; e.g. the hand or the foot. We must grasp, then, the kinds of differentiae (for these will be the principles of the being of things), e.g. the things characterized by the more and the less, or by the dense and the rare, and by other such 35 qualities; for all these are characterized by excess and defect. And everything that is characterized by shape or by smoothness and roughness, is determined by the straight and the curved. And for other things their being will mean their being 1034ᵃ1 mixed, and their not being will mean the opposite. It is clear then from these facts that if its substance is the cause of each thing's being, we must seek in these differentiae the cause of the being of each of these things. Now none of these differentiae is substance, even when coupled

5 with matter, yet in each there is something analogous to substance; and as in substances that
which is predicated of the matter is the actuality
itself, in all other definitions also it is what most
resembles full actuality. E.g. if we had to define a
threshold, we should say 'wood or stone in such
and such a position' and a house we should define
as 'bricks and timbers in such and such a position' (or we may name that for the sake of which
as well in some cases), and if we define ice we say
10 'water frozen or solidified in such and such a
way', and harmony is 'such and such a blending
of high and low', and similarly in all other cases.

Obviously then the actuality or the formula
is different when the matter is different; for in
some cases it is the juxtaposition, in others the
mixing, and in others some other of the attributes
we have named. And so, in defining, those who
15 define a house as stones, bricks, and timbers, are
speaking of the potential house, for these are the
matter; but those who define it as a covering for
bodies and chattels, or add some other similar differentia, speak of the actuality; and those who
combine both of these speak of the third kind of
substance, which is composed of matter and form.
20 For the formula that gives the differentiae seems
to be an account of the form and the actuality,
while that which gives the components is rather
an account of the matter. And the same is true
with regard to the definitions which Archytas
used to accept; for they are accounts of the combined form and matter. E.g. what is still weather?
Absence of motion in a large extent of air; air is
the matter, and absence of motion is the actuality
and substance. What is a calm? Smoothness of
sea; the material substratum is the sea, and the
25 actuality or form is smoothness. It is obvious
then, from what has been said, what sensible substance is and how it exists—one kind of it as
matter, another as form or actuality; while the
third kind is that which is composed of these two.

3. We must not forget that sometimes it is
not clear whether a name means the composite
substance, or the actuality or form, e.g. whether
30 'house' is a sign for the composite thing, 'a covering consisting of bricks and stones laid thus and
thus', or for the actuality or form, 'a covering',

and whether a line is twoness in length or
twoness, and whether an animal is a soul in a
body or a soul. For soul is the substance or actuality of some body; but animal might be applied to
35 both, not that both are definable by one formula
but because they refer to the same thing. But this
question, while important for another purpose, is
of no importance for the inquiry into sensible
substance; for the essence certainly attaches to
1043 the form and the actuality. For soul and to be soul
are the same, but to be man and man are not the
same, unless indeed the soul is to be called man;
and thus on one interpretation the thing is the
same as its essence, and on another it is not.

If we consider we find that the syllable is not
5 produced by the letters and juxtaposition, nor is
the house bricks and juxtaposition. And this is
right; for the juxtaposition or mixing is not produced by those things of which it is the juxtaposition or mixing. And the same is true in the
other cases, e.g. if the threshold is characterized
by its position, the position is not produced by
the threshold, but rather the latter is produced by
the former. Nor is man animal and biped, but
10 there must be something besides these, if these are
matter,—something which is neither an element
in the whole nor produced by an element, but is
the substance, which people eliminate and state
the matter. If then this is the cause of the thing's
being, and if the cause of its being is its substance,
they cannot be stating the substance itself.

This, then, must either be eternal or it must
15 be destructible without being ever in course of
being destroyed, and must have come to be without ever being in course of coming to be. But it
has been proved and explained elsewhere that no
one makes or generates the form, but it is a 'this'
that is made, i.e. the complex of form and matter
that is generated. Whether the substances of
destructible things can exist apart, is not yet at
all clear; except that obviously this is impossible
in some cases—in the case of things which can-
20 not exist apart from the individual instances, e.g.
house or utensil. Perhaps neither these things
themselves, nor any of the other things which are
not formed by nature, are substances at all; for one
might say that the nature in natural objects is the
only substance to be found in destructible things.

Therefore the difficulty which was raised by
25 the school of Antisthenes and other such uneducated people has a certain appropriateness. They stated that the 'what' cannot be defined (for the definition so called is a long formula); but of what *sort* a thing, e.g. silver, is, they thought it possible to explain, not saying what it is but that it is like tin. Therefore one kind of substance can be defined and formulated, i.e. the composite kind, whether it be the object of sense or of rea-
30 son; but the primary parts of which this consists cannot be defined, since a definitory formula predicates something of something, and one part of the definition must play the part of matter and the other that of form. . . .

1044ᵃ11 Let this then suffice for an account of the generation and destruction of so-called substances—in what sense it is possible and in what sense impossible—and of the reduction of things to number.

BOOK XII

6. Since there were three kinds of substance, two of them natural and one unmovable, regarding the latter we must assert that it is necessary that there should be an eternal unmovable substance. For substances are the first of existing
5 things, and if they are all destructible, all things are destructible. But it is impossible that movement should either come into being or cease to be; for it must always have existed. Nor can time come into being or cease to be; for there could not be a before and an after if time did not exist. Movement also is continuous, then, in the sense in which time is; for time is either the same thing
10 as movement or an attribute of movement. And there is no continuous movement except movement in place, and of this only that which is circular is continuous.

But if there is something which is capable of moving things or acting on them, but is not actually doing so, there will not be movement; for that which has a capacity need not exercise it. Nothing, then, is gained even if we suppose eternal substances, as the believers in the Forms do,
15 unless there is to be in them some principle which can cause movement; and even this is not

enough, nor is another substance besides the Forms enough; for if it does not *act*, there will be no movement. Further, even if it acts, this will not be enough, if its substance is potentiality; for there will not be *eternal* movement; for that which is potentially may possibly not be. There must, then, be such a principle, whose very sub-
20 stance is actuality. Further, then, these substances must be without matter; for they must be eternal, at least if anything else is eternal. Therefore they must be actuality.

Yet there is a difficulty; for it is thought that everything that acts is able to act, but that not everything that is able to act acts, so that the potentiality is prior. But if this is so, nothing at all will exist; for it is possible for things to be
25 capable of existing but not yet to exist. Yet if we follow the mythologists who generate the world from night, or the natural philosophers who say that all things were together, the same impossible result ensues. For how will there be movement, if there is no actual cause? Matter will surely not move itself—the carpenter's art must act on it;
30 nor will the menstrual fluids nor the earth set themselves in motion, but the seeds and the semen must act on them.

This is why some suppose eternal actuality—e.g. Leucippus and Plato; for they say there is always movement. But why and what this movement is they do not say, nor, if the world moves in this way or that, do they tell us the cause of its doing so. Now nothing is moved at random, but
35 there must always be something present, e.g. as a matter of fact a thing moves in one way by nature, and in another by force or through the influence of thought or something else. Further, what sort of movement is primary? This makes a vast difference. But again Plato, at least, cannot even say what it is that he sometimes supposes to
1072ᵃ1 be the source of movement—that which moves itself; for the *soul* is later, and simultaneous with the heavens, according to his account. To suppose potentiality prior to actuality, then, is in a sense right, and in a sense not; and we have specified these senses.

That actuality is prior is testified by Anaxago-
5 ras (for his thought is actuality) and by Empedocles in his doctrine of love and strife, and by

those who say that there is always movement, e.g. Leucippus.

Therefore chaos or night did not exist for any infinite time, but the same things have always existed (either passing through a cycle of changes or in some way), since actuality is prior to potentiality. If, then, there is a constant cycle, something must always remain, acting in the same 10 way. And if there is to be generation and destruction, there must be something else which is always acting in different ways. This must, then, act in one way in virtue of itself, and in another in virtue of something else—either of a third agent, therefore, or of the first. But it must be in virtue of the first. For otherwise this again causes the motion both of the third agent and of the second. Therefore it is better to say the first. For 15 it was the cause of eternal movement; and something else is the cause of variety, and evidently both together are the cause of eternal variety. This, accordingly, is the character which the motions actually exhibit. What need then is there to seek for other principles?

7. Since this is a possible account of the matter, and if it were not true, the world would 20 have proceeded out of night and 'all things together' and out of non-being, these difficulties may be taken as solved. There is, then, something which is always moved with an unceasing motion, which is motion in a circle; and this is plain not in theory only but in fact. Therefore the first heavens must be eternal. There is therefore also something which moves them. And since that which is moved and moves is intermediate, there is a mover which moves without 25 being moved, being eternal, substance, and actuality. And the object of desire and the object of thought move in this way; they move without being moved. The primary objects of desire and of thought are the same. For the apparent good is the object of appetite, and the real good is the primary object of wish. But desire is consequent on opinion rather than opinion on desire; for the thinking is the starting-point. And thought 30 is moved by the object of thought, and one side of the list of opposites is in itself the object of thought; and in this, substance is first, and in

substance, that which is simple and exists actually. (The one and the simple are not the same; for 'one' means a measure, but 'simple' means that the thing itself has a certain nature.) But the good, also, and that which is in itself desir- 35 able are on this same side of the list; and the first in any class is always best, or analogous to the best.

1072ᵇ1 That that for the sake of which is found among the unmovables is shown by making a distinction; for that for the sake of which is both that *for* which and that *towards* which, and of these the one is unmovable and the other is not. Thus it produces motion by being loved, and it moves the other moving things. Now if something is moved it is capable of being otherwise than as it is. Therefore if the actuality of the heavens is primary motion, then in so far as they 5 are in motion, in *this* respect they are capable of being otherwise,—in place, even if not in substance. But since there is something which moves while itself unmoved, existing actually, this can in no way be otherwise than as it is. For motion in space is the first of the kinds of change, and motion in a circle the first kind of spatial motion; and this the first mover *produces*. 10 The first mover, then, of necessity exists; and in so far as it is necessary, it is good, and in this sense a first principle. For the necessary has all these senses—that which is necessary perforce because it is contrary to impulse, that without which the good is impossible, and that which cannot be otherwise but is *absolutely* necessary.

On such a principle, then, depend the heavens and the world of nature. And its life is such as the best which we enjoy, and enjoy for but a 15 short time. For it is ever in this state (which we cannot be), since its actuality is also pleasure. (And therefore waking, perception, and thinking are most pleasant, and hopes and memories are so because of their reference to these.) And thought in itself deals with that which is best in itself, and that which is thought in the fullest sense with that which is best in the fullest sense. And thought thinks itself because it shares the 20 nature of the object of thought; for it becomes an object of thought in coming into contact with and thinking its objects, so that thought and object of thought are the same. For that which is *capable* of receiving the object of thought, i.e. the substance, is thought. And it is *active* when it *possesses* this object. Therefore the latter rather than the former is the divine element which thought seems to contain, and the act of contemplation is what is most pleasant and best. If, then, God is always in that good state in which we sometimes are, this compels our wonder; and if in 25 a better this compels it yet more. And God *is* in a better state. And life also belongs to God; for the actuality of thought is life, and God is that actuality; and God's essential actuality is life most good and eternal. We say therefore that God is a living being, eternal, most good, so that life and duration continuous and eternal belong 30 to God; for this *is* God.

Those who suppose, as the Pythagoreans and Speusippus do, that supreme beauty and goodness are not present in the beginning, because the beginnings both of plants and of animals are *causes*, but beauty and completeness are in the *effects* of these, are wrong in their opinion. For the seed comes from other individuals which are prior and complete, and the first thing is not seed 1073ª1 but the complete being, e.g. we must say that before the seed there is a man,—not the man produced from the seed, but another from whom the seed comes.

It is clear then from what has been said that there is a substance which is eternal and unmovable and separate from sensible things. It has 5 been shown also that this substance cannot have any magnitude, but is without parts and indivisible. For it produces movement through infinite time, but nothing finite has infinite power. And, while every magnitude is either infinite or finite, it cannot, for the above reason, have finite magnitude, and it cannot have infinite magnitude 10 because there is no infinite magnitude at all. But it is also clear that it is impassive and unalterable; for all the other changes are posterior to change of place. It is clear, then, why the first mover has these attributes.

1073ᵇ **8.** We must not ignore the question whether we have to suppose one such substance or more 15 than one, and if the latter, how many. . . .

We however must discuss the subject, starting from the presuppositions and distinctions we have mentioned. The first principle or primary being is not movable either in itself or acciden- 25 tally, but produces the primary eternal and single movement. And since that which is moved must be moved by something, and the first mover must be in itself unmovable, and eternal movement must be produced by something eternal and a single movement by a single thing, and since we see that besides the simple spatial movement of the universe, which we say the first and unmovable substance produces, there are 30 other spatial movements—those of the planets— which are eternal (for the body which moves in a circle is eternal and unresting; we have proved these points in the *Physics*), each of *these* movements also must be caused by a substance unmovable in itself and eternal. For the nature of the stars is eternal, being a kind of sub- 35 stance, and the mover is eternal and prior to the moved, and that which is prior to a substance must be a substance. Evidently, then, there must be substances which are of the same number as the movements of the stars, and in their nature eternal, and in themselves unmovable, and without magnitude, for the reason 1073ᵇ1 before mentioned.

That the movers are substances, then, and that one of these is first and another second according to the same order as the movements of the stars, is evident. . . .

Evidently there is but one heaven. For if 1074ª31 there are many heavens as there are many men, the moving principles, of which each heaven will have one, will be one in form but in number many. But all things that are many in number have matter. (For one and the same formula applies to *many* things, e.g. the formula of man; but Socrates is *one*.) But the primary essence has 35 not matter; for it is fulfillment. So the unmovable first mover is one both in formula and in number; therefore also that which is moved always and continuously is one alone; therefore there is one 1074ᵇ1 heaven alone.

9. The nature of the divine thought 1074ᵇ15 involves certain problems; for while thought is held to be the most divine of phenomena, the question what it must be in order to have that character involves difficulties. For if it thinks nothing, what is there here of dignity? It is just like one who sleeps. And if it thinks, but this depends on something else, then (as that which is its substance is not the act of thinking, but a 20 capacity) it cannot be the best substance; for it is through thinking that its value belongs to it. Further, whether its substance is the faculty of thought or the act of thinking, what does it think? Either itself or something else; and if something else, either the same always or something different. Does it matter, then, or not, whether it thinks the good or any chance thing? Are there not some things about which it is 25 incredible that it should think? Evidently, then, it thinks that which is most divine and precious, and it does not change; for change would be change for the worse, and this would be already a movement. First, then, if it is not the act of thinking but a capacity, it would be reasonable to suppose that the continuity of its thinking is wearisome to it. Secondly, there would evidently 30 be something else more precious than thought, viz. that which is thought. For both thinking and the act of thought will belong even to one who has the worst of thoughts. Therefore if this ought to be avoided (and it ought, for there are even some things which it is better not to see than to see), the act of thinking cannot be the best of things. Therefore it must be itself that thought thinks (since it is the most excellent of things), and its thinking is a thinking on thinking. . . .

A further question is left—whether the 1075ª5 object of the thought is composite; for if it were, thought would change in passing from part to part of the whole. We answer that everything which has not matter is indivisible. As human thought, or rather the thought of composite objects, is in a certain period of time (for it does not possess the good at this moment or at that, but its best, being something *different* from it, is attained only in a whole period of time), so throughout eternity is the thought which has 10 *itself* for its object.

STUDY QUESTIONS: ARISTOTLE, *METAPHYSICS*

1. What is the purpose of metaphysics?
2. Why do people desire to know?
3. How does memory produce experience? How does art arise from experience?
4. Why do the senses alone not provide wisdom?
5. What is wisdom? What are some of its characteristics?
6. What made it possible for mathematics to arise in Egypt?
7. What are *first causes* and *the principles of things*?
8. What is the difference between material, efficient, and final causes?
9. What critical comments does Aristotle make of the early natural philosophers, such as Empedocles?
10. What critical comments does Aristotle make of Plato's theory of Forms?
11. In Book IV, how exactly does Aristotle formulate the claim that a contradiction is impossible?
12. In what way and why can this principle *not* be demonstrated? However, Aristotle claims that it can be demonstrated negatively. What is that demonstration?
13. In Book V, what are the two senses of 'substance'?
14. In Book V, why does Aristotle call substance that 'which is a "this" and separable'? What does he mean?
15. What does Aristotle mean by 'substratum'?
16. In Book VII, Aristotle says that only substance is definable. What is his reasoning for this assertion?

17. Aristotle says that each primary and self-subsistent thing is the same as its essence. What does this mean?
18. Toward the end of Book VII, how does Aristotle define primary substance?
19. Why is Aristotle so careful in his attempt to define and specify what primary substances are? What does he hope to gain from the investigation?
20. What are the differences between what Aristotle says in Book VII about substance and the distinction he draws between primary and secondary uses of the word 'substance' in the *Categories*?
21. How does Aristotle argue that there must be something that causes eternal movement?
22. How is it possible for something to cause motion without itself moving, according to Aristotle?
23. Why must the unmoved mover be an eternal substance? Why can there be only one of them?
24. What is the special problem regarding the divine thoughts of the unmoved mover? How does Aristotle solve this problem?
25. In what ways does Aristotle's metaphysics differ from Plato's? Does Aristotle's theory avoid some of the problems that Plato's theory faces? What are they? Does Aristotle's theory face its own difficulties?
26. What is the relationship between Aristotle's metaphysics and his theory of the categories?

ON THE SOUL

In Book II, Aristotle claims that every living body is both a form and matter. The soul is the form of the body. The individual person is only one substance. Described as form, the person is psyche or soul identified by its essential functions. Described as matter, this person is flesh and bone. Neither the form nor the matter should be thought of as separate substances. It is a mistake to regard the form as an additional nonmaterial thing, in the way that Plato does. Also, it is an error to try to reduce a substance to its matter, in the way that some of the pre-Socratics would. The English word 'soul' can be misleading, because it conveys the idea of a nonmaterial thing. The relevant Greek word is '*psuché*.'

Aristotle has three related ways to explain form. First, form is the essence of a substance. Note that this means that the psyche *is* an essence; it does not have one. Second, Aristotle says that form stands to matter as actual stands to potential. For example, a piece of bronze (i.e., matter) is only potentially a statue. When it has the form of a statue, then it actually is a statue. In other words, matter is merely potential; the form is actual. In terms of the human soul, a person actually has certain capacities, and, in this way, the soul is the actuality of the body. This requires that a body must have the appropriate organs that allow the person to exercise the relevant capacities. Third, Aristotle explains form in terms of function; he compares a natural body to a tool, and then to the eye. This is closely linked to the earlier reference to organs because organs perform various functions.

In Chapter 3 of Book II, Aristotle describes different levels of the psyche. All living things must have a capacity to feed. Plants, as the simplest form of life, have the powers of nutrition: to eat, grow, decay, and reproduce. Animals also have the power of sense perception and, because of this, they have imagination and desire, which is stimulated by perception and imagination, as well as the capacity to perform actions, to move. These animal functions (perception, desire, and action) are conceptually linked. Perception provides desire with its objects. Perception would have no point without desire, and desire would have no point without the power to pursue or to move.

Chapters 5–12 of Book II explain sense perception. The sense organs receive perceptible forms; they have the capacity to become similar to the thing affecting them, and this similarity is transmitted to a center, which Aristotle thought was the heart. The whole sensory system of an animal is really one. All sense organs converge on the single primary organ because it is the animal or person who touches, sees, hears, and so on.

In Chapter 1 of Book III, Aristotle notes that an explanation of any mental function will identify the relevant object. For instance, the object of sight is the visible, which is color. However, this does not mean that we can only see colors, because the object of sight can be described incidentally, as a person or as some object. In this way, it can be said that we see ordinary objects. Similar points apply to the other sense functions.

In Book III, Chapters 4–5, Aristotle distinguishes passive from active intellect. Passive intellect works by acquiring the form. In this sense, reasoning is like perception; passive reason is like a perceiver of definitions. On the other hand, active reason works by making all things. Aristotle compares it to light, which makes potential colors actual. As such, he suggests that active reason is necessary for passive reason. Aristotle also claims that active reason is immortal, eternal, and divine, and does not depend on matter for its functioning. It is pure form without matter. This seems to contradict the claim that matter and form are inseparable except in account.

BOOK II

412ᵃ3 **1.** Enough has been said of the views about the soul which have been handed down by our predecessors. Let us start again, as it were from the beginning, and try to determine what the soul is and what would be its most comprehensive definition.

412ᵃ6 Now we speak of one particular kind of existent things as substance, and under this heading we so speak of one thing *qua* matter, which in itself is not a particular, another *qua* shape and form, in virtue of which it is then spoken of as a particular, and a third *qua* the product of these two. And matter is potentiality, while form is actuality—and that in two ways, first as knowledge is, and second as contemplation is.

412ᵃ11 It is bodies especially which are thought to be substances, and of these especially natural bodies; for these are sources of the rest. Of natural bodies, some have life and some do not; and it is self-nourishment, growth, and decay that we speak of as life. Hence, every natural body which partakes of life will be a substance, and substance of a composite kind.

412ᵃ16 Since it is indeed a body of such a kind (for it is one having life), the soul will not be body; for the body is not something predicated of a subject, but exists rather as subject and matter. The soul must, then, be substance *qua* form of a natural body which has life potentially. Substance is actuality. The soul, therefore, will be the actuality of a body of this kind.

412ᵃ22 But actuality is so spoken of in two ways, first as knowledge is and second as contemplation is. It is clear then that the soul is actuality as knowledge is; for both sleep and waking depend on the existence of soul, and waking is analogous to contemplation, and sleep to the possession but not the exercise of knowledge. In the same individual knowledge is in origin prior. Hence the soul is the first actuality of a natural body which has life potentially.

412ᵃ28 Whatever has organs will be a body of this kind. Even the parts of plants are organs, although extremely simple ones, e.g. the leaf is a covering for the pod, and the pod for the fruit; while roots are analogous to the mouth, for both take in food.

Aristotle's De Anima, translated by D. W. Hamlyn, 1968. Reprinted by permission of Oxford University Press.

412ᵇ4 If then we are to speak of something common to every soul, it will be the first actuality of a natural body which has organs. Hence too we should not ask whether the soul and body are one, any more than whether the wax and the impression are one, or in general whether the matter of each thing and that of which it is the matter are one. For, while unity and being are so spoken of in many ways, that which is most properly so spoken of is the actuality.

412ᵇ10 It has then been stated in general what the soul is; for it is substance, that corresponding to the principle of a thing. And this is 'what it is for it to be what it was' for a body of such a kind. Compare the following: if an instrument, e.g. an axe, were a natural body, then its substance would be what it is to be an axe, and this would be its soul; if this were removed it would no longer be an axe, except homonymously. But as it is it is an axe; for it is not of this kind of body that the soul is 'what it is for it to be what it was' and the principle, but of a certain kind of natural body having within itself a source of movement and rest.

412ᵇ17 We must consider what has been said in relation to the parts of the body also. For, if the eye were an animal, sight would be its soul; for this is an eye's substance—that corresponding to its principle. The eye is matter for sight, and if this fails it is no longer an eye, except homonymously, just like an eye in stone or a painted eye. We must now apply to the whole living body that which applies to the part; for as the part is to the part, so analogously is perception as a whole to the whole perceptive body as such.

412ᵇ25 It is not that which has lost its soul which is potentially such as to live, but that which possesses it. Seeds and fruit are potentially bodies of this kind.

412ᵇ27 Just, then, as the cutting and the seeing, so too is the waking state actuality, while the soul is like sight and the potentiality of the instrument; the body is that which is this potentially. But just as the pupil and sight make up an eye, so in this case the soul and body make up an animal.

413ᵃ3 That, therefore, the soul or certain parts of it, if it is divisible, cannot be separated from the body is quite clear; for in some cases the actuality is of the parts themselves. Not that anything prevents at any rate *some* parts from being separable, because of their being actualities of no body. Furthermore, it is not clear whether the soul is the actuality of the body in the way that the sailor is of the ship. Let this suffice as a rough definition and sketch about the soul.

413ᵃ11 **2.** Since it is from things which are obscure but more obvious that we arrive at that which is clear and more intelligible in respect of the principle involved, we must try again in this way to treat of the soul; for a defining statement should not only make clear the fact, as the majority of definitions do, but it should also contain and reveal the reason for it. As things are, the statements of the definitions are like conclusions. For example, what is squaring? The construction of an equilateral rectangle equal to one which is not equilateral. But such a definition is a statement of the conclusion; whereas one who says that squaring is the discovery of the mean proportional states the reason for the circumstance.

413ᵃ20 We say, then, making a beginning of our inquiry, that that which has soul is distinguished from that which has not by life. But life is so spoken of in many ways, and we say that a thing lives if but one of the following is present—intellect, perception, movement, and rest in respect of place, and furthermore the movement involved in nutrition, and both decay and growth.

413ᵃ25 For this reason all plants too are thought to live; for they evidently have in them such a potentiality and first principle, through which they come to grow and decay in opposite directions. For they do not grow upwards without growing downwards, but they grow in both directions alike and in every direction—this being so of all that are constantly nourished and continue to live, as long as they are able to receive nourishment. This {form of life} can exist apart from the others, but the others cannot exist apart from it in mortal creatures. This is obvious in the case of plants; for they have no other potentiality of soul.

413ᵇ1 It is, then, because of this first principle that living things have life. But it is because of sense-perception first of all that they will be animal, for even those things which do not move or change their place, but which do have sense-perception, we speak of as animals and not merely as living.

413ᵇ4   First of all in perception all animals have touch. Just as the nutritive faculty can exist apart from touch and from all sense-perception, so touch can exist apart from the other senses. We speak of as nutritive that part of the soul in which even plants share; all animals clearly have the sense of touch. The reason for each of these circumstances we shall state later.

413ᵇ11   For the present let it be enough to say only that the soul is the source of the things above mentioned and is determined by them—by the faculties of nutrition, perception, thought, and by movement. Whether each of these is a soul or a part of a soul, and if a part, whether it is such as to be distinct in definition only or also in place, are questions to which it is not hard to find answers in some cases, although others present difficulty.

413ᵇ16   For, just as in the case of plants some clearly live when divided and separated from each other, the soul in them being actually one in actuality in each plant, though potentially many, so we see this happening also in other varieties of soul in the case of insects when they are cut in two; for each of the parts has sense-perception and motion in respect of place, and if sense-perception, then also imagination and desire. For where there is sense-perception, there is also both pain and pleasure, and where these, there is of necessity also wanting.

413ᵇ24   Concerning the intellect and the potentiality for contemplation the situation is not so far clear, but it seems to be a different kind of soul, and this alone can exist separately, as the everlasting can from the perishable.

413ᵇ27   But it is clear from these things that the remaining parts of the soul are not separable, as some say; although that they are different in definition is clear. For being able to perceive and being able to believe are different, since perceiving too is different from believing; and likewise with each of the other parts which have been mentioned.

413ᵇ32   Moreover, some animals have all these, others only some of them, and others again one alone, and this will furnish distinctions between animals; what is the reason for this we must consider later. Very much the same is the case with the senses; for some animals have them all, others only some, and others again one only, the most necessary one, touch.

414ᵃ4   That by means of which we live and perceive is so spoken of in two ways, as is that by means of which we know (we so speak in the one case of knowledge, in the other of soul, for by means of each of these we say we know). Similarly, we are healthy in the first place by means of health and in the second by means of a part of the body or even the whole. Now, of these knowledge and health are shape and a kind of form and principle, and as it were activity of the recipient, in the one case of that which is capable of knowing, in the other of that which is capable of health (for the activity of those things which are capable of acting appears to take place in that which is affected and disposed). Now the soul is in the primary way that by means of which we live, perceive, and think. Hence it will be a kind of principle and form, and not matter or subject.

414ᵃ14   Substance is so spoken of in three ways, as we have said, and of these cases one is form, another matter, and the third the product of the two; and of these matter is potentiality and form actuality. And since the product of the two is an ensouled thing, the body is not the actuality of soul, but the latter is the actuality of a certain kind of body.

414ᵃ19   And for this reason those have the right conception who believe that the soul does not exist without a body and yet is not itself a kind of body. For it is not a body, but something which belongs to a body, and for this reason exists in a body, and in a body of such and such a kind. Not as our predecessors supposed, when they fitted it to a body without any further determination of what body and of what kind, although it is clear that one chance thing does not receive another. In our way it happens just as reason demands. For the actuality of each thing comes naturally about in that which is already such potentially and in its appropriate matter.

From all this it is clear that the soul is a kind of actuality and principle of that which has the potentiality to be such.

414ᵃ29 **3.** Of the potentialities of the soul which have been mentioned, some existing things have them all, as we have said, others some of them, and certain of them only one. The potentialities which we mentioned are those for nutrition, sense-perception, desire, movement in respect of place, and thought.

414ᵃ32 Plants have the nutritive faculty only; other creatures have both this and the faculty of sense-perception. And if that of sense-perception, then that of desire also; for desire comprises wanting, passion, and wishing: all animals have at least one of the senses, touch, and for that which has sense-perception there is both pleasure and pain and both the pleasant and the painful: and where there are these, there is also wanting: for this is a desire for that which is pleasant.

414ᵇ6 Furthermore, they have a sense concerned with food; for touch is such a sense; for all living things are nourished by dry and moist and hot and cold things, and touch is the sense for these and only incidentally of the other objects of perception; for sound and colour and smell contribute nothing to nourishment, while flavour is one of the objects of touch. Hunger and thirst are forms of wanting, hunger is wanting the dry and hot, thirst wanting the moist and cold; and flavour is, as it were, a kind of seasoning of these. We must make clear about these matters later, but for now let us say this much, that those living things which have touch also have desire.

414ᵇ16 The situation with regard to imagination is obscure and must be considered later. Some things have in addition the faculty of movement in respect of place, and others, e.g. men and anything else which is similar or superior to man, have that of thought and intellect.

414ᵇ20 It is clear, then, that it is in the same way as with figure that there will be one definition of soul; for in the former case there is no figure over and above the triangle and the others which follow it in order, nor in the latter case is there soul over and above those mentioned. Even in the case of figures there could be produced a common definition, which will fit all of them but which will not be peculiar to any one. Similarly too with the kinds of soul mentioned.

414ᵇ25 For this reason it is foolish to seek both in these cases and in others for a common definition, which will be a definition peculiar to no actually existing thing and will not correspond to the proper indivisible species, to the neglect of one which will.

414ᵇ28 The circumstances with regard to soul are similar to the situation over figures; for in the case both of figures and of things which have soul that which is prior always exists potentially in what follows in order, e.g. the triangle in the quadrilateral on the one hand, and the nutritive faculty in that of perception on the other. Hence we must inquire in each case what is the soul of each thing, what is that of a plant, and what is that of a man or a beast.

414ᵇ33 For what reason they are so arranged in order of succession must be considered. For without the nutritive faculty there does not exist that of perception; but the nutritive faculty is found apart from that of perception in plants. Again, without the faculty of touch none of the other senses exists, but touch exists without the others; for many animals have neither sight nor hearing nor sense of smell. And of those which can perceive, some have the faculty of movement in respect of place, while others have not. Finally and most rarely, they have reason and thought; for those perishable creatures which have reason have all the rest, but not all those which have each of the others have reason. But some do not even have imagination, while others live by this alone. The contemplative intellect requires a separate discussion. That the account, therefore, appropriate for each of these is most appropriate for the soul also is clear.

416ᵇ32 **5.** Now that these matters have been determined let us discuss generally the whole of perception. Perception consists in being moved and affected, as has been said; for it is thought to be a kind of alteration. Some say too that the like is affected by like. How this is possible or impossible we have stated in our general account of acting and being affected.

417ª2 There is a problem why perception of the senses themselves does not occur, and why they do not give rise to perception without there being any external objects, although there is in them fire, earth, and the other elements, of which, either in themselves or in respect of their accidents, there is perception. It is clear, then, that the faculty of sense-perception does not exist by way of activity but by way of potentiality only; for this reason the perception does not occur, just as fuel does not burn in and through itself without something that can burn it; otherwise it would burn itself and would need no actually existing fire.

417ª9 Since we speak of perceiving in two ways (for we speak of that which potentially hears and sees as hearing and seeing, even if it happens to be asleep, as well as of that which is actually doing these things); perception too will be so spoken of in two ways, the one as in potentiality, the other as in actuality. Similarly with the object of perception too, one will be potentially, the other actually.

417ª14 First then let us speak as if being affected, being moved, and acting are the same thing; for indeed movement is a kind of activity, although an incomplete one, as has been said elsewhere. And everything is affected and moved by something which is capable of bringing this about and is in actuality. For this reason, in one way, as we said, a thing is affected by like, and in another by unlike; for it is the unlike which is affected, although when it has been affected it is like.

417ª21 But we must make distinctions concerning potentiality and actuality; for at the moment we are speaking of them in an unqualified way. For there are knowers in that we should speak of a man as a knower because man is one of those who are knowers and have knowledge; then there are knowers in that we speak straightaway of the man who has knowledge of grammar as a knower. (Each of these has a capacity but not in the same way—the one because his kind, his stuff, is of this sort, the other because he can if he so wishes contemplate, as long as nothing exter-

nal prevents him.) There is thirdly the man who is already contemplating, the man who is actually and in the proper sense knowing this particular A. Thus, both the first two, <being> potential knowers, <become actual knowers>, but the one by being altered through learning and frequent changes from an opposite disposition, the other by passing in another way from the state of having arithmetical or grammatical knowledge without exercising it to its exercise.

417ᵇ2 Being affected is not a single thing either; it is first a kind of destruction of something by its contrary, and second it is rather the preservation of that which is so potentially by that which is so actually and is like it in the way that a potentiality may be like an actuality. For that which has knowledge comes to contemplate, and this is either not an alteration (for the development of the thing is into itself and into actuality) or a different kind of alteration. For this reason it is not right to say that something which understands is altered when it understands, any more than a builder when he builds. The leading of a thinking and understanding thing, therefore, from being potentially such to actuality should not be called teaching, but should have another name; while that which, starting from being potentially such, learns and acquires knowledge by the agency of that which is actually such and is able to teach either should not be said to be affected, as has been said, or else we should say that there are two kinds of alteration, one a change to conditions of privation, the other to a thing's dispositions and nature.

417ᵇ16 The first change in that which can perceive is brought about by the parent, and when it is born it already has sense-perception in the same way as it has knowledge. Actual sense-perception is so spoken of in the same way as contemplation; but there is a difference in that in sense-perception the things which are able to produce the activity are external, i.e. the objects of sight and hearing, and similarly for the rest of the objects of perception. The reason is that actual perception is of particulars, while knowledge is of universals; and these are somehow in the soul itself. For this reason it is open to us to think when we wish, but perceiving is not similarly open to us; for there must be the object of perception. The situation is similar with sciences dealing with objects of perception, and for the same reason, that objects of perception are particular and external things.

417ᵇ29 But there will be an opportunity later to clarify these matters; for the present let it be enough to have determined this much—that, while that which is spoken of as potential is not a single thing, one thing being so spoken of as we should speak of a boy as a potential general, another as we should so speak of an adult, it is in the latter way with that which can perceive. But since the difference between the two has no name, although it has been determined that they are different and how they are so, we must use 'to be affected' and 'to be altered' as though they were the proper words.

418ᵃ3 That which can perceive is, as we have said, potentially such as the object of perception already is actually. It is not like the object, then, when it is being affected by it, but once it has been affected it becomes like it and is such as it is.

418ᵃ7 **6.** We must speak first of the objects of perception in relation to each sense. But objects of perception are so spoken of in three ways; of these we say that we perceive two in themselves, and one incidentally. Of the two, one is special to each sense, the other common to all.

418ᵃ11 I call special-object whatever cannot be perceived by another sense, and about which it is impossible to be deceived, e.g. sight has colour, hearing sound, and taste flavour, while touch has many varieties of object. But at any rate each judges about these, and is not deceived as to the fact that there is colour or sound, but rather as to what or where the coloured thing is or as to what or where the object which sounds is.

418ᵃ16 Such then are spoken of as special to each, while those that are spoken of as common are movement, rest, number, figure, size; for such as these are not special to any, but common to all. For certain movements are perceptible by both touch and sight.

418ᵃ20 An object of perception is spoken of as incidental, e.g. if the white thing were the son of Diares; for you perceive this incidentally, since this which you perceive is incidental to the white thing. Hence too you are not affected by the object of perception as such.

418ᵃ24 Of the objects which are perceived in themselves it is the special-objects which are objects of perception properly, and it is to these that the essence of each sense is naturally relative.

418ᵃ26 **7.** That of which there is sight, then, is visible. What is visible is colour and also something which may be described in words, but happens to have no name; what we mean will be clear as we proceed. For the visible is colour, and this is that which overlies what is in itself visible—in itself visible not by definition, but because it has in itself the cause of its visibility. Every colour is capable of setting in motion that which is actually transparent, and this is its nature. For this reason it is not visible without light, but the colour of each thing is always seen in light.

418ᵃ3 Hence we must first say what light is. There is, surely, something transparent. And I call transparent what is visible, not strictly speaking visible in itself, but because of the colour of something else. Of this sort are air, water, and many solid bodies; for it is not *qua* water or *qua* air that these are transparent, but because there exists in them a certain nature which is the same in them both and also in the eternal body above. Light is the activity of this, the transparent *qua* transparent. Potentially, wherever this is, there is darkness also. Light is a sort of colour of the transparent, when it is made actually transparent by fire or something such as the body above; for to this too belongs something which is one and the same.

418ᵃ13 What then the transparent is and what light is has been stated, i.e. that it is not fire nor body generally, nor an effluence from any body (for it would be a body in that case also), but the presence of fire of something of that kind in the transparent. For it is impossible for two bodies to be in the same place at the same time, light is thought to be the opposite of darkness, and since darkness is the privation of such a disposition from the transparent, it is clear that the presence of this is light.

418^b20 Empedocles, and anyone else who maintained the same view, was wrong in saying that light travels and arrives at some time between the earth and that which surrounds it, without our noticing it. For this is contrary to the clear evidence of reason and also to the apparent facts; for it might escape our notice over a short distance, but that it does so over the distance from east to west is too big an assumption.

418^b26 It is the colourless which is receptive of colour, and the soundless of sound. And it is the transparent which is colourless, as is also the invisible or barely visible, as dark things seem to be. The transparent is of this kind, not when it is actually transparent, but when it is potentially so; for the same nature is sometimes darkness and sometimes light.

424^a17 **12.** In general, with regard to all sense-perception, we must take it that the sense is that which can receive perceptible forms without their matter, as wax receives the imprint of the ring without the iron or gold, and it takes the imprint which is of gold or bronze, but not *qua* gold or bronze. Similarly too in each case the sense is affected by that which has colour or flavour or sound, but by these not in so far as they are what each of them is spoken of as being, but in so far as they are things of a certain kind and in accordance with their principle. The primary sense-organ is that in which such a potentiality resides. These are then the same, although what it is for them to be such is not the same. For that which perceives must be a particular extended magnitude, while what it is to be able to perceive and the sense are surely not magnitudes, but rather a certain principle and potentiality of that thing.

424^a28 It is clear from all this too why excess in the objects of perception destroys the sense-organs (for if the movement is too violent for the sense-organ its principle is destroyed—and this we saw the sense to be—just as the consonance and pitch of the strings are destroyed when they are struck too violently). It is also clear why plants do not perceive, although they have a part of the soul and are affected by tangible objects; for they are cooled and warmed. The reason is that they

do not have a mean, nor a first principle of a kind such as to receive the forms of objects of perception; rather they are affected by the matter as well.

424^b3 Someone might raise the question whether that which cannot smell might be affected by smell, or that which cannot see by colour; and similarly in the other cases. If the object of smell is smell, then smell must produce, if anything, smelling; hence nothing which is unable to smell can be affected by smell (and the same account applies to the other cases), nor can any of those things which can perceive be so affected except in so far as each is capable of perceiving. This is clear at the same time from the following too. Neither light and darkness nor sound nor smell does anything to bodies, but rather the things that they are in, e.g. it is the air accompanying the thunderbolt which splits the wood. But tangible objects and flavours do affect bodies; for otherwise by what could soulless things be affected and altered? Will those other objects, too, then, affect them? Or is it the case that not every body is affected by smell and sound, and those which are affected are indeterminate and inconstant, like air (for air smells, as if it had been affected)? What then is smelling apart from being affected? Or is smelling also perceiving, whereas the air when affected quickly becomes an object of perception?

BOOK III

424^b22 **1.** That there is no other sense apart from the five (and by these I mean sight, hearing, smell, taste, and touch) one might be convinced by the following considerations. We have even now perception of everything of which touch is the sense (for all the qualities of the tangible, *qua* tangible, are perceptible to us by touch). Also, if we lack any sense we must also lack a sense-organ. Again, all the things which we perceive through direct contact are perceptible by touch, which we in fact have, while all those which we perceive through media and not by direct contact are perceptible by means of the elements (I mean, for example, air and water). And the situation is such that if two things different in kind from each other are perceptible through one thing, then whoever has a sense-organ of this kind must be capable of perceiving both (e.g. if the sense-organ is composed of air, and air is required both for sound and for colour); while if there is more than one medium for the same object, e.g. both air and water for colour (for both are transparent), then he who has one of these alone will perceive whatever is perceptible through both. Now, sense-organs are composed of two of these elements only, air and water (for the pupil of the eye is composed of water, the organ of hearing of air, and the organ of smell of one or other of these), while fire either belongs to none of them or is common to all (for nothing is capable of perceiving without warmth), and earth either belongs to none of them or is a constituent specially and above all of that of touch. So there would remain no sense-organ apart from those of water and air, and these some animals possess even now. It may be inferred then that all the senses are possessed by those animals which are neither imperfect nor maimed (for even the mole apparently has eyes under the skin); hence, unless there is some other body and a property possessed by none of the bodies existing here and now, no sense can be left out.

425ᵃ14 Nor again is it possible for there to be any special sense-organ for the common-objects, which we perceive by each sense incidentally, e.g. movement, rest, figure, magnitude, number, and unity; for we perceive all these through movement, e.g. magnitude through movement (hence also figure, for figure is a particular form of magnitude), what is at rest through absence of movement, number through negation of continuity and also by the special-objects; for each sense perceives one thing. Hence it is clear that it is impossible for there to be a special sense for any of these, e.g. movement. For in that case it would be as we now perceive the sweet by sight; and this we do because we in fact have a perception of both, as a result of which we recognize them at the same time when they fall together. (Otherwise we should perceive them in no other way than incidentally, as we perceive the son of Cleon not because he is the son of Cleon but because he is white, and the white object happens to be the son of Cleon). But for the common-objects we have even now a common sense, not incidentally; there is, then, no special {sense} for them; for if so we should not perceive them otherwise than as stated [that we see the son of Cleon].

425ᵇ30 The senses perceive each other's special-objects incidentally, not in so far as they are themselves but in so far as they form a unity, when sense-perception simultaneously takes place in respect of the same object, e.g. in respect of bile that it is bitter and yellow (for it is not the task of any further {perception} at any rate to say that both are one); hence too one may be deceived, and if something is yellow, one may think that it is bile.

425ᵇ4 One might ask for what purpose we have several senses and not one only. Is it perhaps in order that the common-objects which accompany {the special-objects}, e.g. movement, magnitude, and number, may be less likely to escape our notice? For if there were sight alone, and this was of white, they would be more likely to escape our notice and all things would seem to be the same because colour and magnitude invariably accompany each other. But as things are, since the common-objects are present in the objects of another sense too, this makes it clear that each of them is distinct.

429ᵃ10 **4.** In respect of that part of the soul by which the soul both knows and understands, whether this is distinct or not distinct spatially but only in definition, we must inquire what distinguishing characteristic it has, and how thinking ever comes about.

429ᵃ13 Now, if thinking is akin to perceiving, it would be either being affected in some way by the object of thought or something else of this kind. It must then be unaffected, but capable of receiving the form, and potentially such as it, although not identical with it; and as that which is capable of perceiving is to the objects of perception, so must be the intellect similarly to its objects.

429ᵃ18 It must, then, since it thinks all things, be unmixed, as Anaxagoras says, in order that it may rule, that is in order that it may know; for the intrusion of anything foreign to it hinders and obstructs it; hence too, it must have no other nature than this, that it is potential. That part of the soul, then, called intellect (and I speak of as intellect that by which the soul thinks and supposes) is actually none of existing things before it thinks. Hence too, it is reasonable that it should not be mixed with the body; for in that case it would come to be of a certain kind, either cold or hot, or it would even have an organ like the faculty of perception; but as things are it has none. Those who say, then, that the soul is a place of forms speak well, except that it is not the whole soul but that which can think, and it is not actually but potentially the forms.

429ᵃ29   That the ways in which the faculties of sense-perception and intellect are unaffected are not the same is clear from reference to the sense-organs and the sense. For the sense is not capable of perceiving when the object of perception has been too intense, e.g. it cannot perceive sound after loud sounds, nor see or smell after strong colours or smells. But when the intellect thinks something especially fit for thought, it thinks inferior things not less but rather more. For the faculty of sense-perception is not independent of the body, whereas the intellect is distinct. When the intellect has become each thing in the way that one who actually knows is said to do so (and this happens when he can exercise his capacity by himself), it exists potentially even then in a way, although not in the same way as before it learned or discovered; and then it can think by itself.

429ᵇ10   Since a magnitude and what it is to be a magnitude are different, and water and what it is to be water (and so too for many other things, but not for all; for in some cases they are the same), we judge what it is to be flesh and flesh itself either by means of something different or by the same thing differently disposed. For flesh does not exist apart from matter, but like the snub it is a this in a this. It is, then, with the faculty of sense-perception that we judge the hot and the cold and those things of which flesh is a certain proportion. But it is by something else, either something distinct or something which is to the former as a bent line

is related to itself when straightened out, that we judge what it is to be flesh.

429ᵇ18   Again, in the case of those things which exist in abstraction, the straight corresponds to the snub, for it involves extension; but 'what it is for it to be what it was', if what it is to be straight and the straight are different, is something else; let it be duality. We judge it, then, by something different or by the same thing differently disposed. In general, then, as things are distinct from matter, so it is too with what concerns the intellect.

429ᵇ22   Given that the intellect is something simple and unaffected, and that it has nothing in common with anything else, as Anaxagoras says, someone might raise these questions: how will it think, if thinking is being affected in some way (for it is in so far as two things have something in common that the one is thought to act and the other to be affected)? And can it itself also be thought? For either everything else will have intellect, if it can itself be thought without this being through anything else and if what can be thought is identical in form, or it will have something mixed in it which makes it capable of being thought as the other things are.

429ᵇ29   Now, being affected in virtue of something common has been discussed before—to the effect that the intellect is in a way potentially the objects of thought, although it is actually nothing before it thinks; potentially in the same way as there is writing on a tablet on which nothing actually written exists; that is what happens in the case of the intellect. And it is itself an object of thought, just as its objects are. For, in the case of those things which have no matter, that which thinks and that which is thought are the same; for contemplative knowledge and that which is known in that way are the same. The reason why it does not always think we must consider. In those things which have matter each of the objects of thought is present potentially. Hence, *they* will not have intellect in them (for intellect is a potentiality for being such things without their matter), while *it* will have what can be thought in it.

430ᵃ10   **5.** Since [just as] in the whole of nature there is something which is matter to each kind of thing (and this is what is potentially all of them), while on the other hand there is something else which is their cause and is productive by producing them all—these being related as an art to its material—so there must also be these differences in the soul. And there is an intellect which is of this kind by becoming all things, and there is another which is so by producing all things, as a kind of disposition, like light, does; for in a way light too makes colours which are potential into actual colours. And this intellect is distinct, unaffected, and unmixed, being in essence activity.

430ᵃ18 For that which acts is always superior to that which is affected, and the first principle to the matter. [Actual knowledge is identical with its object; but potential knowledge is prior in time in the individual but not prior even in time in general]; and it is not the case that it sometimes thinks and at other times not. In separation it is just what it is, and this alone is immortal and eternal. (But we do not remember because this is unaffected, whereas the passive intellect is perishable, and without this thinks nothing.)

STUDY QUESTIONS: ARISTOTLE, *ON THE SOUL*

1. What does he mean by 'matter is potentiality, while form is actuality'?
2. How does Aristotle define 'life'? A natural body that has life in it is a substance in what sense of the word?
3. What does it mean to say that the soul is the actuality of a natural body that is alive? How does Aristotle argue for this point?
4. How does he define 'soul' in terms of principle?
5. If an axe were a natural body, what would its soul be? If an eye were a natural body, what would its soul be?
6. Why is the soul inseparable from the body?
7. Why does he say that the soul must be relative to a body?
8. What is the soul of a plant? What is the soul of an animal? Why does Aristotle distinguish them?
9. What is the problem concerning sensation and perception that Aristotle needs to solve?
10. How does Aristotle explain objects of sense? What are common sensibles (Book II Chapter 6)? And incidental objects of sense?
11. What is a sense? How are forms related to sensible things?
12. Why can't plants perceive?
13. How does Aristotle explain thinking? Why is everything a possible object of thought?
14. What is active thinking? Why is it very different from passive thought? Why does Aristotle claim that it is eternal?
15. How is Aristotle's conception of the soul different from that of Plato?
16. Is it correct to call Aristotle a materialist? In what ways is it misleading?

NICOMACHEAN ETHICS

The *Nicomachean Ethics* is one of the greatest works in moral philosophy. Its main aim is to define the good life for a human being. Every natural thing has a nature, which defines the final end of its development. The good of human life is the fulfillment of human nature. The distinctive characteristic of a human is the rational faculty of the soul. The highest good for human life, therefore, consists in the improvement and actualization of rationality.

The work is divided into ten books. In Book I, Aristotle tries to establish that the best life for a human being consists in activity of the soul in accordance with virtue. Aristotle argues that something good is what we aim for. Some things are desired for themselves, and others merely as means. Some activities are ends in themselves. The most general thing people want purely for itself is a happy life. However, note that the Greek term 'eudaimonia' does not have the hedonistic tone of the English word 'happiness;' it is rather a life that is good to live. From I.7, Aristotle tries to discover the good life by specifying the distinctive functions of human beings. These functions define various traits of excellence. Note that the relevant Greek term, 'àreté,' means excellent traits of character, although it is usually translated with the misleading moralistic term 'virtue.' For Aristotle, virtue consists in character traits that enable us to live well.

At the beginning of Book II, Aristotle distinguishes between moral virtues, the theme of Books II–V, and the intellectual virtues, the topic of Book VI. Book II is a general explanation of the moral virtues. Chapter 6 of Book II explains Aristotle's famous doctrine of the mean, according to which virtues, or excellences of character, are a mean between two extremes, which constitute vices. This is not the same as advocating moderation. For example, courage is a mean between cowardice and foolhardiness, but there can be moments that call for great courage. Aristotle also emphasizes the unity of the virtues. A person cannot have generosity and lack courage, because there will be times when generosity requires courage. Within this framework, in Book IV, Aristotle analyzes specific virtues such as generosity, magnanimity, friendliness, and truthfulness.

Book VI contains an important discussion of practical wisdom, or *phronesis*, which guides us to act in the right way. Practical wisdom includes not only the ability to find the best means to certain ends but also the ability to deliberate about ends. A person with such wisdom can deliberate, and he or she understands how happiness or flourishing is formed by the virtues.

The first chapters of Book VII contain a discussion of weakness of the will, or *akrasia*. Aristotle thinks that someone who thinks that X is good is necessarily disposed to choose it. Given this, he must explain how weakness of the will is possible. Books VIII and IX contain an examination of the nature of friendship. In Book X, Aristotle argues that theoretical contemplation is the highest function of a person, corresponding to the activity of the divine-like active intellect.

BOOK I

1. Every art and every investigation, and likewise every practical pursuit or undertaking, seems to aim at some good: hence it has been 2 well said that the Good is That at which all things aim. (It is true that a certain variety is to be observed among the ends at which the arts and sciences aim: in some cases the activity of practising the art is itself the end, whereas in others the end is some product over and above the mere exercise of the art; and in the arts whose ends are certain things beside the practice of the arts themselves, these products are essentially superior in value to the activities.) 3 But as there are numerous pursuits and arts and

From *The Nicomachean Ethics*, translated by H. Rackham, (Loeb Classical Library, 1934).

sciences, it follows that their ends are correspondingly numerous: for instance, the end of the science of medicine is health, that of the art of shipbuilding a vessel, that of strategy victory,
4 that of domestic economy wealth. Now in cases where several such pursuits are subordinate to some single faculty—as bridle-making and the other trades concerned with horses' harness are subordinate to horsemanship, and this and every other military pursuit to the science of strategy, and similarly other arts to different arts again—in all these cases, I say, the ends of the master arts are things more to be desired than all those of the arts subordinate to them; since the latter
5 ends are only pursued for the sake of the former. (And it makes no difference whether the ends of the pursuits are the activities themselves or some other thing beside these, as in the case of the sciences mentioned.)

2. If therefore among the ends at which our actions aim there be one which we wish for its own sake, while we wish the others only for the sake of this, and if we do not choose everything for the sake of something else (which would obviously result in a process *ad infinitum*, so that all desire would be futile and vain), it is clear that this one ultimate End must be the Good,
2 and indeed the Supreme Good. Will not then a knowledge of this Supreme Good be also of great practical importance for the conduct of life? Will it not better enable us to attain what is fitting,
3 like archers having a target to aim at? If this be so, we ought to make an attempt to determine at all events in outline what exactly this Supreme Good is, and of which of the theoretical or practical sciences it is the object.
4   Now it would be agreed that it must be the object of the most authoritative of the sciences—
5 some science which is pre-eminently a master-
6 craft. But such is manifestly the science of Politics; for it is this that ordains which of the sciences are to exist in states, and what branches of knowledge the different classes of the citizens are to learn, and up to what point; and we observe that even the most highly esteemed of the faculties, such as strategy, domestic economy,
7 oratory, are subordinate to the political science.

Inasmuch then as the rest of the sciences are employed by this one, and as it moreover lays down laws as to what people shall do and what things they shall refrain from doing, the end of this science must include the ends of all the others. Therefore, the Good of man must be the end
8 of the science of Politics. For even though it be the case that the Good is the same for the individual and for the state, nevertheless, the good of the state is manifestly a greater and more perfect good, both to attain and to preserve. To secure the good of one person only is better than nothing; but to secure the good of a nation or a state is a nobler and more divine achievement.

This then being its aim, our investigation is in a sense the study of Politics.

3. Now our treatment of this science will be adequate, if it achieves that amount of precision which belongs to its subject matter. The same exactness must not be expected in all departments of philosophy alike, any more than in all the products of the arts and crafts. The subjects
2 studied by political science are Moral Nobility and Justice; but these conceptions involve much difference of opinion and uncertainty, so that they are sometimes believed to be mere conventions and to have no real existence in the nature
3 of things. And a similar uncertainty surrounds the conception of the Good, because it frequently occurs that good things have harmful consequences: people have before now been ruined by wealth, and in other cases courage has
4 cost men their lives. We must therefore be content if, in dealing with subjects and starting from premises thus uncertain, we succeed in presenting a broad outline of the truth: when our subjects and our premises are merely generalities, it is enough if we arrive at generally valid conclusions. Accordingly we may ask the student also to accept the various views we put forward in the same spirit; for it is the mark of an educated mind to expect that amount of exactness in each kind which the nature of the particular subject admits. It is equally unreasonable to accept merely probable conclusions from a mathematician and to demand strict demonstration from an orator.

5 Again, each man judges correctly those matters with which he is acquainted; it is of these that he is a competent critic. To criticize a particular subject, therefore, a man must have been trained in that subject: to be a good critic generally, he must have had an all-round education. Hence the young are not fit to be students of Political Science. For they have no experience of life and conduct, and it is these that supply the premises and subject matter of this branch of phi-
6 losophy. And moreover they are led by their feelings; so that they will study the subject to no purpose or advantage, since the end of this sci-
7 ence is not knowledge but action. And it makes no difference whether they are young in years or immature in character: the defect is not a question of time, it is because their life and its various aims are guided by feeling; for to such persons their knowledge is of no use, any more than it is to persons of defective self-restraint. But Moral Science may be of great value to those who guide their desires and actions by principle.

8 Let so much suffice by way of introduction as to the student of the subject, the spirit in which our conclusions are to be received, and the object that we set before us.

4. To resume, inasmuch as all studies and undertakings are directed to the attainment of some good, let us discuss what it is that we pronounce to be the aim of Politics, that is, what is the highest of all the goods that action can
2 achieve. As far as the name goes, we may almost say that the great majority of mankind are agreed about this; for both the multitude and persons of refinement speak of it as Happiness, and conceive 'the good life' or 'doing well' to be the same thing as 'being happy.' But what constitutes happiness is a matter of dispute; and the popular
3 account of it is not the same as that given by the philosophers. Ordinary people identify it with some obvious and visible good, such as pleasure or wealth or honour—some say one thing and some another, indeed very often the same man says different things at different times: when he falls sick he thinks health is happiness, when he is poor, wealth. At other times, feeling conscious of their own ignorance, men admire those who

propound something grand and above their heads; and it has been held by some thinkers that beside the many good things we have mentioned, there exists another Good, that is good in itself, and stands to all those goods as the cause of their being good.

4 Now perhaps it would be a somewhat fruitless task to review all the different opinions that are held. It will suffice to examine those that are most widely prevalent, or that seem to have some argument in their favour.

5 And we must not overlook the distinction between arguments that start from first principles and those that lead to first principles. It was a good practice of Plato to raise this question, and to enquire whether the right procedure was to start from or to lead up to the first principles, as in a race-course one may run from the judges to the far end of the track or reversely. Now no doubt it is proper to start from the known. But 'the known' has two meanings—'what is known to us,' which is one thing, and 'what is knowable in itself,' which is another. Perhaps then for us at all events it is proper to start from what is known to
6 us. This is why in order to be a competent student of the Right and Just, and in short of the topics of Politics in general, the pupil is bound to have
7 been well trained in his habits. For the starting-point or first principle is the fact that a thing is so; if this be satisfactorily ascertained, there will be no need also to know the reason why it is so. And the man of good moral training knows first principles already, or can easily acquire them. As for the person who neither knows nor can learn, let him hear the words of Hesiod:

> Best is the man who can himself advise;
> He too is good who hearkens to the wise;
> But who, himself being witless, will not heed
> Another's wisdom, is worthless indeed.

5. But let us continue from the point where we digressed. To judge from men's lives, the more or less reasoned conceptions of the Good or Happiness that seem to prevail among them are the following. On the one hand the generality of men and the most vulgar identify the Good with pleasure, and accordingly are content with the

2 Life of Enjoyment—for there are three specially prominent Lives, the one just mentioned, the Life of Politics, and thirdly, the Life of Contem-

3 plation. The generality of mankind then show themselves to be utterly slavish, by preferring what is only a life for cattle; but they get a hearing for their view as reasonable because many persons of high position share the feelings of Sardanapallus.

4 Men of refinement, on the other hand, and men of action think that the Good is honour— for this may be said to be the end of the Life of Politics. But honour after all seems too superficial to be the Good for which we are seeking; since it appears to depend on those who confer it more than on him upon whom it is conferred, whereas we instinctively feel that the Good must be something proper to its possessor and not easy to be taken away from him. Moreover men's motive

5 in pursuing honour seems to be to assure themselves of their own merit; at least they seek to be honoured by men of judgement and by people who know them, that is, they desire to be honoured on the ground of virtue. It is clear therefore that in the opinion at all events of men of action,

6 virtue is a greater good than honour; and one might perhaps accordingly suppose that virtue rather than honour is the end of the Political Life. But even virtue proves on examination to be too incomplete to be the End; since it appears possible to possess it while you are asleep, or without putting it into practice throughout the whole of your life; and also for the virtuous man to suffer the greatest misery and misfortune— though no one would pronounce a man living a life of misery to be happy, unless for the sake of maintaining a paradox. But we need not pursue this subject, since it has been sufficiently treated in the ordinary discussions.

7 The third type of life is the Life of Contemplation, which we shall consider in the sequel.

8 The Life of Money-making is a constrained kind of life, and clearly wealth is not the Good we are in search of, for it is only good as being useful, a means to something else. On this score indeed one might conceive the ends before mentioned to have a better claim, for they are approved for their own sakes. But even they do not really seem to be the Supreme Good; however, many arguments have been laid down in regard to them, so we may dismiss them.

6. But perhaps it is desirable that we should examine the notion of a Universal Good, and review the difficulties that it involves, although such an enquiry goes against the grain because of our friendship for the authors of the Theory of Ideas. Still perhaps it would appear desirable, and indeed it would seem to be obligatory, especially for a philosopher, to sacrifice even one's closest personal ties in defence of the truth. Both are dear to us, yet 'tis our duty to prefer the truth.

2 The originators of this theory, then, used not to postulate Ideas of groups of things in which they posited an order of priority and posteriority (for which reason they did not construct an Idea of numbers in general). But Good is predicated alike in the Categories of Substance, of Quality, and of Relation; yet the Absolute, or Substance, is prior in nature to the Relative, which seems to be a sort of offshoot or 'accident' of Substance; so that there cannot be a common Idea corresponding to the absolutely good and the relatively good.

3 Again, the word 'good' is used in as many senses as the word 'is'; for we may predicate good in the Category of Substance, for instance of God or intelligence; in that of Quality—the excellences; in that of Quantity—moderate in amount; in that of Relation—useful; in that of Time—a favourable opportunity; in that of Place—a suitable 'habitat'; and so on. So clearly good cannot be a single and universal general notion; if it were, it would not be predicable in all the Categories, but only in one.

4 Again, things that come under a single Idea must be objects of a single science; hence there ought to be a single science dealing with all good things. But as a matter of fact there are a number of sciences even for the goods in one Category: for example, opportunity, for opportunity in war comes under the science of strategy, in disease under that of medicine; and the due amount in diet comes under medicine, in bodily exercise under gymnastics.

5   One might also raise the question what precisely they mean by their expression 'the Ideal so-and-so,' seeing that one and the same definition of man applies both to 'the Ideal man' and to 'man,' for in so far as both are man, there will be no difference between them; and if so, no more will there be any difference between 'the Ideal Good' and 'Good' in so far as both are good.

6 Nor yet will the Ideal Good be any more good because it is eternal, seeing that a white thing that lasts a long time is no whiter than one that lasts only a day.

7   The Pythagoreans seem to give a more probable doctrine on the subject of the Good when they place Unity in their column of goods; and indeed Speusippus appears to have followed them. But this subject must be left for another discussion.

8   We can descry an objection that may be raised against our arguments on the ground that the theory in question was not intended to apply to every sort of good, and that only things pursued and accepted for their own sake are pronounced good as belonging to a single species, while things productive or preservative of these in any way, or preventive of their opposites, are said to be good as a means to these, and in a 9 different sense. Clearly then the term 'goods' would have two meanings, (1) things good in themselves and (2) things good as a means to these; let us then separate things good in themselves from things useful as means, and consider whether the former are called good because they 10 fall under a single Idea. But what sort of things is one to class as good in themselves? Are they not those things which are sought after even without any accessory advantage, such as wisdom, sight, and certain pleasures and honours? for even if we also pursue these things as means to something else, still one would class them among things good in themselves. Or is there nothing else good in itself except the Idea? If so, the species will be 11 of no use. If on the contrary the class of things good in themselves includes these objects, the same notion of good ought to be manifested in all of them, just as the same notion of white is manifested in snow and in white paint. But as a matter of fact the notions of honour and wisdom

and pleasure, as being good, are different and distinct. Therefore, good is not a general term corresponding to a single Idea.

12   But in what sense then are different things called good? For they do not seem to be a case of things that bear the same name merely by chance. Possibly things are called good in virtue of being derived from one good; or because they all contribute to one good. Or perhaps it is rather by way of a proportion: that is, as sight is good in the body, so intelligence is good in the soul, and similarly another thing in something else.

13   Perhaps however this question must be dismissed for the present, since a detailed investigation of it belongs more properly to another branch of philosophy. And likewise with the Idea of the Good; for even if the goodness predicated of various things in common really is a unity or something existing separately and absolute, it clearly will not be practicable or attainable by man; but the Good which we are now seeking is a good within human reach.

14   But possibly someone may think that to know the Ideal Good may be desirable as an aid to achieving those goods which are practicable and attainable: having the Ideal Good as a pattern we shall more easily know what things are good for us, and knowing them, obtain them. 15 Now it is true that this argument has a certain plausibility; but it does not seem to square with the actual procedure of the sciences. For these all aim at some good, and seek to make up their deficiencies, but they do not trouble about a knowledge of the Ideal Good. Yet if it were so potent an aid, it is improbable that all the professors of the arts and sciences should not know it, nor 16 even seek to discover it. Moreover, it is not easy to see *how* knowing that same Ideal Good will help a weaver or carpenter in the practice of his own craft, or how anybody will be a better physician or general for having contemplated the absolute Idea. In fact it does not appear that the physician studies even health in the abstract; he studies the health of the human being—or rather of some particular human being, for it is individuals that he has to cure.

Let us here conclude our discussion of this subject.

7. We may now return to the Good which is the object of our search, and try to find out what exactly it can be. For good appears to be one thing in one pursuit or art and another in another: it is different in medicine from what it is in strategy, and so on with the rest of the arts. What definition of the Good then will hold true in all the arts? Perhaps we may define it as that for the sake of which everything else is done. This applies to something different in each different art—to health in the case of medicine, to victory in that of strategy, to a house in architecture, and to something else in each of the other arts; but in every pursuit or undertaking it describes the end of that pursuit or undertaking, since in all of them it is for the sake of the end that everything else is done. Hence if there be something which is the end of all the things done by human action, this will be the practicable Good—or if there be several such ends, the sum of these will be the 2 Good. Thus by changing its ground the argument has reached the same result as before. We must attempt however to render this still more precise.

3   Now there do appear to be several ends at which our actions aim; but as we choose some of them—for instance wealth, or flutes, and instruments generally—as a means to something else, it is clear that not all of them are final ends; whereas the Supreme Good seems to be something final. Consequently if there be some one thing which alone is a final end, this thing—or if there be several final ends, the one among them which is the most final—will be the Good which 4 we are seeking. In speaking of degrees of finality, we mean that a thing pursued as an end in itself is more final than one pursued as a means to something else, and that a thing never chosen as a means to anything else is more final than things chosen both as ends in themselves and as means to that thing; and accordingly a thing chosen always as an end and never as a means we call 5 absolutely final. Now happiness above all else appears to be absolutely final in this sense, since we always choose it for its own sake and never as a means to something else; whereas honour, pleasure, intelligence, and excellence in its various forms, we choose indeed for their own sakes (since we should be glad to have each of them although no extraneous advantage resulted from it), but we also choose them for the sake of happiness, in the belief that they will be a means to our securing it. But no one chooses happiness for the sake of honour, pleasure, etc., nor as a means to anything whatever other than itself.

6   The same conclusion also appears to follow from a consideration of the self-sufficiency of happiness—for it is felt that the final good must be a thing sufficient in itself. The term self-sufficient, however, we employ with reference not to oneself alone, living a life of isolation, but also to one's parents and children and wife, and one's friends and fellow citizens in general, since man is by nature a social being. On the other 7 hand a limit has to be assumed in these relationships; for if the list be extended to one's ancestors and descendants and to the friends of one's friends, it will go on *ad infinitum*. But this is a point that must be considered later on; we take a self-sufficient thing to mean a thing which merely standing by itself alone renders life desirable and lacking in nothing, and such a thing we deem happiness to be. Moreover, we think happi- 8 ness the most desirable of all good things without being itself reckoned as one among the rest; for if it were so reckoned, it is clear that we should consider it more desirable when even the smallest of other good things were combined with it, since this addition would result in a larger total of good, and of two goods the greater is always the more desirable.

Happiness, therefore, being found to be something final and self-sufficient, is the End at which all actions aim.

9   To say however that the Supreme Good is happiness will probably appear a truism; we still require a more explicit account of what consti- 10 tutes happiness. Perhaps then we may arrive at this by ascertaining what is man's function. For the goodness or efficiency of a flute-player or sculptor or craftsman of any sort, and in general of anybody who has some function or business to perform, is thought to reside in that function; and similarly it may be held that the good of man resides in the function of man, if he has a function.

11 Are we then to suppose that, while the carpenter and the shoemaker have definite functions or businesses belonging to them, man as such has none, and is not designed by nature to fulfil any function? Must we not rather assume that, just as the eye, the hand, the foot and each of the various members of the body manifestly has a certain function of its own, so a human being also has a certain function over and above all the functions of his particular members? What 12 then precisely can this function be? The mere act of living appears to be shared even by plants, whereas we are looking for the function peculiar to man; we must therefore set aside the vital activity of nutrition and growth. Next in the scale will come some form of sentient life; but this too appears to be shared by horses, oxen, and 13 animals generally. There remains therefore what may be called the practical life of the rational part of man. (This part has two divisions, one rational as obedient to principle, the other as possessing principle and exercising intelligence). Rational life again has two meanings; let us assume that we are here concerned with the active exercise of the rational faculty, since this seems to be the more proper sense of the term. If 14 then the function of man is the active exercise of the soul's faculties in conformity with rational principle, or at all events not in dissociation from rational principle, and if we acknowledge the function of an individual and of a good individual of the same class (for instance, a harper and a good harper, and so generally with all classes) to be generically the same, the qualification of the latter's superiority in excellence being added to the function in his case (I mean that if the function of a harper is to play the harp, that of a good harper is to play the harp well): if this is so, and if we declare that the function of man is a certain form of life, and define that form of life as the exercise of the soul's faculties and activities in association with rational principle, and say that 15 the function of a good man is to perform these activities well and rightly, and if a function is well performed when it is performed in accordance with its own proper excellence—from these premises it follows that the Good of man is the active exercise of his soul's faculties in conformity with excellence or virtue, or if there be several human excellences or virtues, in con-16 formity with the best and most perfect among them. Moreover this activity must occupy a complete lifetime; for one swallow does not make spring, nor does one fine day; and similarly one day or a brief period of happiness does not make a man supremely blessed and happy.

17 Let this account then serve to describe the Good in outline—for no doubt the proper procedure is to begin by making a rough sketch, and to fill it in afterwards. If a work has been well laid down in outline, to carry it on and complete it in detail may be supposed to be within the capacity of anybody; and in this working out of details Time seems to be a good inventor or at all events coadjutor. This indeed is how advances in the arts have actually come about, since anyone can 18 fill in the gaps. Also the warning given above must not be forgotten; we must not look for equal exactness in all departments of study, but only such as belongs to the subject matter of each, and in such a degree as is appropriate to the particular 19 line of enquiry. A carpenter and a geometrician both seek after a right angle, but in different ways; the former is content with that approximation to it which satisfies the purpose of his work; the latter, being a student of truth, looks for its essence or essential attributes. We should therefore proceed in the same manner in other subjects also, and not allow side issues to outweigh the main task in hand.

20 Nor again must we in all matters alike demand an explanation of the reason why things are what they are; in some cases it is enough if the fact that they are so is satisfactorily established. This is the case with first principles; and the fact is the primary thing—it is a first princi-21 ple. And principles are studied—some by induction, others by perception, others by some form of habituation, and also others otherwise; so we 22 must endeavour to arrive at the principles of each kind in their natural manner, and must also be careful to define them correctly, since they are 23 of great importance for the subsequent course of the enquiry. The beginning is admittedly more

than half of the whole, and throws light at once on many of the questions under investigation.

8. Accordingly we must examine our first principle not only as a logical conclusion deduced from certain premises but also in the light of the current opinions on the subject. For if a proposition be true, all the facts harmonize with it, but if it is false, it is soon found to be discordant with them.

2 Now things good have been divided into three classes, external goods on the one hand, and goods of the soul and of the body on the other; and of these three kinds of goods, those of the soul we commonly pronounce good in the fullest sense and the highest degree. But it is our actions and the soul's active exercise of its functions that we posit (as being Happiness); hence so far as this opinion goes—and it is of long standing, and generally accepted by students of philosophy—it supports the correctness of our definition of Happiness.

3 It also shows it to be right merely in declaring the End to consist in actions or activities of some sort, for thus the End is included among goods of the soul, and not among external goods.

4 Again, our definition accords with the description of the happy man as one who 'lives well' or 'does well'; for it has virtually identified happiness with a form of good life or doing well.

5 And moreover all the various characteristics that are looked for in happiness are found to belong to the Good as we define it. Some people 6 think happiness is goodness or virtue, others prudence, others a form of wisdom; others again say it is all of these things, or one of them, in combination with pleasure, or accompanied by pleasure as an indispensable adjunct; another school include external prosperity as a concomitant factor. Some 7 of these views have been held by many people and from ancient times, others by a few distinguished men, and neither class is likely to be altogether mistaken; the probability is that their beliefs are at least partly, or indeed mainly, correct.

8 Now with those who pronounce happiness to be virtue, or some particular virtue, our definition is in agreement; for 'activity in conformity with 9 virtue' involves virtue. But no doubt it makes a great difference whether we conceive the Supreme Good to depend on possessing virtue or on displaying it—on disposition, or on the manifestation of a disposition in action. For a man may possess the disposition without its producing any good result, as for instance when he is asleep, or has ceased to function from some other cause; but virtue in active exercise cannot be inoperative— it will of necessity act, and act well. And just as at the Olympic games the wreaths of victory are not bestowed upon the handsomest and strongest persons present, but on men who enter for the competitions—since it is among these that the winners are found,—so it is those who *act* rightly who carry off the prizes and good things of life.

10 And further, the life of active virtue is essentially pleasant. For the feeling of pleasure is an experience of the soul, and a thing gives a man pleasure in regard to which he is described as 'fond of' so-and-so: for instance a horse gives pleasure to one fond of horses, a play to one fond of the theatre, and similarly just actions are pleasant to the lover of justice, and acts conforming with virtue generally to the lover of virtue. 11 But whereas the mass of mankind take pleasure in things that conflict with one another, because they are not pleasant of their own nature, things pleasant by nature are pleasant to lovers of what is noble, and so always are actions in conformity with virtue, so that they are pleasant essentially as well as pleasant to lovers of the noble. There- 12 fore their life has no need of pleasure as a sort of ornamental appendage, but contains its pleasure in itself. For there is the further consideration that the man who does not enjoy doing noble actions is not a good man at all: no one would call a man just if he did not like acting justly, nor liberal if he did not like doing liberal things, and similarly with the other virtues. But if so, actions 13 in conformity with virtue must be essentially pleasant.

But they are also of course both good and noble, and each in the highest degree, if the good man judges them rightly; and his judgement is as we have said. It follows therefore that 14 happiness is at once the best, the noblest, and the pleasantest of things: these qualities are not separated as the inscription at Delos makes out—

Justice is noblest, and health is best,
But the heart's desire is the pleasantest—,

for the best activities possess them all; and it is the best activities, or one activity which is the best of all, in which according to our definition happiness consists.

15 Nevertheless it is manifest that happiness also requires external goods in addition, as we said; for it is impossible, or at least not easy, to play a noble part unless furnished with the necessary equipment. For many noble actions require instruments for their performance, in the shape of friends or wealth or political power; also there

16 are certain external advantages, the lack of which sullies supreme felicity, such as good birth, satisfactory children, and personal beauty: a man of very ugly appearance or low birth, or childless and alone in the world, is not our idea of a happy man, and still less so perhaps is one who has children or friends that are worthless, or who has had good ones but lost them by death. As we said

17 therefore, happiness does seem to require the addition of external prosperity, and this is why some people identify it with good fortune (though some identify it with virtue).

9. It is this that gives rise to the question whether happiness is a thing that can be learnt, or acquired by training, or cultivated in some other manner, or whether it is bestowed by some divine dispensation or even by fortune. (1) Now

2 if anything that men have is a gift of the gods, it is reasonable to suppose that happiness is divinely given—indeed of all man's possessions it is most likely to be so, inasmuch as it is the best of them

3 all. This subject however may perhaps more properly belong to another branch of study. Still, even if happiness is not sent us from heaven, but is won by virtue and by some kind of study or practice, it seems to be one of the most divine things that exist. For the prize and end of goodness must clearly be supremely good—it must be something

4 divine and blissful. (2) And also on our view it will admit of being widely diffused, since it can be attained through some process of study or effort by all persons whose capacity for virtue has not

5 been stunted or maimed. (3) Again, if it is better

to be happy as a result of one's own exertions than by the gift of fortune, it is reasonable to suppose that this is how happiness is won; inasmuch as in the world of nature things have a natural tendency to be ordered in the best possible way, and

6 the same is true of the products of art, and of causation of any kind, and especially the highest. Whereas that the greatest and noblest of all things should be left to fortune would be too contrary to the fitness of things.

7 Light is also thrown on the question by our definition of happiness, which said that it is a certain kind of activity of the soul; whereas the remaining good things are either merely indispensable conditions of happiness, or are of the nature of auxiliary means, and useful instrumen-

8 tally. This conclusion moreover agrees with what we laid down at the outset; for we stated that the Supreme Good was the end of political science, but the principal care of this science is to produce a certain character in the citizens, namely to make them virtuous, and capable of performing noble actions.

12. These questions being settled, let us consider whether happiness is one of the things we praise or rather one of those that we honour; for it is at all events clear that it is not a mere potentiality.

2 Now it appears that a thing which we praise is always praised because it has a certain quality and stands in a certain relation to something. For we praise just men and brave men, in fact good men and virtue generally, because of their actions and the results they produce; and we praise the men who are strong of body, swift of foot and the like on account of their possessing certain natural qualities, and standing in a certain relation to something good and excellent. The point is

3 always illustrated by our feeling about praises addressed to the gods: it strakes us as absurd that the gods should be referred to our standards, and this is what praising them amounts to, since praise, as we said, involves a reference of its

4 object to something else. But if praise belongs to what is relative, it is clear that the best things merit not praise but something greater and better: as indeed is generally recognized, since we

speak of the gods as blessed and happy, and also 'blessed' is the term that we apply to the most godlike men; and similarly with good things—no one praises happiness as one praises justice, but we call it 'a blessing,' deeming it something higher and more divine than things we praise.

5 Indeed it seems that Eudoxus took a good line in advocating the claims of pleasure to the prize of highest excellence, when he held that the fact that pleasure, though a good, is not praised, is an indication that it is superior to the things we praise, as God and the Good are, because they are the standards to which everything else is referred.

6 For praise belongs to goodness, since it is this that makes men capable of accomplishing noble deeds, while encomia are for deeds accomplished, whether bodily feats or achievements of the mind. 7 However, to develop this subject is perhaps rather the business of those who have made a study of encomia. For our purpose we may draw the conclusion from the foregoing remarks, that happiness is a thing honoured and perfect. This seems 8 to be borne out by the fact that it is a first principle or starting-point, since all other things that all men do are done for its sake; and that which is the first principle and cause of things good we agree to be something honourable and divine.

13. But inasmuch as happiness is a certain activity of soul in conformity with perfect goodness, it is necessary to examine the nature of goodness. For this will probably assist us in our investigation of the nature of happiness. Also, 2 the true statesman seems to be one who has made a special study of goodness, since his aim is to make the citizens good and law-abiding men— 3 witness the lawgivers of Crete and Sparta, and the other great legislators of history; but if the 4 study of goodness falls within the province of Political Science, it is clear that in investigating goodness we shall be keeping to the plan which we adopted at the outset.

5 Now the goodness that we have to consider is clearly human goodness, since the good or happiness which we set out to seek was human good and human happiness. But human goodness 6 means in our view excellence of soul, not excellence of body; also our definition of happiness is

an activity of the soul. Now if this is so, clearly it 7 behoves the statesman to have some acquaintance with psychology, just as the physician who is to heal the eye or the other parts of the body must know their anatomy. Indeed a foundation of science is even more requisite for the statesman, inasmuch as politics is a higher and more honourable art than medicine; but physicians of the better class devote much attention to the study 8 of the human body. The student of politics therefore as well as the psychologist must study the nature of the soul, though he will do so as an aid to politics, and only so far as is requisite for the objects of enquiry that he has in view: to pursue the subject in further detail would doubtless be more laborious than is necessary for his purpose.

9 Now on the subject of psychology some of the teaching current in extraneous discourses is satisfactory, and may be adopted here: namely that the soul consists of two parts, one irrational and the other capable of reason. (Whether these 10 two parts are really distinct in the sense that the parts of the body or of any other divisible whole are distinct, or whether though distinguishable in thought as two they are inseparable in reality, like the convex and concave sides of a curve, is a question of no importance for the matter in 11 hand.) Of the irrational part of the soul again one division appears to be common to all living things, and of a vegetative nature: I refer to the part that causes nutrition and growth; for we must assume that a vital faculty of this nature exists in all things that assimilate nourishment, including embryos—the same faculty being present also in the fully-developed organism (this is more reasonable than to assume a different nutri- 12 tive faculty in the latter). The excellence of this faculty therefore appears to be common to all animate things and not peculiar to man; for it is believed that this faculty or part of the soul is most active during sleep, but when they are asleep you cannot tell a good man from a bad one (whence the saying that for half their lives there is no difference between the happy and the mis- 13 erable). This is a natural result of the fact that sleep is a cessation of the soul from the activities on which its goodness or badness depends—except that in some small degree certain of the

sense-impressions may reach the soul during sleep, and consequently the dreams of the good are better than those of ordinary men. We need

14 not however pursue this subject further, but may omit from consideration the nutritive part of the soul, since it exhibits no specifically human excellence.

15 But there also appears to be another element in the soul, which, though irrational, yet in a manner participates in rational principle. In self-restrained and unrestrained people we approve their principle, or the rational part of their souls, because it urges them in the right way and exhorts them to the best course; but their nature seems also to contain another element beside that of rational principle, which combats and

16 resists that principle. Exactly the same thing may take place in the soul as occurs with the body in a case of paralysis: when the patient wills to move his limbs to the right they swerve to the left; and similarly in unrestrained persons their impulses run counter to their principle. But whereas in the body we see the erratic member, in the case of the soul we do not see it; nevertheless it cannot be doubted that in the soul also there is an element beside that of principle, which opposes and runs counter to principle (though in what sense the two are distinct does not concern us here). But this second element

17 also seems, as we said, to participate in rational principle; at least in the self-restrained man it obeys the behest of principle—and no doubt in the temperate and brave man it is still more amenable, for all parts of his nature are in harmony with principle.

18 Thus we see that the irrational part, as well as the soul as a whole, is double. One division of it, the vegetative, does not share in rational principle at all; the other, the seat of the appetites and of desire in general, does in a sense participate in principle, as being amenable and obedient to it (in the sense in fact in which we speak of 'paying heed' to one's father and friends, not in the sense of the term 'rational' in mathematics). And that principle can in a manner appeal to the irrational part, is indicated by our practice of admonishing delinquents, and by our employment of rebuke and exhortation generally.

19 If on the other hand it be more correct to speak of the appetitive part of the soul also as rational, in that case it is the rational part which, as well as the whole soul, is divided into two, the one division having rational principle in the proper sense and in itself, the other obedient to it as a child to its father.

20 Now virtue also is differentiated in correspondence with this division of the soul. Some forms of virtue are called intellectual virtues, others moral virtues: Wisdom or intelligence and Prudence are intellectual, Liberality and Temperance are moral virtues. When describing a man's moral character we do not say that he is wise or intelligent, but gentle or temperate; but a wise man also is praised for his disposition, and praiseworthy dispositions we term virtues.

BOOK II

1. Virtue being, as we have seen, of two kinds, intellectual and moral, intellectual virtue is for the most part both produced and increased by instruction, and therefore requires experience and time; whereas moral or ethical virtue is the product of habit (*ethos*), and has indeed derived its

2 name, with a slight variation of form, from that word. And therefore it is clear that none of the moral virtues is engendered in us by nature, for no natural property can be altered by habit. For instance, it is the nature of a stone to move downwards, and it cannot be trained to move upwards, even though you should try to train it to do so by throwing it up into the air ten thousand times; nor can fire be trained to move downwards, nor can anything else that naturally behaves in one way be trained into a habit of behaving in another

3 way. The virtues therefore are engendered in us neither by nature nor yet in violation of nature; nature gives us the capacity to receive them, and this capacity is brought to maturity by habit.

4 Moreover, the faculties given us by nature are bestowed on us first in a potential form; we exhibit their actual exercise afterwards. This is clearly so with our senses: we did not acquire the faculty of sight or hearing by repeatedly seeing or repeatedly listening, but the other way about—because we had the senses we began to use them, we did not

get them by using them. The virtues on the other hand we acquire by first having actually practised them, just as we do the arts. We learn an art or craft by doing the things that we shall have to do when we have learnt it: for instance, men become builders by building houses, harpers by playing on the harp. Similarly we become just by doing just acts, temperate by doing temperate acts, brave by 5 doing brave acts. This truth is attested by the experience of states: lawgivers make the citizens good by training them in habits of right action— this is the aim of all legislation, and if it fails to do this it is a failure; this is what distinguishes a good 6 form of constitution from a bad one. Again, the actions from or through which any virtue is produced are the same as those through which it also is destroyed—just as is the case with skill in the arts, for both the good harpers and the bad ones are produced by harping, and similarly with builders and all the other craftsmen: as you will become a good builder from building well, so you will become a bad one from building badly. Were 7 this not so, there would be no need for teachers of the arts, but everybody would be born a good or bad craftsman as the case might be. The same then is true of the virtues. It is by taking part in transactions with our fellow-men that some of us become just and others unjust; by acting in dangerous situations and forming a habit of fear or of confidence we become courageous or cowardly. And the same holds good of our dispositions with regard to the appetites, and anger; some men become temperate and gentle, other profligate and irascible, by actually comporting themselves in one way or the other in relation to those passions. In a word, our moral dispositions are formed as a result of the corresponding activities. Hence it is incumbent on us 8 to control the character of our activities, since on the quality of these depends the quality of our dispositions. It is therefore not of small moment whether we are trained from childhood in one set of habits or another; on the contrary it is of very great, or rather of supreme, importance.

2. As then our present study, unlike the other branches of philosophy, has a practical aim (for we are not investigating the nature of virtue for the sake of knowing what it is, but in order that we may become good, without which result our investigation would be of no use), we have consequently to carry our enquiry into the region of conduct, and to ask how we are to act rightly; since our actions, as we have said, determine the quality of our dispositions.

2 Now the formula 'to act in conformity with right principle' is common ground, and may be assumed as the basis of our discussion. (We shall speak about this formula later, and consider both the definition of right principle and its relation to the other virtues.)

3 But let it be granted to begin with that the whole theory of conduct is bound to be an outline only and not an exact system, in accordance with the rule we laid down at the beginning, that philosophical theories must only be required to correspond to their subject matter; and matters of conduct and expediency have nothing fixed or invariable about them, any more than have matters of health. And if this is true of the general 4 theory of ethics, still less is exact precision possible in dealing with particular cases of conduct; for these come under no science or professional tradition, but the agents themselves have to consider what is suited to the circumstances on each occasion, just as is the case with the art of medi- 5 cine or of navigation. But although the discussion now proceeding is thus necessarily inexact, we must do our best to help it out.

6 First of all then we have to observe, that moral qualities are so constituted as to be destroyed by excess and by deficiency—as we see is the case with bodily strength and health (for one is forced to explain what is invisible by means of visible illustrations). Strength is destroyed both by excessive and by deficient exercises, and similarly health is destroyed both by too much and by too little food and drink; while they are produced, increased and preserved by suitable 7 quantities. The same therefore is true of Temperance, Courage, and the other virtues. The man who runs away from everything in fear and never endures anything becomes a coward; the man who fears nothing whatsoever but encounters everything becomes rash. Similarly he that indulges in every pleasure and refrains from none turns out a profligate, and he that shuns all pleas-

ure, as boorish persons do, becomes what may be called insensible. Thus Temperance and Courage are destroyed by excess and deficiency, and preserved by the observance of the mean.

8 But not only are the virtues both generated and fostered on the one hand, and destroyed on the other, from and by the same actions, but they will also find their full exercise in the same actions. This is clearly the case with the other more visible qualities, such as bodily strength: for strength is produced by taking much food and undergoing much exertion, while also it is the strong man who will be able to eat most food and endure most exertion. The same holds good with 9 the virtues. We become temperate by abstaining from pleasures, and at the same time we are best able to abstain from pleasures when we have become temperate. And so with Courage: we become brave by training ourselves to despise and endure terrors, and we shall be best able to endure terrors when we have become brave.

3. An index of our dispositions is afforded by the pleasure or pain that accompanies our actions. A man is temperate if he abstains from bodily pleasures and finds this abstinence itself enjoyable, profligate if he feels it irksome; he is brave if he faces danger with pleasure or at all events without pain, cowardly if he does so with pain.

In fact pleasures and pains are the things with which moral virtue is concerned.

For (1) pleasure causes us to do base actions and pain causes us to abstain from doing noble actions. Hence the importance, as Plato points 2 out, of having been definitely trained from childhood to like and dislike the proper things; this is what good education means.

3 (2) Again, if the virtues have to do with actions and feelings, and every feeling and every action is attended with pleasure or pain, this too shows that virtue has to do with pleasure and pain.

4 (3) Another indication is the fact that pain is the medium of punishment; for punishment is a sort of medicine, and it is the nature of medicine to work by means of opposites.

5 (4) Again, as we said before, every formed disposition of the soul realizes its full nature in relation to and in dealing with that class of objects by which it is its nature to be corrupted or improved. But men are corrupted through pleasures and pains, that is, either by pursuing and avoiding the wrong pleasures and pains, or by pursuing and avoiding them at the wrong time, or in the wrong manner, or in one of the other wrong ways under which errors of conduct can be logically classified. This is why some thinkers define the virtues as states of impassivity or tranquillity, though they make a mistake in using these terms absolutely, without adding 'in the right (or wrong) manner' and 'at the right (or wrong) time' and the other qualifications.

6 We assume therefore that moral virtue is the quality of acting in the best way in relation to pleasures and pains, and that vice is the opposite.

7 But the following considerations also will give us further light on the same point.

(5) There are three things that are the motives of choice and three that are the motives of avoidance; namely, the noble, the expedient, and the pleasant, and their opposites, the base, the harmful, and the painful. Now in respect of all these the good man is likely to go right and the bad to go wrong, but especially in respect of pleasure; for pleasure is common to man with the lower animals, and also it is a concomitant of all the objects of choice, since both the noble and the expedient appear to us pleasant.

8 (6) Again, the susceptibility to pleasure has grown up with all of us from the cradle. Hence this feeling is hard to eradicate, being engrained in the fabric of our lives.

(7) Again, pleasure and pain are also the standards by which we all, in a greater or less degree, regulate our actions. On this account 9 therefore pleasure and pain are necessarily our main concern, since to feel pleasure and pain rightly or wrongly has a great effect on conduct.

10 (8) And again, it is harder to fight against pleasure than against anger (hard as that is, as Heracleitus says); but virtue, like art, is constantly dealing with what is harder, since the harder the task the better is success. For this reason also therefore pleasure and pain are necessarily the main concern both of virtue and of political science, since he who comports himself

towards them rightly will be good, and he who does so wrongly, bad.

11 We may then take it as established that virtue has to do with pleasures and pains, that the actions which produce it are those which increase it, and also, if differently performed, destroy it, and that the actions from which it was produced are also those in which it is exercised.

4. A difficulty may however be raised as to what we mean by saying that in order to become just men must do just actions, and in order to become temperate they must do temperate actions. For if they do just and temperate actions, they are just and temperate already, just as, if they spell correctly or play in tune, they are scholars or musicians.

2 But perhaps this is not the case even with the arts. It is possible to spell a word correctly by chance, or because some one else prompts you; hence you will be a scholar only if you spell correctly in the scholar's way, that is, in virtue of the scholarly knowledge which you yourself possess.

3 Moreover the case of the arts is not really analogous to that of the virtues. Works of art have their merit in themselves, so that it is enough if they are produced having a certain quality of their own; but acts done in conformity with the virtues are not done justly or temperately if they themselves are of a certain sort, but only if the agent also is in a certain state of mind when he does them: first he must act with knowledge; secondly he must deliberately choose the act, and choose it for its own sake; and thirdly the act must spring from a fixed and permanent disposition of character. For the possession of an art, none of these conditions is included, except the mere qualification of knowledge; but for the possession of the virtues, knowledge is of little or no avail, whereas the other conditions, so far from being of little moment, are all-important, inasmuch as virtue results from the repeated performance of just and temperate actions. Thus 4 although actions are entitled just and temperate when they are such acts as just and temperate men would do, the agent is just and temperate not when he does these acts merely, but when he does them in the way in which just and temperate men do them. It is correct 5 therefore to say that a man becomes just by doing just actions and temperate by doing temperate actions; and no one can have the remotest chance of becoming good without doing them. 6 But the mass of mankind, instead of doing virtuous acts, have recourse to discussing virtue, and fancy that they are pursuing philosophy and that this will make them good men. In so doing they act like invalids who listen carefully to what the doctor says, but entirely neglect to carry out his prescriptions. That sort of philosophy will no more lead to a healthy state of soul than will the mode of treatment produce health of body.

5. We have next to consider the formal definition of virtue.

A state of the soul is either (1) an emotion, (2) a capacity, or (3) a disposition; virtue therefore must be one of these three things. By the 2 emotions, I mean desire, anger, fear, confidence, envy, joy, friendship, hatred, longing, jealousy, pity; and generally those states of consciousness which are accompanied by pleasure or pain. The capacities are the faculties in virtue of which we can be said to be liable to the emotions, for example, capable of feeling anger or pain or pity. The dispositions are the formed states of character in virtue of which we are well or ill disposed in respect of the emotions; for instance, we have a bad disposition in regard to anger if we are disposed to get angry too violently or not violently enough, a good disposition if we habitually feel a moderate amount of anger; and similarly in respect of the other emotions.

3 Now the virtues and vices are not emotions because we are not pronounced good or bad according to our emotions, but we are according to our virtues and vices; nor are we either praised or blamed for our emotions—a man is not praised for being frightened or angry, nor is he blamed for being angry merely, but for being angry in a certain way—but we are praised or blamed for our virtues and vices. Again, we are 4 not angry or afraid from choice, but the virtues are certain modes of choice, or at all events

involve choice. Moreover, we are said to be 'moved' by the emotions, whereas in respect of the virtues and vices we are not said to be 'moved' but to be 'disposed' in a certain way.

5 And the same considerations also prove that the virtues and vices are not capacities; since we are not pronounced good or bad, praised or blamed, merely by reason of our capacity for emotion. Again, we possess certain capacities by nature, but we are not born good or bad by nature: of this however we spoke before.

6 If then the virtues are neither emotions nor capacities, it remains that they are dispositions.

Thus we have stated what virtue is generically.

6. But it is not enough merely to define virtue generically as a disposition; we must also say what species of disposition it is. It must then 2 be premised that all excellence has a twofold effect on the thing to which it belongs: it not only renders the thing itself good, but it also causes it to perform its function well. For example, the effect of excellence in the eye is that the eye is good *and* functions well; since having good eyes means having good sight. Similarly excellence in a horse makes it a good horse, and also good at galloping, at carrying its rider, and at 3 facing the enemy. If therefore this is true of all things, excellence or virtue in a man will be the disposition which renders him a good man and also which will cause him to perform his function well. We have already indicated what this 4 means; but it will throw more light on the subject if we consider what constitutes the specific nature of virtue.

Now of everything that is continuous and divisible, it is possible to take the larger part, or the smaller part, or an equal part, and these parts may be larger, smaller, and equal either with respect to the thing itself or relatively to us; the equal part being a mean between excess and defi- 5 ciency. By the mean of the thing I denote a point equally distant from either extreme, which is one and the same for everybody; by the mean relative to us, that amount which is neither too much nor too little, and this is not one and the same for everybody. For example, let 10 be many and 2 few; then one takes the mean with respect to 6 the thing if one takes 6; since $6 - 2 = 10 - 6$, and this is the mean according to arithmetical 7 proportion. But we cannot arrive by this method at the mean relative to us. Suppose that 10 lb. of food is a large ration for anybody and 2 lb. a small one: it does not follow that a trainer will prescribe 6 lb., for perhaps even this will be a large ration, or a small one, for the particular athlete who is to receive it; it is a small ration for a Milo, but a large one for a man just beginning to go in for athletics. And similarly with the amount of running or wrestling exercise to be 8 taken. In the same way then an expert in any art avoids excess and deficiency, and seeks and adopts the mean—the mean, that is, not of the thing but relative to us. If therefore the way in 9 which every art or science performs its work well is by looking to the mean and applying that as a standard to its productions (hence the common remark about a perfect work of art, that you could not take from it nor add to it—meaning that excess and deficiency destroy perfection, while adherence to the mean preserves it)—if then, as we say, good craftsmen look to the mean as they work, and if virtue, like nature, is more accurate and better than any form of art, it will follow that virtue has the quality of hitting the mean. I refer to moral virtue, for this is con- 10 cerned with emotions and actions, in which one can have excess or deficiency or a due mean. For example, one can be frightened or bold, feel desire or anger or pity, and experience pleasure and pain in general, either too much or too little, and in both cases wrongly; whereas to feel these 11 feelings at the right time, on the right occasion, towards the right people, for the right purpose and in the right manner, is to feel the best amount of them, which is the mean amount— and the best amount is of course the mark of 12 virtue. And similarly there can be excess, deficiency, and the due mean in actions. Now feelings and actions are the objects with which virtue is concerned; and in feelings and actions excess and deficiency are errors, while the mean amount is praised, and constitutes success; and to be praised and to be successful are both marks 13 of virtue. Virtue, therefore, is a mean state in the

14 sense that it is able to hit the mean. Again, error is multiform (for evil is a form of the unlimited, as in the old Pythagorean imagery, and good of the limited), whereas success is possible in one way only (which is why it is easy to fail and difficult to succeed—easy to miss the target and difficult to hit it); so this is another reason why excess and deficiency are a mark of vice, and observance of the mean a mark of virtue:

Goodness is simple, badness manifold.

15 Virtue then is a settled disposition of the mind determining the choice of actions and emotions, consisting essentially in the observance of the mean relative to us, this being determined by principle, that is, as the prudent man would determine it.

16 And it is a mean state between two vices, one of excess and one of defect. Furthermore, it is a mean state in that whereas the vices either fall short of or exceed what is right in feelings and in actions, virtue ascertains and adopts the mean.

17 Hence while in respect of its substance and the definition that states what it really is in essence virtue is the observance of the mean, in point of excellence and rightness it is an extreme.

18 Not every action or emotion however admits of the observance of a due mean. Indeed the very names of some directly imply evil, for instance malice, shamelessness, envy, and, of actions, adultery, theft, murder. All these and similar actions and feelings are blamed as being bad in themselves; it is not the excess or deficiency of them that we blame. It is impossible therefore ever to go right in regard to them—one must always be wrong; nor does right or wrong in their case depend on the circumstances, for instance, whether one commits adultery with the right woman, at the right time, and in the right manner; the mere commission of any of them is wrong.

19 One might as well suppose there could be a due mean and excess and deficiency in acts of injustice or cowardice or profligacy, which would imply that one could have a medium amount of excess and of deficiency, an excessive amount of excess and a deficient amount of deficiency. But just as there

20 can be no excess or deficiency in temperance and justice, because the mean is in a sense an extreme,

so there can be no observance of the mean nor excess nor deficiency in the corresponding vicious acts mentioned above, but however they are committed, they are wrong; since, to put it in general terms, there is no such thing as observing a mean in excess or deficiency, nor as exceeding or falling short in the observance of a mean.

7. We must not however rest content with stating this general definition, but must show that it applies to the particular virtues. In practical philosophy, although universal principles have a wider application, those covering a particular part of the field possess a higher degree of truth; because conduct deals with particular facts, and our theories are bound to accord with these.

Let us then take the particular virtues from the diagram.

2 The observance of the mean in fear and confidence is Courage. The man that exceeds in fearlessness is not designated by any special name (and this is the case with many of the virtues and vices); he that exceeds in confidence is Rash; he that exceeds in fear and is deficient in confidence

3 is Cowardly. In respect of pleasures and pains—not all of them, and to a less degree in respect of pains—the observance of the mean is Temperance, the excess Profligacy. Men deficient in the enjoyment of pleasures scarcely occur, and hence this character also has not been assigned a name, but we may call it Insensible. In regard to giving

4 and getting money, the observance of the mean is Liberality; the excess and deficiency are Prodigality and Meanness, but the prodigal man and the mean man exceed and fall short in opposite ways to one another: the prodigal exceeds in giving and is deficient in getting, whereas the mean

5 man exceeds in getting and is deficient in giving. For the present then we describe these qualities in outline and summarily, which is enough for the purpose in hand; but they will be more accurately defined later.

6 There are also other dispositions in relation to money, namely, the mode of observing the mean called Magnificence (the magnificent man being different from the liberal, as the former deals with large amounts and the latter with

small ones), the excess called Tastelessness or Vulgarity, and the defect called Paltriness. These are not the same as Liberality and the vices corresponding to it; but the way in which they differ will be discussed later.

7 In respect of honour and dishonour, the observance of the mean is Greatness of Soul, the excess a sort of Vanity, as it may be called, and the deficiency, Smallness of Soul. And just as we 8 said that Liberality is related to Magnificence, differing from it in being concerned with small amounts of money, so there is a certain quality related to Greatness of Soul, which is concerned with great honours, while this quality itself is concerned with small honours; for it is possible to aspire to minor honours in the right way, or more than is right, or less. He who exceeds in these aspirations is called ambitious, he who is deficient, unambitious; but the middle character has no name, and the dispositions of these persons are also unnamed, except that that of the ambitious man is called Ambitiousness. Consequently the extreme characters put in a claim to the middle position, and in fact we ourselves sometimes call the middle person ambitious and sometimes unambitious: we sometimes praise a man for being ambitious, sometimes for being unambi-9 tious. Why we do so shall be discussed later; for the present let us classify the remaining virtues and vices on the lines which we have laid down.

10 In respect of anger also we have excess, deficiency, and the observance of the mean. These states are virtually without names, but as we call a person of the middle character gentle, let us name the observance of the mean Gentleness, while of the extremes, he that exceeds may be styled irascible and his vice Irascibility, and he that is deficient, spiritless, and the deficiency Spiritlessness.

11 There are also three other modes of observing a mean which bear some resemblance to each other, and yet are different; all have to do with intercourse in conversation and action, but they differ in that one is concerned with truthfulness of speech and behaviour, and the other with pleasantness, in its two divisions of pleasantness in social amusement and pleasantness in the general affairs of life. We must then discuss these qualities also, in order the better to discern that

in all things the observance of the mean is to be praised, while the extremes are neither right nor praiseworthy, but reprehensible. Most of these qualities also are unnamed, but in these as in the other cases we must attempt to coin names for them ourselves, for the sake of clearness and so that our meaning may be easily followed.

12 In respect of truth then, the middle character may be called truthful, and the observance of the mean Truthfulness; pretence in the form of exaggeration is Boastfulness, and its possessor a boaster; in the form of understatement, Self-depreciation, and its possessor the self-depreciator.

13 In respect of pleasantness in social amusement, the middle character is witty and the middle disposition Wittiness; the excess is Buffoonery and its possessor a buffoon; the deficient man may be called boorish, and his disposition Boorishness. In respect of general pleasantness in life, the man who is pleasant in the proper manner is friendly, and the observance of the mean is Friendliness; he that exceeds, if from no interested motive, is obsequious, if for his own advantage, a flatterer; he that is deficient, and unpleasant in all the affairs of life, may be called quarrelsome and surly.

14 There are also modes of observing a mean in the sphere of and in relation to the emotions. For in these also one man is spoken of as moderate and another as excessive—for example the bashful man whose modesty takes alarm at everything; while he that is deficient in shame, or abashed at nothing whatsoever, is shameless, and the man of middle character modest. For though Modesty is not a virtue, it is praised, and so is the modest man.

15 Again, Righteous Indignation is the observance of a mean between Envy and Malice, and these qualities are concerned with pain and pleasure felt at the fortunes of one's neighbours. The righteously indignant man is pained by undeserved good fortune; the jealous man exceeds him and is pained by all the good fortune of others; while the malicious man so far falls short of being pained that he actually feels pleasure.

16 These qualities however it will be time to discuss in another place. After them we will treat

Justice, distinguishing its two kinds—for it has more than one sense—and showing in what way each is a mode of observing the mean. [And we will deal similarly with the logical virtues.]

8. There are then three dispositions—two vices, one of excess and one of defect, and one virtue which is the observance of the mean; and each of them is in a certain way opposed to both the others. For the extreme states are the opposite both of the middle state and of each other, and the middle state is the opposite of both
2 extremes; since just as the equal is greater in comparison with the less and less in comparison with the greater, so the middle states of character are in excess as compared with the defective states and defective as compared with the excessive states, whether in the case of feelings or of actions. For instance, a brave man appears rash in contrast with a coward and cowardly in contrast with a rash man; similarly a temperate man appears profligate in contrast with a man insensible to pleasure and pain, but insensible in contrast with a profligate; and a liberal man seems prodigal in contrast with a mean man, mean in
3 contrast with one who is prodigal. Hence either extreme character tries to push the middle character towards the other extreme; a coward calls a brave man rash and a rash man calls him a coward, and correspondingly in other cases.

4 But while all three dispositions are thus opposed to one another, the greatest degree of contrariety exists between the two extremes. For the extremes are farther apart from each other than from the mean, just as great is farther from small and small from great than either from
5 equal. Again some extremes show a certain likeness to the mean—for instance, Rashness resembles Courage, Prodigality Liberality, whereas the extremes display the greatest unlikeness to one another. But it is things farthest apart from each other that logicians define as contraries, so that the farther apart things are the more contrary they are.

6 And in some cases the defect, in others the excess, is more opposed to the mean; for example Cowardice, which is a vice of deficiency, is more

opposed to Courage than is Rashness, which is a vice of excess; but Profligacy, or excess of feeling, is more opposed to Temperance than is Insensibility, or lack of feeling. This results from either
7 of two causes. One of these arises from the thing itself; owing to one extreme being nearer to the mean and resembling it more, we count not this but rather the contrary extreme as the opposite of the mean; for example, because Rashness seems to resemble Courage more than Cowardice does, and to be nearer to it, we reckon Cowardice rather than Rashness as the contrary of Courage; for those extremes which are more remote from the mean are thought to be more contrary to it.
8 This then is one cause, arising out of the thing itself. The other cause has its origin in us: those things appear more contrary to the mean to which we are ourselves more inclined by our nature. For example, we are of ourselves more inclined to pleasure, which is why we are prone to Profligacy [more than to Propriety]. We therefore rather call those things the contrary of the mean, into which we are more inclined to lapse; and hence Profligacy, the excess, is more particularly the contrary of Temperance.

9. Enough has now been said to show that moral virtue is a mean, and in what sense this is so, namely that it is a mean between two vices, one of excess and the other of defect; and that it is such a mean because it aims at hitting the middle
2 point in feelings and in actions. This is why it is a hard task to be good, for it is hard to find the middle point in anything: for instance, not everybody can find the centre of a circle, but only someone who knows geometry. So also anybody can become angry—that is easy, and so it is to give and spend money; but to be angry with or give money to the right person, and to the right amount, and at the right time, and for the right purpose, and in the right way—this is not within everybody's power and is not easy; so that to do these things properly is rare, praiseworthy, and noble.
3 Hence the first rule in aiming at the mean is to avoid that extreme which is the more opposed to the mean, as Calypso advises—

Steer the ship clear of yonder spray and surge.

For of the two extremes one is a more serious error than the other. Hence, inasmuch as to hit 4 the mean extremely well is difficult, the second best way to sail, as the saying goes, is to take the least of the evils; and the best way to do this will be the way we enjoin.

The second rule is to notice what are the errors to which we are ourselves most prone (as different men are inclined by nature to different faults)—and we shall discover what these are by observing the pleasure or pain that we 5 experience—; then we must drag ourselves away in the opposite direction, for by steering wide of our besetting error we shall make a middle course. This is the method adopted by carpenters to straighten warped timber.

6 Thirdly, we must in everything be most of all on our guard against what is pleasant and against pleasure; for when pleasure is on her trial we are not impartial judges. The right course is therefore to feel towards pleasure as the elders of the people felt towards Helen, and to apply their words to her on every occasion; for if we roundly bid her be gone, we shall be less likely to err.

7 These then, to sum up the matter, are the precautions that will best enable us to hit the mean. But no doubt it is a difficult thing to do, and especially in particular cases: for instance, it is not easy to define in what manner and with what people and on what sort of grounds and how long one ought to be angry; and in fact we sometimes praise men who err on the side of defect in this matter and call them gentle, sometimes those who are quick to anger and style 8 them manly. However, we do not blame one who diverges a little from the right course, whether on the side of the too much or of the too little, but one who diverges more widely, for his error is noticed. Yet to what degree and how seriously a man must err to be blamed is not easy to define on principle. For in fact no object of perception is easy to define; and such questions of degree depend on particular circumstances, and the decision lies with perception.

9 Thus much then is clear, that it is the middle disposition in each department of conduct that is to be praised, but that one should lean sometimes to the side of excess and sometimes to that of deficiency, since this is the easiest way of hitting the mean and the right course.

BOOK III

1. Virtue however is concerned with emotions and actions, and it is only voluntary actions for which praise and blame are given; those that are involuntary are condoned, and sometimes even pitied. Hence it seems to be necessary for the student of ethics to define the difference between the Voluntary and the Involuntary; and this will also be of service to the legislator in assigning rewards and punishments.

2 It is then generally held that actions are involuntary when done (a) under compulsion or 3 (b) through ignorance; and that (a) an act is compulsory when its origin is from without, being of such a nature that the agent, who is really passive, contributes nothing to it: for example, when he is carried somewhere by stress of weather, or 4 by people who have him in their power. But there is some doubt about actions done through fear of a worse alternative, or for some noble object—as for instance if a tyrant having a man's parents and children in his power commands him to do something base, when if he complies their lives will be spared but if he refuses they will be put to death. It is open to question whether such actions are voluntary or involuntary. A somewhat 5 similar case is when cargo is jettisoned in a storm; apart from circumstances, no one voluntarily throws away his property, but to save his own life and that of his shipmates any sane man 6 would do so. Acts of this kind, then, are 'mixed' or composite; but they approximate rather to the voluntary class. For at the actual time when they are done they are chosen or willed; and the end or motive of an act varies with the occasion, so that the terms 'voluntary' and 'involuntary' should be used with reference to the time of action; now the actual deed in the cases in question is done voluntarily, for the origin of the movement of the parts of the body instrumental to the act lies in the agent; and when the origin of an action is in oneself, it is in one's own power to do it or not.

Such acts therefore are voluntary, thought perhaps involuntary apart from circumstances—for no one would choose to do any such action in and for itself.

7 Sometimes indeed men are actually praised for deeds of this 'mixed' class, namely when they submit to some disgrace or pain as the price of some great and noble object; though if they do so without any such motive they are blamed, since it is contemptible to submit to a great disgrace with no advantage or only a trifling one in view. In some cases again, such submission though not praised is condoned, when a man does something wrong through fear of penalties that impose too great a strain on human nature, and that no one 8 could endure. Yet there seem to be some acts which a man cannot be compelled to do, and rather than do them he ought to submit to the most terrible death: for instance, we think it ridiculous that Alcmaeon in Euripides' play is compelled by certain threats to murder his 9 mother! But it is sometimes difficult to decide how far we ought to go in choosing to do a given act rather than suffer a given penalty, or in enduring a given penalty rather than commit a given action; and it is still more difficult to abide by our decision when made, since in most of such dilemmas the penalty threatened is painful and the deed forced upon us dishonourable, which is why praise and blame are bestowed according as we do or do not yield to such compulsion.

10 What kind of actions then are to be called 'compulsory'? Used without qualification, perhaps this term applies to any case where the cause of the action lies in things outside the agent, and when the agent contributes nothing. But when actions intrinsically involuntary are yet in given circumstances deliberately chosen in preference to a given alternative, and when their origin lies in the agent, these actions are to be pronounced intrinsically involuntarily but voluntary in the circumstances, and in preference to the alternative. They approximate however rather to the voluntary class, since conduct consists of particular things done, and the particular things done in the cases in question are voluntary. But it is not easy to lay down rules for deciding which of two alternatives is to be chosen, for particular cases differ widely.

11 To apply the term 'compulsory' to acts done for the sake of pleasure or for noble objects, on the plea that these exercise constraint on us from without, is to make every action compulsory. For (1) pleasure and nobility between them supply the motives of all actions whatsoever. Also (2) to act under compulsion and unwillingly is painful, but actions done for their pleasantness or nobility are done with pleasure. And (3) it is absurd to blame external things, instead of blaming ourselves for falling an easy prey to their attractions; or to take the credit of our noble deeds to ourselves, while putting the blame for our disgraceful ones upon the temptations of pleasure. It 12 appears therefore that an act is compulsory when its origin is from outside, the person compelled contributing nothing to it.

13 (b) An act done through ignorance is in every case not voluntary, but it is involuntary only when it causes the agent pain and regret: since a man who has acted through ignorance and feels no compunction at all for what he has done, cannot indeed be said to have acted voluntarily, as he was not aware of his action, yet cannot be said to have acted involuntarily, as he is not sorry for it. Acts done through ignorance therefore fall into two classes: if the agent regrets the act, we think that he as acted involuntarily; if he does not regret it, to mark the distinction we may call him a 'non-voluntary' agent—for as the case is different it is better to give it a special 14 name. Acting *through* ignorance however seems to be different from acting *in* ignorance; for when a man is drunk or in a rage, his actions are not thought to be done through ignorance but owing to one or other of the conditions mentioned, though he does act without knowing, and *in* ignorance. Now it is true that all wicked men are ignorant of what they ought to do and refrain from doing, and that this error is the cause of injustice and of vice in general. But the term 15 'involuntary' does not really apply to an action when the agent is ignorant of his true interests. The ignorance that makes an act blameworthy is not ignorance displayed in moral choice (that

sort of ignorance constitutes vice)—that is to say, it is not general ignorance (because that is held to be blameworthy), but particular ignorance, ignorance of the circumstances of the act and of the things affected by it; for in this case the act is pitied and forgiven, because he who acts in ignorance of any of these circumstances is an involuntary agent.

16 Perhaps then it will be as well to specify the nature and number of these circumstances. They are (1) the agent, (2) the act, (3) the thing that is affected by or is the sphere of the act; and sometimes also (4) the instrument, for instance, a tool with which the act is done, (5) the effect, for instance, saving a man's life, and (6) the manner, for instance, gently or violently.

17 Now no one, unless mad, could be ignorant of all these circumstances together; nor yet, obviously, of (1) the agent—for a man must know who he is himself. But a man may be ignorant of (2) what he is doing, as for instance when people say 'it slipped out while they were speaking,' or 'they were not aware that the matter was a secret,' as Aeschylus said of the Mysteries; or that 'they let it off when they only meant to show how it worked' as the prisoner pleaded in the catapult case. Again (3) a person might mistake his son for an enemy, as Merope does; or (4) mistake a sharp spear for one with a button on it, or a heavy stone for a pumice-stone; or (5) one might kill a man by giving him medicine with the intention of saving his life; or (6) in loose wrestling hit him a blow

18 when meaning only to grip his hand. Ignorance therefore being possible in respect of all these circumstances of the act, one who has acted in ignorance of any of them is held to have acted involuntarily, and especially so if ignorant of the most important of them; and the most important of the circumstances seem to be the nature of the act itself and the effect it will produce.

19 Such then is the nature of the ignorance that justifies our speaking of an act as involuntary, given the further condition that the agent feels sorrow and regret for having committed it.

20 An involuntary action being one done under compulsion or through ignorance, a voluntary act would seem to be an act of which the origin lies in the agent, who knows the particular circumstances in which he is acting. For it is

21 probably a mistake to say that acts caused by anger or by desire are involuntary. In the first

22 place, (1) this will debar us from speaking of any of the lower animals as acting voluntarily, or

23 children either. Then (2) are none of our actions that are caused by desire or anger voluntary, or are the noble ones voluntary and the base involuntary? Surely this is an absurd distinction when one person is the author of both. Yet perhaps it is

24 strange to speak of acts aiming at things which it is right to aim at as involuntary; and it is right to feel anger at some things, and also to feel desire for some things, for instance health, knowledge.

25 Also (3) we think that involuntary actions are

26 painful and actions that gratify desire pleasant. And again (4) what difference is there in respect of their involuntary character between wrong acts committed deliberately and wrong acts done in anger? Both are to be avoided; and also we

27 think that the irrational feelings are just as much a part of human nature as the reason, so that the actions done from anger or desire also belong to the human being who does them. It is therefore strange to class these actions as involuntary.

BOOK VI

1. We have already said that it is right to choose the mean and to avoid excess and deficiency, and that the mean is prescribed by the right principle. Let us now analyse the latter notion.

In the case of each of the moral qualities or dispositions that have been discussed, as with all the other virtues also, there is a certain mark to aim at, on which the man who knows the principle involved fixes his gaze, and increases or relaxes the tension accordingly; there is a certain standard determining those modes of observing the mean which we define as lying between excess and defect, being in conformity with the

2 right principle. This bare statement however, although true, is not at all enlightening. In all departments of human endeavour that have been reduced to a science, it is true to say that effort ought to be exerted and relaxed neither too much

nor too little, but to the medium amount, and as the right principle decides. Yet a person knowing this truth will be no wiser than before: for example, he will not know what medicines to take merely from being told to take everything that medical science or a medical expert would prescribe. Hence with respect to the qualities of the soul also, it is not enough merely to have established the truth of the above formula; we also have to define exactly what the right principle is, and what is the standard that determines it.

4 Now we have divided the Virtues of the Soul into two groups, the Virtues of the Character and the Virtues of the Intellect. The former, the Moral Virtues, we have already discussed. Our account of the latter must be prefaced by some remarks about psychology.

5 It has been said before that the soul has two parts, one rational and the other irrational. Let us now similarly divide the rational part, and let it be assumed that there are two rational faculties, one whereby we contemplate those things whose first principles are invariable, and one whereby we contemplate those things which admit of variation: since, on the assumption that knowledge is based on a likeness or affinity of some sort between subject and object, the parts of the soul adapted to the cognition of objects that are of different kinds must themselves differ 6 in kind. These two rational faculties may be designated the Scientific Faculty and the Calculative Faculty respectively; since calculation is the same as deliberation, and deliberation is never exercised about things that are invariable, so that the Calculative Faculty is a separate part of the rational half of the soul.

7 We have therefore to ascertain what disposition of each of these faculties is the best, for that will be the special virtue of each.

But the virtue of a faculty is related to the special function which that faculty performs.

2. Now there are three elements in the soul which control action and the attainment of truth: namely, Sensation, Intellect, and Desire.

2 Of these, Sensation never originates action, as is shown by the fact that animals have sensation but are not capable of action.

Pursuit and avoidance in the sphere of Desire correspond to affirmation and denial in the sphere of the Intellect. Hence inasmuch as moral virtue is a disposition of the mind in regard to choice, and choice is deliberate desire, it follows that, if the choice is to be good, both the principle must be true and the desire right, and that desire must pursue the same things as principle affirms. We are here speaking of practical 3 thinking, and of the attainment of truth in regard to action; with speculative thought, which is not concerned with action or production, right and wrong functioning consist in the attainment of truth and falsehood respectively. The attainment of truth is indeed the function of every part of the intellect, but that of the practical intelligence is the attainment of truth corresponding to right desire.

4 Now the cause of action (the efficient, not the final cause) is choice, and the cause of choice is desire and reasoning directed to some end. Hence choice necessarily involves both intellect or thought and a certain disposition of character [for doing well and the reverse in the sphere of action necessarily involve thought and character].

5 Thought by itself however moves nothing, but only thought directed to an end, and dealing with action. This indeed is the moving cause of productive activity also, since he who makes something always has some further end in view: the act of making is not an end in itself, it is only a means, and belongs to something else. Whereas a thing done is an end in itself: since doing well (welfare) is the End, and it is at this that desire aims.

Hence Choice may be called either thought related to desire or desire related to thought; and man, as an originator of action, is a union of desire and intellect.

6 (Choice is not concerned with anything that has happened already: for example, no one chooses to have sacked Troy; for neither does one deliberate about what has happened in the past, but about what still lies in the future and may happen or not; what has happened cannot be made not to have happened. Hence Agathon is right in saying

This only is denied even to God,
The power to make what has been done undone.)

The attainment of truth is then the function of both the intellectual parts of the soul. Therefore their respective virtues are those dispositions which will best qualify them to attain truth.

3. Let us then discuss these virtues afresh, going more deeply into the matter.

Let it be assumed that there are five qualities through which the mind achieves truth in affirmation or denial, namely Art or technical skill, Scientific Knowledge, Prudence, Wisdom, and Intelligence. Conception and Opinion are capable of error.

2 The nature of Scientific Knowledge (employing the term in its exact sense and disregarding its analogous uses) may be made clear as follows. We all conceive that a thing which we know scientifically cannot vary; when a thing that can vary is beyond the range of our observation, we do not know whether it exists or not. An object of Scientific Knowledge, therefore, exists of necessity. It is therefore eternal, for everything existing of absolute necessity is external; and what is eternal does not come into existence or perish. Again, it is held that all 3 Scientific Knowledge can be communicated by teaching, and that what is scientifically known must be learnt. But all teaching starts from facts previously known, as we state in the *Analytics*, since it proceeds either by way of induction, or else by way of deduction. Now induction supplies a first principle or universal, deduction works *from* universals; therefore there are first principles from which deduction starts, which cannot be proved by deduction; therefore they are 4 reached by induction. Scientific Knowledge, therefore, is the quality whereby we demonstrate, with the further qualifications included in our definition of it in the *Analytics*, namely, that a man knows a thing scientifically when he possesses a conviction arrived at in a certain way, and when the first principles on which that conviction rests are known to him with certainty— for unless he is more certain of his first principles than of the conclusion drawn from them he will

only possess the knowledge in question accidentally. Let this stand as our definition of Scientific Knowledge.

4. The class of things that admit of variation includes both things made and actions done. 2 But making is different from doing (a distinction we may accept from extraneous discourses). Hence the rational quality concerned with doing is different from the rational quality concerned with making. Nor is one of them a part of the other, for doing is not a form of making, nor making a form of doing. Now architectural skill, 3 for instance, is an art, and it is also a rational quality concerned with making; nor is there any art which is not a rational quality concerned with making, nor any such quality which is not an art. It follows that an art is the same thing as a rational quality, concerned with making, that 4 reasons truly. All Art deals with bringing something into existence; and to pursue an art means to study how to bring into existence a thing which may either exist or not, and the efficient cause of which lies in the maker and not in the thing made; for Art does not deal with things that exist or come into existence of necessity, or according to nature, since these have their efficient cause in themselves. But as doing and mak- 5 ing are distinct, it follows that Art, being concerned with making, is not concerned with doing. And in a sense Art deals with the same objects as chance, as Agathon says:

Chance is beloved of Art, and Art of Chance.

6 Art, therefore, as has been said, is a rational quality, concerned with making, that reasons truly. Its opposite, Lack of Art, is a rational quality, concerned with making, that reasons falsely. Both deal with that which admits of variation.

5. We may arrive at a definition of Prudence by considering who are the persons who we call prudent. Now it is held to be the mark of a prudent man to be able to deliberate well about what is good and advantageous for himself, not in some one department, for instance what is good for his health or strength, but what is advantageous as a means to the good life in general. This is proved

2 by the fact that we also speak of people as prudent or wise in some particular thing, when they calculate well with a view to attaining some particular end of value (other than those ends which are the object of an art); so that the prudent man in general will be the man who is good at deliberating in general.

3 But no one deliberates about things that cannot vary, nor about things not within his power to do. Hence inasmuch as scientific knowledge involved demonstration, whereas things whose fundamental principles are variable are not capable of demonstration, because everything about them is variable, and inasmuch as one cannot deliberate about things that are of necessity, it follows that Prudence is not the same as Science. Nor can it be the same as Art. It is not Science, because matters of conduct admit of variation; and not Art, because doing and making are generically different, since making aims at an end distinct from the act of making, whereas in doing the end cannot be other than the act itself: doing well is in itself the end. It 4 remains therefore that it is a truth-attaining rational quality, concerned with action in relation to things that are good and bad for human beings.

5 Hence men like Pericles are deemed prudent, because they possess a faculty of discerning what things are good for themselves and for mankind; and that is our conception of an expert in Domestic Economy or Political Science.

(This also accounts for the word Temperance, which signifies 'preserving prudence.' And 6 Temperance does in fact preserve our belief as to our own good; for pleasure and pain do not destroy or pervert all beliefs, for instance, the belief that the three angles of a triangle are, or are not, together equal to two right angles, but only beliefs concerning action. The first principles of action are the end to which our acts are means; but a man corrupted by a love of pleasure or fear of pain, entirely fails to discern any first principle, and cannot see that he ought to choose and do everything as a means to this end, and for its sake; for vice tends to destroy the sense of principle.)

It therefore follows that Prudence is a truth-attaining rational quality, concerned with action in relation to the things that are good for human beings.

7 Moreover, we can speak of excellence in Art, but not of excellence in Prudence. Also in Art voluntary error is not so bad as involuntary, whereas in the sphere of Prudence it is worse, as it is in the sphere of the virtues. It is therefore clear that Prudence is an excellence or virtue, and not an Art.

8 Of the two parts of the soul possessed of reason, Prudence must be the virtue of one, namely, the part that forms opinions; for Opinion deals with that which can vary, and so does Prudence. But yet Prudence is not a rational quality merely, as it shown by the fact that a purely rational faculty can be forgotten, whereas a failure in Prudence is not a mere lapse of memory.

6. Scientific Knowledge is a mode of conception dealing with universals and things that are of necessity; and demonstrated truths and all scientific knowledge (since this involves reasoning) are derived from first principles. Consequently the first principles from which scientific truths are derived cannot themselves be reached by Science; nor yet are they apprehended by Art, nor by Prudence. To be matter of Scientific Knowledge a truth must be demonstrated by deduction from other truths; while Art and Prudence are concerned only with things that admit of variation. Nor is Wisdom the knowledge of first principles either: for the philosopher has to arrive at some things by demonstration.

2 If then the qualities whereby we attain truth, and are never led into falsehood, whether about things invariable or things variable, are Scientific Knowledge, Prudence, Wisdom, and Intelligence, and if the quality which enables us to apprehend first principles cannot be any one among three of these, namely Scientific Knowledge, Prudence, and Wisdom, it remains that first principles must be apprehended by Intelligence.

7. The term Wisdom is employed in the arts to denote those men who are the most perfect masters of their art, for instance, it is applies to Pheidias as a sculptor and to Polycleitus as a statuary. In this use then Wisdom merely signifies artistic excellence. But we also think that some 2 people are wise in general and not in one department, not 'wise in something else,' as Homer says in the *Margites*:

> *Neither a delver nor a ploughman him*
> *The Gods had made, nor wise in aught beside.*

Hence it is clear that Wisdom must be the most 3 perfect of the modes of knowledge. The wise man therefore must not only know the conclusions that follow from his first principles, but also have a true conception of those principles themselves. Hence Wisdom must be a combination of Intelligence and Scientific Knowledge: it must be a consummated knowledge of the most exalted objects.

For it is absurd to think that Political Science or Prudence is the loftiest kind of knowledge, inasmuch as man is not the highest thing · in the world. And as 'wholesome' and 'good' 4 mean on thing for men and another for fishes, whereas 'white' and 'straight' mean the same thing always, so everybody would denote the same thing by 'wise' but not by 'prudent'; for each kind of beings will describe as prudent , and will entrust itself to, one who can discern its own particular welfare; hence even some of the lower animals are said to be prudent, namely those which display a capacity for forethought as regards their own lives.

It is also clear that Wisdom cannot be the same thing as Political Science; for if we are to call knowledge of our own interests wisdom, there will be a number of different kinds of wisdom, one for each species: there cannot be a single such wisdom dealing with the good of all living things, any more than there is one art of medicine for all existing things. It may be argued that man is superior to the other animals, but this makes no difference: since there exist other things far more divine in their nature than man, for instance, to mention the most visible, the things of which the celestial system is composed. 5 These considerations therefore show that Wisdom is both Scientific Knowledge and Intu-

itive Intelligence as regards the things of the most exalted nature. This is why people say that men like Anaxagoras and Thales 'may be wise but are not prudent,' when they see them display ignorance of their own interests; and while admitting them to possess a knowledge that is rare, marvellous, difficult and even superhuman, they yet declare this knowledge to be useless, because these sages do not seek to know the things that are good for human beings.

6 Prudence on the other hand is concerned with the affairs of men, and with things that can be the object of deliberation. For we say that to deliberate well is the most characteristic function of the prudent man; but no one deliberates about things that cannot vary nor yet about variable things that are not a means to some end, and that end a good attainable by action; and a good deliberator in general is a man who can arrive by calculation at the best of the goods attainable by man.

7 Nor is Prudence a knowledge of general principles only: it must also take account of particular facts, since it is concerned with action, and action deals with particular things. This is why men who are ignorant of general principles are sometimes more successful in action than others who know them: for instance, if a man knows that light meat is easily digested and therefore wholesome, but does not know what kinds of meat are light, he will not be so likely to restore you to health as a man who merely knows that chicken is wholesome; and in other matters men of experience are more successful than theorists. And Prudence is concerned with action, so one requires both forms of it, or indeed knowledge of particular facts even more than knowledge of general principles. Here too however there must be some supreme directing faculty.

8. Prudence is indeed the same quality of 2 mind as Political Science, though their essence is different. Of Prudence as regards the state, one kind, as supreme and directive, is called Legislative Science; the other, as dealing with particular occurrences, has the name, Political Science, that really belongs to both kinds. The latter is concerned with action and deliberation (for a parliamentary enactment is a thing to be done, being the last step in a deliberative process), and this is why it is only those persons who deal with particular facts who are spoken of as 'taking part in politics,' because it is only they who perform actions, like the workmen in an industry. Prudence also is ₃ commonly understood to mean especially that kind of wisdom which is concerned with oneself, the individual; and this is given the name, Prudence, which really belongs to all the kinds, while the others are distinguished as Domestic Economy, Legislature, and Political Science, the latter being subdivided into Deliberative Science and ₄ Judicial Science. Now knowledge of one's own interest will certainly be one kind of Prudence; though it is very different from the other kinds, and people think that the man who knows and minds his own business is prudent, and that politicians are busybodies: thus Euripides writes—

> Would that be prudent? when I might have lived
> A quiet life, a cipher in the crowd,
> Sharing the common fortune . . .
> Restless, aspiring, busy men of action . . .

For people seek their own good, and suppose that it is right to do so. Hence this belief has caused the word 'prudent' to mean those who are wise in their own interest. Yet probably as a matter of fact a man cannot pursue his own welfare without Domestic Economy and even Politics. Moreover, even the proper conduct of one's own affairs is a difficult problem, and requires consideration.

₅ A further proof of what has been said is, that although the young may be experts in geometry and mathematics and similar branches of knowledge, we do not consider that a young man can have Prudence. The reason is that Prudence includes a knowledge of particular facts, and this is derived from experience, which a young man does not possess; for experience is the fruit of ₆ years. (One might indeed further enquire why it is that, though a boy may be a mathematician, he cannot be a metaphysician or a natural philosopher. Perhaps the answer is that Mathematics deals with abstractions, whereas the first principles of Metaphysics and Natural Philosophy are derived from experience: the young can only repeat them without conviction of their truth, whereas the formal concepts of Mathematics are ₇ easily understood.) Again, in deliberation there is a double possibility of error: you may go wrong either in your general principle or in your particular fact: for instance, either in asserting that all heavy water is unwholesome, or that the particular water in question is heavy.

₈ And it is clear that Prudence is not the same as Scientific Knowledge: for as has been said, it apprehends ultimate particular things, since the thing to be done is an ultimate particular thing.

₉ Prudence then stands opposite to Intelligence; for Intelligence apprehends definitions, which cannot be proved by reasoning, while Prudence deals with the ultimate particular thing, which cannot be apprehended by Scientific Knowledge, but only by perception: not the perception of the special senses, but the sort of intuition whereby we perceive that the ultimate figure in mathematics is a triangle; for there, too, there will be a stop. But the term perception applies in a fuller sense to mathematical intuition than to Prudence; the practical intuition of the latter belongs to a different species.

9. We ought also to ascertain the nature of Deliberative Excellence, and to discover whether it is a species of Knowledge, or of Opinion, or skill in Conjecture, or something different from these in kind.

₂ Now it is not Knowledge: for men do not investigate matters about which they know, whereas Deliberative Excellence is one form of deliberation, and deliberating implies investigating and calculating. But deliberation is not the same as investigation: it is the investigation of a particular subject.

Nor yet is it skill in Conjecture: for this operates without conscious calculation, and rapidly, whereas deliberating takes a long time, and there is a saying that execution should be swift but deliberation slow. Again, Deliberative Excel-₃lence is not the same as Quickness of mind, which is a form of skill in Conjecture.

Nor yet is Deliberative Excellence any form of Opinion.

But inasmuch as a bad deliberator makes mistakes and a good deliberator deliberates correctly, it is clear that Deliberative Excellence is some form of correctness; though it is not correctness of Knowledge, nor of Opinion. Correctness cannot be predicated of Knowledge, any more than can error, and correctness of Opinion is truth; and also any matter about which one has an opinion has been settled already; [then again Deliberative Excellence necessarily involves conscious calculation. It remains therefore that Deliberative Excellence is correctness in thinking, for thought has not reached the stage of affirmation;] for Opinion has passed beyond the stage of investigation and is a form of affirmation, whereas a man deliberating, whether he deliberates well or badly, is investigating and calculating something.

4 But Deliberative Excellence is a form of correctness in deliberation [so that we have first to investigate what deliberation is, and what object it deals with]. However, 'correctness' in this connexion is ambiguous, and plainly it is not every kind of correctness in deliberation that constitutes Deliberative Excellence. A man of deficient self-restraint or a bad man may as a result of calculation arrive at the object he proposes as the right thing to do, so that he will have deliberated correctly, although he will have gained something extremely evil; whereas to have deliberated well is felt to be a good thing. Therefore it is this kind of correctness in deliberation that is Deliberative Excellence, namely being correct in the sense of arriving at something good.

5 But it is possible to arrive at a good conclusion, as well as at a bad one, by a false process of reasoning; one may arrive at what is the right thing to do, but not arrive at it on the right grounds, but by means of a wrong middle term. This quality then, which leads one to arrive at the right conclusion, but not on the right grounds, is still not Deliberative Excellence.

6 Again, one man may arrive at the right conclusion by prolonged deliberation, while another may do so quickly. The former case also then does not amount to Deliberative Excellence; this is correctness of deliberation as regards what is advantageous, arriving at the right conclusion on the right grounds at the right time.

7 Again, a man can be said to have deliberated well either generally, or in reference to a particular end. Deliberative Excellence in general is therefore that which leads to correct results with reference to the end in general, while correctness of deliberation with a view to some particular end is Deliberative Excellence of some special kind.

If therefore to have deliberated well is a characteristic of prudent men, Deliberative Excellence must be correctness of deliberation with regard to what is expedient as a means to the end, a true conception of which constitutes Prudence.

12. But the further question may be raised, What is the use of these intellectual virtues? Wisdom does not consider the means to human happiness at all, for it does not ask how anything comes into existence. Prudence, it must be granted, does do this; but what do we need it for? seeing that it studies that which is just and noble and good for man, but these are the things that a good man does by nature. Knowing about them does not make us any more capable of doing them, since the virtues are qualities of character; just as is the case with the knowledge of what is healthy and vigorous—using these words to mean not productive of health and vigour but resulting from them: we are not rendered any more capable of healthy and vigorous action by knowing the science of medicine or of physical training.

2 If on the other hand we are to say that Prudence is useful not in helping us to act virtuously but in helping us to become virtuous, then it is of no use to those who are virtuous already. Nor is it of any use either to those who are not, since we may just as well take the advice of others who possess Prudence as possess Prudence ourselves. We may be content to do as we do in regard to our health; we want to be healthy, yet we do not learn medicine.

3 Moreover it would seem strange if Prudence, which is inferior to Wisdom, is nevertheless to have greater authority than Wisdom: yet the faculty that creates a thing governs and gives orders to it.

Let us now therefore discuss these difficulties, which so far have only been stated.

4   First then let us assert that Wisdom and Prudence, being as they are the virtues of the two parts of the intellect respectively, are necessarily desirable in themselves, even if neither produces any effect.

5   Secondly, they do in fact produce an effect: Wisdom produces Happiness, not in the sense in which medicine produces health, but in the sense in which healthiness is the cause of health. For Wisdom is a part of Virtue as a whole, and therefore by its possession, or rather by its exercise, renders a man happy.

6   Also Prudence as well as Moral Virtue determines the complete performance of man's proper function: Virtue ensures the rightness of the end we aim at, Prudence ensures the rightness of the means we adopt to gain that end.

(The fourth part of the soul on the other hand, the nutritive faculty, has no virtue contributing to the proper function of man, since it has no power to act or not to act.)

7   But we must go a little deeper into the objection that Prudence does not render men more capable of performing noble and just actions. Let us start with the following consideration. As some people, we maintain, perform just acts and yet are not just men (for instance, those who do what the law enjoins but do it unwillingly, or in ignorance, or for some ulterior object, and not for the sake of the actions themselves, although they are as a matter of fact doing what they ought to do and all that a good man should), on the other hand, it appears, there is a state of mind in which a man may do these various acts with the result that he really is a good man: I mean when he does them from choice, and for the sake of the acts them-
8 selves. Now rightness in our choice of an end is secured by Virtue; but to do the actions that must in the nature of things be done in order to attain the end we have chosen, is not a matter for Virtue but for a different faculty.

We must dwell on this point to make it more
9 clear. There is a certain faculty called Cleverness, which is the capacity for doing the things aforesaid that conduce to the aim we propose, and so attaining that aim. If the aim is noble, this is a praiseworthy faculty: if base, it is mere knavery; this is how we come to speak of both prudent

men and knaves as clever. Now this faculty is not
10 identical with Prudence, but Prudence implies it. But that eye of the soul of which we spoke cannot acquire the quality of Prudence without possessing Virtue. This we have said before, and it is manifestly true. For deductive inferences about matters of conduct always have a major premise of the form 'Since the End or Supreme Good is so and so' (whatever it may be, since we may take it as anything we like for the sake of the argument); but the Supreme Good only appears good to the good man: vice perverts the mind and causes it to hold false views about the first principles of conduct. Hence it is clear that we cannot be prudent without being good.

13. We have therefore also to reconsider the nature of Virtue. The fact is that the case of Virtue is closely analogous to that of Prudence in relation to Cleverness. Prudence and Cleverness are not the same, but they are similar; and natural virtue is related in the same way to Virtue in the true sense. All are agreed that the various moral qualities are in a sense bestowed by nature: we are just, and capable of temperance, and brave, and possessed of the other virtues from the moment of our birth. But nevertheless we expect to find that true goodness is something different, and that the virtues in the true sense come to belong to us in another way. For even children and wild animals possess the natural dispositions, yet without Intelligence these may manifestly be harmful. This at all events appears to be a matter of observation, that just as a man of powerful frame who has lost his sight meets with heavy falls when he moves about, because he cannot see, so it also happens in the moral sphere;
2 whereas if a man of good natural disposition acquires Intelligence, then he excels in conduct, and the disposition which previously only resembled Virtue, will now be Virtue in the true sense. Hence just as with the faculty of forming opinions there are two qualities, Cleverness and Prudence, so also in the moral part of the soul there are two qualities, natural virtue and true
3 Virtue; and true Virtue cannot exist without Prudence. Hence some people maintain that all the virtues are forms of Prudence; and Socrates'

line of enquiry was right in one way, though wrong in another; he was mistaken in thinking that all the virtues are forms of Prudence, but right in saying that they cannot exist without 4 Prudence. A proof of this is that everyone, even at the present day, in defining Virtue, after saying what disposition it is and specifying the things with which it is concerned, adds that it is a disposition determined by the right principle; and the right principle is the principle determined by Prudence. It appears therefore that everybody in some sense divines that Virtue is a disposition of this nature, namely regulated by Prudence. 5 This formula however requires a slight modification. Virtue is not merely a disposition conforming to right principle, but one co-operating with right principle; and Prudence is right principle in matters of conduct. Socrates then thought that the virtues *are* principles, for he said that they are all of them forms of knowledge. We on the other hand say that the virtues *co-operate with* principle.

6 These considerations therefore show that it is not possible to be good in the true sense without Prudence, nor to be prudent without Moral Virtue.

(Moreover, this might supply an answer to the dialectical argument that might be put forward to prove that the virtues can exist in isolation from each other, on the ground that the same man does not possess the greatest natural capacity for all of them, so that he may have already attained one when he has not yet attained another. In regard to the natural virtues this is possible; but it is not possible in regard to those virtues which entitle a man to be called good without qualification. For if a man have the one virtue of Prudence he will also have all the Moral Virtues together with it.)

7 It is therefore clear that, even if Prudence had no bearing on conduct, it would still be needed, because it is the virtue of that part of the intellect to which it belongs; and also that our choice of actions will not be right without Prudence any more than without Moral Virtue, since, while Moral Virtue enables us to achieve the end, Prudence makes us adopt the right means to the end.

8 But nevertheless it is not really the case that Prudence is in authority over Wisdom, or over the higher part of the intellect, any more than medical science is in authority over health. Medical science does not control health, but studies how to procure it; hence it issues orders *in the interests of* health, but not *to* health. And again, one might as well say that Political Science governs the gods, because it gives orders about everything in the State.

BOOK VII

1. Let us next begin a fresh part of the subject by laying down that the states of moral character to be avoided are of three kinds—Vice, Unrestraint, and Bestiality. The opposite dispositions in the case of two of the three are obvious: one we call Virtue, the other Self-restraint. As the opposite of Bestiality it will be most suitable to speak of Superhuman Virtue, or goodness on a heroic or divine scale; just as Homer has represented Priam as saying of Hector, on account of his surpassing valour—

> *nor seemed to be*
> *The son of mortal man, but of a god.*

2 Hence if, as men say, surpassing virtue changes men into gods, the disposition opposed to Bestiality will clearly be some quality more than human; for there is no such thing as Virtue in the case of a god, any more than there is Vice or Virtue in the case of a beast: divine goodness is something more exalted than Virtue, and bestial 3 badness is different in kind from Vice. And inasmuch as it is rare for a man to be divine, in the sense in which that word is commonly used by the Lacedaemonians as a term of extreme admiration—'Yon mon's divine,' they say—, so a bestial character is rare among human beings; it is found most frequently among barbarians, and some cases also occur as a result of disease or arrested development. We sometimes also use 'bestial' as a term of opprobrium for a surpassing degree of human vice.

4 But the nature of the bestial disposition will have to be touched on later; and of Vice we have spoken already. We must however discuss Unrestraint and Softness or Luxury, and also Self-restraint and Endurance. Neither of these two

classes of character is to be conceived as identical with Virtue and Vice, nor yet as different in kind from them.

5   Our proper course with this subject as with others will be to present the various views about it, and then, after first reviewing the difficulties they involve, finally to establish if possible all or, if not all, the greater part and the most important of the opinions generally held with respect to these states of mind; since if the discrepancies can be solved, and a residuum of current opinion left standing, the true view will have been sufficiently established.

6   Now the following opinions are held: (*a*) that Self-restraint and Endurance are good and praiseworthy dispositions, Unrestraint and Softness bad and blameworthy; (*b*) that the self-restrained man is the man who abides by the results of his calculations, the unrestrained, one who readily abandons the conclusion he has reached; (*c*) that the unrestrained man does things that he knows to be evil, under the influence of passion, whereas the self-restrained man, knowing that his desires are evil, refuses to follow them on principle; (*d*) that the temperate man is always self-restrained and enduring; but that the converse is invariably the case some deny, although others affirm it: the latter identify the unrestrained with the profligate and the profligate with the unrestrained promiscuously, the former distinguish between them. 7 (*e*) Sometimes it is said that the prudent man cannot be unrestrained, sometimes that some prudent and clever men are unrestrained. (*f*) Again, men are spoken of as unrestrained in anger, and in the pursuit of honour and of gain. These then are the opinions advanced.

    2. The difficulties that may be raised are the following. (*c*) How can a man fail in self-restraint when believing correctly that what he does is wrong? Some people say that he cannot do so when he *knows* the act to be wrong; since, as Socrates held, it would be strange if, when a man possessed Knowledge, some other thing should overpower it, and 'drag it about like a slave.' In fact Socrates used to combat the view altogether, implying that there is no such thing as Unrestraint, since no one, he

held, acts contrary to what is best, believing what he does to be bad, but only through igno-2 rance. Now this theory is manifestly at variance with plain facts; and we ought to investigate the state of mind in question more closely. If failure of self-restraint is caused by ignorance, we must examine what sort of ignorance it is. For it is clear that the man who fails in self-restraint does not think the action right before he comes under the influence of passion.—But 3 some thinkers accept the doctrine in a modified form. They allow that nothing is more powerful than knowledge, but they do not allow that no one acts contrary to what he *opines* to be the better course; and they therefore maintain that the unrestrained man when he succumbs to the temptations of pleasure possesses not Knowledge but only Opinion. And yet if it is really 4 Opinion and not Knowledge—not a strong belief that offers resistance but only a weak one (like that of persons in two minds about something)—, we could forgive a man for not keeping to his opinions in opposition to strong desires; but we do not forgive vice, nor any other blameworthy quality.—(*e*) Is it then when desire is opposed by Prudence that we blame a man for yielding? for Prudence is extremely strong. But this is strange, for it means that the same person can be at once prudent and unrestrained; yet no one could possibly maintain that the prudent man is capable of doing voluntarily the basest actions. And furthermore it has already been shown that Prudence displays itself in action (for it is concerned with ultimate particulars), and implies the possession of the other Virtues as well.

6   Again (*d*) if Self-restraint implies having strong and evil desires, the temperate man cannot be self-restrained, nor the self-restrained man temperate; for the temperate man does not have excessive or evil desires. But a self-restrained man must necessarily have strong and evil desires; since if a man's desires are good, the disposition that prevents him from obeying them will be evil, and so Self-restraint will not always be good; while if his desires are weak and not evil, there is nothing to be proud of in resisting them; nor is it anything remarkable if they are evil and weak.

7 Again (*a, b*) if Self-restraint makes a man steadfast in *all* his opinions, it may be bad, namely, if it makes him persist even in a false opinion. And if Unrestraint makes him liable to abandon *any* opinion, in some cases Unrestraint will be good. Take the instance of Neoptolemus in the *Philoctetes* of Sophocles. Neoptolemus abandons a resolution that he has been persuaded by Odysseus to adopt, because of the pain that it gives him to tell a lie: in this case inconstancy is praiseworthy.

8 Again (*a, c*) there is the difficulty raised by the argument of the sophists. The sophists wish to show their cleverness by entrapping their adversary into a paradox, and when they are successful, the resultant chain of reasoning ends in a deadlock: the mind is fettered, being unwilling to stand still because it cannot approve the conclusion reached, yet unable to go forward because it can-
9 not untie the knot of the argument. Now one of their arguments proves that Folly combined with Unrestraint is a virtue. It runs as follows: if a man is foolish and also unrestrained, owing to his unrestraint he does the opposite of what he believes that he ought to do; but he believes that good things are bad, and that he ought not to do them; therefore he will do good things and not bad ones.

10 Again (*b, d*) one who does and pursues what is pleasant from conviction and choice, might be held to be a better man than one who acts in the same way not from calculation but from unrestraint, because he is more easy to cure, since he may be persuaded to alter his conviction; whereas the unrestrained man comes under the proverb that says 'when water chokes you, what are you to drink to wash it down?' Had he been convinced that what he does is right, a change of conviction might have caused him to desist; but as it is he is convinced that he ought to do one thing and nevertheless does another thing.

11 Again (*f*) if Self-restraint and Unrestraint can be displayed with reference to anything, what is the meaning of the epithet 'unrestrained' without qualification? No one has every form of unrestraint, yet we speak of some men as simply 'unrestrained.'

12 Such, more or less, are the difficulties that arise. Part of the conflicting opinions we have to clear out of the way, but part to leave standing; for to solve a difficulty is to find the answer to a problem.

3. We have then to consider, first (i) whether men fail in self-restraint knowing what they do is wrong, or not knowing, and if knowing, knowing in what sense; and next (ii) what are to be set down as the objects with which Self-restraint and Unrestraint are concerned: I mean, are they concerned with pleasure and pain of all sorts, or only with certain special pleasures and pains? and (iii) is Self-restraint the same as Endurance or distinct from it? and so on with (iv) the other questions akin to this subject.

2 A starting-point for our investigation is to ask whether the *differentia* of the self-restrained man and the unrestrained is constituted by their objects, or by their dispositions: I mean, whether a man is called unrestrained solely because he fails to restrain himself with reference to certain things, or rather because he has a certain disposition, or rather for both reasons combined. A second question is, can Self-restraint and Unrestraint be displayed in regard to everything, or not? When a man is said to be 'unrestrained' without further qualification, it does not mean that he is so in relation to everything, but to those things in regard to which a man can be profligate; and also it does not mean merely that he is concerned with these things (for in that case Unrestraint would be the same thing as Profligacy), but that he is concerned with them in a particular manner. The profligate yields to his appetites from choice, considering it right always to pursue the pleasure that offers, whereas the man of defective self-restraint does not think so, but pursues it all the same.

3 (i) Now the suggestion that it is not Knowledge, but True Opinion, against which unrestrained men act, is of no importance for our argument. Some men hold their opinions with absolute certainty, and take them for positive
4 knowledge; so that if weakness of conviction be the criterion for deciding that men who act against their conception of what is right must be said to *opine* rather than to *know* the right, there will really be no difference in this respect between

Opinion and Knowledge; since some men are just as firmly convinced of what they opine as others are of what they know: witness Heracleitus.

5 (1) But the word *know* is used in two senses. A man who has knowledge but is not exercising it is said to know, and so is a man who is actually exercising his knowledge. It will make a difference whether a man does wrong having the knowledge that it is wrong but not consciously thinking of his knowledge, or with the knowledge consciously present to his mind. The latter would be felt to be surprising; but it is not surprising that a man should do what he knows to be wrong if he is not conscious of the knowledge at the time.

6 (2) Again, reasoning on matters of conduct employs premises of two forms. Now it is quite possible for a man to act against knowledge when he knows both premises but is only exercising his knowledge of the universal premise and not of the particular; for action has to do with particular things. Moreover, there is a distinction as regards the universal term: one universal is predicated of the man himself, the other of the thing; for example, he may know and be conscious of the knowledge that dry food is good for every man and that he himself is a man, or even that food of a certain kind is dry, but either not possess or not be actualizing the knowledge whether the particular food before him is food of that kind. Now clearly the distinction between these two ways of knowing will make all the difference in the world. It will not seem at all strange that the unrestrained man should 'know' in one way, but it would be astonishing if he knew in another way.

7 (3) Again, it is possible for men to 'have knowledge' in yet another way besides those just discussed; for even in the state of having knowledge without exercising it we can observe a distinction: a man may in a sense both have it and not have it; for instance, when he is asleep, or mad, or drunk. But persons under the influence of passion are in the same condition; for it is evident that anger, sexual desire, and certain other passions, actually alter the state of the body, and in some cases even cause madness. It is clear therefore that we must pronounce the unrestrained to 'have knowledge' only in the same

way as men who are asleep or mad or drunk.

8 Their using the language of knowledge is no proof that they possess it. Persons in the states mentioned repeat propositions of geometry and verses of Empedocles; students who have just begun a subject reel off its formulae, though they do not yet know their meaning, for knowledge has to become part of the tissue of the mind, and this takes time. Hence we must conceive that men who fail in self-restraint talk in the same way as actors speaking a part.

9 (4) Again, one may also study the cause of Unrestraint scientifically, thus: In a practical syllogism, the major premise is an opinion, while the minor premise deals with particular things, which are the province of perception. Now when the two premises are combined, just as in theoretic reasoning the mind is compelled to *affirm* the resulting conclusion, so in the case of practical premises you are forced at once to *do* it. For example, given the premises 'All sweet things ought to be tasted' and 'Yonder thing is sweet'—a particular instance of the general class—, you are bound, if able and not prevented, immediately to

10 taste the thing. When therefore there is present in the mind on the one hand a universal judgement forbidding you to taste and on the other hand a universal judgement saying 'All sweet things are pleasant,' and a minor premise 'Yonder thing is sweet' (and it is this minor premise that is active), and when desire is present at the same time, then, though the former universal judgement says 'Avoid that thing,' the desire leads you to it (since desire can put the various parts of the body in motion). Thus it comes about that when men fail in self-restraint, they act in a sense under the influence of a principle or opinion, but an opinion not in itself but only accidentally opposed to the right principle (for it is the desire,

11 and not the opinion, that is really opposed). Hence the lower animals cannot be called unrestrained, if only for the reason that they have no power of forming universal concepts, but only mental images and memories of particular things.

12 If we ask how the unrestrained man's ignorance is dissipated and he returns to a state of knowledge, the explanation is the same as in the case of drunkenness and sleep, and is not peculiar

to failure of self-restraint. We must go for it to physiology.

13 But inasmuch as the last premise, which originates action, is an opinion as to some object of sense, and it is this opinion which the unrestrained man when under the influence of passion either does not possess, or only possesses in a way which as we saw does not amount to knowing it but only makes him repeat it as the drunken man repeats the maxims of Empedocles, and since the ultimate term is not a universal, and is not deemed to be an object of Scientific Knowledge in the same way as a universal term is, we do seem to be led to the conclusion which Socrates sought to 14 establish. For the knowledge which is present when failure of self-restraint occurs is not what is held to be Knowledge in the true sense, nor is it true Knowledge which is dragged about by passion, but knowledge derived from sense-perception.

So much for the question whether failure of self-restraint can go with knowledge or not, and with knowledge in what sense.

BOOK VIII

1. Our next business after this will be to discuss Friendship. For friendship is a virtue, or involves virtue; and also it is one of the most indispensable requirements of life. For no one would choose to live without friends, but possessing all other good things. In fact rich men, rulers and potentates are thought especially to require friends, since what would be the good of their prosperity without an outlet for beneficence, which is displayed in its fullest and most praiseworthy form towards friends? and how could such prosperity be safeguarded and preserved without friends? for the greater it is, the greater is its insecurity. And 2 in poverty or any other misfortune men think friends are their only resource. Friends are an aid to the young, to guard them from error; to the elderly, to tend them, and to supplement their failing powers of action; to those in the prime of life, to assist them in noble deeds—

When twain together go—

for two are better able both to plan and to exe-
3 cute. And the affection of parent for offspring

and of offspring for parent seems to be a natural instinct, not only in man but also in birds and in most animals; as also is friendship between member of the same species; and this is especially strong in the human race; for which reason we praise those who love their fellow men. Even when travelling abroad one can observe that a natural affinity and friendship exist between 4 man and man universally. Moreover, friendship appears to be the bond of the state; and lawgivers seem to set more store by it than they do by justice, for to promote concord, which seems akin to friendship, is their chief aim, while faction, which is enmity, is what they are most anxious to banish. And if men are friends, there is no need of justice between them; whereas merely to be just is not enough—a feeling of friendship also is necessary. Indeed the highest form of justice seems to have an element of friendly feeling in it.

5 And friendship is not only indispensable as a means, it is also noble in itself. We praise those who love their friends, and it is counted a noble thing to have many friends; and some people think that a true friend must be a good man.

6 But there is much difference of opinion as to the nature of friendship. Some define it as a matter of similarity; they say that we love those who are like ourselves: whence the proverbs 'Like finds his like,' 'Birds of a feather flock together,' and so on. Others on the contrary say that with men who are alike it is always a case of 'two of a trade.' Some try to find more profound and scientific explanation of the nature of affection. Euripides writes that 'Earth yearneth for the rain' when dried up, 'And the majestic Heaven when filled with rain Yearneth to fall to Earth.' Heracleitus says, 'Opposition unites,' and 'The fairest harmony springs from difference,' and ''Tis strife that makes the world go on.' Others maintain the opposite view, notably Empedocles, who declares that 'Like seeks after like.'

7 Dismissing then these scientific speculations as not germane to our present enquiry, let us investigate the human aspect of the matter, and examine the question that relate to man's character and emotions: for instance, whether all men are capable of friendship, or bad men cannot be friends; and whether there is only one sort

of friendship or several. Those who hold that friendship is of the same kind because friendship admits of degree, are relying on an insufficient proof, for things of different kinds also can differ in degree. But this has been discussed before.

2. Perhaps the answer to these questions will appear if we ascertain what sort of things arouse liking or love. It seems that not everything is loved, but only what is lovable, and that this is either what is good, or pleasant, or useful. But useful may be taken to mean productive of some good or of pleasure, so that the class of 2 things lovable as ends is reduced to the good and the pleasant. Then, do men like what is really good, or what is good for them? for sometimes the two may be at variance; and the same with what is pleasant. Now it appears that each person loves what is good for himself, and that while what is really good is lovable absolutely, what is good for a particular person is lovable for that person. Further, each person loves not what is really good for himself, but what appears to him to be so; however, this will not affect our argument, for 'lovable' will mean 'what appears lovable.'

3   There being then three motives of love, the term Friendship is not applied to love for inanimate objects, since here there is no return of affection, and also no wish for the good of the object—for instance, it would be ridiculous to wish well to a bottle of wine: at the most one wishes that it may keep well in order that one may have it oneself; whereas we are told that we ought to wish our friend well for his own sake. But persons who wish another good for his own sake, if the feeling is not reciprocated, are merely said to feel goodwill for him: only when mutual is 4 such goodwill termed friendship. And perhaps we should also add the qualification that the feeling of goodwill must be known to its object. For a man often feels goodwill towards persons whom he has never seen, but whom he believes to be good or useful, and one of these persons may also entertain the same feeling towards him. Here then we have a case of two people mutually well-disposed, whom nevertheless we cannot speak of as friends, because they are not aware of each other's regard. To be friends therefore, men must

(1) feel goodwill for each other, that is, wish each other's good, and (2) be aware of each other's goodwill, and (3) the cause of their goodwill must be one of the lovable qualities mentioned above.

3. Now these qualities differ in kind; hence the affection or friendship they occasion may differ in kind also. There are accordingly three kinds of friendship, corresponding in number to the three lovable qualities; since a reciprocal affection, known to either party, can be based on each of the three, and when men love each other, they wish each other well in respect of the quality which is the ground of their friendship. Thus friends whose affection is based on utility do not love each other in themselves, but in so far as some benefit accrues to them from each other. And similarly with those whose friendship is based on pleasure: for instance, we enjoy the society of witty people not because of what they are in themselves, but because they are agreeable to 2 us. Hence in a friendship based on utility or on pleasure men love their friend for their own good or their own pleasure, and not as being the person loved, but as useful or agreeable. And therefore these friendships are based on an accident, since the friend is not loved for being what he is, but as affording some benefit or pleasure as the case may 3 be. Consequently friendships of this kind are easily broken off, in the event of the parties themselves changing, for if no longer pleasant or useful to each other, they cease to love each other. And utility is not a permanent quality; it differs at times. Hence when the motive of the friendship has passed away, the friendship itself is dissolved, having existed merely as a means to that end.

Friendships of Utility seem to occur most frequently between the old, as in old age men do not pursue pleasure but profit; and between those persons in the prime of life and young people whose object in life is gain. Friends of this kind do not indeed frequent each other's company much, for in some cases they are not even pleasing to each other, and therefore have no use for friendly intercourse unless they are mutually profitable; since their pleasure in each other goes no further than their expectations of advantage.

With these friendships are classed family ties or hospitality with foreigners.

5 With the young on the other hand the motive of friendship appears to be pleasure, since the young guide their lives by emotion, and for the most part pursue what is pleasant to themselves, and the object of the moment. And the things that please them change as their age alters; hence they both form friendships and drop them quickly, since their affections alter with what gives them pleasure, and the tastes of youth change quickly. Also the young are prone to fall in love, as love is chiefly guided by emotion, and grounded on pleasure; hence they form attachments quickly and give them up quickly, often changing before the day is out.

The young do desire to pass their time in their friend's company, for that is how they get the enjoyment of their friendship.

6 The perfect form of friendship is that between the good, and those who resemble each other in virtue. For these friends wish each alike the other's good in respect of their goodness, and they are good in themselves; but it is those who wish the good of their friends for their friends' sake who are friends in the fullest sense, since they love each other for themselves and not accidentally. Hence the friendship of these lasts as long as they continue to be good; and virtue is a permanent quality. And each is good relatively to his friend as well as absolutely, since the good are both good absolutely and profitable to each other. And each is pleasant in both ways also, since good men are pleasant both absolutely and to each other; for everyone is pleased by his own actions, and therefore by actions that resemble his own, and the actions of all good men are the 7 same or similar.—Such friendship is naturally permanent, since it combines in itself all the attributes that friends ought to possess. All affection is based on good or on pleasure, either absolute or relative to the person who feels it, and is prompted by similarity of some sort; but this friendship possesses all these attributes in the friends themselves, for they are alike, et cetera, in that way. Also the absolutely good is pleasant absolutely as well; but the absolutely good and pleasant are the chief objects of affection; there-fore it is between good men that affection and friendship exist in their fullest and best form.

8 Such friendships are of course rare, because such men are few. Moreover they require time and intimacy: as the saying goes, you cannot get to know a man until you have consumed the proverbial amount of salt in his company; and so you cannot admit him to friendship or really be friends, before each has shown the other that he is worthy of friendship and has won his confidence. 9 People who enter into friendly relations quickly have the wish to be friends, but cannot really be friends without being worthy of friendship, and also knowing each other to be so; the wish to be friends is a quick growth, but friendship is not.

4. This form of friendship is perfect both in point of duration and of the other attributes of friendship; and in all respects either party receives from the other the same or similar benefits, as it is proper that friends should do.

Friendship based on pleasure has a similarity to friendship based on virtue, for good men are pleasant to one another; and the same is true of friendship based on utility, for good men are useful to each other. In these cases also the friendship is most lasting when each friend derives the same benefit, for instance pleasure, from the other, and not only so, but derives it from the same thing, as in a friendship between two witty people, and not as in one between a lover and his beloved. These do not find their pleasure in the same things: the lover's pleasure is in gazing at his beloved, the loved one's pleasure is in receiving the attentions of the lover; and when the loved one's beauty fades, the friendship sometimes fades too, as the lover no longer finds pleasure in the sight of his beloved, and the loved one no longer receives the attentions of the lover; though on the other hand many do remain friends if as a result of their intimacy they have come to love each other's characters, both being alike in char- 2 acter. But when a pair of lovers exchange not pleasure for pleasure but pleasure for gain, the friendship is less intense and less lasting.

A friendship based on utility dissolves as soon as its profit ceases; for the friends did not love each other, but what they got out of each other.

Friendships therefore based on pleasure and on utility can exist between two bad men, between one bad man and one good, and between a man neither good nor bad and another either good, bad, or neither. But clearly only good men can be friends for what they are in themselves; since bad men do not take pleasure in each other, save as they get some advantage from each other.

3 Also friendship between good men alone is proof against calumny; for a man is slow to believe anybody's word about a friend whom he has himself tried and tested for many years, and with them there is the mutual confidence, the incapacity ever to do each other wrong, and all the other characteristics that are required in true friendship. Whereas the other forms of friendship are liable to be dissolved by calumny and suspicion.

4 But since people do apply the term 'friends' to persons whose regard for each other is based on utility, just as states can be 'friends' (since expediency is generally recognized as the motive of international alliances), or on pleasure, as children make friends, perhaps we too must call such relationships friendships; but then we must say that there are several sorts of friendship, that between good men, as good, being friendship in the primary and proper meaning of the term, while the other kinds are friendships in an analogical sense, since such friends are friends in virtue of a sort of goodness and of likeness in them: insomuch as pleasure is good in the eyes of
5 pleasure-lovers. But these two secondary forms of friendship are not very likely to coincide: men do not make friends with each other both for utility and for pleasure at the same time, since accidental qualities are rarely found in combination.

6 Friendship then being divided into these species, inferior people will make friends for pleasure or for use, if they are alike in that respect, while good men will be friends for each other's own sake, since they are alike in being good. The latter therefore are friends in an absolute sense, the former accidentally, and through their similarity to the latter.

5. It is with friendship as it is with virtues; men are called good in two senses, either as having a virtuous disposition or as realizing virtue in action, and similarly friends when in each other's company derive pleasure from and confer benefits on each other, whereas friends who are asleep or parted are not actively friendly, yet have the disposition to be so. For separation does not destroy friendship absolutely, though it prevents its active exercise. If however the absence be prolonged, it seems to cause the friendly feeling itself to be forgotten: hence the poet's remark

Full many a man finds friendship end
For lack of converse with his friend.

2 The old and the morose do not appear to be much given to friendship, for their capacity to please is small, and nobody can pass his days in the company of one who is distasteful to him, or not pleasing, since it seems to be one of the strongest instincts of nature to shun what is painful and seek what is pleasant. And when persons approve
3 of each other without seeking such other's society, this seems to be goodwill rather than friendship. Nothing is more characteristic of friends than that they seek each other's society: poor men desire their friends' assistance, and even the most prosperous wish for their companionship (indeed they are the last people to adopt the life of a recluse); but it is impossible for men to spend their time together unless they give each other pleasure, or have common tastes. The latter seems to be the bond between the members of a comradeship.

4 Friendship between good men then is the truest friendship, as has been said several times before. For it is agreed that what is good and pleasant absolutely is lovable and desirable strictly, while what is good and pleasant for a particular person is lovable and desirable relatively to that person; but the friendship of good men for each other rests on both these grounds.

5 Liking seems to be an emotion, friendship a fixed disposition, for liking can be felt even for inanimate things, but reciprocal liking involves deliberation choice, and this springs from a fixed disposition. Also, when men wish the good of those they love for their own sakes, their goodwill does not depend on emotion but on a fixed disposition. And in loving their friend they love their own good, for the good man in becoming dear to another becomes that other's good. Each

party therefore both loves his own good and also makes an equivalent return by wishing the other's good, and by affording him pleasure; for there is a saying, 'Amity is equality,' and this is most fully realized in the friendships of the good.
7 The degrees of friendship between other relatives vary correspondingly.

The friendship between husband and wife appears to be a natural instinct; since man is by nature a pairing creature even more than he is a political creature, inasmuch as the family is an earlier and more fundamental institution than the State, and the procreation of offspring a more general characteristic of the animal creation. So whereas with the other animals the association of the sexes aims only at continuing the species, human beings cohabit not only for the sake of begetting children but also to provide the needs of life; for with the human race division of labour begins at the outset, and man and woman have different functions; thus they supply each other's wants, putting their special capacities into the common stock. Hence the friendship of man and wife seems to be one of utility and pleasure combined. But it may also be based on virtue, if the partners be of high moral character; for either sex has its special virtue, and this may be the ground of attraction. Children, too, seem to be a bond of union, and therefore childless marriages are more easily dissolved; for children are a good possessed by both parents in common, and common property holds people together.

8 The question what rules of conduct should govern the relations between husband and wife, and generally between friend and friend, seems to be ultimately a question of justice. There are different claims of justice between friends and strangers, between members of a comradeship and schoolfellows.

13. There are then, as we said at the outset, three kinds of friendship, and in each kind there are both friends who are on an equal footing and friends on a footing of disparity; for two equally good men may be friends, or one better man and one worse; and similarly with pleasant friends and with those who are friends for the sake of utility, who may be equal or may differ in the amount of the benefits which they confer. Those who are equals must make matters equal by loving each other, etc., equally; those who are unequal by making a return proportionate to the superiority of whatever kind on the one side.

2 Complaints and recriminations occur solely or chiefly in friendships of utility, as is to be expected. In a friendship based on virtue each party is eager to benefit the other, for this is characteristic of virtue and of friendship; and as they vie with each other in giving and not in getting benefit, no complaints nor quarrels can arise, since nobody is angry with one who loves him and benefits him, but on the contrary, if a person of good feeling, requites him with service in return; and the one who outdoes the other in beneficence will not have any complaint against his friend, since he gets what he desires, and 3 what each man desires is the good. Nor again are complaints likely to occur between friends whose motive is pleasure either; for if they enjoy each other's company, both alike get what they wish for; and indeed it would seem ridiculous to find fault with somebody for not being agreeable to you, when you need not associate with him if you do not want to do so. But a friendship whose 4 motive is utility is liable to give rise to complaints. For here the friends associate with each other for profit, and so each always wants more, and thinks he is getting less than his due; and they make it a grievance that they do not get as much as they want and deserve; and the one who is doing a service can never supply all that the one receiving it wants.

5 It appears that, as justice is of two kinds, one unwritten and the other defined by law, so the friendship based on utility may be either moral or legal. Hence occasions for complaint chiefly occur when the type of friendship in view at the conclusion of the transaction is not the same as when the relationship was formed. Such a con-6 nexion when on stated terms is one of the legal type, whether it be a purely business matter of exchange on the spot, or a more liberal accommodation for future repayment, though still with an agreement as to the *quid pro quo*; and in the latter case the obligation is clear and cannot cause dispute, though there is an element of

friendliness in the delay allowed, for which reason in some states there is no action at law in these cases, it being held that the party to a contract involving credit must abide by the conse-⁷quences. The moral type on the other hand is not based on stated terms, but the gift or other service is given as to a friend, although the giver expects to receive an equivalent or greater return, as though it had not been a free gift but a loan; and as he ends the relationship in a different spirit from that in which he began it, he will complain. The reason of this is that all men, or ⁸most men, wish what is noble but choose what is profitable; and while it is noble to render a service not with an eye to receiving one in return, it is profitable to receive one. One ought therefore, ⁹if one can, to return the equivalent of services received, and to do so willingly; for one ought not to make a man one's friend if one is unwilling to return his favours. Recognizing therefore that one has made a mistake at the beginning and accepted a service from a wrong person—that is, a person who was not a friend, and was not acting disinterestedly—one should accordingly end the transaction as if one had accepted the service on stated terms. Also, one would agree to repay a service if able to do so (and if one were not able, the giver on his side too would not have expected repayment); hence, if possible, one ought to make a return. But one ought to consider at the beginning from whom one is receiving the service, and on what terms, so that one may accept it on those terms or else decline it.

¹⁰ Dispute may arise however as to the value of the service rendered. Is it to be measured by the benefit to the recipient, and the return made on that basis, or by the cost to the doer? The recipient will say that what he received was only a trifle to his benefactor, or that he could have got it from someone else: he beats down the value. The other on the contrary will protest that it was the most valuable thing he had to give, or that it could not have been obtained from anybody else, or that it was bestowed at a time of danger or in some similar emergency. Perhaps then we may ¹¹say that, when the friendship is one of utility, the measure of the service should be its value to the recipient, since it is he who wants it, and the

other comes to his aid in the expectation of an equivalent return; therefore the degree of assistance rendered has been the amount to which the recipient has benefited, and so he ought to pay back as much as he has got out of it; or even more, for that will be more noble.

In friendships based on virtue, complaints do not arise, but the measure of the benefit seems to be the intention of the giver; for intention is the predominant factor in virtue and in character.

BOOK IX

4. The forms which friendly feeling for our neighbours takes, and the marks by which the different forms of friendship are defined, seem to be derived from the feelings of regard which we entertain for ourselves. A friend is defined as (a) one who wishes, and promotes by action, the real or apparent good of another for that other's sake; or (b) one who wishes the existence and preservation of his friend for the friend's sake. (This is the feeling of mothers towards their children, and of former friends who have quarrelled.) Others say that a friend is (c) one who frequents another's society, and (d) who desires the same things as he does, or (e) one who shares his friend's joys and sorrows. (This too is very characteristic of mothers.) Friendship also is defined ²by one or other of these marks. But each of them is also found in a good man's feelings towards himself (and in those of all other men as well, in so far as they believe themselves to be good; but, as has been said, virtue and the virtuous man seem to be the standard in everything). ³For (d) the good man is of one mind with himself, and desires the same things with every part of his nature. Also (a) he wishes his own good, real as well as apparent, and seeks it by action (for it is a mark of the good man to exert himself actively for the good); and he does so for his own sake (for he does it on account of the intellectual part of himself, and this appears to be a man's real self). Also (b) he desires his own life and security, and especially that of his rational part. ⁴For existence is good for the virtuous man; and everyone wishes his own good: no one would choose to possess every good in the world on condition of becoming somebody else (for God possesses the good even as it is), but only while remaining himself, whatever he may be; and it would appear that the thinking part is the real self, or is so more than anything else. And (c) the 5 good man desires his own company; for he enjoys being by himself, since he has agreeable memories of the past, and good hopes for the future, which are pleasant too; also his mind is stored with subjects for contemplation. And (e) he is keenly conscious of his own joys and sorrows; for the same things give him pleasure or pain at all times, and not different things at different times, since he is not apt to change his mind.

It is therefore because the good man has these various feelings towards himself, and because he feels towards his friend in the same way as towards himself (for a friend is another self), that friendship also is thought to consist in one or the other of these feelings, and the possession of them is thought to be the test of a friend.

6 Whether a man can be said actually to feel friendship for himself is a question that may be dismissed for the present; though it may be held that he can do so in so far as he is a dual or composite being, and because very intense friendship resembles self-regard.

7 As a matter of fact, the feelings of self-regard described appear to be found in most people, even though they are of inferior moral worth. Perhaps men share them in so far as they have their own approval and believe in their own virtue; since the utterly worthless and criminal never possess them, or even have the appearance of doing so. 8 Indeed it may almost be said that no morally inferior persons possess them. For (d) such persons are at variance with themselves, desiring one thing and wishing another: this is the mark of the unrestrained, who choose what is pleasant but harmful instead of what they themselves think to be good. (a) Others again, out of cowardice and idleness, neglect to do what they think best for their own interests. And (b) men who have committed a number of crimes, and are hated for their wickedness, actually flee from life 9 and make away with themselves. Also (c) bad men constantly seek the society of others and shun their own company, because when they are by themselves they recall much that was unpleasant in the past and anticipate the same in the future, whereas with other people they can forget. Moreover they feel no affection for themselves, because they have no lovable qualities. Hence (e) such men do not enter into their own joys and sorrows, as there is civil war in their souls; one part of their nature, owing to depravity, is pained by abstinence from certain indulgences while another part is pleased by it; one part pulls them one way and another the other, as if dragging them asunder. Or if it be impossible 10 to feel pain and pleasure at the same time, at all events after indulging in pleasure they regret it a little later, and wish they had never acquired a taste for such indulgences; since the bad are always changing their minds.

Thus a bad man appears to be devoid even of affection for himself, because he has nothing lovable in his nature. If then such a state of mind is utterly miserable, we should do our utmost to shun wickedness and try to be virtuous. That is the way both to be friends with ourselves and to win the friendship of others.

5. Goodwill appears to be an element of friendly feeling, but it is not the same thing as friendship; for it can be felt towards strangers, and it can be unknown to its object, whereas friendship cannot. But that has been discussed already.

Neither is goodwill the same as affection. For it has no intensity, nor does it include desire, but these things are necessarily involved in affection. Also affection requires intimate acquain-2 tance, whereas goodwill may spring up all of a sudden, as happens for instance in regard to the competitors in a contest; the spectators conceive goodwill and sympathy for them, though they would not actively assist them, for as we said, their goodwill is a sudden growth, and the kindly feeling is only superficial.

3 Goodwill seems therefore to be the beginning of friendship, just as the pleasure of the eye is the beginning of love. No one falls in love without first being charmed by beauty, but one may delight in another's beauty without necessarily being in love: one is in love only if one longs for the beloved

when absent, and eagerly desires his presence. Similarly men cannot be friends without having conceived mutual goodwill, though well-wishers are not necessarily friends: they merely desire the good of those whose well-wishers they are, and would not actively assist them to attain it, nor be put to any trouble on their behalf. Hence extending the meaning of the term friendship we may say that goodwill is inoperative friendship, which when it continues and reaches the point of intimacy may become friendship proper—not the sort of friendship whose motive is utility or pleasure, for these do not arouse goodwill. Goodwill is indeed rendered in return for favours received, but this is merely the payment of a due; and that desire for another's welfare which springs from the anticipation of favours to come does not seem really to show goodwill for one's benefactor, but rather for oneself; just as to court a man for 4 some interested motive is not friendship. Speaking generally, true goodwill is aroused by some kind of excellence or moral goodness: it springs up when one person thinks another beautiful or brave or the like, as in the case we mentioned of competitors in a contest.

6. Concord also seems to be a friendly feeling. Hence it is not merely agreement of opinion, for this might exist even between strangers. Nor yet is agreement in reasoned judgements about any subject whatever, for instance astronomy, termed concord; to agree about the facts of astronomy is not a bond of friendship. Concord is said to prevail in a state, when the citizens agree as to their interests, adopt the same policy, and carry their common resolves into execution. Concord 2 then refers to practical ends, and practical ends of importance, and able to be realized by both or all the parties: for instance, there is concord in the state when the citizens unanimously decree that the offices of state shall be elective, or that an alliance shall be made with Sparta, or that Pittacus shall be dictator (when Pittacus was himself willing to be dictator). When each of two persons wishes himself to rule, like the rivals in the *Phoenissae*, there is discord; since men are not of one mind merely when each thinks the same thing (whatever this may be), but when each thinks the

same thing in relation to the same person: for instance, when both the common people and the upper classes wish that the best people shall rule; for only so can all parties get what they desire.

Concord appears therefore to mean friendship between citizens, which indeed is the ordinary use of the term; for it refers to the interests and concerns of life.

3 Now concord in this sense exists between good men, since these are of one mind both with themselves and with one another, as they always stand more or less on the same ground; for good men's wishes are steadfast, and do not ebb and flow like the tide, and they wish for just and expedient ends, which they strive to attain in 4 common. The base on the other hand are incapable of concord, except in some small degree, as they are of friendship, since they try to get more than their share of advantages, and take less than their share of labours and public burdens. And while each desires this for himself, he spies on his neighbour to prevent him from doing likewise; for unless they keep watch over one another, the common interests go to ruin. The result is discord, everybody trying to make others do their duty but refusing to do it themselves.

7. Benefactors seem to love those whom they benefit more than those who have received benefits love those who have conferred them; and it is asked why this is so, as it seems to be unreasonable. The view most generally taken is that it is because the one party is in the position of a debtor and the other of a creditor; just as therefore in the case of a loan, whereas the borrowed would be glad to have his creditor out of the way, the lender actually watches over his debtor's safety, so it is thought that the conferrer of a benefit wishes the recipient to live in order that he may receive a return, but the recipient is not particularly anxious to make a return. Epicharmus no doubt would say that people who give this explanation are 'looking at the seamy side' of life; but all the same it appears to be not untrue to human nature, for most men have short memories, and are more desirous of receiving benefits than of bestowing them.

2 But it might be held that the real reason lies deeper, and that the case of the creditor is not

really a parallel. With him it is not a matter of affection, but only of wishing his debtor's preservation for the sake of recovering his money; whereas a benefactor feels friendship and affection for the recipient of his bounty even though he is not getting anything out of him and is never likely to do so.

3 The same thing happens with the artist: every artist loves his own handiwork more than that handiwork if it were to come to life would love him. This is perhaps especially true of poets, who have an exaggerated affection for their own poems and love them as parents love their chil-
4 dren. The position of the benefactor then resembles that of the artist; the recipient of his bounty is his handiwork, and he therefore loves him more than his handiwork loves its maker. The reason of this is that all things desire and love existence; but we exist in activity, since we exist by living and doing; and in a sense one who has made something exists actively, and so he loves his handiwork because he loves existence. This is in fact a fundamental principle of nature: what a thing is potentially, that its work reveals in actuality.

5 Moreover for the benefactor there is an element of nobility in the act, and so he feels pleased with the person who is its object; but there is nothing noble for the recipient of the benefit in his relation to his benefactor: at most, it is profitable; and what is profitable is not so pleasant or lovable as what is noble. The doer's
6 achievement therefore remains, for nobility or beauty is long-lived, but its utility to the recipient passes away. But while the actuality of the present, the hope of the future, and the memory of the past are all pleasant, actuality is the most pleasant of the three, and the most loved. Also whereas the memory of noble things is pleasant, that of useful ones is hardly at all so, or at least less so; although with anticipation the reverse seems to be the case.

Again, loving seems to be an active experience, being loved a passive one; hence affection and the various forms of friendly feeling are naturally found in the more active party to the relationship.

7 Again, everybody loves a thing more if it has cost him trouble: for instance those who have made money love money more than those who have inherited it. Now to receive a benefit seems to involve no labour, but to confer one is an effort. (This is why mothers love their children more than fathers, because parenthood costs the mother more trouble [and the mother is more certain that the child is her own].) This also then would seem to be a characteristic of benefactors.

8. The question is also raised whether one ought to love oneself or someone else most. We censure those who put themselves first, and 'lover of self' is used as a term of reproach. And it is thought that a bad man considers himself in all he does, and the more so the worse he is—so it is a complaint against him for instance that 'he never does a thing unless you make him'—whereas a good man acts from a sense of what is noble, and the better he is the more he so acts, and he considers his friend's interest, disregarding his own.

2 But the facts do not accord with these theories; nor is this surprising. For we admit that one should love one's best friend most; but the best friend is he that, when he wishes a person's good, wishes it for that person's own sake, even though nobody will ever know of it. Now this condition is most fully realized in a man's regard for himself, as indeed are all the other attributes that make up the definition of a friend; for it has been said already that all the feelings that constitute friendship for others are an extension of regard for self. Moreover, all the proverbs agree with this; for example, 'Friends have one soul between them,' 'Friends' goods are common property,' 'Amity is equality,' 'The knee is nearer than the shin.' All of these sayings will apply most fully to oneself; for a man is his own best friend. Therefore he ought to love himself most.

So it is naturally debated which of these two views we ought to adopt, since each of them has some plausibility.

3 Now where there is a conflict of opinion the proper course is doubtless to get the two views clearly distinguished, and to define how far and in what way each of them is true. So probably the matter may become clear if we ascertain what meaning each side attaches to the term 'self-love.'

4   Those then who make it a term of reproach call men lovers of self when they assign to themselves the larger share of money, honours, or bodily pleasures; since these are the things which most men desire and set their hearts on as being the greatest goods, and which accordingly they compete with each other to obtain. Now those who take more than their share of these things are men who indulge their appetites, and generally their passions and the irrational part of their souls. But most men are of this kind. Accordingly the use of the term 'lover of self' as a reproach has arisen from the fact that self-love of the ordinary kind is bad. Hence self-love is rightly censured in those who are lovers of self in this sense.

5 And that it is those who take too large a share of things of this sort whom most people usually mean when they speak of lovers of self, is clear enough. For if a man were always bent on outdoing everybody else in acting justly or temperately or in displaying any other of the virtues, and in general were always trying to secure for himself moral nobility, no one will charge him with love

6 of self nor find any fault with him. Yet as a matter of fact such a man might be held to be a lover of self in an exceptional degree. At all events he takes for himself the things that are noblest and most truly good. Also it is the most dominant part of himself that he indulges and obeys in everything. But (a) as in the state it is the sovereign that is held in the fullest sense to *be* the state, and in any other composite whole it is the dominant part that is deemed especially to be that whole, so it is with man. He therefore who loves and indulges the dominant part of himself is a lover of self in the fullest degree. Again (b), the terms 'self-restrained' and 'unrestrained' denote being restrained or not by one's intellect, and thus imply that the intellect is the man himself. Also (c) it is our reasoned acts that are felt to be in the fullest sense *our own* acts, *voluntary* acts. It is therefore clear that a man is or is chiefly the dominant part of himself, and that a good man values this part of himself most. Hence the good man will be a lover of self in the fullest degree, though in another sense than the lover of self so-called by way of reproach, from whom he differs as much as living by principle differs from living by passion, and aiming at what is noble

7 from aiming at what seems expedient. Persons therefore who are exceptionally zealous in noble actions are universally approved and commended; and if all men vied with each other in moral nobility and strove to perform the noblest deeds, the common welfare would be fully realized, while individuals also could enjoy the greatest of goods, inasmuch as virtue is the greatest good.

Therefore the good man ought to be a lover of self, since he will then both benefit himself by acting nobly and aid his fellows; but the bad man ought not to be a lover of self, since he will follow his base passions, and so injure both himself and

8 his neighbours. With the bad man therefore, what he does is not in accord with what he ought to do, but the good man does what he ought, since intelligence always chooses for itself that which is best, and the good man obeys his intelligence.

9   But it is also true that the virtuous man's conduct is often guided by the interests of his friends and of his country, and that he will if necessary lay down his life in their behalf. For he will surrender wealth and power and all the goods that men struggle to win, if he can secure nobility for himself; since he would prefer an hour of rapture to a long period of mild enjoyment, a year of noble life to many years of ordinary existence, one great and glorious exploit to many small successes. And this is doubtless the case with those who give their lives for others; thus they choose great nobility for themselves. Also the virtuous man is ready to forgo money if by that means his friends may gain more money; for thus, though his friend gets money, he himself achieves nobility, and so he assigns the greater good to his

10 own share. And he behaves in the same manner as regards honours and offices also: all these things he will relinquish to his friend, for this is noble and praiseworthy for himself. He is naturally therefore thought to be virtuous, as he chooses moral nobility in preference to all other things. It may even happen that he will surrender to his friend the performance of some achievement, and that it may be nobler for him to be the cause of his friend's performing it than to perform it himself.

11   Therefore in all spheres of praiseworthy conduct it is manifest that the good man takes the

larger share of moral nobility for himself. In this sense, then, as we said above, it is right to be a lover of self, though self-love of the ordinary sort is wrong.

9. Another debated question is whether friends are necessary or not for happiness. People say that the supremely happy are self-sufficing, and so have no need of friends: for they have the good things of life already, and therefore, being complete in themselves, require nothing further; whereas the function of a friend, who is a second self, is to supply things we cannot procure for ourselves. Hence the saying

When fortune favours us, what need of friends?

2 But it seems strange that if we attribute all good things to the happy man we should not assign him friends, which we consider the greatest of external goods. Also if it be more the mark of a friend to give than to receive benefits, and if beneficence is a function of the good man and of virtue, and it is nobler to benefit friends than strangers, the good man will need friends as the objects of his beneficence.

Hence the further question is asked: Are friends more needed in prosperity or in adversity? It is argued that the unfortunate need people to be kind to them, but also that the prosperous need people to whom they may be kind.

3 Also perhaps it would be strange to represent the supremely happy man as a recluse. Nobody would choose to have all possible good things on the condition that he must enjoy them alone; for man is a social being, and designed by nature to live with others; accordingly the happy man must have society, for he has everything that is naturally good. And it is obviously preferable to associate with friends and with good men than with strangers and chance companions. Therefore the happy man requires friends.

4 What then do the upholders of the former view mean, and in what sense is it true? Perhaps the explanation of it is that most men think of friends as being people who are useful to us. Now it is true that the supremely happy man will have no need for friends of that kind, inasmuch as he is supplied with good things already. Nor yet will

he want friends of the pleasant sort, or only to a very small extent, for his life is intrinsically pleasant and has no need of adventitious pleasure. And as he does not need useful or pleasant friends, it is assumed that he does not require friends at all.

5 But perhaps this inference is really untrue. For as we said at the beginning, happiness is a form of activity, and an activity clearly is something that comes into being, not a thing that we possess all the time, like a piece of property. But if happiness consists in life and activity, and the activity of a good man, as was said at the beginning, is good and so pleasant in itself, and if the sense that a thing is our own is also pleasant, yet we are better able to contemplate our neighbours than ourselves, and their actions than our own, and thus good men find pleasure in the actions of other good men who are their friends, since those actions possess both these essentially pleasant qualities, it therefore follows that the supremely happy man will require good friends, insomuch as he desires to contemplate actions that are good and that are his own, and the actions of a good man that is his friend are such. Also men think that the life of the happy man ought to be pleasant. Now a solitary man has a hard life, for it is not easy to keep up continuous activity by oneself; it is easier to do so with the aid of and in 6 relation to other people. The good man's activity therefore, which is pleasant in itself, will be more continuous if practiced with friends; and the life of the supremely happy should be continuously pleasant (for a good man, in virtue of his goodness, enjoys actions that conform with virtue and dislikes those that spring from wickedness, just as a skilled musician is pleased by good music and 7 pained by bad). Moreover the society of the good may supply a sort of training in goodness, as Theognis remarks.

Again, if we examine the matter more fundamentally, it appears that a virtuous friend is essentially desirable for a virtuous man. For as has been said above, that which is essentially good is good and pleasing in itself to the virtuous man. And life is defined, in the case of animals, by the capacity for sensation; in the case of man, by the capacity for sensation and thought. But a capacity is referred to its activity, and in this its full reality consists. It appears therefore that life in the full sense is sensation or thought. But life is a thing good and pleasant in itself, for it is definite, and definiteness is a part of the essence of goodness, and what is essentially good is good for the good 8 man, and hence appears to be pleasant to all men. We must not argue from a vicious and corrupt life, or one that is painful, for such a life is indefinite, like its attributes. (The point as to pain will be 9 clearer in the sequel.) But if life itself is good and pleasant (as it appears to be, because all men desire it, and virtuous and supremely happy men most of all, since their way of life is most desirable and their existence the most blissful); and if one who sees is conscious that he sees, one who hears that he hears, one who walks that he walks, and similarly for all the other human activities there is a faculty that is conscious of their exercise, so that whenever we perceive, we are conscious that we perceive, and whenever we think, we are conscious that we think, and to be conscious that we are perceiving or thinking is to be conscious that we exist (for existence, as we saw, is sense-perception or thought); and if to be conscious one is alive is a pleasant thing in itself (for life is a thing essentially good, and to be conscious that one possesses a good thing is pleasant); and if life is desirable, and especially so for good men, because existence is good for them, and so pleasant (because they are pleased by the perception of 10 what is intrinsically good); and if the virtuous man feels towards his friend in the same way as he feels towards himself (for his friend is a second self)— then, just as a man's own existence is desirable for him, so, or nearly so, is his friend's existence also desirable. But, as we saw, it is the consciousness of oneself as good that makes existence desirable, and such consciousness is pleasant in itself. Therefore a man ought also to share his friend's consciousness of his existence, and this is attained by their living together and by conversing and communicating their thoughts to each other; for this is the meaning of living together as applied to human beings, it does not mean merely feeding in the same place, as it does when applied to cattle.

If then to the supremely happy man existence is desirable in itself, being good and pleas-

ant essentially, and if his friend's existence is almost equally desirable to him, it follows that a friend is one of the things to be desired. But that which is desirable for him he is bound to have, or else his condition will be incomplete in that particular. Therefore to be happy a man needs virtuous friends.

10. Ought we then to make as many friends as possible? or, just as it seems a wise saying about hospitality—

Neither with troops of guests nor yet with none—

so also with friendship perhaps it will be fitting neither to be without friends nor yet to make friends in excessive numbers. This rule would 2 certainly seem applicable to those friends whom we choose for their utility; for it is troublesome to have to repay the services of a large number of people, and life is not long enough for one to do it. Any more therefore than are sufficient for the requirements of one's own life will be superfluous, and a hindrance to noble living, so one is better without them. Of friends for pleasure also a few are enough, just as a small amount of sweets is enough in one's diet. But should one have as 3 many good friends as possible? or is there a limit of size for a circle of friends, as there is for the population of a state? Ten people would not make a city, and with a hundred thousand, it is a city no longer; though perhaps the proper size is not one particular number, but any number between certain limits. So also the number of one friends must be limited, and should perhaps be the largest number with whom one can constantly associate; since, as we saw, to live together is the 4 chief mark of friendship, but it is quite clear that it is not possible to live with and to share oneself among a large number of people. Another essential is that one's friends must also be the friends of one another, if they are all to pass the time in each other's company; but for a large number of people all to be friends is a difficult matter. 5 Again, it is difficult to share intimately in the joys and sorrows of many people; for one may very likely be called upon to rejoice with one and to mourn with another at the same time.

Perhaps therefore it is a good rule not to seek to have as many friends as possible, but only as many as are enough to form a circle of associates. Indeed it would appear to be impossible to be very friendly with many people, for the same reason as it is impossible to be in love with several people. Love means friendship in the superlative degree, and that must be with one person only; so also warm friendship is only possible with a few.

BOOK X

1. Our next business after this is doubtless to discuss Pleasure. For pleasure is thought to be especially congenial to mankind; and this is why pleasure and pain are employed in the education of the young, as means whereby to steer their course. Moreover, to like and to dislike the right things is thought to be a most important element in the formation of a virtuous character. For pleasure and pain extend throughout the whole of life, and are of great moment and influence for virtue and happiness; since men choose what is pleasant and avoid what is painful.

2   It would therefore seem by no means proper to omit so important a subject, especially as there is much difference of opinion about it. Some people maintain that pleasure is the Good. Others on the contrary say that it is altogether bad: some of them perhaps from a conviction that it is really so, but others because they think it to be in the interests of morality to make out that pleasure is bad, even if it is not, since most men (they argue) have a bias towards it, and are the slaves of their pleasures, so that they have to be driven in the opposite direction in order to arrive at the due mean.

3   Possibly however this view is mistaken. In matters of emotion and of action, words are less convincing than deeds; when therefore our theories are at variance with palpable facts, they provoke contempt, and involve the truth in their own discredit. If one who censures pleasure is seen sometimes to desire it himself, his swerving towards it is thought to show that he really believes that all pleasure is desirable; for the mass of mankind cannot discriminate. Hence it appears

4 that true theories are the most valuable for conduct as well as for science; harmonizing with the facts, they carry conviction, and so encourage those who understand them to guide their lives by them.

With so much by way of introduction, let us now review the theories about pleasure that have been advanced.

4. We may ascertain the nature and quality of pleasure more clearly if we start again from the beginning.

Now the act of sight appears to be perfect at any moment of its duration; it does not require anything to supervene later in order to perfect its specific quality. But pleasure also appears to be a thing of this nature. For it is a whole, and one cannot at any moment put one's hand on a pleasure which will only exhibit its specific quality perfectly if its duration be prolonged.

2   It follows also that pleasure is not a form of motion. For every motion or process of change involves duration, and is a means to an end, for instance the process of building a house; and it is perfect when it has effected its end. Hence a motion is perfect either when viewed over the whole time of its duration, or at the moment when its end has been achieved. The several motions occupying portions of the time of the whole are imperfect, and different in kind from the whole and from each other. For instance, in building a temple the fitting together of the stones is a different process from the fluting of a column, and both are different from the construction of the temple as a whole; and whereas the building of the temple is a perfect process, for nothing more is required to achieve the end proposed, laying the foundation and constructing the triglyphs are imperfect processes, since each produces only a part of the design; they are therefore specifically different from the construction of the whole, and it is not possible to lay one's finger on a motion specifically perfect at any moment of the process of building, but only, if at all, in the whole of its duration.

3   And the same is true of walking and the other forms of locomotion. For if locomotion is motion from one point in space to another, and if this is of different kinds, flying, walking, leaping and the like, and not only so, but if there are also differences in walking itself (for the

terminal points of a racecourse are not the same as those of a portion of the course, nor are those of one portion the same as those of another; nor is traversing this line the same as traversing that one, for the runner does not merely travel along a certain line but travels along a line that is in a certain place, and this line is in a different place from that)—however, for a full treatment of the subject of motion I must refer to another work, but it appears that a motion is not perfect at every moment, but the many movements which make up the whole are imperfect; and different from each other in kind, inasmuch as the terminal points of a movement constitute a specific quality. 4 The specific quality of pleasure on the contrary is perfect at any moment. It is clear therefore that pleasure is not the same as motion, and that it is a whole and something perfect.

This may also be inferred from the fact that a movement necessarily occupies a space of time, whereas a feeling of pleasure does not, for every moment of pleasurable consciousness is a perfect whole.

These considerations also show that it is a mistake to speak of pleasure as the result of a motion or of a process of generation. For we cannot so describe everything, but only such things as are divided into parts and are not wholes. Thus an act of sight, a geometrical point, an arithmetical unit are not the result of a process of generation (nor is any of them a motion or process). Pleasure therefore also is not the result of a motion or process; for pleasure is a whole.

5 Again, inasmuch as each of the senses acts in relation to its object, and acts perfectly when it is in good condition and directed to the finest of the objects that belong to it (for this seems to be the best description of perfect activity, it being assumed to make no difference whether it be the sense itself that acts or the organ in which the sense resides), it follows that the activity of any of the senses is at its best when the sense-organ being in the best condition is directed to the best of its objects; and this activity will be the most perfect and the pleasantest. For each sense has a corresponding pleasure, as also have thought and speculation, and its activity is pleasantest when it is most perfect, and most perfect when the organ is in good condition and when it is directed to the most excellent of its objects; and the pleasure 6 perfects the activity. The pleasure does not however perfect the activity in the same way as the object perceived and the sensory faculty, if good, perfect it; just as health and the physician are not in the same way the cause of being healthy.

7 (It is clear that each of the senses is accompanied by pleasure, since we apply the term pleasant to sights and sounds; and it is also clear that the pleasure is greatest when the sensory faculty is both in the best condition and acting in relation to the best object; and given excellence in the perceived object and the percipient organ, there will always be pleasure when an object to cause it and a subject to feel it are both present.)

8 But the pleasure perfects the activity, not as the fixed disposition does, by being already present in the agent, but as a supervening perfection, like the bloom of health in the young and vigorous.

So long therefore as both object thought of or perceived, and subject discerning or judging, are such as they should be, there will be pleasure in the activity; since while both the passive and the active parties to a relationship remain the same in themselves and unaltered in their relation to one another, the same result is naturally produced.

9 How is it then that no one can feel pleasure continuously? Perhaps it is due to fatigue, since no human faculty is capable of uninterrupted activity, and therefore pleasure also is not continuous, because it accompanies the activity of the faculties. It is for the same reason that some things please us when new, but cease to give so much pleasure later; this is because at first the mind is stimulated, and acts vigorously in regard to the object, as in the case of sight when we look at something intently; but afterwards the activity is less vigorous and our attention relaxes, and consequently the pleasure also fades.

10 It might be held that all men seek to obtain pleasure, because all men desire life. Life is a form of activity, and each man exercises his activity upon those objects and with those faculties which he likes the most: for example, the musician exercises his sense of hearing upon musical tunes, the student his intellect upon problems of

philosophy, and so on. And the pleasure of these activities perfects the activities, and therefore perfects life, which all men seek. Men have good 11 reason therefore to pursue pleasure, since it perfects for each his life, which is a desirable thing. The question whether we desire life for the sake of pleasure or pleasure for the sake of life, need not be raised for the present. In any case they appear to be inseparably united; for there is no pleasure without activity, and also no perfect activity without its pleasure.

5. This moreover is the ground for believing that pleasures vary in specific quality. For we feel that different kinds of things must have a different sort of perfection. We see this to be so with natural organisms and the productions of art, such as animals, trees, a picture, a statue, a house, a piece of furniture. Similarly we think that that which perfects one kind of activity must differ in kind from that which perfects another kind. Now the 2 activities of the intellect differs from those of the senses, and from one another, in kind: so also therefore do the pleasures that perfect them.

This may also be seen from the affinity which exists between the various pleasures and the activities which they perfect. For an activity is augmented by the pleasure that belongs to it; since those who work with pleasure always work with more discernment and with greater accuracy—for instance, students who are fond of geometry become proficient in it, and grasp its various problems better, and similarly lovers of music, architecture or the other arts make progress in their favourite pursuit because they enjoy it. An activity then is augmented by its pleasure; and that which augments a thing must be akin to it. But things that are akin to things of different kinds must themselves differ in kind.

3 A still clearer proof may be drawn from the hindrance that activities receive from the pleasure derived from other activities. For instance, persons fond of the flute cannot give their attention to a philosophical discussion when they overhear someone playing the flute, because they enjoy music more than the activity in which they are engaged; therefore the pleasure afforded by the music of the flute impairs the activity of

4 study. The same thing occurs in other cases when a man tries to do two things at once; the pleasanter activity drives out the other, the more so if it is much more pleasant, until the other activity ceases altogether. Hence, when we enjoy something very much, we can hardly do anything else; and when we find a thing only mildly agreeable, we turn to some other occupation; for instance, people who eat sweets at the theatre do so espe- 5 cially when the acting is bad. And since our activities are sharpened, prolonged and improved by their own pleasure, and impaired by the pleasures of other activities, it is clear that pleasures differ widely from each other. In fact alien pleasures have almost the same effect on the activities as their own pains; since, when an activity causes pain, this pain destroys it, for instance, if a person finds writing or doing sums unpleasant and irksome; for he stops writing or doing sums, because the activity is painful. Activities then are affected in opposite ways by the pleasures and the pains that belong to them, that is to say, those that are intrinsically due to their exercise. Alien pleasure, as has been said, have very much the same effect as pain, for they destroy an activity, only not to the same degree.

Again, since activities differ in moral value, 6 and some are to be adopted, others to be avoided, and others again are neutral, the same is true also of their pleasures: for each activity has a pleasure of its own. Thus the pleasure of a good activity is morally good, that of a bad one morally bad; for even desires for noble things are praised and desires for base things blamed; but the pleasures contained in our activities are more intimately connected with them than the appetites which prompt them, for the appetite is both separate in time and distinct in its nature from the activity, whereas the pleasure is closely linked to the activity indeed so inseparable from it as to raise a doubt whether the activity is not the same things as the 7 pleasure. However, we must not regard pleasure as really being a thought or a sensation—indeed this is absurd, though because they are inseparable they seem to some people to be the same.

As then activities are diverse, so also are their pleasures. Sight excels touch in purity, and hearing and smell excel taste; and similarly the pleasures of the intellect excel in purity the pleasures of sensation, while the pleasure of either class differ among themselves in purity.

8 And it is thought that every animal has its own special pleasure, just as it has its own special function: namely, the pleasure of exercising that function. This will also appear if we consider the different animals one by one: the horse, the dog, man, have different pleasures—as Heracleitus says, an ass would prefer chaff to gold, since to asses food gives more pleasure than gold. Different species therefore have different kinds of pleasures. On the other hand it might be supposed that there is no variety among the pleas-
9 ures of the same species. But as a matter of fact in the human species at all events there is a great diversity of pleasures. The same things delight some men and annoy others, and things painful and disgusting to some are pleasant and attractive to others. This also holds good of things sweet to the taste: the same things do not taste sweet to a man in a fever as to one in good health; nor does the same temperature feel warm to an invalid and to a person of robust constitution. The same holds good of other things as well.

10 But we hold that in all such cases the thing really is what it appears to be to the good man. And if this rule is sound, as it is generally held to be, and if the standard of everything is goodness, or the good man, *qua* good, then the things that seem to him to be pleasures are pleasures, and the things he enjoys are pleasant. Nor need it cause surprise that things disagreeable to the good man should seem pleasant to some men; for mankind is liable to many corruptions and diseases, and the things in question are not really pleasant, but only pleasant to these particular persons, who are in a condition to think them so.

11 It is therefore clear that we must pronounce the admittedly disgraceful pleasures not to be pleasures at all, except to the depraved.

But among the pleasures considered respectable, which class of pleasures or which particular pleasure is to be deemed the distinctively human pleasure? Perhaps this will be clear from a consideration of man's activities. For pleasures correspond to the activities to which they belong; it is therefore that pleasure, or those pleasures, by which the activity, or the activities, of the perfect and supremely happy man are perfected, that must be pronounced human in the fullest sense. The other pleasures are so only in a secondary or some lower degree, like the activities to which they belong.

6. Having now discussed the various kinds of Virtue, of Friendship and of Pleasure, it remains for us to treat in outline of Happiness, inasmuch as we count this to be the End of human life. But it will shorten the discussion if we recapitulate what has been said already.

2 Now we stated that happiness is not a certain disposition of character; since if it were it might be possessed by a man who passed the whole of his life asleep, living the life of a vegetable, or by one who was plunged in the deepest misfortune. If then we reject this as unsatisfactory, and feel bound to class happiness rather as some form of activity, as has been said in the earlier part of this treatise, and if activities are of two kinds, some merely necessary means and desirable only for the sake of something else, others desirable in themselves, it is clear that happiness is to be classed among activities desirable in themselves, and not among those desirable as a means to something else; since happiness lacks nothing, and is self-sufficient.

3 But those activities are desirable in themselves which do not aim at any result beyond the mere exercise of the activity. Now this is felt to be the nature of actions in conformity with virtue; for to do noble and virtuous deeds is a thing desirable for its own sake.

But agreeable amusements also are desirable for their own sake; we do not pursue them as a means to something else, for as a matter of fact they are more often harmful than beneficial, causing men to neglect their health and their estates. Yet persons whom the world counts happy usually have recourse to such pastimes; and this is why adepts in such pastimes stand in high favour with princes, because they make themselves agreeable in supplying what their patrons desire, and what they want is amusement. So it is supposed that amusements are a component part of happiness, because princes and potentates devote their leisure to them.

4 But (i) perhaps princes and potentates are not good evidence. Virtue and intelligence, which are the sources of man's higher activities, do not depend on the possession of power; and if these persons, having no taste for pure and liberal pleasure, have recourse to the pleasures of the body, we must not on that account suppose that bodily pleasures are the more desirable. Children imagine that the things they themselves value are actually the best; it is not surprising therefore that, as children and grown men have different standards of value, so also should the worthless and the virtuous.

5 Therefore, as has repeatedly been said, those things are actually valuable and pleasant which appear so to the good man; but each man thinks that activity most desirable which suits his particular disposition, and therefore the good man

6 thinks virtuous activity most desirable. It follows therefore that happiness is not to be found in amusements.

(ii) Indeed it would be strange that amusement should be our End—that we should toil and moil all our life long in order that we may amuse ourselves. For virtually every object we adopt is pursued as a means to something else, excepting happiness, which is an end in itself; to make amusement the object of our serious pursuits and our work seems foolish and childish to excess: Anacharsis's motto, Play in order that you may work, is felt to be the right rule. For amusement is a form of rest; but we need rest because we are not able to go on working without a break, and therefore it is not an end, since we take it as a means to further activity.

(iii) And the life that conforms with virtue is thought to be a happy life; but virtuous life involves serious purpose, and does not consist in amusement.

7 (iv) Also we pronounce serious things to be superior to things that are funny and amusing; and the nobler a faculty or a person is, the more serious, we think, are their activities; therefore, the activity of the nobler faculty or person is itself superior, and therefore more productive of happiness.

8 (v) Also anybody can enjoy the pleasures of the body, a slave no less than the noblest of mankind; but no one allows a slave any measure of happiness, any more than a life of his own. Therefore happiness does not consist in pastimes and amusements, but in activities in accordance with virtue, as has been said already.

7. But if happiness consists in activity in accordance with virtue, it is reasonable that it should be activity in accordance with the highest virtue; and this will be the virtue of the best part of us. Whether then this be the intellect, or whatever else it be that is thought to rule and lead us by nature, and to have cognizance of what is noble and divine, either as being itself also actually divine, or as being relatively the divinest part of us, it is the activity of this part of us in accordance with the virtue proper to it that will constitute perfect happiness; and it has been stated already that this activity is the activity of contemplation.

2 And that happiness consists in contemplation may be accepted as agreeing both with the results already reached and with the truth. For contemplation is at once the highest form of activity (since the intellect is the highest thing in us, and the objects with which the intellect deals are the highest things that can be known), and also it is the most continuous, for we can reflect more continuously than we can carry on

3 any form of action. And again we suppose that happiness must contain an element of pleasure; now activity in accordance with wisdom is admittedly the most pleasant of the activities in accordance with virtue: at all events it is held that philosophy or the pursuit of wisdom contains pleasures of marvellous purity and permanence, and it is reasonable to suppose that the enjoyment of knowledge is a still pleasanter occupation than the pursuit of it. Also the activ-

4 ity of contemplation will be found to possess in the highest degree the quality that is termed self-sufficiency; for while it is true that the wise man equally with the just man and the rest requires the necessaries of life, yet, these being adequately supplied, whereas the just man needs other persons towards whom or with whose aid he may act justly, and so likewise do the temperate man and the brave man and the others, the wise man on

the contrary can also contemplate by himself, and the more so the wiser he is; no doubt he will study better with the aid of fellow-workers, but still he is the most self-sufficient of men. Also 5 the activity of contemplation may be held to be the only activity that is loved for its own sake: it produces no result beyond the actual act of contemplation, whereas from practical pursuits we look to secure some advantage, greater or smaller, beyond the action itself. Also happiness is 6 thought to involve leisure; for we do business in order that we may have leisure, and carry on war in order that we may have peace. Now the practical virtues are exercised in politics or in warfare; but the pursuits of politics and war seem to be unleisured—those of war indeed entirely so, for no one desires to be at war for the sake of being at war, nor deliberately takes steps to cause a war: a man would be thought an utterly bloodthirsty character if he declared war on a friendly state for the sake of causing battles and massacres. But the activity of the politician also is unleisured, and aims at securing something beyond the mere participation in politics—positions of authority and honour, or, if the happiness of the politician himself and of his fellow-citizens, this happiness conceived as something distinct from political activity (indeed we are 7 clearly investigating it as so distinct). If then among practical pursuits displaying the virtues, politics and war stand out pre-eminent in nobility and grandeur, and yet they are unleisured, and directed to some further end, not chosen for their own sakes: whereas the activity of the intellect is felt to excel in serious worth, consisting as it does in contemplation, and to aim at no end beyond itself, and also to contain a pleasure peculiar to itself, and therefore augmenting its activity: and if accordingly the attributes of this activity are found to be self-sufficiency, leisuredness, such freedom from fatigue as is possible for man, and all the other attributes of blessedness: it follows that it is the activity of the intellect that constitutes complete human happiness—provided it be granted a complete span of life, for nothing that belongs to happiness can be incomplete.

8 Such a life as this however will be higher than the human level: not in virtue of his humanity will a man achieve it, but in virtue of something within him that is divine; and by as much as this something is superior to his composite nature, by so much is its activity superior to the exercise of the other forms of virtue. If then the intellect is something divine in comparison with man, so is the life of the intellect divine in comparison with human life. Nor ought we to obey those who enjoin that a man should have man's thoughts and a mortal the thoughts of mortality, but we ought so far as possible to achieve immortality, and do all that man may to live in accordance with the highest thing in him; for though this be small in bulk, in power and value it far surpasses all the rest.

9 It may even be held that this is the true self of each, inasmuch as it is the dominant and better part; and therefore it would be a strange thing if a man should choose to live not his own life but the life of some other than himself.

Moreover what was said before will apply here also: that which is best and most pleasant for each creature is that which is proper to the nature of each; accordingly the life of the intellect is the best and the pleasantest life for man, inasmuch as the intellect more than anything else is man; therefore this life will be the happiest.

8. The life of moral virtue, on the other hand, is happy only in a secondary degree. For the moral activities are purely human: Justice, I mean, Courage and the other virtues we display in our intercourse with our fellows, when we observe what is due to each in contracts and services and in our various actions, and in our emotions also; and all of these things seem to be purely human affairs. And some moral actions 2 are thought to be the outcome of the physical constitution, and moral virtue is thought to have a close affinity in many respects with the 3 passions. Moreover, Prudence is intimately connected with Moral Virtue, and this with Prudence, inasmuch as the first principles which Prudence employs are determined by the Moral Virtues, and the right standard for the Moral

Virtues is determined by Prudence. But these being also connected with the passions are related to our composite nature; now the virtues of our composite nature are purely human; so therefore also is the life that manifests these virtues, and the happiness that belongs to it. Whereas the happiness that belongs to the intellect is separate: so much may be said about it here, for a full discussion of the matter is beyond the scope of our present purpose. And such hap-
4 piness would appear to need but little external equipment, or less than the happiness based on moral virtue. Both, it may be granted, require the mere necessaries of life, and that in an equal degree (though the politician does as a matter of fact take more trouble about bodily requirements and so forth than the philosopher); for in this respect there may be little difference between them. But for the purpose of their special activities their requirements will differ widely. The liberal man will need wealth in order to do liberal actions, and so indeed will the just man in order to discharge his obligations (since mere intentions are invisible, and even the unjust pretend to wish to act justly); and the brave man will need strength if he is to perform any action displaying his virtue; and the temperate man opportunity for indulgence: otherwise how can he, or the possessor of any other virtue, show that he is
5 virtuous? It is disputed also whether purpose or performance is the more important factor in virtue, as it is alleged to depend on both; now the perfection of virtue will clearly consist in both; but the performance of virtuous actions requires much outward equipment, and the more so the greater and more noble the actions are. But the
6 student, so far as the pursuit of his activity is concerned, needs no external apparatus: on the contrary, worldly goods may almost be said to be a hindrance to contemplation; though it is true that, being a man and living in the society of others, he chooses to engage in virtuous action, and so will need external goods to carry on his life as a human being.
7   The following considerations also will show that perfect happiness is some form of contemplative activity. The gods, as we conceive them,

enjoy supreme felicity and happiness. But what sort of actions can we attribute to them? Just actions? but will it not seem ridiculous to think of them as making contracts, restoring deposits and the like? Then brave actions—enduring terrors and running risks for the nobility of so doing? Or liberal actions? but to whom will they give? Besides, it would be absurd to suppose that they actually have a coinage or currency of some sort! And temperate actions—what will these mean in their case? surely it would be derogatory to praise them for not having evil desires! If we go through the list we shall find that all forms of virtuous conduct seem trifling and unworthy of the gods. Yet nevertheless they have always been conceived as, at all events, living, and therefore living actively, for we cannot suppose they are always asleep like Endymion. But for a living being, if we eliminate action, and *a fortiori* creative action, what remains save contemplation? It follows that the activity of God, which is transcendent in blessedness, is the activity of contemplation; and therefore among human activities that which is most akin to the divine activity of contemplation will be the greatest source of happiness.
8   A further confirmation is that the lower animals cannot partake of happiness, because they are completely devoid of the contemplative activity. The whole of the life of the gods is blessed, and that of man is so in so far as it contains some likeness to the divine activity; but none of the other animals possess happiness, because they are entirely incapable of contemplation. Happiness therefore is co-extensive in its range with contemplation: the more a class of beings possesses the faculty of contemplation, the more it enjoys happiness, not as an accidental concomitant of contemplation but as inherent in it, since contemplation is valuable in itself. It follows that happiness is some form of contemplation.
9   But the philosopher being a man will also need external well-being, since man's nature is not self-sufficient for the activity of contemplation, but he must also have bodily health and a supply of food and other requirements. Yet if

supreme blessedness is not possible without external goods, it must not be supposed that happiness will demand many or great possessions; for self-sufficiency does not depend on excessive abundance, nor does moral conduct, and it is

10 possible to perform noble deeds even without being ruler of land and sea: one can do virtuous acts with quite moderate resources. This may be clearly observed in experience: private citizens do not seem to be less but more given to doing virtuous actions than princes and potentates. It is sufficient then if moderate resources are forthcoming; for a life of virtuous activity will be essentially a happy life.

11 Solon also doubtless gave a good description of happiness, when he said that in his opinion those men were happy who, being moderately equipped with external goods, had performed noble exploits and had lived temperately; for it is possible for a man of but moderate possessions to do what is right. Anaxagoras again does not seem to have conceived the happy man as rich or powerful, since he says that he would not be surprised if he were to appear a strange sort of person in the eyes of the many; for most men judge by externals, which are all that they can perceive.

12 So our theories seem to be in agreement with the opinions of the wise.

Such arguments then carry some degree of conviction; but it is by the practical experience of life and conduct that the truth is really tested, since it is there that the final decision lies. We must therefore examine the conclusions we have advanced by bringing them to the test of the facts of life. If they are in harmony with the facts, we may accept them; if found to disagree, we must deem them mere theories.

13 And it seems likely that the man who pursues intellectual activity, and who cultivates his intellect and keeps that in the best condition, is also the man most beloved of the gods. For if, as is generally believed, the gods exercise some superintendence over human affairs, then it will be reasonable to suppose that they take pleasure in that part of man which is best and most akin to themselves, namely the intellect, and that they recompense with their favours those men

who esteem and honour this most, because these care for the things dear to themselves, and act rightly and nobly. Now it is clear that all these attributes belong most of all to the wise man. He therefore is most beloved by the gods; and if so, he is naturally most happy. Here is another proof that the wise man is the happiest.

9. If then we have sufficiently discussed in their outlines the subjects of Happiness and of Virtue in its various forms, and also Friendship and Pleasure, may we assume that the investigation we proposed is now complete? Perhaps however, as we maintain, in the practical sciences the end is not to attain a theoretic knowledge of the

2 various subjects, but rather to carry out our theories in action. If so, to know what virtue is is not enough; we must endeavour to possess and to practise it, or in some other manner actually ourselves to become good.

3 Now if discourses on ethics were sufficient in themselves to make men virtuous, 'large fees and many' (as Theognis says) 'would they win,' quite rightly, and to provide such discourse would be all that is wanted. But as it is, we see that although theories have power to stimulate and encourage generous youths, and, given an inborn nobility of character and a genuine love of what is noble, can make them susceptible to the influence of virtue, yet they are powerless to stimulate the mass of mankind to moral nobility. For it is

4 the nature of the many to be amenable to fear but not to a sense of honour, and to abstain from evil not because of its baseness but because of the penalties it entails; since, living as they do by passion, they pursue the pleasures akin to their nature, and the things that will procure those pleasures, and avoid the opposite pains, but have not even a notion of what is noble and truly pleasant, having never tasted true pleasure.

5 What theory then can reform the natures of men like these? To dislodge by argument habits long firmly rooted in their characters is difficult if not impossible. We may doubtless think ourselves fortunate if we attain some measure of virtue when all the things believed to make men virtuous are ours.

6   Now some thinkers hold that virtue is a gift of nature; others think we become good by habit, others that we can be taught to be good. Natural endowment is obviously not under our control; it is bestowed on those who are fortunate, in the true sense, by some divine dispensation. Again, theory and teaching are not, I fear, equally efficacious in all cases: the soil must have been previously tilled if it is to foster the seed, the mind of the pupil must have been prepared by the cultivation of habits, so as to like and dislike aright.
7 For he that lives at the dictates of passion will not hear nor understand the reasoning of one who tries to dissuade him; but if so, how can you change his mind by argument?

And, speaking generally, passion seems not to be amenable to reason, but only to force.

8   We must therefore by some means secure that the character shall have at the outset a natural affinity for virtue, loving what is noble and hating what is base. And it is difficult to obtain a right education in virtue from youth up without being brought up under right laws; for to live temperately and hardily is not pleasant to most men, especially when young; hence the nurture and exercises of the young should be regulated by law, since temperance and hardiness will not be
9 painful when they have become habitual. But doubtless it is not enough for people to receive the right nurture and discipline in youth; they must also practise the lessons they have learnt, and confirm them by habit, when they are grown up. Accordingly we shall need laws to regulate the discipline of adults as well, and in fact the whole life of the people generally; for the many are more amenable to compulsion and punishment than to reason and to moral ideals.

22   As then the question of legislation has been left uninvestigated by previous thinkers, it will perhaps be well if we consider it for ourselves, together with the whole question of the constitution of the State, in order to complete as far as possible our philosophy of human affairs.

23   We will begin then by attempting a review of any pronouncements of value contributed by our predecessors in this or that branch of the subject; and then on the basis of our collection of constitutions we will consider what institutions are preservative and what destructive of states in general, and of the different forms of constitution in particular, and what are the reasons which cause some states to be well governed and others the contrary. For after studying these questions we shall perhaps be in a better position to discern what is the best constitution absolutely, and what are the best regulations, laws, and customs for any given form of constitution. Let us then begin our discussion.

STUDY QUESTIONS: ARISTOTLE, NICOMACHEAN ETHICS

1. How does Aristotle define 'good' in the *Nicomachean Ethics*?
2. What are the three prominent types of life? Why does Aristotle draw this distinction?
3. How does Aristotle first characterize *eudaimonia*, or happiness?
4. How does Aristotle define *eudaimonia* in terms of excellence? Why does he add the phrase 'in a complete life'? How does this definition of *eudaimonia* relate to the pleasant?
5. What is *àreté*, or excellence? What is human excellence? How does it relate to proper function?
6. What are the irrational elements of the soul? And how do they relate to happiness?
7. What are the two kinds of excellence, or virtue?
8. How do we acquire moral virtue, or excellence?
9. How does Aristotle argue that the excellences are not emotions? That they are not capacities? If they are not emotions or capacities, what are they?
10. What does Aristotle mean when he claims that the moral excellences or virtues are a mean? What examples of such a mean does he provide? Why do some actions and passions not have a mean?

11. How does Aristotle characterize the involuntary? For what purpose does he do this?
12. What are the two parts of the soul that possess reason?
13. How does Aristotle characterize choice at Book VI, Chapter 2?
14. What is intellectual excellence?
15. What are the five ways in which a person may possess the truth by way of affirmation? How does he distinguish these?
16. Why does Aristotle claim that 'prudence is not the same as art or science' (Book VI, Chapter 5)?
17. What is *phronesis*, or prudence? How does it guide us?
18. What does Aristotle mean by 'deliberation'?
19. What is *akrasia*, or unrestraint? What was the view of Socrates and Plato regarding incontinence? How does their view of incontinence relate to their definition of moral virtue?
20. What reasons does Aristotle give for thinking that friendship is important?
21. How many kinds of friendship are there? How does Aristotle distinguish them?
22. Why is perfect friendship the best type of friendship?
23. How does Aristotle characterize the good person's relation to himself?
24. For what purposes does Aristotle distinguish different uses of the phrase 'lover of self'? What distinctions does he draw?
25. What is Aristotle's account of pleasure?
26. What is the highest excellence?
27. In what way is the active intellect divine-like?
28. How does Aristotle's account of the happy life in Book I compare with his conclusions in Book X?

POLITICS

For Aristotle, politics is a part of ethics. The individual's aim of achieving the good is impossible outside of the state, more specifically, the best kind of state, a city-state or *polis*. Citizens need to employ their practical wisdom by participating in the government of a self-governing community. In other words, a *polis* should be a participatory democracy.

The simplest political unit is the household, a natural development of which is the village, and the natural extension of which is the *polis*. As individuals, people lack self-sufficiency, and so they combine to form increasingly complex associations, until the only self-sufficient community is reached, namely, the *polis*. Additionally, Aristotle stresses that the good life is a social life, and he claims that the state exists for the sake of the good life of its citizens.

In Books IV–VI, Aristotle examines the best form of government given economic and other limitations. Wealth is the primary political determinant: if the rich minority has power, the government is oligarchic, and if power resides with the poor majority, then there is democracy. Aristotle favors a mixed system because this will promote best the common interest.

Aristotle argues that theoretical contemplation is the most valuable form of activity for humans and, ideally, a political organization should make that activity available as much as possible. However, this seems to be possible only because the women, the slaves, and the people who are not citizens, such as traders, do all the work in the *polis*. Those sufficiently intelligent or well educated, the 'natural masters,' should govern the rest, the 'natural slaves.'

BOOK I

1. Every state is a community of some kind, and every community is established with a view to some good; for everyone always acts in order to obtain that which they think good. But, if all communities aim at some good, the state or political community, which is the highest of all, 5 and which embraces all the rest, aims at good in a greater degree than any other, and at the highest good.

Some people think that the qualifications of a statesman, king, householder, and master are the same, and that they differ, not in kind, but 10 only in the number of their subjects. For example, the ruler over a few is called a master; over more, the manager of a household; over a still larger number, a statesman or king, as if there were no difference between a great household and a small state. The distinction which is made between the king and the statesman is as follows: When the government is personal, the ruler is a 15 king; when, according to the rules of the political science, the citizens rule and are ruled in turn, then he is called a statesman.

But all this is a mistake, as will be evident to any one who considers the matter according to the method which has hitherto guided us. As in other departments of science, so in politics, the compound should always be resolved into the simple elements or least parts of the whole. We must therefore look at the elements of which the state is composed, in order that we may see in 20 what the different kinds of rule differ from one another, and whether any scientific result can be attained about each one of them.

2. He who thus considers things in their first growth and origin, whether a state or anything else, will obtain the clearest view of them. In the 25 first place there must be a union of those who cannot exist without each other; namely, of male and female, that the race may continue (and this is a union which is formed, not of choice, but because, in common with other animals and with plants, mankind have a natural desire to leave behind them an image of themselves), and of 30 natural ruler and subject, that both may be preserved. For that which can foresee by the exercise of mind is by nature lord and master, and that which can with its body give effect to such foresight is a subject, and by nature a slave; hence master and slave have the same interest. Now nature has distinguished between the female and 1252ᵇ1 the slave. For she is not niggardly, like the smith who fashions the Delphian knife for many uses; she makes each thing for a single use, and every instrument is best made when intended for one and not for many uses. But among barbarians no 5 distinction is made between women and slaves, because there is no natural ruler among them: they are a community of slaves, male and female. That is why the poets say,—

> It is meet that Hellenes should rule over barbarians;

as if they thought that the barbarian and the slave were by nature one.

Out of these two relationships the first thing 10 to arise is the family, and Hesiod is right when he says,—

> First house and wife and an ox for the plough,

for the ox is the poor man's slave. The family is the association established by nature for the supply of men's everyday wants, and the members of it are called by Charondas, 'companions of the cupboard', and by Epimenides the Cretan, 'companions of the manger'. But when several families are united, and the association aims at something more than the supply of daily needs, the first society to be formed is the village. And the most natural form of the village appears to be that of a colony from the family, composed of the children and grandchildren, who are said to be 'suckled with the same milk'. And this is the reason why

Hellenic states were originally governed by kings; because the Hellenes were under royal rule before they came together, as the barbarians still are. Every family is ruled by the eldest, and therefore in the colonies of the family the kingly form of government prevailed because they were of the same blood. As Homer says:

> *Each one gives law to his children and to his wives.*

For they lived dispersedly, as was the manner in ancient times. That is why men say that the Gods have a king, because they themselves either are or were in ancient times under the rule of a king. For they imagine not only the forms of the Gods but their ways of life to be like their own.

When several villages are united in a single complete community, large enough to be nearly or quite self-sufficing, the state comes into existence, originating in the bare needs of life, and continuing in existence for the sake of a good life. And therefore, if the earlier forms of society are natural, so is the state, for it is the end of them, and the nature of a thing is its end. For what each thing is when fully developed, we call its nature, whether we are speaking of a man, a horse, or a family. Besides, the final cause and end of a thing is the best, and to be self-sufficing is the end and the best.

Hence it is evident that the state is a creation of nature, and that man is by nature a political animal. And he who by nature and not by mere accident is without a state, is either a bad man or above humanity; he is like the

> *Tribeless, lawless, hearthless one,*

whom Homer denounces—the natural outcast is forthwith a lover of war; he may be compared to an isolated piece at draughts.

Now, that man is more of a political animal than bees or any other gregarious animals is evident. Nature, as we often say, makes nothing in vain, and man is the only animal who has the gift of speech. And whereas mere voice is but an indication of pleasure or pain, and is therefore found in other animals (for their nature attains to the perception of pleasure and pain and the intimation of them to one another, and no fur-

ther), the power of speech is intended to set forth the expedient and inexpedient, and therefore likewise the just and the unjust. And it is a characteristic of man that he alone has any sense of good and evil, of just and unjust, and the like, and the association of living beings who have this sense makes a family and a state.

Further, the state is by nature clearly prior to the family and to the individual, since the whole is of necessity prior to the part; for example, if the whole body be destroyed, there will be no foot or hand, except homonymously, as we might speak of a stone hand; for when destroyed the hand will be no better than that. But things are defined by their function and power; and we ought not to say that they are the same when they no longer have their proper quality, but only that they are homonymous. The proof that the state is a creation of nature and prior to the individual is that the individual, when isolated, is not self-sufficing; and therefore he is like a part in relation to the whole. But he who is unable to live in society, or who has no need because he is sufficient for himself, must be either a beast or a god: he is no part of a state. A social instinct is implanted in all men by nature, and yet he who first founded the state was the greatest of benefactors. For man, when perfected, is the best of animals, but, when separated from law and justice, he is the worst of all; since armed injustice is the more dangerous, and he is equipped at birth with arms, meant to be used by intelligence and excellence, which he may use for the worst ends. That is why, if he has not excellence, he is the most unholy and the most savage of animals, and the most full of lust and gluttony. But justice is the bond of men in states; for the administration of justice, which is the determination of what is just, is the principle of order in political society.

3. Seeing then that the state is made up of households, before speaking of the state we must speak of the management of the household. The parts of household management correspond to the persons who compose the household, and a complete household consists of slaves and freemen. Now we should begin by examining

everything in its fewest possible elements; and
5 the first and fewest possible parts of a family are
master and slave, husband and wife, father and
children. We have therefore to consider what
each of these three relations is and ought to
be:—I mean the relation of master and servant,
the marriage relation (the conjunction of man
and wife has no name of its own), and thirdly,
10 the paternal relation (this also has no proper
name). And there is another element of a household, the so-called art of getting wealth, which,
according to some, is identical with household
management, according to others, a principal
part of it; the nature of this art will also have to
be considered by us.

Let us first speak of master and slave, looking
15 to the needs of practical life and also seeking to
attain some better theory of their relation than
exists at present. For some are of the opinion that
the rule of a master is a science, and that the
management of a household, and the mastership
of slaves, and the political and royal rule, as I was
saying at the outset, are all the same. Others
20 affirm that the rule of a master over slaves is contrary to nature, and that the distinction between
slave and freeman exists by convention only, and
not by nature, and being an interference with
nature is therefore unjust.

4. Property is a part of the household, and
the art of acquiring property is a part of the art of
managing the household; for no man can live
25 well, or indeed live at all, unless he is provided
with necessaries. And as in the arts which have a
definite sphere the workers must have their own
proper instruments for the accomplishment of
their work, so it is in the management of a household. Now instruments are of various sorts; some
are living, others lifeless; in the rudder, the pilot
of a ship has a lifeless, in the look-out man, a living instrument; for in the arts the servant is a
30 kind of instrument. Thus, too, a possession is an
instrument for maintaining life. And so, in the
arrangement of the family, a slave is a living possession, and property a number of such instruments; and the servant is himself an instrument
for instruments. For if every instrument could
accomplish its own work, obeying or anticipating

the will of others, like the statues of Daedalus, or
35 the tripods of Hephaestus, which, says the poet,

*of their own accord entered the assembly of the
Gods;*

if, in like manner, the shuttle would weave and
the plectrum touch the lyre, chief workmen
would not want servants, nor masters slaves.
1254ª1 Now the instruments commonly so called are
instruments of production, whilst a possession is
an instrument of action. From a shuttle we get
something else besides the use of it, whereas of a
garment or of a bed there is only the use. Further,
5 as production and action are different in kind,
and both require instruments, the instruments
which they employ must likewise differ in kind.
But life is action and not production, and therefore the slave is the minister of action. Again, a
possession is spoken of as a part is spoken of; for
the part is not only a part of something else, but
10 wholly belongs to it; and this is also true of a possession. The master is only the master of the
slave; he does not belong to him, whereas the
slave is not only the slave of his master, but
wholly belongs to him. Hence we see what is the
nature and office of a slave; he who is by nature
not his own but another's man, is by nature a
15 slave; and he may be said to be another's man
who, being a slave, is also a possession. And a
possession may be defined as an instrument of
action, separable from the possessor.

5. But is there anyone thus intended by
nature to be a slave, and for whom such a condition is expedient and right, or rather is not all
slavery a violation of nature?

There is no difficulty in answering this ques-
20 tion, on grounds both of reason and of fact. For
that some should rule and others be ruled is a
thing not only necessary, but expedient; from the
hour of their birth, some are marked out for subjection, others for rule.

And there are many kinds both of rulers and
subjects (and that rule is the better which is exer-
25 cised over better subjects—for example, to rule
over men is better than to rule over wild beasts;
for the work is better which is executed by better
workmen, and where one man rules and another

is ruled, they may be said to have a work); for in all things which form a composite whole and which are made up of parts, whether, continuous 30 or discrete, a distinction between the ruling and the subject element comes to light. Such a duality exists in living creatures, originating from nature as a whole; even in things which have no life there is a ruling principle, as in a musical mode. But perhaps this is matter for a more popular investigation. A living creature consists in the first place of soul and body, and of these two, the one is by nature the ruler and the other the 35 subject. But then we must look for the intentions of nature in things which retain their nature, and not in things which are corrupted. And therefore we must study the man who is in the most perfect state both of body and soul, for in him we shall see the true relation of the two; although in bad or corrupted natures the body will often appear 1254ʰ1 to rule over the soul, because they are in an evil and unnatural condition. At all events we may firstly observe in living creatures both a despotical and a constitutional rule; for the soul rules the body with a despotical rule, whereas the 5 intellect rules the appetites with a constitutional and royal rule. And it is clear that the rule of the soul over the body, and of the mind and the rational element over the passionate, is natural and expedient; whereas the equality of the two or the rule of the inferior is always hurtful. The same holds good of animals in relation to men; 10 for tame animals have a better nature than wild and all tame animals are better off when they are ruled by man; for then they are preserved. Again, the male is by nature superior, and the female inferior; and the one rules, and the other is ruled; this principle, of necessity, extends to all mankind. Where then there is such a difference 15 as that between soul and body, or between men and animals (as in the case of those whose business is to use their body, and who can do nothing better), the lower sort are by nature slaves, and it is better for them as for all inferiors that they 20 should be under the rule of a master. For he who can be, and therefore is, another's, and he who participates in reason enough to apprehend, but not to have, is a slave by nature. Whereas the lower animals cannot even apprehend reason;

they obey their passions. And indeed the use made of slaves and of tame animals is not very different; for both with their bodies minister to the needs of life. Nature would like to distinguish 25 between the bodies of freemen and slaves, making the one strong for servile labour, the other upright, and although useless for such services, 30 useful for political life in the arts both of war and peace. But the opposite often happens—that some have the souls and others have the bodies of freemen. And doubtless if men differed from one another in the mere forms of their bodies as 35 much as the statues of the Gods do from men, all would acknowledge that the inferior class should be slaves of the superior. And if this is true of the body, how much more just that a similar distinction should exist in the soul? But the beauty of the body is seen, whereas the beauty of the soul is not seen. It is clear, then, that some men are by 1255ª1 nature free, and others slaves, and that for these latter slavery is both expedient and right.

6. But that those who take the opposite view have in a certain way right on their side, may be easily seen. For the words slavery and 5 slave are used in two senses. There is a slave or slavery by convention as well as by nature. The convention is a sort of agreement—the convention by which whatever is taken in war is supposed to belong to the victors. But this right many jurists impeach, as they would an orator who brought forward an unconstitutional measure: they detest the notion that, because one man has the power of doing violence and is supe- 10 rior in brute strength, another shall be his slave and subject. Even among philosophers there is a difference of opinion. The origin of the dispute, and what makes the views invade each other's territory, is as follows: in some sense excellence, when furnished with means, has actually the greatest power of exercising force: and as superior 15 power is only found where there is superior excellence of some kind, power seems to imply excellence, and the dispute to be simply one about justice (for it is due to one party identifying justice with goodwill, while the other identifies it with the mere rule of the stronger). If these views are thus set out separately, the other views have

20 no force or plausibility against the view that the superior in excellence ought to rule, or be master. Others, clinging, as they think, simply to a principle of justice (for convention is a sort of justice), assume that slavery in accordance with the custom of war is just, but at the same moment they deny this. For what if the cause of the war be unjust? And again, no one would ever say that he 25 is a slave who is unworthy to be a slave. Were this the case, men of the highest rank would be slaves and the children of slaves if they or their parents chanced to have been taken captive and sold. That is why people do not like to call themselves slaves, but confine the term to foreigners. Yet, in using this language, they really mean the natural slave of whom we spoke at first; for it must be admitted that some are slaves everywhere, others 30 nowhere. The same principle applies to nobility. People regard themselves as noble everywhere, and not only in their own country, but they deem foreigners noble only when at home, thereby implying that there are two sorts of nobility and freedom, the one absolute, the other relative. 35 The Helen of Theodectes says:

> Who would presume to call me servant who am
> on both sides sprung from the stem of the Gods?

What does this mean but that they distinguish freedom and slavery, noble and humble birth, by the two principles of good and evil? They think 1255ᵇ1 that as men and animals beget men and animals, so from good men a good man springs. Nature intends to do this often but cannot.

5 We see then that there is some foundation for this difference of opinion, and that all are not either slaves by nature or freemen by nature, and also that there is in some cases a marked distinction between the two classes, rendering it expedient and right for the one to be slaves and the others to be masters: the one practising obedience, the others exercising the authority and lordship which nature intended them to have. 10 The abuse of this authority is injurious to both; for the interests of part and whole, of body and soul, are the same, and the slave is a part of the master, a living but separated part of his bodily frame. Hence, where the relation of master and slave between them is natural they are friends and

have a common interest, but where it rests merely on convention and force the reverse is true.

7. The previous remarks are quite enough 15 to show that the rule of a master is not a constitutional rule, and that all the different kinds of rule are not, as some affirm, the same as each other. For there is one rule exercised over subjects who are by nature free, another over subjects who are by nature slaves. The rule of a household is a monarchy, for every house is under one head: whereas constitutional rule is a 20 government of freemen and equals. The master is not called a master because he has science, but because he is of a certain character, and the same remark applies to the slave and the freeman. Still there may be a science for the master and a science for the slave. The science of the slave would 25 be such as the man of Syracuse taught, who made money by instructing slaves in their ordinary duties. And such a knowledge may be carried further, so as to include cookery and similar menial arts. For some duties are of the more necessary, others of the more honourable sort; as the proverb says, 'slave before slave, master before 30 master'. But all such branches of knowledge are servile. There is likewise a science of the master, which teaches the use of slaves; for the master as such is concerned, not with the acquisition, but with the use of them. Yet this science is not anything great or wonderful; for the master need only know how to order that which the slave 35 must know how to execute. Hence those who are in a position which places them above toil have stewards who attend to their households while they occupy themselves with philosophy or with politics. But the art of acquiring slaves, I mean of justly acquiring them, differs both from the art of the master and the art of slave, being a species of hunting or war. Enough of the distinction between master and slave.

BOOK III

1. He who would inquire into the essence and attributes of various kinds of government must first of all determine what a state is. At present this is a disputed question. Some say that the

35 state has done a certain act; others, not the state, but the oligarchy or the tyrant. And the legislator or statesman is concerned entirely with the state, a government being an arrangement of the inhabitants of a state. But a state is composite, 40 like any other whole made up of many parts— these are the citizens, who compose it. It is evident, therefore, that we must begin by asking, Who is the citizen, and what is the meaning of 1275ᵃ1 the term? For here again there may be a difference of opinion. He who is a citizen in a democracy will often not be a citizen in an oligarchy. Leaving out of consideration those who have 5 been made citizens, or who have obtained the name of citizen in any other accidental manner, we may say, first, that a citizen is not a citizen because he lives in a certain place, for resident aliens and slaves share in the place; nor is he a citizen who has legal rights to the extent of suing and being sued; for this right may be enjoyed 10 under the provisions of a treaty. Resident aliens in many places do not possess even such rights completely, for they are obliged to have a patron, so that they do but imperfectly participate in the community, and we call them citizens only in a qualified sense, as we might apply the term to children who are too young to be on the register, 15 or to old men who have been relieved from state duties. Of these we do not say quite simply that they are citizens, but add in the one case that they are not of age, and in the other, that they are past the age, or something of that sort; the precise expression is immaterial, for our meaning is clear. Similar difficulties to those which I have mentioned may be raised and answered about disfranchised citizens and about exiles. But the citizen whom we are seeking to define is a citizen in the strictest sense, against whom no such exception can be taken, and his special charac- 20 teristic is that he shares in the administration of justice, and in offices. Now of offices some are discontinuous, and the same persons are not 25 allowed to hold them twice, or can only hold them after a fixed interval; others have no limit of time—for example, the office of juryman or member of the assembly. It may, indeed, be argued that these are not magistrates at all, and

that their functions give them no share in the government. But surely it is ridiculous to say that those who have the supreme power do not govern. Let us not dwell further upon this, which is a 30 purely verbal question; what we want is a common term including both juryman and member of the assembly. Let us, for the sake of distinction, call it 'indefinite office', and we will assume that those who share in such office are citizens. This is the most comprehensive definition of a citizen, and best suits all those who are generally so called.

35 But we must not forget that things of which the underlying principles differ in kind, one of them being first, another second, another third, have, when regarded in this relation, nothing, or hardly anything, worth mentioning in common. Now we see that governments differ in kind, and that some of them are prior and that others are 1275ᵇ1 posterior; those which are faulty or perverted are necessarily posterior to those which are perfect. (What we mean by perversion will be hereafter explained.) The citizen then of necessity differs under each form of government; and our definition is best adapted to the citizen of a democracy; 5 but not necessarily to other states. For in some states the people are not acknowledged, nor have they any regular assembly, but only extraordinary ones; and law-suits are distributed by sections among the magistrates. At Lacedaemon, for instance, the Ephors determine suits about con- 10 tracts, which they distribute among themselves, while the elders are judges of homicide, and other causes are decided by other magistrates. A similar principle prevails at Carthage; there certain magistrates decide all causes. We may, indeed, modify our definition of the citizen so as to include these states. In them it is the holder of 15 a definite, not an indefinite office, who is juryman and member of the assembly, and to some or all such holders of definite offices is reserved the right of deliberating or judging about some things or about all things. The conception of the citizen now begins to clear up.

He who has the power to take part in the deliberative or judicial administration of any 20 state is said by us to be a citizen of that state; and, speaking generally, a state is a body of citizens sufficing for the purposes of life. . . .

6. Having determined these questions, we have next to consider whether there is only one form of government or many, and if many, what they are, and how many, and what are the differences between them.

A constitution is the arrangement of magistracies in a state, especially of the highest of all. The government is everywhere sovereign in the 10 state, and the constitution is in fact the government. For example, in democracies the people are supreme, but in oligarchies, the few; and, therefore, we say that these two constitutions also are different: and so in other cases.

15 First, let us consider what is the purpose of a state, and how many forms of rule there are by which human society is regulated. We have already said, in the first part of this treatise, when discussing household management and the rule of a master, that man is by nature a political animal. And therefore, men, even when they do not require one another's help, desire to live 20 together; not but that they are also brought together by their common interests in so far as they each attain to any measure of well-being. This is certainly the chief end, both of individuals and of states. And mankind meet together 25 and maintain the political community also for the sake of mere life (in which there is possibly some noble element so long as the evils of existence do not greatly overbalance the good). And we all see that men cling to life even at the cost of enduring great misfortunate, seeming to find 30 in life a natural sweetness and happiness.

There is no difficulty in distinguishing the various kinds of rule; they have been often defined already in our popular discussions. The rule of a master, although the slave by nature and the master by nature have in reality the same interests, is nevertheless exercised primarily with 35 a view to the interest of the master, but accidentally considers the slave, since, if the slave perish, the rule of the master perishes with him. On the other hand, the government of a wife and children and of a household, which we have called

household management, is exercised in the first instance for the good of the governed or for the common good of both parties, but essentially for the good of the governed, as we see to be the case 1279ª1 in medicine, gymnastic, and the arts in general, which are only accidentally concerned with the good of the artists themselves. For there is no reason why the trainer may not sometimes practise gymnastics, and the helmsman is always one of the crew. The trainer or the helmsman considers the good of those committed to his care. But, 5 when he is one of the persons taken care of, he accidentally participates in the advantage, for the helmsman is also a sailor, and the trainer becomes one of those in training. And so in politics: when the state is framed upon the principle of equality and likeness, the citizens think that they ought to hold office by turns. Formerly, as is 10 natural, everyone would take his turn of service; and then again, somebody else would look after his interest, just as he, while in office, had looked after theirs. But nowadays, for the sake of the advantage which is to be gained from the public revenues and from office, men want to be always in office. One might imagine that the rulers, being sickly, were only kept in health while they 15 continued in office; in that case we may be sure that they would be hunting after places. The conclusions is evident: that governments which have a regard to the common interest are constituted in accordance with strict principles of justice, and are therefore true forms; but those 20 which regard only the interest of the rulers are all defective and perverted forms, for they are despotic, whereas a state is a commonly of freemen.

7. Having determined these points, we have next to consider how many forms of government there are, and what they are; and in the first place what are the true forms, for when they are determined the perversions of them will at once be 25 apparent. The words constitution and government have the same meaning, and the government, which is the supreme authority in states, must be in the hands of one, or of a few, or of the many. The true forms of government, therefore, are those in which the one, or the few, or the many, govern with a view to the common interest; but governments which rule with a view to the private interest, whether of the one, or of the few, or of the many, are perversions. For the members of a state, if they are truly citizens, ought to participate in its advantages. Of forms of government in which one rules, we call that which regards the common interest, kingship; that in which more than one, but not many, rule, aristocracy; and it is so called, either because the rulers are the best men, or because they have at heart the best interests of the state and of the citizens. But when the many administer the state for the common interest, the government is called by the generic name—a constitution. And there is a reason for this use of language. One man or a few may excel in excellence; but as the number increases it becomes more difficult for them to attain perfection in every kind of excellence, though they may in military excellence, for this is found in the masses. Hence in a constitutional government the fighting-men have the supreme power, and those who possess arms are the citizens.

Of the above-mentioned forms, the perversions are as follows:—of kingship, tyranny; of aristocracy, oligarchy; of constitutional government, democracy. For tyranny is a kind of monarchy which has in view the interest of the monarch only; oligarchy has in view the interest of the wealthy; democracy, of the needy: none of them the common good of all.

8. But there are difficulties about these forms of government, and it will therefore be necessary to state a little more at length the nature of each of them. For he who would make a philosophical study of the various sciences, and is not only concerned with practice, ought not to overlook or omit anything, but to set forth the truth in every particular. Tyranny, as I was saying, is monarchy exercising the rule of a master over the political society; oligarchy is when men of property have the government in their hands; democracy, the opposite, when the indigent, and not the men of property, are the rulers. And here arises the first of our difficulties, and it relates to the distinction just drawn. For democracy is said

to be the government of the many. But when if the many are men of property and have the power in their hands? In like manner oligarchy is said to be the government of the few; but what if the poor are fewer than the rich, and have the power in their hands because they are stronger? In these cases the distinction which we have drawn between these different forms of government would no longer hold good.

Suppose, once more, that we add wealth to the few and poverty to the many, and name the governments accordingly—an oligarchy is said to be that in which the few and the wealthy, and a democracy that in which the many and the poor are the rulers—there will still be a difficulty. For, if the only forms of government are the ones already mentioned, how shall we describe those other governments also just mentioned by us, in which the rich are the more numerous and the poor are the fewer, and both govern in their respective states?

The argument seems to show that, whether in oligarchies or in democracies, the number of the governing body, whether the greater number, as in a democracy, or the smaller number, as in an oligarchy, is an accident due to the fact that the rich everywhere are few, and the poor numerous. But if so, there is a misapprehension of the causes of the difference between them. For the real difference between democracy and oligarchy is poverty and wealth. Wherever men rule by reason of their wealth, whether they be few or many, that is an oligarchy, and where the poor rule, that is a democracy. But in fact the rich are few and the poor many; for few are well-to-do, whereas freedom is enjoyed by all, and wealth and freedom are the grounds on which the two parties claim power in the state.

9. Let us begin by considering the common definitions of oligarchy and democracy, and what is oligarchical and democratic justice. For all men cling to justice of some kind, but their conceptions are imperfect and they do not express the whole idea. For example, justice is thought by them to be, and is, equality—not, however, for all, but only for equals. And inequality is thought to be, and is, justice; neither is this for all, but only for unequals. When the persons are omitted, then men judge erroneously. The reason is that they are passing judgement on themselves, and most people are bad judges in their own case. And whereas justice implies a relation to persons as well as to things, and a just distribution, as I have already said in the *Ethics*, implies the same ratio between the persons and between the things, they agree about the equality of the things, but dispute about the equality of the persons, chiefly for the reason which I have just given—because they are bad judges in their own affairs; and secondly, because both the parties to the argument are speaking of a limited and partial justice, but imagine themselves to be speaking of absolute justice. For the one party, if they are unequal in one respect, for example wealth, consider themselves to be unequal in all; and the other party, if they are equal in one respect, for example free birth, consider themselves to be equal in all. But they leave out the capital point. For if men met and associated out of regard to wealth only, their share in the state would be proportioned to their property, and the oligarchical doctrine would then seem to carry the day. It would not be just that he who paid one mina should have the same share of a hundred minae, whether of the principal or of the profits, as he who paid the remaining ninety-nine. But a state exists for the sake of a good life, and not for the sake of life only: if life only were the object, slaves and brute animals might form a state, but they cannot, for they have no share in happiness or in a life based on choice. Nor does a state exist for the sake of alliance and security from injustice, nor yet for the sake of exchange and mutual intercourse; of then the Tyrrhenians and the Carthaginians, and all who have commercial treaties with one another, would be the citizens of one state. True, they have agreements about imports, and engagements that they will do no wrong to one another, and written articles of alliance. But there are no magistracies common to the contracting parties; different states have each their own magistracies. Nor does one state take care that the citizens of the other are such as they ought to be, nor see that those who come under the terms of the treaty do no wrong or

wickedness at all, but only that they do no injustice to one another. Whereas, those who care for good government take into consideration political excellence and defect. Whence it may be further inferred that excellence must be the care of a state which is truly so called, and not merely enjoys the name: for without this end the community becomes a mere alliance which differs only in place from alliances of which the members live apart; and law is only a convention, 'a surety to one another of justice', as the sophist Lycophron says, and has no real power to make the citizens good and just.

This is obvious; for suppose distinct places, such as Corinth and Megara, to be brought together so that their walls touched, still they would not be one city, not even if the citizens had the right to intermarry, which is one of the rights peculiarly characteristic of states. Again, if men dwelt at a distance from one another, but not so far off as to have no intercourse, and there were laws among them that they should not wrong each other in their exchanges, neither would this be a state. Let us suppose that one man is a carpenter, another a farmer, another a shoemaker, and so on, and that their number is ten thousand: nevertheless, if they have nothing in common but exchange, alliance, and the like, that would not constitute a state. Why is this? Surely not because they are at a distance from one another; for even supposing that such a community were to meet in one place, but that each man had a house of his own, which was in a manner his state, and that they made alliance with one another, but only against evil-doers; still an accurate thinker would not deem this to be a state, if their intercourse with one another was of the same character after as before their union. It is clear then that a state is not a mere society, having a common place, established for the prevention of mutual crime and for the sake of exchange. These are conditions without which a state cannot exist; but all of them together do not constitute a state, which is a community of families and aggregations of families in well-being, for the sake of a perfect and self-sufficing life. Such a community can only be established among those who live in the same place and intermarry.

Hence there arise in cities family connexions, brotherhoods, common sacrifices, amusements which draw men together. But these are created by friendship, for to choose to live together is friendship. The end of the state is the good life, and these are the means towards it. And the state is the union of families and villages in a perfect 1281ᵃ1 and self-sufficing life, by which we mean a happy and honourable life.

Our conclusion, then, is that political society exists for the sake of noble actions, and not of living together. Hence they who contribute most to such a society have a greater share in it than those who have the same or a greater free-5 dom or nobility of birth but are inferior to them in political excellence; or than those who exceed them in wealth but are surpassed by them in excellence.

From what has been said it will be clearly seen that all the partisans of different forms of 10 government speak of a part of justice only.

10. There is also a doubt as to what is to be the supreme power in the state:—Is it the multitude? Or the wealthy? Or the good? Or the one best man? Or a tyrant? Any of these alternatives seems to involve disagreeable consequences. If the poor, for example, because they are more in 15 number, divide among themselves the property of the rich—is not this unjust? No, by heaven (will be the reply), for the supreme authority justly willed it. But if this is not extreme injustice, what is? Again, when in the first division all has been taken, and the majority divide anew the property of the minority, is it not evident, if this goes on, that they will ruin the state? Yet surely, excellence is not the ruin of those who possess it, nor is justice destructive of a state; and therefore 20 the law of confiscation clearly cannot be just. If it were, all the acts of tyrant must of necessity be just; for he only coerces other men by superior power, just as the multitude coerce the rich. But is it just then that the few and the wealthy should be the rulers? And what if they, in like manner, rob and plunder the people—is this just? 25 If so, the other case will likewise be just. But there can be no doubt that all these things are wrong and unjust.

Then ought the good to rule and have supreme power? But in that case everybody else, being excluded from power, will be dishonoured. 30 For the offices of a state are posts of honour; and if one set of men always hold them, the rest must be deprived of them. Then will it be well that the one best man should rule? That is still more oligarchical, for the number of those who are dishonoured is thereby increased. Someone may say that it is bad in any case for a man, subject as he 35 is to all the accidents of human passion, to have the supreme power, rather than the law. But what if the law itself be democratic or oligarchical, how will that help us out of our difficulties? Not at all; the same consequences will follow.

11. Most of these questions may be reserved 40 for another occasion. The principle that the multitude ought to be in power rather than the few best might seem to be solved and to contain some difficulty and perhaps even truth. For the many, of whom each individual is not a good 1281ᵇ1 man, when they meet together may be better than the few good, if regarded not individually but collectively, just as a feast to which many contribute is better than a dinner provided out of single purse. For each individual among the many has a share of excellence and practical wisdom, and when they meet together, just as they 5 become in a manner one man, who has many feet, and hands, and senses, so too with regard to their character and thought. Hence the many are better judges than a single man of music and poetry; for some understand one part, and some another, and among them they understand the whole. There is a similar combination of qualities 10 in good men, who differ from any individual of the many, as the beautiful are said to differ from those who are not beautiful, and works of art from realities because in them the scattered elements are combined, although, if taken separately, the eye of one person or some other feature in another person would be fairer than in 15 the picture. Whether this principle can apply to every democracy, and to all bodies of men, is not clear. Or rather, by heaven, in some cases it is impossible to apply; for the argument would equally hold about brutes; and wherein, it will be

20 asked, do some men differ from brutes? But there may be bodies of men about whom our statement is nevertheless true. And if so, the difficulty which has been already raised, and also another which is akin to it—viz. what power should be assigned to the mass of freemen and citizens, who are not rich and have no personal merit—are 25 both solved. There is still a danger in allowing them to share the great offices of state, for their folly will lead them into error, and their dishonesty into crime. But there is a danger also in not letting them share, for a state in which many poor men are excluded from office will necessarily be full of enemies. The only way of escape is 30 to assign to them some deliberative and judicial functions. For this reason Solon and certain other legislator give them the power of electing of offices, and of calling the magistrates to account, but they do not allow them to hold office singly. When they meet together their perceptions are 35 quite good enough, and combined with the better class they are useful to the state (just as impure food when mixed with what is pure sometimes make the entire mass more wholesome than small quantity of the pure would be), but each individual, left to himself, forms an imperfect judgement. On the other hand, the popular form of government involves certain difficulties. In the first place, it might be objected that he who can judge of the healing of a sick man would be one 40 who could himself heal his disease, and make him whole—that is, in other words, the physician; and so in all professions and arts. As, then, the 1282·1 physician ought to be called to account by physicians, so ought men in general to be called to account by their peers. But physicians are of three kinds:—there is the ordinary practitioner, and there is the master physician, and thirdly the man educated in the art: in all arts there is such a class; and we attribute the power of judging to them 5 quite as much as to professors of the art. Secondly, does not the same principle apply to elections? For a right election can only be made by those who have knowledge; those who know geometry, for example, will choose a geometrician rightly, and those who know how to steer, a pilot; and, even if there be some occupations and 10 arts in which private persons share in the ability

to choose, they certainly cannot choose better than those who know. So that, according to this argument, neither the election of magistrates, nor the calling of them to account, should be entrusted to the many. Yet possibly these objections are to a great extent met by our old answer, 15 that if the people are not utterly degraded, although individually they may be worse judges than those who have special knowledge, as a body they are as good or better. Moreover, there are some arts whose products are not judge of solely, or best, by the artists themselves, namely those arts whose products are recognized even by those who do not posses the art; for example, the 20 knowledge of the house is not limited to the builder only; the user, or, in other words, the master, of the house will actually be a better judge than the builder, just as the pilot will judge better of a rubber than the carpenter, and the guest will judge better of a feast than the cook.

This difficulty seems now to be sufficiently answered, but there is another akin to it. That inferior persons should have authority in greater 25 matters than the good would appear to be strange thing, yet the election and calling to account of the magistrates is the greater of all. And these, as I was saying, are functions which in some states are assigned to the people, for the assembly is supreme in all such matters. Yet persons of any age, and having but a small property qualifica- 30 tion, sit in the assembly and deliberate and judge, although for the great officers of state, such as treasurers and generals, a high qualification is required. This difficulty may be solved in the same manner as the preceding, and the present practice of democracies may be really defensible. For the power does not reside in the juryman, or counsellor, or member of the assem- 35 bly, but in the court, and the council, and the assembly, of which the aforesaid individuals— counsellor, assemblyman, juryman—are only parts or members. And for this reason the many may claim to have a higher authority than the few; for the people, and the council, and the courts consist of many persons, and their property collectively is greater than the property of 40 one or of a few individuals holding great offices. But enough of this.

1282ᵇ1 The discussion of the first question shows nothing so clearly as that laws, when good, should be supreme; and that the magistrate or magistrates should regulate those matters only on which the laws are unable to speak with precision owing to the difficulty of any general principle embracing all particulars. But what are good laws 5 has not yet been clearly explained; the old difficulty remains. The goodness or badness, justice or injustice, of laws varies of necessity with the constitutions of states. This, however, is clear, that the laws must be adapted to the constitu- 10 tions. But, if so, true forms of government will of necessity have just laws, and perverted forms of government will have unjust laws.

12. In all sciences and arts the end is a good, and the greatest good and in the highest degree a good in the most authoritative of all— 15 this is the political science of which the good is justice, in other words, the common interest. All men think justice to be a sort of equality; and to a certain extent they agree with what we have 20 said in our philosophical works about ethics. For they say that what is just is just *for* someone and that it should be equal for equals. But there still remains a question: equality or inequality of what? Here is a difficulty which calls for political speculation. For very likely some persons will say that offices of state ought to be unequally distributed according to superior excellence, in whatever respect, of the citizen, although there is no 25 other difference between him and the rest of the community: for those who differ in any one respect have different rights and claims. But, surely, if this is true, the complexion or height of a man, or any other advantage, will be reason for his obtaining a greater share of political rights. The error here lies upon the surface, and may be 30 illustrated from the other arts and sciences. When a number of flute-players are equal in their art, there is no reason why those of them who are better born should have better flutes given to them; for they will not play any better on the flute, and the superior instrument should be reserved for him who is the superior artist. If 35 what I am saying is still obscure, it will be made clearer as we proceed. For if there were a superior flute-player who was far inferior in birth and beauty, although either of these may be a greater good than the art of flute-playing and may excel 40 flute-playing in a greater ratio than he excels the others in his art, still he ought to have the best flutes given to him, unless the advantages of 1283ᵃ1 wealth and birth contribute to excellence in flute-playing, which they do not. Moreover, upon this principle any good may be compared with 5 any other. For if a given height my be measured against wealth and against freedom, height in general may be so measured. Thus if A excels in height more than B in excellence, even if excellence in general excels height still more, all goods will be comparable; for if a certain amount is better than some other, it is clear that some other will be equal. But since no such comparison can be made, it is evident that there is good 10 reason why in politics men do not ground their claim to office on every sort of inequality. For if some be slow, and others, swift, that is no reason why the one should have little and the others much; it is in gymnastic contests that such excellence is rewarded. Whereas the rival claims of candidates for office can only be based on the possession of elements which enter into the com- 15 position of a state. And therefore the well-born, or free-born, or rich, may with good reason claim office; for holders of offices must be freemen and tax-payers; a state can be no more composed entirely of poor men than entirely of slaves. But if wealth and freedom are necessary elements, justice and valour are equally so; for without the 20 former qualities a state cannot exist at all, without the latter not well.

13. If the existence of the state is alone to be considered, then it would seem that all, or some at least, of these claims are just; but, if we take into account a good life, then, as I have already said, education and excellence have 25 superior claims. As, however, those who are equal in one thing ought not to have an equal share in all, nor those who are unequal in one thing to have an unequal share in all, it is certain that all forms of government which rest on either of these principles are perversions. All men have a claim in a certain sense, as I have already

30 admitted, but not all have an absolute claim. The rich claim because they have a greater share in the land, and land is the common element of the state; also they are generally more trustworthy in contracts. The free claim under the same title as the well-born; for they are nearly akin. For the 35 well-born are citizens in a truer sense than the low-born, and good birth is always valued in a man's own home. Another reason is, that those who are sprung from better ancestors are likely to be better men, for good birth is excellence of race. Excellence, too, may be truly said to have a claim, for justice has been acknowledged by us to be a social excellence, and it implies all others. Again, the many may urge their claim against 40 the few; for, when taken collectively, and compared with the few, they are stronger and richer and better. But, what if the good, the rich, the well-born, and the other classes who make up a 1283ᵇ1 state, are all living together in the same city, will there, or will there not, be any doubt who shall rule?—No doubt at all in determining who ought 5 to rule in each of the above-mentioned forms of government. For states are characterized by differences in their governing bodies—one of them has a government of the rich, another of the good, and so on. But a difficulty arises when these elements coexist. How are we to decide? Suppose the good to be very few in number: may 10 we consider their numbers in relation to their duties, and ask whether they are enough to administer the state, or so many as will make up a state? Objections may be urged against all the aspirants to political power. For those who found their claims on wealth or family might be thought to have no basis of justice; on this principle, if 15 any one person were richer than all the rest, it is clear that he ought to be ruler of them. In like manner he who is very distinguished by his birth ought to have the superiority over all those who claim on the ground that they are free-born. In 20 an aristocracy a like difficulty occurs about excellence; for if one citizen is better than the other members of the government, however good they may be, he too, upon the same principle of justice, should rule over them. And if the people are to be supreme because they are stronger than the few, then if one man, or more than one, but not a

25 majority, is stronger than the many, they ought to rule, and not the many.

All these considerations appear to show that none of the principles on which men claim to rule and to hold all other men in subjection to them are right. To those who claim to be masters of the government on the ground of their excel- 30 lence or their wealth, the many might fairly answer that they themselves are often better and richer than the few—I do not say individually, but collectively. And another problem which is sometimes put forward may be met in a similar 35 manner. Some persons doubts whether the legislator who desires to make the justest laws ought to legislate with a view to the good of the better or of the many, when the case which we have mentioned occurs. Now what is right must be 40 construed as equally right, and what is equally right is to be considered with reference to the advantage of the state, and the common good of the citizens. And a citizen is one who shares in governing and being governed. He differs under 1284ᵃ1 different forms of government, but in the best state he is one who is able and choose to be governed and to govern with a view to the life of excellence.

If, however, there be some one person, or more than one, although not enough to make up the full complement of a state, whose excellence is so pre-eminent that the excellence or the political capacity of all the rest admit of no com- 5 parison with his or theirs, he or they can be no longer regarded as part of a state; for justice will not be done to the superior, if he is reckoned only as the equal of those who are so far inferior to him in excellence and in political capacity. 10 Such a man may truly be deemed a God among men. Hence we see that legislation is necessarily concerned only with those who are equal in birth and in capacity; and that for men of pre-eminent excellence there is no law—they are themselves a law. Anyone would be ridiculous who attempted to make laws for them: they would 15 probably retort what, in the fable of Antisthenes, the lions said to the hares, when in the council of the beasts the latter began haranguing and claiming equality for all. And for this reason democratic states have instituted ostracism; equality is

above all things their aim, and therefore they ostracized and banished from the city for a time those who seemed to predominate too much
20 through their wealth, or the number of their friends, or through any other political influence. Mythology tells us that the Argonauts left Heracles behind for a similar reason; the ship Argo would not take him because she feared that he would have been too much for the rest of the
25 crew. That is why those who denounce tyranny and blame the counsel which Periander gave to Trasybulus cannot be held altogether just in their censure. The story is that Periander, when the herald was sent to ask counsel of him, said nothing, but only cut off the tallest ears of corn till he
30 had brought the field to a level. The herald did not know the meaning of the action, but came and reported what he had seen to Thrasybulus, who understood that he was to cut off the principal men in the state; and this is a policy not only expedient for tyrants or in practice confined to them, but equally necessary in oligarchies and
35 democracies. Ostracism is a measure of the same kind, which acts by disabling and banishing the most prominent citizens. Great powers do the same to whole cities and nations, as the Athenians did to the Samians, Chians, and Lesbians; no
40 sooner had they obtained a firm grasp of the empire, than they humbled their allies contrary to treaty; and the Persian king has repeatedly crushed the Medes, Babylonians, and other
1284ᵇ1 nations, when their spirit has been stirred by the recollection of their former greatness.

The problem is a universal one, and equally concerns all forms of government, true as well as false; for, although perverted forms with a view to
5 their own interests may adopt this policy, those which seek the common interest do so likewise. The same thing may be observed in the arts and sciences; for the painter will not allow the figure to have a foot which, however beautiful, is not in
10 proportion, nor will the ship-builder allow the stern or any other part of the vessel to be unduly large, any more than the chorus-master will allow anyone who sings louder or better than all the rest to sing in the choir. Monarchs, too, may practice compulsion and still live in harmony with their cities, if their own government is for the interest

15 of the state. Hence where there is an acknowledged superiority the argument in favour of ostracism is based upon a kind of political justice. It would certainly be better that the legislator should from the first so order his state as to have no need of such a remedy. But if the need arises, the next best thing is that he should endeavour to correct the evil by this or some similar measure.
20 The principle, however, has not been fairly applied in states; for, instead of looking to the good of their own constitution, they have used ostracism for factious purposes. It is true that under perverted forms of government, and from their special point of view, such a measure is just and expedient, but it is also clear that it is not
25 absolutely just. In the perfect state there would be great doubts about the use of it, not when applied to excess in strength, wealth, popularity, or the like, but when used against someone who is preeminent in excellence—what is to be done with him? People will not say that such a man is to be
30 expelled and exiled; on the other hand, he ought not to be a subject—that would be as if mankind should claim to rule over Zeus, dividing his offices among them. The only alternative is that all should happily obey such a ruler, according to what seems to be the order of nature, and that men like him should be kings in their state for life.

35　　**14.** The preceding discussion, by a natural transition, leads to the consideration of kingship, which we say is one of the true forms of government. Let us see whether in order to be well governed a state or country should be under the rule of a king or under some other form of government; and whether monarchy, although good for some, may not be bad for others. But first we must determine whether there is one species of kingship or many. It is easy to see that there are
1285ᵃ1 many, and that the manner of government is not the same in all of them.

Of kingships according to law, the Lacedaemonian is thought to be the best example; but there the royal power is not absolute, except when
5 the kings go on an expedition, and then they take the command. Matters of religion are likewise committed to them. The kingly office is in truth a kind of generalship, sovereign and perpetual. The

king has not the power of life and death, except in certain cases, as for instance, in ancient times, he had it when upon a campaign, by right of force. This custom is described in Homer. For Agamemnon puts up with it when he is attacked in the assembly, but when the army goes out to battle he has the power even of life and death. Does he not say: 'When I find a man skulking apart from the battle, nothing shall save him from the dogs and vultures, for in my hands is death'?

This, then, is one form of kingship—a generalship for life; and of such kingships some are hereditary and others elective.

There is another sort of monarchy not uncommon among foreigners, which nearly resembles tyranny. But this is both legal and hereditary. For foreigners, being more servile in character than Hellenes, and Asiatics than Europeans, do not rebel against a despotic government. Such kingships have the nature of tyrannies because the people are by nature slaves; but there is no danger of their being overthrown, for they are hereditary and legal. For the same reason, their guards are such as a king and not such as a tyrant would employ, that is to say, they are composed of citizens, whereas the guards of tyrants are mercenaries. For kings rule according to law over voluntary subjects, but tyrants over involuntary; and the one are guarded by their fellow-citizens, the others are guarded against them.

These are two forms of monarchy, and there was a third which existed in ancient Hellas, called an Aesymnetia. This may be defined generally as an elective tyranny, which, like foreign monarchy, is legal, but differs from it in not being hereditary. Sometimes the office was held for life, sometimes for a term of years, or until certain duties had been performed.

BOOK VII

1. He who would duly inquire about the best form of a state ought first to determine which is the most eligible life; while this remains uncertain the best form of the state must also be uncertain; for, in the natural order of things, those men may be expected to lead the best life who are governed in the best manner of which their circumstances admit. We ought therefore to ascertain, first of all, which is the most generally eligible life, and then whether the same life is or is not best for the state and for individuals.

Assuming that enough has been already said in discussions outside the school concerning the best life, we will now only repeat what is contained in them. Certainly no one will dispute the propriety of that partition of goods which separates them into three classes, viz. external goods, goods of the body, and goods of the soul, or deny that the happy man must have all three. For no one would maintain that he is happy who has not in him a particle of courage or temperance or justice or practical wisdom, who is afraid of every insect which flutters past him, and will commit any crime, however great, in order to gratify his lust for meat or drink, who will sacrifice his dearest friend for the sake of half a farthing, and is as feeble and false in mind as a child or a madman. These propositions are almost universally acknowledged as soon as they are uttered, but men differ about the degree or relative superiority of this or that good. Some think that a very moderate amount of excellence is enough, but set no limit to their desires for wealth, property, power, reputation, and the like. To them we shall reply by an appeal to facts, which easily prove that mankind does not acquire or preserve the excellences by the help of external goods, but external goods by the help of the excellences, and that happiness, whether consisting in pleasure or excellence, or both, is more often found with those who are most highly cultivated in their mind and in their character, and have only a moderate share of external goods, than among those who possess external goods to a useless extent but are deficient in higher qualities; and this is not only a matter of experience, but, if reflected upon, will easily appear to be in accordance with reason. For, whereas external goods have a limit, like any other instrument, and all things useful are useful for a purpose, and where there is too much of them they must either do harm, or at any rate be of no use, to their possessors, every good of the soul, the greater it is, is also of greater use, if the epithet useful as well as noble is appropriate to such subjects. No proof is required to show that the best state of one thing in relation to another corresponds in degree of excellence to the interval between the natures of which we say that these very states are states: so that, if the soul is more noble than our possessions or our bodies, both absolutely and in relation to us, it must be admitted that the best state of either has a similar ratio to the other. Again, it is for the sake of the soul that goods external and goods of the body are desirable at all, and all wise men ought to choose them for the sake of the soul, and not the soul for the sake of them.

Let us acknowledge them that each one has just so much of happiness as he has of excellence and wisdom, and of excellent and wise action. The gods are a witness to us of this truth, for they are happy and blessed, not by reason of any external good, but in themselves and by reason of their own nature. And herein of necessity lies the difference between good fortune and happiness; for external goods come of themselves, and chance is the author of them, but no one is just or temperate by or through chance. In like manner, and by a similar train of argument, the happy state may be shown to be that which is best and which acts rightly; and it cannot act rightly without doing right actions, and neither individual nor state can do right actions without excellence and wisdom. Thus the courage, justice, and wisdom of a state have the same form and nature as the qualities which give the individual who possesses them the name of just, wise or temperate.

Thus much may suffice by may of preface: for I could not avoid touching upon these questions, neither could I go through all the arguments affecting them; these are the business of another science.

Let us assume then that the best life, both for individuals and states, is the life of excellence, when excellence has external goods enough for the performance of good actions. If there are any who dispute our assertion, we will in this treatise pass them over, and consider their objections hereafter. . . .

13. Returning to the constitution itself, let us seek to determine out of what and what sort of elements the state which is to be happy and well-governed should be composed. There are two things in which all well-being consists: one of them is the choice of a right end and aim of action, and the other the discovery of the actions which contribute towards it; for the means and the end may agree or disagree. Sometimes the right end is set before men, but in practice they fail to attain it; in other cases they are successful in all the contributory factors, but they propose to themselves a bad end; and sometimes they fail in both. Take, for example, the art of medicine; physicians do not always understand the nature of health, and also the means which they use may not effect the desired end. In all arts and sciences both the end and the means should be equally within our control.

The happiness and well-being which all men manifestly desire, some have the power of attaining, but to others, from some accident or defect of nature, the attainment of them is not granted; for a good life requires a supply of external goods, in a less degree when men are in a good state, in a greater degree when they are in a lower state. Others again, who possess the conditions of happiness, go utterly wrong from the first in the pursuit of it. But since our object is to discover the best form of government, that, namely, under which a city will be best governed, and since the city is best governed which has the greatest opportunity of obtaining happiness, it is evident that we must clearly ascertain the nature of happiness.

We maintain, and have said in the *Ethics*, if the arguments there adduced are of any value, that happiness is the realization and perfect exercise of excellence, and this not conditional, but absolute. And I use the term 'conditional' to express that which is indispensable, and 'absolute' to express that which is good in itself. Take the case of just actions; just punishments and chastisements do indeed spring from a good principle, but they are good only because we cannot do without them—it would be better that neither individuals nor states should need anything of the sort—but actions which aim at honour and advantage are absolutely the best. The condi-

tional action is only the choice of a lesser evil; whereas these are the foundation and creation of good. A good man may make the best even of poverty and disease, and the other ills of life; but he can only attain happiness under the oppo-
20 site conditions (for this also has been determined in the *Ethics*, that the good man is he for whom, because he is excellent, the things that are absolutely good are good; it is also plain that his use of these goods must be excellent and in the absolute sense good). This makes men fancy
25 that external goods are the cause of happiness, yet we might as well say that a brilliant performance on the lyre was to be attributed to the instrument and not to the skill of the performer.

It follows then from what has been said that some things the legislator must find ready to his hand in a state, others he must provide. And
30 therefore we can only say: may our state be constituted in such a manner as to be blessed with the goods of which fortune disposes (for we acknowledge her power): whereas excellence and goodness in the state are not a matter of chance but the result of knowledge and choice. A city can be excellent only when the citizens who have a share in the government are excellent, and in
35 our state all the citizens share in the government; let us then inquire how a man becomes excellent. For even if we could suppose the citizen body to be excellent, without each of them being so, yet the latter would be better, for in the excellence of each the excellence of all is involved.

There are three things which make men good and excellent; these are nature, habit, rea-
40 son. In the first place, every one must be born a man and not some other animal; so, too, he must have a certain character, both of body and soul.
1332ᵇ1 But some qualities there is no use in having at birth, for they are altered by habit, and there are some gifts which by nature are made to be turned by habit to good or bad. Animals lead for the most part a life of nature, although in lesser particulars some are influenced by habit as well. Man
5 has reason, in addition, and man only. For this reason nature, habit, reason must be in harmony with one another; for they do not always agree; men do many things against habit and nature, if

reason persuades them that they ought. We have already determined what natures are likely to be
10 most easily moulded by the hands of the legislator. All else is the work of education; we learn some things by habit and some by instruction.

14. Since every political society is composed of rulers and subjects, let us consider whether the relations of one to the other should interchange or be permanent. For the education
15 of the citizens will necessarily vary with the answer given to this question. Now, if some men excelled other in the same degree in which gods and heroes are supposed to excel mankind in general (having in the first place a great advantage even in their bodies, and secondly in their minds), so that the superiority of the governors
20 was undisputed and patent to their subjects, it would clearly be better that once for all the one class should rule and the others serve. But since this is unattainable, and kings have no marked superiority over their subjects such as Scylax
25 affirms to be found among the Indians, it is obviously necessary on many grounds that all the citizens alike should take their turn of governing and being governed. Equality consists in the same treatment of similar persons, and no government can stand which is not founded upon justice. For if the government is unjust everyone
30 in the country unites with the governed in the desire to have a revolution, and it is an impossibility that the members of the government can be so numerous as to be stronger than all their enemies put together. Yet that governors should be better than their subjects is undeniable. How all this is to be effected, and in what way they will respectively share in the government, the
35 legislator has to consider. The subject has been already mentioned. Nature herself has provided the distinction when she made a difference between old and young within the same species, of whom she fitted the one to govern and the other to be governed. No one takes offence at being governed when he is young, nor does he think himself better than his governors, espe-
40 cially if he will enjoy the same privilege when he reaches the required age.

We conclude that from one point of view governors and governed are identical, and from another different. And therefore their education must be the same and also different. For he who would learn to command well must, as men say, first of all learn to obey. As I observed in the first part of this treatise, there is one rule which is for the sake of the rulers and another rule which is for the sake of the ruled; the former is a despotic, the latter a free government. Some commands differ not in the thing commanded, but in the intention with which they are imposed. That is why many apparently menial offices are an honour to the free youth by whom they are performed; for actions do not differ as honourable or dishonorable in themselves so much as in the end and intention of them. But since we say that the excellence of the citizen and ruler is the same as that of the good man, and that the same person must first be a subject and then a ruler, the legislator has to see that they become good men, and by what means this may be accomplished, and what is the end of the perfect life.

Now the soul of man is divided into two parts, one of which has a rational principle in itself, and the other, not having a rational principle in itself, is able to obey such a principle. And we call a man in any way good because he has the excellences of these two parts. In which of them the end is more likely to be found is no matter of doubt to those who adopt our division; for in the world both of nature and of art the inferior always exists for the sake of the superior, and the superior is that which has a rational principle. This principle, too, in our ordinary way of making the division, is divided into two kinds, for there is a practical and a speculative principle. This part, then, must evidently be similarly divided. And there must be a corresponding division of actions; the actions of the naturally better part are to be preferred by those who have it in their power to attain to two out of the three or to all, for that is always to everyone the most desirable which is the highest attainable by him. The whole of life is further divided into two parts, business and leisure, war and peace, and of actions some aim at what is necessary and useful, and some at what is honourable. And the preference given to one or the other class of actions must necessarily be like the preference given to one or other part of the soul and its actions over the other; there must be war for the sake of peace, business for the sake of leisure, things useful and necessary for the sake of things honourable. All these points the statesman should keep in view when he frames his laws; he should consider the parts of the soul and their functions, and above all the better and the end; he should also remember the diversities of human lives and actions. For men must be able to engage in business and go to war, but leisure and peace are better; they must do what is necessary and indeed what is useful, but what is honourable is better. On such principles children and persons of every age which requires education should be trained. Whereas even the Greeks of the present day who are reputed to be best governed, and the legislators who gave them their constitutions, do not appear to have framed their governments with a regard to the best end, or to have given them laws and education with a view to all the excellences, but in a vulgar spirit have fallen back on those which promised to be more useful and profitable. Many modern writers have taken a similar view; they commend the Lacedaemonian constitution, and praise the legislator for making conquest and war his sole aim, a doctrine which may be refuted by argument and has long ago been refuted by facts. For most men desire empire in the hope of accumulating the goods of fortune; and on this ground Thibron and all those who have written about the Lacedaemonian constitution have praised their legislator, because the Lacedaemonians, by being trained to meet dangers, gained great power. But surely they are not a happy people now that their empire has passed away, nor was their legislator right. How ridiculous is the result, if, while they are continuing in the observance of his laws and no one interferes with them, they have lost the better part of life! These writers further err about the sort of government which the legislator should approve, for the government of freemen is nobler and implies more excellence than despotic government. Neither is a city to be deemed happy or a legislator

30 to be praised because he trains his citizens to conquer and obtain dominion over their neighbours, for there is great harm in this. On a similar principle any citizen who could, should obviously try to obtain the power in his own state—the crime which the Lacedaemonians 35 accuse king Pausanias of attempting, although he had such great honour already. No such principle and no law having this object is either statesmanlike or useful or right. For the same things are best both for individuals and for states, and these are the things which the legislator ought to implant in the minds of his citizens. Neither should men study war with a view to the enslavement of those who do not deserve to be 40 enslaved; but first of all they should provide against their own enslavement, and in the second place obtain empire for the good of the governed, and not for the sake of exercising a 1334ᵃ1 general despotism, and in the third place they should seek to be masters only over those who deserve to be slaves. Facts, as well as arguments, prove that the legislator should direct all his military and other measures to the provision of 5 leisure and the establishment of peace. For most of these military states are safe only while they are at war, but fall when they have acquired their empire; like unused iron they lose their edge in time of peace. And for this the legislator is to 10 blame, he never having taught them how to lead the life of peace.

15. Since the end of individuals and of states is the same, the end of the best man and of the best constitution must also be the same; it is therefore evident that there ought to exist in both of them the excellences of leisure; for peace, 15 as has been often repeated, is the end of war, and leisure of toil. But leisure and cultivation may be promoted not only by those excellences which are practiced in leisure, but also by some of those which are useful to business. For many necessaries of life have to be supplied before we can have leisure. Therefore a city must be temperate 20 and brave, and able to endure: for truly, as the proverb says, 'There is no leisure for slaves,' and those who cannot face danger like men are the slaves of any invader. Courage and endurance are required for business and philosophy for leisure, 25 temperance and justice for both, and more especially in times of peace and leisure, for war compels men to be just and temperate, whereas the enjoyment of good fortune and the leisure which comes with peace tend to make them insolent. 30 Those then who seem to be the best-off and to be in the possession of every good, have special need of justice and temperance—for example, those (if such there be, as the poets say) who dwell in the Islands of the Blest; they above all will need philosophy and temperance and justice, and all the more the more leisure they have, 35 living in the midst of abundance. There is no difficulty in seeing why the state that would be happy and good ought to have these excellences. If it is disgraceful in men not to be able to use the goods of life, it is peculiarly disgraceful not to be able to use them in time of leisure—to show excellent qualities in action and war, and when they have peace and leisure to be no better than slaves. That is why we should not practise excel-40 lence after the manner of the Lacedaemonians. For they, while agreeing with other men in their conception of the highest goods, differ from the rest of mankind in thinking that they are to be 1334ᵇ1 obtained by the practice of a single excellence. And since these goods and the enjoyment of them are greater than the enjoyment derived from the excellences . . . and that for its own sake, is evident from what has been said; we must 5 now consider how and by what means it is to be attained.

We have already determined that nature and habit and reason are required, and, of these, the proper nature of the citizens has also been defined by us. But we have still to consider whether the training of early life is to be that of 10 reason or habit, for these two must accord, and when in accord they will then form the best of harmonies. Reason may be mistaken and fail in attaining the highest ideal of life, and there may be a like influence of habit. Thus much is clear in the first place, that, as in all other things, birth implies an antecedent beginning, and that there 15 are beginnings whose end is relative to a further end. Now, in men reason and mind are the end towards which nature strives, so that the birth

and training in custom of the citizens ought to be ordered with a view to them. In the second place, as the soul and body are two, we see also that
20 there are two parts of the soul, the rational and the irrational, and two corresponding states—reason and appetite. And as the body is prior in order of generation to the soul, so the irrational is prior to the rational. The proof is that anger

and wishing and desire are implanted in children from their very birth, but reason and understanding are developed as they grow older. For this rea-
25 son, the care of the body ought to precede that of the soul, and the training of the appetitive part should follow: none the less our care of it must be for the sake of the reason, and our care of the body for the sake of the soul.

STUDY QUESTIONS: ARISTOTLE, *POLITICS*

1. What are the main aims of Aristotle's *Politics?*
2. What is the smallest community?
3. What are Aristotle's views on slavery?
4. How does Aristotle characterize the state?
5. What are the purposes of the state? Among these, what is the chief end?
6. What are the true forms of government? What distinguishes these from what Aristotle calls 'perversions'? What are the perversions?
7. Why should good laws be supreme?
8. Aristotle distinguishes three kinds of goods. What are they? How does he define the best life?
9. What is necessary for a city to be excellent?
10. For what ends must a legislator make laws? And what must he keep in view when he frames the laws?

POETICS

Aristotle's aim is to investigate the poetic craft, its power, and how plots should be composed. The *Poetics* is concerned with the fictional or dramatic work of the time, especially the epic and the tragedy. The work begins with a survey of different kinds of poetry (Chapters 1–3) and a history of their development. Most of the work is concerned with tragedy (Chapters 6–22). There follows a discussion of the epic (Chapters 23–4), literary criticism (Chapter 25), and a comparison of epic and tragedy. Part of the work is lost, including a section on comedy.

1447ª10 **1.** I propose to speak not only of poetry in general but also of its species and their respective capacities; of the structure of plot required for a good poem; of the number and nature of the constituent parts of a poem; and likewise of any other matters in the same line of inquiry. Let us follow the natural order and begin with first principles.

Epic poetry and tragedy, as also comedy, dithyrambic poetry, and most flute-playing and

lyre-playing, are all, viewed as a whole, modes of
15 imitation. But they differ from one another in three ways, either in their means, or in their objects, or in the manner of their imitations.

Just as colour and form are used as means by some, who (whether by art or constant practice) imitate and portray many things by their aid, and
20 the voice is used by others; so also in the above-mentioned group of arts, the means with them as a whole are rhythm, language, and harmony—

used, however, either singly or in certain combinations. A combination of harmony and rhythm alone is the means in flute-playing and lyre-25 playing, and any other arts there may be of the same description, e.g. imitative piping. Rhythm alone, without harmony, is the means in the dancer's imitations; for even he, by the rhythms of his attitudes, may represent men's characters, as well as what they do and suffer. There is further an art which imitates by language alone, and one which imitates by metres, either one or a plurality of metres. . . .

There are, lastly, certain other arts, which combine all the means enumerated, rhythm, 25 melody, and verse, e.g. dithyrambic and nomic poetry, tragedy and comedy; with this difference, however, that the three kinds of means are in some of them all employed together, and in others brought in separately, one after the other. These elements of difference in the above arts I term the means of their imitation.

1448ª1 **2.** The objects the imitator represents are actions, with agents who are necessarily either good men or bad—the diversities of human character being nearly always derivative from this primary distinction, since it is by badness and excellence men differ in character. It follows, therefore, that the agents represented must be either above our own level of goodness, or beneath it, or just such as we are; in the same way as, with the painters, the personages of Polygno-5 tus are better than we are, those of Pauson worse, and those of Dionysius just like ourselves. It is clear that each of the above-mentioned arts will admit of these differences, and that it will become a separate art by representing objects with this point of difference. . . .

15 This difference it is that distinguishes Tragedy and Comedy also; the one would make its personages worse, and the other better, than the men of the present day.

3. A third difference in these arts is in the manner in which each kind of object is represented. Given both the same means and the 20 same kind of object for imitation, one may either speak at one moment in narrative and at another in an assumed character, as Homer does; or one may remain the same throughout, without any such change; or the imitators may represent the whole story dramatically, as though they were actually doing the things described.

As we said at the beginning, therefore, the differences in the imitation of these arts come under three heads, their means, their objects, 25 and their manner.

So that as an imitator Sophocles will be on one side akin to Homer, both portraying good men; and on another to Aristophanes, since both present their personages as acting and doing. This in fact, according to some, is the reason for plays being termed dramas, because in a play the personages act the story.

4. It is clear that the general origin of 5 poetry was due to two causes, each of them part of human nature. Imitation is natural to man from childhood, one of his advantages over the lower animals being this, that he is the most imitative creature in the world, and learns at first by imitation. And it is also natural for all to delight in works of imitation. The truth of this second point is shown by experience: though the objects themselves may be painful to see, we 10 delight to view the most realistic representations of them in art, the forms for example of the lowest animals and of dead bodies. The explanation is to be found in a further fact: to be learning something is the greatest of pleasures not only to the philosopher but also to the rest of mankind, however small their capacity for it; 15 the reason of the delight in seeing the picture is that one is at the same time learning—gathering the meaning of things, e.g. that the man there is so-and-so; for if one has not seen the thing before, one's pleasure will not be in the picture as an imitation of it, but will be due to the execution or colouring or some similar 20 cause. Imitation, then, being natural to us—as also the sense of harmony and rhythm, the metres being obviously species of rhythms—it was through their original aptitude, and by a series of improvements for the most part gradual on their first efforts, that they created poetry out of their improvisations.

Poetry, however, soon broke up into two kinds according to the differences of character in the individual poets; for the graver among them ²⁵ would represent noble actions, and those of noble personages; and the meaner sort the actions of the ignoble. The latter class produced invectives at first, just as others did hymns and panegyrics. We know of no such poem by any of the pre-Homeric poets, though there were probably many such writers among them; instances, however, may be found from Homer downwards, ³⁰ e.g. his *Margites*, and the similar poems of others. In this poetry of invective its natural fitness brought an iambic metre into use; hence our present term 'iambic', because it was the metre of their 'iambs' or invectives against one another. The result was that the old poets became some of them writers of heroic and others of iambic verse. Homer, just as he was in the serious style the poet of poets, standing alone not only through the ³⁵ excellence, but also through the dramatic character of his imitations, so also was he the first to outline for us the general forms of comedy by producing not a dramatic invective, but a dramatic picture of the ridiculous; his *Margites* in fact stands in the same relation to our comedies as the *Iliad* and *Odyssey* to our tragedies. As soon, 1449ᵃ1 however, as tragedy and comedy appeared in the field, those naturally drawn to the one line of poetry became writers of comedies instead of iambs, and those naturally drawn to the other, writers of tragedies instead of epics, because these ⁵ new modes of art were grander and of more esteem than the old.

If it be asked whether tragedy is now all that it need be in its formative elements, to consider that, and decide it theoretically and in relation to the theatres, is a matter for another inquiry.

¹⁰ It certainly began in improvisations—as did also comedy; the one originating with the authors of the dithyramb, the other with those of the phallic songs, which still survive as institutions in many of our cities. And its advance after that was little by little, through their improving on whatever they had before them at each stage.

It was in fact only after a long series of changes that the movement of tragedy stopped on its attaining to its natural form. The number of ¹⁵ actors was first increased to two by Aeschylus, who curtailed the business of the Chorus, and made the dialogue take the leading part in the play. A third actor and scenery were due to Sophocles. Tragedy acquired also its magnitude. Discarding short stories and a ludicrous diction, ²⁰ through its passing out of its satyric stage, it assumed, though only at a late point in its progress, a tone of dignity; and its metre changed then from trochaic to iambic. The reason for their original use of the trochaic tetrameter was that their poetry was satyric and more connected with dancing than it now is. As soon, however, as a spoken part came in, the very nature of the thing found the appropriate metre. The iambic, ²⁵ we know, is the most speakable of metres, as is shown by the fact that we very often fall into it in conversation, whereas we rarely talk hexameters, and only when we depart from the speaking tone of voice. Another change was a plurality of episodes. As for the remaining matters, the embellishments and the account of their introduction, these must be taken as said, as it would ³⁰ probably be a long piece of work to go through the details.

9. From what we have said it will be seen that the poet's function is to describe, not the thing that has happened, but a kind of thing that might happen, i.e. what is possible as being probable or necessary. The distinction between historian and poet is not in the one writing 1451ᵇ1 prose and the other verse—you might put the work of Herodotus into verse, and it would still be a species of history; it consists really in this, that the one describes the thing that has been, and the other a kind of thing that might be. Hence poetry is something more philosophic ⁵ and of graver import than history, since its statements are of the nature rather of universals, whereas those of history are singulars. By a universal statement I mean one as to what such or such a kind of man will probably or necessarily say or do—which is the aim of poetry, though it

affixes proper names to the characters; by a sin-
10 gular statement, one as to what, say, Alcibiades
did or had done to him. In comedy this has
become clear by this time; it is only when their
plot is already made up of probable incidents
that they give it a basis of proper names, choosing for the purpose any names that may occur to
them, instead of writing like the old iambic
poets about particular persons. In Tragedy, how-
15 ever, they still adhere to the historic names; and
for this reason: what convinces is the possible;
now whereas we are not yet sure as to the possibility of that which has not happened, that
which has happened is manifestly possible, otherwise it would not have happened. Nevertheless even in tragedy there are some plays with
20 but one or two known names in them, the rest
being inventions; and there are some without a
single known name, e.g. Agathon's *Antheus*, in
which both incidents and names are of the
poet's invention; and it is no less delightful on
that account. So that one must not aim at a rigid
adherence to the traditional stories on which
tragedies are based. It would be absurd, in fact,
25 to do so, as even the known stories are only
known to a few, though they are a delight none
the less to all.

It is evident from the above that the poet
must be more the poet of his plots than of his
verses, inasmuch as he is a poet by virtue of the
imitative element in his work, and it is actions
that he imitates. And if he should come to take a
subject from actual history, he is none the less a
30 poet for that; since some historic occurrences may
very well be in the probable order of things; and it
is in that aspect of them that he is their poet.

Of simple plots and actions the episodic are
the worst. I call a plot episodic when there is neither probability nor necessity in the sequence of
35 its episodes. Actions of this sort bad poets construct through their own fault, and good ones on
account of the players. His work being for public
performance, a good poet often stretches out a
plot beyond its capabilities, and is thus obliged to
1452ᵃ1 twist the sequence of incident.

Tragedy, however, is an imitation not only of
a complete action, but also of incidents arousing
pity and fear. Such incidents have the very greatest effect on the mind when they occur unex-
pectedly and at the same time in consequence of
one another; there is more of the marvellous in
5 them than if they happened of themselves or by
mere chance. Even matters of chance seem most
marvellous if there is an appearance of design as
it were in them; as for instance the statue of
Mitys at Argos killed the author for Mitys' death
by falling down on him when he was looking at
it; for incidents like that we think to be not without a meaning. A plot, therefore, of this sort is
10 necessarily finer than others.

13. The next points after what we have said
above will be these: what is the poet to aim at,
and what is he to avoid, in constructing his
Plots? and what are the conditions on which the
30 tragic effect depends?

We assume that, for the finest form of
tragedy, the plot must be not simple but complex; and further, that it must imitate actions
arousing fear and pity, since that is the distinctive function of this kind of imitation. It follows, therefore, that there are three forms of
plot to be avoided. A good man must not be
seen passing from good fortune to bad, or a bad
man from bad fortune to good. The first situa-
35 tion is not fear-inspiring or piteous, but simply
odious to us. The second is the most untragic
that can be; it has no one of the requisites of
tragedy; it does not appeal either to the human
feeling in us, or to our pity, or to our fears. Nor,
1453ᵃ1 on the other hand, should an extremely bad
man be seen falling from good fortune into bad.
Such a story may arouse the human feeling in
us, but it will not move us to either pity or fear;
pity is occasioned by undeserved misfortune,
and fear by that of one like ourselves; so that
there will be nothing either piteous or fear-
5 inspiring in the situation. There remains, then,
the intermediate kind of personage, a man not
preeminently virtuous and just, whose misfortune, however, is brought upon him not by vice
and depravity but by some fault, of the number
10 of those in the enjoyment of great reputation
and prosperity; e.g. Oedipus, Thyestes, and the

men of note of similar families. The perfect plot, accordingly, must have a single, and not (as some tell us) a double issue; the change in the subject's fortunes must be not from bad fortune to good, but on the contrary from good to bad;

15 and the cause of it must lie not in any depravity, but in some great fault on his part; the man himself being either such as we have described, or better, not worse, than that. Fact also confirms our theory. Though the poets began by accepting any tragic story that came to hand, in these days the finest tragedies are always on the story of some few houses, on that of Alcmeon, Oedipus, Orestes, Meleager, Thyestes, Telephus,

20 or any others that may have been involved, as either agents or sufferers, in some deed of horror. The theoretically best tragedy, then, has a plot of this description. The critics, therefore, are wrong who blame Euripides for taking this line in his tragedies, and giving many of them an unhappy ending. It is, as we have said, the right

25 line to take. The best proof is this: on the stage, and in the public performances, such plays, properly worked out, are seen to be the most truly tragic; and Euripides, even if his execution be faulty in every other point, is seen to be nevertheless the most tragic certainly of the dramatists. After this comes the construction of plot

30 which some rank first, one with a double story (like the *Odyssey*) and an opposite issue for the good and the bad personages. It is ranked as first only through the weakness of the audiences; the poets merely follow their public,

35 writing as its wishes dictate. But the pleasure here is not that of tragedy. It belongs rather to comedy, where the bitterest enemies in the piece (e.g. Orestes and Aegisthus) walk off good friends at the end, with no slaying of any one by any one.

14. The tragic fear and pity may be aroused 1453ᵇ1 by the spectacle; but they may also be aroused by the very structure and incidents of the play— which is the better way and shows the better poet. The plot in fact should be so framed that, even without seeing the things take place, he who simply hears the account of them shall be filled with horror and pity at the incidents;

5 which is just the effect that the mere recital of the story in *Oedipus* would have on one. To produce this same effect by means of the spectacle is less artistic, and requires extraneous aid. Those, however, who make use of the spectacle to put before us that which is merely monstrous and not productive of fear, are wholly out of touch with tragedy; not every kind of pleasure should be required of a tragedy, but only its own proper

10 pleasure.

The tragic pleasure is that of pity and fear, and the poet has to produce it by a work of imitation; it is clear, therefore, that the causes should be included in the incidents of his story. Let us see, then, what kinds of incident strike one as horrible, or rather as piteous. In a deed of

15 this description the parties must necessarily be either friends, or enemies, or indifferent to one another. Now when enemy does it on enemy, there is nothing to move us to pity either in his doing or in his meditating the deed, except so far as the actual pain of the sufferer is concerned; and the same is true when the parties are indifferent to one another. Whenever the tragic deed, however, is done among friends— when murder or the like is done or meditated by brother on brother, by son on father, by mother

20 on son, or son on mother—these are the situations the poet should seek after. The traditional stories, accordingly, must be kept as they are, e.g. the murder of Clytaemnestra by Orestes and of Eriphyle by Alcmeon. At the same time even

25 with these there is something left to the poet himself; it is for him to devise the right way of treating them. Let us explain more clearly what we mean by 'the right way'. The deed of horror may be done by the doer knowingly and consciously, as in the old poets, and in Medea's murder of her children in Euripides. Or he may do

30 it, but in ignorance of his relationship, and discover that afterwards, as does the Oedipus in Sophocles. Here the deed is outside the play; but it may be within it, like the act of the Alcmeon in Astydamas, or that of the Telegonus in *Ulysses Wounded*. A third possibility is for one meditating some deadly injury to another, in

ignorance of his relationship, to make the dis-
35 covery in time to draw back. These exhaust the
possibilities, since the deed must necessarily be
either done or not done, and either knowingly
or unknowingly.

The worst situation is when the personage is
with full knowledge on the point of doing the
deed, and leaves it undone. It is odious and also
(through the absence of suffering) untragic;
hence it is that no one is made to act thus except
in some few instance, e.g. Haemon and Creon in
1454ª1 *Antigone*. Next after this comes the actual perpe-
tration of the deed meditated. A better situation
than that, however, is for the deed to be done in
ignorance, and the relationship discovered afterwards, since there is nothing odious in it, and the
discovery will serve to astound us. But the best of

all is the last; what we have in *Cresphontes*, for
5 example, where Merope, on the point of slaying
her son, recognizes him in time, in *Iphigenia*,
where sister and brother are in a like position;
and in *Helle*, where the son recognizes his
mother, when on the point of giving her up to
her enemy.

This will explain why our tragedies are
restricted (as we said just now) to such a small
number of families. It was accident rather than art
10 that led the poets in quest of subjects to embody
this kind of incident in their plots. They are still
obliged, accordingly, to have recourse to the families in which such honours have occurred.

On the construction of the plot, and the
kind of plot required for tragedy, enough has now
15 been said.

STUDY QUESTIONS: ARISTOTLE, POETICS

1. Modes of imitation can differ in which three ways?
2. What is the origin of poetry, according to Aristotle?
3. Why is poetry more philosophical than history, according to Aristotle?
4. What is a tragedy?
5. What sort of plot should the best tragedy have ideally? What sort of effect should the tragedy have?
6. Why is Euripides seen as the most tragic of the dramatists?

Philosophical Bridges: The Aristotelian Influence

As with Plato, it is difficult to overestimate the influence of Aristotle on the history of thought. It is so pervasive and persistent that it is impossible to recount in a short space, except in very general terms.

One of the most historically decisive early influences of Aristotle was on Jewish and especially Arab philosophy. During the period from 750 to 900, Arab scholars translated many Greek texts into Arabic, including those of Aristotle, some of which had been lost to the European world. The Moors living in Spain reintroduced Aristotle into the European tradition. Ibn Sina or Avicenna (980–1037) wrote influential works that drew much inspiration from Aristotle, and Ibn Rushd or Averroës (1126–1198) wrote several commentaries on Aristotle, as did Al Farabi (878–950). In his famous work *The Guide for the Perplexed*, the Spanish Jewish philosopher Moses ben Maimon (Maimonides, 1135–1204) also draws on Aristotle. Since much of Aristotle's work had been unknown in Europe for many centuries, this rediscovery gave a new direction and impetus to medieval European learn-ing, especially because these works emphasized the importance of observation, experiment, and logical argument as opposed to abstract speculation, an emphasis that had been lacking in the earlier Roman-Platonic tradition.

By the end of the thirteenth century, Aristotle was considered the giant of medieval philosophy. His *Organon* was *the* textbook for the definition of scientific methodology until the modern period. His physics and astronomy were considered definitive until the time of Copernicus and Galileo. His work in other scientific areas, such as biology, dominated the field until the nineteenth century. His logic overshadowed the field until the nineteenth-century works of Gottlob Frege and George Boole, among others. Furthermore, St. Thomas Aquinas (1225–1274) attempted to fuse the teachings of Aristotle with those of Christianity and thereby defined what was to become the orthodoxy of the Roman Catholic Church. In other words, Catholic philosophy today still contains important elements of Aristotle's thought. Since the Church dominated European culture throughout the medieval period, up until around 1450, to be a philosopher was to be an Aristotelian. Aristotle was known as *the* philosopher.

Aristotle's influence is so pervasive, and he introduced so many new concepts into western thought, that we can only highlight a few central points. First, Aristotle observed nature in a systematic way and used these observations to classify natural things into different kinds. His insistence on the importance of observation makes Aristotle the precursor of Empiricism, even though it would be anachronistic and misleading to think of him as an Empiricist.

Second, Aristotle's method that combines synthesis and analysis set a new standard for philosophical reflection for future generations. Consider how he summarizes carefully the views of various pre-Socratic philosophers and tries to separate what can be learned from what should be rejected in their views. Consider, for instance, the debate between Parmenides' thesis that reality is unchanging and Heraclitus' assertion that reality is in constant flux. By analyzing different kinds of change and distinguishing form and matter, Aristotle argues that every event has both a permanent and a changing aspect. In this way, he is able to challenge the specifics of Parmenides' argument in a very direct way. Consider also how he analyzes different uses of crucial words such as 'to be' and 'cause,' and employs these analyses to define the basic categories of human thought and to construct a metaphysic. Aristotle's claim that things can be said to be in many ways provides one of the greatest insights in philosophy, showing how careful attention to language can help resolve philosophical problems.

Third, based on such analyses, Aristotle formulates a three-way distinction between substance, form, and matter, so as to transcend the debate between the pre-Socratics and Plato. Form and matter constitute two inseparable aspects of individual substances, such as a tree and an animal. Neither form nor matter has priority; both are necessary for a substance, and neither is itself a substance. Just as Plato is wrong to conceive form as a substance, so the pre-Socratics were mistaken to treat matter as substance. In this way, Aristotle revolutionized the conception of the soul, rejecting both the reductionism inherent in naturalistic early Milesian thought and the dualism of Plato.

In these general terms, Aristotle's analysis is influential today. In the philosophy of mind, Aristotle's form/matter distinction provides an alternative to dualism while avoiding reductionism. In other words, the assertions that form cannot be reduced to matter but that it is not a substance distinct from matter seem to imply an interesting version of nonreductive materialism when applied to mental states. For example, Hilary Putnam and Martha Nussbaum argued that Aristotle advanced a form of functionalism. In a similar vein, contemporary thinkers working in the field of the nature of universals and properties have employed Aristotle's form/matter distinction to reject Platonic realism without accepting strong forms of nominalism.

Allied to this distinction between substance, form, and matter, Aristotle also distinguished different kinds of explanation or cause; this is the precursor to the contemporary debate concerning whether the types of causal explanations employed in the natural sciences are also appropriate for the social sciences.

Fourth, Aristotle formulated the ideas of metaphysical necessity and essence. Not all the properties of a substance are on the same footing. Some are accidental, and others constitute the essence of a substance. This idea had a tremendous impact on medieval philosophy and became a foundation stone of Scholasticism. In a very different vein, some contemporary thinkers claim that the universe contains natural kinds and individual substances that have a real essence. These are broadly Aristotelian views emanating from his view of essence.

Fifth, Aristotle invented many of the notions that form part of our modern conception of God. For instance, he argued for the necessity of a first cause or unmoved mover. He also conceived of the divine as the end to which all things strive. As mentioned earlier, Aquinas tried to reconcile Christian doctrine with Aristotle's metaphysics, and in the process made much Christian thought Aristotelian. As a consequence, as mentioned above, aspects of Aristotle's metaphysics are alive today as a part of the official doctrine of the Roman Catholic Church.

Finally, Aristotle introduced several key ideas into ethics, which several thinkers draw inspiration from today. In recent years, there has been a renewed interest in virtue theory as an alternative to Kantian and utilitarian action-based approaches to morality. Aristotle's *Ethics* is considered as the primary text in this field, influencing recent writers such as Philippa Foot and Alasdair MacIntyre.

BIBLIOGRAPHY

Primary

Aristotle, *The Complete Works*, 2 vols., ed. J. Barnes, Princeton University Press, 1984

Secondary

Ackrill, J. L., *Aristotle the Philosopher*, Oxford University Press, 1981

Allan, D. J., *The Philosophy of Aristotle*, Oxford University Press, 1970

Barnes, Jonathan, *Aristotle*, Oxford University Press, 1982

———, ed., *The Cambridge Companion to Aristotle*, Cambridge University Press, 1995

Barnes, J., Schofield, M., and Sorabji, R., *Articles on Aristotle*, 4 vols., Duckworth, 1975

Furley, David, *From Aristotle to Augustine*, Routledge History of Philosophy, vol. 2, Routledge, 1999

Gill, M., *Aristotle on Substance: The Paradox of Unity*, Princeton University Press, 1989

Graham, D., *Aristotle's Two Systems*, Oxford University Press, 1987

Hardie, W., *Aristotle's Ethical Theory*, Oxford University Press, 1980

Irwin, Terence, *Aristotle's First Principles*, Clarendon Press, 1988

Jaeger, Werner, *Aristotle: Fundamental of the History of His Development*, Clarendon Press, 1948

Lear, Jonathan, *Aristotle: The Desire to Understand*, Cambridge University Press, 1988

Lloyd, G. E. R., *Aristotle: The Growth and Structure of His Thought*, Cambridge University Press, 1968

Nussbaum, Martha, *The Fragility of Goodness*, Cambridge University Press, 1986

Rorty, A., *Essays on Aristotle's Ethics*, University of California Press, 1980

Ross, Sir David, *Aristotle*, Methuen, 1923

Thomson, G., and Missner, M., *On Aristotle*, Wadsworth, 2000

Veatch, Henry, *Aristotle: A Contemporary Appreciation*, Indiana University Press, 1974

✦ HELLENISTIC AND ✦
ROMAN PHILOSOPHY

PROLOGUE

In 323 B.C., Alexander the Great died. A year later, Aristotle passed away. In nine years, Alexander, who had been Aristotle's best-known pupil, conquered much of the known world, as far as India. These events mark the end of the classical Greek period and the demise of Greece as a collection of autonomous city-states. It is the beginning of the so-called Hellenistic period, which lasted until the first century B.C. By 188 B.C., Rome was the center of the Mediterranean, and, in 146 B.C., Greece became a protectorate of Rome.

Although the schools established by Plato (the Academy) and Aristotle (the Lyceum) continued their work, Hellenistic philosophy consists of thought that is in some ways independent of Plato and Aristotle, and it has three main branches that are of great interest: Epicureanism, Stoicism, and Skepticism. These schools continued to attract followers in the Roman period. Stoicism in particular had great influence on the thought and social life of Rome; in some ways, it became a religion in Rome. These three schools concentrate less on metaphysics and more on explaining the importance for the individual of attaining inner peace.

By the time Augustus established the Roman Empire in 30 B.C., the initial period of Hellenistic philosophy was at an end. Soon afterward, Christianity began to spread over the empire. Plotinus (204–270 A.D.) developed a new interpretation of Plato, which became known as neo-Platonism, and which became a rival to Christianity in the fourth century. By the third century A.D., the cities, which were once the cultural centers of the Roman Empire, began to collapse economically due to the pressures of financing constant military campaigns. Many of the wealthier citizens fled to escape the steadily rising taxes; health standards began to deteriorate, and, within a fairly short period, about a third of the population died from either wars or the plague. The militaristic elements of the Roman Empire gained supreme power, even over the emperors. This disintegration of the empire was due largely to the continuous attacks by German tribes from the north and the Persians from the east. These events mark the transition to the next volume in this series. Finally, in

529, Justinian closed the four philosophical schools in Athens (the Academy, the Lyceum, the Garden, and the Stoa), which were already only remnants of a bygone age.

EPICUREANISM
PROLOGUE

After the demise of Athenian democracy, Greek philosophy took a new turn. In a less liberal political climate, thinkers were forced to search for conceptions of the ethical life that were divorced from political ideals. For example, Epicureanism is a philosophy dedicated to the pursuit of individual happiness through the cultivation of a state of tranquility achieved through freedom from desire. Another feature of early Hellenistic philosophy is that science and metaphysics acquire a more peripheral role compared to in earlier periods. For instance, drawing inspiration from the early atomists, such as Democritus, Epicurus argued for materialism, but mainly for the reason that this is required to free persons from superstitious fears. Philosophy should not try to explain the world, but rather help the individual attain happiness. Epicureanism became popular in Greece and to some extent in Rome, and its most famous exponent was the great Latin poet Lucretius (99–55 B.C.), whose poem *On the Nature of Things* preserved and popularized Epicurus' ideas.

Epicurus (341–270 B.C.)

Biographical History

Epicurus was born in Samos, the birthplace of Pythagoras. At the age of 18, he moved to Athens to serve for two years in the military, after which he taught near his hometown. In 307 B.C., at the age of 35, he returned to Athens to establish a philosophical school, known as the 'Garden,' which was open to women and persons from all social classes. It was not only an academic institution but also a community of persons dedicated to living in accordance with Epicurean principles. He remained in the city until his death, living simply and quietly. He was a prodigious writer, but only a few letters and fragments remain of his work.

Philosophical Overview

Epicurus' philosophy covers three broad areas: a hedonistic ethic, a materialist metaphysics, and an empiricist theory of knowledge. Epicurus believed that philosophy should be primarily the search for individual happiness and that science, virtue, and knowledge are subservient to this search. He himself was supposed to have attained a state of real happiness and freedom from anxiety. He was considered by his followers to be 'a god among men' and the founder of a new religion.

Epicurus created a curious philosophy that combined an atomistic materialism and empiricism with a set of ethical principles designed to liberate humanity from the superstitious terrors of traditional Greek religion. He did not deny the existence of the gods, but he argued that they have no influence at all over human lives and indeed the rest of the universe. His argument is that the traditional description of the gods as perfectly ha⟋ requires that they be in a perfect state of tranquility, which is incompatible with be⟋ concerned about human affairs.

The main aim of Epicurus' philosophy is to aid the individual in finding a ha⟋⟋, His metaphysics and theory of knowledge serve this end. His ontology that postulates the existence of only material atoms and the void is supposedly sufficient to explain natural events and psychological phenomena, without the need of religious superstition and more extravagant metaphysics. Furthermore, he argues that this materialism requires denying the possibility of life after death, and thus it removes the fear and anxiety of divine punishment, which is one of the principal causes of unhappiness.

>Metaphysics: Epicurus affirms that everything is composed of atoms and void. Since nothing can come from nothing, the basic constituents of the universe have always existed. These atoms must be indivisible even conceptually; they cannot have parts. The void must exist because if all space were occupied, then solid objects would have no space to move into. All atoms move at the same speed, but when they collide and deflect each other's motions, they conjoin to form a solid object. Such compound bodies have properties, which the atoms out of which they are made do not possess. Atoms have only shape, weight, and size. According to Epicurus, the soul is composed of physical atoms; it is finely structured and diffused throughout the whole body. It is born, grows, and dies with the body. He argues that the soul must be physical, because otherwise it would be void or nothing. Since it is changed by and affects changes in physical things, it cannot be immaterial.

>Theory of Knowledge: To avoid false belief, we should believe truths based on perception. Sensation consists in the conscious reception of the atoms emanated from the solid bodies around us. These atoms preserve the shape and other properties of the bodies. Consequently, as long as we do not add anything to this stimulus, our perceptions will be reliable. Therefore, we should not confuse perception with fallible interpretation. Reason itself is founded on the senses. If one follows this theory of knowledge, then one will not quarrel with the senses and will have the confidence of a person who has well-formed conceptions.

LETTER TO HERODOTUS

Epicurus describes this letter as 'an epitome of the whole system' (i.e., the Epicurean philosophy) for those who are unable to work through the details. He says that the outline is based on certain general principles. You will notice that Epicurus recommends continuous study of nature to his student because 'with this sort of activity more than any other, I bring calm to my life.' First, Epicurus points out the need for a clear definition for each word. He proceeds to explain the principles of physics, such as the principles that nothing can come from nothing and that everything is composed of atoms and void. Afterward, he turns to the production of images and the nature of perception (46–55). Then he discusses the magnitude of bodies, arguing against infinite indivisibility of things with mass, and also their motion (55–62). Returning to the theme of perception (63), he argues that the soul is material. In sections 75–76, he discusses the origin of language.

35 For those who are unable, Herodotus, to work in detail through all that I have written about nature, or to peruse the larger books which I have composed, I have already prepared at sufficient length an epitome of the whole system, that they may keep adequately in mind at least the most general principles in each department, in order that as occasion arises they may be able to assist themselves on the most important points, in so far as they undertake the study of nature. But those also who have made considerable progress in the survey of the main principles ought to bear in mind the scheme of the whole system set forth in its essentials. For we have frequent need of the general view, but not so often of the 36 detailed exposition. Indeed it is necessary to go back on the main principles, and constantly to fix in one's memory enough to give one the most essential comprehension of the truth. And in fact the accurate knowledge of details will be fully discovered, if the general principles in the various departments are thoroughly grasped and borne in mind; for even in the case of one fully initiated the most essential feature in all accurate knowledge is the capacity to make a rapid use of observation and mental apprehension, and (this can be done if everything) is summed up in elementary principles and formulae. For it is not possible for any one to abbreviate the complete course through the whole system, if he cannot embrace in his own mind by means of short formulae all that might be set out with accuracy in detail. 37 Wherefore since the method I have described is valuable to all those who are accustomed to the investigation of nature, I who urge upon others the constant occupation in the investigation of nature, and find my own peace chiefly in a life so occupied, have composed for you another epitome on these lines, summing up the first principles of the whole doctrine.

First of all, Herodotus, we must grasp the ideas attached to words, in order that we may be able to refer to them and so to judge the inferences of opinion or problems of investigation or reflection, so that we may not either leave every-

thing uncertain and go on explaining to infinity 38 or use words devoid of meaning. For this purpose it is essential that the first mental image associated with each word should be regarded, and that there should be no need of explanation, if we are really to have a standard to which to refer a problem of investigation or reflection or a mental inference. And besides we must keep all our investigations in accord with our sensations, and in particular with the immediate apprehensions whether of the mind or of any one of the instruments of judgement, and likewise in accord with the feelings existing in us, in order that we may have indications whereby we may judge both the problem of sense-perception and the unseen.

Having made these points clear, we must now consider things imperceptible to the senses. First of all, that nothing is created out of that which does not exist: for if it were, everything 39 would be created out of everything with no need of seeds. And again, if that which disappears were destroyed into that which did not exist, all things would have perished, since that into which they were dissolved would not exist. Furthermore, the universe always was such as it is now, and always will be the same. For there is nothing into which it changes: for outside the universe there is nothing which could come into it and bring about the change.

Moreover, the universe is (bodies and space): for that bodies exist, sense itself witnesses in the experience of all men, and in accordance with the evidence of sense we must of necessity 40 judge of the imperceptible by reasoning, as I have already said. And if there were not that which we term void and place and intangible existence, bodies would have nowhere to exist and nothing through which to move, as they are seen to move. And besides these two nothing can even be thought of either by conception or on the analogy of things conceivable such as could be grasped as whole existences and not spoken of as the accidents or properties of such existences. Furthermore, among bodies some are compounds, and others those of which compounds 41

From *Epicurus—The Extant Remains*, translated by Cyril Bailey, 1926. Reprinted by permission of Oxford University Press.

are formed. And these latter are indivisible and unalterable (if, that is, all things are not to be destroyed into the non-existent, but something permanent is to remain behind at the dissolution of compounds): they are completely solid in nature, and can by no means be dissolved in any part. So it must needs be that the first-beginnings are indivisible corporeal existences.

Moreover, the universe is boundless. For that which is bounded has an extreme point: and the extreme point is seen against something else. So that as it has no extreme point, it has no 42 limit; and as it has no limit, it must be boundless and not bounded. Furthermore, the infinite is boundless both in the number of the bodies and in the extent of the void. For if on the one hand the void were boundless, and the bodies limited in number, the bodies could not stay anywhere, but would be carried about and scattered through the infinite void, not having other bodies to support them and keep them in place by means of collisions. But if, on the other hand, the void were limited, the infinite bodies would not have room wherein to take their place.

Besides this the indivisible and solid bodies, out of which too the compounds are created and into which they are dissolved, have an incomprehensible number of varieties in shape: for it is not possible that such great varieties of things should arise from the same (atomic) shapes, if they are limited in number. And so in each shape the atoms are quite infinite in number, but their differences of shape are not quite infinite, but only incomprehensible in number.

43 And the atoms move continuously for all time, some of them (falling straight down, others swerving, and others recoiling from their collisions. And of the latter, some are borne on) separating to a long distance from one another, while others again recoil and recoil, whenever they chance to be checked by the interlacing with 44 others, or else shut in by atoms interlaced around them. For on the one hand the nature of the void which separates each atom by itself brings this about, as it is not able to afford resistance, and on the other hand the hardness which belongs to the atoms makes them recoil after collision to as

great a distance as the interlacing permits separation after the collision. And these motions have no beginning, since the atoms and the void are the cause.

45 These brief sayings, if all these points are borne in mind, afford a sufficient outline for our understanding of the nature of existing things.

Furthermore, there are infinite worlds both like and unlike this world of ours. For the atoms being infinite in number, as was proved already, are borne on far out into space. For those atoms, which are of such nature that a world could be created out of them or made by them, have not been used up either on one world or on a limited number of worlds, nor again on all the worlds which are alike, or on those which are different from these. So that there nowhere exists an obstacle to the infinite number of the worlds.

46' Moreover, there are images like in shape to the solid bodies, far surpassing perceptible things in their subtlety of texture. For it is not impossible that such emanations should be formed in that which surrounds the objects, nor that there should be opportunities for the formation of such hollow and thin frames, nor that there should be effluences which preserve the respective position and order which they had before in the solid bodies: these images we call idols.

47' Next, nothing among perceptible things contradicts the belief that the images have unsurpassable fineness of texture. And for this reason they have also unsurpassable speed of motion, since the movement of all their atoms is uniform, and besides nothing or very few things hinder their emission by collisions, whereas a body composed of many or infinite atoms is at 48 once hindered by collisions. Besides this (nothing contradicts the belief) that the creation of the idols takes place as quick as thought. For the flow of atoms from the surface of bodies is continuous, yet it cannot be detected by any lessening in the size of the object because of the constant filling up of what is lost. The flow of images preserves for a long time the position and order of the atoms in the solid body, though it is occasionally confused. Moreover compound idols are quickly formed in the air around, because it is not necessary for their substance to be filled in deep inside: and besides there are certain other methods in which existences of this sort are produced. For not one of these beliefs is contradicted by our sensations, if one looks to see in what way sensation will bring us the clear visions from external objects, and in what way again the corresponding sequence of qualities and movements.

49 Now we must suppose too that it is when something enters us from external objects that we not only see but think of their shapes. For external objects could not make on us an impression of the nature of their own colour and shape by means of the air which lies between us and them, nor again by means of the rays or effluences of any sort which pass from us to them—nearly so well as if models, similar in colour and shape, leave the objects and enter according to

50 their respective size either into our sight or into our mind; moving along swiftly, and so by this means reproducing the image of a single continuous thing and preserving the corresponding sequence of qualities and movements from the original object as the result of their uniform contact with us, kept up by the vibration of the atoms deep in the interior of the concrete body.

And every image which we obtain by an act of apprehension on the part of the mind or of the sense-organs, whether of shape or of properties, this image is the shape (or the properties) of the concrete object, and is produced by the constant repetition of the image or the impression it has left. Now falsehood and error always lie in the addition of opinion with regard to (what is waiting) to be confirmed or not contradicted, and

51 then is not confirmed (or is contradicted). For the similarity between the things which exist, which we call real, and the images received as a likeness of things and produced either in sleep or through some other acts of apprehension on the part of the mind or the other instruments of judgement, could never be, unless there were some effluences of this nature actually brought into contact with our senses. And error would not exist unless another kind of movement too were produced inside ourselves, closely linked to the apprehension of images, but differing from it;

and it is owing to this, supposing it is not confirmed, or is contradicted, that falsehood arises;

52 but if it is confirmed or not contradicted, it is true. Therefore we must do our best to keep this doctrine in mind, in order that on the one hand the standards of judgement dependent on the clear visions may not be undermined, and on the other error may not be as firmly established as truth and so throw all into confusion.

Moreover, hearing too results when a current is carried off from the object speaking or sounding or making a noise, or causing in any other way a sensation of hearing. Now this current is split up into particles, each like the whole, which at the same time preserve a correspondence of qualities with one another and a unity of character which stretches right back to the object which emitted the sound: this unity it is which in most cases produces comprehension in the recip-

53 ient, or, if not, merely makes manifest the presence of the external object. For without the transference from the object of some correspondence of qualities, comprehension of this nature could not result. We must not then suppose that the actual air is moulded into shape by the voice which is emitted or by other similar sounds—for it will be very far from being so acted upon by it—but that the blow which takes place inside us, when we emit our voice, causes at once a squeezing out of certain particles, which produce a stream of breath, of such a character as to afford us the sensation of hearing.

Furthermore, we must suppose that smell too, just like hearing, could never bring about any sensation, unless there were certain particles carried off from the object of suitable size to stir this sense-organ, some of them in a manner disorderly and alien to it, others in a regular manner and akin in nature.

54 Moreover, we must suppose that the atoms do not possess any of the qualities belonging to perceptible things, except shape, weight, and size, and all that necessarily goes with shape. For every quality changes; but the atoms do not change at all, since there must needs be something which remains solid and indissoluble at the dissolution of compounds, which can cause

changes; not changes into the non-existent or from the non-existent, but changes effected by the shifting of position of some particles, and by the addition or departure of others. For this reason it is essential that the bodies which shift their position should be imperishable and should not possess the nature of what changes, but parts and configuration of their own. For thus much 55 must needs remain constant. For even in things perceptible to us which change their shape by the withdrawal of matter it is seen that shape remains to them, whereas the qualities do not remain in the changing object, in the way in which shape is left behind, but are lost from the entire body. Now these particles which are left behind are sufficient to cause the differences in compound bodies, since it is essential that some things should be left behind and not be destroyed into the non-existent.

Moreover, we must not either suppose that every size exists among the atoms, in order that the evidence of phenomena may not contradict us, but we must suppose that there are some variations of size. For if this be the case, we can give 56 a better account of what occurs in our feelings and sensations. But the existence of atoms of every size is not required to explain the differences of qualities in things, and at the same time some atoms would be bound to come within our ken and be visible; but this is never seen to be the case, nor is it possible to imagine how an atom could become visible.

Besides this we must not suppose that in a limited body there can be infinite parts or parts of every degree of smallness. Therefore, we must not only do away with division into smaller and smaller parts to infinity, in order that we may not make all things weak, and so in the composition of aggregate bodies be compelled to crush and squander the things that exist into the non-existent, but we must not either suppose that in limited bodies there is a possibility of continuing 57 to infinity in passing even to smaller and smaller parts. For if once one says that there are infinite parts in a body or parts of any degree of smallness, it is not possible to conceive how this should be, and indeed how could the body any

longer be limited in size? (For it is obvious that these infinite particles must be of some size or other; and however small they may be, the size of the body too would be infinite.) And again, since the limited body has an extreme point, which is distinguishable, even though not perceptible by itself, you cannot conceive that the succeeding point to it is not similar in character, or that if you go on in this way from one point to another, it should be possible for you to proceed to infinity 58 marking such points in your mind. We must notice also that the least thing in sensation is neither exactly like that which admits of progression from one part to another, nor again is it in every respect wholly unlike it, but it has a certain affinity with such bodies, yet cannot be divided into parts. But when on the analogy of this resemblance we think to divide off parts of it, one on the one side and another on the other, it must needs be that another point like the first meets our view. And we look at these points in succession starting from the first, not within the limits of the same point nor in contact part with part, but yet by means of their own proper characteristics measuring the size of bodies, more in a 59 greater body and fewer in a smaller. Now we must suppose that the least part in the atom too bears the same relation to the whole; for though in smallness it is obvious that it exceeds that which is seen by sensation, yet it has the same relations. For indeed we have already declared on the ground of its relation to sensible bodies that the atom has size, only we placed it far below them in smallness. Further, we must consider these least indivisible points as boundary-marks, providing in themselves as primary units the measure of size for the atoms, both for the smaller and the greater, in our contemplation of these unseen bodies by means of thought. For the affinity which the least parts of the atom have to the homogeneous parts (of sensible things) is sufficient to justify our conclusion to this extent: but that they should ever come together as bodies with motion is quite impossible.

60 [Furthermore, in the infinite we must not speak of 'up' or 'down', as though with reference to an absolute highest or lowest—and indeed we

must say that, though it is possible to proceed to infinity in the direction above our heads from wherever we take our stand, the absolute highest point will never appear to us—nor yet can that which passes beneath the point thought of to infinity be at the same time both up and down in reference to the same thing: for it is impossible to think this. So that it is possible to consider as one single motion that which is thought of as the upwards motion to infinity and as another the downward motion, even though that which passes from us into the regions above our heads arrives countless times at the feet of beings above and that which passes downwards from us at the head of beings below; for none the less the whole motions are thought of as opposed, the one to the other, to infinity.]

61 Moreover, the atoms must move with equal speed, when they are borne onwards through the void, nothing colliding with them. For neither will the heavy move more quickly than the small and light, when, that is, nothing meets them: nor again the small more quickly than the great, having their whole course uniform, when nothing collides with them either: nor is the motion upwards or sideways owing to blows (quicker), nor again that downwards owing to their own weight. For as long as either of the two motions prevails, so long will it have a course as quick as thought, until something checks it either from outside or from its own weight counteracting the 46ᵇ force of that which dealt the blow. Moreover, their passage through the void, when it takes place without meeting any bodies which might collide, accomplishes every comprehensible distance in an inconceivably short time. For it is collision and its absence which take the outward 62 appearance of slowness and quickness. Moreover, it will be said that in compound bodies too one atom is faster than another, though as a matter of fact all are equal in speed: this will be said because even in the least period of continuous time all the atoms in aggregate bodies move towards one place, even though in moments of time perceptible only by thought they do not move towards one place but are constantly jostling one against another, until the continuity

of their movement comes under the ken of sensation. For the addition of opinion with regard to the unseen, that the moments perceptible only by thought will also contain continuity of motion, is not true in such cases; for we must remember that it is what we observe with the senses or grasp with the mind by an apprehension 47ᵇ that is true. Nor must it either be supposed that in moments perceptible only by thought the moving body too passes to the several places to which its component atoms move (for this too is unthinkable, and in that case, when it arrives all together in a sensible period of time from any point that may be in the infinite void, it would not be taking its departure from the place from which we apprehend its motion); for the motion of the whole body will be the outward expression of its internal collisions, even though up to the limits of perception we suppose the speed of its motion not to be retarded by collision. It is of advantage to grasp this first principle as well.

63 Next, referring always to the sensations and the feelings (for in this way you will obtain the most trustworthy ground of belief), you must consider that the soul is a body of fine particles distributed throughout the whole structure, and most resembling wind with a certain admixture of heat, and in some respects like to one of these and in some to the other. There is also the part which is many degrees more advanced even than these in fineness of composition, and for this reason is more capable of feeling in harmony with the rest of the structure as well. Now all this is made manifest by the activities of the soul and the feelings and the readiness of its movements and its processes of thought and by what we lose at the moment of death. Further, you 64 must grasp that the soul possesses the chief cause of sensation: yet it could not have acquired sensation, unless it were in some way enclosed by the rest of the structure. And this in its turn having afforded the soul this cause of sensation acquires itself too a share in this contingent capacity from the soul. Yet it does not acquire all the capacities which the soul possesses: and therefore when the soul is released from the body, the body no longer has sensation. For it

never possessed this power in itself, but used to afford opportunity for it to another existence, brought into being at the same time with itself: and this existence, owing to the power now consummated within itself as a result of motion, used spontaneously to produce for itself the capacity of sensation and then to communicate it to the body as well, in virtue of its contact and 65 correspondence of movement, as I have already said. Therefore, so long as the soul remains in the body, even though some other part of the body be lost, it will never lose sensation; nay more, whatever portions of the soul may perish too, when that which enclosed it is removed either in whole or in part, if the soul continues to exist at all, it will retain sensation. On the other hand the rest of the structure, though it continues to exist either as a whole or in part, does not retain sensation, if it has once lost that sum of atoms, however small it be, which together goes to produce the nature of the soul. Moreover, if the whole structure is dissolved, the soul is dispersed and no longer has the same powers nor performs its movements, so that it 66 does not possess sensation either. For it is impossible to imagine it with sensation, if it is not in this organism and cannot effect these movements, when what encloses and surrounds it is no longer the same as the surroundings in which 67 it now exists and performs these movements. Furthermore, we must clearly comprehend as well, that the incorporeal in the general acceptation of the term is applied to that which could be thought of as such as an independent existence. Now it is impossible to conceive the incorporeal as a separate existence, except the void: and the void can neither act nor be acted upon, but only provides opportunity of motion through itself to bodies. So that those who say that the soul is incorporeal are talking idly. For it would not be able to act or be acted on in any respect, if it were of this nature. But as it is, both 68 these occurrences are clearly distinguished in respect of the soul. Now if one refers all these reasonings about the soul to the standards of feeling and sensation and remembers what was said at the outset, he will see that they are suffi-

ciently embraced in these general formulae to enable him to work out with certainty on this basis the details of the system as well.

Moreover, as regards shape and colour and size and weight and all other things that are predicated of body, as though they were concomitant properties either of all things or of things visible or recognizable through the sensation of these qualities, we must not suppose that they are either independent existences (for it is impossi-69 ble to imagine that), nor that they absolutely do not exist, nor that they are some other kind of incorporeal existence accompanying body, nor that they are material parts of body: rather we should suppose that the whole body in its totality owes its own permanent existence to all these, yet not in the sense that it is composed of properties brought together to form it (as when, for instance, a larger structure is put together out of the parts which compose it, whether the first units of size or other parts smaller than itself, whatever it is), but only, as I say, that it owes its own permanent existence to all of them. All these properties have their own peculiar means of being perceived and distinguished, provided always that the aggregate body goes along with them and is never wrested from them, but in virtue of its comprehension as an aggregate of qualities acquires the predicate of body.

70   Furthermore, there often happen to bodies and yet do not permanently accompany them (accidents, of which we must suppose neither that they do not exist at all nor that they have the nature of a whole body), nor that they can be classed among unseen things nor as incorporeal. So that when according to the most general usage we employ this name, we make it clear that accidents have neither the nature of the whole, which we comprehend in its aggregate and call body, nor that of the qualities which permanently accompany it, without which a given body cannot be conceived. But as the result of certain acts of apprehension, provided the aggre-71 gate body goes along with them, they might each be given this name, but only on occasions when each one of them is seen to occur, since accidents are not permanent accompaniments. And we

must not banish this clear vision from the realm of existence, because it does not possess the nature of the whole to which it is joined nor that of the permanent accompaniments, nor must we suppose that such contingencies exist independently (for this is inconceivable both with regard to them and to the permanent properties), but, just as it appears in sensation, we must think of them all as accidents occurring to bodies, and that not as permanent accompaniments, or again as having in themselves a place in the ranks of material existence; rather they are seen to be just what our actual sensation shows their proper character to be.

72 Moreover, you must firmly grasp this point as well; we must not look for time, as we do for all other things which we look for in an object, by referring them to the general conceptions which we perceive in our own minds, but we must take the direct intuition, in accordance with which we speak of 'a long time' or 'a short time', and examine it, applying our intuition to time as we do to other things. Neither must we search for expressions as likely to be better, but employ just those which are in common use about it. Nor again must we predicate of time anything else as having the same essential nature as this special perception, as some people do, but we must turn our thoughts particularly to that only with which 73 we associate this peculiar perception and by which we measure it. For indeed this requires no demonstration, but only reflection, to show that it is with days and nights and their divisions that we associate it, and likewise also with internal feelings or absence of feeling, and with movements and states of rest; in connexion with these last again we think of this very perception as a peculiar kind of accident, and in virtue of this we call it time.

And in addition to what we have already said we must believe that worlds, and indeed every limited compound body which continuously exhibits a similar appearance to the things we see, were created from the infinite, and that all such things, greater and less alike, were separated off from individual agglomerations of matter; and that all are again dissolved, some more

quickly, some more slowly, some suffering from 74 one set of causes, others from another. And further we must believe that these worlds were neither (created) all of necessity with one configuration (nor yet with every kind of shape. Furthermore, we must believe that in all worlds there are living creatures and plants and other things we see in this world;) for indeed no one could prove that in a world of one kind there might or might not have been included the kinds of seeds from which living things and plants and all the rest of the things we see are composed, and that in a world of another kind they could not have been.

75 Moreover, we must suppose that human nature too was taught and constrained to do many things of every kind merely by circumstances; and that later on reasoning elaborated what had been suggested by nature and made further inventions, in some matters quickly, in others slowly, at some epochs and times (making great advances), and lesser again at others. And so names too were not at first deliberately given to things, but men's natures according to their different nationalities had their own peculiar feelings and received their peculiar impressions, and so each in their own way emitted air formed into shape by each of these feelings and impressions, according to the differences made in the 76 different nations by the places of their abode as well. And then later on by common consent in each nationality special names were deliberately given in order to make their meanings less ambiguous to one another and more briefly demonstrated. And sometimes those who were acquainted with them brought in things hitherto unknown and introduced sounds for them, on some occasions being naturally constrained to utter them, and on others choosing them by reasoning in accordance with the prevailing mode of formation, and thus making their meaning clear.

Furthermore, the motions of the heavenly bodies and their turnings and eclipses and risings and settings, and kindred phenomena to these, must not be thought to be due to any being who 77 controls and ordains or has ordained them and at the same time enjoys perfect bliss together with immortality (for trouble and care and anger and kindness are not consistent with a life of blessedness, but these things come to pass where there is weakness and fear and dependence on neighbours). Nor again must we believe that they, which are but fire agglomerated in a mass, possess blessedness, and voluntarily take upon themselves these movements. But we must preserve their full majestic significance in all expressions which we apply to such conceptions, in order that there may not arise out of them opinions contrary to this notion of majesty. Otherwise this very contradiction will cause the greatest disturbance in men's souls. Therefore we must believe that it is due to the original inclusion of matter in such agglomerations during the birth-process 78 of the world that this law of regular succession is also brought about.

Furthermore, we must believe that to discover accurately the cause of the most essential facts is the function of the science of nature, and that blessedness for us in the knowledge of celestial phenomena lies in this and in the understanding of the nature of the existences seen in these celestial phenomena, and of all else that is akin to the exact knowledge requisite for our happiness: in knowing too that what occurs in several ways or is capable of being otherwise has no place here, but that nothing which suggests doubt or alarm can be included at all in that which is naturally immortal and blessed. Now 79 this we can ascertain by our mind is absolutely the case. But what falls within the investigation of risings and settings and turnings and eclipses, and all that is akin to this, is no longer of any value for the happiness which knowledge brings, but persons who have perceived all this, but yet do not know what are the natures of these things and what are the essential causes, are still in fear, just as if they did not know these things at all: indeed, their fear may be even greater, since the wonder which arises out of the observation of these things cannot discover any solution or realize the regulation of the essentials. And for this very reason, even if we discover several causes for turnings and settings and risings and eclipses and

80 the like, as has been the case already in our investigation of detail, we must not suppose that our inquiry into these things has not reached sufficient accuracy to contribute to our peace of mind and happiness. So we must carefully consider in how many ways a similar phenomenon is produced on earth, when we reason about the causes of celestial phenomena and all that is imperceptible to the senses; and we must despise those persons who do not recognize either what exists or comes into being in one way only, or that which may occur in several ways in the case of things which can only be seen by us from a distance, and further are not aware under what conditions it is impossible to have peace of mind. If, therefore, we think that a phenomenon probably occurs in some such particular way, and that in circumstances under which it is equally possible for us to be at peace, when we realize that it may occur in several ways, we shall be just as little disturbed as if we know that it occurs in some such particular way.

81 And besides all these matters in general we must grasp this point, that the principal disturbance in the minds of men arises because they think that these celestial bodies are blessed and immortal, and yet have wills and actions and motives inconsistent with these attributes; and because they are always expecting or imagining some everlasting misery, such as is depicted in legends, or even fear the loss of feeling in death as though it would concern them themselves; and, again, because they are brought to this pass not by reasoned opinion, but rather by some irrational presentiment, and therefore, as they do not know the limits of pain, they suffer a disturbance equally great or even more extensive than 82 if they had reached this belief by opinion. But peace of mind is being delivered from all this, and having a constant memory of the general and most essential principles.

Wherefore we must pay attention to internal feelings and to external sensations in general and in particular, according as the subject is general or particular, and to every immediate intuition in accordance with each of the standards of judgement. For if we pay attention to these, we shall rightly trace the causes whence arose our mental disturbance and fear, and, by learning the true causes of celestial phenomena and all other occurrences that come to pass from time to time, we shall free ourselves from all which produces the utmost fear in other men.

83 Here, Herodotus, is my treatise on the chief points concerning the nature of the general principles, abridged so that my account would be easy to grasp with accuracy. I think that, even if one were unable to proceed to all the detailed particulars of the system, he would from this obtain an unrivalled strength compared with other men. For indeed he will clear up for himself many of the detailed points by reference to our general system, and these very principles, if he stores them in his mind, will constantly aid him. For such is their character that even those who are at present engaged in working out the details to a considerable degree, or even completely, will be able to carry out the greater part of their investigations into the nature of the whole by conducting their analysis in reference to such a survey as this. And as for all who are not fully among those on the way to being perfected, some of them can from this summary obtain a hasty view of the most important matters without oral instruction so as to secure peace of mind.

STUDY QUESTIONS: EPICURUS, *LETTER TO HERODOTUS*

1. How does Epicurus argue for the thesis that nothing can come from what is not?
2. What is the universe composed of?
3. Why is the universe unlimited? What does that mean?
4. What characteristics do atoms have?
5. How do atoms form compounds?
6. What does Epicurus say about images?
7. How does one perceive external objects, according to Epicurus?
8. How does he explain falsehood and error?
9. Why can there not be an unlimited number of masses?
10. How does Epicurus explain the fact that compounds move at different speeds?
11. What is the soul?
12. How does the study of physics and nature contribute to the ethical goals of Epicurean teaching?

LETTER TO MENOECEUS

In his *Letter to Menoeceus*, Epicurus asserts that we should always seek pleasure. Although today the term 'Epicurean' is associated with sensual indulgence, Epicurus argues that desire is a major cause of suffering. He claims that the pursuit of pleasure requires prudence, virtue, wisdom, and, above all, tranquility. For this reason, Epicurus argues vigorously against the claim that the gods interfere in worldly events. Such superstitious beliefs cause fear and anxiety. Furthermore, the gods themselves are sublimely happy, and such happiness requires tranquility, which is incompatible with any involvement in the world. Furthermore, he argues that there is no reason for us to fear death because if we are alive, then death is not present, and when death is present, we do not exist. Either way, it is irrelevant.

Epicurus distinguishes two kinds of pleasure, the most valuable of which is simply the absence of mental and physical pain. This he called static pleasure. Pain is a disturbance from our natural state of pleasure, and freedom from such disturbances can be attained only through a state of nearly perfect rest. In contrast, active pleasure, which comes from satisfying one's desires, is less perfect. In sum, pleasure caused by the satisfaction of desire is less perfect than that caused by the absence of desire. There are three types of desires: (1) natural and indispensable, (2) natural and dispensable, and (3) imaginary, which are neither natural nor indispensable. We cannot live without the first. Without the second, we cannot be happy, but we can discard the third, which we should resist because of the disturbance they cause.

122 Let no one when young delay to study philosophy, nor when he is old grow weary of his study. For no one can come too early or too late to secure the health of his soul. And the man who says that the age for philosophy has either not yet come or has gone by is like the man who says that the age for happiness is not yet come to him, or has passed away. Wherefore both when young and old a man must study philosophy, that as he grows old he may be young in blessings through the grateful recollection of what has been, and that in youth he may be old as well, since he will know no fear of what is to come. We must then meditate on the things that make our happiness, seeing that when that is with us we have all, but when it is absent we do all to win it.

123 The things which I used unceasingly to commend to you, these do and practice, considering them to be the first principles of the good life. First of all believe that god is a being immortal and blessed, even as the common idea of a god is engraved on men's minds, and do not assign to him anything alien to his immortality or ill-suited to his blessedness: but believe about him everything that can uphold his blessedness and immortality. For gods there are, since the knowledge of them is by clear vision. But they are not such as the many believe them to be: for indeed they do not consistently represent them as they believe them to be. And the impious man is not he who denies the gods of the many, 124 but he who attaches to the gods the beliefs of the many. For the statements of the many about the gods are not conceptions derived from sensation, but false suppositions, according to

which the greatest misfortunes befall the wicked and the greatest blessings (the good) by the gift of the gods. For men being accustomed always to their own virtues welcome those like themselves, but regard all that is not of their nature as alien.

Become accustomed to the belief that death is nothing to us. For all good and evil consists in sensation, but death is deprivation of sensation. And therefore a right understanding that death is nothing to us makes the mortality of life enjoyable, not because it adds to it an infinite span of time, but because it takes away the crav- 125 ing for immortality. For there is nothing terrible in life for the man who has truly comprehended that there is nothing terrible in not living. So that the man speaks but idly who says that he fears death not because it will be painful when it comes, but because it is painful in anticipation. For that which gives no trouble when it comes, is but an empty pain in anticipation. So death, the most terrifying of ills, is nothing to us, since so long as we exist, death is not with us; but when death comes, then we do not exist. It does not then concern either the living or the dead, since for the former it is not, and the latter are no more.

But the many at one moment shun death as the greatest of evils, at another (yearn for it) as a 126 respite from the (evils) in life. (But the wise man neither seeks to escape life) nor fears the cessation of life, for neither does life offend him nor does the absence of life seem to be any evil. And just as with food he does not seek simply the larger share and nothing else, but rather the most

From *Epicurus—The Extant Remains*, translated by Cyril Bailey, 1926. Reprinted by permission of Oxford University Press.

pleasant, so he seeks to enjoy not the longest period of time, but the most pleasant.

And he who counsels the young man to live well, but the old man to make a good end, is foolish, not merely because of the desirability of life, but also because it is the same training which teaches to live well and to die well. Yet much worse still is the man who says it is good not to be born, but

127 'once born make haste to pass the gates of Death'. For if he says this from conviction why does he not pass away out of life? For it is open to him to do so, if he had firmly made up his mind to this. But if he speaks in jest, his words are idle among men who cannot receive them.

We must then bear in mind that the future is neither ours, nor yet wholly not ours, so that we may not altogether expect it as sure to come, nor abandon hope of it, as if it will certainly not come.

We must consider that of desires some are natural, others vain, and of the natural some are necessary and others merely natural; and of the necessary some are necessary for happiness, oth-

128 ers for the repose of the body, and others for very life. The right understanding of these facts enables us to refer all choice and avoidance to the health of the body and (the soul's) freedom from disturbance, since this is the aim of the life of blessedness. For it is to obtain this end that we always act, namely, to avoid pain and fear. And when this is once secured for us, all the tempest of the soul is dispersed, since the living creature has not to wander as though in search of something that is missing, and to look for some other thing by which he can fulfil the good of the soul and the good of the body. For it is then that we have need of pleasure, when we feel pain owing to the absence of pleasure; (but when we do not feel pain), we no longer need pleasure. And for this cause we call pleasure the

129 beginning and end of the blessed life. For we recognize pleasure as the first good innate in us, and from pleasure we begin every act of choice and avoidance, and to pleasure we return again,

using the feeling as the standard by which we judge every good.

And since pleasure is the first good and natural to us, for this very reason we do not choose every pleasure, but sometimes we pass over many pleasures, when greater discomfort accrues to us as the result of them: and similarly we think many pains better than pleasures, since a greater pleasure comes to us when we have endured pains for a long time. Every pleasure then because of its natural kinship to us is good, yet

130 not every pleasure is to be chosen: even as every pain also is an evil, yet not all are always of a nature to be avoided. Yet by a scale of comparison and by the consideration of advantages and disadvantages we must form our judgement on all these matters. For the good on certain occasions we treat as bad, and conversely the bad as good.

And again independence of desire we think a great good—not that we may at all times enjoy but a few things, but that, if we do not possess many, we may enjoy the few in the genuine persuasion that those have the sweetest pleasure in luxury who least need it, and that all that is natural is easy to be obtained, but that which is superfluous is hard. And so plain savours bring us a

131 pleasure equal to a luxurious diet, when all the pain due to want is removed; and bread and water produce the highest pleasure, when one who needs them puts them to his lips. To grow accustomed therefore to simple and not luxurious diet gives us health to the full, and makes a man alert for the needful employments of life, and when after long intervals we approach luxuries disposes us better towards them, and fits us to be fearless of fortune.

When, therefore, we maintain that pleasure is the end, we do not mean the pleasures of profligates and those that consist in sensuality, as is supposed by some who are either ignorant or disagree with us or do not understand, but freedom from pain in the body and from trouble in the

132 mind. For it is not continuous drinkings and revellings, nor the satisfaction of lusts, nor the enjoyment of fish and other luxuries of the wealthy table, which produce a pleasant life, but sober reasoning, searching out the motives for all

choice and avoidance, and banishing mere opinions, to which are due the greatest disturbance of the spirit.

Of all this the beginning and the greatest good is prudence. Wherefore prudence is a more precious thing even than philosophy: for from prudence are sprung all the other virtues, and it teaches us that it is not possible to live pleasantly without living prudently and honourably and justly, (nor, again, to live a life of prudence, honour, and justice) without living pleasantly. For the virtues are by nature bound up with the 133 pleasant life, and the pleasant life is inseparable from them. For indeed who, think you, is a better man than he who holds reverent opinions concerning the gods, and is at all times free from fear of death, and has reasoned out the end ordained by nature? He understands that the limit of good things is easy to fulfil and easy to attain, whereas the course of ills is either short in time or slight in pain: he laughs at (destiny), whom some have introduced as the mistress of all things. (He thinks that with us lies the chief power in determining events, some of which happen by necessity) and some by chance, and some are within our control; for while necessity cannot be called to account, he sees that chance is inconstant, but

that which is in our control is subject to no master, and to it are naturally attached praise and 134 blame. For, indeed, it were better to follow the myths about the gods than to become a slave to the destiny of the natural philosophers: for the former suggests a hope of placating the gods by worship, whereas the latter involves a necessity which knows no placation. As to chance, he does not regard it as a god as most men do (for in a god's acts there is no disorder), nor as an uncertain cause (of all things): for he does not believe that good and evil are given by chance to man for the framing of a blessed life, but that opportu- 135 nities for great good and great evil are afforded by it. He therefore thinks it better to be unfortunate in reasonable action than to prosper in unreason. For it is better in a man's actions that what is well chosen (should fail, rather than that what is ill chosen) should be successful owing to chance.

Meditate therefore on these things and things akin to them night and day by yourself, and with a companion like to yourself, and never shall you be disturbed waking or asleep, but you shall live like a god among men. For a man who lives among immortal blessings is not like to a mortal being.

STUDY QUESTIONS: EPICURUS, *LETTER TO MENOECEUS*

1. What are the three main branches of Hellenistic philosophy?
2. Why, according to Epicurus, should we always seek pleasure?
3. What are the two different kinds of pleasure? Which is the most valuable, and why?
4. What are the three types of desires? Why can we not live without the first? Why can we not be happy without the second? Why should we discard the third?

PRINCIPAL DOCTRINES

Epicurus' ethical theory is fundamentally different from Plato and Aristotle's. Whereas they regard living in a community as part and parcel of the virtuous life, Epicurus' view is individualistic; ethics is a question of individual pleasure. For this reason, Epicurus regards the basis of a society as a social contract, and he denies that justice is a good in itself. In other words, people do not have a moral obligation to act justly; rather, justice is a question of obeying rules that advance the happiness of all concerned. Rules or laws that satisfy this criterion of usefulness are just, and the wise person will obey them in order to secure tranquility.

The *Principal Doctrines* also make it clear that Epicurus' philosophy is not egoistic despite its individualism. It recognizes the interests of others and extols the virtues and great importance of friendship (XXVII). In another context, Epicurus claims that 'it is more pleasant to confer a benefit than to receive it.'

The *Principal Doctrines* also contains a clear exposition of the three kinds of desire, which were mentioned in the Philosophical Overview (see also section XXIX), as well as a brief outline of his theory of knowledge and its importance for the life of tranquility (XXII–XXV).

139   **I.** The blessed and immortal nature knows no trouble itself nor causes trouble to any other, so that it is never constrained by anger or favour. For all such things exist only in the weak.

II. Death is nothing to us: for that which is dissolved is without sensation; and that which lacks sensation is nothing to us.

III. The limit of quantity in pleasures is the removal of all that is painful. Wherever pleasure is present, as long as it is there, there is neither pain of body nor of mind, nor of both at once.

140   **IV.** Pain does not last continuously in the flesh, but the acutest pain is there for a very short time, and even that which just exceeds the pleasure in the flesh does not continue for many days at once. But chronic illnesses permit a predominance of pleasure over pain in the flesh.

V. It is not possible to live pleasantly without living prudently and honourably and justly, [nor again to live a life of prudence, honour, and justice] without living pleasantly. And the man who does not possess the pleasant life, is not living prudently and honourably and justly, [and the man who does not possess the virtuous life], cannot possibly live pleasantly.

VI. To secure protection from men anything is a natural good, by which you may be able to attain this end.

141   **VII.** Some men wished to become famous and conspicuous, thinking that they would thus win for themselves safety from other men. Wherefore if the life of such men is safe, they have obtained the good which nature craves; but if it is not safe, they do not possess that for which they strove at first by the instinct of nature.

VIII. No pleasure is a bad thing in itself: but the means which produce some pleasures bring with them disturbances many times greater than the pleasures.

142   **IX.** If every pleasure could be intensified so that it lasted and influenced the whole organism or the most essential parts of our nature, pleasures would never differ from one another.

X. If the things that produce the pleasures of profligates could dispel the fears of the mind about the phenomena of the sky and death and its pains, and also teach the limits of desires (and of pains), we should never have cause to blame them; for they would be filling themselves full with pleasures from every source and never have pain of body or mind, which is the evil of life.

XI. If we were not troubled by our suspicions of the phenomena of the sky and about death, fearing that it concerns us, and also by our failure to grasp the limits of pains and desires, we should have no need of natural science.

143   **XII.** A man cannot dispel his fear about the most important matters if he does not know what is the nature of the universe but suspects the truth of some mythical story. So that without natural science it is not possible to attain our pleasures unalloyed.

XIII. There is no profit in securing protection in relation to men, if things above and things beneath the earth and indeed all in the boundless universe remain matters of suspicion.

XIV. The most unalloyed source of protection from men, which is secured to some extent by a certain force of expulsion, is in fact the

From *Epictetus—Encheiridion (Manual)*, translated by W. A. Oldfather. The Loeb Classic Library, 1928.

immunity which results from a quiet life and the retirement from the world.

144   **XV.** The wealth demanded by nature is both limited and easily procured; that demanded by idle imaginings stretches on to infinity.

    XVI. In but few things chance hinders a wise man, but the greatest and most important matters reason has ordained and throughout the whole period of life does and will ordain.

    XVII. The just man is most free from trouble, the unjust most full of trouble.

    XVIII. The pleasure in the flesh is not increased, when once the pain due to want is removed, but is only varied: and the limit as regards pleasure in the mind is begotten by the reasoned understanding of these very pleasures and of the emotions akin to them, which used to cause the greatest fear to the mind.

145   **XIX.** Infinite time contains no greater pleasure than limited time, if one measures by reason the limits of pleasure.

    XX. The flesh perceives the limits of pleasure as unlimited and unlimited time is required to supply it. But the mind, having attained a reasoned understanding of the ultimate good of the flesh and its limits and having dissipated the fears concerning the time to come, supplies us with the complete life, and we have no further need of infinite time; but neither does the mind shun pleasure, nor, when circumstances begin to bring about the departure from life, does it approach its end as though it fell short in any way of the best life.

146   **XXI.** He who has learned the limits of life knows that that which removes the pain due to want and makes the whole of life complete is easy to obtain; so that there is no need of actions which involve competition.

    XXII. We must consider both the real purpose and all the evidence of direct perception, to which we always refer the conclusions of opinion; otherwise, all will be full of doubt and confusion.

    XXIII. If you fight against all sensations, you will have no standard by which to judge even those of them which you say are false.

147   **XXIV.** If you reject any single sensation and fail to distinguish between the conclusion of opinion as to the appearance awaiting confirma-

tion and that which is actually given by the sensation or feeling, or each intuitive apprehension of the mind, you will confound all other sensations as well with the same groundless opinion, so that you will reject every standard of judgement. And if among the mental images created by your opinion you affirm both that which awaits confirmation and that which does not, you will not escape error, since you will have preserved the whole cause of doubt in every judgement between what is right and what is wrong.

148   **XXV.** If on each occasion instead of referring your actions to the end of nature, you turn to some other nearer standard when you are making a choice or an avoidance, your actions will not be consistent with your principles.

    XXVI. Of desires, all that do not lead to a sense of pain, if they are not satisfied, are not necessary, but involve a craving which is easily dispelled, when the object is hard to procure or they seem likely to produce harm.

    XXVII. Of all the things which wisdom acquires to produce the blessedness of the complete life, far the greatest is the possession of friendship.

    XXVIII. The same conviction which has given us confidence that there is nothing terrible that lasts for ever or even for long, has also seen the protection of friendship most fully completed in the limited evils of this life.

149   **XXIX.** Among desires some are natural (and necessary, some natural) but not necessary, and others neither natural nor necessary, but due to idle imagination.

    XXX. Wherever in the case of desires which are physical, but do not lead to a sense of pain, if they are not fulfilled, the effort is intense, such pleasures are due to idle imagination, and it is not owing to their own nature that they fail to be dispelled, but owing to the empty imaginings of the man.

150   **XXXI.** The justice which arises from nature is a pledge of mutual advantage to restrain men from harming one another and save them from being harmed.

    XXXII. For all living things which have not been able to make compacts not to harm one another or be harmed, nothing ever is either just or unjust; and likewise too for all tribes of men which have been unable or unwilling to make compacts not to harm or be harmed.

XXXIII. Justice never is anything in itself, but in the dealings of men with one another in any place whatever and at any time it is a kind of compact not to harm or be harmed.

151   **XXXIV.** Injustice is not an evil in itself, but only in consequence of the fear which attaches to the apprehension of being unable to escape those appointed to punish such actions.

XXXV. It is not possible for one who acts in secret contravention of the terms of the compact not to harm or be harmed, to be confident that he will escape detection, even if at present he escapes a thousand times. For up to the time of death it cannot be certain that he will indeed escape.

XXXVI. In its general aspect justice is the same for all, for it is a kind of mutual advantage in the dealings of men with one another: but with reference to the individual peculiarities of a country or any other circumstances the same thing does not turn out to be just for all.

152   **XXXVII.** Among actions which are sanctioned as just by law, that which is proved on examination to be of advantage in the requirements of men's dealings with one another, has the guarantee of justice, whether it is the same for all or not. But if a man makes a law and it does not turn out to lead to advantage in men's dealings with each other, then it no longer has the essen-

tial nature of justice. And even if the advantage in the matter of justice shifts from one side to the other, but for a while accords with the general concept, it is none the less just for that period in the eyes of those who do not confound themselves with empty sounds but look to the actual facts.

153   **XXXVIII.** Where, provided the circumstances have not been altered, actions which were considered just, have been shown not to accord with the general concept in actual practice, then they are not just. But where, when circumstances have changed, the same actions which were sanctioned as just no longer lead to advantage, there they were just at the time when they were of advantage for the dealings of fellow-citizens with one another; but subsequently they are no longer just, when no longer of advantage.

154   **XXXIX.** The man who has best ordered the element of disquiet arising from external circumstances has made those things that he could akin to himself and the rest at least not alien: but with all to which he could not do even this, he has refrained from mixing, and has expelled from his life all which it was of advantage to treat thus.

XL. As many as possess the power to procure complete immunity from their neighbours, these also live most pleasantly with one another, since they have the most certain pledge of security, and after they have enjoyed the fullest intimacy, they do not lament the previous departure of a dead friend, as though he were to be pitied.

STUDY QUESTIONS: EPICURUS, *PRINCIPAL DOCTRINES*

1. Why does Epicurus think that death is nothing to us? Is this a reasonable claim?
2. According to Epicurus, what is required to live pleasantly?
3. Why is justice required to live a pleasant life? How does Epicurus define justice? Would Plato agree with Epicurus' claim about justice?
4. What is required to dispel fear?
5. What is Epicurus' main claim about desires?

LUCRETIUS (99–55 B.C.)

Biographical History

Titus Lucretius Carus, the great Latin poet, is the most famous Epicurean. Little is known of his life except that he came from a wealthy Roman family, and that he may have committed suicide as the result of insanity due to the consumption of a love potion. The main aim of his poem *De Rerum Natura* (*On the Nature of Things*), which is divided into six books, is to liberate people from superstitious fears of the gods and of death, and thereby help them to attain peace of mind. Such liberation requires a proper understanding of nature.

Philosophical Overview

Book I is devoted to explaining how the boundless universe consists of only indestructible atoms and void. Book II explains how the motion of these atoms constitutes the world and its observable qualities, such as color, heat, and smell. In Book III, Lucretius argues that the human soul is composed of matter and that the fear of death is irrational because death itself is not bad. Since one's nonexistence prior to birth is not bad, neither is nonexistence after death. Book IV advocates an Epicurean view of knowledge as sense-perception. Visual images consist of thin films emanating from the surfaces of objects. Book V contains Lucretius' view of the origin of the earth and of the development of species and human institutions. These provide an alternative account of history to those advanced by Plato. The sixth book, which shows signs of being unfinished, discusses a wide range of topics, such as the nature of thunder, magnets, and volcanoes.

ON THE NATURE OF THINGS

Lucretius' poem is the most complete statement of Epicurean philosophy and probably reflects well the thought of Epicurus himself despite the gap of over 200 years. Lucretius dedicates Book III of his verse to explaining the nature of mind and spirit, and to dispelling the fear of Acheron, or Death, which troubles the life of man so deeply. Lucretius argues that the mind, or intelligence, is focused in the chest because this is where we feel fear and joy. The rest of the spirit is suffused throughout the whole body, because the whole body can be moved by it. Because it can influence the body, Lucretius argues that the mind must be physical. Because of its great speed in reacting, he concludes that it must be composed of tiny particles. Lucretius turns next to reasons for believing that the spirit or mind is mortal. Finally, he explains how this mortality should liberate us from the fear of death, contrary to what many suppose. Our nonexistence prior to birth is not a cause of distress. Consequently, one has no reason to fear nonexistence after life.

BOOK I

46–99 I will essay to discourse to you of the most high system of heaven and the gods and will open up the first beginnings of things, out of which nature gives birth to all things and increase and nourishment, and into which nature likewise dissolves them back after their destruction. These we are accustomed in explaining their reason to call matter and begetting bodies of things and to name seeds of things and also to term first bodies, because from them as first elements all things are.

When human life to view lay foully prostrate upon earth crushed down under the weight of religion, who showed her head from the quarters of heaven with hideous aspect lowering upon mortals, a man of Greece ventured first to lift up his mortal eyes to her face and first to withstand her to her face. Him neither story of gods nor thunderbolts nor heaven with threatening roar could quell: they only chafed the more the eager courage of his soul, filling him with desire to be the first to burst the fast bars of nature's portals. Therefore the living force of his soul gained the day: on he passed far beyond the flaming walls of the world and traversed throughout in mind and spirit the immeasurable universe; whence he returns a conqueror to tell us what can, what cannot come into being; in short on what principle each thing has its powers defined, its deepest boundary mark. Therefore religion is put under foot and trampled upon in turn; us his victory brings level with heaven.

This is what I fear herein, lest haply you should fancy that you are entering on unholy grounds of reason and treading the path of sin; whereas on the contrary often and often that very religion has given birth to sinful and unholy deeds.

99–154   This terror then and darkness of mind must be dispelled not by the rays of the sun and glittering shafts of day, but by the aspect and the law of nature; the warp of whose design we shall begin with this first principle, nothing is ever gotten out of nothing by divine power. Fear in sooth holds so in check all mortals, because they see many operations go on in earth and heaven, the causes of which they can in no way understand, believing them therefore to be done by power 154-205 divine. For these reasons when we shall have seen that nothing can be produced from nothing, we shall then more correctly ascertain that which we are seeking, both the elements out of which every thing can be produced and the manner in which all things are done without the hand of the gods.

If things came from nothing, any kind might be born of any thing, nothing would require seed. Men for instance might rise out of the sea, the scaly race out of the earth, and birds might burst out of the sky; horned and other herds, every kind of wild beasts would haunt with changing brood tilth and wilderness alike. Nor would the same fruits keep constant to trees, but would change; any tree might bear any fruit. For if there were not begetting bodies for each, how could things have a fixed unvarying mother? But in fact because things are all produced from fixed seeds, each thing is born and goes forth into the borders of light out of that in which resides its matter and first bodies; and for this reason all things cannot be gotten out of all

things, because in particular things resides a distinct power. . . .

187-207   No nor would time be required for the growth of things after the meeting of the seed, if they could increase out of nothing. Little babies would at once grow into men and trees in a moment would rise and spring out of the ground. But none of these events it is plain ever comes to pass, since all things grow step by step at a fixed time, as is natural, since they all grow from a fixed seed and in growing preserve their kind; so that you may be sure that all things increase in size and are fed out of their own matter. Furthermore without fixed seasons of rain the earth is unable to put forth its gladdening produce, nor again if kept from food could the nature of living things continue its kind and sustain life; so that you may hold with greater truth that many bodies are common to many things, as we see letters common to different words, than that any thing could come into being without first-beginnings. Again why could not nature have produced men of such a size and strength as to be able to wade on foot across the sea and rend great mountains with their hands and outlive many generations of living men, if not because an unchanging matter has been assigned for begetting things and what can arise out of this matter is fixed? We must admit therefore that nothing can come from nothing, since things require seed before they can severally be born and be brought out into the buxom fields of air. . . .

219-227   Moreover nature dissolves every thing back into its first bodies and does not annihilate things. For if aught were mortal in all its parts alike, the thing in a moment would be snatched away to destruction from before our eyes; since no force would be needed to produce disruption among its parts and undo their fastenings. Whereas in fact, as all things consist of an imperishable seed, nature suffers the destruction of nothing to be seen, until a force has encountered it sufficient to dash things to pieces by a blow or to pierce through the void places within them and break them up. . . .

247-251   But in fact, because the fastenings of first-beginnings one with the other are unlike and matter is everlasting, things continue with body uninjured, until a force is found to encounter them strong enough to overpower the texture of each. A thing therefore never returns to nothing, but all things after disruption go back into the first bodies of matter. . . .

265–269   Now mark me: since I have taught that things cannot be born from nothing, cannot when begotten be brought back to nothing, that you may not haply yet begin in any shape to mistrust my words, because the first-beginnings of things cannot be seen by the eyes. . . .

319–341   Lastly the bodies which time and nature add to things by little and little, constraining them to grow in due measure, no exertion of the eyesight can behold; and so too wherever things grow old by age and decay, and when rocks hanging over the sea are eaten away by the gnawing salt spray, you cannot see what they lose at any given moment. Nature therefore works by unseen bodies.

And yet all things are not on all sides jammed together and kept in by body: there is also void in things. To have learned this will be good for you on many accounts; it will not suffer you to wander in doubt and be to seek in the sum of things and distrustful of our words. If there were not void, things could not move at all; for that which is the property of body, to let and hinder, would be present to all things at all times; nothing therefore could go on, since no other thing would be the first to give way. But in fact throughout seas and lands and the heights of heaven we see before our eyes many things move in many ways for various reasons, which things, if there were no void, I need not say would lack and want restless motion: they never would have been begotten at all since matter jammed on all sides would have been at rest. . . .

418–453   But now to resume the thread of the design which I am weaving in verse: all nature then, as it exists by itself, is founded on two things: there are bodies and there is void in which these bodies are placed and through which they move about. For that body exists by itself the general feeling of mankind declares; and unless at the very first belief in this be firmly grounded, there will be nothing to which we can appeal on hidden things in order to prove anything by reasoning of mind. Then again, if room and space which we call void did not exist, bodies could not be placed anywhere nor move about at all to any side; as we have demonstrated to you a little before. Moreover there is nothing which you can affirm to be at once separate from all body and quite distinct from void, which would so to say count as the discovery of a third nature. For whatever shall exist, this of itself must be something or other. Now if it shall admit of touch in however slight and small a measure, it will, be it with a large or be it with a little addition, provided it do exist, increase the amount of body and join the sum. But if it shall be intangible and unable to hinder any thing from passing through it on any side, this you are to know will be that which we call empty void. Again whatever shall exist by itself, will either do something or will itself suffer by the action of other things, or will be of such a nature as things are able to exist and go on in. But no thing can do and suffer without body, nor aught furnish room except void and vacancy. Therefore beside void and bodies no third nature taken by itself can be left in the number of things, either such as to fall at any time under the ken of our senses or such as any one can grasp by the reason of his mind. . . .

504–527   So universally there is found to be nothing solid in things. But yet because true reason and the nature of things constrains, attend until we make clear in a few verses that there are such things as consist of solid and everlasting body, which we teach are seeds of things and first-beginnings, out of which the whole sum of things which now exists has been produced.

First of all then since there has been found to exist a two-fold and widely dissimilar nature of two things, that is to say of body and of place in which things severally go on, each of the two must exist for and by itself and quite unmixed. For wherever there is empty space which we call void, there body is not; wherever again body maintains itself, there empty void no wise exists. First bodies therefore are solid and without void. Again since there is void in things begotten, solid matter must exist about this void, and no thing can be proved by true reason to conceal in its body and have within it void, unless you choose to allow that that which holds it in is solid. Again that can be nothing but a union of matter which can keep in the void of things. Matter therefore, which consists of a solid body, may be everlasting, though all things else are dissolved. Moreover if there were no empty void, the universe would be solid; unless on the other hand there were certain bodies to fill up whatever places they occupied, the existing universe would be empty and void space. Therefore sure enough body and void are marked off in alternate layers, since the universe is neither of a perfect fullness nor a perfect void. . . .

950–965 But since I have taught that most solid bodies of matter fly about for ever unvanquished through all time, mark now, let us unfold whether there is or is not any limit to their sum; likewise let us clearly see whether that which has been found to be void, or room and space, in which things severally go on, is all of it altogether finite or stretches without limits and to an unfathomable depth.

Well then the existing universe is bounded in none of its dimensions; for then it must have had an outside. Again it is seen that there can be an outside of nothing, unless there be something beyond to bound it, so that that is seen, farther than which the nature of this our sense does not follow the thing. Now since we must admit that there is nothing outside the sum, it has no outside, and therefore is without end and limit. And it matters not in which of its regions you take your stand; so invariably, whatever position any one has taken up, he leaves the universe just as infinite as before in all directions. . . .

990–1006 Again if all the space of the whole sum were enclosed within fixed borders and were bounded, in that case the store of matter by its solid weights would have streamed together from all sides to the lowest point nor could anything have gone on under the canopy of heaven, no nor would there have been a heaven nor sunlight at all, inasmuch as all matter, settling down through infinite time past, would lie together in a heap. But as it is, sure enough no rest is given to the bodies of the first-beginnings because there is no lowest point at all, to which they might stream together as it were, and where they might take up

their positions. All things are ever going on in ceaseless motion on all sides and bodies of matter stirred to action are supplied from beneath out of infinite space. Therefore the nature of room and the space of the unfathomable void are such as bright thunderbolts cannot race through in their course though gliding on through endless tract of time, no nor lessen one jot the journey that remains to go by all their travel: so huge a room is spread out on all sides for things without any bounds in all directions round. . . .

1015–1039 For verily not by design did the first-beginnings of things station themselves each in its right place guided by keen intelligence, nor did they bargain sooth to say what motions each should assume, but because many in number and shifting about in many ways throughout the universe they are driven and tormented by blows during infinite time past, after trying motions and unions of every kind at length they fall into arrangements such as those out of which this our sum of things has been formed, and by which too it is preserved through many great years when once it has been thrown into the appropriate motions, and causes the streams to replenish the greedy sea with copious river waters and the earth, fostered by the heat of the sun, to renew its produce, and the race of living things to come up and flourish, and the gliding fires of ether to live: all which these several things could in no wise bring to pass, unless a store of matter could rise up from infinite space, out of which store they are wont to make up in due season whatever has been lost. . . .

1079–1088 For there can be no centre where the universe is infinite; no nor, even if there were a centre, could anything take up a position there any more on that account than for some quite different reason be driven away. For all room and space, which we term void, must through centre, through no-centre alike give place to heavy bodies, in whatever directions their motions tend. Nor is there any spot of such a sort that when bodies have reached it, they can lose their force of gravity and stand upon void; and that again which is void must not serve to support anything, but must, as its nature craves, continually give place. Things cannot therefore in such a way be held in union, o'ermastered by love of a centre.

BOOK II

215-263 This point too herein we wish you to apprehend: when bodies are borne downwards sheer through void by their own weights, at quite uncertain times and uncertain spots they push themselves a little from their course: you just and only just can call it a change of inclination. If they were not used to swerve, they would all fall down, like drops of rain, through the deep void, and no clashing would have been begotten nor blow produced among the first-beginnings: thus nature never would have produced aught.

But if haply any one believes that heavier bodies, as they are carried more quickly sheer through space, can fall from above on the lighter and so beget blows able to produce begetting motions, he goes most widely astray from true reason. For whenever bodies fall through water and thin air, they must quicken their descents in proportion to their weights, because the body of water and subtle nature of air cannot retard everything in equal degree, but more readily give way, overpowered by the heavier: on the other hand empty void cannot offer resistance to anything in any direction at any time, but must, as its nature craves, continually give way; and for this reason all things must be moved and borne along with equal velocity though of unequal weights through the unresisting void. Therefore heavier things will never be able to fall from above on lighter nor of themselves to beget blows sufficient to produce the varied motions by which nature carries on things. Wherefore again and again I say bodies must swerve a little; and yet not more than the least possible; lest we be found to be imagining oblique motions and this the reality should refute. For this we see to be plain and evident, that weights, so far as in them is, cannot travel obliquely, when they fall from above, at least so far as you can perceive; but that nothing swerves in any case from the straight course, who is there that can perceive?

Again if all motion is ever linked together and a new motion ever springs from another in a fixed order and first-beginnings do not by swerving make some commencement of motion to break through the decrees of fate, that cause follow not cause from everlasting, whence have all living creatures here on earth, whence, I ask, has been wrested from the fates the power by which we go forward whither the will leads each, by which likewise we change the direction of our motions neither at a fixed time nor fixed place; but when and where the mind itself has prompted? For beyond a doubt in these things his own will makes for each a beginning and from this beginning motions are welled through the limbs. . . .

286-294 Wherefore in seeds too you must admit the same, admit that besides blows and weights there is another cause of motions, from which this power of free action has been begotten in us, since we see that nothing can come from nothing. For weight forbids that all things be done by blows through as it were an outward force; but that the mind itself does not feel an internal necessity in all its actions and is not as it were overmastered and compelled to bear and put up with this, is caused by a minute swerving of first-beginnings at no fixed part of space and no fixed time.

BOOK III

34-41 And now since I have shown what-like the beginnings of all things are and how diverse with varied shapes as they fly spontaneously driven on in everlasting motion, and how all things can be severally produced out of these, next after these questions the nature of the mind and soul should methinks be cleared up by my verses and that dread of Acheron be driven headlong forth, troubling as it does the life of man from its inmost depths and overspreading all things with the blackness of death, allowing no pleasure to be pure and unalloyed. . . .

91-107 This terror therefore and darkness of mind must be dispelled not by the rays of the sun and glittering shafts of day, but by the aspect and law of nature.

First then I say that the mind which we often call the understanding, in which dwells the directing and governing principle of life, is no less part of the man, than hand and foot and eyes are parts of the whole living creature. Some however affirm that the sense of the mind does not dwell in a distinct part, but is a certain vital state of the body, which the Greeks call harmonia, because by it, they say, we live with sense, though the understanding is in no one part; just as when good health is said to belong to the body, though yet it is not any one part of the man in health. In this way they do not assign a distinct part to the sense of the mind; in all which they appear to me to be grievously at fault in

115-124 more ways than one.... Now that you may know that the soul as well is in the limbs and that the body is not wont to have sense by any harmony, this is a main proof: when much of the body has been taken away, still life often stays in the limbs; and yet the same life, when a few bodies of heat have been dispersed abroad and some air has been forced out through the mouth, abandons at once the veins and quits the bones: by this you may perceive that all bodies have not functions of like importance nor alike uphold existence, but rather that those seeds which constitute wind and heat, cause life to stay in the limbs. Therefore vital heat and wind are within the body and abandon our frame at death....

138-147 Now I assert that the mind and the soul are kept together in close union and make up a single nature, but that the directing principle which we call mind and understanding, is the head so to speak and reigns paramount in the whole body. It has a fixed seat in the middle region of the breast: here throb fear and apprehension, about these spots dwell soothing joys; therefore here is the understanding or mind. All the rest of the soul disseminated through the whole body obeys and moves at the will and inclination of the mind. It by itself alone knows for itself, rejoices for itself, at times when the impression does not move either soul or body together with it....

160-166 This same principle teaches that the nature of the mind and soul is bodily; for when it is seen to push the limbs, rouse the body from sleep, and alter the countenance and guide and turn about the whole man, and when we see that none of these effects can take place without touch nor touch without body, must we not admit that the mind and the soul are of a bodily nature?...

281-291 I will now go on to explain in my verses of what kind of body the mind consists and out of what it is formed. First of all I say that it is extremely fine and formed of exceedingly minute bodies. That this is so you may, if you please to attend, clearly perceive from what follows: nothing that is seen takes place with a velocity equal to that of the mind when it starts some suggestion and actually sets it agoing; the mind therefore is stirred with greater rapidity than any of the things whose nature stands out visible to sight. But that which is so passing nimble, must consist of seeds exceedingly round and exceedingly minute, in order to be stirred and set in motion by a small moving power.

236-251 We are not however to suppose that this nature is single. For a certain subtle spirit mixed with heat quits men at death, and then the heat draws air along with it; there being no heat which has not air too mixed with it: for since its nature is rare, many first-beginnings of air must move about through it. Thus the nature of the mind is proved to be threefold; and yet these things all together are not sufficient to produce sense; since the fact of the case does not admit that any of these can produce sense-giving motions and the thoughts which a man turns over in mind. Thus some fourth nature too must be added to these: it is altogether without name; than it nothing exists more nimble or more fine, or of smaller of smoother elements: it first transmits the sense giving motions through the frame; for it is first stirred, made up as it is of small particles; next the heat and the unseen force of the spirit receive the motions, then the air; then all things are set in action, the blood is stirred, every part of the flesh is filled with sensation; last of all the feeling is transmitted to the bones and marrow, whether it be one of pleasure or an opposite excitement....

257-291 Now though I would fain explain in what way these are mixed up together, by what means united, when they exert their powers, the poverty of my native speech deters me sorely against my will: yet will I touch upon them and in summary fashion to the best of my ability: the first-beginnings by their mutual motions are interlaced in such a way that none of them can be separated by itself, nor can the function of any go on divided from the rest by any interval; but they are so to say the several powers of one body. Even so in any flesh of living creature you please without exception there is smell and some colour and a savour, and yet out of all these is made up one single bulk of body. Thus the heat and the air and the unseen power of the spirit mixed together produce a single nature, together with that nimble force which transmits to them from itself the origin of motion; by which means sense-giving motion first takes its rise through the fleshly frame. For this nature lurks secreted in its inmost depths, and nothing in our body is farther beneath all ken than it, and more than this it is the very soul of the whole soul. Just in the same way as the power of the mind and the function of the soul are latent in our limbs and throughout our body, because they are each formed of small and few bodies: even so, you are to know, this nameless power made of minute bodies is concealed and is moreover the very soul so to say of the whole soul, and reigns supreme in the whole body. On a like principle the spirit and air and heat must, as they exert their powers, be mixed up together through the frame, and one must ever be more out of view or more prominent than another, that a single substance may be seen to be formed from the union of all, lest the heat and spirit apart by themselves and the power of the air apart by itself should destroy sense and dissipate it by their disunion. . . .

416-423 Now mark me: that you may know that the minds and light souls of living creatures have birth and are mortal, I will go on to set forth verses worthy of your attention, got together by long study and invented with welcome effort. Do you mind to link to one name both of them alike, and when for instance I shall choose to

speak of the soul, showing it to be mortal, believe that I speak of the mind as well, inasmuch as both make up one thing and are one united substance. . . .

530-535 Again we often see a man pass gradually away and limb by limb lose vital sense; first the toes of his feet and the nails turn livid, then the feet and shanks die, then next the steps of chilly death creep with slow pace over the other members. Therefore since the nature of the soul is rent and passes away and does not at one time stand forth in its entireness, it must be reckoned mortal. . . .

620-628 Again if the nature of the soul is immortal and can feel when separated from our body, methinks we must suppose it to be provided with five senses; and in no other way can we picture to ourselves souls below flitting about Acheron. Painters therefore and former generations of writers have thus represented souls provided with senses. But neither eyes nor nose nor hand can exist for the soul apart from the body nor can tongue, nor can ears perceive by the sense of hearing or exist for the soul by themselves apart from the body. . . .

667-674 Again if the nature of the soul is immortal and makes its way into our body at the time of birth, why are we unable to remember besides the time already gone, and why do we retain no traces of past actions? If the power of the mind has been so completely changed, that all remembrance of past things is lost, that methinks differs not widely from death; therefore you must admit that the soul which was before has perished and that which now is has now been formed. . . .

754-773 For the assertion that an immortal soul is altered by a change of body is advanced on a false principle. What is changed is dissolved, and therefore dies: the parts are transposed and quit their former order; therefore they must admit of being dissolved too throughout the frame, in order at last to die one and all together with the body. But if they shall say that souls of men always go into human bodies, I yet will ask how it is a soul can change from wise to foolish, and no child has discretion, and why the mare's foal is not so well trained as the powerful strength of the horse. You may be sure they will fly to the subterfuge that the mind grows weakly in a weakly body. But granting this is so, you must admit the soul to be mortal, since changed so completely throughout the frame it loses its former life and sense. Then too in what way will it be able to grow in strength uniformly with its allotted body and reach the coveted flower of age, unless it shall be its partner at its first beginning? Or what means it by passing out from the limbs when decayed with age? Does it fear to remain shut up in a crumbling body, fear that its tenement, worn out by protracted length of days, bury it in its ruins? Why an immortal being incurs no risks.

831–842   Death therefore to us is nothing, concerns us not a jot, since the nature of the mind is proved to be mortal; and as in time gone by we felt no distress, when the Poeni from all sides came together to do battle, and all things shaken by war's troublous uproar shuddered and quaked beneath high heaven, and mortal men were in doubt which of the two people it should be to whose empire all must fall by sea and land alike, thus when we shall be no more, when there shall have been a separation of body and soul, out of both of which we are each formed into a single being, to us, you may be sure, who then shall be no more, nothing whatever can happen to excite sensation, not if earth shall be mingled with sea and sea with heaven. . . .

844–870   And if time should gather up our matter after our death and put it once more into the position in which it now is, and the light of life be given to us again, this result even would concern us not at all, when the chain of our self-consciousness has once been snapped asunder. So now we give ourselves no concern about any self which we have been before, nor do we feel any distress on the score of that self. For when you look back on the whole past course of immeasurable time and think how manifold are the shapes which the motions of matter take, you

may easily credit this too, that these very same seeds of which we now are formed, have often before been placed in the same order in which they now are; and yet we cannot recover this in memory: a break in our existence has been interposed, and all the motions have wandered to and fro far astray from the sensations they produced. For he whom evil is to befall, must in his own person exist at the very time it comes, if the misery and suffering are haply to have any place at all; but since death precludes this, and forbids him to be, upon whom the ills can be brought, you may be sure that we have nothing to fear after death, and that he who exists not, cannot become miserable, and that it matters not a whit whether he has been born into life at any other time, when immortal death has taken away his mortal life.

918–928   What folly! no one feels the want of himself and life at the time when mind and body are together sunk in sleep; for all we care this sleep might be everlasting, no craving whatever for ourselves then moves us. And yet by no means do those first-beginnings throughout our frame wander at that time far away from their sense-producing motions, at the moment when a man starts up from sleep and collects himself. Death therefore must be thought to concern us much less, if less there can be than what we see to be nothing; for a greater dispersion of the mass of matter follows after death, and no one wakes up, upon whom the chill cessation of life has once come. . . .

972–983   Think too how the bygone antiquity of everlasting time before our birth was nothing to us. Nature therefore holds this up to us as a mirror of the time yet to come after our death. Is there aught in this that looks appalling, aught that wears an aspect of gloom? Is it not more untroubled than any sleep?. . .

    Nor by prolonging life do we take one tittle from the time past in death nor can we fret anything away, whereby we may haply be a less long time in the condition of the dead. Therefore you may complete as many generations as you please during you life; none the less however will that everlasting death await you; and for no less long a time will he be no more in being, who beginning with to-day has ended his life, than the man who has died many months and years ago.

BOOK IV

32–39 And now that I have taught what the nature of the mind is and out of what things it is formed into one quickened being with the body, and how it is dissevered and returns into its first-beginnings, I will attempt to lay before you a truth which most nearly concerns these questions, the existence of things which we call idols of things: these, like films peeled off from the surface of things, fly to and fro through the air. . . .

48–53 I say then that pictures of things and thin shapes are emitted from things off their surface, to which an image serves as a kind of film, or name it if you like a rind, because such image bears an appearance and form like to the thing whatever it is from whose body it is shed and wanders forth. This you may learn however dull of apprehension from what follows. . . .

100–109 Lastly in the case of all idols which show themselves to us in mirrors, in water or any other shining object, since their outsides are possessed of an appearance like to the things they represent, they must be formed of emitted images of things. There are therefore thin shapes and pictures like to the things, which, though no one can see them one at a time, yet when thrown off by constant and repeated reflexion give back a visible image from the surface of mirrors; and in no other way it would seem can they be kept so entire that shapes are given back so exceedingly like each object.

144–159 Now I will proceed to show with what ease and celerity they are begotten and how incessantly they flow and fall away from things. The outermost surface is ever streaming off from things and admits of being discharged: when this reaches some things, it passes through them, glass especially. But when it reaches rough stones or the matter of wood, it is then so torn that it cannot give back any idol. But when objects at once shining and dense have been put in its way, a mirror especially, none of these results has place: it can neither pass through it, like glass, nor can it be torn either; such perfect safety the polished surface minds to ensure. In consequence of this idols stream back to us from such objects; and however suddenly at any moment you place any thing opposite a mirror, an image shows itself: hence you may be sure that thin textures and thin shapes of things incessantly stream from their surface. Therefore many idols are begotten in a short time, so that the birth of such things is with good reason named a rapid one. . . .

469–500 Again if a man believe that nothing is known, he knows not whether this even can be known, since he admits he knows nothing. I will therefore decline to argue the case against him who places himself with head where his feet should be. And yet granting that he knows this, I would still put this question, since he has never yet seen any truth in things, whence he knows what knowing and not knowing severally are, and what it is that has produced the knowledge of the true and the false and what has proved the doubtful to differ from the certain. You will find that from the senses first has proceeded the knowledge of the true and that the senses cannot be refuted. For that which is of itself to be able to refute things false by true things must from the nature of the case be proved to have the higher certainty. Well then what must fairly be accounted of higher certainty than sense? Shall reason founded on false sense be able to contradict them, wholly founded as it is on the senses? And if they are not true, then all reason as well is rendered false. Or shall the ears be able to take the eyes to task, or the touch the ears? Again shall the taste call in question this touch, or the nostrils refute or the eyes controvert it? Not so, I guess; for each apart has its own distinct office, each its own power; and therefore we must perceive what is soft and cold or hot by one distinct faculty, by another perceive the different colours of things and thus see all objects which are conjoined with colour. Taste too has its faculty apart; smells spring from one source, sounds from another. It must follow therefore that any one sense cannot confute any other. No nor can any sense take itself to task, since equal credit must be assigned to it at all times.

STUDY QUESTIONS: LUCRETIUS, ON *THE NATURE OF THINGS*

1. According to Lucretius, what is the relationship between the mind and the body?
2. What reasons does he give in favor of this view?
3. How does Lucretius argue against the idea of immortality?
4. Why should one's death not matter to one, according to Lucretius?

Philosophical Bridges: The Influence of Epicureanism

Like the earlier atomism of Democritus, the materialism of the Epicureans had an important impact on the thinking of the scientific philosophers of the Renaissance. When these ancient texts were rediscovered, materialism was unknown and alien to the Scholastic thinkers of the medieval period; however, it was nourishment for the very early scientific philosophers who were struggling to break free of Scholasticism. For example, the great philosopher rebel Giordano Bruno (1548–1600), who was burned at the stake for his heresy, was inspired by the materialism of the Epicurean Lucretius. Galileo noted that Lucretius had challenged Aristotle's claim that a body falls in proportion to its weight. The very existence of such ancient traditions helped to embolden the early scientific thinkers in their rather solitary attempts to challenge the Scholastic mainstream.

Epicurean thinking reached the zenith of its influence through the French philosopher Pierre Gassendi, who wrote three major works on Epicurus from 1647 to 1649, which were read by Thomas Hobbes, Locke, and Isaac Newton, and which continued to have an important impact up to the French Enlightenment of the late eighteenth century.

STOICISM

PROLOGUE

Around 300 B.C., Zeno of Citium began teaching from a *stoa*, or porch, in the marketplace of Athens and founded the philosophical movement Stoicism, which lasted six centuries. In part, Stoicism can be regarded as a reaction to the popular misunderstanding of Epicureanism as advocating a life of pleasure. However, like Epicurus' philosophy, it too is dedicated almost exclusively to the ethical question 'What is the good life?' The Stoic answer draws on a metaphysical view of the material universe as rationally governed and organized by a divine aspect or element. The good life consists in living virtuously, and, since humans are part of the material universe, this requires following the dictates of nature as reflected in our divine-like reason. It does not consist in the pursuit of pleasure but rather in adapting our own ends to the rational laws of nature. It requires us to follow reason, become free of the passions, and be indifferent to all misfortune.

After his death, Zeno's work was continued by Cleanthes, who lived in ascetic poverty, and also by the learned and prolific Chrysippus, after whom Stoicism spread widely in the ancient world. Stoic views appealed to all classes, from slaves to rulers, and it exerted a great influence upon the Roman Empire; one of its greatest adherents was the Roman Emperor Marcus Aurelius.

The history of Stoicism is divided into three phases: Early, Middle, and Late. The well-known Stoic writings of Marcus Aurelius, Epictetus, and Seneca all come from the later Roman period. No complete Stoic work survives from the Early and Middle periods (i.e., from Zeno and Panaetius [150 B.C.]). Most of our knowledge of these two periods comes secondhand from the reports of later writers, such as Cicero (45 B.C.) and Diogenes Laertius (third century A.D.). In order to provide the reader with an idea of these earlier periods, we have included some selections from these Stoic fragments, as well as the later Stoic writings of Epictetus and Marcus Aurelius.

ZENO OF CITIUM (334–262 B.C.)

Biographical History

Zeno was born in Citium, on the island of Cyprus. In 314 B.C., the young man moved to Athens, possibly to work as a merchant. At the time, the city was still a flourishing philosophical center: Plato's Academy was thriving, and Theophrastus was in charge of the Lyceum, Aristotle's school. There were Pythagorean thinkers and many Cynic philosophers, who claimed to be followers of Socrates. Zeno was attracted to philosophy when, after losing his fortune in a shipwreck, he sat by a bookstall reading the description of Socrates in Xenophon's *Memorabilia*. It is said that he asked to meet someone like Socrates and that, at this moment, Crates, a Cynic, was passing by. Zeno enrolled in Crates' school. He studied there for 14 years, but was also influenced by the ideas of Socrates and Heraclitus. In 300 B.C., Zeno founded his own school, discussing philosophy with students under the porch in the marketplace of Athens. He taught in the Stoa for nearly 40 years. He became famous as the living embodiment of his own teachings, and the Athenian Assembly honored him with a golden crown and statue.

Philosophical Overview

Stoic philosophy has three branches: logic, physics, and ethics. However, these categories should be understood broadly: logic relates to *logos*, or to language, thought, and rationality, and physics pertains to the study of nature. According to the Stoics, the universe is composed of the four elements, earth, water, air, and fire. Fire is the most divine of the four elements, and represents an intelligent, ever-present, guiding force in the universe. It is symbolized as the power of Zeus. The divine element explains the following: the cohesion of the universe as a whole, the organizational structure of things, and, finally, the soul (*psuchê*) of animals as well as the reason (*logos*) of persons. Since this divine element is the organizing power of the whole cosmos, Stoics often identified God with the whole universe, and, because of this, everything that we perceive as separate, including ourselves, is really a part of the organized cosmos as a whole. This conclusion has important ethical implications.

The Stoics understood logic to include all studies of language and reasoning. For instance, they incorporated the practices of both public speaking and discovering truth within their broad conception of rhetoric, thereby bringing the rhetoric of the Sophists closer to Socrates' dialectical method. The Stoics' interest in logic was motivated largely by the idea that the proper use of reason has great ethical importance.

For the Stoics, ethics is the study of the good life. According to Zeno, we humans are part of the cosmos as a whole. Like the macrocosm, the human microcosm is governed by the divine element of fire, or reason. Because of this, the good life consists in living in agreement with nature, which implies following the dictates of reason. In general, something good is beneficial in a lasting way, and the only thing that is beneficial in all circumstances is virtue. Reason guides us to live virtuously by teaching us to adapt our ends to the nature of the world, and this alone can bring happiness that is secure against misfortune. This requires us to cultivate a firm and noble indifference to the many vicissitudes of life. The natural desire for self-preservation includes a commitment to develop our rationality, and, given this, the Stoic conception of ethics is based on the dictates of reason.

The Stoics accepted the Socratic theory of the unity of the virtues, as well as the claim that the virtues are based on knowledge of what is good and bad. They defined the passions as the irrational and excessive movements of the soul. Passions usually cloud our judgment and bring us into conflict with nature and reason. However, this does not mean that the Stoics characterized all feeling as unhealthy; indeed, they claimed that all functions of the soul have both a cognitive and an affective, or emotive, element. However, the truly wise person uses knowledge to achieve independence from both the external world of social and political forces, and the internal world of his or her own passions and emotions.

FRAGMENTS
Zeno

Zeno founded Stoicism in 300 B.C. However, the only remaining full-length Stoic works, such as those of Epictetus and Marcus Aurelius, are from the second century A.D., the later of the three periods of Stoicism. By this time, Stoicism had become largely a set of doctrines and practices akin to a religion. From these later writers, we can appreciate how it was to live and understand the world as a Stoic but not the full range of philosophical concerns of Stoicism. For this reason, we have selected some of the fragments that preserve the ideas of Zeno and other early Stoics. We have organized them into three sections: philosophy and logic, physics, and ethics.

STOICISM LOGIC

1.

They say that philosophical theory [logos] is tripartite. For one part of it concerns nature [i.e., physics], another concerns character [i.e., ethics] and another concerns rational discourse [i.e., logic]. Zeno of Citium first gave this division in his book On Rational Discourse [logos] and so did Chrysippus in book one of On Rational Discourse and book one of his Physics and so did Apollodorus and Syllos in the first books of their respective Introductions to Doctrine; and so too

did Eudromus in his Outline of Ethics; and so too did Diogenes of Babylon and Posidonius. Apollodorus calls these parts 'topics'; Chrysippus and Eudromus call them 'species'; others call them 'kinds'.

(Diogenes Laertius 7.39)

2.

So they include the [study] of canons and criteria in order to discover the truth. For it is in this study that they straighten out the differences among presentations; and similarly [they include] the definitional part for the purpose of recognizing the truth. For objects are grasped by means of conceptions. And rhetorical knowledge is about speaking well in expository speeches, while dialectical knowledge is about conversing correctly in speeches of question and answer form. And that is why they also define it thus, as a knowledge of what is true and false and neither.

(Diogenes Laertius 7.42)

3.

They say that the study of syllogisms is extremely useful; for it indicates what is demonstrative, and this makes a big contribution towards correcting one's opinions; and orderliness and good memory indicate attentive comprehension. And an argument itself is a complex [made up of] premises and a conclusion; and a syllogism is a syllogistic argument [made up] of these. And demonstration is an argument which by means of things more [clearly] grasped concludes to something which is less [clearly] grasped.

(Diogenes Laertius 7.45)

4.

According to Diogenes, a noun is a part of rational discourse which signifies a common quality, for example 'man', 'horse'; a name is a part of rational discourse which reveals an individual quality, for example 'Diogenes', 'Socrates'; a verb as Diogenes says, is a part of rational discourse which signifies an incomposite predicate, or as others [say], it is an undeclined element of rational discourse which signifies something put together with [lit. of] some thing or things, for example 'write', 'speak'; a conjunction is an undeclined part of rational discourse which joins together the parts of rational discourse; an article is a declined element of rational discourse which distinguishes the genders and numbers of names, for example *ho, he, to, hoi, hai, ta*.

(Diogenes Laertius 7.58)

5.

A concept is a phantasm of the intellect, and is neither a something nor a qualified thing, but [rather] a quasi-something and a quasi-qualified thing; for example, there arises an impression of a horse even when no horse is present.

A species is that which is included by a genus, as man is included in animal. The most generic is that which, being a genus, does not have a genus, i.e., being; the most specific is that which, being a species, does not have a species, for example, Socrates.

Division is the cutting of a genus into its immediate species, for example: of animals, some are rational and some are irrational. Counter-division is a division of the genus into a species in virtue of its opposite, as when things are divided by negation, for example: of beings, some are good and some are not good. Subdivision is a division following on a division, for example: of beings some are good and some are not good, and of things not good some are bad and some are indifferent.

(Op. cit 7.61)

6.

And this is what the Stoics are like in logical matters, so that they can maintain that the wise man is always a dialectician. For *everything* is seen through consideration of it in arguments: both what belong to the topic of physics and again what belongs to ethics. For if the logician is supposed to say something about the correct use of terms, how could he fail to say what are the proper names for things? There are two customary facets of the virtue [i.e. dialectic]; one considers what each existent thing is, the other what it is called. And this is what their logic is like.

(Op. cit 83)

STOICISM PHYSICS

7.

They believe that there are two principles of the universe, the active and the passive. The passive, then, is unqualified substance, i.e., matter, while the active is the rational principle [*logos*] in it, i.e., god. For he, being eternal and [penetrating] all of matter, is the craftsman of all things. Zeno of Citium propounds this doctrine in his *On Substance*, Cleanthes in his *On Atoms*, Chrysippus towards the end of book one of his *Physics*, Archedemus in his *On Elements* and Posidonius in book two of his *Account of Physics*. They say that there is a difference between principles and elements. For the former are ungenerated and indestructible, while the elements are destroyed in the [universal] conflagration. And the principles are bodies and without form, while the elements are endowed with form.

(Diogenes Laertius 7.134)

8.

An element is that from which generated things are first generated and that into which they are dissolved in the end. **137.** The four elements together are unqualified substance, i.e., matter; and fire is the hot, water the wet, air the cold, and earth the dry. Nevertheless, there is still in the air the same part. Anyway, fire is the highest, and this is called aither; in this is produced first the sphere of the fixed stars, and then the sphere of the planets. Next comes the air, then the water, and, as the foundation for everything, the earth, which is in the middle of absolutely everything.

(Diogenes Laertius 7.136–37)

9.

[They say] that the cosmos is one, and limited at that, having a spherical shape; for that sort of thing is most fit for movement, as Posidonius, in book five of his *Account of Physics*, and the followers of Antipater, in their treatises on the cosmos, say.

Spread around the outside of it is the unlimited void, which is incorporeal. And the void is what can be occupied by bodies but is not occupied. Inside the cosmos there is no void, but it is [fully] unified. For this is necessitated by the sympathy and common tension of heavenly things in relation to earthly things.

(Op. cit 140)

10.

The cosmos comes into being when substance turns from fire through air to moisture, and then the thick part of it is formed into earth and the thin part is rarefied and this when made even more thin produces fire. Then by a mixing from these are made plants and animals and the rest of the [natural] kinds. Zeno, then, speaks about the generation and destruction in his *On the Universe*.

(Op. cit 142)

11.

God is an animal, immortal, rational, perfect in happiness, immune to everything bad, providentially [looking after] the cosmos and the things in the cosmos; but he is not anthropomorphic. [God] is the craftsman of the universe and as it were a father of all things, both in general and also that part of him which extends through everything; he is called by many names in accordance with its powers. They say

that *Dia* [a grammatical form of the name Zeus] is the one 'because of whom' all things are; they call [god] *Zena* [a grammatical form of the name Zeus] in so far as he is cause of life or because he penetrates life.

(Op. cit 147)

12.

Zeno says that the entire cosmos and the heaven are the substance of god, and so does Chrysippus in book one of his *On Gods* and Posidonius in book one of *On Gods*. And Antipater, in book seven of *On the Cosmos*, says that his substance is airy. Boethus [says] in his *On Nature* that the sphere of the fixed stars is the substance of god.

(Op. cit 148)

13.

They say that primary matter is the substance of all things which exist, as Chrysippus says in book one of his *Physics* and [so too does] Zeno. Matter is that from which anything at all can come into being. And it has two names, 'substance' and 'matter', both as the matter of all things [as a whole], and as the matter of individual things. The matter of all things [as a whole] does not become greater or smaller, but the matter of the individual things does. Substance is, according to the Stoics, body, and it is limited, according to Antipater in book two of *On Substance* and Apollodorus in his *Physics*.

(Op. cit 150)

14.

They believe that nature is a craftsmanlike fire, proceeding methodically to generation, i.e., a fiery and craftsmanly *pneuma*. And soul is a <nature> capable of sense perception. And this [soul] is the inborn *pneuma* in us. Therefore, it is a body and lasts after death. It is destructible, but the soul of the universe, of which the souls in animals are parts, is indestructible. **157.** Zeno of Citium and Antipater in their treatises *On the Soul* and Posidonius [say] that the soul is a warm *pneuma*. For by means of this we live and breathe and by this we are moved. So Cleanthes says that all [souls] last until <the> conflagration, but Chrysippus says that only those of the wise do so.

(Diogenes Laertius 7.155)

15.

When these doctrines are expounded in a fuller and more flowing fashion, as I intend to do, they more easily escape the captious criticisms of the Academy; but when they are demonstrated in the manner of Zeno, in shorter and more cramped syllogisms, then they are more open to attack; for just as a flowing river is virtually free of the risk of pollution while a confined body of water is polluted quite readily, in the same way the reproaches of a critic are diluted by a flowing oration while a cramped syllogistic demonstration cannot easily protect itself.

Zeno used to compress the arguments which we expand upon, in the following manner. **21.** "That which is rational is better than that which is not rational; but nothing is better than the cosmos; therefore, the cosmos is rational." It can be proven in a similar manner that the cosmos is wise, happy and eternal, since all of these are better than things which lack them, and nothing is better than the world. From all of this it will be proven that the cosmos is a god. Zeno also used this argument: **22.** "If something lacks the ability to perceive, no part of it can have the ability to perceive; but some parts of the cosmos have the ability to perceive; therefore, the cosmos does not lack the ability to perceive." He goes on and presses his point even more compactly. He says, "nothing which lacks life and reason can produce from itself something which is alive and rational; but the cosmos produces from itself things which are alive and rational; therefore, the cosmos is alive and rational." He also argues by means of a comparison, as he often does, as follows: "If flutes playing tunefully grew on olive trees, surely you would not doubt that the olive tree possessed some knowledge of flute playing? What if plane trees bore lyres playing melodiously? surely you would also decide that there was musical ability in plane trees. Why, then, is the cosmos not judged to be alive and wise, when it produces from itself creatures which are alive and wise?"

(Cicero, *On the Nature of the Gods* 2, 1a, 20)

16.

Indeed, they also think that the food one eats makes a difference to one's mental acuity. So, it is plausible that the stars should have exceptional intelligence, since they inhabit the aitherial part of the cosmos and are nourished by moisture from the land and sea which is rarified by the great distance it has travelled. The orderliness and regularity of the heavenly bodies is the clearest indication of their powers of sense-perception and intelligence. For nothing can move rationally and with measure except by the use of intelligence, which contains nothing haphazard or random or accidental. But the orderliness and perpetual consistency of the heavenly bodies does not indicate a merely natural process (for it is full of rationality) nor one produced by chance, which tends to produce haphazard change and is hostile to consistency.

(Cicero, Op. cit 43)

17.

82. And there are also those who use the term 'nature' to refer to everything, like Epicurus, who makes the following division: the nature of all things which exist is bodies and void and their attributes. But since we say that the cosmos is constituted and governed by nature, we do not mean that it is like some lump of mud, piece of stone or anything else with only a natural power of cohesion, but rather, that it is like a tree or animal. For nothing is random in them; rather, it is evident that they posses a certain orderliness and craftsmanlike quality.

(Op. cit 82)

18.

154. It remains for me to come to my conclusion at last by showing that everything in this cosmos which is of use to men was in fact made and provided for their sake. First of all, the cosmos itself was made for the sake of gods and men, and the things in it were provided and discovered for the use of men. For the cosmos is like a common home for gods and men, or a city which both [gods and men] inhabit.

(Op. cit 154)

STOICISM ETHICS

19.

They divide the ethical part of philosophy into these topics: on impulse, on good and bad things, on passions, on virtue, on the goal, on primary value, on actions, on appropriate actions, on encouragements and discouragements to actions. This is the sub-division given by the followers of Chrysippus, Archedemus, Zeno of Tarsus, Apollodorus, Diogenes, Antipater and Posidonius. For Zeno of Citium and Cleanthes, as might be expected from earlier thinkers, made less elaborate distinctions in their subject matter. But they did divide both logic and physics.

(Diogenes Laertius 7.84)

20.

87. Thus Zeno first, in his book *On the Nature of Man*, said that the goal was to live in agreement with nature, which is to live according to virtue. For nature leads us to virtue. And similarly Cleanthes in *On Pleasure* and Posidonius and Hecaton in their books *On the Goal*.

Again, "to live according to virtue" is equivalent to living according to the experience of events which occur by nature, as Chrysippus says in book one of his *On Goals*. **88.** For our natures are parts of the nature of the universe. Therefore, the goal becomes "to live consistently with nature", i.e., according to one's own nature and that of the universe, doing nothing which is forbidden by the common law, which is right reason, penetrating all things, being the same as Zeus who is the leader of the administration of things. And this itself is the virtue of the happy man and a smooth flow of life, whenever all things are done according to the harmony of the daimon in each of us with the will of the administrator of the universe. So Diogenes says explicitly that the goal is reasonable behaviour in the selection of things according to nature, and Archedemus [says it is] to live carrying out all the appropriate acts.

(Diogenes Laertius 7.87)

21.

Virtue in one sense is generally a sort of completion [or: perfection] for each thing, for example, of a statue. And there is also non-intellectual virtue, for example, health; and intellectual virtue, for example, prudence.

(Diogenes Laertius 7.90)

22.

Good is in general that from which there is something beneficial; in particular it is either the same as or not different from benefit. Hence, virtue itself and

the good, which participates in it, are spoken of in these three ways: [1] the good is that *from which* being benefited is a characteristic result; [2] it is that *according to which* [being benefited] is a characteristic result, for example, action according to virtue; [3] it is he *by whom* [being benefited is a characteristic result]; and "by whom" means, for example, the virtuous man who participates in virtue.

They give another particular definition of the good, as follows: "that which is perfectly in accord with nature for a rational being, qua rational". And virtue is such a thing, so that virtuous actions and virtuous men participate [in it]; and its supervenient byproducts are joy and good spirits and the like.

(Diogenes Laertius 7.94)

23.

Preferred things are those which also have value; for example, among things of the soul, natural ability, skill, [moral] progress and similar things; among bodily things life, health, strength, good condition, soundness, beauty and the like; among external things wealth, reputation, noble birth, and similar things.

(Diogenes Laertius 7.106)

24.

Again, of preferred things, some are preferred for themselves, some because of other things, and some both for themselves and because of other things. For themselves, natural ability, [moral] progress and similar things; because of other things, wealth, noble birth, and similar things; for themselves and because of other things, strength, good perceptual abilities, soundness. [Those which are preferred] for themselves [are preferred] because they are according to nature; [those which are preferred] because of other things, [are preferred] because they produce a significant amount of utility; the same applies to the rejected conversely.

(Diogenes Laertius 7.107)

25.

Appropriate [actions], then, are those which reason constrains [us] to do, such as honouring our parents, brothers, fatherland, and spending time with friends. Inappropriate are those which reason constrains [us] not [to do], such as things like this: neglecting our parents, ignoring our brothers, being out of sympathy with our friends, overlooking [the interests of] our fatherland and such things. **109.** Neither appropriate nor inappropriate are those which reason neither constrains us to perform nor forbids, such as picking up a small stick, holding a writing instrument or scraper and things similar to these.

(Diogenes Laertius 7.108–9)

26.

Desire is an irrational striving, and these [forms] are ranged under it: want, hatred, quarrelsomeness, anger, sexual love, wrath, spiritedness. Want is an unsuccessful desire and is as though it were separated from its object yet vainly straining for and drawn to it; hatred is a progressive and increasing desire for things to go badly for someone.

(Diogenes Laertius 7.113)

27.

There are also three good states [of the soul], joy, caution, and wish. And joy is opposite to pleasure, being a reasonable elation; and caution to fear, being a reasonable avoidance. For the wise man will not be afraid in any way, but will be cautious. They say that wish is opposite to desire, being a reasonable striving.

(Diogenes Laertius 7.116)

28.

127. They believe that there is nothing in between virtue and vice, while the Peripatetics say that [moral] progress is between virtue and vice. For, they say, just as a stick must be either straight or crooked, so must a man be either just or unjust and neither 'more just' nor 'more unjust'; and the same for the other virtues.

(Diogenes Laertius 7.127)

29.

There being three ways of life, the theoretical, the practical, and the rational, they say that the third is to be chosen; for the rational animal was deliberately made by nature for theory and action.

(Diogenes Laertius 7.130)

30.

1. Consider who you are. First of all a man, i.e., you have nothing more authoritative than your power of moral choice and all else is subordinate to it, but it itself is free and independent. **2.** Consider, then, what you are separate from in virtue of your rationality. You are separate from wild beasts and from sheep. **3.** And in addition you are a citizen of the cosmos and a part of it—not one of the servile parts but one of its principal parts. For you are able to follow the divine administration and figure out what comes next. **4.** So, what is the role of a citizen? To have no private advantage, not to deliberate about anything as though one were a separate part, but just as if the hand or foot had reasoning power and were able to follow the arrangements of nature, they would never have sought or desired anything except after referring to the whole.

(Epictetus *Discourses* 2.10.1–4)

STUDY QUESTIONS: ZENO, FRAGMENTS

1. How did the Stoics divide philosophy?
2. According to the Stoics, what is an argument?
3. According to Diogenes, how did the Stoics distinguish between a noun, a name, and a verb?
4. What is a concept, according to the Stoic view?
5. Why did the Stoics think that logic is important?
6. What are the active and passive principles of the universe?
7. What do the Stoics say about the cosmos and its shape?
8. How did the natural kinds arise, according to Zeno?
9. According to Zeno, what is the relation between God and the cosmos?

Epictetus (55–135 A.D.)

Biographical History

Epictetus was born as a Roman slave in Hieropolis, in Asia Minor. As a youth, he was passed from one owner to another. Finally, a member of Nero's court, Epaphroditus, purchased Epictetus and allowed him to study with the Stoic philosopher Musonius Rufus. Epictetus soon surpassed his teacher, and his philosophical abilities so impressed his master that he was freed. Afterward, he founded his own Stoic school. One of his students, Arrian, transcribed and published his lectures as *The Encheiridion* (or *The Manual*) and *The Discourses*. Despite being physically weak and lame from his period as a slave, Epictetus developed a large following, even among the early Christians. In 90 A.D., when the Emperor Domitian banned the philosophers, Epictetus fled. In later life, he married and adopted a baby that he had rescued from exposure.

Philosophical Overview

According to Epictetus, the purpose of philosophy is to train us to achieve inner peace through a proper understanding of the world. A person should mold his or her life and actions so that his or her happiness depends as little as possible on external contingencies. Natural changes are governed by the Logos, which manifests itself in human reason. Consequently, one can attain inner peace by conforming to the nature of the world rather than by trying to make the world conform to one's own prejudices and wishes. This path of reason has three stages: mastering one's desires, performing one's duties, and thinking correctly about oneself and the world.

ENCHEIRIDION (THE MANUAL)

Epictetus expresses full confidence that a person has adequate control over his or her happiness. This is because we are able to evaluate the significance of all impressions and thoughts that enter our minds and correct any tendency to interpret them in a way that detracts from our inner peace. The *Encheiridion* provides different methods for interpreting all external impressions and thoughts wisely and beneficially. For instance, if something is not under one's control, then one must accept it as it is and not complain. Paragraph 17 says that one is responsible for playing the role assigned to one admirably, but not for the selection of the role, which is determined by the divine Playwright. On the other hand, one must not relinquish what is under one's own control. For example, Epictetus says that if someone irritates you, be assured that it is really your judgment that is making you irritated (20).

1. Some things are under our control, while others are not under our control. Under our control are conception, choice, desire, aversion, and in a word, everything that is our own doing; not under our control are our body, our property, reputation, office and, in a word, everything that is not our own doing. Furthermore, the things under our control are by nature free, unhindered, and unimpeded; while the things

From *Epictetus—Encheiridion (Manual)*, translated by W. A. Oldfather. The Loeb Classic Library, 1928.

not under our control are weak, servile, subject to hindrance, and not our own. Remember, therefore, that if what is naturally slavish you think to be free, and what is not your own to be your own, you will be hampered, will grieve, will be in turmoil, and will blame both gods and men; while if you think only what is your own to be your own, and what is not your own to be, as it really is, not your own, then no one will ever be able to exert compulsion upon you, no one will hinder you, you will blame no one, will find fault with no one, will do absolutely nothing against your will, you will have no personal enemy, no one will harm you, for neither is there any harm that can touch you.

With such high aims, therefore, remember that you must bestir yourself with no slight effort to lay hold of them, but you will have to give up some things entirely, and defer others for the time being. But if you wish for these things also, and at the same time for both office and wealth, it may be that you will not get even these latter, because you aim also at the former, and certainly you will fail to get the former, which alone bring freedom and happiness.

Make it, therefore, your study at the very outset to say to every harsh external impression, "You are an external impression and not at all what you appear to be." After that examine it and test it by these rules which you have, the first and most important of which is this: Whether the impression has to do with the things which are under our control, or with those which are not under our control; and, if it has to do with some one of the things not under our control, have ready to hand the answer, "It is nothing to me."

2. Remember that the promise of desire is the attainment of what you desire, that of aversion is not to fall into what is avoided, and that he who fails in his desire is unfortunate, while he who falls into what he would avoid experiences misfortune. If, then, you avoid only what is unnatural among those things which are under your control, you will fall into none of the things which you avoid; but if you try to avoid disease, or death, or poverty, you will experience misfortune. Withdraw, therefore, your aversion from all the matters that are not under our control, and transfer it to what is unnatural among those which are under our control. But for the time being remove utterly your desire; for if you desire some one of the

things that are not under our control you are bound to be unfortunate; and, at the same time, not one of the things that are under our control, which it would be excellent for you to desire, is within your grasp. But employ only choice and refusal, and these too but lightly, and with reservations, and without straining.

3. With everything which entertains you, is useful, or of which you are fond, remember to say to yourself, beginning with the very least things, "What is its nature?" If you are fond of a jug, say, "I am fond of a jug"; for when it is broken you will not be disturbed. If you kiss your own child or wife, say to yourself that you are kissing a human being; for when it dies you will not be disturbed.

4. When you are on the point of putting your hand to some undertaking, remind yourself what the nature of that undertaking is. If you are going out of the house to bathe, put before your mind what happens at a public bath—those who splash you with water, those who jostle against you, those who vilify you and rob you. And thus you will set about your undertaking more securely if at the outset you say to yourself, "I want to take a bath, and, at the same time, to keep my moral purpose in harmony with nature." And so do in every undertaking. For thus, if anything happens to hinder you in your bathing, you will be ready to say, "Oh, well, this was not the only thing that I wanted, but I wanted also to keep your moral purpose in harmony with nature; and I shall not so keep it if I am vexed at what is going on."

5. It is not the things themselves that disturb men, but their judgements about these things. For example, death is nothing dreadful, or else Socrates too would have thought so, but the judgement that death is dreadful, *this* is the dreadful thing. When, therefore, we are hindered, or disturbed, or grieved, let us never blame anyone but ourselves, that means, our own judgements. It is the part of an uneducated person to blame others where he himself fares ill; to blame himself is the part of one whose education has begun; to blame neither another nor his own self is the part of one whose education is already complete.

6. Be not elated at any excellence which is not your own. If the horse in his elation were to say, "I am beautiful," it could be endured; but when you say in your elation, "I have a beautiful horse," rest assured that you are elated at something good which belongs to a horse. What then, is your own? The use of external impressions. Therefore, when you are in harmony with nature in the use of external impressions, then be elated; for then it will be some good of your own at which you will be elated.

7. Just as on a voyage, when your ship has anchored, if you should go on shore to get fresh water, you may pick up a small shell-fish or little bulb on the way, but you have to keep your attention fixed on the ship, and turn about frequently for fear lest the captain should call; and if he calls, you must give up all these things, if you would escape being thrown on board all tied up like the sheep. So it is also in life: If there be given you, instead of a little bulb and a small shell-fish, a little wife and child, there will be no objection to that; only, if the Captain calls, give up all these things and run to the ship, without even turning around to look back. And if you are an old man, never even get very far away from the ship, for fear that when He calls you may be missing.

8. Do not seek to have everything that happens happen as you wish, but wish for everything to happen as it actually does happen, and your life will be serene.

9. Disease is an impediment to the body, but not to the moral purpose, unless that consents. Lameness is an impediment to the leg, but not to the moral purpose. And say this to yourself at each thing that befalls you; for you will find the thing to be an impediment to something else, but not to yourself.

10. In the case of everything that befalls you, remember to turn to yourself and see what faculty you have to deal with it. If you see a handsome lad or woman, you will find continence the faculty to employ here; if hard labour is laid upon you, you will find endurance; in this fashion, your external impressions will not run away with you.

11. Never say about anything, "I have lost it," but only "I have given it back." Is your child dead? It has been given back. Is your wife dead? She has been given back. "I have had my farm taken away." Very well, this too has been given back. "Yet it was a rascal who took it away." But what concern is it of yours by whose instrumentality the Giver called for its return? So long as He gives it to you, take care of it as of a thing that is not your own, as travellers treat their inn.

12. If you wish to make progress, dismiss all reasoning of this sort: "If I neglect my affairs, I shall have nothing to live on." "If I do not punish my slave-boy he will turn out bad." For it is better to die of hunger, but in a state of freedom from grief and fear, than to live in plenty, but troubled in mind. And it is better for your slave-boy to be bad than for you to be unhappy. Begin, therefore, with the little things. Your paltry oil gets spilled, your miserable wine stolen; say to yourself, "This is the price paid for a calm spirit, this the price for peace of mind." Nothing is got without a price. And when you call your slave-boy, bear in mind that it is possible he may not heed you, and again, that even if he does heed, he may not do what you want done. But he is not in so happy a condition that your peace of mind depends upon him.

13. If you wish to make progress, then be content to appear senseless and foolish in externals, do not make it your wish to give the appearance of knowing anything; and if some people think you to be an important personage, distrust yourself. For be assured that it is no easy matter to keep your moral purpose in a state of conformity with nature, and, at the same time, to keep externals; but the man who devotes his attention to one of these two things must inevitably neglect the other.

14. If you make it your will that your children and your wife and your friends should live forever, you are silly; for you are making it your will that things not under your control should be under your control, and that what is not your own should be your own. In the same way, too, if you make it your will that your slave-boy be free from faults, you are a fool; for you are making it your will that vice be not vice, but something else. If, however, it is your will not to fail in what you desire, this is in your power. Wherefore, exercise yourself in that which is in your power. Each man's master is the person who has the authority over what the man wishes or does not wish, so as to secure it, or take it away. Whoever, therefore, wants to be free, let him neither wish for anything, nor avoid anything, that is under the control of others; or else he is necessarily a slave.

15. Remember that you ought to behave in life as you would at a banquet. As something is being passed around it comes to you; stretch out your hand and take a portion of it politely. It passes on; do not detain it. Or it has not come to you yet; do not project your desire to meet it, but wait until it comes in

front of you. So act toward children, so toward a wife, so toward office, so toward wealth; and then some day you will be worthy of the banquets of the gods. But if you do not take these things even when they are set before you, but despise them, then you will not only share the banquet of the gods, but share also their rule. For it was by so doing that Diogenes and Heracleitus, and men like them, were deservedly divine and deservedly so called.

16. When you see someone weeping in sorrow, either because a child has gone on a journey, or because he has lost his property, beware that you be not carried away by the impression that the man is in the midst of external ills, but straightway keep before you this thought: "It is not what has happened that distresses this man (for it does not distress another), but his judgement about it." Do not, however, hesitate to sympathize with him so far as words go, and, if occasion offers, even to groan with him; but be careful not to groan also in the centre of your being.

17. Remember that you are an actor in a play, the character of which is determined by the Playwright: if He wishes the play to be short, it is short; if long, it is long; if He wishes you to play the part of a beggar, remember to act even this role adroitly; and so if your role be that of a cripple, an official, or a layman. For this is your business, to play admirably the role assigned you; but the selection of that role is Another's.

18. When a raven croaks inauspiciously, let not the external impression carry you away, but straightway draw a distinction in your own mind, and say, "None of these portents are for me, but either for my paltry body, or my paltry estate, or my paltry opinion, or my children, or my wife. But for me every portent is favourable, if I so wish; for whatever be the outcome, it is within my power to derive benefit from it."

19. You can be invincible if you never enter a contest in which victory is not under your control. Beware lest, when you see some person preferred to you in honour, or possessing great power, or otherwise enjoying high repute, you are ever carried away by the external impression, and deem him happy. For if the true nature of the good is one of the things that are under our control, there is no place for either envy or jealousy; and you yourself will not wish to be a praetor, or a senator, or a consul, but a

free man. Now there is but one way that leads to this, and that is to despise the things that are not under our control.

20. Bear in mind that it is not the man who reviles or strikes you that insults you, but it is your judgement that these men are insulting you. Therefore, when someone irritates you, be assured that it is your own opinion which has irritated you. And so make it your first endeavour not to be carried away by the external impression; for if once you gain time and delay, you will more easily become master of yourself.

21. Keep before your eyes day by day death and exile, and everything that seems terrible, but most of all death; and then you will never have any abject thought, nor will you yearn for anything beyond measure.

22. If you yearn for philosophy, prepare at once to be met with ridicule, to have many people jeer at you, and say, "Here he is again, turned philosopher all of a sudden," and "Where do you suppose he got that high brow?" But do you not put on a high brow, and do you so hold fast to the things which to you seem best, as a man who has been assigned by God to this post; and remember that if you abide by the same principles, those who formerly used to laugh at you will later come to admire you, but if you are worsted by them, you will get the laugh on yourself twice.

23. If it should ever happen to you that you turn to externals with a view to pleasing someone, rest assured that you have lost your plan of life. Be content, therefore, in everything to be a philosopher, and if you wish also to be taken for one, show to yourself that you are one, and you will be able to accomplish it.

24. Let not these reflections oppress you: "I shall live without honour, and be nobody anywhere." For, if lack of honour is an evil, you cannot be in evil through the instrumentality of some other person, any more than you can be in shame. It is not your business, is it, to get office, or to be invited to a dinner-party? Certainly not. How, then, can this be any longer a lack of honour? And how is it that you will be "nobody anywhere," when you ought to be somebody only in those things which are under your control, wherein you are privileged to be a man of the very greatest honour? But your friends will be without assistance? What do you mean by being "without assistance"?

They will not have paltry coin from you, and you will not make them Roman citizens. Well, who told you that these are some of the matters under our control, and not rather things which others do? And who is able to give another what he does not himself have? "Get money, then," says some friend, "in order that we too may have it." If I can get money and at the same time keep myself self-respecting, and faithful, and high-minded, show me the way and I will get it. But if you require me to lose the good things that belong to me, in order that you may acquire the things that are not good, you can see for yourselves how unfair and inconsiderate you are. And which do you really prefer? Money, or a faithful and self-respecting friend? Help me, therefore, rather to this end, and do not require me to do those things which will make me lose these qualities.

"But my country," says he, "so far as lies in me, will be without assistance." Again I ask, what kind of assistance do you mean? It will not have loggias or baths of your providing. And what does that signify? For neither does it have shoes provided by the blacksmith, nor has it arms provided by the cobbler; but it is sufficient if each man fulfil his own proper function. And if you secured for it another faithful and self-respecting citizen, would you not be doing it any good? "Yes." Very well, and then you also would not be useless to it. "What place, then, shall I have in the State?" says he. Whatever place you can have, and at the same time maintain the man of fidelity and self-respect that is in you. But if, through your desire to help the State, you lose these qualities, of what good would you become to it, when in the end you turned out to be shameless and unfaithful?

25. Has someone been honoured above you at a dinner-party, or in salutation, or in being called in to give advice? Now if these matters are good, you ought to be happy that he got them; but if evil, be not distressed because you did not get them; and bear in mind that, if you do not act the same way that others do, with a view to getting things which are not under our control, you cannot be considered worthy to receive an equal share with others. Why, how is it possible for a person who does not haunt some man's door, to have equal shares with the man who does? For the man who does not do escort duty, with the

man who does? For the man who does not praise, with the man who does? You will be unjust, therefore, and insatiable, if, while refusing to pay the price for which such things are bought, you want to obtain them for nothing. Well, what is the price for heads of lettuce? An obol, perhaps. If, then, somebody gives up his obol and gets his heads of lettuce, while you do not give your obol, and do not get them, do not imagine that you are worse off than the man who gets his lettuce. For as he has his heads of lettuce, so you have your obol which you have not given away.

Now it is the same way also in life. You have not been invited to somebody's dinner-party? Of course not; for you didn't give the host the price at which he sells his dinner. He sells it for praise; he sells it for personal attention. Give him the price, then, for which it is sold, if it is to your interest. But if you wish both not to give up the one and yet to get the other, you are insatiable and a simpleton. Have you, then, nothing in place of the dinner? Indeed you have; you have not had to praise the man you did not want to praise; you have not had to put up with the insolence of his doorkeepers.

26. What the will of nature is may be learned from a consideration of the points in which we do not differ from one another. For example, when some other person's slave-boy breaks his drinking-cup, you are instantly ready to say, "That's one of the things which happen." Rest assured, then, that when your own drinking-cup gets broken, you ought to behave in the same way that you do when the other man's cup is broken. Apply now the same principle to the matters of greater importance. Some other person's child or wife has died; no one but would say, "Such is the fate of man." Yet when a man's own child dies, immediately the cry is, "Alas! Woe is me!" But we ought to remember how we feel when we hear of the same misfortune befalling others.

27. Just as a mark is not set up in order to be missed, so neither does the nature of evil arise in the universe.

28. If someone handed over your body to any person who met you, you would be vexed; but that you hand over your mind to any person that comes along, so that, if he reviles you, it is disturbed and troubled—are you not ashamed of that?

29. In each separate thing that you do, consider the matters which come first and those which follow

after, and only then approach the thing itself. Otherwise, at the start you will come to it enthusiastically, because you have never reflected upon any of the subsequent steps, but later on, when some difficulties appear, you will give up disgracefully. Do you wish to win an Olympic victory? So do I, by the gods! for it is a fine thing. But consider the matters which come before that, and those which follow after, and only when you have done that, put your hand to the task. You have to submit to discipline, follow a strict diet, give up sweet cakes, train under compulsion, at a fixed hour, in heat or in cold; you must not drink cold water, nor wine just whenever you feel like it; you must have turned yourself over to your trainer precisely as you would to a physician. Then when the contest comes on, you have to "dig in" beside your opponent, and sometimes dislocate your wrist, sprain your ankle, swallow quantities of sand, sometimes take a scourging, and along with all that get beaten. After you have considered all these points, go on into the games, if you still wish to do so; otherwise, you will be turning back like children. Sometimes they play wrestlers, again gladiators, again they blow trumpets, and then act a play. So you too are now an athlete, now a gladiator, then a rhetorician, then a philosopher, yet with your whole soul nothing; but like an ape you imitate whatever you see, and one thing after another strikes your fancy. For you have never gone out after anything with circumspection, nor after you had examined it all over, but you act haphazard and half-heartedly.

In the same way, when some people have seen a philosopher and have heard someone speaking like Euphrates (though, indeed, who can speak like him?), they wish to be philosophers themselves. Man, consider first the nature of the business, and then learn your own natural ability, if you are able to bear it. Do you wish to be a contender in the pentathlon, or a wrestler? Look to your arms, your thighs, see what your loins are like. For one man has a natural talent for one thing, another for another. Do you suppose that you can eat in the same fashion, drink in the same fashion, give way to impulse and to irritation, just as you do now? You must keep vigils, work hard, abandon your own people, be despised by a paltry slave, be laughed to scorn by those who meet you, in everything get the worst of it, in honour, in office, in court, in every paltry affair. Look these drawbacks

over carefully, if you are willing at the price of these things to secure tranquillity, freedom, and calm. Otherwise, do not approach philosophy; don't act like a child—now a philosopher, later on a tax-gatherer, then a rhetorician, then a procurator of Caesar. These things do not go together. You must be one person, either good or bad; you must labour to improve either your own government principle or externals; you must work hard either on the inner man, or on things outside; that is, play either the rôle of a philosopher or else that of a layman.

30. Our duties are in general measured by our social relationships. He is a father. One is called upon to take care of him, to give way to him in all things, to submit when he reviles or strikes you. "But he is a bad father." Did nature, then, bring you into relationship with a *good* father? No, but simply with a father. "My brother does me wrong." Very well, then, maintain the relation that you have toward him; and do not consider what he is doing, but what you will have to do, if your moral purpose is to be in harmony with nature. For no one will harm you without your consent; you will have been harmed only when you think you are harmed. In this way, therefore, you will discover what duty to expect of your neighbour, your citizen, your commanding officer, if you acquire the habit of looking at your social relations with them.

31. In piety towards the gods, I would have you know, the chief element is this, to have right opinions about them—as existing and as administering the universe well and justly—and to have set yourself to obey them and to submit to everything that happens, and to follow it voluntarily, in the belief that it is being fulfilled by the highest intelligence. For if you act in this way, you will never blame the gods, nor find fault with them for neglecting you. But this result cannot be secured in any other way than by withdrawing your idea of the good and the evil from the things which are not under our control, and placing it in those which are under our control, and in those alone. Because, if you think any of those former things to be good or evil, then, when you fail to get what you want and fall into what you do not want, it is altogether inevitable that you will blame and hate those who are responsible for these results. For this is the nature of every living creature, to flee from and to turn aside from the things that appear harmful, and all that produces them, and to pursue after and to

admire the things that are helpful, and all that produces them. Therefore, it is impossible for a man who thinks that he is being hurt to take pleasure in that which he thinks is hurting him, just as it is also impossible for him to take pleasure in the hurt itself. Hence it follows that even a father is reviled by a son when he does not give his child some share in the things that seem to be good; and this it was which made Polyneices and Eteocles enemies of one another, the thought that the royal power was a good thing. That is why the farmer reviles the gods, and so also the sailor, and the merchant, and those who have lost their wives and their children. For where a man's interest lies, there is also his piety. Wherefore, whoever is careful to exercise desire and aversion as he should, is at the same time careful also about piety. But it is always appropriate to make libations, and sacrifices, and to give of the firstfruits after the manner of our fathers, and to do all this with purity, and not in a slovenly or careless fashion, nor, indeed, in a miserly way, nor yet beyond our means.

32. When you have recourse to divination, remember that you do not know what the issue is going to be, but that you have come in order to find this out from the diviner; yet if you are indeed a philosopher, you know, when you arrive, what the nature of it is. For if it is one of the things which are not under our control, it is altogether necessary that what is going to take place is neither good nor evil. Do not, therefore, bring to the diviner desire or aversion, and do not approach him with trembling, but having first made up your mind that every issue is indifferent and nothing to you, but that, whatever it may be, it will be possible for you to turn it to good use, and that no one will prevent this. Go, then, with confidence to the gods as to counsellors; and after that, when some counsel has been given you, remember whom you have taken as counsellors, and whom you will be disregarding if you disobey. But go to divination as Socrates thought that men should go, that is, in cases where the whole inquiry has reference to the outcome, and where neither from reason nor from any other technical art are means vouchsafed for discovering the matter in question. Hence, when it is your duty to share the danger of a friend or of your country, do not ask of the diviner whether you ought to share that danger. For if the diviner fore-

warns you that the omens of sacrifice have been unfavourable, it is clear that death is portended, or the injury of some member of your body, or exile; yet reason requires that even at this risk you are to stand by your friend, and share the danger with your country. Wherefore, give heed to the greater diviner, the Pythian Apollo, who cast out of his temple the man who had not helped his friend when he was being murdered.

33. Lay down for yourself, at the outset, a certain stamp and type of character for yourself, which you are to maintain whether you are by yourself or are meeting with people. And be silent for the most part, or else make only the most necessary remarks, and express these in few words. But rarely, and when occasion requires you to talk, talk, indeed, but about no ordinary topics. Do not talk about gladiators, or horse-races, or athletes, or things to eat or drink—topics that arise on all occasions; but above all, do not talk about people, either blaming, or praising, or comparing them. If, then, you can, by your own conversation bring over that of your companions to what is seemly. But if you happen to be left alone in the presence of aliens, keep silence.

Do not laugh much, nor at many things, nor boisterously.

Refuse, if you can, to take an oath at all, but if that is impossible, refuse as far as circumstances allow.

Avoid entertainments given by outsiders and by persons ignorant of philosophy; but if an appropriate occasion arises for you to attend, be on the alert to avoid lapsing into the behaviour of such laymen. For you may rest assured, that, if a man's companion be dirty, the person who keeps close company with him must of necessity get a share of his dirt, even though he himself happens to be clean.

In things that pertain to the body take only as much as your bare need requires, I mean such things as food, drink, clothing, shelter, and household slaves; but cut down everything which is for outward show or luxury.

In your sex-life preserve purity, as far as you can, before marriage, and, if you indulge, take only those privileges which are lawful. However, do not make yourself offensive, or censorious, to those who do indulge, and do not make frequent mention of the fact that you do not yourself indulge.

If someone brings you word that So-and-so is speaking ill of you, do not defend yourself against what has been said, but answer, "Yes, indeed, for he did not know the rest of the faults that attach to me; if he had, these would not have been the only ones he mentioned."

It is not necessary, for the most part, to go to the public shows. If, however, a suitable occasion ever arises, show that your principal concern is for none other than yourself, which means, wish only for that to happen which does happen, and for him only to win who does win; for so you will suffer no hindrance. But refrain utterly from shouting, or laughter at anyone, or great excitement. And after you have left, do not talk a great deal about what took place, except in so far as it contributes to your own improvement; for such behaviour indicates that the spectacle has aroused your admiration.

Do not go rashly or readily to people's public reading, but when you do go, maintain your own dignity and gravity, and at the same time be careful not to make yourself disagreeable.

When you are about to meet somebody, in particular when it is one of those men who are held in very high esteem, propose to yourself the question, "What would Socrates or Zeno have done under these circumstances?" and then you will not be at a loss to make proper use of the occasion. When you go to see one of those men who have great power, propose to yourself the thought that you will not find him at home, that you will be shut out, that the door will be slammed in your face, that he will pay no attention to you. And if, despite all this, it is your duty to go, go and take what comes, and never say to yourself, "It was not worth all the trouble." For this is characteristic of the layman, that is, a man who is vexed at externals.

In your conversation avoid making mention at great length and excessively of your own deeds or dangers, because it is not as pleasant for others to hear about your adventures, as it is for you to call to mind your own dangers.

Avoid also raising a laugh, for this is a kind of behaviour that slips easily into vulgarity, and at the same time is calculated to lessen the respect which your neighbours have of you. It is dangerous also to lapse into foul language. When, therefore, anything of the sort occurs, if the occasion be suitable, go even so far as to reprove the person who has made such a lapse; if, however, the occasion does not arise, at all events show by keeping silence, and blushing, and frowning, that you are displeased by what has been said.

34. When you get an external impression of some pleasure, guard yourself, as with impressions in general, against being carried away by it; nay, let the matter wait upon your leisure, and give yourself a little delay. Next think of the two periods of time, first, that in which you will enjoy your pleasure, and second, that in which, after the enjoyment is over, you will later repent and revile your own self; and set over against these two periods of time how much joy and self-satisfaction you will get if you refrain. However, if you feel that a suitable occasion has arisen to do the deed, be careful not to allow its enticement, and sweetness, and attractiveness to overcome you; but set over against all this the thought, how much better is the consciousness of having won a victory over it.

35. When you do a thing which you have made up your mind ought to be done, never try not to be seen doing it, even though most people are likely to think unfavourably about it. If, however, what you are doing is not right, avoid the deed itself altogether; but if it is right, why fear those who are going to rebuke you wrongly?

36. Just as the propositions, "It is day," and "it is night," are full of meaning when separated, but meaningless if united; so also, granted that for you to take the larger share at a dinner is good for your body, still, it is bad for the maintenance of the proper kind of social feeling. When, therefore, you are eating with another person, remember to regard, not merely the value for your body of what lies before you, but also to maintain your respect for your host.

37. If you undertake a role which is beyond your powers, you both disgrace yourself in that one, and at the same time neglect the role which you might have filled with success.

38. Just as you are careful, in walking about, not to step on a nail or to sprain your ankle, so be careful also not to hurt your governing principle. And if we observe this rule in every action, we shall be more secure in setting about it.

39. Each man's body is a measure for his property, just as the foot is a measure for his shoe. If, then, you abide by this principle, you will maintain the proper measure, but if you go beyond it, you cannot help but fall headlong over a precipice, as it were, in the end. So also in the case of your shoe; if once you go beyond the foot, you get first a gilded shoe, then a purple one, then an embroidered one. For once you go beyond the measure there is no limit.

40. Immediately after they are fourteen, women are called "ladies" by men. And so when they see that they have nothing else but only to be the bedfellows of men, they begin to beautify themselves, and put all their hopes in that. It is worthwhile for us to take pains, therefore, to make them understand that they are honoured for nothing else but only for appearing modest and self-respecting.

41. It is a mark of an ungifted man to spend a great deal of time in what concerns his body, as in much exercise, much eating, much drinking, much evacuating of the bowels, much copulating. But these things are to be done in passing; and let your whole attention be devoted to the mind.

42. When someone treats you ill or speaks ill of you, remember that he acts or speaks thus because he thinks it is incumbent upon him. That being the case, it is impossible for him to follow what appears good to you, but what appears good to himself; whence it follows that, if he gets a wrong view of things, the man that suffers is the man that has been deceived. For if a person thinks a true composite judgement to be false, the composite judgement does not suffer, but the person who has been deceived. If, therefore, you start from this point of view, you will be gentle with the man who reviles you. For you should say on each occasion, "He thought that way about it."

43. Everything has two handles, by one of which it ought to be carried and by the other not. If your brother wrongs you, do not lay hold of the matter by the handle of the wrong that he is doing, because this is the handle by which the matter ought not to be carried; but rather by the other handle— that he is your brother, that you were brought up together, and then you will be laying hold of the matter by the handle by which it ought to be carried.

44. The following statements constitute a *non sequitur*: "I am richer than you are, therefore I am superior to you"; or, "I am more eloquent than you

are, therefore I am superior to you." But the following conclusions are better: "I am richer than you are, therefore my property is superior to yours"; or, "I am more eloquent than you are, therefore my elocution is superior to yours." But *you* are neither property nor elocution.

45. Somebody is hasty about bathing; do not say that he bathes badly, but that he is hasty about bathing. Somebody drinks a good deal of wine; do not say that he drinks badly, but that he drinks a good deal. For until you have decided what judgement prompts him, how do you know that what he is doing is bad? And thus the final result will not be that you receive convincing sense-impressions of some things, but give your assent to others.

46. On no occasion call yourself a philosopher, and do not, for the most part, talk among laymen about your philosophic principles, but do what follows from your principles. For example, at a banquet do not say how people ought to eat, but eat as a man ought. For remember how Socrates had so completely eliminated the thought of ostentation, that people came to him when they wanted him to introduce them to philosophers, and he used to bring them along. So well did he submit to being overlooked. And if talk about some philosophic principle arises among laymen, keep silence for the most part for there is great danger that you will spew up immediately what you have not digested. So when a man tells you that you know nothing, and you, like Socrates, are not hurt, then rest assured that you are making a beginning with the business you have undertaken. For sheep, too, do not bring their fodder to the shepherds and show how much they have eaten, but they digest their food within them, and on the outside produce wool and milk. And so do you, therefore, make no display to the laymen of your philosophical principles, but let them see the results which come from these principles when digested.

47. When you have become adjusted to simple living in regard to your bodily wants, do not preen yourself about the accomplishment; and so likewise, if you are a water-drinker, do not on every occasion say that you are a water-drinker. And if ever you want to train to develop physical endurance, do it by yourself and not for outsiders to behold; do not throw your arms around statues, but on occasion, when you are very thirsty, take cold water into your mouth, and then spit it out, without telling anybody.

48. This is the position and character of a layman: He never looks for either help or harm from himself, but only from externals. This is the position and character of the philosopher: He looks for all his help or harm from himself.

Signs of one who is making progress are: He censures no one, praises no one, blames no one, finds fault with no one, says nothing about himself as though he were somebody or knew something. When he is hampered or prevented, he blames himself. And if anyone compliments him, he smiles to himself at the person complimenting; while if anyone censures him, he makes no defence. He goes about like an invalid, being careful not to disturb, before it has grown firm, any part which is getting well. He has put away from himself his every desire, and has transferred his aversion to those things only, of what is under our control, which are contrary to nature. He exercises no pronounced choice in regard to anything. If he gives the appearance of being foolish or ignorant he does not care. In a word, he keeps guard against himself as though he were his own enemy lying in wait.

49. When a person gives himself airs because he can understand and interpret the books of Chrysippus, say to yourself, "If Chrysippus had not written obscurely, this man would have nothing about which to give himself airs."

But what is it I want? To learn nature and to follow her. I seek, therefore, someone to interpret her; and having heard that Chrysippus does so, I go to him. But I do not understand what he has written; I seek, therefore, the person who interprets Chrysippus. And down to this point there is nothing to justify pride. But when I find the interpreter, what remains is to put his precepts into practice; this is the only thing to be proud about. If, however, I admire the mere act of interpretation, what have I done but turned into a grammarian instead of a philosopher? The only difference, indeed, is that I interpret Chrysippus instead of Homer. Far from being proud, therefore, when somebody says to me, "Read me Chrysippus," I blush the rather, when I am unable to show him such deeds as match and harmonize with his words.

50. Whatever principles are set before you, stand fast by these like laws, feeling that it would be impiety for you to transgress them. But pay no attention to what somebody says about you, for this is, at length, not under your control.

51. How long will you still wait to think yourself worthy of the best things, and in nothing to transgress against the distinctions set up by the reason? You have received the philosophical principles which you ought to accept, and you have accepted them. What sort of a teacher, then, do you still wait for, that you should put off reforming yourself until he arrives? You are no longer a lad, but already a full-grown man. If you are now neglectful and easy-going, and always making one delay after another, and fixing first one day and then another, after which you will pay attention to yourself, then without realizing it you will make no progress, but, living and dying, will continue to be a layman throughout. Make up your mind, therefore, before it is too late, that the fitting thing for you to do is to live as a mature man who is making progress, and let everything which seems to you to be best be for you a law that must not be transgressed. And if you meet anything that is laborious, or sweet, or held in high repute, or in no repute, remember that now is the contest, and here before you are the Olympic games, and that it is impossible to delay any longer, and that it depends on a single day and a single action, whether progress is lost or saved. This is the way Socrates became what he was, by paying attention to nothing but his reason in everything that he encountered. And even if you are not yet a Socrates, still you ought to live as one who wishes to be a Socrates.

52. The first and most necessary division in philosophy is that which has to do with the application of the principles, as, for example, Do not lie. The second deals with the demonstrations, as, for example, How comes it that we ought not to lie? The third confirms and discriminates between these processes, as, for example, How does it come that this is a proof? For what is a proof, what is logical consequence, what contradiction, what truth, what falsehood? Therefore, the third division is necessary because of the second, and the second because of the first; while the most necessary of all, and the one in which we ought to rest, is the first. But we do the opposite; for we spend our time in the third division, and all our zeal is devoted to it, while we utterly neglect the first. Wherefore, we lie, indeed, but are ready with the arguments which prove that one ought not to lie.

53. Upon every occasion we ought to have the following thoughts at our command:

> Lead thou me on, O Zeus, and Destiny,
> To that goal long ago to me assigned.
> I'll follow and not falter; if my will
> Prove weak and craven, still I'll follow on.

Cleanthes

> Whoso has rightly with necessity complied, We count him wise, and skilled in things divine.

Euripides

> Well, O Crito, if so it is pleasing to the gods, so let it be.

Socrates [Crito, 43D]

> Anytus and Meletus can kill me, but they cannot hurt me.

Socrates [Apology, 30C]

STUDY QUESTIONS: EPICTETUS, ENCHEIRIDION (MANUAL)

1. What things are under our control, and what things are not? Why is this distinction important, according to Epictetus?
2. What is the most important thing one should say to a harsh external impression?
3. Why does one have to remind oneself of the nature of an undertaking?
4. What disturbs us? What insults us?
5. 'Do no seek to have everything that happens to you happen as you wish.' Instead, what should we wish for, and why?
6. Why does Epictetus advise us to remember that we are actors in a play?
7. Why does Epictetus say that everything has two handles? How does this analogy relate to his point about external impressions?
8. What are the signs of making progress in becoming a philosopher?
9. How is Stoicism related to Epicureanism? In what ways are they similar? How are they most different?

MARCUS AURELIUS (121–180 A.D.)

Biographical History

Marcus Aurelius was born to a prominent Spanish family in Rome. When Aurelius was only 3 months old, his father died, and he went to live with his grandfather, who was consul. The Emperor Hadrian knew the child well and thought that he was a born leader. Marcus received an excellent education. By the age of 12, he was mastering geometry, music, mathematics, painting, literature, and, most of all, philosophy. He showed so much promise and talent that when the Emperor Hadrian chose Marcus' uncle Antoninus as his successor, he also specified that Antoninus should designate Marcus to be the next emperor. Despite being the heir apparent to the imperial throne of Rome, Marcus Aurelius lived the simple life of a Stoic. In 161, at the age of 39, he became the fourteenth Roman emperor. During his 19-year reign, he brought about many legal, social, educational, and economic reforms. He championed the poor, improved the condition of slaves, and initiated programs to aid young children. After years of peace, it was Marcus Aurelius' misfortune that, during his reign, the Roman Empire came under attack from many quarters. He successfully resisted the threats of invasion in Syria, Spain, Egypt, Britain, and Italy, as well as from the Germanic tribes along the Rhine-Danube frontier. He appointed his son, Commodus, as his successor.

Philosophical Overview

During the tumult of war, Marcus Aurelius wrote *The Meditations*, probably for personal reasons rather than for other readers, in order to nourish himself with noble thoughts during a seven-year military campaign. The book reveals the eloquence of a Stoic philosopher on a path of self-discovery and enlightenment through a regime of self-examination and self-discipline. The overarching theme of *The Meditations* is that there is only one thing to keep a person free: philosophy. *The Meditations* constitute a structured reflection that puts this claim into practice, as well as being an exercise in self-discipline.

THE MEDITATIONS

Marcus Aurelius articulates two fundamental principles of Stoicism from the outset: first, external matters do not affect the soul; and second, everything changes. Several sections elaborate and draw out the implications of these two principles. For example, the first principle is amplified at section 7, where Aurelius says that if one discards the thought of injury, the injury will be gone. It is our judgment of events that harms us rather than the events themselves (39). The second principle is expounded in various ways. For instance, at 17, Marcus Aurelius reminds himself that his life is short as a spur to practice virtue diligently. There are several passages where Aurelius emphasizes that he is a being with reason (e.g., 13 and 14). Reason can grasp the order in all changes, and in this way a person can be in tune with the universe rather than being a stranger (e.g., 22, 27, 29, and 36).

However, these two principles do not capture the entire metaphysical basis of Aurelius' Stoic ethics. For example, there is also the principle that all things are one (40).

IV

That which rules within, when it is according to nature, is so affected with respect to the events which happen, that it always easily adapts itself to that which is possible and is presented to it. For it requires no definite material, but it moves towards its purpose, under certain conditions however; and it makes a material for itself out of that which opposes it, as fire lays hold of what falls into it, by which a small light would have been extinguished: but when the fire is strong, it soon appropriates to itself the matter which is heaped on it, and consumes it, and rises higher by means of this very material.

2. Let no act be done without a purpose, nor otherwise than according to the perfect principles of art.

3. Men seek retreats for themselves, houses in the country, seashores, and mountains; and thou too art wont to desire such things very much. But this is altogether a mark of the most common sort of men, for it is in thy power whenever thou shalt choose to retire into thyself. For nowhere, either with more

quiet or more freedom from trouble, does a man retire than into his own soul, particularly when he has within him such thoughts that by looking into them he is immediately in perfect tranquillity; and I affirm that tranquillity is nothing else than the good ordering of the mind. Constantly then give to thyself this retreat, and renew thyself; and let thy principles be brief and fundamental, which, as soon as thou shalt recur to them, will be sufficient to cleanse the soul completely, and to send thee back free from all discontent with the things to which thou returnest. For with what art thou discontented? With the badness of men? Recall to thy mind this conclusion, that rational animals exist for one another, and that to endure is a part of justice, and that men do wrong involuntarily; and consider how many already, after mutual enmity, suspicion, hatred, and fighting, have been stretched dead, reduced to ashes; and be quiet at last.—But perhaps thou art dissatisfied with that which is assigned to thee out of the universe.—Recall to thy recollection this alternative; either there is providence or atoms [fortuitous concurrence of things]; or remember the arguments by which it has been proved that the world is a kind of political community [and be quiet at last].—But perhaps corporeal things will still fasten upon thee.—Consider then further that the mind mingles not with the breath, whether moving gently or violently, when it has once drawn itself apart and discovered its own power, and think also of all that thou hast heard and assented to about pain and pleasure [and be quiet at last].—But perhaps the desire of the thing called fame will torment thee.—See how soon everything is forgotten, and look at the chaos of infinite time on each side of [the present], and the emptiness of applause, and the changeableness and want of judgment in those who pretend to give praise, and the narrowness of the space within which it is circumscribed [and be quiet at last]. For the whole earth is a point, and how small a nook in it is this thy dwelling, and how few are there in it, and what kind of people are they who will praise thee.

This then remains: Remember to retire into this little territory of thy own, and, above all, do not distract or strain thyself, but be free, and look at things as a man, as a human being, as a citizen, as a mortal.

But among the things readiest to thy hand to which thou shalt turn, let there be these, which are two. One is that things do not touch the soul, for they are external and remain immovable; but our perturbations come only from the opinion which is within. The other is that all these things, which thou seest, change immediately and will no longer be; and constantly bear in mind how many of these changes thou hast already witnessed. The universe is transformation: life is opinion.

4. If our intellectual part is common, the reason also, in respect of which we are rational beings, is common: if this is so, common also is the reason which commands us what to do, and what not to do; if this is so, there is a common law also; if this is so, we are fellow-citizens; if this is so, we are members of some political community; if this is so, the world is in a manner a state. For of what other common political community will any one say that the whole human race are members? And from thence, from this common political community comes also our very intellectual faculty and reasoning faculty and our capacity for law; or whence do they come? For as my earthly part is a portion given to me from certain earth, and that which is watery from another element, and that which is hot and fiery from some peculiar source (for nothing comes out of that which is nothing, as nothing also returns to nonexistence), so also the intellectual part comes from some source.

5. Death is such as generation is, a mystery of nature; a composition out of the same elements, and a decomposition into the same; and altogether not a thing of which any man should be ashamed, for it is not contrary to [the nature of] a reasonable animal, and not contrary to the reason of our constitution.

6. It is natural that these things should be done by such persons, it is a matter of necessity; and if a man will not have it so, he will not allow the fig-tree to have juice. But by all means bear this in mind, that within a very short time both thou and he will be dead; and soon not even your names will be left behind.

7. Take away thy opinion, and then there is taken away the complaint, "I have been harmed." Take away the complaint, "I have been harmed," and the harm is taken away.

8. That which does not make a man worse than he was, also does not make his life worse, nor does it harm him either from without or from within.

9. The nature of that which is [universally] useful has been compelled to do this.

10. Consider that everything which happens, happens justly, and if thou observest carefully, thou wilt find it to be so. I do not say only with respect to the continuity of the series of things, but with respect to what is just, and as if it were done by one who assigns to each thing its value. Observe then as thou hast begun; and whatever thou doest, do it in conjunction with this, the being good, and in the sense in which a man is properly understood to be good. Keep to this in every action.

11. Do not have such an opinion of things as he has who does thee wrong, or such as he wishes thee to have, but look at them as they are in truth.

12. A man should always have these two rules in readiness; the one, to do only whatever the reason of the ruling and legislating faculty may suggest for the use of men; the other, to change thy opinion, if there is any one at hand who sets thee right and moves thee from any opinion. But this change of opinion must proceed only from a certain persuasion, as of what is just or of common advantage, and the like, not because it appears pleasant or brings reputation.

13. Hast thou reason? I have.—Why then dost not thou use it? For if this does its own work, what else dost thou wish?

14. Thou hast existed as a part. Thou shalt disappear in that which produced thee; but rather thou shalt be received back into its seminal principle by transmutation.

15. Many grains of frankincense on the same altar: one falls before, another falls after; but it makes no difference.

16. Within ten days thou wilt seem a god to those to whom thou art now a beast and an ape, if thou wilt return to thy principles and the worship of reason.

17. Do not act as if thou wert going to live ten thousand years. Death hangs over thee. While thou livest, while it is in thy power, be good.

18. How much trouble he avoids who does not look to see what his neighbour says or does or thinks, but only to what he does himself, that it may be just and pure; or, as Agathon says, look not round at the depraved morals of others, but run straight along the line without deviating from it.

19. He who has a vehement desire for posthumous fame does not consider that every one of those who remember him will himself also die very soon; then again also they who have succeeded them, until the whole remembrance shall have been extinguished as it is transmitted through men who foolishly admire and perish. But suppose that those who will remember are even immortal, and that the remembrance will be immortal, what then is this to thee? And I say not, what is it to the dead? but, what is it to the living? What is praise, except indeed so far as it has a certain utility? For thou now rejectest unseasonably the gift of nature, clinging to something else. . . .

20. Everything which is in any way beautiful is beautiful in itself, and terminates in itself, not having praise as part of itself. Neither worse then nor better is a thing made by being praised. I affirm this also of the things which are called beautiful by the vulgar; for example, material things and works of art. That which is really beautiful has no need of anything; not more than law, not more than truth, not more than benevolence or modesty. Which of these things is beautiful because it is praised, or spoiled by being blamed? Is such a thing as an emerald made worse than it was, if it is not praised? or gold, ivory, purple, a lyre, a little knife, a flower, a shrub?

21. If souls continue to exist, how does the air contain them from eternity?—But how does the earth contain the bodies of those who have been buried from time so remote? For as here the mutation of these bodies after a certain continuance, whatever it may be, and their dissolution make room for other dead bodies; so the souls which are removed into the air after subsisting for some time are transmuted and diffused, and assume a fiery nature by being received into the seminal intelligence of the universe, and in this way make room for the fresh souls which come to dwell there. And this is the answer which a man might give on the hypothesis of souls continuing to exist. But we must not only think of the number of bodies which are thus buried, but also of the number of animals which are daily eaten by us and the other animals. For what a number is consumed, and thus in a manner buried in the bodies of those who feed on them! And nevertheless this earth receives them by reason of the changes [of these bodies] into blood, and the transformations into the aërial or the fiery element.

What is the investigation into the truth in this matter? The division into that which is material and that which is the cause of form [the formal] (vii. 29).

22. Do not be whirled about, but in every movement have respect to justice, and on the occasion of every impression maintain the faculty of comprehension [or understanding].

23. Everything harmonizes with me which is harmonious to thee, O Universe. Nothing for me is too early nor too late, which is in due time for thee. Everything is fruit to me which thy seasons bring, O Nature: from thee are all things, in thee are all things, to thee all things return. The poet says, Dear city of Cecrops; and wilt not thou say, Dear city of Zeus?

24. Occupy thyself with few things, says the philosopher, if thou wouldst be tranquil.—But consider if it would not be better to say, Do what is necessary, and whatever the reason of the animal which is naturally social requires, and as it requires. For this brings not only the tranquillity which comes from doing well, but also that which comes from doing few things. For the greatest part of what we say and do being unnecessary, if a man takes this away, he will have more leisure and less uneasiness. Accordingly on every occasion a man should ask himself, Is this one of the unnecessary things? Now a man should take away not only unnecessary acts but also unnecessary thoughts, for thus superfluous acts will not follow after.

25. Try how the life of the good man suits thee, the life of him who is satisfied with his portion out of the whole, and satisfied with his own just acts and benevolent disposition.

26. Hast thou seen those things? Look also at these. Do not disturb thyself. Make thyself all simplicity. Does any one do wrong? It is to himself that he does the wrong. Has anything happened to thee? Well, out of the universe from the beginning everything which happens has been apportioned and spun out to thee. In a word, thy life is short. Thou must turn to profit the present by the aid of reason and justice. Be sober in thy relaxation.

27. Either it is a well arranged universe or a chaos huddled together, but still a universe. But can a certain order subsist in thee, and disorder in the All?

And this, too, when all things are so separated and diffused and sympathetic.

28. A black character, a womanish character, a stubborn character, bestial, childish, animal, stupid, counterfeit, scurrilous, fraudulent, tyrannical.

29. If he is a stranger to the universe who does not know what is in it, no less is he a stranger who does not know what is going on in it. He is a runaway, who flies from social reason; he is blind, who shuts the eyes of the understanding; he is poor, who has need of another, and has not from himself all things which are useful for life. He is an abscess on the universe, who withdraws and separates himself from the reason of our common nature through being displeased with the things which happen, for the same nature produces this, and has produced thee too; he is a piece rent asunder from the state, who tears his own soul from that of reasonable animals, which is one.

30. The one is a philosopher without a tunic, and the other without a book: here is another half naked: Bread I have not, he says, and I abide by reason. And I do not get the means of living out of my learning, and I abide [by my reason].

31. Love the art, poor as it may be, which thou hast learned, and be content with it; and pass through the rest of life like one who has intrusted to the gods with his whole soul all that he has, making thyself neither the tyrant nor the slave of any man.

32. Consider, for example, the times of Vespasian. Thou wilt see all these things, people marrying, bringing up children, sick, dying, warring, feasting, trafficking, cultivating the ground, flattering, obstinately arrogant, suspecting, plotting, wishing for some to die, grumbling about the present, loving, heaping up treasure, desiring consulship, kingly power. Well, then, that life of these people no longer exists at all. Again, remove to the times of Trajan. Again, all is the same. Their life, too, is gone. In like manner view also the other epochs of time and of whole nations, and see how many after great efforts soon fell and were resolved into the elements. But chiefly thou shouldst think of those whom thou hast thyself known distracting themselves about idle things, neglecting to do what was in accordance with their proper constitution, and to hold firmly to this and to be content with it. And herein it is necessary to remember that the attention given to everything has its proper value and proportion. For thus thou wilt not be dissatisfied, if thou appliest thyself to smaller matters no further than is fit.

33. The words which were formerly familiar are now antiquated; so also the names of those who were famed of old, are now in a manner antiquated: Camillus, Cæso, Volesus, Leonnatus, and a little after also Scipio and Cato, then Augustus, then also Hadrianus and Antoninus. For all things soon pass away and become a mere tale, and complete oblivion soon buries them. And I say this of those who have shone in a wondrous way. For the rest, as soon as they have breathed out their breath, they are gone, and no man speaks of them. And, to conclude the matter, what is even an eternal remembrance? A mere nothing. What, then, is that about which we ought to employ our serious pains? This one thing, thoughts just, and acts social, and words which never lie, and a disposition which gladly accepts all that happens, as necessary, as usual, as flowing from a principle and source of the same kind.

34. Willingly give thyself up to Clotho [one of the fates], allowing her to spin thy thread into whatever things she pleases.

35. Everything is only for a day, both that which remembers and that which is remembered.

36. Observe constantly that all things take place by change, and accustom thyself to consider that the nature of the Universe loves nothing so much as to change the things which are and to make new things like them. For everything that exists is in a manner the seed of that which will be. But thou art thinking only of seeds which are cast into the earth or into a womb: but this is a very vulgar notion.

37. Thou wilt soon die, and thou art not yet simple, nor free from perturbations, nor without suspicion of being hurt by external things, nor kindly disposed towards all; nor dost thou yet place wisdom only in acting justly.

38. Examine men's ruling principles, even those of the wise, what kind of things they avoid, and what kind they pursue.

39. What is evil to thee does not subsist in the ruling principle of another; nor yet in any turning and mutation of thy corporeal covering. Where is it then? It is in that part of thee in which subsists the power of forming opinions about evils. Let this power then not form [such] opinions, and all is well. And if that which is nearest to it, the poor body, is cut,

burnt, filled with matter and rottenness, nevertheless let the part which forms opinions about these things be quiet, that is, let it judge that nothing is either bad or good which can happen equally to the bad man and the good. For that which happens equally to him who lives contrary to nature and to him who lives according to nature, is neither according to nature nor contrary to nature.

40. Constantly regard the universe as one living being, having one substance and one soul; and observe how all things have reference to one perception, the perception of this one living being; and how all things act with one movement; and how all things are the cooperating causes of all things which exist; observe too the continuous spinning of the thread and the contexture of the web.

41. Thou art a little soul bearing about a corpse, as Epictetus used to say (1. c. 19).

42. It is no evil for things to undergo change, and no good for things to subsist in consequence of change.

43. Time is like a river made up of the events which happen, and a violent stream; for as soon as a thing has been seen, it is carried away, and another comes in its place, and this will be carried away too.

44. Everything which happens is as familiar and well known as the rose in spring and the fruit in summer; for such is disease, and death, and calumny, and treachery, and whatever else delights fools or vexes them.

45. In the series of things those which follow are always aptly fitted to those which have gone before; for this series is not like a mere enumeration of disjointed things, which has only a necessary sequence, but it is a rational connection: and as all existing things are arranged together harmoniously, so the things which come into existence exhibit no mere succession, but a certain wonderful relationship (vi. 38; vii. 9; vii. 75, note).

46. Always remember the saying of Heraclitus, that the death of earth is to become water, and the death of water is to become air, and the death of air is to become fire, and reversely. And think too of him who forgets whither the way leads, and that men quarrel with that with which they are most constantly in communion, the reason which governs the universe; and the things which they daily meet with seem to them strange: and consider that we ought not to act and speak as if we were asleep, for even in sleep we seem to act and speak; and that we ought not, like children who learn from their parents, simply to act and speak as we have been taught.

47. If any god told thee that thou shalt die to-morrow, or certainly on the day after to-morrow, thou wouldst not care much whether it was on the third day or on the morrow, unless thou wast in the highest degree mean-spirited—for how small is the difference?—so think it no great thing to die after as many years as thou canst name rather than to-morrow.

48. Think continually how many physicians are dead after often contracting their eyebrows over the sick; and how many astrologers after predicting with great pretensions the deaths of others; and how many philosophers after endless discourses on death or immortality; how many heroes after killing thousands; and how many tyrants who have used their power over men's lives with terrible insolence as if they were immortal; and how many cities are entirely dead, so to speak, Helice and Pompeii and Herculaneum, and others innumerable. Add to the reckoning all whom thou hast known, one after another. One man after burying another has been laid out dead, and another buries him; and all this in a short time. To conclude, always observe how ephemeral and worthless human things are, and what was yesterday a little mucus, to-morrow will be a mummy or ashes. Pass then through this little space of time conformably to nature, and end thy journey in content, just as an olive falls off when it is ripe, blessing nature who produced it, and thanking the tree on which it grew.

49. Be like the promontory against which the waves continually break, but it stands firm and tames the fury of the water around it.

Unhappy am I, because this has happened to me.—Not so, but Happy am I, though this has happened to me, because I continue free from pain, neither crushed by the present nor fearing the future. For such a thing as this might have happened to every man; but every man would not have continued free from pain on such an occasion. Why, then, is that rather a misfortune than this a good fortune? And dost thou in all cases call that a man's misfortune, which is not a deviation from man's nature? And does a thing seem to thee to be a deviation from man's nature, when it is not contrary to the will of man's nature? Well, thou knowest the will of nature. Will then this which has happened prevent thee from being just, magnanimous, temperate, prudent, secure against inconsiderate opinions and falsehood; will it prevent thee from having modesty, freedom, and everything else, by the presence of which man's nature obtains all that is its own? Remember, too, on every occasion which leads thee to vexation to apply this principle: not that this is a misfortune, but that to bear it nobly is good fortune.

50. It is a vulgar but still a useful help towards contempt of death, to pass in review those who have tenaciously stuck to life. What more then have they gained than those who have died early? Certainly they lie in their tombs somewhere at last, Cadicianus, Fabius, Julianus, Lepidus, or any one else like them, who have carried out many to be buried, and then were carried out themselves. Altogether the interval is small [between birth and death]; and consider with how much trouble, and in company with what sort of people, and in what a feeble body this interval is laboriously passed. Do not then consider life a thing of any value. For look to the immensity of time behind thee, and to the time which is before thee, another boundless space. In this infinity then what is the difference between him who lives three days and him who lives three generations?

51. Always run to the short way; and the short way is the natural: accordingly say and do everything in conformity with the soundest reason. For such a purpose frees a man from trouble, and warfare, and all artifice and ostentatious display.

STUDY QUESTIONS: AURELIUS, *THE MEDITATIONS*

1. Aurelius recommends retreating to the quietude of one's own soul. Why does he recommend that? What does he mean?
2. What are the two foremost principles that one will find if one is able to be free?
3. Aurelius says, 'That which does not make a man worse than he was, also does not make his life worse.' What does this mean? How would he defend this claim?

4. 'Thou hast existed as a part' (14). For what reason does Aurelius point this out? What does he think are the ethical implications of this thesis?
5. What is the proper function of reason, according to Aurelius?
6. How does Aurelius explain the idea of the order of the universe? Why does that order have an ethical importance for the way we live?
7. How does Aurelius characterize the person who is a stranger to the universe? As a runaway? A beggar? An abscess?
8. Why and how is it ethically important to understand that everything changes?

Philosophical Bridges: The Influence of Stoicism

According to Stoicism, the universe is entirely material but, at the same time, it has a divine aspect. Because we humans are part of this greater whole, we should aim to live in accordance with the laws of nature, which reflect its divine aspect. These ideas had an influence on the seventeenth-century philosopher Spinoza, whose work the *Ethics* develops an understanding of human ethical development based on a nondualist metaphysics that has some striking similarities to Stoicism. In particular, they both are pantheistic, deterministic, and nondualistic in their metaphysics, and both stress the proper understanding of things as the way to liberate oneself from negative passions.

During the Roman Empire, Stoicism was a popular philosophy of life, almost a religion. Roman Stoicism was mainly an ethics to live by that required control of the emotions. It required one to want nothing that would make one's happiness and peace hostage to external events.

The early Church in Rome adopted elements of Stoicism, which made Christianity more palatable to the Romans. For instance, the Stoics stressed that the divine *Logos*, which is the source of the natural order of things, is also present in human reason. This idea is similar to the Christian claim that the soul is divine, like a spark of God inside each of us.

More recently, the Stoic writer Seneca had an important influence on the French thinker Michel Montaigne, whose *Essays* express the humanistic spirit of the Renaissance. For early modern thinkers, such as Montaigne, Stoicism represented a noble ethical vision of human life that was free from Church doctrine. In this way, it encouraged such philosophers to think outside the limits of Christianity and medieval Scholaticism.

SKEPTICISM
PROLOGUE

Today, the English word 'skeptic' means roughly 'doubter.' However, the Greek term '*skepsis*' meant inquiry, and the Pyrrhonean Skeptics were thinkers who argued for persistence in inquiry. They claimed that one should not accept anything as true until it has been subjected to exhaustive and rigorous scrutiny. Pyrrho of Elis (367–275 B.C.), who refused to pass judgment on any claim, inspired the movement that has his name.

Pyrrhonism may be contrasted with the Academic Skepticism developed in Plato's Academy under Arcesilas (315–241 B.C.) and Carneades (213–129 B.C.). At first, the

Academics tried to refute the arguments in favor of particular philosophies, especially Stoicism. Later, around the first century B.C., the Academics began arguing that nothing at all can be known.

In contrast, according to the Pyrrhonean, such a claim is itself too dogmatic. Such finality is premature: we do not know that nothing can be known. Instead, we should merely suspend judgment, without affirming or denying anything. Things appear a certain way, and the Pyrrhonean Skeptic accepts this without judging whether reality is as it seems. The Pyrrhonean suspends judgment about everything that is not immediately evident. Such a suspension of belief, according to Pyrrho, leads not to insecurity and anxiety but, rather, to a tranquil and liberating state of indifference about the world.

SEXTUS EMPIRICUS (175–225 A.D.)

Biographical History

Sextus Empiricus (175–225 A.D.) is the only Pyrhonnean Skeptic whose writings have survived. He was trained as a medical doctor and teacher, and he became the last leader of the Pyrrhonean movement. His written works provide an overview of the arguments worked out by previous Skeptics. *Against the Mathematicians* and *Against the Dogmatists* contain detailed arguments against the claim to knowledge in the liberal arts (such as grammar, geometry, astronomy, and music), as well as in philosophy. Ironically, these works are two important sources of knowledge about the early history of astronomy, geometry, grammar, and Stoic theology.

Philosophical Overview

Sextus begins his *Outlines of Pyrrhonism* by dividing those who inquire into three groups. First, there are those who claim to have found the answer, such as the Stoics. Second, there are thinkers who claim that questions cannot be answered, such as the Academic Skeptics. Finally, there are those who think that questions have not yet been answered, the Pyrrhoneans. Only this third group carries on with the relevant inquiries. This is philosophically the healthiest position: not to draw premature and final conclusions.

OUTLINES OF PYRRHONISM

The *Outlines of Pyrrhonism* is a general summary of the various Pyrrhonean arguments organized as a philosophical method to aid the Skeptic to maintain his healthy and quiet skeptical attitude of neither affirming nor denying anything beyond the immediate sense impressions that 'induce our assent involuntarily' (x, 19).

Just as medical doctors use varying remedies of different strengths to cure the sick depending on the severity of their illness, so the skeptical philosopher must use arguments of appropriate strength and measure to cure the philosophical ills of dogmatic belief. The strongest skeptical arguments should be applied to the more entrenched beliefs with the aim of showing that one does not really know what one thinks one knows. The *Outlines of Pyrrhonism* helps the Skeptic to apply the appropriate skeptical reasoning at the right time.

The ultimate aim of this skeptical attitude is to achieve tranquility or quietude. This state requires the suspension of judgment because the person who judges that anything is by nature good or bad is always being disquieted (12).

BOOK I

Chapter I.—Of the Main Difference between Philosophic Systems

1 The natural result of any investigation is that the investigators either discover the object of search or deny that it is discoverable and confess it to be inapprehensible or persist in their search. 2 So, too, with regard to the objects investigated by philosophy, this is probably why some have claimed to have discovered the truth, others have asserted that it cannot be apprehended, while others again go on inquiring. Those who 3 believe they have discovered it are the "Dogmatists," specially so called—Aristotle, for example, and Epicurus and the Stoics and certain others; Cleitomachus and Carneades and other Academics treat it as inapprehensible: the Sceptics 4 keep on searching. Hence it seems reasonable to hold that the main types of philosophy are three—the Dogmatic, the Academic, and the Sceptic. Of the other systems it will best become others to speak: our task at present is to describe in outline the Sceptic doctrine, first premising that of none of our future statements do we positively affirm that the fact is exactly as we state it, but we simply record each fact, like a chronicler, as it appears to us at the moment.

Chapter II.—Of the Arguments of Scepticism

5 Of the Sceptic philosophy one argument (or branch of exposition) is called "general," the other "special." In the general argument we set forth the distinctive features of Scepticism, stating its purport and principles, its logical methods, criterion, and end or aim; the "Tropes," also, or "Modes," which lead to suspension of judgement, and in what sense we adopt the Sceptic formulae, and the distinction between Scepticism and the philosophies which stand next to it. In the special 6 argument we state our objections regarding the several divisions of so-called philosophy. Let us, then, deal first with the general argument, beginning our description with the names given to the Sceptic School.

Chapter III.—Of the Nomenclature of Scepticism

7 The Sceptic School, then, is also called "Zetetic" from its activity in investigation and inquiry, and "Ephectic" or Suspensive from the state of mind produced in the inquirer after his search, and "Aporetic" or Dubitative either from its habit of doubting and seeking, as some say, or from its indecision as regards assent and denial, and "Pyrrhonean" from the fact that Pyrrho appears to us to have applied himself to Scepticism more thoroughly and more conspicuously than his predecessors.

Chapter IV.—What Scepticism Is

8 Scepticism is an ability, or mental attitude, which opposes appearances to judgements in any way whatsoever, with the result that, owing to the equipollence of the objects and reasons thus opposed, we are brought firstly to a state of mental suspense and next to a state of "unperturbedness" or quietude. Now we call it an "ability" not 9 in any subtle sense, but simply in respect of its "being able." By "appearances" we now mean the objects of senseperception, whence we contrast them with the objects of thought or "judgements." The phrase "in any way whatsoever" can be connected either with the word "ability," to make us take the word "ability," as we said, in its simple sense, or with the phrase "opposing appearances to judgements"; for inasmuch as we oppose these in a variety of ways—appearances

From *Sextus Empiricus-Outlines of Pyrrhonism*, translated by Rev. R. Bury, (The Loeb Classical Library, 1933).

to appearances, or judgements to judgements, or *alternando* appearances to judgements,—in order to ensure the inclusion of all these antitheses we employ the phrase "in any way whatsoever." Or, again, we join "in any way whatsoever" to "appearances and judgements" in order that we may not have to inquire how the appearances appear or how the thought-objects are judged, but may take these terms in the simple sense. The

10 phrase "opposed judgements" we do not employ in the sense of negations and affirmations only but simply as equivalent to "conflicting judgements." "Equipollence" we use of equality in respect of probability and improbability, to indicate that no one of the conflicting judgements takes precedence of any other as being more probable. "Suspense" is a state of mental rest owing to which we neither deny nor affirm anything. "Quietude" is an untroubled and tranquil condition of soul. And how quietude enters the soul along with suspension of judgement we shall explain in our chapter (XII.) "Concerning the End."

Chapter V.—Of the Sceptic

11 In the definition of the Sceptic system there is also implicitly included that of the Pyrrhonean philosopher: he is the man who participates in this "ability."

Chapter VI.—Of the Principles of Scepticism

12 The originating cause of Scepticism is, we say, the hope of attaining quietude. Men of talent, who were perturbed by the contradictions in things and in doubt as to which of the alternatives they ought to accept, were led on to inquire what is true in things and what false, hoping by the settlement of this question to attain quietude. The main basic principle of the Sceptic system is that of opposing to every proposition an equal proposition; for we believe that as a consequence of this we end by ceasing to dogmatize.

Chapter VII.—Does the Sceptic Dogmatize?

13 When we say that the Sceptic refrains from dogmatizing we do not use the term "dogma," as some do, in the broader sense of "approval of a thing" (for the Sceptic gives assent to the feelings which are the necessary results of sense-impressions, and he would not, for example, say when feeling hot or cold "I believe that I am not hot or cold"); but we say that "he does not dogmatize" using "dogma" in the sense, which some give it, of "assent to one of the non-evident objects of scientific inquiry"; for the Pyrrhonean philosopher assents to nothing that is non-evident. Moreover,

14 even in the act of enunciating the Sceptic formulae concerning things non-evident—such as the formula "No more (one thing than another)," or the formula "I determine nothing," or any of the others which we shall presently mention,—he does not dogmatize. For whereas the dogmatizer posits the things about which he is said to be dogmatizing as really existent, the Sceptic does not posit these formulae in any absolute sense; for he conceives that, just as the formula "All things are false" asserts the falsity of itself as well as of everything else, as does the formula "Nothing is true," so also the formula "No more" asserts that itself, like all the rest, is "No more (this than that)," and thus cancels itself along with the rest. And

15 of the other formulae we say the same. If then, while the dogmatizer posits the matter of his dogma as substantial truth, the Sceptic enunciates his formulae so that they are virtually cancelled by themselves, he should not be said to dogmatize in his enunciation of them. And, most important of all, in his enunciation of these formulae he states what appears to himself and announces his own impression in an undogmatic way, without making any positive assertion regarding the external realities.

Chapter VIII.—Has the Sceptic a Doctrinal Rule?

16 We follow the same lines in replying to the question "Has the Sceptic a doctrinal rule?" For if one defines a "doctrinal rule" as "adherence to a number of dogmas which are dependent both on one another and on appearances," and defines "dogma" as "assent to a non-evident proposition," then we shall say that he has not a doctri-

17 nal rule. But if one defines "doctrinal rule" as

"procedure which, in accordance with appearance, follows a certain line of reasoning, that reasoning indicating how it is possible to seem to live rightly (the word 'rightly' being taken, not as referring to virtue only, but in a wider sense) and tending to enable one to suspend judgement," then we say that he has a doctrinal rule. For we follow a line of reasoning which, in accordance with appearances, points us to a life conformable to the customs of our country and its laws and institutions, and to our own instinctive feelings.

Chapter IX.—Does the Sceptic Deal with Physics?

18 We make a similar reply also to the question "Should the Sceptic deal with physical problems?" For while, on the one hand, so far as regards making firm and positive assertions about any of the matters dogmatically treated in physical theory, we do not deal with physics; yet, on the other hand, in respect of our mode of opposing to every proposition an equal proposition and of our theory of quietude we do treat of physics. This, too, is the way in which we approach the logical and ethical branches of so-called "philosophy."

Chapter X.—Do the Sceptics Abolish Appearances?

19 Those who say that "the Sceptics abolish appearances," or phenomena, seem to me to be unacquainted with the statements of our School. For, as we said above, we do not overthrow the affective sense-impressions which induce our assent involuntarily; and these impressions are "the appearances." And when we question whether the underlying object is such as it appears, we grant the fact that it appears, and our doubt does not concern the appearance itself but the account given of that appearance,—and that is a different thing from questioning the appearance itself. For 20 example, honey appears to us to be sweet (and this we grant, for we perceive sweetness through the senses), but whether it is also sweet in its essence is for us a matter of doubt, since this is not an appearance but a judgement regarding the appearance. And even if we do actually argue against the appearances, we do not propound such arguments with the intention of abolishing appearances, but by way of pointing out the rashness of the Dogmatists; for if reason is such a trickster as to all but snatch away the appearances from under our very eyes, surely we should view it with suspicion in the case of things non-evident so as not to display rashness by following it.

Chapter XI.—Of the Criterion of Scepticism

21 That we adhere to appearances is plain from what we say about the Criterion of the Sceptic School. The word "Criterion" is used in two senses: in the one it means "the standard regulating belief in reality or unreality," (and this we shall discuss in our refutation); in the other it denotes the standard of action by conforming to which in the conduct of life we perform some actions and abstain from others; and it is of the 22 latter that we are now speaking. The criterion, then, of the Sceptic School is, we say, the appearance, giving this name to what is virtually the sense-presentation. For since this lies in feeling and involuntary affection, it is not open to question. Consequently, no one, I suppose, disputes that the underlying object has this or that appearance; the point in dispute is whether the object is in reality such as it appears to be.

23 Adhering, then, to appearances we live in accordance with the normal rules of life, undogmatically, seeing that we cannot remain wholly inactive. And it would seem that this regulation of life is fourfold, and that one part of it lies in the guidance of Nature, another in the constraint of the passions, another in the tradition of laws and customs, another in the instruction of 24 the arts. Nature's guidance is that by which we are naturally capable of sensation and thought; constraint of the passions is that whereby hunger drives us to food and thirst to drink; tradition of customs and laws, that whereby we regard piety in the conduct of life as good, but impiety as evil; instruction of the arts, that whereby we are not inactive in such arts as we adopt. But we make all these statements undogmatically.

Chapter XII.—What Is the End of Scepticism?

25 Our next subject will be the End of the Sceptic system. Now an "End" is "that for which all actions or reasonings are undertaken, while it exists for the sake of none"; or, otherwise, "the ultimate object of appetency." We assert still that the Sceptic's End is quietude in respect of matters of opinion and moderate feeling in respect of things unavoidable. For the Sceptic, having set 26 out to philosophize with the object of passing judgement on the sense-impressions and ascertaining which of them are true and which false, so as to attain quietude thereby, found himself involved in contradictions of equal weight, and being unable to decide between them suspended judgement; and as he was thus in suspense there followed, as it happened, the state of quietude 27 in respect of matters of opinion. For the man who opines that anything is by nature good or bad is for ever being disquieted: when he is without the things which he deems good he believes himself to be tormented by things naturally bad and he pursues after the things which are, as he thinks, good; which when he has obtained he keeps falling into still more perturbations because of his irrational and immoderate elation, and in his dread of a change of fortune he uses every endeavour to avoid losing the things which he deems good. On the other 28 hand, the man who determines nothing as to what is naturally good or bad neither shuns nor pursues anything eagerly; and, in consequence, he is unperturbed.

The Sceptic, in fact, had the same experience which is said to have befallen the painter Apelles. Once, they say, when he was painting a horse and wished to represent in the painting the horse's foam, he was so unsuccessful that he gave up the attempt and flung at the picture the sponge on which he used to wipe the paints off his brush, and the mark of the sponge produced 29 the effect of a horse's foam. So, too, the Sceptics were in hopes of gaining quietude by means of a decision regarding the disparity of the objects of sense and of thought, and being unable to effect this they suspended judgement; and they found that quietude, as if by chance, followed upon their suspense, even as a shadow follows its sub-

stance. We do not, however, suppose that the Sceptic is wholly untroubled; but we say that he is troubled by things unavoidable; for we grant that he is cold at times and thirsty, and suffers various affections of that kind. But even in these 30 cases, whereas ordinary people are afflicted by two circumstances,—namely, by the affections themselves and, in no less a degree, by the belief that these conditions are evil by nature,—the Sceptic, by his rejection of the added belief in the natural badness of all these conditions, escapes here too with less discomfort. Hence we say that, while in regard to matters of opinion the Sceptic's End is quietude, in regard to things unavoidable it is "moderate affection." But some notable Sceptics have added the further definition "suspension of judgement in investigations."

Chapter XIII.—Of the General Modes Leading to Suspension of Judgement

31 Now that we have been saying that tranquillity follows on suspension of judgement, it will be our next task to explain how we arrive at this suspension. Speaking generally, one may say that it is the result of setting things in opposition. We oppose either appearances to appearances or objects of thought to objects of thought or *alternando*. For 32 instance, we oppose appearances to appearances when we say "The same tower appears round from a distance, but square from close at hand"; and thoughts to thoughts, when in answer to him who argues the existence of Providence from the order of the heavenly bodies we oppose the fact that often the good fare ill and the bad fare well, and draw from this the inference that Providence does 33 not exist. And thoughts we oppose to appearances, as when Anaxagoras countered the notion that snow is white with the argument, "Snow is frozen water, and water is black; therefore snow also is black." With a different idea we oppose things present sometimes to things present, as in the foregoing examples, and sometimes to things past or future, as, for instance, when someone propounds to us a theory which we are unable to 34 refute, we say to him in reply, "Just as, before the birth of the founder of the School to which you belong, the theory it holds was not as yet apparent as a sound theory, although it was really in

existence, so likewise it is possible that the opposite theory to that which you now propound is already really existent, though not yet apparent to us, so that we ought not as yet to yield assent to this theory which at the moment seems to be valid."

35 But in order that we may have a more exact understanding of these antitheses I will describe the Modes by which suspension of judgement is brought about, but without making any positive assertion regarding either their number or their validity; for it is possible that they may be unsound or there may be more of them than I shall enumerate.

Chapter XIV.—Concerning the Ten Modes

36 The usual tradition amongst the older Sceptics is that the "modes" by which "suspension" is supposed to be brought about are ten in number; and they also give them the synonymous names of "arguments" and "positions." They are these: the first, based on the variety in animals; the second, on the differences in human beings; the third, on the different structures of the organs of sense; the fourth, on the circumstantial conditions; the fifth, on positions and intervals and locations; 37 the sixth, on intermixtures; the seventh, on the quantities and formations of the underlying objects; the eighth, on the fact of relativity; the ninth, on the frequency or rarity of occurrence; the tenth, on the disciplines and customs and laws, the legendary beliefs and the dogmatic convictions. This order, however, we adopt without 38 prejudice.

As superordinate to these there stand three Modes—that based on the subject who judges, that on the object judged, and that based on both. The first four of the ten Modes are subordinate to the Mode based on the subject (for the subject which judges is either an animal or a man or a sense, and existent in some condition): the seventh and tenth Modes are referred to that based on the object judged: the fifth, sixth, eighth and ninth are referred to the Mode based 39 on both subject and object. Furthermore, these three Modes are also referred to that of relation, so that the Mode of relation stands as the highest genus, and the three as species, and the ten as

subordinate sub-species. We give this as the probable account of their numbers.

Chapter XV.—Of the Five Modes

164 The later Sceptics hand down Five Modes leading to suspension, namely these: the first based on discrepancy, the second on regress ad infinitum, the third on relativity, the fourth on hypothesis, the fifth on circular reasoning. That 165 based on discrepancy leads us to find that with regard to the object presented there has arisen both amongst ordinary people and amongst the philosophers an interminable conflict because of which we are unable either to choose a thing or reject it, and so fall back on suspension. The 166 Mode based upon regress ad infinitum is that whereby we assert that the thing adduced as a proof of the matter proposed needs a further proof, and this again another, and so on ad infinitum, so that the consequence is suspension, as we 167 possess no starting-point for our argument. The Mode based upon relativity, as we have already said, is that whereby the object has such or such an appearance in relation to the subject judging and to the concomitant percepts, but as to its real nature we suspend judgement. We have the 168 Mode based on hypothesis when the Dogmatists, being force to recede ad infinitum, take as their starting-point something which they do not establish by argument but claim to assume as granted simply and without demonstration. The 169 Mode of circular reasoning is the form used when the proof itself which ought to establish the matter of inquiry requires confirmation derived from that matter; in this case, being unable to assume either in order to establish the other, we suspend judgement about both.

That every matter of inquiry admits of being brought under these Modes we shall show briefly 170 in this way. The matter proposed is either a sense-object of a thought-object, but whichever it is, it is an object of controversy; for some say that only sensibles are true, others only intelligibles, others that some sensible and some intelligible objects are true. Will they then assert that the controversy can or cannot be decided? If they say it cannot, we have it granted that we must suspend judgement; for concerning matters of dispute which admit of no decision it is impossible to make an assertion. But if they say that it can be decided, we ask by what is it to be decided. For example, in the case of

171 the sense-object (for we shall base our argument on it first), is it to be decided by a sense-object or a thought-object? For if they say by a sense-object, since we are inquiring about sensibles that object itself also will require another to confirm it; and if that too is to be a sense-object, it likewise will require another for its confirmation, and so on *ad infinitum*. And if the sense-object shall have to

172 be decided by a thought-object, then, since thought-objects also are controverted, this being an object of thought will need examination and confirmation. Whence then will it gain confirmation? If from an intelligible object, it will suffer a similar regress *ad infinitum*; and if from a sensible object, since an intelligible was adduced to establish the sensible and a sensible to establish the intelligible, the Mode of circular reasoning is brought in.

173   If, however, our disputant, by way of escape from this conclusion, should claim to assume as granted and without demonstration some postulate for the demonstration of the next steps of his argument, then the Mode of hypothesis will be brought in, which allows no escape. For if the author of the hypothesis is worthy of credence, we shall be no less worthy of credence every time that we make the opposite hypothesis. Moreover, if the author of the hypothesis assumes what is true he causes it to be suspected by assuming it by hypothesis rather than after proof; while if it is false, the foundation of his argument will be rot-

174 ten. Further, if hypothesis conduces at all to proof, let the subject of inquiry itself be assumed and not some other thing which is merely a means to establish the actual subject of the argument; but if it is absurd to assume the subject of inquiry, it will also be absurd to assume that upon which it depends.

175   It is also plain that all sensible are relative; for they are relative to those who have the sensations. Therefore it is apparent that whatever sensible object is presented can easily be referred to one of the Five Modes. And concerning the intelligible object we argue similarly. For if it should be said that it is a matter of unsettled con-

troversy, the necessity of our suspending judge-
176 ment will be granted. And if, on the other hand, the controversy admits of decision, then if the decision rests on an intelligible object we shall be driven to the regress *ad infinitum*, and to circular reasoning if it rests on a sensible; for since the sensible again is controverted and cannot be decided by means of itself because of the regress *ad infinitum*, it will require the intelligible object, just as also the intelligible will require the sensi-
177 ble. For these reasons, again, he who assumes anything by hypothesis will be acting illogically. Moreover, objects of thought, or intelligibles, are relative; for they are so named on account of their relation to the person thinking, and if they had really possessed the nature they are said to possess, there would have been no controversy about them. Thus the intelligible also is referred to the Five Modes, so that in all cases we are compelled to suspend judgement concerning the object presented.

   Such then are the Five Modes handed down amongst the later Sceptics; but they propound these not by way of superseding the Ten Modes but in order to expose the rashness of the Dogmatists with more variety and completeness by means of the Five in conjunction with the Ten.

Chapter XVIII.—Of the Sceptic Expressions or Formulae

187 And because when we make use of these Modes and those which lead to suspension of judgement we give utterance to certain expressions indicative of out skeptical attitude and tone of mind—such as "Not more," "Nothing must be determined," and others of the kind—it will be our next task to discuss these in order. So let us begin with the expression "Not more."

Chapter XIX.—Of the Expression "Not more"

188 This expression, then, we sometimes enunciate in the form I have stated but sometimes in the form "Nowise more." For we do not, as some suppose, adopt the form "Not more" in specific inquiries and "Nowise more" in generic inquiries, but we enunciate both "Not more" and "Nowise

more" indifferently, and we shall discuss them now as identical expressions. This expression, then, is elliptical. For just as when we say "a double" we are implicitly saying "a double hearth," and when we say "a square" we are implicitly saying "a square roadway," so when we say "Not more" we are implicitly saying "Not this more than that, up than down." Some of the Sceptics, 189 however, in place of the "Not" adopt the form "(For) what this more than that," taking the "what" to denote, in this case, cause, so that the meaning is "For what reason this more than that?" And it is a common practice to use questions instead of assertion, as for example—"The bride of Zeus, what mortal knows her not?" And also assertions in the place of questions; for instance— "I am inquiring where Dion lives," and "I ask you what reason there is for showing surprise at a poet." And further, the use of "What" instead of "For what reason" is found in Menander, "(For) 190 what was I left behind?" And the expression "Not more this than that" indicated also our feeling, whereby we come to end in equipoise because of the equipollence of the opposed objects; and by "equipollence" we mean equality in respect of what seems probable to us, and by "opposed" we mean in general conflicting, and by "equipoise" refusal of assent to either alternative.

191 Then as to the formula "Nowise more," even though it exhibits the character of a form of assent or of denial, we do not employ it in this way, but we take it in a loose and inexact sense, either in place of a question or in place of the phrase "I know not to which of these things I ought to assent, and to which I ought not." For our aim is to indicate what appears to us; while as to the expression by which we indicate this we are indifferent. This point, too, should be noticed—that we utter the expression "Nowise more" not as positively affirming that it really is true and certain, but as stating in regard to it also what appears to us.

Chapter XX.—Of "Aphaisa" or Non-assertion

192 Concerning non-assertion what we say is this. The term "assertion" has two senses, general and special; used in the general sense it indicates affirmation or negation, as for example "It is day."

"It is not day"; in its special sense it indicates affirmation only, and in this sense negations are not termed assertions. Non-assertion, then, is avoidance of assertion in the general sense in which it is said to include both affirmation and negation, so that non-assertion is a mental condition of ours because of which we refuse either 193 to affirm or to deny anything. Hence it is plain that we adopt non-assertion also not as though things are in reality of such a kind as wholly to induce non-assertion, but as indicating that we now, at the time of uttering it, are in this condition regarding the problems now before use. It must also be borne in mind that what, as we say, we neither posit nor deny, is some one of the dogmatic statements made about what is non-apparent; for we yield to those things which move us emotional and drive us compulsorily to assent.

Chapter XXI.—Of the Expressions "Perhaps," "Possibly," and "Maybe"

194 The formulae "perhaps" and "perhaps not," and "possibly" and "possibly not," and "maybe" and "maybe not," we adopt in place of "perhaps it is and perhaps it is not," and "possible it is and possibly it is not," and "maybe it is and maybe it is not," so that for the sake of conciseness we adopt the phrase "possibly not" instead of "possibly it is not," and "maybe not" instead of "maybe it is not," and "perhaps not" instead of "perhaps it 195 is not." But here again we do not fight about phrases nor do we inquire whether the phrases indicate realities, but we adopt them, as I said, in a loose sense. Still it is evident, as I think, that these expressions are indicative of non-assertion. Certainly the person who says "perhaps it is" is implicitly affirming also the seemingly contradictory phrase "perhaps it is not" by his refusal to make the positive assertion that "it is." And the same applies to all the other cases.

Chapter XXII.—Of the Expression "I suspend Judgement"

196 The phrase "I suspend judgement" we adopt in place of "I am unable to say which of the objects presented I ought to believe and which I ought to disbelieve," indicating that the objects appear to

us equal as regards credibility and incredibility. As to whether they are equal we make no positive assertion; but what we state is what appears to us in regard to them at the time of observation. And the term "suspension" is derived from the fact of the mind being held up or "suspended" so that it neither affirms nor denies anything owing to the equipollence of the matters in question.

Chapter XXIII.—Of the Expression "I determine Nothing"

197 Regarding the phrase "I determine nothing" this is what we say. We hold that "to determine" is not simply to state a thing but to put forward something non-evident combined with assent. For in this sense, no doubt, it will be found that the Sceptic determines nothing, not even the very proposition "I determine nothing"; for this is not a dogmatic assumption, that is to say assent to something non-evident, but an expression indicative of our own mental condition. So whenever the Sceptic says "I determine nothing," what he means is "I am now in such a state of mind as neither to affirm dogmatically nor deny any of the matters now in question." And this he says simply by way of announcing undogmatically what appears to himself regarding the matters presented, not making any confident declaration, but just explaining his own state of mind.

Chapter XXIV.—Of the Expression "All Things are Undetermined"

198 Indetermination is a state of mind in which we neither deny nor affirm any of the matters which are subjects of dogmatic inquiry, that is to say, non-evident. So whenever the Sceptic says "All things are undetermined," he takes the word "are" in the sense of "appear to him," and by "all things" he means not existing things but such of the non-evident matters investigated by the Dogmatists as he has examined, and by "undetermined" he means not examined, and by "undetermined" he means not superior in point of credibility or incredibility to things opposed, or 199 in any way conflicting. And just as the man who says "(I) walk about" is potentially saying "I walk about," so he who says "All are undetermined" conveys also, as we hold, the meaning "so far as

relates to me," or "as appears to me," so that the statement amounts to this—"All the matters of dogmatic inquiry which I have examined appear to me to be such that no one of them is preferable to the one in conflict with it in respect of credibility or incredibility."

Chapter XXV.—Of the Expression "All Things are Non-apprehensible"

200 We adopt a similar attitude when we say "All things are non-apprehensible." For we give a similar explanation to the word "all," and we similarly supply the words "to me," so that the meaning conveyed is this—"All the non-apparent matters of dogmatic inquiry which I have investigated appear to me non-apprehensible." And this is the utterance not of one who is positively asserting that the matters investigated by the Dogmatists are really of such a nature as to be non-apprehensible, but of one who is announcing his own state of mind, "wherein," he says, "I conceive that up till now I myself have apprehended nothing owing to the equipollence of the opposites; and therefore also nothing that is brought forward to overthrow our position seems to me to have any bearing on what we announce."

Chapter XXVI.—Of the Expressions "I am Non-apprehensive" and "I apprehend not"

201 Both the expressions "I am non-apprehensive" and "I apprehend not" are indicative of a personal state of mind, in which the Sceptic, for the time being, avoids affirming or denying any non-evident matter of inquiry, as is obvious from what we have said above concerning the other expressions.

Chapter XXVII.—Of the Phrase "To every Argument an Equal Argument is Opposed"

202 When we say "To every argument an equal argument is opposed," we mean "to every argument" that has been investigated by us, and the word "argument" we use not in its simple sense, but of that which establishes a point dogmatically (that is to say with reference to what is non-evident) and establishes it by any method, and not necessarily by means of premises and conclusion. We

say "equal" with reference to credibility or incredibility, and we employ the word "opposed" in the general sense of "conflicting"; and we supply therewith in thought the phrase "as appears 203 to me." So whenever I say "To every argument an equal argument is opposed," what I am virtually saying is "To every argument investigated by me which establishes a point dogmatically, it seems to me there is opposed another argument, establishing a point dogmatically, which is equal to the first in respect of credibility and incredibility"; so that the utterance of the phrase is not a piece of dogmatism, but the announcement of a human state of mind which is apparent to the person experiencing it.

204   But some also utter the expression in the form "To every argument an equal argument is to be opposed," intending to give the injunction "To every argument which establishes a point dogmatically let us oppose an argument which investigates dogmatically, equal to the former in respect of credibility and incredibility, and conflicting therewith"; for they mean their words to be addressed to the Sceptic, although they use the infinitive form "to be opposed" instead of the 205 imperative "let us oppose." And they address this injunction to the Sceptic lest haply, though being misled by the Dogmatist, he may give up the Sceptic search, and through precipitancy miss the "quietude" approved by the Sceptics, which they—as we said above—believe to be dependent on universal suspension of judgement.

Chapter XXVIII.—Supplementary Notes on the Sceptic Expressions

206 In a preliminary outline it will be sufficient to have explained the expressions now set forth, especially since it is possible to explain the rest by deductions from the foregoing. For, in regard to all the Sceptic expressions, we must grasp first the fact that we make no positive assertion respecting their absolute truth, since we say that they may possibly be confuted by themselves, seeing that they themselves are included in the things to which their doubt applies, just as aperient drugs do not merely eliminate the humours from the body, but also expel themselves along with the humours. And we also say that we 207 employ them not by way of authoritatively explaining the things with reference to which we adopt them, but without precision and, if you like, loosely; for it does not become the Sceptic to wrangle over expressions, and besides it is to our advantage that even to these expressions no absolute significance should be ascribed, but one that is relative to the Sceptics. Besides 208 this we must also remember that we do not employ them universally about all things, but about those which are non-evident and are objects of dogmatic inquiry; and that we state what appears to us and do not make any positive declarations as to the real nature of external objects; for I think that, as a result of this, every sophism directed against a Sceptic expression can be refuted.

And now that we have reviewed the idea or 209 purpose of Scepticism and its divisions, and the criterion and the end, and the modes, too, of suspension, and have discussed the Sceptic expressions, and have thus made clear the character of Scepticism, our next task is, we suppose, to explain briefly the distinction which exists between it and the philosophic systems which lie next to it, in order that we may more clearly understand the "suspensive" Way of thought. Let us begin with the Heracleitean philosophy.

STUDY QUESTIONS: EMPIRICUS, *OUTLINES OF PYRRHONISM*

1. What does the Greek term *skepsis* mean?
2. How does Sextus Empiricus distinguish the Stoics, the Academic Skeptics, and the Pyrrhoneans? Which method is healthiest, and why?
3. Do Pyrrhonean skeptics hold beliefs? What is the standard of skepticism?
4. What is the aim of Pyrrhonean skepticism?
5. What is meant by suspension of judgment? When and how is it applied, and what is its importance?

6. What does Sextus mean by the evident? How does he distinguish the evident and the nonevident? Why is this distinction important?

7. What are the five modes of skeptical argument? How does Sextus Empiricus argue for the claim that every inquiry can be brought under these modes?

Philosophical Bridges: The Influence of Skepticism

Pyrrhonian Skepticism had a liberating effect on early modern thought. In his popular *Essays* (1580), the French Renaissance thinker Montaigne takes his reader on a tour of ancient philosophy. Initially, he finds wisdom in the ethics of Stoicism, but, as the *Essays* proceed, he is drawn increasingly toward Skepticism. Like Pyrrho, Montaigne decides to suspend all judgment and simply to observe. His *Essays* present Skepticism with a very human and reasonable face; they oppose any religious dogmatism and articulate the humanism and the freedom of thought of the Renaissance.

Descartes, who knew of Pyrrhonism through Montaigne's *Essays*, revolutionized philosophy with his method of doubt. Descartes argued that it was reasonable to suspend judgment as to the veracity of our perceptions basically because there is no independent way to check them. Descartes' skeptical arguments set a fundamental problem that many later philosophers have tried to solve: how can we have justified knowledge of the external world?

Philosophical Bridges: The Ancient Influence

Medieval philosophy was dominated by the influence of the ancients, especially Plato and Aristotle. However, this influence includes much more than the towering figures of Plato and Aristotle. Around 1340, Plutarch and Boccaccio acquired a passion for Greek literature and culture, which were largely unknown to a Latin-dominated Europe. Their passion ignited Europe and initiated the Italian Renaissance a century later. The study of Greek culture gave rise to the central idea of humanism that the proper study of humankind is itself. This idea had a tremendous effect on art and literature, as well as philosophy. It was the first step in a long process that liberated European thought and politics from the dominating influence of the all-powerful Church. The rediscovery of ancient Greece had an effect on western culture at least as profound as the 'discovery' of the Americas of around the same time.

Humanism dominated western culture for a century. In this process, it freed the European mind from the otherworldliness of Christian doctrine and, thereby, permitted the development of science after the year 1550. However, the birth of science required two other elements: scientific instruments, such as the telescope, and the influence of the naturalistic philosophies of the ancient world, especially atomism and Epicureanism, as well as the mathematical ideas of Pythagoras and neo-Platonism. We have already described the impact of the materialism of Epicurus and Lucretius on the growth of modern science, and also outlined the importance of Pythagoras and neo-Platonism. In many ways, the early modern scientists can be regarded as continuing the rich ancient tradition of natural philosophy.

BIBLIOGRAPHY

GENERAL

Primary

Inwood, Brad, and Gerson, L. P., *Hellenistic Philosophy*, Hackett, 1988

Irwin, Terence, *Hellenistic Philosophy*, Garland Publishing, 1995

Long, A. A., and Sedley, D. N, *The Hellenistic Philosophers*, vols. 1 and 2, Cambridge University Press, 1987

Oates, Whitney, ed., *The Stoic and Epicurean Philosophers: The Complete Extant Writings of Epicurus, Epictetus, Lucretius and Marcus Aurelius*, Random House, 1940

Secondary

Annas, Julia, *The Morality of Happiness*, Oxford University Press, 1993

Furley, David, *From Aristotle to Augustine*, Routledge History of Philosophy, vol. 2, Routledge, 1999

Long, A. A., *Hellenistic Philosophy, Stoics, Epicureans and Sceptics*, University of California Press, 1986

Sharples, R. W., *Stoics, Epicureans, and Sceptics*, Routledge, 1996

EPICUREANISM

Primary

Lucretius, *On the Nature of Things*, trans. by W. Rouse and M. Smith, Loeb edition, Cambridge University Press, 1975

Secondary

Diskin, Clay, *Lucretius and Epicurus*, Cornell University Press, 1983

Kenny, E. J., *Lucretius*, Oxford University Press, 1977

Rist, J. M., *Epicurus: An Introduction*, Cambridge University Press, 1972

THE STOICS

Primary

Epictetus, *The Discourses*, ed. C. J. Gill and J. M. Dent, Everyman and Sons, 1995

———, *Encheiridion*, trans. W. A. Oldfather, Loeb Version, Harvard University Press, 1928

Marcus Aurelius, *Meditations*, trans. Maxwell Standford, Penguin, 1964

The Meditations of the Emperor Marcus Aurelius, ed. A. S. L. Farquharson, Clarendon Press, 1944

Secondary

Long, A., *Problems in Stoicism*, Althone Press, 1971

——— ed., *Stoic Studies*, Cambridge University Press, 1996

Rutherford, R. B., *The Meditations of Marcus Aurelius: A Study*, Oxford University Press, 1989

Xenakis, J., *Epictetus: Philosopher—Therapist*, E. J. Brill, 1969

THE SKEPTICS

Primary

Sextus Empiricus, *Outlines of Pyrrhonism*, trans. J. Annas and J. Barnes, Cambridge University Press, 1994

Secondary

Annas, J., and Barnes, J., *The Modes of Scepticism*, Cambridge University Press, 1985

Harkinson, R., *The Sceptics*, Routledge, 1995

Mates, Benson, *The Skeptic Way: Sextus Empiricus's Outlines of Pyrrhonism*, Oxford University Press, 1995

◆ SOURCES ◆

SECTION I: PRE-SOCRATICS

Note: All references quoted as 'B' followed by a number refer to the *Ancilla*. The sources of all other references are given.

Page 7: Thales translated by J. Barnes, *Early Greek Philosophy*, Harmondsworth, 1987: Aristotle, *Metaphysics*, 983b6–11; 17–27; Aristotle, *On the Heavens*, 294a28–34; Diogenes Laertius, *Lives of the Philosophers*, I, 22–28; Aristotle, *On the Soul*, 411a7–8; Aristotle, *On the Soul*, 405a19–21; and Diogenes Laertius, *Lives of the Philosophers*, I, 33–40.

Page 10: Anaximander translated by J. Barnes, op. cit: Hippolytus, *Refutation of All Heresies*, I vi 1–7; Aristotle, *Physics* 203 b6–11, 13–30; Simplicius, *Commentary on the Physics*, 24.13–25; Plutarch, Miscellanies fragment 179,2 in Eusebius, *Preparation for the Gospel*, I, vii, 16; Hippolytus, *Refutation of All Heresies*, I vi 1–7; Aristotle, *On the Heavens*, 295b11–16; and Plutarch, *On the Scientific Beliefs of the Philosophers*, 908D.

Page 12: Anaximenes translated by J. Barnes, op. cit: Hippolytus, *Refutation of All Heresies*, I vii 1–9; Plutarch, *On the Scientific Beliefs of the Philosophers*, 876ab (B2); Plutarch, *The Primary Cold*, 947f (B1); and Hippolytus, *Refutation of All Heresies*, I vii 1–9.

Page 15: Pythagoras, translated by Robin Waterfield, *The First Philosophers: The Presocratics and Sophists*, Oxford University Press, 2000. Philolaus fr.14, Clement, Miscellanies 2.203.11; Philolaus fr.1, Diogenes Laertius, *Lives of the Philosophers*, 8.85.13–14; Philolaus fr.4, John of Stobi, *Anthology*, 1.21.7b; Philolaus fr.6, John of Stobi, *Anthology*, 1.21.7d; Herodotus, *Histories*, 2.123, 2–3; Aristotle, *On the Soul*, 407b20–3; Diogenes Laertius, *Lives of the Philosophers*, 8.4–5; Diogenes Laertius, *Lives of the Philosophers*, 8.34.1–35.2; op.cit, 8.11.10–12.5; Porphyry, *Commentary on Ptolemy's Harmonics*, 30.1–6; Isocrates, *Busiris*, 28.5–29.9; Sextus Empiricus, *Against the Professors*, 7.94–6; Aristotle, *Metaphysics*, 985b23–986a26; Aristotle, op. cit, 987a13–19; Aristotle, op. cit, 1090a20–5; Aristotle, op. cit, 1080b16–21; and Aristotle, *On the Soul*, 407b27–32;

Page 20: Heraclitus, translated by C. Kahn, *The Art and Thought of Heraclitus*, Cambridge University Press, 1979: Fragments 1–22, 25–33, 35–42, 43b, 44–48a, and 49–125. *Ancilla* numbering: B1, B34, B2, B17, B71–73, B89, B18, B22, B35, B123, B47, A23, B74, B55, B101a, B107, B19, B40, B57, B106, B42, B56, B129, B81, B108, B101, B116, B114, B113, B112, B93, B45, B50, B30, B31a, B31b, B90, B76, B100, A5, B99, B3, B6, B126, B12, B91, B84a, B84b, B41, B78, B82–83, B79, B70, B104, B87, B97, B49, B44, B33, B110–11, B102, B23, B61, B9, B13, B58, B59, B8, B11, B125, B51, B48, B54, A22, B80, B53, B27, B28a, B86, B28b, B96, B21, B26, B75, B63, B88, B52, A19, B29, B25, B20, B103, B24, B115, B36, B60, B43, B85, B117, B95, B77, B118, B63, B98, B7, A15, B87, B15, B5, B32, B64, B65, B66, B16, B67, B10, and B124.

Page 30: Parmenides, translated by D. Gallup, *Fragments*, University of Toronto Press, 1984. Fragments 1–19; Cornford's fragment.

Page 37: Zeno, translated by J. Barnes, op. cit: Plato, *Parmenides*, 127a–128d; Aristotle, *Physics*, 239b5–240a18; Simplicius, *Commentary on the Physics*, 138. 3–6, 138.29–140.6; 140.18–141.11; Simplicius, *Commentary on the Physics*, 562.3–6, 563.17–20; and Aristotle's *Physics*, 210b22–25.

Page 43: *Empedocles*, translated by M. R. Wright, *Empedocles: The Extant Fragments*, Yale University Press, 1981.
1. *On Nature*: B2, B3, B1, B4, B6, B17, B12, B13, B16, B8, B9, B21, B23, B26, B25, B36, B27, B29, B28, B30, B31, B22, B20, B38, B54, B37, B52, B39, B35, B59, B62, B71, B89, B109, B107, B103, B98, B100, B132, B133, B134, and B100.
2. *Purifications*: B112, B114, B11, B113, B15, B117, B118, B121, B124, B120, B139, B136, B137, B127, and B146.

Page 49: Anaxagoras, translated by Barnes op. cit: B1–B9, B11–B17, B21; Diogenes Laertius, *Lives of the Philosophers*, II 6–14; Aristotle, *Metaphysics*, 984b15–18; Plato, *Phaedo* 97bc, 98bc; and Scholiast to Gregory of Nazianzus, *Patrologia Graeca*, XXXVI, 911 BC.

Page 53: Democritus, translated by J. Barnes, op. cit:
1. Atomism: Simplicius, *Commentary on the Heavens*, 294.30–295.22; Aristotle, *Metaphysics*, 985b4–20; Aristotle, *On Generation and Corruption*, 316a13–b16; and Plutarch, *Against Colotes*, 1110f–1111a.
2. Knowledge: Sextus Empiricus, *Against the Mathematicians*, VII 135–140 (contains B125, B9, B10, B6, B7, B8, and B11); Diogenes Laertius, *Lives of the Philosophers*, IX 72 (B125); Galen, *On Medical Experience*, XV 7–8; Galen, *The Elements According to Hippocrates*, I 417–418k; B165; and Theophrastus, *On the Senses*, 49–50; B118.

3. Ethics: B3, B159, B170, B172, B173, B183, B187, B188, B189, B191, B219, B233, B234, B235, B236, B264, B284, B289, and B290.
4. Maxims: B37, B40, B41, B42, B43, B45, B46, B50, B54, B55, B57, B59, B60, B61, B62, B63, B64, B68, B69, B70, B71, B72, B73, B74, B77, B81, B83, B86, B89, B94, B96, B98, B99, and B103.
5. Politics: B49, B267, B270, and B283.

Page 63: *Protagoras*, translated by Robin Waterfield, op. cit: Diogenes Laertius, *Lives of the Philosophers*, 9.51–53; Plato, *Protagoras*, 316b8–319a7; Aristotle, *Metaphysics*, 1062b13–19; Didymus the Blind, *Commentary on the Psalms*; Plato, *Protagoras*, 334a3–c2; and Diogenes of Oenoanda, fr.11, John of Stobi, *Anthology*, 3.29.80.

Page 65: *Gorgias*, translated by Robin Waterfield, op. cit. Diodorus of Sicily, *Universal History*, 12.53, 2–5; Cicero, *Brutus*, 12.47.1–5; and Plato, *Philebus*, 58a7–b2; B3.

SECTION II: PLATO

Page 75: *Euthyphro*, translated by Thomas and Grace West, Cornell University Press, 1984–complete.

Page 86: *Apology*, translated by Thomas and Grace West, Cornell University Press, 1984–complete.

Page 103: *Crito*, translated by Thomas and Grace West, Cornell University Press, 1984–complete.

Page 112: *Protagoras*, translated by C. C. Taylor, Clarendon, 1976: 328d4–330c4; 357b5–362a3.

Page 117: *Gorgias*, translated by T. Irwin, Oxford, 1979: 447b–c8; 448a1–b4; 449c9–451a2; 453a1–b4; 453d8–12; 453e1–451b7; 454c–455a7; 456d–458c4; 460e3–461d4; 462a5–d3; 462e7–463d7; 464b3–466a4; 466b5–c5; 466e5–467a10; 474c3–d3; 475b7–e5; 477c5–478b3; 478d–479a4; 480a1–b5; 480e5–481c4; 481e1–482b5; 482c5–486c4; 486d7–e5; 487e1–5; 488b1–9; 488d5–8; 489d1–7; 489e4–490a8; 491b1–492b2; 492d1–494c4; 495a2–7; 495c5–9; 496e5–497b3; 497d2–9; 499b5–510a2; and 520e3–522e5.

Page 139: *Meno*, translated by Benjamin Jowett, Library of Liberal Arts, Bobbs-Merrill, 1949.

Page 159: *Phaedo*, translated by D. Gallup, Oxford University Press, 1994: 57a1–60c7; 63b1–68c3; 69e6–72a12; 74a4–75d6; 78c10–80a9; 104c7–107b10; and 114d1–118a17.

Page 173: *Symposium*, translated by R. Waterfield, Oxford University Press, 1994: 201d–223d.

Page 188: *Republic*, translated by R. Waterfield, Oxford University Press, 1993:
Book I: 327a–c; 328d–329a; 329b7–329e; 330d; 331a–b4; 331c–d5; 336b8–d4; 336e–337b4; 337c6–338a4; 338c1–340a7; 340c1–d2; and 341c–343a2.
Book II: 357a–362c; 368c2–370c5; 372e–375a1; 376d–379e; and 380c.
Book III: 412b8–414b8; and 416d3–417b.
Book IV: 419a–421c7; and 427d–442d10.

Book V: 451c4–452c2; 453a6–457a7; 457b–c8; 458b7–460d7; 461e4–462d8; 463a–464e3; and 471c3–480a.
Book VI: 484a–489d6; and 503b6–511e.
Book VII: 514a–521c1; and 531d–535a1.
Book VIII: 543a–545d5; 546a; 546d–547a3; 547b2–549a1; 549c1–e; 550a1–553a4; 554a1–554b5; 556a1–a7; 561b7–c7; 562a3–563b6; 563d4–e4; 563e7–**564a9**; 565c8–d5; 565**e3**–**566b7**; 566d4–567d9; and 569b7–c8.
Book IX: 571a–573**e2**; 575**e2**–576d6; 577e–578a5; 578d1–579b5; 579d7–e6; 580a7–582d5; 583a1–584c3; and 584d1–587b.
Book X: 595a–b; 596a–e; 597c–598d; 608c–609c; 609d–610c; 610d–611a; 612a–c; 613d–614el; 615a2–615c2; 616b–616c4; 617b3–620a1; and 620d5–621d.

Page 241: *Phaedrus*, translated by J. C. Rowe, Aris and Philips, 1986: 245c7–256e4.

Page 249: *Parmenides*, translated by Kenneth Sayre, University of Notre Dame Press, 1996: 127d7–135d6.

Page 255: *Theaetetus*, translated by John McDowell, Oxford University Press, 1977: 151d4–152c4; 184b4–187c8; 200c3–201d3; and 208c1–210d5.

Page 262: *Timaeus*, translated by F. M. Cornford, Routledge, 1937: 29D–32C; 35C–36A; and 37C–38B.

Page 266: *Letter VII*, translated by L. A. Post, from *Plato: The Collected Dialogues*, ed. Hamilton E. and H. Cairns, 323e–324b3; and 339d5–344d1.

SECTION III: ARISTOTLE

Page 276: *Categories*, translated by J. L. Ackrill: chs. 1–5.

Page 281: *On Interpretation*, translated by J. L. Ackrill: chs. 1–4 and 9.

Page 285: *Prior Analytics*, translated by A. J. Jenkinson: Book I, chs. 1 and 4.

Page 289: *Posterior Analytics*, translated by J. Barnes: Book I, chs. 1–4; and Book II, ch. 1–2, 8–10, and 19.

Page 299: *Physics*, translated by H. Apostle, Indiana University Press, 1969: Book I: ch. 1; ch. 2, 184b15–185b11, 185b16–186a4; ch. 5; and chs. 7–8; Book II: chs. 1–3 and 7–8; Book III: chs. 1, ch. 4: 203b16–204a7; ch. 5: 204a8–24, 204b1–205a7, 206a8; ch. 6, 206a9–207a14; and ch. 7, 207b26–34; and Book VIII: ch. 5, 256a4–2256b3, 258b4–9; and ch. 6.

Page 320: *Metaphysics*, translated by W. D. Ross: Book I: chs. 1–2; ch. 3, 983a24–983b18, 983b20, 984a5–9, 984a17–984b1; ch. 4, 985a3–28, 985b21–2; ch. 6; ch. 9, 990a33–991b8; and ch. 10, 993a11–17. Book IV: chs. 1–3; ch. 4, 1005b35–1006a33, 1006b11–35, 1007b19–24, 1008a29–1008b2. Book V: ch. 8. Book VI: ch. 1. Book VII: chs. 1–3, ch. 4, 1029b12–16, 1029b23–1030a24, 1030a27–30; ch. 5, 1031a1–14; ch. 6, 1031a15–26, 1031a28–1031b21, 1031b27–1032a5; ch. 13, 1038b1–1039a3; and ch. 17. Book VIII: ch. 1–2; ch. 3,

1043a29–1043b32; and 1044a11–14. Book XII: ch. 6–7; ch. 8, 1073b14–15, 1073b23–1073b3, 1074a31–38; and ch. 9, 1074b15–34, 1075a5–10.

Page 348: *On the Soul,* from *Aristotle's De Anima,* translated by D. W. Hamlyn, Clarendon Press, 1968; Book II, chs. 1–3, 5–6, and 12; and Book III, chs. 1, 4–5.

Page 358: *Nicomachean Ethics,* translated by H. Rackham, Loeb Classical Library, Harvard University Press, 1934:
Book I, chs. 1–8, 9: 1099b9–30, 12–13.
Book II, chs. 1–9.
Book III, ch1.
Book VI, chs. 1–9, 12–13.
Book VII, chs. 1–3.
Book VIII, chs. 1–5 and 13.
Book IX, chs. 4–9, 10: 1170b20–1171a12.
Book X, chs. 1, 4–8, and 9: 1179a–1180a5 and 1181b11–23.

Page 412: *Politics* translated by B. Jowett, Book I, chs. 1–7; Book III: ch. 1 and 6–13; and Book VII, chs. 1 and 13–15.

Page 432: *Poetics* translated by I. Bywater: ch. 1, 147a10–29 and 1447b24–29; ch. 2, 1448a1–8 and 15–18; ch. 3, 1448a19–29; ch. 4; ch. 6; ch. 9; and chs. 13–14.

Unless stated otherwise, the above selections are from Aristotle, *The Complete Works,* ed. J. Barnes, 2 vols., Princeton University Press, 1984.

SECTION IV: HELLENISTIC AND ROMAN PHILOSOPHY

EPICUREANISM

Page 442: Epicurus, *The Extant Remains,* translated by Cyril Bailey, Clarendon Press, 1926.
1. *Letter to Herodotus*—complete
2. *Letter to Menoeceus*—complete
3. *Principal Doctrines*—complete

Page 458: Lucretius, translated by H. A. J. Munroe, in *The Stoic and Epicurean Philosophers,* ed. Whitney J. Oates, Random House, 1940: *On the Nature of Things* (selections).

STOICISM

Page 469: Zeno of Citium, selections, translated by Brad Inwood and L. P. Gerson, *Hellenistic Philosophy,* Hackett, 1997:
1. Philosophy and Logic: Diogenes Laertius 7: 39, 42, 45, 58, 61, and 83.
2. Physics: Diogenes Laertius 7: 134, 135, 140, 142, 147, 148, 150, 155, and 157.
3. Ethics: Diogenes Laertius 7: 84, 87, 90, 94, 106, 107, 108, 113, 116, 127, and 130; Epictetus, *Discourses,* 2.10.1–4; and Cicero, *On the Nature of the Gods,* 2: 20, 21, 22, 43, 82, and 154.

Page 476: Epictetus, *Encheiridion (The Manual),* translated by W. A. Oldfather, Loeb Classical Library, Harvard University Press, 1928–complete.

Page 486: Marcus Aurelius, *Meditations,* Book IV, translated by George Long, *The Harvard Classics,* ed. Charles Elliot, Grolier Enterprises, 1907.

SKEPTICISM

Page 494: Sextus Empiricus, *Outlines of Pyrrhonism,* translated by Rev. R. Bury, Loeb Classical Library, Harvard University Press, 1933, Book I, chs. 1–13, 14: lines 36–39, 15, and 18–28.